MW01064696

Inside
RavenDB 4.0

Inside RavenDB 4.0

Oren Eini

Hibernating Rhinos

Table of Contents

Dedicated to Rachel and Tamar,
with all my love.

I. Introduction

1. Welcome to RavenDB

RavenDB is a high performance, distributed, NoSQL document database. Phew, that is a mouthful. But it probably hits all the right buzzwords. What does this actually *mean*?

Let me try to explain those terms in reverse order. A document database is a database that stores "documents", meaning structured information in the form of self-contained data (as opposed to Word or Excel documents). A document is usually in JSON or XML format. RavenDB is, essentially, a database for storing and working with JSON data. You can also store binary data and a few other types, but you'll primarily use RavenDB for JSON documents.

RavenDB can run on a single node (suitable for development or for small applications) or on a cluster of nodes (which gives you high availability, load balancing, geo distribution of data and work, etc.). A single cluster can host multiple databases, each of which can span some or all of the nodes in the cluster.

With RavenDB 4.0, the team has put a major emphasis on extremely high performance. I am going to assume I don't need to tell you why that's a good thing :-). Throughout this book, I'm going to explain how that decision has impacted both the architecture and implementation of RavenDB.

In addition to the tagline, RavenDB is also an ACID database, unlike many other NoSQL databases. ACID stands for atomic, consistent, isolated and durable and is a fancy way to say that RavenDB has *real* transactions. Per document, across multiple documents in the same collection, across multiple documents in multiple collections; it's all there, the kinds of transactions developers can rely on. If you send work to RavenDB, you can be assured that either it will be done completely and persist to disk or it will fail completely (and let you know about the failure); no half-way measures and no needing to roll your own "transactions."

This seems silly to mention, I'm aware, but there are databases out there that don't have this. Given how much work we've put into this particular feature, I can empathize with the wish to just drop ACID behavior, because making a database that is both high performance and fully transactional is anything but trivial. That said, I think this should be one of the most basic requirements of a database, and RavenDB has it out of the box.

There are certain things that a database should provide; transactions are one, but you also need manageability and a certain degree of ease of use. A common thread we'll explore in this book is how RavenDB was designed to reduce the load on the operations team by dynamically adjusting to load, environment and the kind of work it is running. Working with a database should be easy and obvious, and to a large extent, RavenDB facilitates that.

This book isn't meant to provide documentation; RavenDB has quite a bit of documentation that tells you exactly how to use it. While informative, documentation tends to be dry and it hardly makes for good reading (or for an interesting time writing it). A blog post, on the other hand, tells a story – even if most of mine are technical stories. I like writing them, and I've been pleasantly surprised that a large number of people also seem to like reading them.

I'm a developer at heart. That means that one of my favorite activities is writing code. Writing documentation, on the other hand, is so far down the list of my favorite activities that one could say it isn't even on the list. I do like writing blog posts, and I've been maintaining an active blog for close to fifteen years.[1]

1.1. About this book

What you're reading now is effectively a book-length blog post. The main idea here is that I want to give you a way to *grok* RavenDB.[2] This means not only gaining knowledge of what RavenDB does, but also all the reasoning behind the bytes. In effect, I want you to understand all the *whys* of RavenDB.

Although blog posts and books have very different structures, audiences and purposes, I'll still aim to give you the same easy-reading feeling of your favorite blogger. If I've accomplished what I've set out to do, this will be neither dry documentation nor a reference book. If you need either, you can read the online RavenDB documentation. This is not to say that the book is purely my musings; the content is also born from the training course we've been teaching for the past decade and the formalization of our internal onboarding training.

By the end of this book, you're going to have a far better understanding of how and why RavenDB is put together the way it is. More importantly, you'll have the knowledge and skills needed to make efficient use of RavenDB in your systems.

---

1   You can find it at http://ayende.com/blog

2   Grok means "to understand so thoroughly that the observer becomes a part of the observed – to merge, blend, intermarry, lose identity in group experience." From Robert A. Heinlein, *Stranger in a Strange Land*.

1.1.1. ACKNOWLEDGMENTS

This book has been written and re-written several times. In fact, looking at the commit logs, I started writing it in July of 2014. Writing something of this scope, and at the same time pushing the product itself forward is not easy and would not have been possible without the help of many people.

On the technical side, I want to thank Adi Avivi, Dan Bishop, Maxim Buryak, Danielle Greenberg, Judah Himango, Karmel Indych, Elemar Junior, Grisha Kotler, Rafał Kwiatkowski, Grzegorz Lachowski, Marcin Lewandowski, Jonathan Matheus, Tomasz Opalach, Arkadiusz Paliński, Paweł Pekról, Aviv Rahmany, Idan Ben Shalom, Efrat Shenhar, Tal Weiss, Michael Yarichuk, Fitzchak Yitzchaki and Iftah Ben Zaken.

The editors, who had the harsh task of turning raw text into a legible book. Erik Dietrich, Laura Lattimer, Katherine Mechling and Amanda Muledy. All the errors you find were inserted by myself after the last round of edits, I assure you.

The early readers of this book, who had gone above merely giving feedback and actively contributed to making this better. Andrej Krivulcik, Jason Ghent, Bobby Johnson, Sean Killeen, Gabriel Schmitt Kohlrausch, Cathal McHale, Daniel Palme, Alessandro Riolo, Clinton Sheppard, Jan Ove Skogheim, Daniel Wonisch and Stephen Zeng.

Thanks you all, it would have been much harder, and likely not possible, without you.

1.2. Who is this for?

I've tried to make this book useful for a broad category of users. Developers will come away with an understanding of how to best use RavenDB features to create awesome applications. Architects will gain the knowledge required to design and guide large-scale systems with RavenDB clusters at their cores. Operations teams will learn how to monitor, support and nurture RavenDB in production.

Regardless of who you are, you'll come away from this book with a greater understanding of all the moving pieces and how you can mold RavenDB to meet your needs.

This book mostly used C# as the language for code samples, though RavenDB can be used with .NET, Java, Go, Node.js, Python, Ruby and PHP, among others. Most things discussed in the book are applicable even if you aren't writing code in C#.

All RavenDB official clients follow the same model adjusted to match different platform expectations and API standards. So regardless of the platform you use to connect to RavenDB, this book should still be useful.

1.3. Who am I?

My name in Oren Eini and over a decade ago, I got frustrated working with relational databases. At the time, I was working mostly as a consultant for companies looking to improve the performance of data-driven applications. I kept seeing customer after customer really struggle with this, not because they were unqualified for the task, but because they kept using the wrong tools for the job.

At some point I got so frustrated that I sat down and wrote a blog post about what I thought an ideal datastore for OLTP applications (online transaction processing applications, a fancy way to say business applications) should look like. That blog post turned into a series of blog posts and then into some weekend hacking. Fast-forward a few months, and I had the skeleton of what would eventually become RavenDB and a burning desire to make it a reality.

At some point, building RavenDB felt not like I was creating something from scratch, but like I was merely letting out something that was already fully formed. As I mentioned, that was over a decade ago, and RavenDB has been running production systems ever since.

In that decade, we have learned a lot about what it takes to really make a database that *just works* and doesn't force you to jump through so many hoops. In particular, I came from a Microsoft-centric world, and that world had a big impact on the design of RavenDB. Most NoSQL solutions (especially at the time) had a very different mental model for how they should operate. They put a lot of attention on speed, scale out or esoteric data models, often at the severe expense of ease of use, operational simplicity and what I consider to be fundamental features such as transactions.

I wanted to have a database that would *make sense* for building web applications and business systems; you know, the bread and butter of our industry. I wanted a database that would be ACID, because a database without transactions just didn't make sense to me. I wanted to get rid of the limitations of the rigid schema of relational databases but keep working on domain-driven systems. I wanted something that is fast but at the same time could just be thrown on a production server and would work without having to pay for an on-call babysitter.

A lot of the design of RavenDB was heavily influenced by the Release It! book, which I *highly* recommend. We tried to get a lot of things right from the get go, and with a decade in production to look back at, I think we did a good job there.

That doesn't mean that we always hit the bullseye. Almost a decade in production – deployed to hundreds of thousands of machines (of sometimes dubious origin) and used by teams of wildly different skill levels – will teach you a *lot* about what works in theory, what the real world can tolerate and what is really needed.

For the RavenDB 4.0 release, we took the time to look back at what worked and what didn't and made certain to actually *use* all of that experience and knowhow to build a much better end result.

I'm insanely proud of what came out of the door as a result of it. RavenDB 4.0 is a really cool database capable of doing amazing things, and I'm really glad I have the chance to write this book and explore with you all the things you can do with it.

1.4. In this book...

One of the major challenges in writing this book was figuring out how to structure it. There are so many concepts that interweave with another and trying to understand them in isolation can be difficult. For example, we can't talk about modeling documents before we understand the kind of features that are available for us to work with. Considering this, I'm going to introduce concepts in stages.

1.4.1. PART I – THE BASICS OF RAVENDB

Focus: Developers

This is the part you will want new hires to read before starting to work with RavenDB, as it contains a practical discussion on how to build an application using RavenDB. We'll skip over theory, concepts and background information in favor of getting things done; the more theoretical concepts will be discussed later in the book.

We'll cover setting up RavenDB on your machine, opening up the RavenDB Studio in the browser and connecting to the database from your code. After we get beyond the "hello world" stage, we'll introduce some of the basic concepts that you need to know in order to work with RavenDB: building a simple CRUD application, learning how to perform basic queries and in general working with the client API.

After covering the basics, we'll move into modeling documents in RavenDB; how to build your application so that it meshes well with document-based modeling; what sort of features you need to be aware of when designing the domain model and how to deal with common modeling scenarios; concurrency control and dealing with data that doesn't always match the document model (binary data, for example).

Following on this high level discussion, we'll dive into the client API and explore the advanced options RavenDB offers: from lazy requests to reduce network traffic, perform partial document updates and see how caching is an integral part of the client API.

We'll conclude the first part of the book with an overview of batch processing in RavenDB and how you can use highly available, reliable subscriptions to manage all sorts of background tasks in your application in a quite elegant fashion.

1.4.2. PART II – DISTRIBUTED RAVENDB

Focus: Architects

This part focuses on the theory of building robust and high performance systems using RavenDB. We'll go directly to working with a cluster of RavenDB nodes on commodity hardware, discuss data and work distribution across the cluster and learn how to best structure systems to take advantage of what RavenDB brings to the table.

We'll begin by dissecting RavenDB's dual-distributed nature. RavenDB is using both a consensus protocol and a gossip protocol to build two layers of communication between the various nodes in the cluster. We'll learn why we use this dual-mode and how it adds tremendously to RavenDB's robustness in the presence of failures.

After going over the theory, we'll get practical: setting up RavenDB clusters, explore different topologies and study how clients interact with a cluster of RavenDB nodes. We'll cover distributed work, load balancing and ensuring high availability and zero downtime for your applications.

One key reason you'll want to use a distributed system is to handle bigger load. We'll cover how you can grow your cluster and even run RavenDB in a geo-distributed deployment with nodes all around the world. RavenDB clusters aren't just collections of machines. They are self-managing entities, sharing load and distributing tasks among the various nodes. We'll talk about how clusters are self-monitoring and self-healing and how RavenDB takes active steps to ensure the safety of your data at all times.

Modern systems are rarely composed of a stand-alone application. So to finish up this section, we'll explore how RavenDB integrates with other systems and databases. RavenDB was explicitly designed to make such integration easier. We'll go over how to create data flow that automatically synchronizes data to different destinations, be they RavenDB instances or even relational databases.

1.4.3. PART III – QUERYING AND INDEXING

Focus: Developers and architects

This part discusses RavenDB indexes data to allow for quick retrieval of information, whether a single document or aggregated data spanning years. We'll cover all the different indexing methods in RavenDB and how each of them can be used to implement the features you want in your systems.

RavenDB has very rich querying and indexing support. We'll start by exploring the RavenDB Query Language (RQL) and the kind of queries that you can perform. We'll look at how RavenDB processes and optimizes your queries to answer them as fast as possible.

Then we'll get to the really fun stuff. RavenDB's queries can answer a lot more than just `where Status = 'Active'`. We'll look at full text queries, querying multiple collections at once and faceted search. We'll look at how RavenDB can find similar documents and suggest to the user different queries to try as the user tries to find a particular nugget of information.

Spatial queries (searching based on geographical data) will be covered in depth. We'll also cover how you can find documents not based on their own data, but on related documents' data. Similar to, but simpler and faster than `JOIN` from relational databases, the ability to efficiently find documents using related documents can greatly simplify and speed up your queries. One of the strengths of RavenDB is that it is schema-less by nature, and that doesn't stop at data storage. RavenDB also has very powerful capabilities for querying over dynamic data and user-generated content.

MapReduce in RavenDB is a very important feature. It allows RavenDB to perform lightning-fast aggregation queries over practically any dataset, regardless of size. We'll explore exactly how this feature works, the kind of behaviors it enables and what you can do with what are effectively free aggregation queries.

Finally, we'll go over the care and feeding of indexes in RavenDB: how you can create, deploy, monitor and manage them yourself. We'll talk about how the RavenDB query optimizer interacts with your indexes and how to move them between environments.

1.4.4. PART IV – SECURITY

Focus: Operations and architects

RavenDB is used to store business-critical data such as medical information and financial transactions. In this part, we'll go over all the steps that have been taken to ensure that your data is safe, the communication channels are secure and only authorized users are able to access your database.

We'll cover how to set up RavenDB securely. RavenDB's security model is binary in nature. Either you run RavenDB in an unsecured mode (only useful for development) or you run it in a secured mode. There are no half measures or multiple steps to take.

Setting up RavenDB securely is easy – although making it easy was certainly not easy – and once set up, RavenDB takes care of all aspects of securing your data. Data in transit is encrypted, and clients and servers mutually authenticate themselves. We'll discuss how RavenDB handles authentication and authorization, as well as how you can control who gets to the database and what they can access.

We'll also cover securing your data at rest. RavenDB supports full database encryption, ensuring that not even a single byte of your data is ever saved to disk in plain text. Instead, RavenDB will encrypt all data and indexes using 256-bit encryption. Your data will be decrypted on the fly as needed and only kept in memory for the duration of an active transaction.

We'll also cover other aspects of running an encrypted database: how you should manage encryption keys and how to back up and restore encrypted databases.

1.4.5. PART V – RUNNING IN PRODUCTION

Focus: Operations

This part deals with running and supporting a RavenDB cluster or clusters in production, from spinning a new cluster, to decommissioning a downed node, to tracking down performance problems. We'll learn all you need (plus a bit more) in order to understand how RavenDB works and how to customize its behavior to fit your own environment.

We'll go over the details you'll need to successfully deploy to production, like how to plan ahead for the resources you'll need to handle expected load (and how to handle *unexpected* load) and the kind of deployment topologies you can choose from and their implications. We'll also go over the network, firewall and operating system configurations that can make or break a production environment.

Just getting to production isn't good enough; we are also going to cover how you can *stay* in production and stay there healthily. We'll discuss monitoring and troubleshooting, what sort of details you need to keep an eye on and how RavenDB surfaces potential issues early on. We'll discover how you can dig into RavenDB and see exactly what is going on inside the engine. We'll go over the kinds of self-optimizations RavenDB routinely applies and how you can take advantage of them.

We'll cover common issues and how to troubleshoot them, diagnosing and resolving problems while keeping the cluster up and functioning. We'll learn how to plan for disaster recovery and actually apply the plan if (and when) disaster strikes.

We'll spend a whole chapter discussing backups and restores. RavenDB supports several options for backing up your data: offsite hot spares, full binary snapshots of your data and highly compressed backups meant for long term storage. We'll discuss backup strategies and options, including backing up directly to the cloud. More importantly, we'll cover how you can define and execute a restore strategy, a critical – though often (sadly) overlooked – part of your overall backup strategy.

Finally, we are going to close this book with a set of operational recipes. These are ready-made answers to specific scenarios that you might run into in production. These are meant to serve both as a series of steps for you to follow if you run into a particular scenario and as a way to give you better insight into the process of working with RavenDB in production.

1.5. Summary

So there's a lot going on in this book, and I hope you'll find it both interesting and instructive. But remember, the one thing it *isn't* meant to do is replace the documentation. The purpose of this book is to give you a full background on and greater understanding of how RavenDB works. I'm not covering the nitty-gritty details of every API call and what parameters should be passed to it.

In many cases, I have elected to discuss a feature, give one or two examples of its use and where it's best utilized and leave the reader with the task of reading up on the full details in the documentation.

This book is meant to be more than API listing. It is meant to tell a story, the story of how you can make the best use of RavenDB in your applications and environment. So, without further ado, turn the page and let's get started.

2. Zero to RavenDB

The very first step we need to take in our journey to understand RavenDB is to get it running on our machine so we can actually get things done. I'm deferring discussion on what RavenDB is and how it works to a later part of this book because I think having a live version that you can play with will make it much easier to understand.

2.1. Setting RavenDB on your machine

For this section, I'm assuming that you're a developer trying to get a RavenDB instance so you can explore it. I'm going to ignore everything related to actual production deployments in favor of getting you set up in as few steps as possible. A full discussion on how to deploy, secure and run RavenDB in production is available in the "Production Deployments" chapter.

I'm going to go over a few quick install scenarios, and you can select whichever one makes the most sense for your setup. After that, you can skip to the next section, where we'll actually start using RavenDB.

2.1.1. RUNNING ON DOCKER

The easiest way to get RavenDB is probably via Docker. If you already have Docker installed, all you need to do is run the following command (using PowerShell):

```
$rvn_args = "--Setup.Mode=None --License.Eula.Accepted=true"
docker run `
  -p 8080:8080 `
  -e RAVEN_ARGS=$rvn_args `
  ravendb/ravendb
```

Docker will now get the latest RavenDB version and spin up a new container to host it. Note that we run it in developer mode, without any authentication.

The output of this command should look something like Listing 2.1.

Listing 2.1 *RavenDB Server Output*

```
   _____                               _____   ____
  |  __ \                             |  __ \ |  _ \
  | |__) |__ __   ___    _____ _ __   | |  | | | |_) |
  |  _  // _` \ \ / / _ \ '_ \| | | | |  _ <
  | | \ \ (_| |\ V /  __/| | | | |__| | | |_) |
  |_|  \_\__,_| \_/ \___|_| |_|_____/|_____/


        Safe by default, optimized for efficiency

   Build 40038, Version 4.0, SemVer 4.0.4-patch-40038, Commit 4837206
   PID 7, 64 bits, 2 Cores, Phys Mem 1.934 GBytes, Arch: X64
   Source Code (git repo): https://github.com/ravendb/ravendb
   Built with love by Hibernating Rhinos and awesome contributors!
  +-----------------------------------------------------------+
  Using GC in server concurrent mode retaining memory from the OS.
  Server available on: http://a698a4246832:8080
  Tcp listening on 172.17.0.2:38888
  Server started, listening to requests...
  TIP: type 'help' to list the available commands.
  ravendb> End of standard input detected, switching to server mode...
  Running non-interactive.
```

You can now access your RavenDB instance using `http://localhost:8080`. If something is already holding port 8080 on your machine, you can map it to a different one using the `-p 8080:8081` option.

2.1.2. RUNNING ON WINDOWS

To set up RavenDB on Windows, you'll need to go to https://ravendb.net/download, select the appropriate platform (Windows x64, in this case) and download the `zip` file containing the binaries.

Extract the file to a directory and then run the `Start.cmd` script or `Server\Raven.Server.exe` executable. This will run RavenDB in interactive mode, inside a console application, and you can access the server by going to http://localhost:8080 in your browser.

If something is already using port 8080, RavenDB will fail to start and give you an "address in use" error (more specifically, EADDRINUSE). You can customize the port and host from the command line by issuing this command:

```
Server\Raven.Server.exe --ServerUrl=http://localhost:8081
```

That will run RavenDB on port 8081, avoiding the conflicting port issue. You might need to try another port as well if port 8081 is also taken on your machine, of course.

2.1.3. RUNNING ON LINUX

To set up RavenDB on Linux, you'll need to go to https://ravendb.net/download, select the appropriate platform (Linux x64, most likely) and download the tar.bz2 file containing the binaries.

Extract the file to a directory and then run the run.sh script or ./Server/Raven.Server executable. This will run RavenDB in interactive mode, inside a console application, and you can access the server by going to http://localhost:8080 in your browser.

If something is already using port 8080, RavenDB will fail to start and give you an "address in use" error (more specifically, EADDRINUSE). You can customize the port and host from the command line by issuing this command:

```
./Server/Raven.Server.exe --ServerUrl=http://localhost:8081
```

That will run RavenDB on port 8081, avoiding the conflicting port issue. You might need to try another port as well if port 8081 is also taken on your machine, of course.

2.1.4. USING THE LIVE DEMO INSTANCE

Without installing anything, you can point your browser to http://live-test.ravendb.net and access the public demo instance that we have available. This is useful for quick checks and verifications, but it isn't meant for anything more serious than that.

Obviously, all data in the live instance is public, and there are no guarantees about availability. We use this instance to try out the latest versions, so you should take that into consideration. In short, if you need to verify something small, go ahead and hit that instance. Otherwise, you'll need your own version.

2.2. Your first database

At this point, you've already set up an instance of RavenDB to work with, and you've loaded the RavenDB Studio in your browser. For simplicity's sake, I'm going to assume from now on that you're running RavenDB on the local machine on port 8080. Point your browser to `http://localhost:8080`, and you should be greeted with an empty RavenDB instance. You can see how it looks in Figure 2.1.

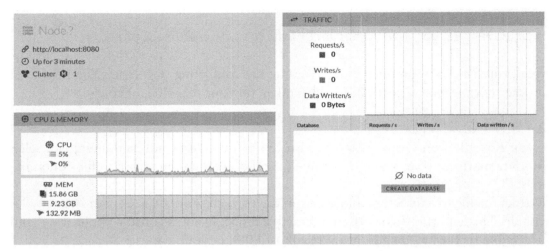

Figure 2.1. *Empty RavenDB node*

What we have right now is a RavenDB node that is a self-contained cluster.[1] Now that we have a running node, the next step is to create a new database on this node.

You can do that by clicking the `Create Database` button, naming the new database `Northwind` and accepting all the defaults in the dialog. We'll discuss what all of those mean later in this book. Click the `Create` button, and that's pretty much it. Your new database is ready. Click on the `Databases` button on the left to see what this looks, as shown in Figure 2.2.

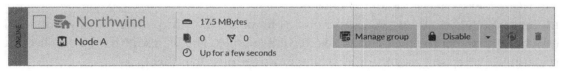

Figure 2.2. *New empty database*

2.2.1. CREATING SAMPLE DATA

Of course, this new database contains no data, which makes it pretty hard to work with. We'll use the `sample data` feature in RavenDB to have some documents to experiment with. Go to `Create Sample Data` under `Tasks` in the left menu and click the `Create` button.

Clicking this button will populate the database with the sample `Northwind` dataset. For those not familiar with Northwind, it's a sample dataset of an online store, and it includes

---

1   Actually, that's not exactly the case, but the details on the state of a newly minted node are a bit complex and covered in more detail in Chapter 6.

common concepts such as orders, customers and products. Let's explore this dataset inside of RavenDB.

On the left menu, select Documents, and you'll see a view similar to what's pictured in Figure 2.3, showing the recently created documents and collections.

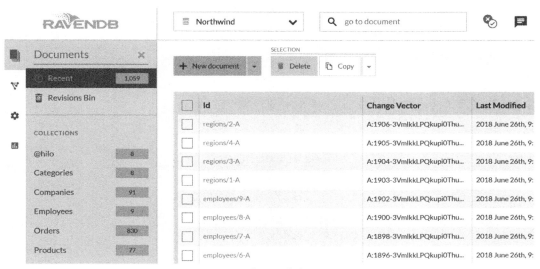

Figure 2.3. *Northwind documents view*

Collections are the basic building blocks inside RavenDB. Every document belongs to exactly one collection, and the collection typically holds similar documents (though it doesn't have to). These documents are most often based on the entity type of the document in your code. It's very similar to tables in a relational database, but unlike tables, there's no requirement that documents within the same collection will share the same structure or have any sort of schema.

Collections are very important to the way data is organized and optimized internally within RavenDB. We'll frequently use collections to group similar documents together and apply an operation to them (subscribing to changes, indexing, querying, ETL, etc.).

2.2.2. OUR FIRST REAL DOCUMENT

Click on the Orders collection and then on the first document in the listing, which should be orders/830-A. The result is shown in Figure 2.4. For the first time, we're looking at a real JSON document inside of RavenDB.

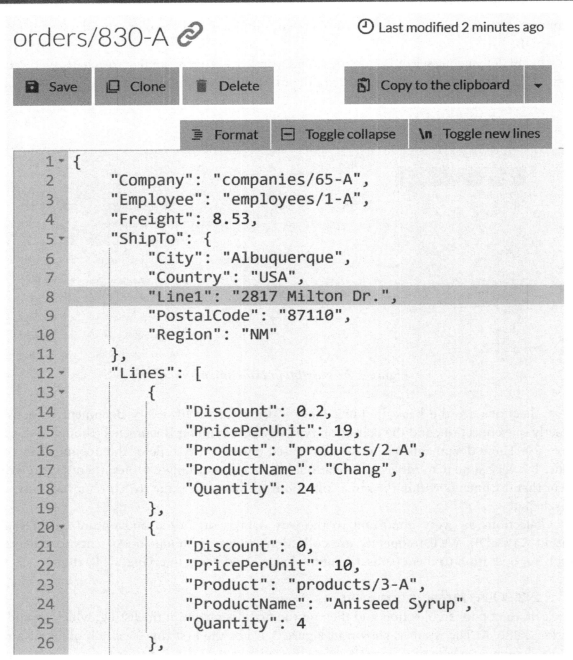

Figure 2.4. *An Orders document*

If you're used to working with non-relational databases, this is pretty obvious and not too exciting. But if you're mostly used to relational databases, there are several things to note here.

In RavenDB, we're able to store arbitrarily complex data as a single unit. If you look closely at Figure 2.4, you'll see that instead of just storing a few columns, we can store rich information and work with nested objects (the ShipTo property) or arrays of complex types (the Lines property).

This means that we don't have to split our data to satisfy the physical constraints of our storage. A whole object graph can be stored in a single document. Modeling will be further discussed in Chapter 3, but for now I'll just mention that the basic modeling method in RavenDB is based around root aggregates.

In the meantime, you can explore the different collections and the sample data in the Studio. We spent a lot of time and effort on the RavenDB Studio. Though it's pretty, I'll be the first to admit that looking at a syntax highlighted text editor isn't really *that* impressive. So let's see what kind of things we can do with the data as a database.

2.3. Working with the RavenDB Studio

This section will cover the basics of working with data within RavenDB Studio. If you're a developer, you're probably anxious to start seeing code. We'll get into that in the next section – no worries.

2.3.1. CREATING AND EDITING DOCUMENTS

When you look at a particular document, you can edit the JSON and click Save, and the document will be saved. There isn't really much to it, to be honest. Creating new documents is a bit more interesting. Let's create a new category document.

Go to Documents in the left menu, click Categories under Collections and select New document in current collection, as shown in Figure 2.5.

Figure 2.5. *New document in current collection*

This will open the editor with an empty, new document that's based on one of the existing categories. Note that the document ID is set to categories/. Fill in some values for the properties in the new document and save it. RavenDB will assign the document ID automatically for you.

One thing that may not be obvious is that while the Studio generates an empty document based on the existing ones, there is no such thing as schema in RavenDB, and you are free to add or remove properties and values and modify the structure of the document however you like. This feature makes evolving your data model and handling more complex data much easier.

2.3.2. PATCHING DOCUMENTS

The first thing we'll learn is how to do bulk operations inside the Studio. Go to `Documents` on the left menu and click the `Patch` menu item. You'll be presented with the screen shown in Figure 2.6.

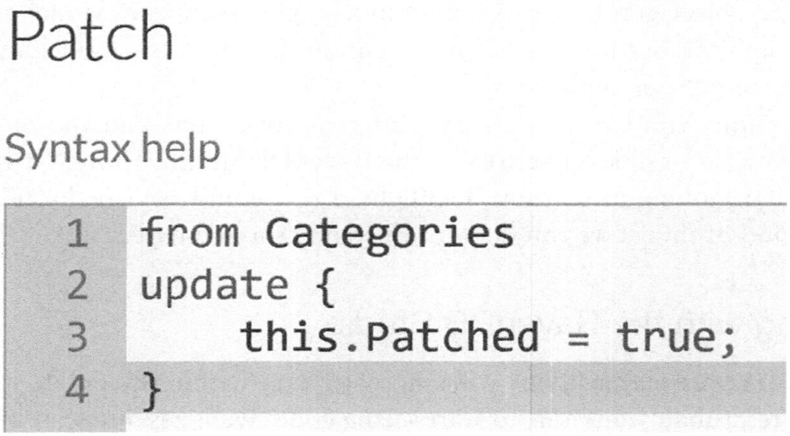

Patch

Syntax help

```
1  from Categories
2  update {
3      this.Patched = true;
4  }
```

Figure 2.6. *Adding field 'Patched' to all documents in the Categories Collection*

Patching allows you to write a query that executes a JavaScript transformation that can modify the matching documents. To try this out, let's run a non-trivial transformation on the `categories` documents. Using a patch script, we'll add localization support – the ability to store the category name and description in multiple languages.

Start by adding the code in Listing 2.2 to the query text.

Listing 2.2 *Patching categories for internationalization support*

```
from Categories
update {
    this.Name = [
      {"Lang": "en-us", "Text": this.Name }
    ];
    this.Description = [
      {"Lang": "en-us", "Text": this.Description }
    ];
}
```

Click the `Test` button, and you can see the results of running this operation: a category document. You can also select which specific document this test will be tested on. The before-and-after results of running this script on `categories/4-A` are shown in Figure 2.7.

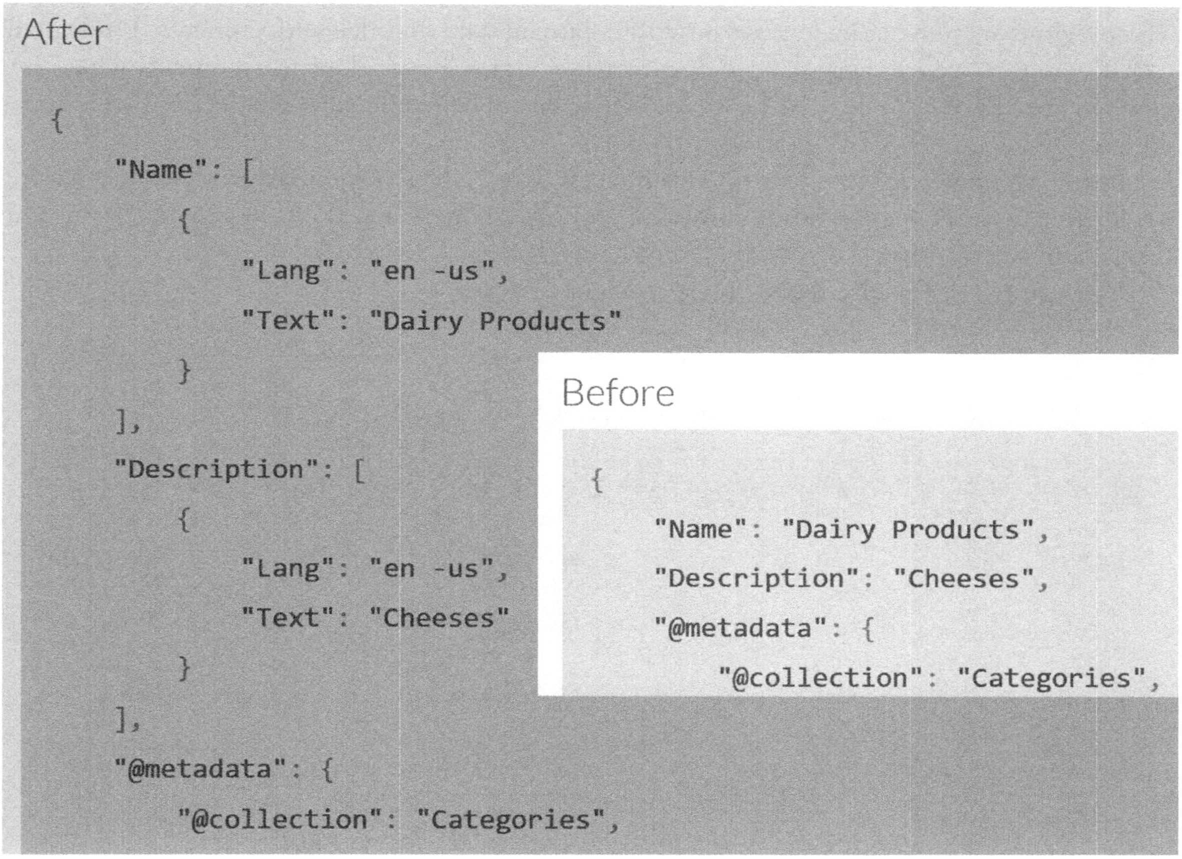

```
After

{
    "Name": [
        {
            "Lang": "en -us",
            "Text": "Dairy Products"
        }
    ],
    "Description": [
        {                          Before
            "Lang": "en -us",
            "Text": "Cheeses"       {
        }                              "Name": "Dairy Products",
    ],                                 "Description": "Cheeses",
    "@metadata": {                     "@metadata": {
        "@collection": "Categories",       "@collection": "Categories",
```

Figure 2.7. *Categories localization with JavaScript patching*

Patch scripts allow us to modify our documents en masse, and they are very useful when you need to reshape existing data. They can be applied on a specific document, a whole collection or all documents matching a specific query.

It's important to mention that for performance reasons, such bulk operations can be composed of multiple, independent and concurrent transactions instead of spanning a single large transaction. Each such independent transaction processes some portion of the data with full ACID properties (while the patch operation as a whole does not).

2.3.3. DELETING DOCUMENTS

If you want to delete a particular document in the Studio, you can simply go to the document and hit the Delete button. You can delete a whole collection by going to the collection page (in the left menu, choose Documents and then select the relevant collection in the Collections menu), selecting all the documents in the header row and clicking Delete.

2.3.4. QUERYING DOCUMENTS

The previous sections talked about how to create, update and delete documents. But for full CRUD support, we still need to read documents. So far, we've looked at documents whose IDs were already known to us, and we've looked at entire collections. In this section, we'll focus on querying documents based on their data.

In the left menu, go to Indexes and then to Query. This is the main screen for querying documents in the RavenDB Studio. Enter the following query and then click the query button:
`from Companies where Address.Country = 'UK'`

You can see the results of this query in Figure 2.8.

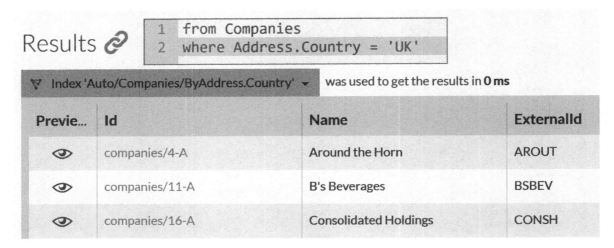

Figure 2.8. *All companies in the UK query results*

The overview in this section was not meant to be a thorough walk-through of all options in RavenDB Studio, but only show you some basic usage so that you can get familiar with the Studio and be able to see the results of the coding done in the next section within the Studio.

2.4. Your first RavenDB program

We're finally at the good parts, where we can start slinging code around. For simplicity's sake, I'm going to use a simple console application to explore the RavenDB API. Typically, RavenDB is used in web/backend applications, so we'll also explore some of the common patterns of organizing your RavenDB usage in your application later in this chapter.

The code samples in this book use C#, but the documentation can guide you on how to achieve the same results with any supported client.

Create a new console application with RavenDB, as shown Listing 2.3.

Listing 2.3 *Installing RavenDB Client NuGet package*

```
dotnet new console --name Rvn.Ch02
dotnet add .\Rvn.Ch02\ package RavenDB.Client --version 4.*
```

This will setup the latest client version for RavenDB 4.0 on the project. The next step is to add a namespace reference by adding using Raven.Client.Documents; to the top of the Program.cs file.

And now we're ready to start working with the client API. The first thing we need to do is to set up access to the RavenDB cluster that we're talking to. This is done by creating an instance of DocumentStore and configuring it as shown in Listing 2.4.

Listing 2.4 *Creating a document store pointed to a local instance*

```
var store = new DocumentStore
{
    Urls = new[] { "http://localhost:8080" },
    Database = "Tasks"
};

store.Initialize();
```

This code sets up a new DocumentStore instance and lets it know about a single node – the one running on the local machine – and that we are going to be using the Tasks database. The document store is the starting location for all communication with the RavenDB cluster. It holds the configuration, topology, cache and any customizations that you might have applied.

Typically, you'll have a single instance of a document store per application (singleton pattern) and use that same instance for the lifetime of the application. However, before we can continue, we need to go ahead and create the Tasks database in the Studio so we'll have a real database to work with.

The document store is the starting location for all RavenDB work, but the real workhorse is the session. The session is what will hold our entities, talk with the server and, in general, act as the front man to the RavenDB cluster.

2.4.1. Defining entities and basic CRUD

Before we can actually start using the session, we need *something* to actually store. It's possible to work with completely dynamic data in RavenDB, but that's a specific scenario covered in the documentation. Most of the time, you're working with your entities. For the purpose of this chapter, we'll use the notion of tasks to build a simple list of things to do.

Listing 2.5 shows what a class that will be saved as a RavenDB document looks like.

Listing 2.5 *Entity class representing a task*

```
public class ToDoTask
{
    public string Id { get; set; }
    public string Task { get; set; }
    public bool Completed { get; set; }
    public DateTime DueDate { get; set; }
}
```

This is about as simple as you can get, but we're only starting, so that's good. Let's create a new task inside RavenDB, reminding us that we need to pick up a bottle of milk from the store tomorrow. The code to perform this task (pun intended) is shown in Listing 2.6.

Listing 2.6 *Saving a new task to RavenDB*

```
using (var session = store.OpenSession())
{
    var task = new ToDoTask
    {
        DueDate = DateTime.Today.AddDays(1),
        Task = "Buy milk"
    };
    session.Store(task);
    session.SaveChanges();
}
```

We opened a new session and created a new ToDoTask. We then stored the task in the session and called SaveChanges to save all the changes in the session to the server. You can see the results of this in Figure 2.9.

ToDoTasks/1

Save   Clone   Delete

```
1 ▾ {
2       "Completed": false,
3       "DueDate": "2017-05-14T00:00:00.0000000",
4       "Task": "Buy milk",
5 ▾     "@metadata": {
6           "@collection": "ToDoTasks",
7           "Raven-Clr-Type": "Tryouts.ToDoTask, Tryouts"
8       }
9   }
```

Figure 2.9. *The newly created task document in the Studio*

As it so happened, I was able to go to the store today and get some milk, so I need to mark this task as completed. Listing 2.7 shows the code required to handle updates in RavenDB.

Listing 2.7 *Loading, modifying and saving a document*

```
using (var session = store.OpenSession())
{
    var task = session.Load<ToDoTask>("ToDoTasks/1-A");
    task.Completed = true;
    session.SaveChanges();
}
```

Several interesting things can be noticed even in this very small sample. We loaded the document and modified it, and then we called SaveChanges. We didn't need to call Store again. Because the task instance was loaded via the session, it was also tracked by the session, and any changes made to it would be sent back to the server when SaveChanges was called. Conversely, if the Completed property was already set to true, the RavenDB client would detect that and do nothing since the state of the server and the client match.

The document session implements the Unit of Work and Identity Map design patterns. This makes it much easier to work with complex behaviors since you don't need to manually track changes to your objects and decide what needs to be saved and what doesn't. It also means that the only time the RavenDB client will send updates to the server is when you call SaveChanges. That, in turn, means you'll experience a reduced number of network calls. All of the changes will be sent as a single batch to the server. And because RavenDB is transactional, all those changes will happen as a single transaction, either completing fully or not at all.

Let's expand on that and create a few more tasks. You can see how this works in Listing 2.8.

Listing 2.8 *Creating multiple documents in a single transaction*

```
using (var session = store.OpenSession())
{
    for (int i = 0; i < 5; i++)
    {
        session.Store(new ToDoTask
        {
            DueDate = DateTime.Today.AddDays(i),
            Task = "Take the dog for a walk"
        });
    }

    session.SaveChanges();
}
```

Figure 2.10 shows the end result of all this playing around we've done. We're creating five new tasks and saving them in the same SaveChanges call, so they will be saved as a single transactional unit.

	Id	Completed	DueDate	Task
☐	ToDoTasks/6	false	2017-05-18T...	Take the dog for a walk
☐	ToDoTasks/5	false	2017-05-17T...	Take the dog for a walk
☐	ToDoTasks/4	false	2017-05-16T...	Take the dog for a walk
☐	ToDoTasks/3	false	2017-05-15T...	Take the dog for a walk
☐	ToDoTasks/2	false	2017-05-14T...	Take the dog for a walk
☐	ToDoTasks/1	false	2017-05-15T...	Buy milk

Figure 2.10. *All the current task documents*

2.4.2. QUERYING RAVENDB

Now that we have all these tasks, we want to start querying the data. Before we get to querying these tasks from code, I want to show you how to query the data from the Studio. Go to Indexes and then Query in the Studio and you'll see the query page. Let us find all the tasks we still have to do, we can do that using the following query: from ToDoTasks where Completed = false. You can see the results of this in Figure 2.11.

```
1  from ToDoTasks
2  where Completed  = false
```

Id	Task	Completed
ToDoTasks/1	Buy milk	false
ToDoTasks/2	Take the dog for a walk	false
ToDoTasks/3	Take the dog for a walk	false
ToDoTasks/4	Take the dog for a walk	false
ToDoTasks/5	Take the dog for a walk	false

Figure 2.11. *Querying for incomplete tasks in the Studio*

We'll learn all about querying RavenDB in Part III. For now, let's concentrate on getting results, which means looking at how we can query RavenDB from code. Let's say I want to know what kind of tasks I have for the next couple of days. In order to get that information, I can use the query in Listing 2.9. (Remember to add using System.Linq; to the top of the Program.cs file.)

Listing 2.9 *Querying upcoming tasks using LINQ*

```
using (var session = store.OpenSession())
{
    var tasksToDo =
        from t in session.Query<ToDoTask>()
        where t.DueDate >= DateTime.Today &&
              t.DueDate <= DateTime.Today.AddDays(2) &&
              t.Completed == false
        orderby t.DueDate
        select t;
    Console.WriteLine(tasksToDo.ToString());

    foreach (var task in tasksToDo)
    {
        Console.WriteLine($"{task.Id} - {task.Task} - {task.DueDate}");
    }
}
```

Running the code in Listing 2.9 gives the following output:

```
from ToDoTasks where DueDate between $p0 and $p1
  and Completed = $p2 order by DueDate

ToDoTasks/2-A - Take the dog for a walk - 5/14/2017 12:00:00 AM
ToDoTasks/3-A - Take the dog for a walk - 5/15/2017 12:00:00 AM
ToDoTasks/4-A - Take the dog for a walk - 5/16/2017 12:00:00 AM
```

The query code sample shows us using LINQ to perform queries against RavenDB with very little hassle and no ceremony whatsoever. There is actually a *lot* going on behind the scenes, but we'll leave all of that to Part III. You can also see that we can call `.ToString()` on the query to get the query text from the RavenDB client API.

Let's look at an aggregation query. The code in Listing 2.10 gives us the results of all the tasks per day.

If you're familiar with LINQ, there isn't much to say about the code in Listing 2.10. It works, and it's obvious and easy to understand. If you *aren't* familiar with LINQ and working with the .NET platform, I strongly recommend learning it. From the consumer side, Linq is quite beautiful. Now, if you were to implement querying using LINQ, it's utterly atrocious – take it from someone who's done it a few times. But lucky for you, that isn't *your* problem. It's ours.

Listing 2.10 *Aggregation query on tasks*

```
using (var session = store.OpenSession())
{
    var tasksPerDay =
        from t in session.Query<ToDoTask>()
        group t by t.DueDate into g
        select new
        {
            DueDate = g.Key,
            TasksPerDate = g.Count()
        };

    // from ToDoTasks
    // group by DueDate
    // select key() as DueDate, count() as TasksPerDate
    Console.WriteLine(tasksPerDay.ToString());

    foreach (var tpd in tasksPerDay)
    {
        Console.WriteLine($"{tpd.DueDate} - {tpd.TasksPerDate}");
    }
}
```

So far, we've explored the RavenDB API a bit, saved documents, edited a task and queried the tasks in various ways. This was intended to familiarize you with the API and how to work with RavenDB. The client API was designed to be very simple, focusing on the common CRUD scenarios. Deleting a document is as easy as calling `session.Delete`, and all the complex options that you would need are packed inside the `session.Advanced` property.

Now that you have a basic understanding of how to write a `Hello World` in RavenDB, we're ready to dig deeper and see the client API in all its glory.

2.5. The client API

We've already used a document store to talk with a RavenDB server. At the time, did you wonder what its purpose is? The document store is the main entry point for the whole client API. It holds the server URLs, for one. (So far we used only a single server, but in many cases, our data can span across multiple nodes.) It also holds the default database we will want to operate on, as well as the X509 client certificate that will be used to authenticate ourselves to the server. Its importance goes beyond connection management, so let's take a closer look at it.

2.5.1. THE DOCUMENT STORE

The document store holds all the client-side configuration, including serialization configuration, failover behavior, caching options and much more. In a typical application, you'll have a single document-store instance per application (singleton). Because of that, the document store is thread safe, with an initialization pattern that typically looks like the code in Listing 2.11.

Listing 2.11 *Common pattern for initialization of the DocumentStore*

```
public class DocumentStoreHolder
{
    private readonly static Lazy<IDocumentStore> _store =
        new Lazy<IDocumentStore>(CreateDocumentStore);

    private static IDocumentStore CreateDocumentStore()
    {
        var documentStore = new DocumentStore
        {
            Urls = // urls of the nodes in the RavenDB Cluster
            {
                "https://ravendb-01:8080",
                "https://ravendb-02:8080",
                "https://ravendb-03:8080",
            },
            Certificate =
                new X509Certificate2("tasks.pfx"),
            Database = "Tasks",
        };

        documentStore.Initialize();
        return documentStore;
    }

    public static IDocumentStore Store
    {
        get { return _store.Value; }
    }
}
```

The use of "Lazy" ensures that the document store is only created once, without you having to worry about double locking or explicit thread safety issues. And you can configure the document store as you see fit. The rest of the code can access the document store using `DocumentStoreHolder.Store`. That should be relatively rare since, apart from configuring the document store, the majority of the work is done using sessions.

Listing 2.11 shows how to configure multiple nodes, set up security and select the appropriate database. We'll learn about how to work with a RavenDB cluster in Chapter 6. We still have a lot to cover on the document store without getting to clusters, though.

2.5.1.1. Conventions

The client API, just like the rest of RavenDB, aims to *just work*. To that end, it's based on the notion of conventions: a series of policy decisions that have already been made for you. Those decisions range from which property holds the document ID to how the entity should be serialized to a document.

For the most part, we expect that you'll not have to touch the conventions. A lot of thought and effort has gone into ensuring you'll have little need to do that. But there's simply no way that we can foresee the future or anticipate every need. That's why most of the client API parts are customizable.

Customizations can be applied by changing various settings and behaviors via the `DocumentStore.Conventions` property. For example, by default, the client API will use a property named Id (case sensitive) to store the document ID. But there are users who want to use the entity name as part of the property name. So they'll have OrderId for orders, ProductId for products, etc. [2]

Here's how we tell the client API to apply the TypeName + Id policy:

```
documentStore.Conventions.FindIdentityProperty =
    prop => prop.Name == prop.DeclaringType.Name + "Id";
```

Don't worry. We won't go over all of the available options, since there are quite a few of them. Please refer to the online documentation to get the full list of available conventions and their effects. It might be worth your time to go over and quickly study them just to know what's available to you, even if they aren't something that you'll touch all that often (or ever).

Beside the conventions, there are certain settings available directly from the document store level that you should be aware of, like default request timeouts, caching configuration and event handlers. We'll cover all of those later on. But for now, let's focus on authentication.

---

2   I'll leave aside Id vs. ID, since it's handled in the same manner.

2.5.1.2. Authentication

A database holds a lot of information. Usually, it's pretty important that you have control over who can access that information and what they can do with it. RavenDB fully supports this notion.

In development mode, you'll most commonly work in an unsecured mode, which implies that any connection will be automatically granted cluster administrator privileges. This reduces the number of things that you have to do upfront. But as easy as that is for development, for production, you'll want to run in a secure fashion. After doing so, all access to the server is restricted to authenticated users only.

> **Caution: unsecured network-accessible databases are bad for you.**
>
> By default, RavenDB will refuse to listen to anything but `localhost` in an unsecured mode. This is done for security reasons, to prevent admins from accidentally exposing RavenDB without authentication over the network. If you attempt to configure a non-localhost URL with authentication disabled, RavenDB will answer all requests with an error page explaining the situation and giving instructions on how to fix the issue.
>
> You can let RavenDB know this is something you actually want, if you're running on a secure and isolated network. It requires an additional and explicit step to make sure this is your conscious choice and not an admin oversight.

RavenDB uses `X509` client certificates for authentication. The good thing about certificates is that they're *not* users. They're not tied to a specific person or need to be managed as such. Instead, they represent specific access that was granted to the database for a particular reason. I find that this is a much more natural way to handle authentication, and typically `X509` client certificates are granted on a per application / role basis.

A much deeper discussion of authentication, managing certificates and security in general can be found in the Chapter 13.

2.5.2. THE DOCUMENT SESSION

The session (also called "document session", but we usually shorten it to just "session") is the primary way your code interacts with RavenDB. If you're familiar with Hibernate (Java), Entity Framework (.NET) or Active Record (Ruby), you should feel right at home. The RavenDB session was explicitly modeled to make it easy to work with.

> **Terminology**
>
> We tend to use the term "document" to refer both to the actual documents on the server and to manipulating them, on the client side. It's common to say, "load that document and then…" But occasionally, we need to be more precise.

We make a distinction between a document and an entity (or aggregate root). A document is the server-side representation, while an entity is the client-side equivalent. An entity is the deserialized document that you work with in the client-side and save back to the database to become an updated server-side document.

We've already gone over the basics previously in this chapter, so you should be familiar with basic CRUD operations using the session. Let's look at the session with a bit more scrutiny. One of the main design forces behind RavenDB was the idea that it should *just work*. And the client API reflects that principle. If you look at the surface API for the session, here are the following high level options:

- Load()
- Include()
- Delete()
- Query()
- Store()
- SaveChanges()
- Advanced

Those are the most common operations that you'll run into on a day-to-day basis. And more options are available under the Advanced property.

Disposing the session

The .NET implementation of the client API holds resources that must be freed. Whenever you make use of the session, be sure to wrap the variable in a using statement or else do something to ensure proper disposal. Not doing so can force the RavenDB client to clean up using the finalizer thread, which can in turn increase the time it takes to release the acquired resources.

2.5.2.1. Load

Even though we called Load<ToDoTask>("ToDoTasks/1-A") twice, there's only a single remote call to the server and only a single instance of the ToDoTask class. Whenever you load a document, it's added to an internal dictionary that the session manages, and the session checks the dictionary to see if the document is already there. If so, it will return the existing instance immediately. This helps avoid aliasing issues and also generally helps performance.

As the name implies, this gives you the option of loading a document or a set of documents into the session. A document loaded into the session is managed by the session. Any changes made to the document would be persisted to the database when you call SaveChanges. A document can only be loaded once in a session. Let's look at the following code:

```
var t1 = session.Load<ToDoTask>("ToDoTasks/1-A");
var t2 = session.Load<ToDoTask>("ToDoTasks/1-A");

Assert.True(Object.ReferenceEquals(t1, t2));
```

For those of you who deal with patterns, the session implements the Unit of Work and Identity Map patterns. This is most obvious when talking about the Load operation, but it also applies to Query and Delete.

Load can also be used to read more than a single document at a time. For example, if I wanted three documents, I could use:

```
Dictionary<string, ToDoTask> tasks = session.Load<ToDoTask>(
    "ToDoTasks/1-A",
    "ToDoTasks/2-A",
    "ToDoTasks/3-A"
);
```

This will result in a dictionary with all three documents in it, retrieved in a single remote call from the server. If a document we tried to load wasn't found on the server, the dictionary will contain null for that document ID.

Budgeting remote calls

Probably the easiest way to kill your application performance is to make a lot of remote calls. And a likely culprit is the database. It's common to see a web application making dozens of calls to the database to service a single request, usually for no good reason. In RavenDB, we've done several things to mitigate that problem. The most important among them is to allocate a budget for every session. Typically, a session would encompass a single operation in your system. An HTTP request or the processing of a single message is usually the lifespan of a session.

A session is limited by default to a maximum of 30 calls to the server. If you try to make more than 30 calls to the server, an exception is thrown. This serves as an early warning that your code is generating too much load on the system and is a circuit breaker.[3]

You can increase the budget, of course, but just having that warning in place ensures that you'll think about the number of remote calls you're making.

---

3   See Release It!, a wonderful book that heavily influenced the RavenDB design.

The limited number of calls allowed per session also means that RavenDB has a lot of options to reduce the number of calls. When you call SaveChanges(), you don't need to make a separate call per changed entity; you can go to the database once. In the same manner, we also allow you to batch read calls. We'll discuss the Lazy feature in more depth in Chapter 4.

The client API is pretty smart about it. If you try to load a document that was already loaded (directly or via Include), the session can serve it directly from the session cache. And if the document doesn't exist, the session will also remember that it couldn't load that document and will immediately return null rather than attempt to load the document again.

2.5.2.2. *Working with multiple documents*

We've seen how to work with a single document, and we even saved a batch of several documents into RavenDB in a single transaction. But we haven't actually worked with anything more complex than a ToDoTask. That's pretty limiting, in terms of the amount of complexity we can express. Listing 2.12 lets us add the notion of people who can be assigned tasks to the model.

Listing 2.12 *People and Tasks model in RavenDB*

```
public class Person
{
    public string Id { get; set; }
    public string Name { get; set; }
}

public class ToDoTask
{
    public string Id { get; set; }
    public string Task { get; set; }
    public bool Completed { get; set; }
    public DateTime DueDate { get; set; }

    public string AssignedTo { get; set; }
    public string CreatedBy { get; set; }
}
```

From looking at the model in Listing 2.12, we can learn a few interesting tidbits. First, we can see that each class stands on its own. We don't have a Person property on ToDoTask or a Tasks collection on Person. We'll learn about modeling more extensively in Chapter 3, but the gist of modeling in RavenDB is that each document is independent, isolated and coherent.

What does this mean? It means we should be able to take a single document and work with it successfully without having to look at or load additional documents. The easiest way to conceptualize this is to think about physical documents. With a physical document, I'm able to pick it up and read it, and it should make sense. References to other locations may be frequent, but there will usually be enough information in the document itself that I don't *have* to go and read those references.

In the case of the ToDoTask, I can look at my tasks, create new tasks or mark them as completed without having to look at the Person document. This is quite a shift from working with relational databases, where traversing between rows and tables is very common and frequently required.

Let's see how we can create a new task and assign it to a person. Listing 2.13 shows an interesting feature of RavenDB. Take a look and see if you can find the oddity.

Listing 2.13 *Creating a new person document*

```
using (var session = store.OpenSession())
{
    var person = new Person
    {
        Name = "Oscar Arava"
    };
    session.Store(person);
    Console.WriteLine(person.Id);
    session.SaveChanges();
}
```

RavenDB is transactional, and we only send the request to the server on SaveChanges. So how could we print the person.Id property before we called SaveChanges? Later in this chapter, we'll cover document identifiers and how they're generated, but the basic idea is that the moment we returned from Store, the RavenDB client ensured that we had a valid ID to use with this document. As you can see with Listing 2.14, this can be quite important when you're creating two documents at the same time, with references between them.

Now that we know how to write multiple documents and create associations between documents, let's see how we read them back. There's a catch, though. We want to do it efficiently.

Listing 2.14 *Creating a new person and assigning him a task at the same time*

```
using (var session = store.OpenSession())
{
    var person = new Person
    {
        Name = "Oscar Arava"
    };
    session.Store(person);

    var task = new ToDoTask
    {
        DueDate = DateTime.Today.AddDays(1),
        Task = "Buy milk",
        AssignedTo = person.Id,
        CreatedBy = person.Id
    };
    session.Store(task);
    session.SaveChanges();
}
```

2.5.2.3. Includes

RavenDB doesn't actually *have* references in the usual sense. There's no such thing as foreign keys, like you might be used to. A reference to another document is just a string property that happens to contains the ID of another document. What does this mean for working with the data? Let's say that we want to print the details of a particular task, including the name of the person assigned to it. Listing 2.15 shows the obvious way to do this.

This code works, but it's inefficient. We're making *two* calls to the server here, one to fetch the task and another to fetch the assigned user. The last line of Listing 2.15 prints how many requests we made to the server. This is part of the budgeting and awareness program RavenDB has, aimed at reducing the number of remote calls and speeding up your applications.

Error handling

Listing 2.15 really bugged me when I wrote it, mostly because there's a lot of error handling that isn't being done: the task ID being empty, the task document not existing, the task not being assigned to anyone…you get the drift. I just wanted to mention that most code samples in this book will contain as little error handling as possible so as not to distract from the code that actually *does* things.

Listing 2.15 *Displaying the details of a task (and its assigned person)*

```
using (var session = store.OpenSession())
{
    string taskId = Console.ReadLine();

    ToDoTask task = session.Load<ToDoTask>(taskId);
    Person assignedTo = session.Load<Person>(task.AssignedTo);

    Console.WriteLine(
        $"{task.Id} - {task.Task} by {assignedTo.Name}");

    // will print 2
    Console.WriteLine(session.Advanced.NumberOfRequests);
}
```

Having to go to the database twice is a pity because the server already knows the value of the AssignedTo property, and it could send the document that matches the value of that property at the same time it's sending us the task. RavenDB's Includes functionality, which handles this in one step, is a favorite feature of mine because I still remember how excited I was when we finally figured out how to do this in a clean fashion. Look at Listing 2.16 to see how it works, and compare it to Listing 2.15.

The only difference between the two code listings is that in Listing 2.16 we're calling to Include before the Load. The Include method gives instructions to RavenDB: when it loads the document, it should look at the AssignedTo property. If there's a document with the document ID that's stored in the AssignedTo property, it should send it to the client immediately.

However, we didn't change the type of the task variable. It remains a ToDoTask. So what exactly did this Include method do here? What happened is that the session got a reply from the server, saw that there are included documents, and put them in its Identity Map. When we request the Person instance that was assigned to this task, we already have that information in the session and can avoid going back to the server to fetch the same document we already have.

The API is almost the same – and except for that call, everything else remains the same – but we managed to significantly cut the number of remote calls we make. You can Include multiple properties to load several referenced documents (or even a collection of them) efficiently. This is similar to a JOIN in a relational database, but it's much more efficient since you don't have to deal with Cartesian products and it doesn't modify the shape of the results.

Listing 2.16 *Task and assigned person - single roundtrip*

```
using (var session = store.OpenSession())
{
    string taskId = Console.ReadLine();

    ToDoTask task = session
              .Include<ToDoTask>(x => x.AssignedTo)
              .Load(taskId);

    Person assignedTo = session.Load<Person>(task.AssignedTo);

    Console.WriteLine(
      $"{task.Id} - {task.Task} by {assignedTo.Name}");

    // will print 1
    Console.WriteLine(session.Advanced.NumberOfRequests);
}
```

Includes aren't joins

It's tempting to think about includes in RavenDB as similar to a join in a relational database. And there are similarities, but there are also fundamental differences. A join will modify the shape of the output. It combines each matching row from one side with each matching row on the other, sometimes creating Cartesian products that can cause panic attacks for your DBAs.

And the more complex your model, the more joins you'll have, the wider your result sets become and the slower your application will become. In RavenDB, there's very little cost to adding includes. That's because they operate on a different channel than the results of the operation and don't change the shape of the returned data.

Includes are also important in queries. There, they operate *after* paging has applied, instead of before, like joins.

The end result is that includes don't modify the shape of the output, don't have a high cost when you use more than one of them and don't suffer from problems like Cartesian products.

Include cannot, however, be used to include documents that are referenced by included documents. In other words, Include is not recursive. This is quite intentional because allowing includes on included documents will lead to complex requests, both for the user to write and understand

and for the server to execute. You *can* actually do recursive includes in RavenDB, but that feature is exposed differently (via the declare function mode, which we'll cover in Chapter 9).

Using multiple Includes on the same operation, however, is just fine. Let's load a task, and with it we'll include both the assigned to person and the one who created the task. This can be done using the following snippet:

```
ToDoTask task = session.Include<ToDoTask>(x => x.AssignedTo)
                       .Include(x => x.CreatedBy)
                       .Load(taskId);
```

Now I can load both the AssignedTo person and the CreatedBy one, and there's still only a single round trip to the server. What about when both of them are pointing at the same document? RavenDB will return just a single copy of the document, even if it was included multiple times. On the session side of things, you'll get the same instance of the entity when you load it multiple times.

> **Beware of relational modeling inside of RavenDB**
>
> As powerful as the Include feature is, one of *the* most common issues we run into with RavenDB is people using it with a relational mindset – trying to use RavenDB as if it was a relational database and modeling their entities accordingly. Include can help push you that way because it lets you get associated documents easily.

We'll talk about modeling in a lot more depth in the next chapter, when you've learned enough about the kind of environment that RavenDB offers to make sense of the choices we'll make.

2.5.2.4. Delete

Deleting a document is done through the appropriately named Delete method. This method can accept an entity instance or a document ID. The following are various ways to delete a document:

```
var task = session.Load<ToDoTask>("ToDoTasks/1-A");
session.Delete(task); // delete by instance

session.Delete("ToDoTasks/1-A"); // delete by ID
```

It's important to note that calling Delete doesn't actually delete the document. It merely marks that document as deleted in the session. It's only when SaveChanges is called that the document will be deleted.

2.5.2.5. Query

Querying is a large part of what RavenDB does. Not surprisingly, queries strongly relate to indexes, and we'll talk about those extensively in Part III. You've already seen some basic queries in this chapter, so you know how we can query to find documents that match a particular predicate, using LINQ.

Like documents loaded via the `Load` call, documents that were loaded via a `Query` are managed by the session. Modifying them and calling `SaveChanges` will result in their update on the server. A document that was returned via a query and was loaded into the session explicitly via `Load` will still have only a single instance in the session and will retain all the changes that were made to it.[4]

Queries in RavenDB don't behave like queries in a relational database. RavenDB doesn't allow computation during queries, and it doesn't have problems with table scans or slow queries. We'll touch on exactly why and cover details about indexing in Part III, but for now you can see that most queries will *just work* for you.

2.5.2.6. Store

The `Store` command is how you associate an entity with the session. Usually, this is done because you want to create a new document. We've already seen this method used several times in this chapter, but here's the relevant part:

```
var person = new Person
{
  Name = "Oscar Arava"
};
session.Store(person);
```

Like the `Delete` command, `Store` will only save the document to the database when `SaveChanges` is called. However, it will give the new entity an ID immediately, so you can refer to it in other documents that you'll save in the same batch.

Beyond saving a new entity, `Store` is also used to associate entities of existing documents with the session. This is common in web applications. You have one endpoint that sends the entity to the user, who modifies that entity and then sends it back to your web application. You have a live entity instance, but it's not loaded by a session or tracked by it.

At that point, you can call `Store` on that entity, and because it doesn't have a null document ID, it will be treated as an existing document and overwrite the previous version on the database side. This is instead of having to load the database version, update it and then save it back.

---

4   You can call `session.Advanced.Refresh` if you want to force the session to update the state of the document from the server.

Store can also be used in optimistic concurrency scenarios, but we'll talk about this in more detail in Chapter 4.

2.5.2.7. SaveChanges

The SaveChanges call will check the session state for all deletions and changes. It will then send all of those to the server as a single remote call that will complete transactionally. In other words, either all the changes are saved as a single unit or none of them are.

Remember that the session has an internal map of all loaded entities. When you call SaveChanges, those loaded entities are checked against the entity as it was when it was loaded from the database. If there are any changes, that entity will be saved to the database.

It's important to understand that any change would force the entire entity to be saved. We don't attempt to make partial document updates in SaveChanges. An entity is always saved to a document as a single full change.

The typical way one would work with the session is:

```
using (var session = documentStore.OpenSession())
{
    // do some work with the session

    session.SaveChanges();
}
```

So SaveChanges is usually only called once per session, although there's nothing wrong with calling it multiple times. If the session detects that there have been no changes to the entities, it will skip calling the server entirely.

With this, we conclude the public surface area of the session. Those methods allow us to do about 90% of everything you could wish for with RavenDB. For the other 10%, we need to look at the Advanced property.

2.5.2.8. Advanced

The surface area of the session was carefully designed so that the common operations were just a method call away from the session, and that there would be few of them. But while this covers many of the most common scenarios, it isn't enough to cover them all.

All of the extra options are hiding inside the Advanced property. You can use them to configure the behavior of optimistic concurrency on a per-session basis using:

```
session.Advanced.UseOptimisticConcurrency = true;
```

Or you can define it once globally by modifying the conventions:

```
documentStore.Conventions.UseOptimisticConcurrency = true;
```

You can force a reload of an entity from the database to get the changes made since the entity was last loaded:

```
session.Advanced.Refresh(product);
```

And you can make the session forget about an entity completely (it won't track it, apply changes, etc.):

```
session.Advanced.Evict(product);
```

I'm not going to go over the `Advanced` options here. There are quite a few, and they're covered in the documentation quite nicely. It's worth taking the time to read about, even if you'll rarely need the extra options.

Hiding the session: avoid the `IRepository` mess

A common problem we see with people using the client API is that they frequently start by defining their own data access layer, usually named `IRepository` or something similar.

This is generally a bad idea. We've only started to scratch the surface of the client API, and you can already see there are plenty of valuable features (`Includes`, optimistic concurrency, change tracking). Hiding behind a generic interface typically results in one of two situations:

- ❖ Because a generic interface doesn't expose the relevant (and useful) features of RavenDB, you're stuck with using the lowest common denominator. That means you give up a lot of power and flexibility, and in 99% of cases, the interface won't allow you to switch between data store implementations.[5]
- ❖ The second situation is that, because of issues mentioned in the previous point, you expose the RavenDB features behind the `IRepository`. In this case, you're already tied to the RavenDB client, but you added another layer that doesn't do much but increase code complexity. This can make it hard to understand what's actually going on.

The client API is meant to be easy to use and high level enough that you'll not need to wrap it for convenience's sake. In all likelihood, if you do wrap it, you'll just wind up forwarding calls back and forth.

One thing that's absolutely wrong to do, however, is to have methods like `T IRepository.Get<T>(string id)` that will create and dispose of a session

---

5   The 1% case where it will help is the realm of demo apps with little to no functionality

within the scope of the Get method call. That cancels out a *lot* of optimizations, behaviors and functionality,[6] and it would be a real shame for you to lose these features of RavenDB.

2.5.3. THE ASYNC SESSION

So far, we've shown only synchronous work with the client API. But async support is crucial for high performance applications. That's why RavenDB has full support for it. In fact, that's the recommended mode, and the synchronous version is actually built on top of the async version. The async API is exposed via the async session. In all respects, it's identical to the sync version.

Listing 2.17 *Working with the async session*

```
using (var session = documentStore.OpenAsyncSession())
{
    var person = new Person
    {
        Name = "Oscar Arava"
    };
    await session.StoreAsync(person);
    await session.SaveChangesAsync();
}
using (var session = documentStore.OpenAsyncSession())
{
    var tasksPerDayQuery =
        from t in session.Query<ToDoTask>()
        group t by t.DueDate into g
        select new
        {
            DueDate = g.Key,
            TasksPerDate = g.Count()
        };
    List<ToDoTask> tasksToDo = await tasksPerDayQuery.ToListAsync();

    foreach (var task in tasksToDo)
    {
        Console.WriteLine($"{task.Id} - {task.Task} - {task.DueDate}");
    }
}
```

6   Unit of Work won't work. Neither will change tracking, optimistic concurrency you'll have to deal with manually, etc.

Listing 2.17 shows a few examples of working with the async session. For the rest of the book, we'll use both the async and synchronous sessions to showcase features and behavior of RavenDB.

RavenDB splits the sync and async API because their use cases are quite different, and having separate APIs prevents you from doing some operations synchronously and some operations asynchronously. Because of that, you can't mix and use the synchronous session with async calls or vice versa. You can use either mode in your application, depending on the environment you're using. Aside from the minor required API changes, they're completely identical.

The async support is deep – all the way to the I/O issued to the server. In fact, as I mentioned earlier, the synchronous API is built on top of the async API and async I/O.

We covered the basics of working with the client API in this section, but that was mostly mechanics. We'll dive deeper into using RavenDB in the next chapter, where we'll also learn how it's all put together.

2.5.4. GOING BELOW THE SESSION

"Ogres are like onions," said Shrek. In a way, so is the client API. At the top, and what you'll usually interact with, are the document store and the document session. They, in turn, are built on top of the notion of `Operations` and `Commands`. An `Operation` is a high level concept, such as loading a document from the server.

> **Deep dive note**
>
> I'm going to take a small detour to explain how the client API is structured internally. This shouldn't have an impact on how you're *using* the client API, but it might help you better understand how the client is put together. Feel free to skip this section for now and come back to it at a later date.

The `LoadOperation` is the canonical example of this. A session `Load` or `LoadAsync` will translate into a call to the `LoadOperation`, which will run all the associated logic (`Identity Map`, `Include` tracking, etc.) up to the point where it will make a call to the server. That portion is handled by the `GetDocumentCommand`, which knows how to ask the server for a document (or a set of documents) and how to parse the server reply.

The same `GetDocumentCommand` is also used by the `session.Advanced.Refresh` method to get an updated version of the document from the server. You won't typically be using any of that directly, going instead through the session. Occasions to use an `Operation` directly usually arise when you're writing some sort of management code, such as Listing 2.18, which creates a new database on the cluster.

Listing 2.18 *Creating a database named 'Orders' using Operation*

```
var dbRecord = new DatabaseRecord("Orders");
var createDbOp = new CreateDatabaseOperation(dbRecord);
documentStore.Admin.Server.Send(createDbOp);
```

A lot of the management functionality (creating and deleting databases, assigning   sions, changing configuration, etc.) is available as operations that can be invoked in such a manner.

In other cases, you can use an `Operation` to run something that doesn't make sense in the context of a session. For example, let's say I wanted to delete all of the tasks in the database. I could do it with the following code:

```
store.Operations.Send(new DeleteByQueryOperation(
    new IndexQuery { Query = "from ToDoTasks" }
));
```

The reason that the tasks are exposed to the user is that the RavenDB API, at all levels, is built with the notion of layers. The expectation is that you'll usually work with the highest layer: the session API. But since we can't predict all things, we also provide access to the lower level API, on top of which the session API is built, so you can use it if you need to.

2.6. Document identifiers in RavenDB

The document ID is a unique string that globally identifies a document inside a RavenDB database. A document ID can be any UTF8 string up to 2025 bytes, although getting to those sizes is extremely rare. You've already seen document IDs used in this chapter – `people/1-A`, `ToDoTasks/4-A` and the like. Using a `Guid` like `92260D13-A032-4BCC-9D18-10749898AE1C` is possible but not recommended because it's opaque and hard to read/work with.

By convention, we typically use the collection name as the prefix, a slash and then the actual unique portion of the key. But you can also call your document `hello/world` or `what-a-wonderful-world`. For the adventurous, Unicode is also a valid option. The character U+1F426 is a valid document ID, and trying to use it in RavenDB is possible, as you can see in Figure 2.12. Amusingly enough, trying to include a raw emoji character broke the build for this book.

While going full-on emoji for document identifiers might be going too far[7], using Unicode for document IDs means that you don't have to worry if you need to insert a Unicode character (such as someone's name).

---

7   Although, when you think about it, there's a huge untapped market of teenage developers…

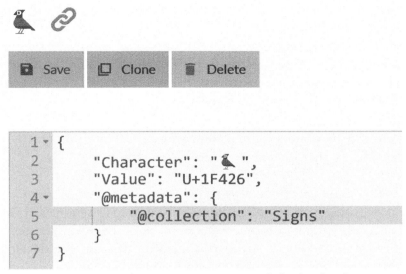

Figure 2.12. *Unicode gave us Emojis, and the birdie document*

RavenDB and Unicode

I hope it goes without saying that RavenDB has full support for Unicode. Storing and retrieving documents, querying on Unicode data and pretty much any related actions are supported. I haven't talked about it so far because it seems like an obvious requirement, but I think it's better to state this support explicitly.

So RavenDB document IDs are Unicode strings up to 2025 bytes in length, which must be globally unique in the scope of the database. This is unlike a relational database, in which a primary key must only be unique in the scope of its table. This has never been a problem because we typically use the collection name as the prefix to the document key. Usually, but not always, there's no requirement that a document in a specific collection will use the collection name prefix as the document key. There are a few interesting scenarios that open up because of this feature, discussed later in this section.

Human-readable document IDs

Usually, we strongly recommend to have document IDs that are human-readable (ToDoTasks/123-A, people/oscar@arava.example). We often use identifiers for many purposes. Debugging and troubleshooting are not the least of those.

A simple way to generate IDs is to just generate a new Guid, such as 92260D13-A032-4BBC-9D18-10749898AE1C. But if you've ever had to read a Guid over the phone, keep track of multiple Guids in a log file or just didn't realize that the Guid in this paragraph and the one at the start of this section aren't, in fact, the same Guid...

If you're anything like me, you went ahead and compared the two Guids to see if they actually didn't match. Given how hard finding the difference is, I believe the point is made. Guids are not friendly, and we want to avoid having to deal with them on an ongoing basis if we can avoid it.

So pretty much the only thing we require is some way to generate a unique ID as the document ID. Let's see the strategies that RavenDB uses to allow that.

2.6.1. SEMANTIC (EXTERNAL) DOCUMENT IDENTIFIERS

The most obvious way to get an identifier is to ask the user to generate it. This is typically done when you want an identifier that's of some meaningful value. For example, accounts/591-192 or people/oscar@arava.example are two document IDs that the developer can choose. Listing 2.19 shows how you can provide an external identifier when creating documents.

Listing 2.19 *Saving a new person with an externally defined document ID*

```
using (var session = store.OpenSession())
{
    var person = new Person
    {
        Name = "Oscar Arava"
    };
    session.Store(person, "people/oscar@arava.example");
    session.SaveChanges();
}
```

The people/oscar@arava.example example, which uses an email address in the document identifier, is a common technique to generate a human-readable document identifier that makes it easy to locate a document based on a user provided value (the email). While the accounts/591-192 example uses a unique key that's defined in another system. This is common if you're integrating with existing systems or have an external feed of data into your database.

2.6.2. NESTED DOCUMENT IDENTIFIERS

A special case of external document naming is when we want to handle nested documents. Let's consider a financial system that needs to track accounts and transactions on those accounts. We have our account document accounts/591-192, but we also have all the financial transactions concerning this account that we need to track.

We'll discuss this exact scenario in the next chapter, where we'll talk about modeling, but for now I'll just say that it isn't practical to hold all the transactions directly inside the account document. So we need to put the transactions in separate documents. We *could* identify those documents using `transactions/1234-A`, `transactions/1235-A`, etc. It would work, but there are better ways.

We're going to store the transaction information on a per-day basis, using identifiers that embed both the owner account and the time of the transactions: `accounts/591-192/txs/2017-05-17`. This document holds all the transactions for the 591-192 account for May 17th, 2017.

RavenDB doesn't care about your document IDs

RavenDB treats the document IDs as opaque values and doesn't attach any meaning to a document whose key is the prefix of other documents. In other words, as far as RavenDB is concerned, the only thing that `accounts/591-192` and `accounts/591-192/txs/2017-05-17` have in common is that they're both documents.

In practice, the document IDs are stored in a sorted fashion inside RavenDB, and it allows for efficient scanning of all documents with a particular prefix quite cheaply. But this is a secondary concern. What we're really trying to achieve here is to make sure our document IDs are very clear about their contents.

You might recall that I mentioned that RavenDB doesn't require documents within a given collection to be have an ID with the collection prefix. This is one of the major reasons why – because it allows you to nest document IDs to get yourself a clearer model of your documents.

2.6.3. CLIENT-SIDE IDENTIFIER GENERATION (HILO)

External identifiers and nesting document IDs are nice, but they tend to be the exception rather than the rule. For the most part, when we create documents, we don't want to have to think about what IDs we should be giving them. We want RavenDB to just handle that for us.

RavenDB is a distributed database

A minor wrinkle in generating identifiers with RavenDB is that the database is distributed and capable of handling writes on any of the nodes without requiring coordination between them. On the plus side, it means that in the presence of failures we stay up and are able to process requests and writes. On the other hand, it can create non-trivial complexities.

If two clients try to create a new document on two nodes in parallel, we need to ensure that they will not accidentally create documents with the same ID.[8]

---

8   If the user explicitly specified the document ID, there's nothing that RavenDB *can* do here. But for IDs that are being generated by RavenDB (client or server), we can do better than just hope that we'll have no collisions.

It's important to note, even at this early date, that such conflicts are part of life in any distributed database, and RavenDB contains several ways to handle them (this is discussed in Chapter 6 in more detail).

Another wrinkle that we need to consider is that we really want to be able to generate document IDs on the client, since that allows us to write code that creates a new document and uses its ID immediately, in the same transaction. Otherwise, we'll need to call to the server to get the ID, then make use of this ID in a separate transaction.

RavenDB handles this by using an algorithm called `hilo`. The concept is pretty simple. The first time you need to generate an identifier, you reserve a *range* of identifiers from the server. The server is responsible for ensuring it will only provide that range to a single client. Multiple clients can ask for ranges at the same time, and they will receive different ranges. Each client can then safely generate identifiers within the range it was given, without requiring any further coordination between client and server.

This is extremely efficient, and it scales nicely. RavenDB uses a dynamic range allocation scheme, in which the ranges provided to the client can expand if the client is very busy and generates a lot of identifiers very quickly (thus consuming the entire range quickly).

This is the default approach in RavenDB and the one we've used so far in this book. There's still another wrinkle to deal with, though. What happens if two clients request ID ranges from two different nodes at the same time? At this point, each node is operating independently (indeed, a network failure might mean that we aren't *able* to talk to other nodes). In order to handle this scenario properly, each range is also stamped with the ID of the node that assigned that range. This way, even if those two clients have managed to get the same range from each node, the generated IDs will be unique.

Let's assume the first client got the range 128 - 256 from node A and the second client got the same range from node B. The `hilo` method on the first client will generate document IDs like `people/128-A`, `people/129-A`, and on the second client, it will generate `people/128-B`, `people/129-B`, etc. These are different documents. Using shorthand to refer to documents using just the numeric portion of the ID is common, but pay attention to the full ID as well.

It's important to note that this scenario rarely occurs. Typically, the nodes can talk to one another and share information about the provided ID ranges. Even if they can't, all clients will typically try to use the same server for getting the ranges, so you need multiple concurrent failures to cause this. If it *does* happen, RavenDB will handle it smoothly, and the only impact is that you'll have a few documents with similar IDs. A minor consideration indeed.

2.6.4. SERVER-SIDE IDENTIFIER GENERATION

Hilo is quite nice, as it generates human-readable and predictable identifiers. However, it requires both client and server to cooperate to get to the end result. This is not an issue if you're using any of the client APIs, but if you're writing documents directly (using the RavenDB Studio, for example) or don't care to assign the IDs yourself, there are additional options.

You can ask RavenDB to assign a document ID to a new document when it is saved. You do that by providing a document ID that ends with the slash (/). Go into the RavenDB Studio and create a new document. Enter in the ID the value `tryouts/` and then click on the `Save` button. The generated document ID should look something like Figure 2.13.

tryouts/0000000000000000021-A

Figure 2.13. *Server side generated document ID (tryouts/0000000000000000021-A)*

When you save a document whose ID ends with a slash, RavenDB will generate the ID for you by appending a numeric value (the only guarantee you have about this value is that it's always increasing) and the node ID.

> **Don't generate similar IDs manually**
>
> Due to the way we implement server-side identifier generation, we can be sure that RavenDB will never generate an ID that was previously generated. That allows us to skip some checks in the save process (avoid a B+Tree lookup). Since server-side generation is typically used for large batch jobs, this can have a significant impact on performance.
>
> What this means is that if you manually generate a document ID with a pattern that matches the server-side generated IDs, RavenDB will not check for that and may *overwrite* the existing document. That's partly why we're putting all those zeros in the ID – to make sure that we aren't conflicting with any existing document by accident.

This kind of ID plays quite nicely with how RavenDB actually stores the information on disk, which is convenient. We'll give this topic a bit more time further down in the chapter. This is the recommended method if you just need to generate a large number of documents, such as in bulk insert scenarios, since it will generate the least amount of work for RavenDB.

2.6.5. IDENTITY GENERATION STRATEGY

All the ID generation strategies we've outlined so far have one problem: they don't give you any promises with regards to the end result. What they do give you is an ID you can be sure will be unique, but that's all. In the vast majority of cases, this is all you need. But sometimes you need a bit more.

If you really need to have consecutive IDs, you can use the identity option. Identity, just like in a relational database (also called sequence), is a simple always-incrementing value. Unlike the `hilo` option, you always have to go to the server to generate such a value.

Generating identities is very similar to generating server-side IDs. But instead of using the slash (/) at the end of the document, you use a pipe symbol (|). In the Studio, try to save a document with the document ID `tryouts|`. The pipe character will be replaced by a slash (/) and a document with the ID `tryouts/1` will be created. Doing so again will generate `tryouts/2`, and so on.

Invoices and other tax annoyances

For the most part, unless you're using semantic IDs (covered earlier in this chapter), you shouldn't care what your document ID is. The one case you care about is when you have an outside requirement to generate absolute consecutive IDs. One such common case is when you need to generate invoices.

Most tax authorities have rules about not missing invoice numbers, to make it just a tad easier to audit your system. But an invoice document's *identifier* and the invoice *number* are two very different things.

It's entirely possible to have the document ID of `invoices/843-C` for invoice number 523. And using an identity doesn't protect you from skipping values because documents have been deleted or a failed transaction consumed the identity and now there's a hole in the sequence.

For people coming from a relational database background, the identity option usually seems to be the best one, since it's what they're most familiar with. But updating an identity happens in a *separate transaction* from the current one. In other words, if we try to save a document with the ID `invoices|` and the transaction fails, the identity value is still incremented. So even though identity generated consecutive numbers, it might still skip identifiers if a transaction has been rolled back.

Except for very specific requirements, such as a legal obligation to generate consecutive numbers, I would strongly recommend not using identity. Note my wording here. A legal obligation doesn't arise because someone wants consecutive IDs since they are easier to grasp. Identity has a real cost associated with it.

The biggest problem with identities is that generating them in a distributed database requires us to do a lot more work than one might think. In order to prevent races, such as two clients generating the same identity on two different servers, part of the process of generating a new identity requires the nodes to coordinate with one another.[9]

That means we need to go over the network and talk to the other members in the cluster to guarantee we have the next value of the identity. That can increase the cost of saving a new document with identity. What's worse is that, under failure scenarios, we might not be able to

---

9   This is done using the Raft consensus protocol, which covered in Chapter 6.

communicate with a sufficient number of nodes in our cluster. This means we'll also be unable to generate the requested identity.

Because we *guarantee* that identities are always consecutive across the cluster, if there's a failure scenario that prevents us from talking to a majority of the nodes, we'll not be able to generate the identity at all, and we'll fail to save the new document. All the other ID generation methods can work without issue when we're disconnected from the cluster, so unless you truly need consecutive IDs, use one of the other options.

2.6.6. PERFORMANCE IMPLICATIONS OF DOCUMENT IDENTIFIERS

We've gone over a lot of options for generating document identifiers, and each of them have their own behaviors and costs. There are also performance differences among the various methods that I want to talk about.

> **Premature optimization warning**
>
> This section is included because it's important at scale, but for most users, there's no need to consider it at all. RavenDB is going to accept whatever document IDs you throw at it, and it's going to be *very* fast when doing so. My strong recommendation is that you use whatever document ID generation that best matches *your* needs, and only consider the performance impact if you notice an observable difference – or have crossed the hundreds of millions of documents per database mark.

RavenDB keeps track of the document IDs by storing them inside a B+Tree. If the document IDs are very big, it will mean that RavenDB can pack less of them in a given space.[10]

The `hilo` algorithm generates document IDs that are lexically sortable, up to a degree (`people/2-A` is sorted after `people/100-A`). But with the exception of when we add a digit to the number[11], values are nicely sorted. This means that for the most part we get nice trees and very efficient searches. It also generates the most human-readable values.

The server-side method using the slash (`/`) generates the best values in terms of suitability for storage. They're a bit bigger than the comparable `hilo` values, but they make up for it by being always lexically sorted and predictable as far as the underlying storage is concerned. This method is well suited for large batch jobs and contains a number of additional optimizations in its codepath. (We can be sure this is a new value, so we can skip a B+Tree lookup, which matters if you are doing that a *lot*.)

Semantic IDs (`people/oscar@arava.example` or `accounts/591-192/txs/2017-05-17`) tend to be unsorted, and sometimes that can cause people to want to avoid them. But this is

---

10   RavenDB is using B+Tree for on disk storage, and uses pages of 8KB in size. Bigger document IDs means that we can fit less entries in each page, and need to traverse down the tree, requiring us to do a bit more work to find the right document. The same is true for saving unsorted document IDs, which can cause page splits and increase the depth of the tree. In nearly all cases, that doesn't really matter.

11   Rolling from 99 to 100 or from 999 to 1000.

rarely a good reason to do so. RavenDB can easily handle a large number of documents with semantic identifiers without any issue.

Running the numbers

If you're familiar with database terminology, then you're familiar with terms like B+Tree and page splits. In the case of RavenDB, we're storing document IDs separately from the actual document data, and we're making sure to coalesce the pages holding the document keys so we have a good locality of reference.

Even with a database that holds a hundred million documents, the whole of the document ID data is likely to be memory resident, which makes the cost of finding a particular document extremely cheap.

The one option you need to be cautious of is the identity generation method. Be careful not to use it without careful consideration and analysis. Identity requires network round trips to generate the next value, and it will become unavailable if the node cannot communicate with a majority of the nodes the cluster.

2.7. Document metadata

Document data is composed of whatever it is that you're storing in the document. For the order document, that would be the shipping details, the order lines, who the customer is, the order priority, etc. You also need a place to store additional information that's unrelated to the document itself but is rather *about* the document. This is where metadata comes into play.

The metadata is also in JSON format, just like the document data itself. RavenDB reserves for its own use metadata property names that start with @ , but you're free to use anything else. By convention, users' custom metadata properties use Pascal-Case capitalization. In other words, we separate words with a dash, and the first letter of each word is capitalized while everything else is in lower case. RavenDB's internal metadata properties use the @ prefix, all lower cased, with words separated by a dash (e.g., @last-modified).

RavenDB uses the metadata to store several pieces of information about the document that it keeps track of:

◆ The collection name – stored in the @collection metadata property and determines where RavenDB will store the document. If the collection isn't set, the document will be placed in the @empty collection. The client API will automatically assign an entity to a collection based on its type. (You can control exactly how using the conventions.)

◆ The last modified date – stored in the @last-modified metadata property in UTC format.

◆ The client-side type – This is a client-side metadata property. So for .NET, it will be named `Raven-Clr-Type`; for a Java client, it will be `Raven-Java-Class`; for Python, `Raven-Python-Type` and…you get the point. This is used solely by the clients to deserialize the entity into the right client-side type.

You can use the metadata to store your own values. For example, `Last-Modified-By` is a common metadata property that's added when you want to track who changed a document. From the client side, you can access the document metadata using the code in Listing 2.20.

Listing 2.20 *Modifying the metadata of a document*

```
using (var session = store.OpenSession())
{
    var task = session.Load<ToDoTask>("ToDoTasks/1-A");
    var metadata = session.Advanced.GetMetadataFor(task);
    metadata["Last-Modified-By"] = person.Name;
    session.SaveChanges();
}
```

Note that there will be no extra call to the database to fetch the metadata. Whenever you load the document, the metadata is fetched as well. That metadata is embedded inside the document and is an integral part of it.

Changing a document collection

RavenDB does *not* support changing collections, and trying to do so will raise an error. You *can* delete a document and then create a new document with the same ID in a different collection, but that tends to be confusing, so it's best to be avoided if you can.

Once you have the metadata, you can modify it as you wish, as seen in Listing 2.20. The session tracks changes to both the document and its metadata, and changes to either one of those will cause the document to be updated on the server once `SaveChanges` has been called.

Modifying the metadata in this fashion is possible, but it's pretty rare to do so explicitly in your code. Instead, you'll usually use event handlers (covered in Chapter 4) to do this sort of work.

2.8. Distributed compare-exchange operations with RavenDB

RavenDB is meant to be run in a cluster. You can run it in single-node mode, but the most common (and recommended) deployment option is with a cluster. You already saw some of the impact this has had on the design of RavenDB. Auto-generated document IDs contain the node ID that generated them to avoid conflicts between concurrent work on different nodes in the cluster.

One of the challenges of any distributed system is how to handle coordination across all the nodes in the cluster. RavenDB uses several strategies for this, discussed in Part II of this book. At this point, I want to introduce one of the tools RavenDB provides specifically in order to allow users to manage the distributed state correctly.

If you've worked with multi-threaded applications, you are familiar with many of the same challenges. Different threads can be doing different things at the same time. They may be acting on stale information or modifying the shared state. Typically, such systems use locks to coordinate the work between threads. That leads to a whole separate issue of lock contention, deadlock prevention, etc. With distributed systems, you have all the usual problems of multiple threads with the added complication that you may be operating in a partial failure state. Some of the nodes may not be able to talk to other nodes (but can still talk to *some*).

RavenDB offers a simple primitive to handle such a scenario: the compare-exchange feature. A very common primitive with multi-thread solutions is the atomic compare-and-swap operation. From code, this will be `Interlocked.CompareExchange` when using C#. Because this operation is so useful, it's supported at the hardware level with the `CMPXCHG` assembly instruction. In a similar way, RavenDB offers a distributed compare-exchange feature.

Let's take a look at Listing 2.21, for a small sample of what this looks like in code.

Listing 2.21 *Using compare exchange to validate unique username in a distributed system*

```
var cmd = new PutCompareExchangeValueOperation<string>(
    key: "names/john",
    value: "users/1-A",
    index: 0);
var result = await store.Operations.SendAsync(cmd);
if (result.Successful)
{
    // users/1-A now owns the username 'john'
}
```

The code in Listing 2.21 uses `PutCompareExchangeValueOperation` to submit a compare-exchange operation to the cluster at large. This operation compares the existing index for names/john with the expected index (in this case, 0, meaning we want to create a new value). If successful, the cluster will store the value users/1-A for the key names/john. However, if there is already a value for the key and the index does not match, the operation will fail. You'll get the existing index and the current value and can decide how to handle things from that point (show an error to the user, try writing again with the new index, etc.).

Figure 2.14. *Viewing the compare exchange values in the Studio*

The most important aspect of this feature is the fact that this is a cluster-wide, distributed operation. It is guaranteed to behave properly even if you have concurrent requests going to separate nodes. This feature is a low-level one; it is meant to be built upon by the user to provide more sophisticated features. For example, in Listing 2.21, we ensure a unique username for each user using a method that is resilient to failures, network partitions, etc.

You can see how this is exposed in the Studio in Figure 2.14.

We'll talk more about compare-exchange values in Chapter 6. For now, it's good to remember that they're there and can help you make distributed decisions in a reliable manner. A compare-exchange value isn't limited to just a string. You can also use a complex object, a counter, etc. However, remember that these are *not* documents. You can read the current value of compare-exchange value using the code in Listing 2.22. Aside from checking the current value of the key, you get the current index, which you can then use in the next call to PutCompareExchangeValueOperation.

Listing 2.22 *Reading an existing compare exchange value by name*

```
var cmd = new GetCompareExchangeValueOperation<string>("names/john");
var result = await store.Operations.SendAsync(cmd);
```

Aside from getting the value by key, there is no other way to query for the compare-exchange values. Usually you already know what the compare-exchange key will be (as in the case of creating a new username and checking the name isn't already taken). Alternatively, you can store the compare-exchange key in a document that you'll query and then use the key from the document to make the compare-exchange operation.

If you know the name of the compare-exchange value, you can use it directly in your queries, as shown in Listing 2.23.

Listing 2.23 *Querying for documents using cmpxchg() values*

```
from Users
where id() == cmpxchg('names/john')
```

The query in Listing 2.23 will find a document whose ID is located in the names/john compare-exchange value. We'll discuss this feature again in Chapter 6. This feature relies on some of the low-level details of RavenDB distributed flow, and it will make more sense once we have gone over that.

2.9. Testing with RavenDB

This chapter is quite long, but I can't complete the basics without discussing testing. When you build an application, it's important to be able to verify that your code works. That has become an accepted reality, and an application using RavenDB is no exception.

In order to aid in testing, RavenDB provides the Raven.TestDriver NuGet package. Using the test driver, you can get an instance of an IDocumentStore that talks to an in-memory database. Your tests will be very fast, they won't require you to do complex state setup before you start and they will be isolated from one another.

Listing 2.24 shows the code for a simple test that saves and loads data from RavenDB. There are two interesting things happening in the code in Listing 2.24. The code inherits from the RavenTestDriver<RavenExecLocator> class, and it uses the GetDocumentStore method to get an instance of the document store. Let's break apart what's going on.

The RavenTestDriver<T> class is the base test driver, which is responsible for setting up and tearing down databases. All your RavenDB tests will use this class as a base class.[12] Most importantly, from your point of view, is that the RavenTestDriver<T> class provides the GetDocumentStore method, which generates a new in-memory database and is responsible for tearing it down at the end of the test. Each call to the GetDocumentStore method will generate a *new* database. It will run purely in memory, but other then that, it's fully functional and behaves in the same manner as a typical RavenDB server.

Listing 2.24 *Basic CRUD test using RavenDB Test Driver*

```
public class BasicCrud : RavenTestDriver<RavenExecLocator>
{
    public class Play
    {
        public string Id { get; set; }
        public string Name { get; set; }
        public string Author { get; set; }
    }
```

---

12   Not strictly necessary, but this is the easiest way to build tests.

```
    [Fact]
    public void CanSaveAndLoad()
    {
        using (var store = GetDocumentStore())
        {
            string id;
            using (var session = store.OpenSession())
            {
                var play = new Play
                {
                    Author = "Shakespeare",
                    Name = "As You Like It"
                };
                session.Store(play);
                id = play.Id;
                session.SaveChanges();
            }

            using (var session = store.OpenSession())
            {
                var play = session.Load<Play>(id);
                Assert.Equal("Shakespeare", play.Author);
                Assert.Equal("As You Like It", play.Name);
            }
        }
    }
}
```

If you've been paying attention, you might have noticed the difference between RavenTestDriver<RavenExecLocator> and RavenTestDriver<T>. What's that about? The RavenTestDriver<T> uses its generic argument to find the Raven.Server.exe executable. Listing 2.25 shows the implementation of RavenExecLocator.

Listing 2.25 *Letting the RavenTestDriver know where the Raven.Server exec is located*

```
public class RavenExecLocator : RavenTestDriver.Locator
{
    public override string ExecutablePath =>
        @"d:\RavenDB\Raven.Server.exe";
}
```

The code in Listing 2.24 is using `xunit` for testing, but there's no dependency on the testing framework from `Raven.TestDriver`. You can use whatever testing framework you prefer.

How does Raven.TestDriver work?

In order to provide fast tests and reduce environment noise, the test driver runs a single instance of the RavenDB server using an in-memory-only node binding to `localhost` and a dynamic port. Each call to the `GetDocumentStore` method will then create a new database on that single-server instance.

When the test is closed, we'll delete the database, and when the test suite is over, the server instance will be closed. This provides you with a test setup that's both very fast and that runs the exact same code as you will run in production.

2.9.1. DEBUGGING TESTS

Sometimes a test fails and you need to figure out what happened. This is easy if you're dealing with in-memory state only, but it can be harder if your state resides elsewhere. The RavenDB test driver provides the `WaitForUserToContinueTheTest` method to make that scenario easier. Calling this method will pause the current test and open the RavenDB Studio, allowing you to inspect, validate and modify the content of the in-memory database (while the test is *still running*). After you've looked at the database state, you can resume the test and continue execution.

This makes it much easier to figure out what's going on because you can just *look*. Let's test this out. Add the following line between the two sessions in the code in Listing 2.24 and then run the test:

```
WaitForUserToContinueTheTest(store);
```

When the test reaches this line, a magical thing will happen, as shown in Figure 2.15. The Studio will open, and you'll be able to see and interact with everything that's going on inside RavenDB. One nice feature I like for complex cases is the ability to just export the entire database to a file, which lets me import it into another system later on for further analysis.

Figure 2.15. *Peeking into running test instance mid-test*

At this time, the rest of the test is suspended, waiting for you to confirm you're done peeking inside. You can do that by clicking the button shown in Figure 2.16, after which your test will resume normally and (hopefully) turn green.

Figure 2.16. *Press this to continue the test*

The test driver can do quite a bit more (configure the database to your specifications, create relevant indexes, load initial data, etc.). You can read all about its features in the online documentation.

2.10. Summary

At this point in the book, we've accomplished quite a lot. We started by setting up a development instance of RavenDB on your machine.[13] And we learned how to set up a new database and played a bit with the provided sample database.

We then moved to the most common tasks you'll do with RavenDB:

◆ Creating/editing/deleting documents via the Studio.
◆ Querying for documents in the Studio.

The idea was to get you familiar with the basics of working with the Studio so you can see the results of your actions and learn to navigate the Studio well enough that it's useful. We'll talk more about working with the Studio throughout the rest of the book, but remember that the details are covered extensively in the online documentation and are unlikely to need additional verbiage.

Things got more interesting when we started working with the RavenDB API and wrote our first document via code. We looked at the very basics of defining entities to work with RavenDB (the next chapter will cover this exact topic in depth). We learned about creating and querying documents and were able to remind ourselves to buy some milk using RavenDB.

We dove deeper and discussed the architecture of the RavenDB client, as well as the use of `Document Store` and `Document Session` to access the cluster and a specific database, respectively. As a reminder, the document store is the single access point to a particular RavenDB cluster, and it allows you to globally configure a wide range of behaviors by changing the default conventions.

The session is a single `Unit of Work` that represents a single business transaction against a particular database and is the most commonly used API to talk to RavenDB. It was designed

---

13   The steps outlined in this chapter are meant to be quick and hassle-free, rather than an examination of proper production deployments. Check Chapter 15 for details on those.

explicitly to make it easy to handle 90% of pure CRUD scenarios, and more complex scenarios are possible by accessing the `session.Advanced` functionality.

From the client API, we moved to discussing how RavenDB deals with the crucial task of properly generating document identifiers. We looked at a few of RavenDB's identifier generation strategies and how they work in a distributed cluster:

◆ The hilo algorithm: generates the identifier on the client by collaborating with the server to reserve identifier ranges that can be exclusively generated by a particular client.

◆ Server-side: generates the identifier on the server side, optimized for very large tasks. It allows each server to generate human-readable, unique identifiers independently of each other.

◆ Identity: generates a consecutive numeric value using a consensus of the entire cluster. Typically the slowest method to use and only useful if you *really* need to generate consecutive IDs for some reason.

You can also generate the document ID yourself, which we typically call a semantic ID. Semantic IDs are identifiers that have meaning: maybe it's an external ID brought over from another system, or maybe it's a naming convention that implies the content of the document.

We briefly discussed document metadata and how it allows you to store out-of-band information about the document (auditing details, workflow steps, etc.) without impacting the document's structure. You can modify such metadata seamlessly on the client side (and access it on the server). RavenDB makes use of metadata to hold critical information such as the document collection, when it was last modified, etc.

Last but certainly not least, we discussed testing your applications and how the RavenDB test driver allows you to easily set up in-memory instances that will let you run your code against them. The test driver even allows you to stop a test midway through and inspect the running RavenDB instance using the Studio.

In this chapter, we started building the foundation of your RavenDB knowledge. In the next one, we'll build even further on that foundation. We'll discuss modeling data and documents inside RavenDB and how to best structure your system to take advantage of what RavenDB has to offer.

3. Document Modeling

Modeling your data is crucially important as different modeling decisions will have a different impact on your data and the amount of work that needs to be done by the database. It requires your understanding of how RavenDB, or any other database, is actually storing information and what features it has available for you to utilize.

If you get it wrong, you may be forcing the database to do an exponential amount of additional work. On the other hand, if you play to the database's strengths, you can get a robust and easy-to-build system. So, overall, no pressure whatsoever.

Relational-based modeling is so frequently encountered that, in most cases, you don't even see people talk about the relational part. They refer to relational data modeling as just "data modeling." But when you try to apply a relational modeling solution to a non-relational system, the end result is usually...suboptimal.

Documents aren't flat

Documents, unlike a row in a relational database, aren't flat. You aren't limited to just storing keys and values. Instead, you can store complex object graphs as a single document. That includes arrays, dictionaries and trees. Unlike a relational database, where a row can only contain simple values and more complex data structures need to be stored as relations, you don't need to work hard to map your data into a document database.

That gives you a major advantage. It simplifies a lot of common tasks, as you'll see in this chapter.

The problem is that this is extremely well-entrenched behavior, to the point where most people don't even realize they're making decisions based on what would work best for a relational database. So the first section of this chapter is going to deal with how to get away from the relational mindset, and the second part will focus on how to model data for RavenDB.

3.1. Beyond relational data modeling

You've likely used a relational database in the past. That means you've learned about normalization and how important it is. Words like "data integrity" are thrown around quite often. But the original purpose of normalization had everything to do with reducing duplication to the maximum extent.

A common example of normalization is addresses. Instead of storing a customer's address on every order that he has, we can simply store the address ID in the order, and we've saved ourselves the need to update the address in multiple locations. You can see a sample of such a schema in Figure 3.1.

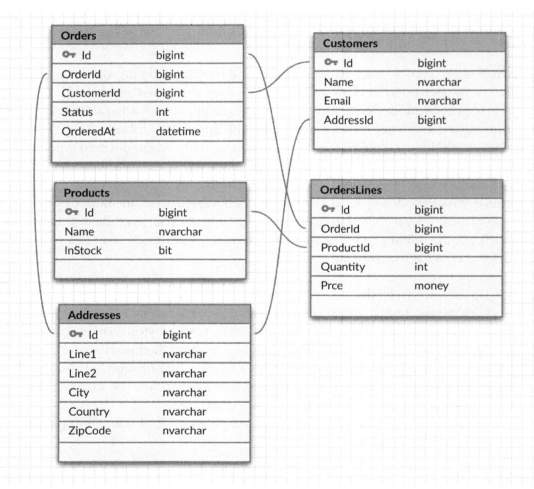

Figure 3.1. *A simple relational schema for orders*

You've seen (and probably written) such schemas before. And at a glance, you'll probably agree that this is a reasonable way to structure a database for order management. Now, let's explore what happens when the customer wishes to change his address. The way the database is set up, we can just update a single row in the addresses table. Great, we're done.

Well, it *would* be great...except we've just introduced a subtle but deadly data corruption to our database. If that customer had existing orders, both those orders and the customer information now point at the same address. Updating the address for the customer therefore will also update the address for *all of its orders*. When we look at one of those orders, we won't see the address it was shipped to but rather the *current* customer address.

> **When a data modeling error means calling the police**
>
> In the real world, I've seen such things happen with payroll systems and paystubs (or "payslips," across the pond). An employee had married and changed her bank account information to a new shared bank account with her husband. The couple also wanted to purchase a home, so they applied for a mortgage. As part of that, they had to submit paystubs from the past several months. The employee asked her HR department to send over her most recent stubs. When the bank saw paystubs made to an account that didn't exist, they suspected fraud. The mortgage was denied and the police were called. An unpleasant situation all around.[1]

It's common for this issue to be blamed on bad modeling decisions (and I agree). The problem is that a more appropriate model is complex to build and work with, expensive to query and hard to reason about in general.

A lot of the wisdom about data modeling is limited by only seeing the world through relational eyes. The relation model offers us tables, rows and columns to store our data, and it's up to us to hammer the data into the right shape so the relational database can accept it. Along the way, we have to deal with an impedance mismatch between how software (and our minds) model the data and how we're forced to store it to the relational database.

A document database like RavenDB doesn't solve this problem completely. It's entirely possible to construct models that would be a poor fit for the way RavenDB stores data. However, the way most business applications (and in general OLTP systems) think about their data is an excellent fit for RavenDB.

You can read more about this by looking at `Domain Driven Design`[2] and, in particular, about the concept of an `Aggregate Root`.

---

1   This ended up being sorted out eventually by uttering the magic words: "computer error." But it was very exciting for a while there.
2   The book is a bit dry, but I remember being very impressed when I read it the first time.

What are aggregates?

One of the best definitions I've read is Martin Fowler's:

A DDD aggregate is a cluster of domain objects that can be treated as a single unit. An example may be an order and its line items. These will be separate objects, but it's useful to treat the order (together with its line items) as a single aggregate.

An aggregate will have one of its component objects be the aggregate root. Any references from outside the aggregate should only go to the aggregate root. The root can thus ensure the integrity of the aggregate as a whole.

In the context of RavenDB, this is highly relevant since every RavenDB document is an aggregate and every aggregate is a document. Modeling techniques for aggregates work well for document-oriented design, and that gives you a great resource for modeling in the real world.

But before we can start running, we need to learn to walk. So let's start by learning how to use RavenDB with the most basic of modeling techniques: none.

3.2. Using RavenDB as a key/value store

RavenDB is a document database, but it's also quite good at being just a key/value store. That's mostly accidental, but as part of making sure we have a fast database, we also significantly reduced the cost of storing and loading documents without any of the other benefits of RavenDB.

With the restriction that the data must be JSON, using RavenDB as a key/value store makes a lot of sense. It also makes sense to use RavenDB to cache information, to store the shopping cart during the purchase process or just to hold on to the user session data – all classic models for key/value stores.

RavenDB doesn't impose any additional costs on storing/loading documents by default, so you get to use a fast database with the simplest of all access models. Typically, complexity in key/value modeling resides in generating the appropriate key and in what sort of operations you can do on it.

For the purpose of using RavenDB as a key/value store, it's likely the following features will be most relevant:

- You can generate the document identifier independently of the collection used.
- Loading saved document(s) can be done in a single call by providing the ID(s) to load.
- RavenDB provides automatic expiration for documents, which you can use with caching/session data.
- You can perform searches using document identifiers as a prefix (and even using glob-like searches).
- Includes can be used to fetch related data without having to make multiple remote calls.

The nice thing about using RavenDB as a key/value store for such information is that you aren't *limited* to just those key/value operations. If you're storing shopping cart data inside RavenDB, you can also start pulling data from there. You can see the most popular item being purchased or do projections on inventory or any of a whole host of things that will provide you with useful knowledge.

In a typical key/value store (Redis, for example), you'll have to manually track such things. However, RavenDB allows you to query and aggregate the data very easily.

But using RavenDB just for key/value data is somewhat of a waste, given what it's capable of doing with your data. So, without further ado, let's dive into document modeling in RavenDB.

3.3. Modeling considerations in RavenDB

The reason we cover modeling in this chapter is that I want you to get a feel for some of RavenDB's capabilities before we start discussing modeling techniques. The kind of features that RavenDB has to offer are directly relevant to the models you'll write.

> **RavenDB as the application database**
>
> A common bad practice is to integrate between different applications using a shared database. This has been looked down upon for quite a while. RavenDB makes no attempt to cater to those who use it as shared database. Instead, it shines in its role as an application database.
>
> Typically, shared database solutions suffer because they attempt to force disparate applications to treat the data in the same manner. This is a pretty bad idea, since different applications tend to treat even very similar concepts in a variety of ways. The most common example is a billing application and a fulfillment application. Both have the concept of a customer, and both actually refer to the same thing when they talk about a customer. But the fulfillment application needs to keep track of very different data from the billing application. What will the fulfillment app do with the CreditScore field, and what can the billing app gain from looking at the ShippingManifest details?
>
> Each application should model its data independently and evolve it as it needs to. Keeping everything in a shared database leads to required coordination between the various application teams. That results in increased complexity in evolving the data model as the various applications are being worked on.
>
> However, even though the different applications are separate, they still need to share data between them. How do you do that with RavenDB? We'll talk about that a lot more in Chapter 8, but the answer is that each application has its own database, and we can set up information flow between the servers by using RavenDB's built-in ETL capabilities.

In this way, each application is independent and can evolve and grow on its own, with well-defined boundaries and integration points to its siblings.

We typically encourage you to use DDD techniques for modeling in RavenDB since they fit so well. A core design principle for modeling documents is that they should be independent, isolated and coherent, or more specifically,

- *Independent*, meaning a document should have its own separate existence from any other documents.
- *Isolated*, meaning a document can change independently from other documents.
- *Coherent*, meaning a document should be legible on its own, without referencing other documents.

These properties are easier to explain using negation. First, a document isn't independent if it can't stand up on its own. A good example of a dependent document is the `OrderLine`. An `OrderLine` doesn't really have a meaning outside the scope of an `Order`, so it should be a `Value Object` inside the `Order` document. An `Entity` is defined as something with a distinct and independent existence. And that's how you treat documents: as entities. If a document exists only as part of a larger whole, then the whole thing should be re-factored/re-modeled to a single document.

Second, a document isn't isolated if changing one document requires you to also update additional documents. For example, if updating the `CustomerBilling` document necessitates updating the `Customer` document, they aren't isolated. A document should be able to change independently from other documents. Otherwise, there's an unclear transaction boundary involved. With each document isolated, the transaction boundary (meaning what can change together) is much clearer. It's drawn at the document level.

Lastly, a document isn't coherent if it's not possible to make sense of it with just the information it contains. If you need to go and look up additional state or information from other documents, the document isn't coherent. A good example is the `Order` document and the `ShippingMethod`. If, to ship an order, we need to go and look at the `Customer` document, then the `Order` document is not coherent.

3.3.1. Looking at physical documents

A great trick for document modeling is to consider the data as, well...documents. What I mean by that is *physical* documents – the kind you can actually hold in your hand and get a paper cut from. A lot of the same considerations that apply in the real world apply to document modeling.

If I hand you a document and tell you that you need to fill out *this* form and then go and update *that* form, you'll rightly consider the process a normal government behavior/

bureaucratic/Kafkaesque.[3] If I gave you a form and told you that, in order to understand it, you had to consult another document…you get my point.

When modeling, I find that it helps to picture the document in its printed form. If it makes sense as a printed page, it's probably valid in terms of document modeling.

3.3.2. DENORMALIZATION AND OTHER SCARY BEASTS

Anyone taking a relational modeling course knows that "store a fact only once" is a mantra that's just short of being sacred (or maybe not even short). The basic idea is that if you store a fact only a single time, you are preventing update anomalies, such as when you updated a person's date of birth in the employee record but forgot to update it on the "send a card" listing.

I wholeheartedly agree with this statement in principle. But the problem is that sometimes this isn't the same fact at all, even if it looks the same. Let's consider the notion of a `Customer`, an `Order` and what the `Address` property means in this case. The `Customer` entity has an `Address` property that holds the address of the customer, and the `Order` has a `ShipTo` property.

Why are we duplicating this information? Well, this isn't actually the same information, even if the content is the same. On the one hand, we have the `Customer.Address`, which represents the customer's *current* address. On the other hand, we have the `Order.ShipTo` which represents a *point-in-time* copy of the customer address, captured at the time we created the order. Those are important distinctions.

One of the more common objections to the kind of modeling advice found in this chapter is that the data is denormalized. And that's true. But for the most part, even if the same data appears in multiple locations, it doesn't have the same semantic meaning. And the notion of point-in-time data is important in many fields.

RavenDB has quite a few features that help in working with normalized data (`LoadDocument` and projections are the two main ones, and they're covered in Part III), but you need to consider whether it make sense to traverse document references in your model or whether you're breaking document coherency.

The most useful question you can ask yourself in this situation is whether you're looking at the *current* value (in which case you need normalization) or the *point-in-time* value (in which case you'd use a copy).

And with all of this information now in our heads, we can turn to concrete modeling scenarios and see how to deal with them.

---

3   Circle the appropriate choice

3.4. Common modeling scenarios

Giving you advice on how to model your application is beyond the scope of this book. While I highly recommend the DDD book in general, it isn't always the best choice. Proper DDD modeling takes a lot of discipline and hard work, and it's most appropriate only in specific parts of your system (typically the most highly valued ones). RavenDB doesn't have any requirement regarding how you should model your data in your application. You can use DDD, you can use business objects or data transfer objects – it doesn't matter to RavenDB.

What matters is how you *structure* the data inside RavenDB, and that's what we'll be talking about for the rest of this chapter. We'll focus on concrete scenarios rather than generic modeling advice. Instead of trying to advise you on how to model your entire system, I'm going to focus on giving you the tools to build the model as you need it to be, so it will play best with RavenDB.

To make things interesting, we're going to use a kindergarten as our data model. As you can expect, we have the concepts of children, parents, registrations, etc. On the face of it, this is a pretty simple model. We can model it using the code in Listing 3.1.

Listing 3.1 *Simple kindergarten model*

```
public class Parent
{
    public string Name { get; set; }
}

public class Registration
{
    public DateTime EnrolledAt { get; set; }
    public EnrollmentType Type { get; set; }
}

public class Child
{
    public string Name { get; set; }
    public DateTime Birthday { get; set; }
    public Parent Father { get; set; }
    public Parent Mother { get; set; }
    public Registration Registration { get; set; }
}
```

The code in Listing 3.1 is obviously a simplified model, but it's a good place to start our discussion. A core tenet of modeling in RavenDB is that we need to identify what pieces of information belong together and what pieces are independent of one another. Recall our discussion on the basics of document modeling design. A good document model has documents that are independent, isolated and coherent.

With the basic model in Listing 3.1 and our understanding of a kindergarten, we can now proceed to explore aspects of document modeling. We'll start with the most obvious one. In this model, we don't have documents, we have *a* document: just a single one per child. That's because we're embedding all information about the child in the document itself. Why would we do that?

3.4.1. EMBEDDED DOCUMENTS

A document model is very different from a relational model. It would be typical in a relational model to have a separate table for each class shown in Listing 3.1. A concrete example might work better, and Listing 3.2 shows how this model works for registering Alice to our kindergarten.

Listing 3.2 *Kindergarten record of Alice in Wonderland*

```
// children/alice-liddell
{
    "Name": "Alice Liddell",
    "Birthday": "2012-05-04T00:00:00.0000000Z",
    "Mother": {
        "Name": "Lorina Hanna Liddell",
    },
    "Father": {
        "Name": "Henry Liddell"
    },
    "Registration": {
        "EnrolledAt": "2014-11-24T00:00:00.0000000Z",
        "Type": "FullDay"
    }
}
```

All of the information is in one place. For the document ID you can see that we used a semantic ID, children/alice-liddell, which includes the child name. This works well for data that's well known and predictable. The data itself is centrally located and easy to access. Looking at the data, it's easy to see all relevant information about our Alice.[4]

For the most part, embedding information is our default approach because it leads us to more coherent documents, which contain all the information relevant to processing them. We aren't limited by format of schema; we can represent arbitrarily complex data without any issue, and we want to take full advantage of that.

---

4   Except maybe which rabbit hole she wandered down…

So if the default approach is to embed data, when *wouldn't* we want to do that? There are a few cases. One is when the data doesn't belong to the same document because it's owned by another entity. A good document model gives each document a single reason to change, and that's the primary force for splitting the document apart.

In the case of the kindergarten record, the obvious example here are the parents. Henry and Lorina are independent entities and are not fully owned by the Alice record. We need to split them into independent documents. On the other side of things, Henry and Lorina have more children than just Alice: there's also Harry and Edith.[5] So we need to consider how to model such information.

3.4.2. MANY-TO-ONE RELATIONSHIP

How do we model a kindergarten where Alice, Harry and Edith are all the children of Henry and Lorina? The technical term for this relationship is many to one. Unlike the previous example, where we embedded the parents inside the child document, now we want to model the data so there's a distinct difference between the different entities. You can see the document model as JSON in Listing 3.3.

Listing 3.3 *Many to one modeling with children and parents*

```
// children/alice-liddell
{
    "Name": "Alice Liddell",
    "MotherId": "parents/1923-A",
    "FatherId": "parents/1921-A",
}

// children/henry-liddell
{
    "Name": "Henry Liddell",
    "MotherId": "parents/1923-A",
    "FatherId": "parents/1921-A",
}
```

Listing 3.3 shows[6] both Alice and Henry (you can figure out what Edith's document looks like on your own) with references to their parents. I've intentionally not included semantic IDs for the parents to avoid confusion about what information is stored on the side holding the reference. Alice and Henry (and Edith) only hold the *identifier* for their parents' documents, nothing else.

---

5   The real Harry and Lorina had a total of 10 children, by the way.
6   I removed all extra information from the documents to make it clearer.

How is this model reflected in our code? Let's look at Listing 3.4 to see that (again, with some information redacted to make it easier to focus on the relevant parts).

Listing 3.4 *Child class representing the model*

```
public class Child
{
    public string Name { get; set; }
    public string FatherId { get; set; }
    public string MotherId { get; set; }
}
```

Instead of storing the parent as an embedded document, we just hold the ID to that parent. And when we need to traverse from the child document to the parent document, we do that by following the ID. To make things faster, we'll commonly use the `Include` feature to make sure that we load all those documents in one remote call, but that doesn't impact the data model we use.

What about the other side, when we need to find all of Lorina's children? We use a query, as shown in Listing 3.5.

Listing 3.5 *Loading Lorina and her children*

```
using (var session = store.OpenSession())
{
    var lorina = session.Load<Parent>("parents/1923-A");
    var lorinaChildren = (
        from c in session.Query<Child>()
        where c.MotherId == lorina.Id
        select c
    ).ToList();
}
```

You can also run this query directly in the Studio by going to `Indexes` and then `Query` and using the following query: `from Children where MotherId = 'parents/1923-A'`.

As you can see in Listing 3.4 and 3.5, we're being very explicit when we move between documents. RavenDB doesn't allow you to transparently move between different documents. Each document is a standalone entity. This helps ensure you don't create silent dependencies in your model since each document is clearly delineated.

Using lazy operations

In Listing 3.5, you can see we have to make two separate calls to the server to get all the information we want. When going from a child to a parent, we can use the `Include` feature to reduce the number of calls. Going the other way, `Include` wouldn't work, but we don't have to give up. We have the option of making a few lazy operations and only going to the server once. We'll see exactly how this is possible in the next chapter.

The many-to-one relation is probably the simplest one, and it's incredibly common. However, when using it, you need to carefully consider whether the association should cross a document boundary or remain inside the document. In the case of parents and children, it's obvious that each is a separate entity, but orders and order lines are the reverse. In the case of orders and order lines, it's just as obvious that order lines do *not* belong in a separate document but should be part and parcel of the order document.

There are many cases where that distinction isn't quite so obvious, and you need to give it some thought. The decision can be situational and, frequently, it's highly dependent on the way you *use* the data. An equally valid decision in the kindergarten case would be to embed the parents' information in the child document and duplicate that information if we have two or more siblings in kindergarten at the same time.

It depends what kind of work is done with the parents. If all or nearly all the work is done with the children, there's no point in creating a parent document. (It isn't meaningful inside the domain of the kindergarten outside the scope of the children.) However, if we wanted to keep track of parents as well (for example, maybe we want to note that Mrs. Liddell takes two sugars in her tea), then we'll likely use a separate document.

Children and parents are all well and good, but what about when we ramp the example up a bit and explore the world of grandchildren and grandparents? Now we need to talk about many-to-many relationships.

3.4.3. MANY-TO-MANY RELATIONSHIP

A many-to-many relationship is a lot more complex than a many-to-one relationship because it's usually used differently. In our kindergarten example, let's consider how we can model the grandparents. Each grandchild has multiple grandparents, and each grandparent can have multiple grandchildren.

When we were working with parents and children, it was obvious that we needed to place the association on the children. But how should we model grandparents? One way to do it would be to simply model the hierarchy. A grandparent is the parent of a parent. That seems like an elegant reflection of the relationship, but it will lead to a poor model. Grandparents and grandchildren have an association between them that's completely separate from the one going through the parent, and that deserves to be modeled on its own, not as a side effect.

The next question is where to put the relationship. We can add a `Grandparents` array to the child document, which will hold all the document IDs of the grandparents. We can add a `Grandchildren` array to the grandparent document and store the children IDs there. Or we can do both. What should we choose?

In the context of many-to-many associations, we always place the record of the association on the smaller side. In other words, since a child is likely to have fewer grandparents than a grandparent has children, the association should be kept on the child document.

The users and groups model

A more technical example that frequently comes up within the context of many-to-many associations is the users and groups model. A user can belong to many groups, and a group can have many users. How do we model this?

A user typically belongs to a few groups, but a group can have a *lot* of users. So we record the relationship on the smaller side by having a Groups property on the user document.

Traversing a many-to-many association from the grandchild (smaller) side can be done by simply including and loading the grandparents, as shown in Listing 3.6.

Listing 3.6 *Alice and her grandparents*

```
using (var session = store.OpenSession())
{
    Child alice = session
        .Include<Child>(c => c.Grandparents)
        .Load("children/alice-liddell");
    Dictionary<string, Parent> gradparents =
        session.Load<Parent>(alice.Grandparents);
}
```

Following the association from the other side requires us to query, as shown in Listing 3.7.

Listing 3.7 *Alice and her grandparents*

```
using (var session = store.OpenSession())
{
    Parent grandparent = session.Load<Parent>("parent/1923-A");
    List<Child> grandchildren = (
        from c in session.Query<Child>()
        where c.Grandparents.Contain(grandparent.Id)
        select c
    ).ToList();
}
```

You can also run this query directly in the Studio by going to `Indexes` and then `Query` and using the following query: `from Children where Grandparents[] in ('parents/1923-A')`.

The code in Listing 3.7 will load Alice's mother and all of her grandchildren. In this case, we see a slightly more complex query, but the essence of it remains the same as the one in Listing 3.5. We have separate documents and clear separation between them. In other words, we can query for related data, but we don't just traverse the object graph from one document to another.

3.4.4. ONE-TO-ONE RELATIONSHIP

A one-to-one relationship is a pretty strange sight. If there's a one-to-one relationship, shouldn't it be an embedded document instead of having a separate document? Indeed, in nearly all cases, that would be a better idea.

There are a few reasons why I'd want to store a part of a document in a separate document. Usually this would be the case if we have a document that's conceptually the same but has very different access patterns. In the order example, we might have the order header, which is frequently accessed and looked at. And then there's the full order, which might be very big (lots of line items) and which we don't need to access often.

In this case, it might make sense to create a document just for the order header (call it `orders/2834/header`). But using a projection will be almost as good, and we'll discuss those in Chapter 4. This saves us the need to split our data. The typical way you'll build one-to-one relationships in RavenDB is to utilize document ID postfixes to create a set of related documents (`orders/2834` and `orders/2834/header`, for example).

This tends to result in clearer intent since it's obvious what each part is doing and what it's meant to be. But even so, it's often not advisable. Just putting it all in a single document is easier in most cases.

Another scenario that might require you to split a document is if you have a real need to have concurrent activities on a document. This is generally pretty rare. Since a document is the unit of concurrency in RavenDB, you'll model your documents so they'll have a single reason to change. But sometimes there are reasons to allow concurrent updates on a document – for example, if you have properties on the document that are useful for the application, not the business model.

Case in point, imagine in an order system that we want to add a feature for tracking an order. A customer representative may mark an order for tracking so they can see what kind of steps a particular order goes through and take action at various points in the workflow. Such an action needs to be recorded, but it doesn't actually impact the behavior of the system in any way. It is fine to add or remove tracking on an order at any point in time, including during concurrent updates to the order.

One way to do that would be to always use patching (also discussed in the next chapter) to update the document, but a better way to handle this kind of requirement is to create a dedicated document `orders/2834/tracking` that would hold all the details about the users tracking this order. This makes it an explicit action in your domain instead of just tacking it onto the existing objects.

3.5. Advanced modeling scenarios

The RavenDB modeling techniques that we've explored so far are good for modeling standard business data. You know how to build your entities, how to deal with relationships between them and how to identify whether they should be separate documents or nested in the same document. But there's also a good deal of sophistication we can apply to non-standard scenarios, which is the topic of this section.

3.5.1. REFERENCE DATA

Reference data is common, and it can be anything from a list of states to tax rates to localized text. The common thread for reference data is that it's typically small and not really interesting in isolation. Such data only gets interesting when you start working with a lot of it.

It's typical to ignore the modeling concerns for such items – to just throw them in a pile somewhere and not give it any thought. With the list of states example, the most natural way to do it is to define a document whose ID is states/ny and has a single Name property with the value New York. That would *work*, but it's hardly the best way to go about it.

Going back to basic principles, such a document will hardly be coherent or independent. Indeed, such a document makes little sense on its own. Instead of storing each state and each configuration value as its own document, we'll raise the bar a bit and introduce configuration documents. You can see the example in Listing 3.8.

Listing 3.8 *Storing the states list as a configuration document*

```
// config/states
{
    "AL": "Alabama",
    "AK": "Alaska",
    "AS": "American Samoa",
    ...
    ...
    "WV": "West Virginia",
    "WI": "Wisconsin",
    "WY": "Wyoming"
}
```

Modeling reference data in the manner shown in Listing 3.8 has several advantages. It's much easier to work with the data. Instead of issuing a query, we can just load the document in one shot, and it's ready for our consumption. It means the database has less work to do, and it plays nicely into the way RavenDB caches data. It also means we can reduce deserialization costs and make it easier to edit and work with the reference data.

In fact, because this is a single document, we can also get RavenDB to do some tasks for us, such as the build-in revisions capability. We'll discuss this in more detail in Chapter 4. This can be *very* useful when you're talking about reference or configuration data since it's easy to see what the changes were (or revert them).

3.5.2. HIERARCHICAL INFORMATION

Working with hierarchical data is complex because there are cases where you need to traverse the hierarchy, and that traditionally has been expensive. In many cases, hierarchies are recursive and have no limits to their number of levels (although, in practice, the number is usually known to be small).

We need to make a distinction between several types of hierarchies. The first hierarchy is quite simple and can comfortably fit into a single document. An example of such a hierarchy is comments in a discussion thread. The entire thread is a single document, and all the comments in the thread always reside in that document. In such a case, storing and working with the hierarchical nature of the data is quite trivial since you'll often just traverse the data directly after loading the document from the server.

A commonly-seen example of a hierarchy that doesn't fit the "everything in a single document" model is the company hierarchy. Each employee is an independent entity, and we can't store them all as a single document. Instead, we'll strive to model the hierarchy explicitly as an independent concept from the employees. In this case, we'll have the notion of a department, which will record just the chains of who reports to whom. The idea is that we separate the hierarchy out since the position of an employee in the hierarchy is orthogonal to most aspects of the employee.

The notion of a separated hierarchy document gives us a lot of simplicity. Hierarchical operations and queries (all direct and indirect reports, for example) are easy and natural, and the separated hierarchy document works well with caching and the use of Include.

The final example for modeling hierarchies in RavenDB is when we need to model the hierarchy directly in the model. Departments in an organization might be a good example; their location in the hierarchy is important to what they are. In this case, we'll typically model such a relationship as many to one or many to many, at each individual level. That's the simplest method for handling such a requirement.

This works as long as we only need to handle a single level, but it doesn't handle hierarchical queries. Finding all the departments under R&D, regardless of whether they're directly or indirectly attached, requires a bit more work since we'll need to define indexes that are able to walk through the hierarchy. We haven't talked about complex operations in indexes, so I'll just mention that RavenDB's indexes can use Recurse to work with hierarchical data and leave that topic to Chapter 10, where we'll cover it in depth.

3.5.3. TEMPORAL DATA MODEL

Temporal data is often a challenge because it can really mess with the way you think about information. Despite the fancy name, temporal data is just a way to store data that has a relation to time. The best example I've seen for temporal data is payroll. Consider the notion of a paycheck. An employer and employee have a contract stipulating that, for a given amount of work, a given amount of money will be exchanged.

The problem is that this contract can *change* over time. An employee can get a raise, earn additional vacation days, negotiate better overtime terms or all of the above. For extra fun, you may get some of those changes retroactively. This sort of thing makes it hard to figure out what exactly you're supposed to do. (What if these terms change mid-month? How would you handle overtime calculation on a shift between 8 PM and 4 AM that falls in that switch?)

The way to model temporal data in RavenDB is to embrace its document nature fully, especially because in most temporal domains the notion of documents and views over time is so important. Consider this situation: a paystub was issued on May 1st, and then a retroactive pay raise was given. How is that money counted? It's easy to see that when we model the data as physical documents, we don't try to model a paystub as a mutable entity but rather a point-in-time view. Any changes that were made during the time frame it covered will be reflected in the *next* paystub.

This approach makes it much easier on you. You don't have to keep track of valid time, effective time and bitemporal time all at once. You just store facts and the time at which they were stored, just as if you were keeping all your printed paystubs in a drawer somewhere.

The same applies to contracts and other things that mutate over time. Consider the documents seen in Figure 3.2. They represent the same contract, with modifications over time as things change.

Figure 3.2. *Contract documents and changes over time*

The key is that, when we consider references to this contract, we can select what *kind* of reference we want. When looking at the employee's record, we'll have a reference to `contracts/hourly/1234-A`, which is the current version of the contract. But when issuing a paystub, we'll always reference a fixed revision of this contract, such as `contracts/hourly/1234-A/2013-05-21`. This way, we set ourselves up to choose whether we want the point-in-time information or the current (continuously updated) version.

If this sounds similar to the way we decide if we'll copy data from another document to get a point-in-time snapshot of it or reference it by ID to always get the latest data, that's probably because it *is* similar. And it makes dealing with temporal data significantly simpler.

3.6. Additional considerations for document modeling

A major challenge in modeling data with RavenDB is that different features and behaviors all have a very different impact on the cost of various operations, and that in turn impacts how you'll design and work with your model. In this section, we'll explore a few of the features that we haven't gotten to know yet and their impact on modeling data in RavenDB.

I recommend going over this section briefly now and returning to it when you've finished this book. By then, you'll have the complete picture and will be able to make more informed decisions.

3.6.1. HANDLING UNBOUNDED DOCUMENT GROWTH

What size should a document be? It's an interesting question that frequently comes up with regard to modeling. A good range for a document is somewhere on the order of kilobytes. In other words, if your document is very small (a few dozen bytes), is it really a document? Or is it just a single value that would be better off as a reference data document, as we discussed earlier in this chapter? On the other hand, if you document is multiple megabytes, how easy it is to work with it?

> **Maximum document size**
>
> RavenDB has a hard limit on document sizes, and it's around the 2 GB mark. (Documents are often stored compressed, so a 2 GB JSON document will typically be smaller inside RavenDB.) But the biggest document I recall seeing in the field was about 170 MB. We had a discussion with the customer regarding modeling and about the fact that, while RavenDB is *a* document database, it's perfectly capable of handling *multiple* documents.

RavenDB itself, by the way, is just fine with large documents. The problem is everything else. Consider a page that needs to display a 12 MB document. What are the costs involved in doing this?

- Reading 12 MB over the network.
- Parsing 12 MB of JSON into our entities (this often means using a lot more memory than just the 12 MB of serialized JSON).
- Generating a web page with some or all of the information in the 12 MB document.
- Discarding all of this information and letting it be garbage-collected.

In short, there's a *lot* of work going on, and it can be very expensive. On the other hand, if you have anemic documents, we'll typically need to read many of them to get anything meaningful done, which means a lot of work for the database engine.

Here's the rule of thumb we use: as long as it makes sense to measure the document size in kilobytes, you're good. RavenDB will generate a warning in the Studio when it encounters documents that are too large,[7] but it has no impact whatsoever on the behavior or performance of the system.

There are two common reasons why a document can be very large. Either it holds a single (or a few) very large properties, such as a lot of text, binary data, etc., or it contains a collection whose size is not bounded.

In the first case, we need to consider whether the large amount of data is actually a core part of the document or if it should be stored externally. RavenDB supports the notion of attachments, which allows you to, well, *attach* binary data to a document. If the data can be stored outside the document, regardless of whether it's binary or textual, that's preferable. Attachments in RavenDB don't have a size limit and aren't accessed when loading the document, so that's a net win. We'll learn more about attachments toward the end of this chapter.

The more complex case is if we have a collection or collections inside the document that have no upper bound. Consider the case of an order document. In retail, an order can contain up to a few hundred items, but in business-to-business scenarios, it's not uncommon to have orders that contain tens and hundreds of thousands of items. Putting all of that in a single document is going to lead to problems, as we've already seen.

Who modifies the big documents?

While big documents are typically frowned upon because of the awkwardness of working with large amounts of data (network, parsing and memory costs) there's another, more theoretical aspect to the problems they bring: who owns a very big document?

Remember that good document modeling implies there's only a single reason to change a document. But if an order document contains so many items, that likely means there are multiple sources that add items to the order, such as different departments working with the same supplier. At that point, it isn't a single document we're working with. It's multiple independent orders merged into a single, final shipping/billing order.

Again, falling back to the real-world example, we'd find it strange if a van stopped by our store and started unpacking crates full of pages detailing all the things a customer wanted to purchase. But when we're working on a single document, this is pretty much what we're doing. Instead, we'll typically accept individual requests from each contact person/department and associate them with the appropriate billing/shipping cycle.

In other words, the *reason* we split the document isn't so much to artificially reduce its size but because that's how the business will typically work,

---

7   By default, that's set to 5 MB, and it's configurable.

and doing it any other way is *really* hard. Splitting it so the document structure follows the structure of the business is usually the right thing to do.

So how do we handle large documents? We typically split them into smaller pieces along some sort of business boundary. Let's consider the case of a bank account and the transactions we need to track. Keeping all the transactions inside the account document isn't feasible on a long-term basis. But how are we going to split them? Here, we look at the business and see that the bank itself doesn't look at the account and all its history as a single unit.

Instead, the bank talks about transactions that happened on a particular business day or in a particular month. And we can model our documents accordingly. In the bank example, we'll end up with the following documents:

- accounts/1234 – account details, status, ownership, conditions, etc.
- accounts/1234/txs/2017-05 – the transactions in this account on May 2017
- accounts/1234/txs/2017-04 – the transactions in this account on April 2017

Within a given time frame, we can be reasonably certain that there's going to be an upper bound to the number of transactions in an account. I quite like this approach because it aligns closely with how the business is thinking about the domain and it results in clear separation of documents. But you can't always split things apart on such a convenient boundary. What happens if there isn't a time element that you can use?

At that point, you still split the document, but you do so arbitrarily. You can decide that you'll generate a new document for the items in the collection every N items, for example. Often, that N value is some multiple of the typical page size you have in your system. If we go back to the example of order and items in the order, assuming we don't go the route of splitting the order itself into separate requests, we'll just split the order every 100 items. So, we'll end up with the following documents:

- orders/1234 – the order header, shipping details, billing, etc.
- orders/1234/items/1 – the first 100 items for this order
- orders/1234/items/2 – the second 100 items for this order

The order document will contain the IDs of all the items documents (so we can easily Include them), as well as the ID of the last items document, so we'll know where to add an item to this order.

This approach is a bit clumsier, in my eyes. But if we don't have another alternative natural boundary, this will work fine.

3.6.2. CACHED QUERIES PROPERTIES

A common modeling technique is to keep track of some cached global state inside our entities. The most trivial example I can think of is the `customer.NumberOfOrders` property. I want to call out this behavior specifically because it's common, it makes sense and it's usually a bad idea.

But why? Well, let's consider why we need to have this property in the first place. In most domains, a property such as `NumberOfOrders` doesn't comprise an intrinsic part of the customer. In other words, the information is interesting, but it doesn't *belong* inside the customer document. Moreover, in order to keep this property up to date, we need to update it whenever we add an order, decrement it when an order is deleted, etc. For that matter, what do we do about an order that was returned? Does it count? What about the replacement order?

In other words, this is a pretty hefty business decision. But most of the time, this property is added because we want to show that value in the user interface, and issuing an aggregation query can be expensive. Or, rather, an aggregation query is expensive if you aren't using RavenDB.

With RavenDB, aggregation is handled via MapReduce operations, and you don't pay any cost at all for querying on the results of the aggregation. We dedicated a whole chapter (Chapter 11) to discussing this topic, so I'll go into the details there, but the impact of such a feature is profound. Cheap aggregation means that you can do a lot more of it, and you don't have to manage it yourself.

That frees you from a lot of worries, and it means you can focus on building your model as it's used. You can let RavenDB handle the side channel operations, like calculating exactly how many orders a customer has and in what state.

Another problem with `customer.NumberOfOrders` is how you update it. Two orders generated at once for the same customer may result in lost updates and invalid data. How does RavenDB handle concurrency, and how does it impact your model?

3.6.3. CONCURRENCY CONTROL

RavenDB is inherently concurrent, capable of handling hundreds of thousands[8] of requests per second.

That leads to a set of interesting problems regarding concurrency. What happens if two requests are trying to modify the same document at the same time? That depends on what, exactly, you asked RavenDB to do. If you didn't do anything, RavenDB will execute those two modifications one at a time, and the last one will win. There's no way to control which would be last. Note that *both* operations will execute. That means that in certain cases, it will leave marks. In particular, if you have revisions enabled for this collection, there are going to be two revisions for this document. We'll discuss revisions in the next chapter.

---

8   Not a typo! In our benchmarks, we're always saturating the network long before we saturate any other resource, so the current limit is how fast your network cards are in packet processing.

Change Vectors in RavenDB

RavenDB makes extensive use of the notion of change vectors. A change vector is composed of a list of node IDs and etags. A node ID uniquely identifies a node, while an etag is a 64 bit number that is incremented on every operation in a database. Each time a document is modified, it's associated with the current etag value and a new change vector is generated.

This change vector uniquely marks the specific version of the document globally and is used for optimistic concurrency control, for various internal operations and caching. We'll discuss change vectors in detail in the Chapter 6.

The `last write wins` model is the default option in RavenDB except when you're creating a new document. When the RavenDB client API is generating the ID, it *knows* it intends to create a new document, and it sets the expected change vector accordingly. So if the document already exists, an error will be generated.

What about when you want to take advantage of this feature? You can ask RavenDB to enable optimistic concurrency at several levels. The following code enables optimistic concurrency for all sessions created by this document store.

```
store.Conventions.UseOptimisticConcurrency = true;
```

And you can also enable this on a more selective basis, on a particular session, using the following snippet:

```
session.Advanced.UseOptimisticConcurrency = true;
```

Or you can enable it on a single particular operation:

```
session.Store(entity, changeVector);
```

In all cases, the RavenDB client API will send the expected change vector to the server, which will compare it to the current change vector. If the current change vector does not match the expected change vector, a `ConcurrencyException` will be thrown, aborting the entire transaction.

The first two options use the change vector that the server supplied when the document was loaded. In other words, they would error if the document was modified between the time we fetched it from the server and the time we wrote it back. The third option is a lot more interesting, though.

The ability to specify the change vector on a specific entity is quite important because it allows you to perform offline optimistic concurrency checks. You can render a web page to the user and, along with the document data there, include the change vector that you got when you loaded that document. The user can look at the document, modify it, and then send it back to your application. At that point, you'll store the document with the tag as it was when we rendered the page to the user and call `SaveChanges`. If the document has been modified by anyone in the meantime, the operation will fail.

In this manner, you don't need to keep the session around. You just need to pass the change vector back and forth. As you can see, the change vector is quite important for concurrency, but it also plays another important role with caching.

3.6.4. CACHING

RavenDB uses REST over HTTP for communication between client and server. That means whenever you load a document or perform a query, you're actually sending an HTTP call over the wire. This lets RavenDB take advantage of the nature of HTTP to play some nice tricks.

In particular, the RavenDB client API is capable of using the nature of HTTP to enable transparent caching of all requests from the server, which provides the client API with some assistance. Here's how it works. Each response from the server contains an Etag header. In the case of loading a single document, that ETag header is also the document etag, but if we're querying or loading multiple documents, that ETag header will contain a computed value.

On the client side, we'll cache the request from the server alongside the URL and the ETag value. When a new request comes in for the same URL, we'll send it to server, but we'll also let the server know we have the result of the request with a specific ETag value. On the server side, there are dedicated code paths that can cheaply check if the ETag we have on the client is the same as the current one. If it is, we'll just let the client know that it can use the cached version, and that's it.

We don't have to execute any further code or send anything other than 304 Not Modified to the client. And on the client side, there's no need to download any data from the server. We can access our local copy, already parsed and primed for us. That can represent significant speed savings in some cases because we have to do a lot less work.

If the data has changed, we'll have a different ETag for the request, and the server will process it normally. The client will replace the cached value and the process will repeat. You can take advantage of that when designing your software because you know certain operations are likely to be cached and thus cheap.

RavenDB also has a feature called Aggressive Caching, which allows the RavenDB client API to register for changes from the server. At that point, we don't even need to make a call to the server if we already have a cached value. We can wait for the server to let us know that something has changed and that we need to call back to the database to see what that change was. For certain types of data – config/reference documents in particular – that can provide major performance savings.

3.6.5. REFERENCE HANDLING, INCLUDE AND LOADDOCUMENT

Earlier in this chapter, we looked at various types of relationships between objects and documents, like embedding a value inside a larger document, many-to-one and many-to-many relationships and more. While we were focused on building our model, I skipped a bit on explaining how we work with relationships beyond the diagram stage. I'd like to return to that now.

There are two separate operations that we need to take into account. Fetching related information during a query or a document load can be done using an `Include` call, which we already covered in Zero to RavenDB. I'm pointing this out again because it's a very important feature that deserves more attention (and use). It's an incredibly powerful tool to reduce the number of server requests when working with complex data.

The second operation is querying, or more to the point, when I want to query for a particular document based on the properties of a related document. Going back to the kindergarten example, searching for all the children whose mothers' names are Lorina would be a great example. The child document no longer contains the name of the parent, so how are we going to search for that? RavenDB doesn't allow you to perform joins, but it does allow you to index related data during the indexing phase and then query on that. So querying the children by their mothers' names is quite easy to do, using the `LoadDocument` feature. `LoadDocument` is discussed in full in Chapter 10.

I'm mentioning it here because knowing that it exists has an impact on the way we model data. Be sure to read all about what `LoadDocument` can do and how it works. It can be of great help when deciding how to model related data. In the end, though, the decision almost always comes down to whether we want a point-in-time view of the data or the current value. For the first option, we'll typically copy the value from the source to its own document, and for the second, we can use `LoadDocument` during indexing and querying and `Include` when fetching the data from the server.

3.6.6. ATTACHMENTS AND BINARY DATA

RavenDB is a JSON document database, but not all data can be (or should be) represented in JSON. This is especially true when you consider that a document might reasonably include binary data. For example, when working with an order document, the invoice PDF might be something we need to keep.[9]. If we have a user document, the profile picture is another piece of binary data that is both part of the document and separate from it.

RavenDB's answer to that need is attachments. Attachments are binary data that can be attached to documents. An attachment is always on a document, and beyond the binary data,

---

9   A signed PDF invoice is pretty common, and you're required to keep it for tax purposes and can't just generate it on the fly

there's an attachment name (which must be unique within the scope of the parent document). Attachments are kept on the same storage as the documents, although in a separate location, and can be worked on together with documents.

That means attachments can participate in the same transaction as documents with the same ACID semantics (all in or none at all). There's no size limit for attachments, and a single document can have multiple attachments.

The ability to store binary data easily is important for our modeling, especially because we can treat attachment changes as part of our transaction. That means an operation such as "the lease is signed" can be done in a single transaction that includes both the update of the Lease document and the storage of the signed lease scan in the same operation. That can save you a bit of a headache with error handling.

When modeling, consider which external data is strongly related to the document and should be stored as an attachment. The easiest mental model I have for doing this is to consider attachments in email. Imagine that the document is the email content, and the attachments are just like attachments in email. Typically, such attachments provide additional information about the topic in question, and that's a good use case for attachments in RavenDB.

3.6.7. REVISIONS AND AUDITING

Tracking changes in data over time is a challenging task. Depending on the domain in question,[10] we need to be able to show all changes that happened to a document. RavenDB supports that with its revisions feature.

The database administrator can configure RavenDB to keep track of document revisions. Whenever a document is changed, an immutable revision will be created, which can be used later on to follow all changes that happened to a document. RavenDB can be set to track only specific collections and to only keep track of the last N revisions, but often you'll choose "track everything" since disk space is relatively cheap and those domains need this account-ability. It's better to keep too much than not enough.

Revisions also can apply to deletes, so you can restore a deleted document if you need to. One way of looking at revisions is as a way to have a copy of all changes on a per-document level.[11]

Auditing is a *bit* different. While revisions tell you *what* changed, auditing tells you by *whom* and typically what *for*. RavenDB supports this kind of auditing using client-side listeners, which can provide additional context for the document whenever it's changed. We'll discuss listeners and their use in more depth in Chapter 4.

3.6.8. EXPIRATION

When storing documents inside RavenDB, you can specify that they will expire at a given point in time. RavenDB will periodically remove all the expired documents automatically. This

---

10   This is common in insurance and healthcare, for example.
11   Obviously, this does not alleviate the need to have proper backups.

is a relatively small feature, but it's nice to be able to implement functionality like "the link in this email will expire in 12 hours."

We'll see how to use the expiration feature in Chapter 4. There isn't much to say about it besides that it works, but it should be noted that the expiration is a soft one. In other words, if you specified an expiration time, the document might still be there after that time has passed because RavenDB didn't get around to cleaning it yet. By default, RavenDB will clear expired documents every minute. So the document might live just a bit longer than expected, but not terribly so.

3.7. ACID vs. BASE

The final topic in the modeling chapter is one of the more important ones. ACID stands for atomic, consistent, isolated and durable, while BASE stands for basically available, soft state, eventually consistent. Those are two very different approaches for dealing with data.

RavenDB uses both, in different parts of its operations. In general, ACID is what we always strive for. A fully consistent model makes it easy to build upon and reason about, but it also can be quite expensive to build and maintain. In a distributed system, ensuring atomicity can be quite expensive, since you need to talk to multiple machines for each operation, for example. On the other hand, BASE give us a lot more freedom, and that translates into a lot more optimization opportunities.

In RavenDB, all operations on a document or attachment using its ID (put, modify, delete) are always consistent and run in an ACID transaction. Bulk operations over sets of documents (update all that match a particular query, bulk insert, etc.) are composed of multiple separate transactions instead of one very big one.

By default, when you save a document into RavenDB, we'll acknowledge the write when the data has been saved on one node in a durable fashion.[12] You can also ask the write to be acknowledged only when the write has been made durable on multiple nodes (using the WaitForReplicationAfterSaveChanges method) for additional safety. We discuss all such details in Chapter 6.

One of the typical balancing acts that database administrators have to do is to choose how many indexes they will have. Too many indexes and the write process grinds to a halt. Not enough indexes and your queries are going to require table scans, which are *horrendously* expensive even on moderately sized databases.

The reason for the tradeoff is that a transaction must update all the relevant indexes on every change. That means that index updates are right there in the main pathway for updating data, which explains why they can so severely degrade performance. When designing our indexing implementation, we took a different approach.

---

12   That means that the data has been written to disk and fsync() or the equivalent was called, so the data is safe from power loss.

Indexing in RavenDB is handled as an asynchronous task running in the background whenever there are updates to the database. This means that we don't have to wait for the index to finish updating before completing the write. And that means that we have far better opportunities for optimizations. For example, we can roll up multiple changes that happened in different transactions into the same index update batch.

This also allows us to be able to prioritize certain operations on the fly. If we're under a load of pressure right now, we can reduce the amount of time we spend indexing in order to serve more requests. This follows the idea that we always want to be able to return a result from RavenDB as soon as possible and that, in many cases, a triple-checked answer that came too late is worse than useless.

Indexes in RavenDB are BASE in the sense that they can lag behind the documents they reflect. In practice, indexes are kept up to date and the lag time between a document update and an index update is typically measured in microseconds. The BASE nature of indexes allows us to achieve a number of desirable properties. Adding an index to the system doesn't block anything, and updating an index definition can be done in a side-by-side manner. Various optimizations are possible because of this (mostly related to batching and avoidance of locks).

What are the costs in waiting

Waiting for indexing or waiting for replication is something that you have to explicitly ask for because it costs. But what *are* those costs? In the case of replication, it means waiting for another server (or servers) to get the information and persist it safely to disk. That can add latency in the order of tens of milliseconds when running on a local data center – and hundreds of milliseconds if your cluster is going over the public internet.

For indexing, this is usually a short amount of time since the indexes are updated quickly. If there's a new index, it may take longer because the write will have to wait for the index to catch up not just with this write but also with all the writes that the new index is processing.

We typically measure RavenDB performance in tens or hundreds of thousands of requests per second. Even going with just 10,000 requests per second, that gives us a budget of 1/10 of a millisecond to process a request. Inside RavenDB, requests are handled in an async manner, so it isn't as if we're holding hundreds of threads open. But additional wait time for the request is something we want to avoid.

For the most part, those costs are pretty small, but there are times where they might be higher. If there's a new index running, and we asked to wait for all indexes, we may be waiting for a while. And we want the default behavior to be as predictable as possible. That isn't meant to discourage you from using these features, but we suggest that you give it some thought.

In particular, spraying the waits at any call is possible and it will work, but it's usually not the best solution. You typically want to apply them in specific scenarios: either high-value writes (and you want to make sure that it's saved on multiple nodes) or if you intend to issue a query immediately after the write and want to ensure that it will be included in the results. Otherwise, you should accept the defaults and allow RavenDB the freedom to optimize its operations.

The BASE on indexing behavior is optional. You can ask RavenDB to wait for the indexes to update (using the WaitForIndexesAfterSaveChanges method) so you have the option of choosing. If this is a write you intend to immediately query, you can force a wait. Usually, that isn't required, so you don't need to pay the cost here.

You need to be aware of the distinctions here between queries (which can be BASE and lag a bit[13]) and bulk operations (many small transactions) and operations on specific documents (either one at a time or in groups), which happen as ACID transactions. Taking advantage of the BASE nature of indexing allows you to reduce the cost of querying and writing, as well as selectively apply the decision on a case-by-case basis.

3.8. Summary

Modeling data in RavenDB isn't a trivial topic, and it isn't over just because you finished this chapter. I tried to highlight certain features and their impact on modeling, but I suggest finishing the book and then reading this chapter again, with fresh perspective and a better understanding of how things are playing together.

We started by looking at RavenDB as a simple key/value store. Just throw data in (such as session information, shopping cart, etc.) and access it by a well-known key. That has the advantage of giving us fast operations without hiding the data behind an opaque barrier. We can also use the expiration feature to store time dependent data.

From the trivial model of key/value store, we moved to considering real document models. By looking at how documents in the real world – physical ones – are modeled, we made it much easier to explain document models to the business. Reducing the impedance mismatch between the business and the application is always a good thing, and proper modeling can help there. Of course, don't go too far. Remember that documents are virtual concepts and aren't limited to the physical world. We then looked at the issue of denormalization and noted the difference between the same *value* of the data and the same *meaning* of the data.

The next topic was actual modeling. We looked at how we should structure embedded values to store data that's intrinsically part of the document instead of holding that data outside of the document. We looked at how to model relations and collections, many-to-one and many-to-many associations. Then we covered more advanced modeling techniques, such as

---

13   The typical lag time for indexing is under 1 ms

how to handle references and configuration data and how to deal with temporal information and hierarchical structures.

Next, we went over some of the constraints that we have to take into account when modeling, like how to deal with the growth of a document and what constitutes a good size for a document in RavenDB. We looked at concurrency control and how change vectors are useful for optimistic concurrency and for caching. And we examined why we should avoid caching aggregated data in our model (NumberOfOrders).

We looked at handling binary data with attachments, as well as auditing and change tracking using the revisions feature, and we learned that we can expire documents natively in RavenDB. Reference handling at indexing and query time was briefly covered (we'll cover it in depth in Chapter 9), as it's important to how you model your documents.

A repeating theme was the use of semantic IDs to give you better control over documents and their meaning – not so much for RavenDB's sake[14] but because it increases understanding and visibility in your domain. Using document IDs to "nest" documents such as accounts/1234/tx/2017-05 or having meaningful document IDs such as config/states helps a lot in setting out the structure for your model.

The final topic we covered was ACID vs. BASE in RavenDB. Documents in RavenDB are stored and accessed in an ACID manner, while we default to BASE queries to get higher performance and have more chances for optimizations. This behavior is controlled by the user on a case-by-case basis, so you can select the appropriate mode for each scenario.

Our next chapter is going to cover the client API in depth, going over all the tools that you have to create some really awesome behaviors. After that, we'll get to running clusters of RavenDB and understanding how the distributed portion of RavenDB is handled.

---

14   The database doesn't care what your document IDs look like.

4. Deep Dive Into the RavenDB Client API

In this chapter, we're going to take a deep dive into how the client API works. We're going to show mostly C# code examples, but the same concepts apply to any of the RavenDB client APIs, regardless of platform, with minor changes needed to make things applicable.

There are still some concepts that we haven't gotten around to (clustering or indexing, for example), which will be covered in their own chapters. But the client API is rich and has a lot of useful functionality on its own, quite aside from the server-side behavior.

We already looked into the document store and the document session, the basic building blocks of CRUD in RavenDB. But in this chapter, we're going to look beyond the obvious and into the more advanced features.

One thing we'll *not* talk about in this chapter is querying. We'll cover that extensively in Chapter 9, so let's keep it there. You already know the basics of querying in RavenDB, but there's a *lot* more power for you to discover.

This chapter is going to contain a large number of code examples, and it will discuss the nitty-gritty details of using the client. It's divided into brief sections, each dealing with a specific feature or behavior. I suggest reading this over to note the capabilities of RavenDB and coming back to it as needed in your application.

For the rest of this chapter, we'll use the classes shown in Listing 4.1 as our model, using a simplified help desk as our example.

Listing 4.1 *Simplified Help Desk sample model*

```
public class Customer
{
    public string Id { get; set; }
    public string Name { get; set; }
}
```

```
public class SupportCall
{
    public string Id { get; set; }
    public string CustomerId { get; set; }
    public DateTime Started { get;set; }
    public DateTime? Ended { get;set; }
    public string Issue { get; set; }
    public int Votes { get; set; }
    public List<string> Comments { get; set; }
}
```

4.1. Writing documents

Writing documents in RavenDB is easy, as we saw in "Zero to RavenDB". If we want to create a new support call, we can use the code in Listing 4.2 to do so.

Listing 4.2 *Creating a new support call using the session*

```
using (var session = store.OpenSession())
{
    var call = new SupportCall
    {
        Started = DateTime.UtcNow,
        Issue = customerIssue,
        CustomerId = customerId
    };
    session.Store(call);
    session.SaveChanges();
}
```

This is the basic behavior of RavenDB and how you would typically work with saving data. But there are lot of additional things that we can do when writing data. For example, let's say the user might have sent us some screenshots that we want to include in the support call.

4.1.1. WORKING WITH ATTACHMENTS

You can add attachments to a RavenDB document to store binary data related to that document. Let's assume the user sent us a screenshot of the problem along with the call. Listing 4.3 shows how we can store and retrieve the attachments.

Listing 4.3 *Saving attachments to RavenDB as part of opening the support call*

```
using (var session = store.OpenSession())
{
    var call = new SupportCall
    {
        Started = DateTime.UtcNow,
        Issue = customerIssue,
        CustomerId = customerId
    };
    session.Store(call);

    foreach (var file in attachedFiles)
    {
        session.Advanced.StoreAttachment(call, file.Name,
            file.OpenStream());
    }

    session.SaveChanges();
}
```

Note that we're using the session to store both the support call document and any attachments the user might have sent. An attachment is basically a file name and a stream that will be sent to the server (with an optional content type). When the call to SaveChanges is made, the RavenDB client API will send both the new document and all of its attachments to the server in a single call, which will be treated as a transaction. Both the document and the attachments will be saved, or both will fail.

That was easy enough, but now how do we retrieve the attachments? The list of attachments for a particular document is accessible via the session, as shown in Listing 4.4.

Listing 4.4 *Getting the list of attachments for a support call*

```
using (var session = store.OpenSession())
{
    var call = session.Load<SupportCall>("SupportCalls/238-B");
    var attachments = session.Advanced.GetAttachmentNames(call);

    // render the call and the attachment names
}
```

Calling `GetAttachmentNames` is cheap; the attachments on a document are already present in the document metadata, which we loaded as part of getting the document. There is no server-side call involved. Note that the result of `GetAttachmentNames` doesn't include the *content* of the attachments. To get the attachment itself and not just its name, you need to make an additional call, as shown in Listing 4.5.

Listing 4.5 *Getting an attachment content*

```
using (var session = store.OpenSession())
{
    var call = session.Load<SupportCall>("SupportCalls/238-B");
    var attachments = session.Advanced.GetAttachmentNames(call);

    using (var stream = session.Advanced.GetAttachment(call,
        attachments[0].Name))
    {
        // process the content of the attachment
    }
}
```

Each call to `GetAttachment` will make a separate call to the server to fetch the attachment. If you have a lot of attachments, be aware that fetching all their information can be expensive due to the number of remote calls that are involved.

4.1.2. WORKING WITH THE DOCUMENT METADATA

In the attachments section, we noted that attachment information is stored in the document metadata. RavenDB uses the metadata for a lot of things. Most of them you don't generally care about (etag, change vector, etc.). But the document metadata is also available to you for your own needs and use.

An actual use case for direct use of the document metadata is pretty rare. If you want to store information, you'll typically want to store it in the document itself, not throw it to the metadata sidelines. Typical use cases for storing data in the metadata are cross-cutting concerns. The preeminent one is auditing. You may want to see who edited a document, for example.

In order to demonstrate working with the metadata, we'll consider creating a support call. Handling a support call can be a complex process that has to go through several steps. In this case, we will save the new support call document to RavenDB with a draft status in the metadata. Typical modeling advice would be to model this explicitly in the domain (so you'll have an `IsDraft` or `Status` property on your model), but for this example, we'll use the metadata. You can see the code for setting a draft status in the metadata in Listing 4.6.

Listing 4.6 *Setting a metadata flag as part of creating a new support call*

```
using (var session = store.OpenSession())
{
    var call = new SupportCall
    {
        Started = DateTime.UtcNow,
        Issue = customerIssue,
        CustomerId = customerId
    };
    session.Store(call);

    var metadata = session.Advanced.GetMetadataFor(call);
    metadata["Status"] = "Draft";

    session.SaveChanges();
}
```

We can call GetMetadataFor on any document that has been associated with the session. A document is associated with the session either by loading it from the server or by calling Store. After the document has been associated with the session, we can get its metadata and manipulate it.

Changes to the metadata count as changes to the document and will cause the document to be saved to the server when SaveChanges is called.

4.1.3. CHANGE TRACKING AND SAVECHANGES

The document session implements change tracking on your documents, as you can see in Listing 4.7.

Listing 4.7 *Setting a metadata flag as part of creating a new support call*

```
using (var session = store.OpenSession())
{
    var call = session.Load<SupportCall>("SupportCalls/238-B");

    call.Ended = DateTime.UtcNow;

    session.SaveChanges();
}
```

The session's change tracking (and identity map) means that you don't have to keep track of what changed and manually call `Store`. Instead, when you call `SaveChanges`, all your changes will be sent to the server in a single request.

You have a few knobs available to tweak the process. `session.Advanced.HasChanges` will let you know if calling `SaveChanges` will result in a call to the server. And `session.Advanced.HasChanged(entity)` will tell you when a particular `entity` has changed. You can also take it up a notch and ask RavenDB to tell you *what* changed, using `session.Advanced.WhatChanged()`. This will give you all the changes that happened in the session. The `WhatChanged` feature can be nice if you want to highlight changes for user approval, for example, or if you just want to see what modifications were made to your model after a certain operation.

You can also tell RavenDB not to update a particular instance by calling `session.Advanced.IgnoreChangesFor(entity)`. The document will remain attached to the session and will be part of any identity map operations, but it won't be saved to the server when `SaveChanges` is called. Alternatively, you can call `session.Advanced.Evict(entity)` to make the session completely forget about a document.

These operations tend to be useful only in specific cases, but they are very powerful when utilized properly.

4.1.4. OPTIMISTIC CONCURRENCY

We covered optimistic concurrency in Chapter 3, but only in the most general terms. Now, let's take a look and see how we can use optimistic concurrency in practice. Listing 4.8 shows two simultaneous sessions modifying the same support call.

Listing 4.8 *Concurrent modifications of a support call*

```
using (var sessionOne = store.OpenSession())
using (var sessionTwo = store.OpenSession())
{
    var callOne = sessionOne.Load<SupportCall>("SupportCalls/238-B");
    var callTwo = sessionTwo.Load<SupportCall>("SupportCalls/238-B");

    callOne.Ended = DateTime.Today;
    callTwo.Ended = DateTime.Today.AddDays(1);

    sessionOne.SaveChanges();
    sessionTwo.SaveChanges();
}
```

In the case of the code in Listing 4.8, we're always going to end up with the support call end date set to tomorrow. This is because, by default, RavenDB uses the `Last Write Wins` model. You can change that by setting `store.Conventions.UseOptimisticConcurrency` to "true," which will affect all sessions, or you can change it on a case-by-case basis by setting `session.Advanced.UseOptimisticConcurrency` to "true" on the session directly.

In either case, when this flag is set and `SaveChanges` is called, we'll send the modified documents to the server alongside their change vectors that were received from the server when loading the documents. This allows the server to reject any stale writes. If the flag were set to true, the code in Listing 4.8 would result in a `ConcurrencyException` on the `sessionTwo.SaveChanges()` call.

This ensures that you can't overwrite changes you didn't see, and if you set `UseOptimisticConcurrency`, you need to handle this error in some manner.

4.1.4.1. Pessimistic locking

When changes happen behind our backs to the document we modified, optimistic locking handles it. Pessimistic locking, on the other hand, prevents those changes entirely. RavenDB does *not* support pessimistic locking. And while you really need support from the database engine to properly implement pessimistic locking, we fake it in an interesting way. The following is a recipe for using approximating pessimistic locking in RavenDB. We mention it not so much because it's a good idea, but because it allows us to explore several different features and see how they work together.

Using pessimistic locking, we can lock a document for modification until we release the lock or until a certain amount of time has gone by. We can build a pessimistic lock in RavenDB by utilizing the document metadata and optimistic concurrency. It's easier to explain with code, and you can find the `Lock` and `Unlock` implementations in Listing 4.9.

> **The locks are opt-in**
>
> In RavenDB, both the pessimistic lock explored in this section and the optimistic lock in the previous section are opt-in. That means that you have to explicitly participate in the lock. If you're using `UseOptimisticConcurrency` and another thread isn't, that thread will get the `Last Write Wins` behavior (and might overwrite the changes made by the thread using optimistic concurrency).
>
> In the same manner, the pessimistic lock recipe described here is dependent on all parties following it. If there's a thread that isn't, the lock will not be respected.
>
> In short, when using concurrency control, make sure that you're using it across the board, or it may not hold.

Listing 4.9 *Extension method to add pessimistic locking to the session*

```
public static IDisposable Lock(
    this IDocumentSession session,
    string docToLock)
{
    var doc = session.Load<object>(docToLock);
    if (doc == null)
        throw new DocumentDoesNotExistException("The document " +
            docToLock + " does not exists and cannot be locked");

    var metadata = session.Advanced.GetMetadataFor(doc);
    if (metadata.GetBoolean("Pessimistic-Locked"))
    {
        // the document is locked and the lock is still value
        var ticks = metadata.GetNumber("Pessimistic-Lock-Timeout");
        var lockedUntil = new DateTime(ticks);
        if (DateTime.UtcNow <= lockedUntil)
            throw new ConcurrencyException("Document " +
                docToLock + " is locked using pessimistic");
    }

    metadata["Pessimistic-Locked"] = true;
    metadata["Pessimistic-Lock-Timeout"] =
        DateTime.UtcNow.AddSeconds(15).Ticks;

    // will throw if someone else took the look in the meantime
    session.Advanced.UseOptimisticConcurrency = true;
    session.SaveChanges();

    return new DisposableAction(() =>
    {
        metadata.Remove("Pessimistic-Locked");
        metadata.Remove("Pessimistic-Lock-Timeout");
        Debug.Assert(session.Advanced.UseOptimisticConcurrency);
        session.SaveChanges();
    });
}
```

There's quite a bit of code in Listing 4.9, but there isn't actually a lot that gets done. We load a document and check if its metadata contains the `Pessimistic-Locked` value. If it does, we check if the lock time expired. If it isn't locked, we first update the document metadata, then enable *optimistic* concurrency and finally call `SaveChanges`. If no one else modified the document in the meantime, we'll successfully mark the document as ours, and any other call to `Lock` will fail.

The `Lock` method returns an `IDisposable` instance that handles releasing the lock. This is done by removing the metadata values and then calling `SaveChanges` again. If the lock has timed out and someone took the lock, we'll fail here with a concurrency exception as well.

Avoid your own distributed pessimistic locks

There's a reason why RavenDB does not include a pessimistic lock feature, and I strongly recommend you avoid using the recipe above. It's here to show how you'd use several different features at once to achieve a goal.

Actually handling a distributed lock is a non-trivial issue. Consider a RavenDB cluster with multiple nodes. If two lock requests go to two distinct nodes at the same time, *both* of them will succeed.[1] The two nodes will quickly discover the conflicting updates and generate a conflict. But it isn't guaranteed they'll discover it inside the lock/unlock period.

Another issue is the subject of timing. If two clients have enough of a clock skew, a client might consider a lock to have expired even though it's still valid. Proper distributed locking requires a consensus protocol of some kind, and those aren't trivial to build or use. RavenDB does have a consensus protocol, but pessimistic locking is usually a bad fit for an OLTP environment, and we decided not to implement it.

A typical use for pessimistic locks is to lock a document while a user is editing it. That might sound like a good idea, but experience has shown that, in most cases, it leads to trouble. Consider, for example, version control systems. If you're reading this book, you've likely used a SCM of some kind. If you haven't, I suggest you pick up a book about source control and prioritize it over this one: learning about that is far more foundational.

Early source control systems (SourceSafe is a good example) used locks as their concurrency model, and that led to a lot of problems. Say Joe locks a file and then leaves on vacation. All of his coworkers then have to wait until he gets back before committing code to that file. This is a typical problem that arises in such cases. The same happens when you have pessimistic locks. Implementing pessimistic locks requires you to also implement forced lock release, a feature that tells you who locked the document and a whole slew of management functions around it. Typically, implementing optimistic concurrency or merging is easier and matches most users' expectations.

---

1   We'll discuss in detail how RavenDB clusters work in the next chapter.

4.1.4.2. Offline optimistic concurrency

We looked at online optimistic concurrency in Listing 4.8, where we loaded a document into the session, modified it and then saved. In that time frame, if there was a change, we'd get a concurrency exception. But most software doesn't work like that. In a web application, you aren't going to keep the document session open for as long as the user is on the site. Instead, most likely you'll use a session-per-request model. The user will load a page with the document's content in one request and modify it in another request. There isn't a shared session in sight, so how can we implement optimistic concurrency?

All you need to do is send the change vector of the document to the user and accept it back when the user wants to save the document. Listing 4.10 shows an example using two separate sessions with concurrency handling between them.

Listing 4.10 *Concurrent modifications of a support call*

```
string changeVector;
Supportcall callOne;

using (var sessionOne = store.OpenSession())
using (var sessionTwo = store.OpenSession())
{
    callOne = sessionOne.Load<SupportCall>("SupportCalls/238-B");
    changeVector = sessionOne.Advanced.GetChangeVectorFor(callOne);

    var callTwo = sessionTwo.Load<SupportCall>("SupportCalls/238-B");

    callTwo.Ended = DateTime.Today.AddDays(1);

    sessionTwo.SaveChanges();
}

using (var sessionThree = store.OpenSession())
{
    sessionThree.Advanced.UseOptimisticConcurrency = true;

    callOne.Ended = DateTime.Today;

    sessionThree.Store(callOne, changeVector, callOne.Id);

    sessionThree.SaveChanges(); // will raise ConcurrencyException
}
```

The code in Listing 4.10 first loads the support call in `sessionOne`. Then the code loads it again in `sessionTwo`, modifies the support call and saves it to the server. Both sessions are then closed, and we open a *new* session, `sessionThree`. We call `Store`, passing the entity instance and the change vector that we got from the first session, as well as the document ID.

This gives the RavenDB client API enough information for us to do an optimistic concurrency check from the time we loaded `callOne` in the first session. In a web scenario, you'll typically send the change vector alongside the actual data and get it back from the client to do the check. You might also want to check out the `Changes API`, which is covered a little later in this chapter. This might help you get early change notifications when you need to implement offline optimistic concurrency.

4.1.5. PATCHING DOCUMENTS AND CONCURRENT MODIFICATIONS

The typical workflow with RavenDB is to open a session, load a document, run some business logic and call `SaveChanges`. When you follow those steps, the session will figure out what documents have changed and send them to the server. This model is simple and easy to follow, and it's the recommended way to work.

However, there are a few scenarios in which we don't want to send the entire document back to the server. For example, if our document is very large and we want to make a small change, we can avoid that cost. Another reason to avoid the full document save is a scenario that calls for concurrent work on a document.

Let's consider the `SupportCall.Votes` property. Two users may very well want to vote on the same support call at the same time. One way to handle that is to load the support call, increment the `Votes` property and call `SaveChanges`. In order to handle concurrent modifications, we can utilize optimistic concurrency and retries. But that's quite a lot of work to write, and if the document is large, there's also a lot of data going back and forth over the network for little reason. Listing 4.11 shows how we can do much better.

Listing 4.11 *Incrementing a property using the Patch API*

```
using (var session = store.OpenSession())
{
    session.Advanced.Increment<SupportCall, int>("SupportCalls/238-B",
    c => c.Votes, 1);

    session.SaveChanges();
}
```

What the code in Listing 4.11 does is generate a patch request, rather than load and save the full document. That request is stored in the session, and when `SaveChanges` is called, it will be sent to the server (alongside any other changes/operations made on the session, as usual). On the server side, we'll apply this operation to the document. This patch request is safe to call concurrently, since there's no loss of data when executing patches.

Which is faster, patching or load/save?

The hasty answer is that patching is faster. We send a lot less data, and we need one less round trip to do so. Winning all around, right?

But the real answer is that things are bit more complex. The patch request is actually a JavaScript function that we send. That means we need to parse and run it on the server side, potentially marshal values into the script environment and then marshal it back. Conversely, the code path for loading and saving documents in RavenDB is well trodden and has been optimized plenty. That means in many cases it might be easier to just load and modify the document directly, rather than use a patch.

Patching *isn't* expensive; I want to emphasize that. But at the same time, I've seen codebases where *all* writes had to be made using patching because of perceived performance benefits. That resulted in an extremely hard-to-understand system that was resistant to change. The general recommendation is to utilize patching only when you need to support concurrent modifications.

Note that in most cases concurrent modifications of the same document is *not* the default. A properly modeled document should have a single reason to change, but it's common that documents have additional data on them (like the Votes property or Comments) that are important to save but don't have any real business logic attached to them.

That kind of change is fine to do using patching. If you find yourself trying to run serious business logic in patch scripts (we'll see exactly how to do this in a bit), you should move that into your own business logic.

An important consideration to take into account is that there is no guarantee as to the order in which the patches will run. But, you don't need to worry about concurrency between patches on the same document as there is no concurrent/interleaved execution of the scripts on the same document.

A slightly more complex example of the use of patching is adding a comment to a SupportCall. Just like before, we want to support adding a comment concurrently. But to make things a bit more interesting, we'll add a business rule: a call that has been ended cannot have additional comments added to it. Listing 4.12 shows the obvious way to accomplish this.

Listing 4.12 *Adding a comment to a support call using patch*

```
using (var session = store.OpenSession())
{
    var call = session.Load<SupportCall>("SupportCalls/238-B");
    if (call.Ended != null)
        throw new
            InvalidOperationException("Cannot comment on closed call");

    session.Advanced.Patch(call, c => c.Comments,
        comments => comments.Add("This is important stuff!"));

    session.SaveChanges();
}
```

In Listing 4.12, you can see how we moved from using the simple `Increment` call to the `Patch`, which allows us to either replace a property value completely or add an item to a collection. If you look closely at the code in Listing 4.12, you'll find that there's a hidden race condition there. The business rule is that we can't add comments to a closed call; we're able to load the call, check that its `Ended` property is null and then send the patch request to the server. However, in the meantime, another client could have closed the call, and yet we'd still add the comment.

The seriousness of this issue depends entirely on the domain and the model. It's possible that you *do* want to add comments during that period, or it's possible that allowing it could break important business invariants.

Patch requests are sent as part of `SaveChanges`

It's probably obvious, but I wanted to spell this out explicitly. Calls to `Patch`, `Increment` or `Defer` don't go to the server immediately. Instead, they're added to the list of operations the session needs to execute and will be sent to the server in a single batch (along with any modified documents) when `SaveChanges` is called. If you have multiple patch operations in the same session on the same document, they'll be merged into a single patch. And if there are multiple patches on different documents, they'll all be executed within the same transaction, as a single unit.

There are two ways to avoid the race condition. We can send a change vector to the server asking it to fail with a concurrency exception if the document has been modified since we last saw it. That *works*, but it defeats the whole point of using patches for concurrent modification of the document. The second alternative is to move the invariant check into the script itself. Calls to `Increment` and `Patch` are actually just wrappers around the `Defer` call, which allows you to add work to the session that's to be sent to the server when `SaveChanges` is called.

In Listing 4.13, we're dropping down to using `Defer` directly to manipulate the patch request ourselves, with no wrappers. As you can see, this is a bit involved, but overall it's pretty straightforward.

Listing 4.13 *Using a patch script to maintain call invariants*

```
using (var session = store.OpenSession())
{
    session.Advanced.Defer(new PatchCommandData(
        id: "SupportCalls/238-B",
        changeVector: null,
        patch: new PatchRequest
        {
            Script = @"
                if (this.Ended == null)
                    throw 'Cannot add a comment to a closed call';
                this.Comments.push($comment);
                ",
            Values =
            {
                ["comment"] = "This is important stuff!!"
            }
        },
        patchIfMissing: null));

    session.SaveChanges();
}
```

The code in Listing 4.13 passes a `PatchCommandData`, containing the relevant document ID, to `Defer`. The key part is in the `PatchRequest` itself. We do the check on the document and fail if the call has already been closed. If it hasn't, we add the comment to the call. You can also see that we don't have to deal with string concatenation here since we can pass arguments to the scripts directly. There's also the option to run a script if the document does not exist. This gives you the option to do a "modify or create" style of operation.

Using this method, we can be sure that we'll never violate the rule about adding comments to a closed call. A cautionary word, though: this is more complex than anything we've dealt with before, and I would only recommend doing it if you really must. Running logic in this manner inside the database is a powerful technique, but it's also usually a bad idea because of its potential for abuse. Problems that come with abusing this feature include the scripts being run under a lock, which prevents the database from completing transactions quickly. If you find yourself doing something like this frequently, stop and reconsider.

4.1.6. DEFERRING COMMANDS

In the previous section, we used the `Defer` method to register a `PatchCommandData` on the session, to be executed when `SaveChanges` is called. But `Defer` is more generic then this. It's a general mechanism for the user to register arbitrary commands that will be part of the same transaction as the `SaveChanges`.

The RavenDB API is like an ogre. It has layers

Like the popular character Shrek, RavenDB API is composed of layers. At the top, you have the document store and the document session. Those are built using the operations concept, which you typically won't use directly. And the operations are handled via the request executor, which allows you to generate requests directly to the server (and take advantage of RavenDB's authentication and automatic failover).

The case of `Defer` is a good example. Instead of forcing you to drop down all the way, we expose an extension point in the session so you can plug in a command of your own and piggyback on the session handling of transactions.

The available commands range from putting and deleting documents and attachments to applying patches that delete documents having some prefix. Aside from the patch operation, the rest are only useful in rare cases. The most common use of `Defer` beyond patch is when you need fine-grained control over the operations that will be executed in a single transaction, to the point where you want to control the ordering of the operations.

RavenDB doesn't allow changing the document's collection, you can't just update the `@collection` metadata. So, if you need to do this,[2] you must first delete the old document and then create a new one with the appropriate collection. The session doesn't allow you to both delete and modify a document. And for the purpose of discussion, let's say that we *have* to make this in a single transaction, so no other client sees a point in time where the document was deleted.

To be clear, this is a strange situation, dreamt up specifically to showcase a feature that should be only used in special circumstances. This escape hatch in the API is specifically intended to prevent you from being blocked if you need something we didn't foresee, but I can't emphasize enough that this is probably a bad idea. The emergency exit is important, but you don't want to make it the front door.

Another reason to avoid using `Defer` is that it's lower in the RavenDB client API layers. Instead of dealing with high level concepts like entity, you'll be dealing with the direct manner in which RavenDB is representing JSON, the blittable format (which we'll discuss later in this chapter). That format is meant to be high performance, and things like developer convenience were secondary in its design.

---

2   And this should be a very rare thing indeed.

4.1.7. BULK INSERTING DOCUMENTS TO RAVENDB

RavenDB is fast, *really* fast, but it still needs to face operational realities. The fallacies of distributed computing still apply, and I/O takes a non-trivial amount of time. This means that when you want to get the best speed out of RavenDB, you need to help it achieve that.

> **Stacking the deck**
>
> I'm going to be talking performance numbers in this section, and I wanted to make it clear that I've intentionally chosen the worst possible situation for RavenDB and then compounded the issue by using the wrong approaches. This is so I can show the real costs in a manner that's highly visible.
>
> I'll refer you again to the fallacies of distributed computing. I'm trying to select a scenario that would break as many of those fallacies as possible and show how RavenDB is able to handle them.

Listing 4.14 shows the absolute slowest way to write 10,000 documents into RavenDB.

Listing 4.14 *Writing 10,000 documents, one at a time*

```
var sp = Stopwatch.StartNew();
for (int i = 0; i < 10_000; i++)
{
    using (var session = store.OpenSession())
    {
        session.Store(new Customer
        {
            Name = "Customer #" + i
        });
        session.SaveChanges();
    }
}
Console.WriteLine(sp.Elapsed);
```

For fun, I decided to run the code in Listing 4.14 against the live test instance we have. That instance was in San Francisco, and I was testing this from Israel. The test instance was also running as a container inside an AWS t2.medium machine (two cores and 4 GB of memory, with burst-only mode). In other words, this performance test was heavily biased against RavenDB, and the results were not great. In fact, they were *bad*.

This is because we're running each write as an independent operation, and we have to wait for the previous operation to complete before we can start the new one. What's more, the database server handles just a single request concurrently, which means we have no way to amortize I/O costs across multiple requests. This is the absolute worst way you can write a large amount of documents into RavenDB because most of the time is spent just going back and forth between the client and the application. For each request, we have to make another REST call, send a packet to the server, etc. On the other side, the server accepts a new request, processes it and commits it to disk. During the entire process, it's effectively idle, since most of the time is spent waiting for I/O. That's a big waste all around.

You can see the various times nicely when looking at the Fiddler[3] statistics. Each request takes about 220–260 milliseconds to run. Writing the first 1,000 documents took four minutes and six seconds, and 2,000 requests took eight minutes on the dot. The full 10,000 documents would take 40 minutes or so. Granted, we're intentionally going to a remote server, but still...

What happens when we're running the writes in parallel? The code in Listing 4.15 shows how to do this.

Listing 4.15 *Writing 10,000 documents, with a bit of parallelism thrown in*

```
var sp = Stopwatch.StartNew();
Parallel.For(0, 10_000, i =>
{
    using (var session = store.OpenSession())
    {
        session.Store(new Customer
        {
            Name = "Customer #" + i
        });
        session.SaveChanges();
    }
});
Console.WriteLine(sp.Elapsed);
```

Using the method in Listing 4.15, I was able to write 1,000 documents in 56 seconds. We got to 2,000 in a minute and a half, 3,000 in a minute and 50 seconds, etc. The reason for the speed up is actually related to how thread pooling is handled on the client side. Since we make a lot of blocking requests, the thread pool figures out that we have plenty of blocking work and creates more threads. That means we have the chance to do more concurrent work. So as time goes by, more threads are created and we make additional concurrent requests to RavenDB.

---

3   The Fiddler web proxy is a great debugging tool in general, and is quite useful to peek into the communication between RavenDB's server and clients.

The total time of writing 10,000 documents in this setup was two minutes and 52 seconds. So we've gotten done 20 times faster than we did using sequential writes. The code in Listing 4.15 is still using synchronous calls, which means the client side is spinning threads to handle the load and we're limited by the rate of new thread creation on the client.

RavenDB also supports an async API, which is much more suitable for scale-out scenarios because we aren't holding a thread for the duration of the connection. Listing 4.16 shows how we can write all those documents in parallel, using the async API. The code is a tad complex because we want to control the number of concurrent requests we make. Spinning 10,000 concurrent requests will likely load the network and require careful attention to how they are managed, which is out of scope for this book. Instead, I limited the number of concurrent connections to 128.

Listing 4.16 *Writing 10,000 documents, using async API*

```
var sp = Stopwatch.StartNew();
var semaphore = new SemaphoreSlim(128);

async Task WriteDocument(int i)
{
    using (var session = store.OpenAsyncSession())
    {
        await session.StoreAsync(new Customer
        {
            Name = "Customer #" + i
        });
        await session.SaveChangesAsync();
    }
    semaphore.Release();
}

var tasks = new List<Task>();
for (int i = 0; i < 10_000; i++)
{
    semaphore.Wait();
    tasks.Add(WriteDocument(i));
}

Task.WaitAll(tasks.ToArray());

Console.WriteLine(sp.Elapsed);
```

The code in Listing 4.16 is also using a local method, which is a new C# 7.0 feature. It allows you to package a bit of behavior quite nicely, and it's very useful for small demos and internal async code. This code writes 1,000 documents in just under 10 seconds, and it completes the full 10,000 writes in under 30 seconds (29.6, on my machine). The speed difference is, again, related to the client learning our pattern of behavior and adjusting itself accordingly (creating enough buffers, threads and other resources needed; warming up the TCP connections.[4])

However, we really had to make an effort. We wrote explicit async code and managed it, rate-limited our behavior and jumped through several hoops to get a more reasonable level of performance. Note that we went from over 40 minutes to less than 30 seconds in the span of a few pages. Also note that we haven't actually modified *what* we're doing – we only changed how we're talking to the server – but it had a huge impact on performance.

You can take it as a given that RavenDB is able to process as much data as you can feed it. The typical concern in handling writes is how fast we can get the data to the server, not how fast the server can handle it.

RavenDB contains a dedicated API and behavior that makes it easier to deal with bulk loading scenarios. The bulk insert API uses a single connection to talk to the server and is able to make much better use of the network. The entire process is carefully orchestrated by both the client and the server to optimize performance. Let's look at the code in Listing 4.17 first and then discuss the details.

Listing 4.17 *Using bulk insert to write 100,000 documents, quickly*

```
var sp = Stopwatch.StartNew();

using (var bulkInsert = store.BulkInsert())
{
    for (int i = 0; i < 100_000; i++)
    {
        bulkInsert.Store(new Customer
        {
            Name = "Customer #" + i
        });
    }
}

Console.WriteLine(sp.Elapsed);
```

The code in Listing 4.17 took two minutes and 10 seconds to run on my machine – which is interesting, because it seems slower than the async API usage sample, right? Except there's

---

4   TCP slow start can be a killer on benchmarks.

one problem. I made a typo when writing the code and wrote a *hundred* thousand documents instead of *ten* thousand. If I was writing merely 10,000 documents, it would complete in about 18 seconds. The code is fairly trivial to write, similar to our first sample in Listing 4.14, but the performance is many times faster.

To compare the costs, I ran the same code against a local machine, giving me a total time of 11 seconds to insert 100,000 documents (instead of two minutes remotely). If we wanted to compare apples with apples, then the cost for writing 10,000 documents is shown in Table. 4.1.

Table 4.1. *Bulk insert costs locally and remotely*

	Remote	Local
Session	41 *minutes*	20 seconds
Bulk Insert	18 seconds	6.5 seconds

You can see that while bulk insert is significantly faster in all cases, being over three times faster than the session option (Listing 4.14) locally seems insignificant when considering it's over 130 times faster in the remote case. The major difference, as you can imagine, is the cost of going over the network, but even on the local machine (and we're not even talking about the local network), there's a significant performance benefit for bulk insert.

Amusingly enough, using bulk insert still doesn't saturate the server. For large datasets, it's advisable to have parallel bulk insert operations going at the same time. This gives the server more work to do, and it allows us to do optimizations that increase the ingest rate of the server.

The way bulk insert works is by opening a single long running request to the server and writing the raw data directly into the database. That means we don't need to go back and forth between the client and the server and can rely on a single network roundtrip to do all the work. The server, for its part, will read the data from the network and write it to disk when it's best to do so. In other words, bulk inserts are *not* transactional. A bulk insert is actually composed of many smaller transactions, whose size and scope are determined by the server based on its own calculations, in order to maximize performance.

When the bulk insert is completed, you can rest assured that all the data has been safely committed to disk properly. But during the process, the data is committed incrementally instead of going with a single big-bang approach.

For the most part, RavenDB performance is ruled by how many requests you can send it. The more requests, the higher the degree of parallelism and the more efficiently RavenDB can work. In our internal tests, we routinely bumped into hardware limits (the network card cannot process packets any faster, the disk I/O is saturated, etc.), not software ones.

4.2. Reading documents

We just spent a lot of time learning how we can write documents to RavenDB in all sorts of interesting ways. But for reading, how much is there really to know? We already learned how to load and query a document; we covered that in "Zero to RavenDB." We also covered `Include` and how to use it to effortlessly get referenced documents from the server. What else is there to talk about? As it turns out, quite a bit.

In most applications, reads are far more numerous than writes – often by an order of magnitude. That means RavenDB needs to be prepared to handle a *lot* of reads, and those applications typically have a number of ways in which they access, shape and consume the data. RavenDB needs to be able to provide an answer to all those needs.

The first feature I want to present allows you to dramatically increase your overall performance by being a little lazy.

4.2.1. LAZY REQUESTS

In Section 4.1.7, which dealt with bulk insert, we saw how important the role of the network is. Running the same code on the local network vs. the public internet results in speed differences of 20 seconds to 41 *minutes*, just because of network latencies. On the other hand, moving from many requests to a single bulk insert request is the primary reason we cut our costs by two-thirds on the local machine and over two orders of magnitude in the remote case.

I talked about this a few times already, but it's important. The latency of going to the server and making a remote call is often much higher than the cost of actually processing the request on the server. On the local machine, you'll probably not notice it much. That's normal for running in a development environment. When you go to production, your database is typically going to run on a dedicated machine,[5] so you'll have to go over the network to get it. And that dramatically increases the cost of going to the database.

This problem is well known: it's the fallacies of distributed computing. RavenDB handles the issue in several ways. A session has a budget on the number of remote calls it can make. (This is controlled by `session.Advanced.MaxNumberOfRequestsPerSession`.) If it goes over that limit, an exception is thrown. We had this feature from the get-go, and that led to a lot of thinking about how we can reduce the number of remote calls.

`Include` is obviously one such case. Instead of going to the server multiple times, we let the server know we'll need additional information after this request and tell it to send that immediately. But we can't always do that. Let's take a look at Listing 4.18, showing two queries that we can't optimize using `Include`.

---

5   In fact, it's likely that a database cluster will be used on a set of machines.

Listing 4.18 *Loading a customer and the count of support calls for that customer*

```
using (var session = store.OpenSession())
{
    var customer = session.Load<Customer>("customers/8243-C");
    var countOfCalls = session.Query<SupportCall>()
        .Where(c => c.CustomerId == "customers/8243-C"))
        .Count();

    // show the customer and the number of calls to the user
}
```

A scenario like the one outlined in Listing 4.18 is incredibly common. We have many cases where we need to show the user information from multiple sources, and that's a concern. Each of those calls turns out to be a *remote* call, requiring us to go over the network. There are ways to optimize this specific scenario. We can define a MapReduce index and run a query and Include on it. We haven't yet gone over exactly what this means,[6] but this is a pretty complex solution, and it isn't relevant when you have different types of queries. If we wanted to also load the logged-in user, for example, that wouldn't work.

RavenDB's solution for this issue is the notion of lazy requests. A lazy request isn't actually being executed when you make it. Instead, it's stored in the session, and you get a Lazy<T> instance back. You can make multiple lazy requests, one after another, and no network activity will occur. However, as soon as you access the *value* of one of those lazy instances, all the lazy requests held up by the session will be sent to the server as a single unit.

All those requests will be processed by the server, and all the replies will be sent as a single unit. So no matter how many lazy requests you have, there will only ever be a single network round trip to the server. You can see the code sample in Listing 4.19.

As the code in Listing 4.19 shows, we can define multiple lazy operations. At that stage, they're pending. They're stored in the session but haven't been sent to the server yet. We can either call ExecuteAllPendingLazyOperations to force all pending operations to execute, or we can have that happen implicitly by accessing the Value property on any of the lazy instances we received.

Why do we need ExecuteAllPendingLazyOperations?

The existence of ExecuteAllPendingLazyOperations is strange. It's explicitly doing something that will happen implicitly anyway. So why is it needed? This method exists to allow users to have fine-grained control over the execution of requests. In particular, it allows you to set up a stage in your pipeline

---

6   We'll cover this technique when we discuss MapReduce indexes in Chapter 11.

that will request all the data it's going to need. Then it will call ExecuteAll-
PendingLazyOperations to fetch this explicitly.

The next stage is supposed to operate on the pure in-memory data inside the
session and not require any calls to the server. This is important in advanced scenarios, when you need this level of control and want to prevent the code from
making unexpected remote calls in performance-critical sections of your code.

Listing 4.19 *Lazily loading a customer and their count of support calls*

```
using (var session = store.OpenSession())
{
    Lazy<Customer> lazyCustomer = session.Advanced.Lazily
        .Load<Customer>("customers/8243-C");

    Lazy<int> lazyCountOfCalls = session.Query<SupportCall>()
        .Where(c => c.CustomerId == "customers/8243-C"))
        .CountLazily();

    // no network calls have been made so far

    // force execution of pending lazy operations explicitly
    session.Advanced.Eagerly.ExecuteAllPendingLazyOperations();

    // if ExecuteAllPendingLazyOperations wasn't called, it
    // will be implicitly called here.
    int countOfCalls = lazyCountOfCalls.Value;
    Customer customer = lazyCustomer.Value;

    // show the customer and the number of calls to the user
}
```

The performance gain from Lazy is directly correlated to the number of lazy requests it's able to
batch and how far away the actual server is. The more requests that can be batched and the further away the database server, the faster this method becomes. On the local machine, it's rarely
worth going to the trouble, but once we go to production, this can get you some real benefits.

Note that, as useful as Lazy is, it's limited to requests that you can make with the information you have on hand. If you need to make queries based on the results of another query, you
won't be able to use Lazy for that. For most of those scenarios, you can use Include. And of
course, Lazy and Include can work together, so that will usually suffice.

4.2.2. STREAMING DATA

When dealing with large amounts of data, the typical API we use to talk to RavenDB is not really suitable for the task. Let's consider the case of the code in Listing 4.20.

Listing 4.20 *Query all support calls for a customer*

```
using (var session = store.OpenSession())
{
    List<SupportCall> calls = session.Query<SupportCall>()
        .Where(c => c.CustomerId == "customers/8243-C"))
        .ToList();
}
```

What will happen if this is a particularly troublesome customer that opened a *lot* of calls? If this customer had just 30 calls, it's easy to see that we'll get them all in the list. But what happens if this customer has 30,000 calls? Figure 4.1 shows how a query is processed on the server in this case.

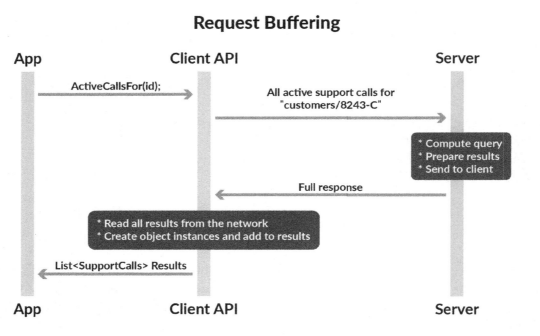

Figure 4.1. *A query using request buffering*

The server will accept the query, find all matches, prepare the results to send and then send them all over the network. On the client side, we'll read the results from the network and batch them all into the list that we'll return to the application.

If there are 30 results in all, that's great, but if we have 30,000, we'll likely suffer from issues. Sending 30,000 results over the network, reading 30,000 results *from* the network and then populating a list of 30,000 (potentially complex) objects is going to take some time. In terms of memory usage, we'll need to hold all those results in memory, possibly for an extended period of time.

Due to the way memory management works in .NET,[7] allocating a list with a lot of objects over a period of time (because we are reading them from the network) will likely push the list instance, and all of its contents, into a higher generation. This means that, when you're done using it, the memory will not be collected without a more expensive Gen1 or even Gen2 round.

In short, for a large number of results, the code in Listing 4.20 will take more time, consume more memory and force more expensive GC in the future. In previous versions of RavenDB, we had guards in place to prevent this scenario entirely. It's easy to start writing code like that in Listing 4.20 and over time have more and more results come in. Our logic was that, at some point, there needed to be a cutoff point where an exception is thrown before this kind of behavior poisoned your application.

As it turned out, our users *really* didn't like this behavior. In many cases, they would rather the application do more work (typically unnecessarily) than to have it throw an error. This allowed them to fix a performance problem rather than a "system is down" issue. As a result of this feedback, this limitation was removed, but we still recommend always using a Take clause in your queries to prevent just this kind of issue.

> **All queries should have a Take clause**
>
> A query that doesn't have a take clause can be a poison pill for your application. As data size grows, the cost of making this query also grows until the entire thing goes down.
>
> The RavenDB client API contains a convention setting called ThrowIfQueryPageSizeIsNotSet, which will force all queries to specify a Take clause and will error otherwise. We recommend that, during development, you set this value to true to ensure your code will always be generating queries that have a limit to the number of results they get.

Very large queries are bad, it seems, but that isn't actually the topic of this section. Instead, it's just the preface explaining why *buffered* large queries are a bad idea. RavenDB also supports the notion of *streaming* queries. You can see what that would look like in Figure 4.2.

---

7   The behavior on the JVM is the same. Other clients environment have different policies.

Request Streaming

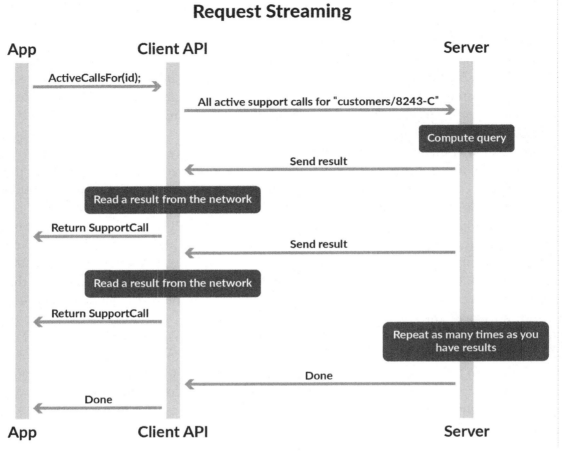

Figure 4.2. *A query using request streaming*

Unlike the previous example, with streaming, neither client nor server need to hold the full response in memory. Instead, as soon as the server has a single result, it sends that result to the client. The client will read the result from the network, materialize the instance and hand it off to the application immediately. In this manner, the application can start processing the results of the query before the server is done sending it, and it doesn't have to wait. You can see the code for that in Listing 4.21.

Instead of getting all the results in one go, the code in Listing 4.21 will pull them from the stream one at a time. This way, the server, the client API and the application can all work in parallel with one another to process the results of the query. This technique is suitable for processing a large number of results (in the millions).

Listing 4.21 *Stream all support calls for a customer*

```
using (var session = store.OpenSession())
{
    var callsQuery = session.Query<SupportCall>()
        .Where(c => c.CustomerId == "customers/8243-C"));

    using (var stream = session.Advanced.Stream(callsQuery))
    {
        while (stream.MoveNext())
        {
            SupportCall current = stream.Current;
            // do something with this instance
        }
    }
}
```

The use of streaming queries requires you to keep a few things in mind:

◆ The results of a streaming query are *not* tracked by the session. Changes made to them will not be sent to the server when SaveChanges is called. This is because we expect streaming queries to have a high number of results, and we don't want to hold all the references for them in the session. If we did, we would prevent the GC from collecting them.

◆ Since streaming is happening as a single large request, there's a limit to how long you can delay before you call MoveNext again. If you wait too long, it's possible for the server to give up sending the rest of the request to you (since you didn't respond in time) and abort the connection. Typically, you'll be writing the results of the stream somewhere (to a file, to the network, etc.).

◆ If you want to modify all the results of the query, don't call session.Store on each as they're pulled from the stream. You'll just generate an excess of work for the session and eventually end up with a truly humongous batch to send to the server. Typically, if you want to read a lot of results and modify them, you'll use a stream and a Bulk Insert at the same time. You'll read from the stream and call Store on the bulk insert for each. This way, you'll have both streaming for the query as you read and streaming via the bulk insert on the write.

When you need to select whether to use a regular (batched) query or a streaming query, consider the number of items that you expect to get from the query and what you intend to do with them. If the number is small, you'll likely want to use a query for its simple API. If you need to process many results, you should use the streaming API.

Note that the streaming API is *intentionally* a bit harder to use. We made sure the API exposes the streaming nature of the operation. You should strive to avoid wrapping that. Streaming should be used on the edge of your system, where you're doing something with the results and passing them directly to the outside in some manner.

4.3. Caching

An important consideration when speeding up an application is caching. In particular, we can avoid expensive operations if we cache the results from the last time we accessed them. Unfortunately, caching is *hard*. Phil Karlton said:

```
There are only two hard things in Computer Science:
cache invalidation and naming things.
```

Caching itself is pretty trivial to get right. The hard part is how you're going to handle cache invalidation. If you're serving stale information from the cache, the results can range from nothing much to critical, depending on what exactly you're doing.

With RavenDB, we decided early on that caching was a complex topic, so we'd better handle it properly. It's done in two parts. The server side generates an etag for all read operations. This etag is computed by the server and can be used by the client later on. The client, on the other hand, is able to cache the request from the server internally. The next time a similar read request is made, the client will send the cached etag to the server alongside the request.

When the server gets such a request with an etag, it follows a dedicated code path, optimized specifically for that, to check whether the results of the operation have changed. If they didn't, the server can return to the client immediately, letting it know that it's safe to use the cached copy. In this manner, we save computation costs on the server and network transfer costs between the server and the client.

Externally, from the API consumer point of view, there's no way to tell that caching happened. Consider the code in Listing 4.22.

The client code doesn't need to change in any way to take advantage of this feature. This is on by default and is always there to try to speed up your requests. Caching is prevalent in RavenDB, so although the example in Listing 4.22 uses queries, loading a document will also use the cache, as will most other read operations.

The cache that's kept on the client side is the already-parsed results, so we saved not only the network round-trip time but also the parsing costs. We keep the data in *unmanaged* memory because it's easier to keep track of the size of the memory and avoid promoting objects into Gen2 just because they've been in the cache for a while. The cache is scoped to the document store, so all sessions from the same document store will share the cache and its benefits.

Listing 4.22 *Query caching in action*

```
using (var session = store.OpenSession())
{
    var calls = session.Query<SupportCall>()
        .Where(c => c.CustomerId == "customers/8243-C"))
        .ToList();
}

using (var session = store.OpenSession())
{
    // this query will result in the server
    // returning a "this is cached" notification
    var calls = session.Query<SupportCall>()
        .Where(c => c.CustomerId == "customers/8243-C"))
        .ToList();
}
```

Time to skip the cache

Caching by default can be a problem with a particular set of queries – those that use the notion of the current time. Consider the case of the following query:

```
session.Query<SupportCall>()
    .Where(c =>
        c.StartedAt >= DateTime.Now.AddDays(-7)
        && c.Ended == null);
```

This query is asking for all opened support calls that are over a week old.

This kind of query is quite innocent looking, but together with the cache, it can have surprising results. Because the query uses `DateTime.Now`, on every call, it will generate a different query. That query will never match any previously cached results, so it will always have to be processed on the server side. What's worse, every instance of this query will sit in the cache, waiting to be evicted, never to be used.

A much better alternative would be to use the following:

```
c.StartedAt >= DateTime.Today.AddDays(-7)
```

By using `Today`, we ensure that we can reuse the cached entry for multiple calls. Even if you need more granularity than that, just truncating the current time to a minute/hour interval can be very beneficial.

The cache works by utilizing HTTP caching behavior. Whenever we make a GET request, we check the cache to see if we previously made a request with the same URL and query string parameters. If we did, we fetch the cached etag for that request and send it to the server. The server will then use that etag to check if the results have changed. If they didn't, the server returns a 304 Not Modified response. The client will then just use the cached response that it already has.

While most read requests are cached, there are a few that aren't. Anything that will always be different, such as stats calls, will never be cached. This is because stats and debug endpoints must return fresh information any time they're called. Attachments are also not cached because they can be very large and are typically handled differently by the application.

4.3.1. AGGRESSIVE CACHING

Caching is great, it would seem. But in order to utilize caching by RavenDB, we still need to go back to the server. That ensures we'll get a server confirmation that the data we're going to return for that request is indeed fresh and valid. However, there are many cases where we don't care much about the freshness of the data.

On a heavily used page, showing data that might be stale for a few minutes is absolutely fine, and the performance benefits gained from not having to go to the server can be quite nice. In order to address this scenario, RavenDB supports the notion of aggressive caching. You can see an example of that in Listing 4.23.

Listing 4.23 *Aggressive caching in action*

```
using (var session = store.OpenSession())
using (session.Advanced.DocumentStore.AggressivelyCache())
{
    var customer = session.Load<SupportCall>(
        "customers/8243-C");
}
```

The code in Listing 4.23 uses aggressive caching. In this mode, if the request is in the cache, the RavenDB client API will *never* even ask the server if it's up to date. Instead, it will immediately serve the request from the cache, skipping all network traffic. This can significantly speed up operations for which you can live with a stale view of the world for a certain period.

However, operating in this mode indefinitely would be pretty bad since you'd never see new results. This leads us back to the problem of cache invalidation. Aggressive caching isn't just going to blindly cache all data at all times. Instead, the first time it encounters an instruction to aggressively cache, the client is going to open a connection to the server and ask the server to let it know whenever something changes in the database. This is done using the Changes API, which is covered in the next section of this chapter.

Whenever the server lets the client know that something has changed, the client will ensure that the next cached request will actually hit the server for the possibly updated value. The client will not be asking specifically for changes it has in its cache. Instead, it will ask for all changes on the server. (Take note of that, as you might be caching a lot of different queries, documents, etc.) The client knows to check with the server for anything in the cache that is older than that notification. When this is done, the cached etag is still being sent, so if that particular response hasn't changed, the server will still respond with a `304 Not Modified` and we'll use the cached value (and update its timestamp).

The idea is that, with this behavior, you get the best of both worlds. If nothing has changed, immediate caching is available without having to go to the server. But if something might have changed, we'll check the server for the most up-to-date response. Given typical behavioral patterns for the application, we'll often be able to use the aggressive cache for quite some time before a write will come in and make us check with the server.

Caching behavior in a cluster

Typically, RavenDB is deployed in a cluster, and a database will reside on multiple machines. How does caching work in this context? The caching is built on the full URL of the request, and that takes into account the particular server that we'll be making the request to. That means that the cache will store a separate result for each server, even if the request is identical otherwise.

For the most part, the etags generated for HTTP requests among servers should be identical for identical data since it uses the change vectors of the documents to compute it. However, different servers may receive documents in a different order, which may result in a difference in the actual results. That shouldn't impact the behavior of the system, but for now we skipped implementing cross node caching.

Why isn't aggressive caching on by default?

Aggressive caching isn't on by default because it may violate a core constraint of RavenDB: that a request will always give you the latest information. With the requirement that aggressive caching must be turned on explicitly, you're aware that there's a period of time where the response you receive might have diverged from the result on the server.

4.4. Changes API

We mentioned the Changes API in the previous section since the aggressive caching is using it. The Changes API is a way for us to connect to the server and ask it to let us know when a particular event has happened. Listing 4.24 shows how we can ask the server to tell us when a particular document has changed.

Listing 4.24 *Getting notified when a document changes*

```
var subscription = store.Changes()
    .ForDocument("customers/8243-C")
    .Subscribe(change => {
        // let user know the document changed
    });

// dispose to stop getting future notifications
subscription.Dispose();
```

Typically, we use the code in Listing 4.24 when implementing an edit page for a document. When the user starts editing the document, we register for notifications on changes to this document. If it does change, we let the user know immediately. That allows us to avoid having to wait for the save action to discover we need to redo all our work.

The Changes API works by opening a WebSocket to the server and letting the server know exactly what kind of changes it's interested in. We can register for a particular document, a collection, documents that start with a particular key, or even global events, such as operations or indexes.

Changes API in a cluster

In a cluster, the Changes API will always connect to one node, and changes must first flow to that node before the changes will be sent to the client. The failure of the node will cause us to reconnect (possibly to a different server) and resume waiting for the changes we're interested in.

The Changes API is meant to get non-critical notifications. It's cheap to run and is pretty simple, but it's possible that a failure scenario will cause you to miss updates. If the connection has been reset, you might lose notifications that happened while you were reconnecting. It's recommended that you use the Changes API for enrichment purposes and not rely on it. For example, you might use it to tell if a document has changed so you can not only give early notification but also ensure you have optimistic concurrency turned on so it will catch the change on save anyway.

Another example of a way you might use the Changes API is with aggressive caching. If we missed a single notification, that isn't too bad. The next notification will put us in the same state. And we'll be fine because the user explicitly chose performance over getting the latest version, in this case. Yet another example of Changes API use might be for monitoring. You want to know what's going on in the server, but it's fine to lose something if there's an error because you're interested in what's happening now, not the full and complete history of actions on the server.

For critical operations – ones where you can't afford to miss even a single change – you can use Subscriptions, which are covered in the next chapter. They're suited for such a scenario, since they guarantee that all notifications will be properly sent and acknowledged.

4.5. Projecting data in queries

In the previous chapter, we talked a lot about modeling and how we should structure our documents to be independent, isolated and coherent. That makes for an excellent system for transaction processing (OLTP) scenarios. But there are quite a few cases where, even in a business application, we have to look at the data differently. Let's take a look at our support case example. If I'm a help desk engineer and I'm looking at the list of open support calls, I want to see all the recent support calls and the customer that opened them.

Based on what we know so far, it would be trivial to write the code in Listing 4.25.

Listing 4.25 *Recent orders and their customers*

```
using (var session = store.OpenSession())
{
    List<SupportCall> recentOrders = session.Query<SupportCall>()
        .Include(c => c.CustomerId) // include customers
        .Where(c => c.Ended == null) // open order
        .OrderByDescending(c => c.Started) // get recent
        .Take(25) // limit the results
        .ToList();
}
```

The code in Listing 4.25 is doing a *lot*. It gets us the 25 most recently opened support calls, and it also includes the corresponding customers. We can now show this to the user quite easily, and we were able to do that in a single request to the server. Under most circumstances, this is exactly what you'll want to do.

However, in order to pull the few fields we need to show to the user in the application, we had to pull the full support calls and customers documents. If those documents are large, that can be expensive. Another way to handle this is by letting the server know exactly what we need returned and then letting it do the work on the server side.

This can be done by specifying a projection during the query. Projections allow us to control exactly what is being returned from the query. On the most basic level it allows us to decide what fields we want to get from the server, but we can actually do a lot more than that.

Let's see how we can use a query to project just the data that we are interested in. You can see the details in Listing 4.26.

Listing 4.26 *Recent orders and their customers, using projection*

```
using (var session = store.OpenSession())
{
  var recentOrders = (
      from call in session.Query<SupportCall>()
      where call.Ended == null // open order
      orderby call.Started descending // get recent
      // fetch customer (happens on the server side)
      let customer = session.Load<Customer>(call.CustomerId)
      select new
      {
          // project just the data that we care about
          // back to the client
          CustomerName = customer.Name,
          call.CustomerId,
          call.Started,
          call.Issue,
          call.Votes
      }
    )
    .Take(25) // limit the results
    .ToList();
}
```

There are a few things to note in Listing 4.26. First, we no longer include the Customer in the query. We don't need that because the result of this query isn't a list of SupportCall documents but a list of projections that already include the CustomerName that we want. The key part, as far as we're concerned, is the call to the session.Load<Customer>() method. This is translated into a server side load operation that fetches the related Customer document and extracts just the Name field from it.[8]

---

[8]   This is possible because we are using a synchronous session and queries. If we were using async queries, we'll need to use RavenQuery.Load<Customer> in the Linq query.

The output of a query like the one in Listing 4.26 is not a document, it is a projection and as a result of that, it isn't tracked by the session. This means that changes to a projection won't be saved back to the server when SaveChanges is called. You *can* call Store on the result of a projection, but be aware that this will create a new document, which is probably isn't what you intended to happen.

4.6. Cross-cutting concerns on the client

The RavenDB client API is quite big. We already discussed the notion of layers in the design of the client API, allowing you to select at what level you want to work at any given point in time. There is quite a lot that you can configure and customize in the client behavior. The most common customization is changing the conventions of the client by providing your own logic.

Most of the decisions that the RavenDB client API makes are actually controlled by the DocumentConventions class. This class allows you to modify all sorts of behaviors, from how RavenDB should treat complex values in queries to selecting what property to use as the document ID in entities.

If you need fine-grained control over the serialization and deserialization of your documents, this is the place to look. The DocumentConventions class holds important configurations, such as the maximum number of requests to allow per server or whether we should allow queries without a Take clause. Listing 4.27 shows an example of controlling what collection an object will find itself in.

Listing 4.27 *Customize the collection to allow polymorphism*

```
store.Conventions.FindCollectionName = type =>
    typeof(Customer).IsAssignableFrom(type)
        ? "Customers"
        : DocumentConventions.DefaultGetCollectionName(type);
```

In Listing 4.27, we're letting RavenDB know that Customer or any derived type should be in the "Customers" collection. That means that we can create a class called VIPCustomer that will have additional properties, but it will still be treated as a Customer by anything else (indexing, queries, etc.). Such options allow you to have absolute control over how RavenDB will work within your environment.

4.6.1. EVENT HANDLERS

Alongside conventions, which are typically reactive, you can use event handlers to perform various operations during the execution of requests by RavenDB. The events are available as events that can be subscribed to at the document store level or at the individual session level.

The following events are available:

◆ OnBeforeStore
◆ OnAfterSaveChanges
◆ OnBeforeDelete
◆ OnBeforeQueryExecuted

This allows us to register to be called whenever a particular event happens, and that in turn gives us a lot of power. Listing 4.28 shows how we can implement auditing with the help of the `OnBeforeStore` event.

Listing 4.28 *Implementing auditing mechanism*

```
store.OnBeforeStore += (sender, args) =>
{
    args.DocumentMetadata["Modified-By"] =
        RequestContext.Principal.Identity.GetUserId();
};
```

Listing 4.28 ensures that whenever the document is modified, we'll register which user has made the modification in the metadata. You can also use this event to handle validation in a cross-cutting fashion. Throwing an error from the event will abort the `SaveChanges` operation and raise the error to the caller.

Another example of using events is to ensure that we always include a particular clause in our queries, as you can see in Listing 4.29.

Listing 4.29 *Never read inactive customer*

```
store.OnBeforeQueryExecuted += (sender, args) =>
{
    if (args.QueryCustomization is IDocumentQuery<Customer> query)
    {
        query.WhereEquals("IsActive", true);
    }
}
```

The code in Listing 4.29 will apply to all queries operating on `Customer` and will ensure that all the results returned have the `IsActive` property set to true. This can also be used in multi-tenancy situations, where you want to add the current tenant ID to all queries.

The full details of what you can do with conventions and listeners are in RavenDB's online documentation. I encourage you to browse the documentation and consider when it might make sense to use listeners in your application. Using them can be quite a time saver because listeners can be applied globally with ease.

4.7. Document revisions

In the previous section, we briefly mentioned auditing. In this section, we're going to take the notion of auditing and dial it up a notch, just to see what will happen. Certain classes of applications have very strict change control requirements for their data. For example, most medical, banking, payroll and insurance applications have strict "never delete since we need to be able to see all changes on the system" rules. One particular system I worked with had the requirement to keep all changes for a minimum of seven years, for example.

With RavenDB, this kind of system is much easier. That's because RavenDB has built-in support for handling revisions. Allow me to walk you through setting up such a system.

Go into the RavenDB Studio in the browser and create a new database, as we have seen in "Zero to RavenDB." Now, go into the database, and on the left side menu, click `Settings` and then `Document Revisions`.

You can configure revisions globally for all collections or a single particular collection. For the purpose of this exercise, we'll define revisions for all collections, as seen in Figure 4.3. You can enable revisions by clicking on `Create default configuration`, accepting the defaults by clicking OK and then `Save`.

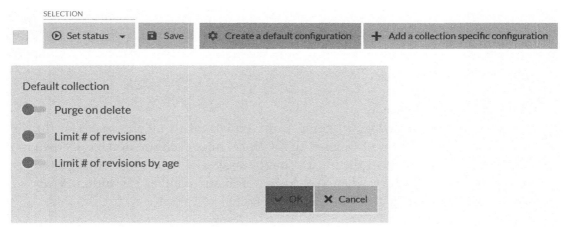

Figure 4.3. *Setting up revisions for all collections*

Now that we've enabled revisions, let's see what this means. Go ahead and create a simple customer document, as seen in Figure 4.4.

You can see that this document has a `@flags` metadata property that is set to `HasRevisions`. And if you look at the right-hand side, you'll see a revisions tab that you can select to see previous revisions of this document. Play around with this document for a bit, modify it, save and see how revisions are recorded on each change.

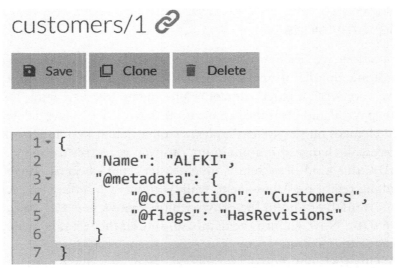

Figure 4.4. *Customer document with revisions enabled*

Documents' revisions in RavenDB are created whenever you have revisions enabled and a document is modified. As part of saving the new document, we create a snapshot of the document (and its metadata, attachments, etc.) and store it as a revision. This allows us to go back in time and look at a previous revision of a document. In a way, this is similar to how we work with code. Every change creates a new revision, and we can go back in time and compare the changes between revisions.

Revisions in a cluster

In a cluster, revisions are going to be replicated to all the nodes in the database. Conflicts cannot occur with revisions, since each revision has its own distinct signature. One of the most common usages of revisions is to store the entire document history when you have automatic conflict resolution. We'll cover this behavior in depth in Chapter 6.

As part of configuring revisions on the database, you can select how many revisions we'll retain and for what period of time. For example, you may choose to keep around 15 revisions for seven days. Under those conditions, RavenDB will delete all revisions that are *both* older than seven days and have more than 15 revisions after them. In other words, if you've made 50 changes to a document in the span of a week, we'll keep all of them and only delete the earliest of them when they're over seven days old.

From the client side, you don't really need to consider revisions at all. This behavior happens purely on the server side and requires no involvement from the client. But you can access the revisions through the client API, as you can see in Listing 4.30.

Listing 4.30 *Getting revisions of a document*

```
List<SupportCall> revisions = session.Advanced
    .GetRevisionsFor<SupportCall>("SupportCalls/238-B");
```

The code in Listing 4.30 will fetch the most recent revisions and provide you with the revisions of the document as it was changed. You can also page through the revision history.

Once a revision has been created, it cannot be changed. This is done to ensure compliance with strict regulatory requirements, since it means you can treat the data in the revision as safe. It cannot be manipulated by the client API or even by the admin.

I've found that some applications, without the regulations requiring versioning, make use of revisions just because they give the users an easy way to look at the changes on an entity over time. That was especially true in one example I can recall, where the user in question was the business expert in charge of the whole system. This feature was very valuable to her since it allowed her to see exactly what happened and who took the action. (The application utilized a listener to implement audits, as shown in Listing 4.29). It was quite interesting to see how much value she got out of this feature.

In terms of cost, revisions obviously increase the amount of disk space required. But given today's disk sizes, that isn't usually a significant concern. Aside from disk space utilization, revisions don't actually have any impact on the system. Revisions are also quite important for ensuring that transaction boundaries are respected when replicating changes in the cluster[9], handling historical subscriptions[10] and ETL processes.

Revisions from an older version of your software

One thing you should note when using the revisions feature is that over time, as your software evolves, you might see revisions from previous versions of your application. As such, the revision document might be missing properties or have properties that have been removed or had their type changed.

Because revisions are immutable, it isn't possible to run migration on them, and you need to take that into account. When working with revisions, you might want to consider working with the raw document, rather than turning it into an instance of an object in your model.

---

9   See "Transaction atomicity and replication" in Chapter 6.
10   See "Versioned Subscriptions" in the next chapter.

4.8. How RavenDB uses JSON

The RavenDB server and the RavenDB C# client API use a dedicated binary format to represent JSON in memory. The details on this format are too low level for this book and generally shouldn't be of much interest to outside parties, but it's worth understanding a bit about how RavenDB handles JSON even at this stage. Typically, you'll work with JSON documents in their stringified form – a set of UTF8 characters with the JSON format. That is human-readable, cheap to parse and simple to work with.

But JSON parsing requires you to work in a streaming manner, which means that to pull up just a few values from a big document, you still need to parse the full document. As it turns out, once a document is inside RavenDB, there are a *lot* of cases where we want to just get a couple of values from it. Indexing a few fields is common, and parsing the JSON each and every time can be incredibly costly. Instead, RavenDB accepts the JSON string on write and turns it into an internal format called blittable.[11]

A blittable JSON document is a format that allows RavenDB random access to any piece of information in the document without having to parse the document, with a traversal cost of (amortised) O(1). Over the wire, RavenDB is sending JSON strings, but internally, it's all blittable. The C# client is also using the blittable format internally since that greatly helps with memory consumption and control. You generally won't see that in the public API, but certain low-level operations may expose you to it.

Blittable documents are immutable once created and *must* be disposed of once you're done with them. Since the document session will typically hold such blittable objects, the session must also be disposed of to make sure all the memory it's holding is released. An important consideration for the overall performance of RavenDB is that blittable documents always reside in native memory. This allows RavenDB fine-grained control over where and how the memory is used and reused, as well as its life cycle.

On the client side, using the blittable format means we have reduced memory consumption and reduced fragmentation. It also reduces the cost of caching significantly.

---

11   I don't like the name, but we couldn't come up with anything better.

4.9. Summary

In this chapter, we've gone over a lot of the advanced features in the client API. We looked at working with attachments and understanding how we can use them to store binary data. Then we moved on to working with the document metadata in general. The document metadata is a convenient place to stash information about our documents that doesn't actually belong to the document itself. Auditing is one such example, and we saw how we can use listeners on the events that the client API exposes to us.

We looked at how change tracking is managed and how we can get detailed information from the session about what exactly changed in our documents. Then we examined how we should handle concurrency in our application. We looked at optimistic concurrency in RavenDB and even implemented *pessimistic* locking.[12] Online optimistic concurrency can be handled for us automatically by the session, or we can send the change vector value to the client and get it back on the next request, thus implementing offline optimistic concurrency.

There's another way to handle concurrency – or just to save yourself the trouble of shuffling lots of data between client and server – and that way is to use patching. The client API offers patching at several levels. Setting a value or incrementing a number is supported by a strongly typed API, but more complex tasks can be handled using `Defer`, which also offers you the ability to write JavaScript code that will be executed on the server to mutate your documents.

We also looked at various ways to get a lot of data into RavenDB, from a sequential `SaveChanges` per document, to running them in parallel, to using the bulk insert API to efficiently push data into RavenDB. We saw that the major limiting factor was typically the cost of going to the database and that different approaches could produce significantly different performance profiles.

After looking at the various ways we could write data to RavenDB, it was time to look at the other side: seeing how we can optimize reads from the server. We had already gone over `Include` in "Zero to RavenDB," and in this chapter we looked at lazy requests, allowing us to combine several different requests to the server into a single round trip.

The mirror image to bulk insert is the streaming feature, suitable for handling an immense amount of data. Streaming allows us to start processing the request from the server immediately, without having to wait for the complete results. This allows us to parallelize the work between client and server and gives us the option to immediately start sending results to the user.

Following the reading and writing of documents, we looked into caching them. The client API has sophisticated caching behaviors, and we delved into exactly how that works, as well as how it reduces the time we need to provide answers to the user. Caching allows us to tell the server we already have the result of a previous call to the same URL. And it allows the

---

12   Although you shouldn't probably use that in real production code.

server to let us know if that hasn't been modified. If that's the case, the server doesn't need to send any results on the wire, and the client can use the cached (parsed and processed) data immediately. RavenDB also supports the notion of aggressive caching, which allows us to skip going to the server entirely. This is done by asking the server to notify the client when things change, and only then go to the server to fetch those changes.

That option is also exposed in the client API, using the changes API. The changes API gives you the ability to ask the server to tell you when a particular document, collection or set of documents with a given prefix has changed. This lets users know that someone has changed the document they're working on, and allows them to implement features such as "this data has changed," etc.

Next, we looked at how we can project the results of queries and document loads on the server side using projections. A projection allows you to modify the shape of the data that RavenDB returns to the client. This can be done by simply returning a subset of the data from the documents – or even by loading additional documents and merging the data from associated documents into a single result.

We looked at cross-cutting concerns on the client and how we can apply behavior throughout the client once. We can modify the client behavior by controlling how RavenDB decides what class belongs in what collection, as well as serialization and deserialization. Listeners allow you to attach behavior to certain actions in the client API, giving you the option to customize certain behaviors. We looked at adding auditing to our application in about three lines of code and even saw how we can limit all the queries on the client to only include active users as a cross-cutting behavior.

Following cross-cutting behaviors, we moved to looking at the revisions feature in RavenDB and how to use it from the client side. The revisions feature asks the server to create a new revision of a document upon each change. Those revisions are immutable and create an audit trail and a change log for the documents in question. While this is primarily a server-side feature, we looked at how we can expose the revisions to the user through the client API and allow the users to view previous revisions of a document.

Our final endeavor was to cover at a high level the native serialization format that RavenDB uses, the blittable format. This format is meant to be extremely efficient in representing JSON. It's typically stored in native memory to reduce managed memory consumption and garbage collection costs down the road. You don't typically need to concern yourself with this, except to remember that it's important to dispose of sessions when you're done with them.

This chapter is a long one, but it still doesn't cover the full functionality. There are plenty of useful features, but they tend to be useful in specific, narrow circumstances or only make sense to talk about in a larger scope. We've barely discussed queries so far, but we'll do so extensively when we get to Chapter 11 and when we discuss indexing.

The next chapter is a good example of this. We'll dedicate that chapter to handling data subscriptions and all the myriad ways they make data processing tasks easier for you.

5. Batch Processing With Subscriptions

RavenDB needs to handle some very different use cases in its day-to-day operations. On the one hand, we have transaction-oriented processing, which typically touches a small number of documents as part of processing a single request. And on the other hand, we have batch processing, which usually operates on large amounts of data. Implementing those kinds of processes with the OLTP mode is possible, but it isn't easy to do.

RavenDB supports a dedicated batch processing mode, using the notion of subscriptions. A subscription is simply a way to register a query with the database and have the database send us all the documents that match the query. An example of this might be, "Give me all the support calls." So far, this sounds very much like the streaming feature, which we covered in the previous chapter. However, subscriptions are *meant* for batch processing. Instead of just getting all the data that matches the criteria, the idea is that we'll keep the subscription open forever.

The first stage in the subscription is to send all the existing data that matches the query. Depending on the amount of data, this can take a while. It's done in batches, and RavenDB will only proceed to send the next batch when the current one has already been acknowledged as successfully processed.

The second stage in the lifetime of a subscription is when it's done going through all the data that's already in the database. This is where things start to get really interesting. At this point, the subscription *isn't* done. Instead, it's kept alive and waiting for new or updated documents that match the query. When that happens, the server will immediately send that document to the subscription. In other words, not only did we get traditional batch processing, but in many cases, we also have *live* batch processes.

Instead of waiting for a nightly process to run, you can keep the subscription open and handle changes as they come in. This keeps you from having to do things like polling and remembering the last items that you read. RavenDB's subscription also includes error handling, high availability and on-the-fly updates.

With subscriptions, work is divided into two distinct operations. First we need to create the subscription. Then we need to open it. Subscriptions aren't like queries; they aren't ephemeral. A subscription is a persistent state of a specific business process. It indicates what documents that particular subscription has processed, the query it is using, etc.

You can create the subscription through the RavenDB Studio. In the same database that we used in the previous chapter, go to `Settings` and then `Manage Ongoing Tasks`, and you'll see the task selection dialog shown in Figure 5.1. Ignore the rest of the tasks and select `Subscription`. You'll see the subscription edit form. Now, name the task "CustomersSubscription" and enter `from Customers` in the query field. That's it. You can save the subscription. The result of this is shown in Figure 5.2.

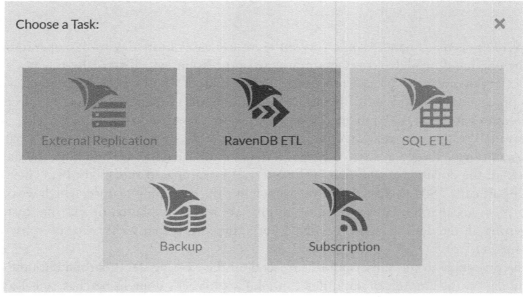

Figure 5.1. *Database tasks selection dialog*

Figure 5.2. *The newly created customers subscription*

You can also do the same through code, as shown in Listing 5.1. Here, you can see how we create a subscription for `Customer` documents.

Listing 5.1 *Creating a subscription to process customers*

```
var options = new SubscriptionCreationOptions
{
    Name = "CustomersSubscription"
};
store.Subscriptions.Create<Customer>(options);
```

Regardless of whether you created the subscription manually or via code, the result is a named subscription. But the question is, what exactly *is* that? In the Studio, if you go to the edit subscription page, you'll see the option to test a subscription. If you select that option, you'll see a result similar to Figure 5.3.

Figure 5.3. *Testing the customers subscription*

Those are the documents in the `Customer` collection, but what does this mean? A subscription is a way to go through all documents that match a query. On its own, it isn't really that interesting because we could see the same details elsewhere in the Studio. But the point of subscriptions isn't for you to manually go to the Studio and inspect things. The point is that RavenDB will send those details to your code. You can see this in Listing 5.2, where we open the subscription and start handling batches of documents on the client.

Listing 5.2 *Opening and using a subscription to process customers*

```
using (var subscription = store.Subscriptions
        .GetSubscriptionWorker<Customer>("CustomersSubscription")))
{
    // wait until the subscription is done
    // typically, a subscription lasts for a very long time
    await subscription.Run(batch => /* redacted */ );
}
```

Listing 5.2 shows the typical way of using a subscription. The subscription is opened with the subscription name that we created previously and then we Run the subscription. The actual batch processing of the documents is done by the lambda that's passed to the Run call on a background thread. I redacted the actual batch processing for now. We'll see what that looks like in the next section.

After calling Run, we wait on the returned task. Why do we do that? In general, a subscription will live for a very long time – typically, the lifetime of the process that's running it. In fact, you'll often have a process dedicated just to running subscriptions (or even a process per subscription). What we're doing in Listing 5.2 is basically waiting until the subscription exits.

There are fewer reasons than you might think for a subscription to exit. Problems with the network will simply cause it to retry or failover to another node, for example. And if it processed all the data that the database had to offer, it will sit there and wait until it has something more to give, rather than exiting. However, there are a few cases where the subscription will actually exit. The first, of course, is if you intentionally close it by disposing the subscription. It's safe to dispose the subscription while it's running, and that's how you typically do an orderly shutdown of a subscription.

Next, we might have been kicked off the subscription for some reason. The admin may have deleted the subscription or the database. Or perhaps the credentials we used were invalid. Maybe the subscription connection was taken over by another client. As you can see, the Run method will return only if you manually disposed the subscription. For most other cases, it will throw when there's no way for it to recover. We'll cover more on this in the subscription deployment section later on in this chapter.

The subscription ID should be persistent, usually stored in configuration or loaded from the database. It's used to represent the state of the subscription and what documents have already been processed by that particular subscription.

You can set your own subscription ID during the Create call, which gives you a well known subscription name to use, or you can ask RavenDB to choose one for you. Note that even if you used your own subscription name, it still needs to be created before you can use it. But why do we have all those moving parts? We create the subscription, open it, run it and wait on the resulting task, and we haven't even gotten to the part where we actually do something using it.

The reason for this is that subscriptions are long-lived processes, which are resilient to failure. Once a subscription is created, a client will open it and keep a connection open to the server, getting fed with all the documents that match the subscription criteria.

Once we've gone over all the documents currently in the database, the subscription will go to sleep but remain connected to the server. Whenever a new or updated document matches the subscription query, it will be sent to the subscription. Errors during this process, either in the network, the server or the client, are tolerated and recoverable. The subscription will ensure that a client will receive each matching document at least once.[1]

Subscription in a cluster

The subscription will connect to *a* server in the cluster, which may redirect the subscription to a more suitable server for that particular subscription. Once the subscription has found the appropriate server, it will open on that server and start getting documents from it. A failure of the client will result in a retry (either from the same client or another one that was waiting to take over). A failure of the server will cause the client to transparently switch over to another server.

The entire process is highly available on both client and server. The idea is that once you set up your subscriptions, you just need to make sure that the processes that open and process your subscriptions are running, and the entire system will hum along, automatically recovering from any failures along the way.

Typically, on a subscription that has already processed all existing documents in the database, the lag time between a new document coming in and the subscription receiving it is a few milliseconds. Under load, when there are many such documents, we'll batch documents and send them to the client for processing as fast as it can handle them. The entire model of subscription is based on the notion of batch processing. While it's true that subscriptions can remain up constantly and get fed with all the changes in the database as they come, that doesn't have to be the case. If a subscription isn't opened, it isn't going to miss anything; once it's re-opened, it will get all the documents that have changed while it was gone.

This allows you to build business processes that can either run continuously or at off-peak times in your system. Your code doesn't change, nor does it matter to RavenDB. A subscription that isn't opened consumes no resources. In fact, a good administrator will know that he can reduce the system load by shutting down subscriptions that are handling non-time-critical information with the knowledge that once the load has passed, starting the subscriptions up again will allow them to catch up from their last processed batch.

This is made possible due to the following flow: on each batch that the client receives, it acknowledges the server once it has successfully completed processing that batch. The server will not move forward and send the next batch until it receives this acknowledgment. It is this acknowledgment that makes this process reliable.

Okay, that's about all we can say about subscriptions without actually showing what they're *doing*. Let's see how RavenDB handles the actual document processing.

---

1   Although errors may cause you to receive the same document multiple times, you're guaranteed to never miss a document.

5.1. Processing a batch of documents in a subscription

We've previously seen the Run method, back in Listing 5.2. But what we haven't seen yet is what's actually going on there. The Run method is simply taking a lambda that will go over the batch of documents. Listing 5.3 shows the code to handle the subscription that was redacted from Listing 5.2.

Listing 5.3 *Processing customers via subscription*

```
await subscription.Run(batch =>
{
    foreach (var item in batch.Items)
    {
        Customer customer = item.Result;
        // do something with this customer
    }
});
```

After all this buildup, the actual code in Listing 5.3 is pretty boring. The lambda we sent gets a batch instance, which has a list of Items that are contained in this batch. And on each of those items, we have a Result property that contains the actual document instance we sent from the server. This code will first get batches of all the customers in the database. Once we have gone through all the customer documents, this subscription will wait, and whenever a new customer comes in or an existing customer is modified, we'll have a new batch with that document. If there are a lot of writes, we might get batches containing several documents that were changed in the time it took us to complete the last batch.

What can we do with this? Well, as it turns out, quite a lot. We can use this to run all sorts of business processes. For example, we may want to check if this customer has a valid address, and if so, record the GPS coordinates so we can run spatial queries on it. Because of the way subscriptions work, we get a full batch of documents from the server, and we can run heavy processing on them. We aren't limited by the data streaming over the network, and unlike streaming, we won't time out. As long as the client remains connected, the server will be happy to keep waiting for the batch to complete. Note that the server will ping the client every now and then to see what its state is and to detect client disconnection at the network level. If that's detected, the connection on the server will be aborted and all resources will be released.

Subscriptions are background tasks

It may be obvious, but I wanted to state this explicitly: subscriptions are background tasks for the server. There's no requirement that a subscription will be opened at any given point in time, and a subscription that wasn't opened will simply get all the documents it needs since the last acknowledged batch.

That means that if a document was modified multiple times, it's possible that the subscription will only be called upon once. See the section about versioned subscriptions if you care about this scenario.

One of the things to be aware of is that right from the subscription lambda itself we can open a new session, modify the document we got from the subscription, `Store` the document and call `SaveChanges` on it. But note that doing so will also put that document right back on the path to be called again with this subscription, so you need to be aware of that and protect against infinite loops. There are also a few other subtle issues that we need to handle with regards to running in a cluster and failover. We'll discuss those issues later in this chapter.

5.2. The subscription script

Subscriptions so far are useful but not really something to get excited about. But the fun part starts now. Subscriptions aren't limited to just fetching all the documents in a particular collection. We can do much better than this. Let's say that we want to send a survey to all customers with whom we had a complex support call. The first step for that is to create a subscription using the code in Listing 5.4.

Listing 5.4 *Creating a subscription for complex calls*

```
var subId = store.Subscriptions.Create<SupportCall>(
    call =>
      call.Comments.Count > 25 &&
      call.Votes > 10 &&
      call.Survey == false
);
```

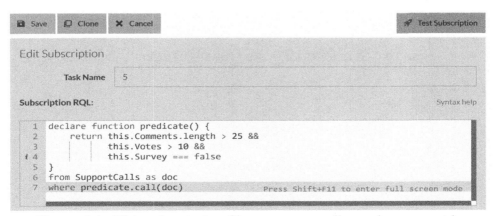

Figure 5.4. *This subscription filters support calls on the server side*

Figure 5.4 shows the newly created subscription on the server side. You can see that the filter we provided on the client side was turned into a server side script that decided whatever a particular `SupportCall` is a match for this subscription.

We've registered for support calls that have more than 10 votes and over 25 comments, and we add a flag to record whether or not we've sent the survey. It's important to note that this filtering is happening on the *server side*, not on the client. Internally we'll transform the conditional into a full query (see Figure 5.4) and send it to the server to be evaluated on each document in turn. Any matching document will be sent to the client for processing. Of course, this is just part of the work. We still need to handle the subscription itself. This is done in Listing 5.5.

Listing 5.5 *Taking surveys of complex calls*

```
await subscription.Run(batch =>
{
    foreach (var item in batch.Items)
    {
        SupportCall call = item.Document;

        var age = DateTime.Today - call.Started;
        if (age > DateTime.FromDays(14))
            return; // no need to send survey for old stuff

        using (var session = batch.OpenSession())
        {
            var customer = session.Load<Customer>(
                call.CustomerId);

            call.Survey = true;

            session.Store(call, item.ChangeVector, item.Id);

            try
            {
                session.SaveChanges();
            }
            catch(ConcurrenyException)
            {
```

```
            // will be retried by the subscription
            return;
        }

        SendSurveyEmailTo(customer, call);
    }
}

});
```

There's a lot going on in Listing 5.5, even though we removed the code that actually opens the subscription. For each item in the batch, we'll create a new session, load the customer for this support call and mark the call as having sent the survey. Then we'll call `Store` and pass it not only the instance that we got from the subscription from but also the change vector and ID for this document. This ensures that when we call `SaveChanges`, if the document has changed in the meantime on the server side, we'll get an error.

> **Don't use the `store.OpenSession` in batch processing**
>
> The code in Listing 5.5 uses `batch.OpenSession` instead of `store.OpenSession`. Why is that? Well, this is where I need to skip ahead a bit and explain some concepts we haven't seen yet. When running in a cluster, RavenDB divides the work between the various nodes in a database. That means that a subscription may run on node B while the cluster as a whole will consider node A as the preferred node to write data to.
>
> RavenDB handles that transparently, by replicating the information across the nodes in the cluster, including optimistic concurrency using the document's change vector, as we discussed in the previous chapter. However, reading from one node and writing to another can lead to subtle concurrency issues. RavenDB can handle these issues, but they can be surprising to users. It's generally better to write back to the same node you're reading from.
>
> In order to avoid that, you should use `batch.OpenSession` (or `batch.OpenAsyncSession`) to create the session. This will ensure that the session you've created will operate against the same node you're reading from and thus will allow us to reason about the state of the system with fewer variables. If your subscription uses include, then the session created via batch will already have the loaded documents in the session cache.

In Listing 5.5, the concurrency exception is an expected error. We can just ignore it and skip processing this document. There's a bit of trickery involved here. Because the document has changed, the subscription will get it again anyway, so we'll skip sending an email about this call for now. But we'll be sending the email later, when we run into the support call again.

Finally, we send the actual email. Note that in a real production code, there's also the need to decide what to do if sending the email has failed. In this case, the code is assuming it cannot fail and favors skipping sending the email rather then sending it twice. Typical mail systems have options to ignore duplicate emails in a certain time period, which is probably how you would solve this in production.

Instead of using explicit concurrency handling, we can also write the code in Listing 5.5 using a `Patch` command, as shown in Listing 5.6.

Listing 5.6 *Taking surveys of complex calls, using patches*

```
await subscription.Run(batch =>
{
    foreach (var item in batch.Items)
    {
        SupportCall call = item.Document;
        var age = DateTime.Today - call.Started;
        if (age > DateTime.FromDays(14))
            return; // no need to send survey for old stuff

        using (var session = batch.OpenSession())
        {
            var customer = session.Load<Customer>(
                call.CustomerId);

            session.Advanced.Patch<SupportCall, bool>(
                result.Id,
                c => c.Survey,
                true);

            SendSurveyEmailTo(customer, call);

            session.SaveChanges();
        }
    }
});
```

In Listing 5.6, we're doing pretty much the same thing we did in Listing 5.5. The difference is that we're using a `Patch` command to do so, which saves us from having to check for concurrency violations. Even if the document has changed between now and the time the server sent it to us, we'll only set the Survey field on it. In Listing 5.6, we're also sending the survey email *before* we set the Survey flag, so a failure to send the email will be thrown all the way to the calling code, which will typically retry the subscription. This is different from the code in Listing 5.5, where we first set the flag and then sent the email.

The main difference here is in what happens in the case of an error being raised when sending the survey email. In Listing 5.5, we've already set the flag and sent it to the server, so the error means that we didn't send the email. The subscription will retry, of course, but the document was already changed and will be filtered from us. In Listing 5.5, if there was an error in sending the email, it won't be sent to the server.

Subscribing to documents on the database we're writing to

There are a few things to remember if you're using the subscription to write back to the same database you're subscribing to:

❖ Avoid the subscription/modify loop. When you modify a document that you're subscribing to, the server will send it to the subscription again. If you modify it every time it's processed, you'll effectively create an infinite loop, with all the costs this entails. You can see in Listing 5.5 and Listing 5.6 that we're careful to avoid this by setting the Survey flag when we process a document and filter on the flag in Listing 5.4.

❖ The document you received may have already been changed on the server. Typically, the lag time between a document being modified and the subscription processing the document is very short. That can lead you to think this happens instantaneously or, even worse, as part of the same operation as modifying the document. Nothing could be further from the truth. A document may be changed between the time the server has sent you the document and the time you finished processing and saving it. In Listing 5.5, we handled that explicitly using optimistic concurrency, and in Listing 5.6, we used patching to avoid having to deal with the issue.

❖ If you're using subscriptions to integrate with other pieces of your infrastructure (such as sending emails), you have to be ready for failure on that end and have a meaningful strategy for handling it. Your options are to either propagate the error up the chain, which will force the subscription to close (and retry from the last successful batch), or you can catch the exception and handle it in some manner.

On the other hand, in Listing 5.6, we first send the email, then set the flag and save it. This means that if there's an error sending the email, we'll retry the document later on. However, if we had an error saving the flag to the server and we already sent the email, we might send it twice. You need to consider what scenario you're trying to prevent: emailing a customer twice or not at all.

Instead of relying on two-phase commit and distributed transactions, a much better alternative is to use the facilities of each system on its own. That topic goes beyond the scope of this book, but both idempotent operations or deduplication of operations can give you a safe path to follow in the presence of errors in a distributed system. If the email system recognizes that this email has already been sent, the code in Listing 5.6 will have no issue. We'll never skip sending an email, and we'll never send the same email twice.

Distributed transactions and RavenDB

The main reason we have to face this issue is that we're forced to integrate between two systems that don't share a transaction boundary. In other words, theoretically speaking, if we could create a transaction covering sending the email and writing to RavenDB, the problem would be solved.

In practice, RavenDB supported distributed transactions with multiple resources up until version 3.x, where we deprecated this feature. Version 4.0 removed it completely. Distributed transactions (also known as two-phase commit or 2PC) *sound* wonderful. Here you have a complex interaction between several different components in your system, and you can use a transaction to orchestrate it all in a nice and simple manner.

But it doesn't actually work like this. Any distributed transaction system that I've worked with had issues related to failure handling and partial success. A distributed transaction coordinator basically requires all participants in the transaction to promise that, if it tells them to commit the transaction, it will be successful. In fact, the way a coordinator usually works is by having one round of promises, and if all participants have been able to make that promise, there will be a second round with confirmations – hence the "two-phase commit" name.

The problem starts when you've gotten a promise from all the participants, you've already confirmed with a few of them that the transaction has been committed and one of the participants fails to commit for whatever reason (hardware failure, for example). In that case, the transaction is in a funny, half-committed state.

The coordinator will tell you this is a bug in the participant – that it shouldn't have made a promise it couldn't keep. And commonly, coordinators will retry such transactions (manually or automatically) and recover from transient errors. But the problem with the line of thinking that deems this an issue with this particular participant and not the coordinator is that those kind of errors are happening in production.

For one project, we had to restart the coordinator and manually resolve hanging transactions on a biweekly basis, and it wasn't a very large or busy website. Joe Armstrong, inventor of Erlang, described[2] the problem far better than I could:

The "Two Generals' Problem" is reality, but the computer industry says it doesn't believe in mathematics: two-phase commit[3] always works!

There's another issue with the code in Listing 5.5 and Listing 5.6. They're incredibly wasteful in the number of remote calls that they're making. One of the key benefits of using batch processing is the fact that we can handle things, well, in a batch. However, both Listing 5.5 and Listing 5.6 will create a session per document in the batch. The default batch size (assuming we have enough documents to send to fill a batch) is on the order of 4,096 items. That means that if we have a full batch, the code in either one of these listings will generate 8,192 remote calls. That's a *lot* of work to send to the server, all of which is handled in a serial fashion.

We can take advantage of the batch nature of subscriptions to do much better. Turn your attention to Listing 5.7, if you would.

Listing 5.7 *Efficiently process the batch*

```
await subscription.Run(batch =>
{
    using (var session = batch.OpenSession())
    {
        var customerIds = batch.Items
            .Select(item => item.Result.CustomerId)
            .Distinct()
            .ToList();

        // force load of all the customers in the batch
        // in a single request to the server
        session.Load<Customer>(customerIds);

        foreach (var item in batch.Items)
        {
            SupportCall call = item.Document;
            var age = DateTime.Today - call.Started;
            if (age > DateTime.FromDays(14))
                return; // no need to send survey for old stuff
```

2 This particular lecture was over a decade ago, but I still vividly remember it. It was *that* good.
3 There's also the *three*-phase commit, which just adds to the fun and doesn't actually solve the issue.

```
        // customer was already loaded into the session
        // no remote call will be made
        var customer = session.Load<Customer>(
            call.CustomerId);

        // register the change on the session
        // no remote call will be made
        session.Advanced.Patch<SupportCall, bool>(
            result.Id,
            c => c.Survey,
            true);

        SendSurveyEmailTo(customer, call);
    }

    // send a single request with all the
    // changes registered on the session
    session.SaveChanges();
    }
});
```

Listing 5.7 and Listing 5.6 are functionally identical. They have the same exact behavior, except Listing 5.6 will generate 8,192 requests and Listing 5.7 will generate only two. Yep, the code in Listing 5.7 is always going to generate just two requests. The first is a bulk load of all the customers in the batch, and the second is a single SaveChanges with all the changes for all the support calls in the batch.

Note that we're relying on the Unit of Work nature of the session. Once we've loaded a document into it, trying to load it again will give us the already loaded version without going to the server. Without this feature, the amount of calls to Load would have probably forced us over the budget of remote calls allowed for the session.[4]

Listing 5.7 takes full advantage of the batch nature of subscriptions. In fact, the whole reason why the batch exposes the Items list property instead of just being an enumerable is to allow you to make those kinds of optimizations. By making it obvious that scanning the list of items per batch is effectively free, we're left with the option of traversing it multiple times and optimizing our behavior.

---

4   Remember, that budget is configurable, but it's mostly there to help you realize that generating so many requests is probably not healthy for you.

5.2.1. COMPLEX CONDITIONALS

We already saw how we can create a subscription that filters documents on the server side: it was shown in Listing 5.4. The code there used a Linq expression, and the client API was able to turn that into a query that was sent to the server. Listing 5.4 was a pretty simple expression, and the code that handles the translation between Linq expressions and queries is quite smart. It's able to handle much more complex conditions.

However, putting a complex condition in a single Linq expression is not a recipe for good code. A better alternative is to skip the convenience of the Linq expression and go directly to the query. In Listing 5.8, we're going to see how we can subscribe to all the support calls that require special attention.

Listing 5.8 *Creating a subscription using JavaScript filtering*

```
var options = new SubscriptionCreationOptions
{
    Name = subscriptionName,
    Query = @"
        declare function isAnnoyedCustomer(call) {
            const watchwords = ['annoy', 'hard', 'silly'];

            const lastIndex =
                        call['@metadata']['Last-Monitored-Index'] || 0;
            for (let i = lastIndex; i < call.Comments.length; i++)
            {
                let comment = call.Comments[i].toLowerCase();
                for (let j = 0; j < watchwords.length; j++)
                {
                    if (comment.indexOf(watchwords[j]) !== -1)
                        return true;
                }
            }
            return false;
        }

        from SupportCalls as call
        where isAnnoyedCustomer(call)"
};
store.Subscriptions.Create(options);
```

The interesting code in Listing 5.8 is in `isAnnoyedCustomer` inside the query. We're defining a few words that we'll watch for, and if we see them in the comments of a support call, we want to give that call some special attention via this subscription. We do that by simply scanning through the array of `Comments` and checking if any comment contains any of the words we're looking for.

Use the subscription test feature

Any time that you need to run non-trivial code, you should consider how you'll debug it. Subscriptions give you a *lot* of power and they can carry the load of significant portions of your business logic. Because of that, it's very important that you will be able to test and play with them while developing.

For this reason, RavenDB has the subscription test feature. This feature will apply the subscription logic on top of the database and allow you to see the results of your filter or transformation scripts. We've already gotten a taste of that in Figure 5.3, but the more complex your queries are, the more useful this feature will become.

There's one item to consider here, though. A subscription test works just like a subscription. It matches all the documents in the particular collection you're operating on and applies the script to each and every one of them, giving you those documents that matched successfully. However, if your script filters out many of the matches and you have a large amount of data, it may take the subscription test a while to find enough documents that match your subscription filter.

You can reduce this time by selecting a document from which the subscription test will start the scanning process. This way it will not have to scan all the documents in the collection. Selecting such a document is done in the `Send Documents From` dropdown. While you'll typically use "Beginning of Time" as the default, you can save some time if you position the subscription directly on the first of the documents you want to process.

The one interesting tidbit is the use of `call['@metadata']['Last-Monitored-Index']`. What's that for? Remember that a subscription will be sent all the documents that match its criteria. And whenever a document is changed, it triggers a check for a match with the subscription. That means that if we didn't have some sort of check to stop it, our subscription would process any support call that had a comment with one of the words we watch for *every single time that call is processed*.

In order to avoid that scenario, we set a metadata value named `Last-Monitored-Index` when we process the subscription. You can see how that works in Listing 5.9.

We are simply setting the `Last-Monitored-Index` to the size of the `Comments` on the call and saving it back to the server. This will ensure that we'll only get the support call again if there are *new* comments with the words we're watching for. The code in Listing 5.9 is going out of its way to be a good citizen and not go to the server any more times than it needs to. This is also a good chance to demonstrate a real use case for `Defer` in production code. The use of `Defer` means two things: one, we don't need to worry about the number of calls and, two, we've handled concurrency.

Listing 5.9 *Escalating problematic calls*

```
await subscription.Run(batch =>
{
    const string script = @"
        var metadata = this['@metadata'];
        var existing = metadata['Last-Monitored-Index'] || 0;
        metadata['Last-Monitored-Index'] = Math.max($idx, existing);
        ";

    using (var session = batch.OpenSession())
    {
        foreach (var item in batch.Items)
        {
            // mark the last index that we
            // already observed using Patch
            session.Advanced.Defer(
                new PatchCommandData(
                    id: item.Id,
                    patch: new PatchRequest
                    {
                        Script = script,
                        Values =
                        {
                            ["idx"] = item.Result.Comments.Count
                        }
                    },
                    patchIfMissing: null,
                );
        }
        // actually escalate the call
        session.SaveChanges();
    }
});
```

Maintaining per-document subscription state

Subscriptions often need to maintain some sort of state on a per-document basis. In the case of Listing 5.9, we needed to keep track of the last monitored index, but other times you'll have much more complex state to track. For example, imagine that we need to kick off a workflow that will escalate a call once it passes a certain threshold. We might need to keep track of the state of the workflow and have that be accounted for in the subscription itself.

Using the metadata to do this works quite nicely if we're talking about small and simple state. However, as the complexity grows, it isn't viable to keep all that in the document metadata, and we'll typically introduce a separate document to maintain the state of the subscription. In it, we'll track support calls, and `SupportCalls/238-B` will have a `SupportCalls/238-B/EscalationState` document that contains the relevant information for the subscription.

Listing 5.8 and Listing 5.9 together show us how a subscription can perform rather complex operations and open up some really interesting options for processing documents. But even so, we aren't done. We can do even more with subscriptions.

5.2.2. COMPLEX SCRIPTS

We've used conditional subscriptions to filter the documents that we want to process, and since this filtering is happening on the server side, it allows us to reduce the number of documents that we have to send to the subscription. This is awesome in itself, but a really interesting feature of subscriptions is that we don't actually *need* to send the full documents to the client. We can select just the relevant details to send.

Say we want to do some processing on highly voted support calls. We don't need to get the full document; we just need the actual issue and the number of votes for that call. Instead of sending the full document over the wire, we can use the code in Listing 5.10 to achieve our goals more efficiently.

Listing 5.10 *Getting just the relevant details in the subscription*

```
var options = new SubscriptionCreationOptions
{
    Name = subscriptionName,
    Query =  @"
        from SupportCalls as call
        where call.Votes >= 10
        select {
            Issue: call.Issue,
            Votes: call.Votes
        }"
};
store.Subscriptions.Create(options);
```

What we're doing in Listing 5.10 is filtering the support calls. If the call has less then 10 votes, we'll just filter it. However, we aren't limited to just filtering the full document. We can also return an object of our own. That object can be built by us and contain just what we want to send directly to the client, and RavenDB will send it.

But there is an issue here. In Listing 5.10, we're creating a subscription on `SupportCall`. However, the value that will be sent to the client for the subscription to process is *not* a `SupportCall` document. It's a projection created during the subscription run. That means that, on the client side, we need to know how to handle such a thing. This requires a bit of a change in how we open the subscription, as you can see in Listing 5.11.

Listing 5.11 *Opening subscription with a different target*

```
public class SupportCallSubscriptionOutput
{
    public string Issue;
    public int Votes;
}

var options = new SubscriptionWorkerOptions(subscriptionName);
var subscription = store.Subscriptions
    .GetSubscriptionWorker<SupportCallSubscriptionOutput>(options);

await subscription.Run(batch =>
{
    foreach (var item in batch.Items)
    {
        SupportCallSubscriptionOutput result = item.Result;
        // do something with the
        // result.Issue, result.Votes
    }
});
```

In order to consume the subscription in a type-safe way, we create a class that matches the output that we'll get from the subscription script, and we'll use that when we open the subscription. Scenarios like the one outlined in Listings 5.10 and 5.11 make this flexibility very useful.

If this was all we could do with the subscription script, it would have been a good way to reduce the amount of data that's sent over the wire. But there are actually more options available for us that we haven't gotten around to yet. Consider Listing 5.6. There, we get the support call and immediately have to load the associated customer. That can lead to a remote call per item in the batch. We've already gone over why this can be a bad idea in terms of overall performance. Even with the optimization we implemented in Listing 5.7, there's still a remote call to do. We can do better.

We can ask RavenDB to handle this as part of the subscription processing directly. Take a look at Listing 5.12, which does just that.

Listing 5.12 *Getting just the relevant details in the subscription*

```
var options = new SubscriptionCreationOptions<SupportCall>
{
    Name = subscriptionName,
    Query = @"
        from SupportCalls as call
        where call.Votes >= 10
        load call.CustomerId as customer
        select {
            Issue: call.Issue,
            Votes: call.Votes,
            Customer: {
                Name: customer.Name,
                Email: customer.Email
            }
        }"
};
store.Subscriptions.Create(options);
```

In Listing 5.12, we're using `load` as part of the processing of the subscription on the server side. This allows us to get the customer instance and send pieces of it back to the client. In order to consume it, we'll need to change the `SupportCallSubscriptionOutput` class that we introduced in Listing 5.11 to add the new fields.

When processing the output of this subscription, we can directly process the results without making any other remote calls, not even to load the associated document. In Listing 5.13, you can see how we'd process such a subscription.

You can see that we use an inner class to scope the meaning of the `Customer` here. This isn't required. It's merely a convention we use to bring some order to the client-side types.

Listing 5.13 *Opening subscription with a different target*

```
public class SupportCallSubscriptionOutput
{
    public class Customer
    {
        public string Name;
        public string Email;
    }
    public string Issue;
    public int Votes;
    public Customer Customer;
}

var options = new SubscriptionWorkerOptions(subscriptionName);
var subscription = store.Subscriptions
    .GetSubscriptionWorker<SupportCallSubscriptionOutput>(options);

await subscription.Run(batch =>
{
    foreach (var item in batch.Items)
    {
        SupportCallSubscriptionOutput result = item.Result;
        SendEscalationEmail(result.Customer, item.Id);
        // other stuff related to processing the call
    }
});
```

5.3. Error handling and recovery with subscriptions

What happens when there's an error in the processing of a document? Imagine that we had code inside the lambda in the Run method and that code threw an exception. Unless you set SubscriptionWorkerOptions.IgnoreSubscriberErrors,[5] we'll abort processing of the subscription and the Run will raise an error. Typical handling in that scenario is to dispose the subscription and immediately open it again.

Assuming the error is transient, we'll start processing from the last batch we received and continue forward from there. If the error isn't transient – for example, some

---

5   And you probably shouldn't do that.

`NullReferenceException` because of a `null` the code didn't check for – the error will repeat itself. You might want to set an upper limit to the number of errors you'll try to recover from in a given time period, choosing to just fail completely afterward. This depends heavily on the kind of error reporting and recovery you're using in your applications.

Note that this applies only to errors that come from the code processing the document. All other errors (connection to server, failover between servers, etc.) are already handled by RavenDB. The reason that we abort the subscription in the case of subscriber error is that there really isn't any good way to recover from it in a safe manner. We don't want to skip processing the document. And just logging the error is possible (in fact, that's exactly what we do if `IgnoreSubscriberErrors` is set), but no one ever reads the log until the problem is already discovered, which is typically very late in the game.

In other words, RavenDB will take care of all the issues related to talking to the database, but the error handling related to your code is on you. In practice, you generally don't have to worry about it. An error thrown during document processing will kill your subscription. We saw in Listing 5.3 that after we call Run, we need to wait on the resulting task. If an error is raised during document processing, the subscription will close and that error will be raised to the caller of the Run method.

The typical manner in which you'll handle errors with subscriptions is to just retry the whole subscription, as shown in Listing 5.14. There's a lot of things going on in this listing, so take the time to carefully read through the error handling.

Listing 5.14 shows a typical way to handle errors in subscriptions. For completion's sake, I've included all the common error conditions that can be raised from the Run method. The first few items involve non-recoverable scenarios. The database doesn't exist, the subscription doesn't exist or is misconfigured, or the credentials we have are invalid. There's no way to recover from those kinds of errors without administrator involvement, so we should just raise this up the stack until we catch the attention of someone who can actually fix this.

The next part handles errors when the subscription was closed explicitly by an administrator. RavenDB will automatically recover from failures and accidental disconnects, but the administrator can also choose to explicitly kill a subscription connection. In this case, we'll report this to the caller, who can decide what to do about it. Simply retrying is probably not a good idea in this case. A subscription can also fail because another client is already holding onto it, or a client came in and kicked our subscription from the subscription. Both of these cases are strongly tied to the deployment mode you have and will be discussed in the next section.

Listing 5.14 *Retrying subscription on error*

```
while (true)
{
    var options = new SubscriptionWorkerOptions(subscriptionName);

    // here we configure that we allow a down time of up to 2 hours
    // and will wait for 2 minutes for reconnecting
    options.MaxErroneousPeriod = TimeSpan.FromHours(2);
    options.TimeToWaitBeforeConnectionRetry = TimeSpan.FromMinutes(2);

    var subscriptionWorker = store.Subscriptions
        .GetSubscriptionWorker<Order>(options);

    try
    {
        // here we are able to be informed of
        // any exception that happens during processing
        subscriptionWorker.OnSubscriptionConnectionRetry +=
          exception =>
        {
            Logger.Error("Error during subscription processing: " +
              subscriptionName, exception);
        };

        await subscriptionWorker.Run(async batch =>
        {
            foreach (var item in batch.Items)
            {
                // we want to force close the subscription processing
                // in that case and let the external code decide
                // what to do with that
                if (item.Result.Company == "companies/832-A")
                    throw new UnsupportedCompanyException("Company
                      Id can't be 'companies/832-A', you must fix this");
                await ProcessOrder(item.Result);
            }
        }, cancellationToken);
```

```
        // Run will complete normally if
        // you have disposed the subscription
        return;
    }
    catch (Exception e)
    {
        Logger.Error("Failure in subscription: " +
          subscriptionName, e);

        if (e is DatabaseDoesNotExistException ||
            e is SubscriptionDoesNotExistException ||
            e is SubscriptionInvalidStateException ||
            e is AuthorizationException)
                    throw; // not recoverable

        if (e is SubscriptionClosedException)
            // closed explicitly by admin, probably
            return;

        if (e is SubscriberErrorException se)
        {
            // for UnsupportedCompanyException type, we want to throw
            // an exception, otherwise we continue processing
            if (se.InnerException is UnsupportedCompanyException)
            {
                throw;
            }

            continue;
        }

        // handle this depending on subscription
        // open strategy (discussed later)
        if (e is SubscriptionInUseException)
            continue;
```

```
        return;
    }
    finally
    {
        subscriptionWorker.Dispose();
    }
}
```

What about subscription script errors?

We've talked plenty about what happens when there are errors on the server side (automatically recover), on the client side (thrown to caller and handled by your code) and the like. However, there's one class of errors that we didn't consider: what would happen if there's an error in the query that we use to evaluate each document?

Consider the following snippet: `select { Rate: 10 / call.Votes) }`. It isn't meant to be meaningful, just to generate an error when the `Votes` property is set to zero. In this case, when evaluating the script on a support call with no votes, we'll get a error attempting to divide by zero. That error will be sent to the client and be part of the batch.

When the client accesses the `item.Result` property on that particular document, the exception will be raised on the client side. In this way, you can select how to handle such errors. You can handle this on the client side in some manner and continue forward normally, or you can let it bubble up as an error in the subscription, which should trigger your error-handling policy, as we saw in Listing 5.14.

All other exceptions would typically be raised from within the batch processing code. A very simple error handling strategy can be to just try an error backoff for retries. So on the first error, you'll retry immediately, if there is still an error, wait for 5 seconds and try again. Keep adding 5 seconds to the sleep time until a certain maximum (such as 1 minute). In many cases, this is enough to handle transient errors without having to get an admin involved in the process.

Exactly how you'll handle error recovery in your system is up to you and the operations teams that will maintain the application in production, and it's tied very closely to how you're using subscriptions and deploying them.

5.4. Subscription deployment patterns

Talking about a single subscription in isolation helps us understand how it works, but we also need to consider how subscriptions are deployed and managed in your systems. Subscriptions are used to handle most batch processing needs in RavenDB, which puts them in an interesting place regarding their use. On the one hand, they're often performing critical business functions. But on the other hand, they aren't visible. (A failing subscription will not cause an error page to be shown to the user.)

Subscriptions are usually deployed in either a batch-and-stop mode or in a continuous run. The continuous run is a process (or a set of processes) that are running your subscriptions constantly. The database will feed any new data to them as soon as it's able, and all processing happens live. That isn't required, mind you. Under load, the administrator is perfectly able to shut down a subscription (or even all of them) to free up processing capacity. When they're started up again, they'll pick up where they left off.

In batch mode, the subscriptions are run on a schedule. When they run out of work to do, they'll shut themselves down until being run again. Listing 5.15 shows how you can write a self-stopping subscription.

Listing 5.15 *Stop the subscription after 15 minutes of inactivity*

```
var options = new SubscriptionWorkerOptions(subscriptionName)
{
    CloseWhenNoDocsLeft = true
}

using (var subscription = store
        .Subscriptions.GetSubscriptionWorker<SupportCall>(options))
{
    await subscription.Run(batch =>
    {
        // process batches until we run out of docs
        // that match the subscription
    });
}
```

The CloseWhenNoDocsLeft option will cause RavenDB to abort the subscription if there are no documents to send. This is useful for processes that start, run through everything that happened since their last run and then shut down again.

Another aspect of subscription deployment is the notion of high availability. On the server side, the cluster will ensure that if there was a failure, we will transparently failover to another node. But who takes care of high availability on the client? Typically you'll want to have at least a couple of machines running subscriptions, so if one of them goes down, the other one will carry on. However, if the same subscription is running concurrently on two machines, that can lead to duplicate processing. Now, your code needs to handle that anyway, since subscriptions guarantee processing at least once and various error conditions can cause a batch to be re-sent. However, there's a major difference between handling that once in a blue moon and having to deal with it constantly, leaving aside the issue that we'll also have higher resource usage because we need to process the subscription on multiple nodes.

Luckily, RavenDB subscriptions don't work like that. Instead, a subscription is always opened by one and only one client. By default, if two clients attempt to open the same subscription, one of them will succeed and the other one will raise an error because it couldn't take hold of the subscription. This is controlled by the `SubscriptionOpeningStrategy` option set on the `Strategy` property. The various options of this property are:

◆ `OpenIfFree` – the default. The client will attempt to open the subscription but will fail if another client is already holding it. This is suitable in cases where you're running subscriptions in batch/schedule mode. If another client is already processing it, there's no need to process anything yourself.

◆ `TakeOver` – the client will attempt to open the subscription even if a client is already connected to it. If there's a connected client, its connection will be closed. This is used to force the subscription open operation to succeed for a particular client. If an incoming subscription tries to take over an existing one, which also has a "take over" strategy, the incoming subscription will "loose" the contest.

◆ `WaitForFree` – the client will attempt to open the subscription, but if there's already a connected client, it will keep trying to acquire the connection. This is suitable for high availability mode, when you have multiple clients attempting to acquire the same subscription and you want one of them to succeed while the rest stand ready in case that one fails.

For high availability processing on the client, you'll set up multiple machines that will run your subscriptions and open them using the `WaitForFree` option. In this way, those clients will compete for the subscriptions. If one of them fails, the other will take over and continue processing them. The use of multiple machines for handling subscriptions also allows you to split your processing between the machines.

Failure conditions in a distributed environment

Failure handling in a distributed environment is *hard*. When both clients and servers are distributed, this makes for some really interesting failure modes. In particular, while we promise that a subscription will only be opened by a single client at a time, it's possible for the network to split in such a way that two clients have successfully connected to two different servers and are trying to process the same subscription from them.

That scenario should be rare, and it will only last for the duration of a single batch, until the next synchronization point for the subscription (which ensures global consistency for the subscription). One of those servers will fail to process the batch acknowledgement and return that error to the client, eventually aborting the connection.

You may decide that you want certain operations to be handled on one worker node[6] and configure those subscriptions to TakeOver on that worker node and WaitForFree on any other worker nodes. This way, a particular subscription has a preferred worker node that it will run on, but if that one fails, it will run on another. In other words, each worker node will run only its own preferred subscriptions unless there's a failure.

When your deployment contains multiple worker nodes that are all processing subscriptions, you need to be even more aware of the fact that you're running in a distributed system and that concurrency in a distributed environment should always be a consideration. We already talked about optimistic concurrency in Chapter 4, but with distributed databases, we also need to take into account eventual consistency and conflicts between machines. We'll start talking about the distributed nature of RavenDB in Chapter 6 in depth.

For subscriptions, we typically don't care about this. The batch processing mode means that we already see the world differently and it doesn't matter if we get a document in a particular batch or in the next. One thing to be aware of is that different subscriptions may be running on different nodes and thus getting the documents in a different order. (All of them will end up getting all the documents. There's just no guaranteed absolute order across the distributed system.)

5.5. Using subscription for queuing tasks

In this section, I want to utilize subscriptions as a processing queue for a few reasons. For one thing, it's a very common scenario for using subscriptions. For another, it lets us explore a lot of the RavenDB functionality and how different pieces are held together. What we want to do is to be able to write an operation to the database and, when we've successfully processed it, automatically delete it.

Going back to the email-sending example, our code will write EmailToSend documents that will be picked up by a subscription and handled. The code for actually doing this is shown in Listing 5.16.

---

6   I'm using the term worker node here to refer to machines that are running business processes, subscriptions, etc. This is to distinguish them from RavenDB nodes.

Listing 5.16 *Delete the emails to send after successful send*

```
using (var subscription =
    store.Subscriptions.GetSubscriptionWorker<EmailToSend>(options))
{
    await subscription.Run(async batch =>
    {
        using (var session = batch.OpenAsyncSession())
        {
            foreach (var item in batch.Items)
            {
                try
                {
                    SendEmail(item.Document);
                }
                catch
                {
                    // logging / warning / etc
                    continue;
                }
                session.Delete(item.Id);
            }
            await session.SaveChangesAsync();
        }
    });
}
```

There's actually a lot going on in Listing 5.16 that may not be obvious. First, we're processing a batch of documents, trying to send each one in turn. If there's an error in sending one of those emails, we'll skip further processing.

However, if we were able to successfully send the email, we'll register the document to be deleted. At the end of the batch, we'll delete all the documents that we've successfully sent. However, we won't touch the documents that we didn't send. The idea is to dedicate the EmailToSend collection for this task only. That means that in the EmailToSend collection, we'll only ever have one of two types of documents:

◆ EmailToSend documents that haven't been processed yet by the subscription and will be sent (and deleted) soon.
◆ Documents that we tried to send but failed to.

Those documents that we fail to send are interesting. Since the subscription has already processed them, we won't be seeing them again. However, we didn't lose any data, and an administrator can compare the current state of the subscription to the state of the `EmailToSend` collection and get all the failed documents.

At that point, the admin can either fix whatever is wrong with those documents (which will cause them to be sent to the subscription again) or they can reset the position of the subscription and have it reprocess all those documents again (for example, if there was some environmental problem). This mode of operation is really nice for processing queues. For simple cases, you can just rely on RavenDB to do it all for you. In fact, given that RavenDB subscriptions can work with failover of both clients and servers, this gives you a robust solution to handle task queues that are local to your application.

One thing to note – RavenDB isn't a queuing solution, and this code doesn't pretend that it is. The code in Listing 5.16 is a great way to handle task queues, but proper queuing systems will offer additional features (like monitoring and built-in error handling) that you might want to consider. For most simple tasks, the fire-and-forget operations, you can use RavenDB in this mode. But for more complex situations, you should at least explore whether a proper queue can offer a better solution.

5.6. Versioned subscriptions

The subscriptions we've used so far are always operating on the current state of the document. Consider the following case:

◆ You create a subscription on the `Customer` collection.
◆ You create a customer document and modify it three times.
◆ You open and run the subscription and observe the incoming items in the batch.

What will the subscription get? It will get the *last* version of the customer document. The same can happen when the subscription is already running. If you've made multiple modifications to a document, when the next batch starts, we'll just grab the current version of the document and send it to the subscription. This can be a problem if your subscription code assumes that you'll always get the document every time it changes.

The good news is that we can utilize another RavenDB feature, revisions (discusssed in Chapter 4), to allow us to see all the changes that were made to a document.

The first step to exploring this feature is to enable revisions on the collection you want. In this case, it's the `Customers` collection. Set the minimum retention time for two weeks, and again make a few modifications to a customer document. When you run your subscription once more, note that you're again getting just the latest version of the `Customer` document.

The reason you only get the latest version of the document is that the subscription, too, needs to let the server know that it's versioned. This is because the data model for versioned subscriptions is different. Let's take a look at Listing 5.17 for an example of a simple versioned subscription that can detect when a customer changed his/her name.

Listing 5.17 *Subscribing to versioned customers*

```
store.Subscriptions.Create<Revision<Customer>>(
    new SubscriptionCreationOptions
    {
        Name = subscriptionName,
    }
);

using (var subscription = store.Subscriptions
        .GetSubscriptionWorker<Revision<Customer>>(
            subscriptionName
    ))
{
    await subscription.Run(batch =>
    {
        foreach (var item in batch.Items)
        {
            Revision<Customer> customer = item.Result;

            if (customer.Previous.Name !=
                customer.Current.Name)
            {
                // report customer name change
            }
        }
    });
}
```

The key parts to the code in Listing 5.17 is the use of `Revision<Customer>` as the type that we're subscribing on. RavenDB recognizes that as a versioned subscription and will feed us each and every revision for the `Customer` collection.

Note that the data model as well has changed. Instead of getting the document itself, we get an object that has `Previous` and `Current` properties, representing the changes that happened to the document. In other words, you're able to inspect the current and previous versions and make decisions based on the changes that happened to the entity.

This feature opens up a *lot* of options regarding analytics because you aren't seeing just a snapshot of the state but all the intermediate steps along the way. This has uses in business analytics, fraud, outliers detection and forensics, in addition to the general benefit of being able to reconstruct the flow of data through your system. The way versioned subscriptions work, we're going to get all the changes that match our criteria, in the same order they happened in the database.[7]

If I wrote to `customers/8243-C`, created a new `customers/13252-B` and then wrote to `customers/8243-C` again, I'll get the changes (either in a single batch or across batches) in the following order:

◆ `customers/8243-C – (Previous -> Current)`
◆ `customers/13252-B – (null -> Current)`
◆ `customers/8243-C – (Previous -> Current)`

This can be useful when running forensics or just when you want to inspect what's going on in your system.

Handling revisioned document creation and deletion

When a new document is created, we'll get it in the versioned subscription with the `Previous` property set to `null` and the `Current` set to the newly created version. Conversely, if the document is deleted, we'll get it with the `Current` set to `null` and the `Previous` set to the last version of the document.

If a document is deleted and recreated, we'll have one entry with (`Previous`, `null`) and then another with (`null`, `Current`). This feature is also useful if you just want to detect the deletion of documents in a subscription.

Just like regular subscriptions, we aren't limited to just getting all the data from the server. We can filter it, as you can see in Listing 5.18.

The code in Listing 5.18 will only send you the `Customer` documents whose names have been changed. The rest of the code in Listing 5.17 can remain the same, but we now don't need to check if the names have changed on the client side. We've done that already on the server.

---

7   Again, different nodes may have observed the events in a different order, but it should roughly match across the cluster.

Listing 5.18 *Setting filters on a versioned subscription*

```
store.Subscriptions.Create(
    new SubscriptionCreationOptions
    {
        Name = subscriptionName,
        Query = @"
            from Customers (Revisions = true)
            where Previous.Name != Current.Name"
    }
);
```

A natural extension of this behavior is to not send the full data to the client but just the data we need. An example of this can be shown in Listing 5.19.

Listing 5.19 *Getting changed names using versioned subscription*

```
store.Subscriptions.Create(
    new SubscriptionCreationOptions<Versioned<Customer>>
    {
        Name = subscriptionName,
        Query = @"
            from Customers (Revisions = true)
            where Previous.Name != Current.Name
            select {
                OldName: this.Previous.Name,
                NewName: this.Current.Name
            }"
    }
);
```

The code in Listing 5.19 isn't that interesting except for what it's actually doing. It's filtering the data on the server side and only sending us the old and new names. The subscription handling code on the client side just needs to take the old name and new name and notify whoever needs to know about the name change.

Versioned subscriptions give you a lot of power to work with your data (and the changes in your data) in an easy way. The ability is of particular interest in reversed event sourcing because you can go over your data, detect a pattern that matches a particular event you want to raise and publish it.

Versioned subscriptions use the document revisions

This might be an obvious statement, but it needs to be explicitly said. The backing store for the versioned subscription is all the revisions that are stored for the documents as they're changed. That means that it's important to know the minimum retention time that's been configured. If you have a weekly subscription run and the versioning is configured to keep data for a day, you're going to miss out on revisions that have already been deleted.

So when using a versioned subscription, the administrator must verify that the revisions retention time matches the subscription run time.

5.7. Subscriptions, background jobs and the role of the admin

Systems typically accrue additional behavior over time. As business processes mature and evolve, so does the demand on our systems. The way we've talked about subscriptions so far is mainly as a core part of the application itself – something that the developers would write, build and manage. But that doesn't have to be the case. In fact, it's common for subscriptions to be used as "aftermarket" entry points for modifying, extending and supporting the system.

Consider the case of wanting to send all new users a welcome email after they've registered. We *could* do that as part of the application itself, but given that this is a self-contained feature, we don't actually *have* to involve the developers. We can write a subscription that would monitor new customers and send them the email.

For flexibility, we don't want to write it in C#. We don't need an application. We just need to be able to run a script to process those documents. I'm using the Python client API in Listing 5.20 to perform this task. (I could have used node.js, Ruby, etc. I'm using Python as the example here because it's a great scripting language, and one I'm very fond of.)

The code is quite similar to the way we would do things in C#. We open a document store, open the subscription and pass a method to process the document batches. The use of Python typically means shorter development time and more freedom for the operations team to modify things. That can be a great thing or a horrible thing.

Subscription in a dynamic language

A major advantage of writing such scripts in a dynamic language is the low overhead and friction. We don't need to define classes. We can just use the shape of the data as it came down the wire. That makes everything simpler.

On the other hand, you need to be aware that doing so requires discipline. You must be sure to version your subscription's code in step with the rest of the code.

Listing 5.20 *Sending welcome emails to new customers*

```python
##!/usr/bin/env python3

from pyravendb import RavenDB

def process_batch(batch):

    with batch.open_session() as session:
        for item in batch.items:
            customer = item.result
            if customer.WelcomeEmailSent:
                continue

            send_welcome_email(customer);
            customer.WelcomeEmailSent = True
            session.store(customer)

        session.save_changes()

store = document_store (
    urls = ["http://rvn-srv-2:8080"],
    database = "HelpDesk"
    )
store.initialize()

with store.Subscriptions.GetSubscriptionWorker(
    subscription_connection_options(
        id = "new-customers-welcome-email"
    )) as subscription:

    subscription.run(process_batch).join()
```

Subscriptions, even if they're written in another platform, are still considered to be a part of your system. RavenDB is meant to be an application database, not a shared database between a multitude of applications using the same data. Even if there are additional processes going on, they should be (eventually, at least) all owned by the application itself.

The beauty in using a scripting language for those kind of tasks is that it allows you to simply set up a subscription without any sort of application, compilation, etc. A single script per business process is usually enough. Since those are background batch processes, it doesn't usually matter if the language isn't very fast. You can trade off convenience for speed in this case with a clear conscience.

One thing that *isn't* in Listing 5.20 is error handling. In previous examples in this chapter, I spent some time discussing error handling, and any subscription scripts you have most certainly do need to have something there. But a conscientious admin will have already set up a watchdog for this, reporting errors and raising alerts accordingly. Any production system is made of a lot of moving parts. Most likely that the infrastructure to manage such scripts, restart them if there is an error and alert you if they haven't recovered is already in place.

I'm mentioning this because it's important that it *is* in place. The nasty side of this kind of approach is that it's easy for what would turn out to be a critical business process to be developed in a completely "Shadow IT" approach; that is, this subscription is running on some server somewhere and will continue to do so until a reboot is done, where stuff breaks and no one really knows what.

5.8. Summary

When RavenDB implemented subscriptions for the first time, it was just a small section: a minor feature that was meant to handle an esoteric scenario that only a single customer had run into. From that modest beginning, this feature has blown up to completely replace most batch processing handling in RavenDB. It's not the first thing you'll use in every situation, but for anything that isn't about responding to a user request, it's usually a match.

In this chapter, we looked into what subscriptions are, how to do batch processes with RavenDB and subscriptions, how to filter and modify the data on the server and how to accept and process the data on the client side and write it back to RavenDB in an optimal fashion. We looked at integrating with external systems via the email-sending example, including how to handle failures and partial failures both in RavenDB and in the external systems.

> **Using subscription for ETL work**
>
> It's tempting to use subscriptions to handle ETL[8] tasks, such as writing to a reporting database. While it *is* possible, RavenDB has better options to handle ETL. See the discussion on this topic in Chapter 8.

We spent a lot of time discussing how to handle errors in subscriptions, how to deploy subscriptions into production and how we can ensure failover and load balancing of the work among both client and server using subscriptions. The subscription open strategies allow us to have a hot standby client for a subscription, ready to take over from a failed node and

---

8   Extract, transform, load – the process of moving data around between different data storage systems.

continue processing. On the server side, RavenDB will automatically failover subscriptions from a failed database node to a healthy one in a completely transparent manner.

Another great use case for subscriptions is implementing task queues. And we looked at that, including error handling and recovery. We also discussed the ability to fix an issue with a document that failed and have it automatically reprocessed by the subscription.

We then looked at versioned subscriptions, where we ask RavenDB to give us a before-and-after snapshot of each and every change for the documents we care about. This is a great help when producing timelines, tracking changes and handling forensics. This feature relies on the revisions configuration on the database and exposes it directly for batch processing needs. We can even write a subscription script that would filter and send just the relevant details from both old and new revisions of the document to the client side.

The next part of the book is going to be exciting. We're going to learn how RavenDB is working in a distributed environment, and we can finally figure out what all those cryptic references to working in a cluster *mean*.

II. Distributed RavenDB

We've looked into RavenDB with an eye to finding out what it can do, but we've only just scratched the surface. We've covered enough for you to be able to write simple CRUD applications, but there's a lot more we haven't covered yet. The chief topics we've yet to cover are running RavenDB in a distributed cluster and querying data.

I struggled to decide the order in which these two topics should show up in the book. Queries are *important*, but RavenDB is quite capable of handling a lot of the decisions around them on its own. And while queries and indexing can have a major impact on coding decisions, the distributed aspect of RavenDB should be a core part of your architecture design. For that reason, I decided to cover RavenDB's distributed nature first. If you only intend to run RavenDB as a single node, you can skip this part and go directly to the next, but I still recommend reading through it to understand what's available to you.

A cluster is always recommended for production deployments for the high availability, fault tolerance and load-balancing features the cluster brings to the table.

You may have noticed that the RavenDB philosophy is to make things as obvious and easy to use as possible. Admittedly, working in a distributed environment is not a trivial task, given the challenges you'll face with your data residing on multiple (sometimes disconnected) nodes, but RavenDB makes it easier than the vast majority of other distributed solutions.

The next chapter will first cover a bit of theory around RavenDB's design. Then we'll set out to build a multi-node cluster on your local machine and see what kind of tricks we can teach it. We'll finish with practical advice on how to best use the distributed nature of RavenDB to your advantage. Following that, we'll dive deep into the innards of the distributed engine inside RavenDB. You'll learn how the sausage is made, knowledge that can be very useful when troubleshooting.

Next, we'll talk about integrating RavenDB with the rest of your environment. RavenDB is rarely deployed on pure greenfield projects that don't have to talk to anything else. We'll discuss integration strategies with the rest of your organization, ETL processes between different systems and how we mesh it all into a single whole.

6. RavenDB Clusters

You might be familiar with the term "murder of crows" as a way to refer to a group of crows.[1] It's been used in literature and the arts many times. Of less renown is the group term for ravens, which is "unkindness." Personally, in the name of all ravens, I'm torn between being insulted and amused.

Professionally, setting up RavenDB as a cluster on a group of machines is a charming exercise (though the term "charm" is actually reserved for finches) that brings a sense of exaltation (a term that's also taken, this time by larks) by how pain-free it is. I'll now end my voyage into the realm of ornithology's etymology and stop speaking in tongues.

On a more serious note, the fact that RavenDB clustering is easy to set up means that it's much more approachable. You don't need an expert on hand at all times to set up a cluster, and it should mostly self-manage. That means the decision to go from a single server to a cluster is much easier, and you can get the benefit of that sooner.

6.1. An overview of a RavenDB cluster

A RavenDB cluster is three or more machines[2] that have been joined together.

But what's the point of doing that? Well, you can create databases on a RavenDB cluster, and you can specify that the cluster should manage them on its own. A database can live on a single node, some number of the nodes or even all the nodes. Each node will then hold a complete copy of the database and will be able to serve all queries, operations and writes.

---

1   If you're interested in learning why, I found this answer fascinating: https://www.quora.com/ Why-is-a-group-of-crows-called-a-murder

2   It doesn't make a lot of sense to have a cluster with just two nodes since we'll require both of the nodes to always be up, in most cases. There are certain advanced scenarios where such topology might make sense, and we'll touch on that briefly in Chapter 7.

The cluster will also distribute work among the various nodes automatically, handle failures and recovery and in general act to make sure that everything is humming along merrily.

Operations in RavenDB are usually divided into cluster-wide operations (including cluster-wide operations that impact only a single database) and internal database operations. For example, creating a new database is a cluster-wide operation, while writing a document to a database only impacts that particular database.

The reason this distinction is important is because RavenDB actually operates two distinct layers in its distributed system. The first, at the cluster level, is composed of nodes working together to achieve the same goal. This is done by using the Raft consensus protocol and having the cluster members vote to select a strong leader among themselves.

This leader, in turn, is responsible for such things as monitoring the cluster's health, selecting the preferred node that clients will use for each database, configuring the databases and making sure there's a consistent way to make decisions at the cluster level. But at the database level, instead of selecting a leader, the nodes are all working together, cooperatively and as equals.

Why would we want that? Wouldn't it be better to have just a single mode of operation? The answer is that it probably would be simpler but not necessarily better. Let's examine the pros and cons of each approach and how they're used by RavenDB.

Cluster consensus with a strong leader (Raft algorithm) provides strong consistency. The leader ensures that, as long as a majority of the nodes are functioning and can talk to one another, we'll remain in operation. The strong consistency mode is quite nice since it means the cluster can make a decision (such as add a database to a node), and we can be sure this decision will either be accepted by the entire cluster (eventually) or we fail to register that decision. That means that each node can operate on its own internal state for most operations, resulting in a more robust system.

The CAP theorem and database design

The CAP theorem, also called Brewer's theorem, states that given consistency, availability and partition tolerance, a system must choose two out of the three. It's not possible to provide all three options.

In practice, since all production systems are vulnerable to partitions, it means you can elect to be either CP (consistent and partition tolerant) or AP (available and partition tolerant). Different database systems have decided to take different design directions to handle this issue.

RavenDB has opted to be CP and AP. That isn't quite as impossible as it sounds. It's just that it isn't trying to be CP and AP on the same layer. With RavenDB, the cluster layer is CP (it's always consistent but may not be available in the presence of a partition), but the database layer is AP (it's always available, even if there's a partition, but it's eventually consistent).

However, if a majority of the nodes aren't available, we can't proceed. This is pretty much par for the course for consensus algorithms. Another issue with consensus algorithms is that they incur additional network round trips for each operation. For cluster maintenance and the configuration of databases, RavenDB uses the Raft consensus protocol. The RavenDB implementation of Raft is codenamed Rachis.[3]

Databases, on the other hand, are treated quite differently. Each node in the cluster has a full copy of the topology, which specifies which nodes host which databases. That information is managed by Rachis, but each node is able to act upon it independently.

The connections between the databases in different nodes do not go through Rachis or any other consensus protocol. Instead, they're direct connections among the various nodes that hold a particular database, and they form a multi-master mesh. A write to any of those nodes will be automatically replicated to all the other nodes.

This design results in a robust system. First, you define your cluster, distribute your databases among the nodes, assign work, etc. Once the cluster is set up, each database instance on the various nodes is independent. That means it can accept writes without consulting the other instances of the same database.

The design of RavenDB was heavily influenced by the Dynamo paper, and one of the key features was the notion that writes are *important*. If a user is writing to the database, you really want to hold on to that data. In order to achieve that, RavenDB uses multi-master replication inside a database, and it's always able to accept writes.

In other words, even if the majority of the cluster is down, as long as a single node is available, we can still process reads and writes.

This is a lot to digest. At this point, it's probably all a bit theoretical for you. We'll get back to the different layers that compose the RavenDB distributed architecture later on. For now, let's get ready to set up our first cluster.

6.2. Your first RavenDB cluster

We've worked with RavenDB before, but only with a single node. What you might not be aware of is that we actually worked with a single node cluster, and it isn't that interesting from the point of view of distributed systems. However, even a single node instance is always running as a cluster. That has the advantage of the same codepaths always being used and exercised.

Another major benefit is that you don't need any special steps to get to a cluster. All you need to do is add a few nodes. Let's see how it works in practice. To do this, close any RavenDB server instances you currently have running and open the command line terminal at the RavenDB folder. We want to reduce the amount of work we have to do per node, so open the `settings.json` file and ensure that it has the following properties:

---

3   Rachis is the central shaft of pennaceous feathers.

```
"Setup.Mode": "None",
"License.Eula.Accepted": true
```

These are needed to skip the setup wizard and EULA acceptance screens, which happen by default when you start a new instance of RavenDB.

Downloading RavenDB

In "Zero To Hero," we went over how to download and set up RavenDB for various environments. If you skipped that step, you can go to the RavenDB download page at https://ravendb.net/download and download the package for your platform. The rest of this chapter assumes that you'll run all commands inside the uncompressed RavenDB directory, after you have updated the settings.json file.

The first thing we want to do is run an instance of RavenDB. I suggest running each RavenDB instance in its own terminal window, since that makes it easy to see the behavior of individual nodes:

```
./Server/Raven.Server.exe `
    --ServerUrl=http://127.0.0.1:8080 `
    --Logs.Path=Logs/A `
    --DataDir=Data/A
```

This command will run a RavenDB instance listening to 127.0.0.1 on port 8080, logging to the Logs/A directory and storing the data in the Data/A directory. You can point your browser to http://127.0.0.1:8080 and see the familiar Studio. Let's create a new database and call it "Spade." The result should look like Figure 6.1.

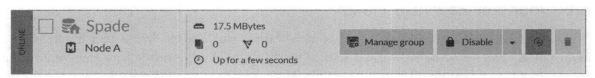

Figure 6.1. *A simple database on a single node*

Let's go into the database and create a couple of documents: "users/1" and "users/2," with your first and last name as the name. We're creating this database and those documents simply so we can see how we can grow a RavenDB cluster.

Now, we need to bring up another RavenDB node. Typically, you'd do that on a separate machine, but to make the demo easier, we'll just run it on the same machine. Open a new terminal session and run the following command:

```
./Server/Raven.Server.exe `
    --ServerUrl=http://127.0.0.2:8080 `
    --Logs.Path=Logs/B `
    --DataDir=Data/B
```

This time, we run the RavenDB instance bound to 127.0.0.2 (note there's a "2" at the end, not a "1") and with the same 8080 port. Logs go to Logs/B, and the data is stored in the Data/B directory. By utilizing the 127.*.*.* local IP range, we can easily run distinct RavenDB instances on the same machine and tell them apart.

You can go to http://127.0.0.2:8080 and see the Studio, as well. However, unlike the instance running in 127.0.0.1:8080, there are no databases in the 127.0.0.2:8080's Studio.

Another difference between the two nodes can be seen at the bottom right, as shown in Figure 6.2.

Figure 6.2. *The node tag in two nodes*

You can see in 127.0.0.2:8080 that the node is marked with a question mark, indicating an unknown node. That's because this is a new node that didn't have any operations made on it. On the other hand, the 127.0.0.1:8080 node had a database created on it and, as such, is a single node cluster marked with the node tag A.

Now, let's add a node to our cluster. Go to 127.0.0.1:8080, Manage server and then to Cluster. The cluster management screen is shown in Figure 6.3.

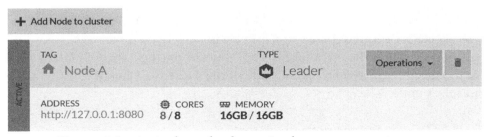

Figure 6.3. *A single node cluster in the management screen*

Click Add Node to Cluster and enter http://127.0.0.2:8080. The new node will show up as a cluster member, as shown in Figure 6.4.

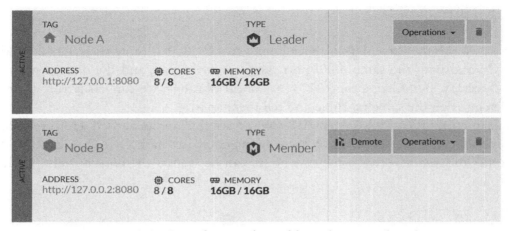

Figure 6.4. *Our cluster after adding the second node*

If you visit 127.0.0.2:8080 in the browser, you'll observe several interesting things. First, at the bottom, you can see 127.0.0.2:8080 is no longer an unknown node. Instead, it has been designated as node B.

Node tags and readability

To simplify matters, RavenDB assigns each node in the cluster a tag. Those tags are used to identify the nodes. They don't replace the node URLs but rather supplement them. Being able to say node B instead of 127.0.0.2:8080 or even WIN-U0RFOJCTPUU is quite helpful. This also helps in more complex network environments where a node may be accessed via several hosts, IPs and names. From now on, I'm going to refer to nodes by their tags instead of continuing to write the IP:Port over and over.

On the databases list view, you can also see that the "Spade" database is marked as offline on node B. This is because this database is only set up to be held on node A. To spread the "Spade" database to node B, click the "Manage group" button on the "Spade" database, which will take you to a page allowing you to add a node to the database. Click the "Add node to group" button and select node B.

HTTP, TCP and the firewall, oh my!

In the configuration we've used so far, we used ServerUrl to specify what interface and port we'll be listening to. However, this applies only to the HTTP interface of RavenDB. There is also a TCP interface, mostly used for direct communication between RavenDB nodes. Because we haven't explicitly specified a `ServerUrl.Tcp` setting, RavenDB will use the `ServerUrl` configuration with a random port. As long as you are running on the local machine (or if you are running in a trusted environment without firewalls blocking connections), that would just work.

When setting up a cluster on multiple machines, remember to set `ServerUrl.Tcp` (you can specify just the port, or a hostname or IP and the port). For example, we could add `--ServerUrl.Tcp=38080` to the server command line. In this case, it will use `127.0.0.1:38080` for TCP communication for node A. For node B, it will use `127.0.0.2:38080`, etc.

You can also set `ServerUrl.Tcp` to a hostname/port combination, such as `rvn-srv-01:38080` or `28.12.4.22:38080` in which case RavenDB will use these. Such a configuration can be a good idea if you are running in the cloud and want to expose HTTP traffic to external parties (binding to the external IP), but intra-cluster communication can be routed through internal IPs (allowing you to use the lower network traffic cost inside the same data center).

That's it. You now have a database that spans two nodes. You can go to node B and see that the status of the "Spade" database has moved from `Offline` to `Online`, and you can enter into the database and see the `users/1` and `users/2` documents that we previously created on node A. RavenDB has automatically moved them to the secondary node.

You can play around for a bit with this setup. Create and update documents on both nodes and see how they flow between the two database instances. Next, we're going to take our cluster and poke it until it squeals, just to see how it handles failure conditions.

6.2.1. KICKING THE TIRES OF YOUR RAVENDB CLUSTER

Running on two nodes is an interesting experience. On the one hand, we now have our data on two separate nodes, and assuming that we've actually run them on two separate machines, we're safe from a single machine going up in flames. However, two nodes aren't actually enough to handle most failure cases.

Let's consider a situation where a node goes down. We can simulate that by killing the RavenDB process running node A (the one running the server on `127.0.0.1:8080`). Now, go to node B (`127.0.0.2:8080`), `Manage server` and then to `Cluster`. You'll see that both nodes are there but none of them is marked as leader. This is because node B is unable to communicate with node A, since we took node A down, and there isn't anyone else in the cluster that it can talk to.

At this point, the cluster is unable to proceed. There's no leader to be found, and there's no way to select one. The *database*, on the other hand, can function just fine. If you go to the "Spade" database on node B and add a new document (`users/3`), you'll observe there's no issue with this at all. The new document was created normally and without issue. This is because each database is independent. Each database instance will cooperate with the other instances, but it isn't dependent on them.

How do clients respond to node failures?

When a node fails, the clients will transparently move to another node that holds the database they're connected to. One of the tasks of the cluster's leader is to maintain the database topology, which clients fetch as part of their initialization (and then keep current). We'll talk more about failover from the client side later in this chapter.

Now, you can re-start the first node by using the following command:

```
./Server/Raven.Server.exe `
    --ServerUrl=http://127.0.0.1:8080 `
    --Logs.Path=Logs/A `
    --DataDir=Data/A
```

The node will start and reconnect into the cluster. If you check the cluster state, you'll see something similar to Figure 6.5.

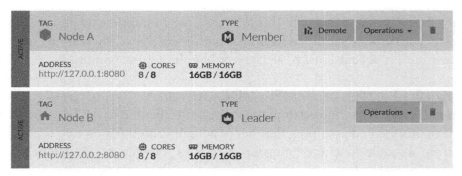

Figure 6.5. *New leader selected after recovery of failed node*

It's possible that in your case, the leader will be node A. There are no guarantees about who the leader will be.

Next, you can check the "Spade" database inside node A. You should see document users/3 inside, as it was replicated from node B.

So, our database remained operational even when we had just a single node available. Our *cluster* was down since it couldn't elect a leader. But what does this mean? Well, it means that during the time we only had node B, we weren't be able to do any cluster-wide operations.

Cluster-wide operations include creating a new database and monitoring the health of other nodes. But a lot of database-specific configuration (anything that impacts all instances of a database) goes through the cluster as well. For example, we won't be able to schedule a backup task with the cluster down,[4] and you'll not be able to deploy new indexes or modify database configurations.

Operations in a failed cluster

The list of operations that you can't perform if the cluster as a whole is down (but isolated nodes are up) seems frightening. However, a closer look at those operations will show you that they're typically not run-of-the-mill operations. These are one-time operations (creating indexes, setting a backup schedule, creating databases, adding nodes to a cluster, etc.).

Normal read/write/query operations from each database instance will proceed normally, and your applications shouldn't failover automatically and immediately. On the other hand, background operations, such as subscriptions or ETL, won't be able to proceed until the cluster is back up, which requires a majority of the nodes to be able to talk to one another.

Remember when I mentioned that running with two nodes in a cluster is strange? That's because any single node going down will result in this half-and-half state. Normally, you'll run three or more nodes, so let's expand our cluster even further.

6.2.2. EXPANDING YOUR CLUSTER

You can probably guess what we're going to do now. In exactly the same way that we previously added node B, we're going to add three new nodes. To do this, execute the following commands:

```
./Server/Raven.Server.exe `
    --ServerUrl=http://127.0.0.3:8080 `
    --Logs.Path=Logs/C `
    --DataDir=Data/C


./Server/Raven.Server.exe `
        --ServerUrl=http://127.0.0.4:8080 `
        --Logs.Path=Logs/D `
        --DataDir=Data/D
```

---

4   Of course, we'll be able to create a backup manually. See the discussion about cluster-wide tasks later in this chapter.

```
./Server/Raven.Server.exe `
    --ServerUrl=http://127.0.0.5:8080 `
    --Logs.Path=Logs/E `
    --DataDir=Data/E
```

Now go to Manage Server, Cluster, in the Studio and add the new nodes (http://127.0.0.3:8080, http://127.0.0.4:8080, http://127.0.0.5:8080). The end result is shown in Figure 6.6.

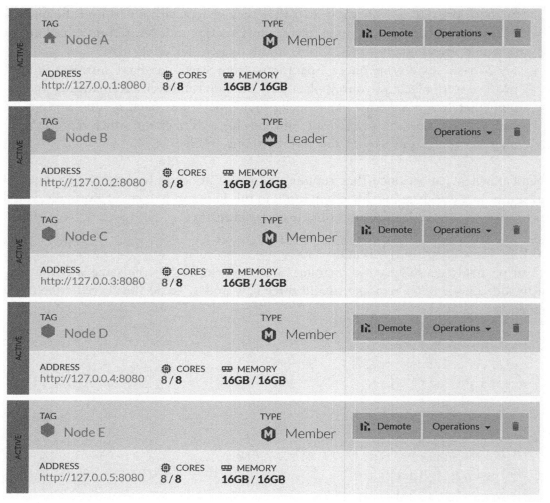

Figure 6.6. *A five nodes cluster*

You can click on the nodes in the cluster to open the Studio on each node. When you do so, look at the tab headers. It will tell you which node you're on, as you can see in Figure 6.7.

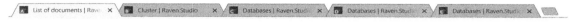

Figure 6.7. *An easy way to know which node you're on is to look at the tab icon*

Now that we have our cluster, we still need to understand the layout of the databases in it. Here's what it looks like when we open the Studio on node D, as shown in Figure 6.8.

Figure 6.8. *The Spade database as seen from node* D

The "Spade" database is marked as remote because it doesn't reside on this node. This leads us to a few important discoveries. For one thing, databases that we manually configured are going to remain on the nodes they've been configured to run on. It also appears that we can see the entire cluster topology from every node.

Now, let's actually use our cluster and create a new database. We'll call it "Pitchfork."[5] Everyone knows that a proper pitchfork has three tines; the four-tine pitchfork is used for shoveling, while a novel three-tine pitchfork is the favorite tool of Poseidon. As such, it's only natural that our "Pitchfork" database will have a replication factor of three. Once that's done, we'll just create the database and observe the results.

Since we didn't explicitly specify the nodes on which the new database will reside, the cluster will distribute the database to three nodes of its choice. This means we now have a five-node cluster with two databases, as you can see in Figure 6.9.

Figure 6.9. *The Spade and Pitchfork databases in our RavenDB cluster*

Figure 6.9 shows the databases from the Studio in node D. So we have Pitchfork on three nodes and Spade on two. You can go ahead and create a few documents on the

---

5   I'm on a garden tools naming streak, it appears.

Pitchfork database and observe how they're spread to the rest of the database instances in the cluster.

6.2.3. APPROPRIATE UTILIZATION OF YOUR CLUSTER

Setting up a five-node cluster just to run a couple of databases seems pretty wasteful. node E doesn't even have a single database to take care of. Why would we do something like this?

Typically, production clusters are set up with either three or five nodes. When a cluster size exceeds five nodes, it'll typically have dozens of databases running in tandem. We'll discuss large clusters later in this chapter. If you have one or two databases, you'll typically deploy a three-node cluster and make sure that the database(s) on it are spread across all the nodes in the cluster.

Sometimes you'll have a five-node cluster with the data replicated five times among the nodes. This is for maximum survivability. But in most cases, when you go to five nodes or higher, you're running a number of databases on the cluster. For instance, consider the situation in Figure 6.10.

In Figure 6.10, you can see that we created eight databases and that they're all spread out throughout the cluster. This means that there's no single point of failure for the cluster. In fact, we can lose any node in the cluster and still remain in full operation.

I intentionally defined some of the databases so they'll only run on two nodes instead of three. In this configuration, it's possible to lose access to a few databases if we kill node A and node B. A proper configuration will have each database reside on three nodes, so you'll have to lose more than half of your servers to lose access to a database.

> **Typical deployment in a cluster**
>
> The normal approach to deployment in a cluster is to decide how important your data is. It's common to require the data to reside on three separate nodes, regardless of the cluster size. In more critical systems, you'll either have this spread out across multiple data centers or have a copy (or copies) of the database being maintained by the cluster in a second data center. We'll discuss this feature in Chapter 7, which covers external replication.

It's important to note that, so far, we're running completely open to the world. This is possible because we're listening on the loopback device, so no external actor can get to those RavenDB servers. This obviously isn't how you'll run in production, and you ought to read about proper deployment and security of your cluster in Chapter 13, before you expose a cluster to the wild wild web.

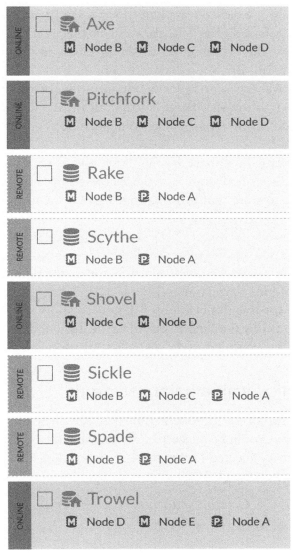

Figure 6.10. *A cluster hosting a whole garden shed of databases*

6.2.4. THE ROLE OF THE DATABASE GROUP

We saw what a cluster looks like and how we can distribute databases among the different nodes in the cluster. This is all well and good, but we still need to understand what we're *doing* with all this data as it's spread out among those nodes. First and foremost, we need to define some shared terminology.

A database can refer to all the individual instances of the database in the cluster, to a specific instance or just to the abstract concept of storing your system data in a database. Because this is confusing, we'll use the following terms to make it clear to what we refer:

◆ Database instance – exists on a single node, usually part of a larger database group. Typically referred to as "the database instance on node A."

◆ Database group – the grouping of all the different instances, typically used to explicitly refer to its distributed nature. For example, "The 'Spade' database group is spread over five servers for maximum availability."

◆ Database topology – the specific nodes that all the database instances in a database group reside on in a particular point in time. For example, "The 'Spade' topology is [B, A]."

◆ Database – the named database we're talking about, regardless of whether we're speaking about a specific instance or the whole group. For example, "We use the 'Spade' database to store that information."

Now that we have a shared vocabulary, let's see if I can explain exactly what's going on. A database group is composed of one or more database instances, each of which holds a full copy of the data in the database. The replication factor on the database group will determine how many copies we hold for that database.

The primary reason for this duplication of data is to allow us high availability. If a node goes down, we still have a copy (and usually two) of the data, and the cluster can shuffle things around so clients can talk to another node without really noticing that anything happened.

6.3. Client interaction with a database group

We'll spend some time exploring the interaction between clients and the database instances because that's usually what you'd be concerned about. We'll describe the behavior of the nodes a bit later. Many elements connected to this topic are intermingled, with both client and server cooperating to get to the best result. We'll start our exploration with the code in Listing 6.1.

Listing 6.1 *Creating a document store to talk to a cluster*

```
var store = new DocumentStore
{
    Urls =
    {
        "http://127.0.01:8080", "http://127.0.02:8080",
        "http://127.0.03:8080", "http://127.0.04:8080",
        "http://127.0.05:8080"
    },
    Database = "Spade"
};

store.Initialize();
```

The code in Listing 6.1 lists all the nodes in our cluster and will talk with the "Spade" database. This is interesting because the "Spade" database only exists on nodes B and A. (You can see the database topology in Figure 6.10.) Why are we listing all the nodes in this manner?

As it turns out, we don't actually need to do so. Listing any node in the cluster is enough to be able to properly connect to the "Spade" database. Each node in the cluster contains the full topology of all the databases hosted in the cluster. And the very first thing that a client will do upon initialization is to query the defined `Urls` and figure out what are actual nodes that it needs to get for the "Spade" database.

Why list all the nodes in the cluster, if any will do?

By listing all the nodes in the cluster, we can ensure that if a single node is down and we bring a new client up, we'll still be able to get the initial topology. If the cluster size is small (three to five nodes), you'll typically list all the nodes in the cluster. But for larger clusters, you'll usually just list enough nodes that having them all go down at once will mean that you have more pressing concerns than a new client coming up.

For extra reliability, the client will also cache the topology on disk, so even if the document store was initialized with a single node that was down at the time the client was restarted, the client will still remember where to look for our database. It's only a completely new client that needs to have the full listing. But it's good practice to list at least a few nodes, just in case.

Once the client gets the database topology, it will use that to talk to the actual database instances themselves. We talked about the different layers of the RavenDB distributed machinery earlier in this chapter. We're now moving from the cluster layer to the database layer, where each database instance works on its own, without relying on its siblings in the group.

That has a lot of implications on how RavenDB works. On the client side, if the client is unable to talk to a node (TCP error, HTTP 503, timeouts, etc.), it will assume that this particular node is down and will switch to the next node in the list. All the clients get their topology from the cluster, and the cluster ensures that we'll always report the same topology to the clients.[6]

By default, all the clients will talk to the first node in the database group topology. We usually call this the preferred node, and any of the other nodes in the topology are called the alternates. A failure of any of the alternates wouldn't even register for the typical client configuration since the client will only talk directly with the preferred node.

A failure of the preferred node will mean that all clients will failover to the same alternate. The cluster will also notice that the node is down and update the topology accordingly. The clients will get the updated topology, which will now have the first alternate as the preferred

---

6   Of course, it's possible that a client has an *outdated view* of the topology, but there are mechanisms in place to ensure that clients will figure out that their topology is out of date and refresh it.

node in the topology. The failed node would be demoted to a standby mode since the cluster doesn't know what state it's in.

Once the failed node comes back up, the cluster will wait for it to catch up and then add it back to the bottom pool of active nodes for this database. Because the failed node is added as the last option in the pool, it won't be usurping the role of the preferred node. This ensures that if the failed node experiences further failures, the cluster won't have to cycle the preferred node each and every time.

The simplest failure mode

While it may seem that an alternate failing (the client isn't even going to notice) or the preferred node failing (cluster will demote, clients will automatically switch to the first alternate) is all that we need to worry about, those are just the simplest and most obvious failure modes that you need to handle in a distributed environment.

More interesting cases include a node that was split off from the rest of the cluster, along with some (but not all) of the clients. In that case, different clients have very different views about who they can talk to. That's why each client is able to failover independently of the cluster. By having the database topology, they know about all the database instances and will try each in turn until they're able to find an available server that can respond to them.

This is completely transparent to your code, and an error will be raised only if we can't reach any of the database instances. While this ensures that we'll always have someone to talk to, it can cause some interesting behavior for our system. We'll discuss this later in this chapter, in the section about conflicts.

From the client point of view, there isn't really much to be said about the cluster. As far as your code is concerned, you operate normally, and RavenDB will take care of everything behind the scenes. However, there are still a few things you need to concern yourself with.

6.3.1. WRITE ASSURANCES FOR HIGH VALUE DATA

Here's how a database group works. Whenever a write is made to any of the database instances, it will disseminate that write to all the other instances in the group. This happens in the background and is continuously running. Most of the time, you don't need to think about it. You write the data to RavenDB, and it shows up in all the nodes on its own.

You *do* need to think about it, however, if you have some writes that are important. It isn't enough to ensure that you wrote that value to a single node (and made sure it hit the disk). You need to be sure that this value resides in more than one machine. You can do that using write assurance, which is available using the `WaitForReplicationAfterSaveChanges` method. An example of that is shown in Listing 6.2.

Listing 6.2 *Saving a very important task to RavenDB, ensuring it resides in multiple nodes*

```
using (var session = store.OpenSession())
{
    var task = new ToDoTask
    {
        DueDate = DateTime.Today.AddDays(1),
        Task = "Buy milk"
    };
    session.Store(task);
    session.Advanced
        .WaitForReplicationAfterSaveChanges(replicas: 1);
    session.SaveChanges();
}
```

The code in Listing 6.2 should look familiar. There isn't much to change when you move from a single node to a cluster. But here we are asking the database instance we wrote to not to confirm that write until it has been replicated at least once.

This increases the time it takes to get a reply from RavenDB, sometimes significantly so. You're now not only paying for the network round trip to the server and then the writing of the data to disk. You're also paying for another network round trip and the disk write cost per each additional replica. Using this frivolously will likely slow your application and introduce problems when you don't have enough replicas. While RavenDB will happily deal with going down to a single node and your application can use that, if you use WaitForReplicationAfterSaveChanges, an error will be raised.

An important aspect of this feature to remember is that when WaitForReplicationAfterSaveChanges is used, it doesn't involve a distributed transaction. In other words, even if we haven't been able to write your value to the number of replicas you wanted, we still wrote it to *some* of them. In the case of Listing 6.2 and the "Spade" database, if node A is down, we'll be able to write to node B. But we'll later fail because we can't replicate the write to node A. The client is going to get an error, but the data *was written to node* B. This is a powerful feature, but you need to be aware of the possible pitfalls of using it.

6.3.2. Load balancing and service level agreements

Earlier in this chapter, I said that by default we have a single preferred node and a few alternates just standing by. This can be a big waste. Our nodes are typically quite similar, and doubling or tripling our processing power just to let most of it go idle is not a good use of resources.

RavenDB allows you to change that behavior as well. Instead of all the clients talking to only the preferred node, you can ask them to load balance all the reads between every node in the group. It's even possible to take timing into account and have each node prefer to read from the fastest node it observed.

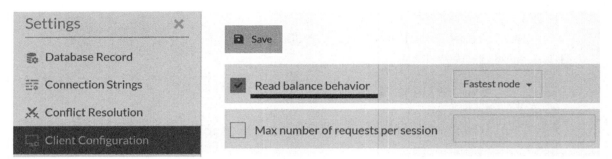

Figure 6.11. *Configuring client read balancing behavior from the server side*

The system administrator can configure such behavior globally, as shown in Figure 6.11, or the client can specify that using the conventions. Updates to the server side configuration will typically be reflected with clients on the next request the client will make (at which point it will learn that it needs to update its configuration). The server side configuration will override any client side setting.

6.4. Replication of data in a database group

We've seen that every node in a database group will have a copy of all the data. This is easiest to reason about when you have a single writer node. However, RavenDB doesn't work in this manner. You can make writes to any node in the database group, and that write will be recorded and replicated to all the other nodes in the database group.

How is this done? Each database instance holds a TCP connection to each of the other database instances in the group. Whenever there's a write on that instance, it will be sent to all the other instances immediately. Note that's not done as part of the write operation but in an async manner. If the database instance is unable to replicate the data, it will still accept that data and send it later.

During normal operations, the lag time between a write on a database instance and it being replicated to all the other nodes is usually around twice the ping time between the machines. Since we don't need to set up a connection just for that write, it's already ready and waiting. This also means you can see at any point the connections that a database instance has opened, which is useful when diagnosing issues. You can see an example of that in Figure 6.12.

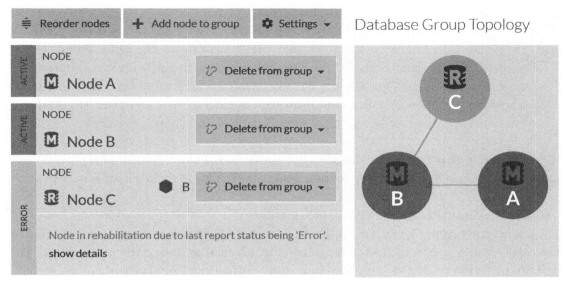

Figure 6.12. *A database group with three nodes, one of which is down*

What about when there are failures? Well, when a node fails for any reason, the cluster will detect that and demote it. When the node comes back up, its database instance will have to wait until it's as up to date as the other database instances in the group. Only then will the cluster let it fully join the group.

In Figure 6.12, you can see that node C is down. The cluster has detected it and designated node B as the mentor node for node C. When node C comes back again, it is node B that will send it all the changes that it missed, and it will only graduate to be a full member in the database group when node B deems it ready.

We commonly talk about document replication, but we're actually replicating more than just documents. All the data inside a database is replicated to every database instance. That obviously includes documents, but it also includes tombstones (which is how we replicate deletes), attachments and revisions. The last inclusion deserves a bit of explanation.

The async nature of replication in RavenDB leads to some interesting questions. For example, what happens if you modify a document several times in short order – fast enough that it was modified several times before the document could be sent to the other database instances? In this case, when we replicate the document to the other siblings, we replicate the latest version that we have and skip replicating all the intermediate revisions.

Sometimes, however, you care about each individual change. For that reason, when you enable revisions on your database, we'll also send them to the other database instances. In this way, you can see the full modification history of your documents, regardless of which server was used to write them and of the speed of replication.

191

Undefined order in a distributed environment

All the database instances are going to end up with the same revisions for the document, but it's not certain that they'll end up in the same order. It's possible that revisions created on different servers will show up in a different order because there's no way for us to determine which came first. Consider it a scaled up version of a race condition. You'll learn more about how RavenDB handles such things in the section about conflicts and change vectors.

Another question that's typically raised with regards to the async nature of replication is how transactions are handled across replication boundaries. This is the topic of our next section.

6.4.1. TRANSACTION ATOMICITY AND REPLICATION

Transactions in RavenDB are *important*. Relying on ACID transactions reduces a lot of the complexity that one has to deal with. However, given that RavenDB transactions are *not* distributed, it's interesting to consider how the transactional guarantees are preserved in a distributed cluster.

Consider for a moment the code in Listing 6.3. It's a simple bank transaction that moves $10 from my account to yours,[7] which I'm sure will be a delightful surprise.

Listing 6.3 *The classic bank transaction example*

```
using (var session = store.OpenSession())
{
    var you = session.Load<Account>("accounts/1234-A");
    var me = session.Load<Account>("accounts/4321-C");

    you.Amount += 10;
    me.Amount -= 10;

    session.SaveChanges();
}
```

There's nothing very interesting about Listing 6.3 in itself. The interesting bit is what will happen over the network, in this case. This is sent to RavenDB as a transaction and persisted as such, but you already knew that. The key here is that it's also *replicated* as a single transaction. In other words, all the other database instances will always have both of those changes replicated to them as a single batch, indivisible.

---

7   This isn't even close to how money transfers really work, of course, but it's a classic example and easy to reason about.

Replication batches

RavenDB isn't actually replicating a single document at a time. When we need to replicate data between nodes, we send a large amount of data at once. The size of the batch and what it includes is decided by RavenDB based on things like the amount of the data that needs to be sent, the number of documents and a few other factors that are implementation dependent (such as the speed of replication).

In most cases, we send everything that's changed since the last successful replication. And during normal operation, we effectively send a replication batch for each transaction. If there are a lot of writes, each batch will likely include data from multiple transactions.

What RavenDB guarantees is that writes made in the same transactions will always be sent to the other database instances in a single batch and won't be broken into separate batches. In other words, we maintain the atomicity property across replication.

This applies to all the changes that you make in a transaction, modifying documents, attachments, etc. They're all going to be sent to the other database instances as a single transaction. There's one caveat, however. Consider the code in Listing 6.4, which transfers money from your account to the tax authority.

Listing 6.4 The classic bank transaction example

```
using (var session = store.OpenSession())
{
    var you = session.Load<Account>("accounts/1234-A");
    var tax = session.Load<Account>("accounts/48879-B");

    you.Amount -= 3;
    tax.Amount += 3;

    session.SaveChanges();
}
```

The code in Listing 6.4 will probably sadden you a bit since no one usually likes to pay the taxman. However, it also exposes an issue with how RavenDB is replicating transactions. In this case, document `accounts/1234-A` is now involved in two separate transactions. Let's assume that we now need to replicate everything from Listing 6.3 onward (meaning my transfer of money to you and your payment of taxes).

We'll further assume that we instructed RavenDB to send the data in as small a unit as possible. When the database instance needs to replicate the documents to another instance, it will replicate them on a per transaction basis. Starting from the transaction that was generated for Listing 6.3, we'll replicate accounts/4321-C but *not* accounts/1234-A. Why is that?

The accounts/1234-A document will not be replicated because, though it was changed in the transaction for Listing 6.3, it was also changed by a later transaction (the one from Listing 6.4). Since we replicate only the current state of the documents and, in this case, we configured RavenDB to send the smallest possible batch size, we'll replicate only the documents that were modified in Listing 6.3 – not documents that were modified in the transaction for Listing 6.3 and then later modified by another transaction.

This means we'll first have a batch-replicated accounts/4321-C document (my transfer of the money) and then another batch with the accounts/1234-A and accounts/48879-B documents (your payment to the taxman). A client reading from another instance may then get an invalid state.

Luckily, everything is not lost. If you need transaction atomicity in a distributed fashion, you have a few options. You can make sure that the documents you care about are always updated together. This will ensure that these documents are always part of the same transaction and sent in the same batch. But this is often awkward to do.

Another option is to use revisions. When you enable revisions on a collection, a revision is written whenever a document is modified. It's written as part of the same transaction, and it flows across replication in the same indivisible batch as any other operation. When RavenDB gets a revision of a document that's newer than the one it has, it will update the document to match the revision. In effect, we'll send the entire transaction in Listing 6.3 as it was so that a client observing a second node can never see a partial transaction.

As you can see, revisions are a very powerful feature, and they're used in more scenarios than might initially be expected. The idea behind relying on revisions to handle transaction consistency is that, in many cases, it doesn't matter. A proper document model follows the isolated, independent and coherent tenets, which usually means you don't *need* this feature. But when you do, and most certainly it will come up,[8] the key here is that you aren't paying for tracking all the intermediate values unless you actually need this.

A lot of RavenDB features use the "pay to play" model, meaning if you aren't using a specific feature, you don't need to pay the performance cost of supporting it.

6.4.2. Change vectors

In the previous section, I mentioned that when a database instance gets a document revision that's newer than its copy of the document, it will update the document to match the revision. This lays the foundation for ensuring transaction boundary consistency across servers. But this doesn't answer an important question: what does "newer" even mean?

---

8   It's not something you'll use for everything, but in most applications there's one or two places where it can be *really* useful.

The easiest way to answer that question is to take a look at the clock. After all, "newer" is a function of time, and we can just check what time the document and revision were modified. But that doesn't actually work when running in a distributed system. Each machine in the cluster may have a slightly different idea about the time, and clock drift is a serious problem. Beyond that, concurrency in the cluster may mean that operations have happened at the exact same time or close enough that we can't tell otherwise.

This is confusing and can cause quite a headache in a distributed system. In order to deal with this, RavenDB uses change vectors (they are sometimes also called vector clocks) to tell when things happened. A change vector is comprised of the node ID and a sequence number (the etag). Whenever a modification happens on a database, a change vector will be generated. Here are a few examples of change vectors:

- A:1
- B:2
- A:3, B:1
- A:3, B:3, C:5

For the purpose of discussion, A/B/C are the node IDs and the numbers are the per-node sequence number. You can see that, with A:1 and B:2, there's no way for us to provide any order. This is because they're local to each node and there's no dependency between them. On the other hand, the A:3, B:1 change vector provides us with more information. We know that it came after A:3 and after B:1. Because of this, we can tell that it's after A:1, but we can't tell whether it happened before or after B:2. On the other hand, it's clear that A:3, B:3, C:5 happened after everything else. In other words, we use change vectors to record the observed state in each node, and we can piece out the timeline from that point onward.

The different nodes in a database group will try to ensure that each database instance is aware of the last etag on each node so they can create a coherent timeline across the cluster. This isn't meant to be a 100 percent foolproof solution, but it's a useful optimization for certain operations. Always having the last etag from the nodes also makes it easier to reason about concurrency in the cluster. You can see for yourself that when you save a document, it will have a change vector entry for the node you saved it on, as well as for all the other nodes in the cluster.

Change vectors and how they come into play are pretty hard concepts to grasp just by talking about them, so let's do some practice. We'll create a new database called "ChangeVectorTrialRun" on two of the nodes in the cluster. Then we'll go into the database and create a document called users/1.

Change this a few times, and we can observe the @change-vector property in the @metadata. Even though we've only modified this document on a single node, you can see that the database instance also includes the change vector from the other instance as well. Take a look at this example in Figure 6.13.

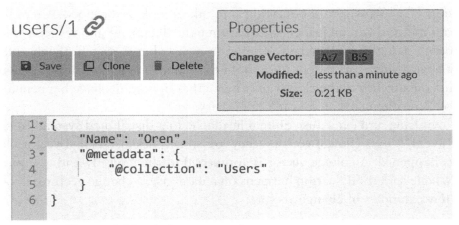

Figure 6.13. *A document change vector in a cluster*

Using this change vector, this document was written at or after etag 7 on node A and at or after etag 5 on node B. We created this document on node A, so how can we have a change vector entry for node B here? The answer is simple: we know what the etag of node B was because it told us on our last replication batch. We'll incorporate this information in future change vectors.

Change vectors are incredibly important inside RavenDB (and in many other distributed systems) because they allow us to know, without relying on a shared clock, when things have happened. This turns out to be quite useful in many cases. For example, let's assume that a database instance received a document via replication but already has this document stored.

How would the database instance know if the document that arrived via replication is an old version of the document that we should ignore or if it's a new version that needs to over-write the existing document? The answer is that it uses the change vector to tell. In this way, even if a document is modified on a different server each time, we can still know whether our version is newer or older than the version we just received via replication.

However, "newer" or "older" aren't the only options that we have. There is also the option of a conflict update.

6.4.3. CONFLICTS

A conflict occurs when the same document is updated on two nodes independently of one another. This can happen because of a network split or because of several client updates that each talked to different nodes faster than we could replicate the information between the nodes.

Let's consider the simplest case. Say we have the document users/1 whose current change vector is A:7, B:5, and we modify it on nodes A and B concurrently. On the database instance on node A, we'll have the change vector A:8, B:5, and on node B we'll have

A:7, B:6. In this case, there's no way for us to tell which version of the document is newer than the other. This is a conflict. In a distributed system, you can either choose to run a consensus (which requires consulting a majority on every decision) or accept the potential for conflicts. For document writes, RavenDB chooses to accept conflicts as a tradeoff of always being able to accept writes.

The question is this – how are we going to handle such a case? Let's generate a conflict manually and see how this is handled. But first, we need to disable automatic conflict resolution so we can observe what is going on behind the scenes. In the Studio, go to Settings, Conflict Resolution. This is where you let RavenDB know how you want it to resolve conflicts when they happen. By default, we resolve conflicts in favor of the most recent version[9]. You can see what this look like in Figure 6.14.

Figure 6.14. *Configuring server side conflict resolution policy in the Studio*

Uncheck the option to automatically resolve to the latest version and click on Save. Now we are ready to create some conflicts. As you'll see shortly, conflicts occur when there is effectively a race in the cluster between modifications to the same document on different nodes. This is a bit hard to reproduce, so we'll take the heavy-handed approach and reproduce a conflicts by shutting down nodes and modifying documents independently on each node. Here's how we'll do it:

◆ Kill node B. (It's running on 127.0.0.2) You can do that by simply closing the console window that's running it.
◆ Modify the users/1 document on node A so its name property will be "John," and save the document. You can see how this will look in Figure 6.15.
◆ Kill node A. (It's running on 127.0.0.1)
◆ Bring up node B by executing
  ```
  ./Server/Raven.Server.exe `
  --ServerUrl=http://127.0.0.2:8080 `
  --Logs.Path=Logs/B `
  --DataDir=Data/B
  ```

---

9   Note that different nodes may have different clocks. RavenDB doesn't attempt to compensate for this and will use the latest timestamp from the conflicts in its automatic resolution.

- Modify the users/1 document on node B so its name property will be "Doe", and save the document. You can see how this will look in Figure 6.16.
- Bring up node A by executing

```
./Server/Raven.Server.exe `
--ServerUrl=http://127.0.0.1:8080 `
--Logs.Path=Logs/A `
--DataDir=Data/A
```

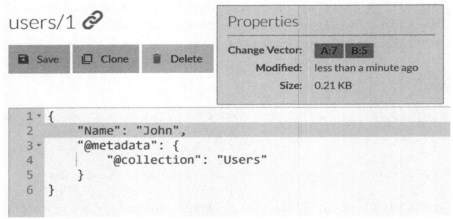

Figure 6.15. *First version of* users/1 *document after modifications on node* B

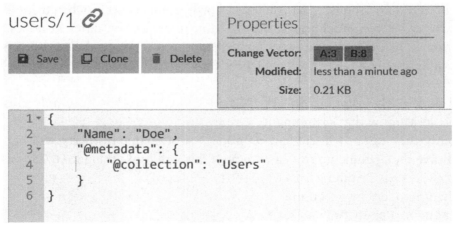

Figure 6.16. *Second version of* users/1 *document after modifications on node* A

At this point, an interesting thing will take place. If you watch the Users collection, you'll notice that it's *empty* and that the Conflicts entry in the Studio is showing there's a conflict. Go to Documents in the Studio and then to Conflicts, and you'll see the missing document.

In fact, you'll see *two* versions of this document, as displayed in Figure 6.17. For developers, the screen shown may look very familiar. It's showing a conflict just as you would get in any source control system. You can also resolve it in the same manner: by deciding what changes to accept and saving. Change the Name property to be "John Doe" and click Save.

Figure 6.17. *Manual conflict resolution in the Studio*

The conflict is now resolved, and you can see the document is back in its proper place – the Users collection. As you could see, getting to the point where we could reliably generate a conflict was a rather involved process. Conflicts aren't expected to happen frequently. At the same time, production systems have a nasty habit of throwing up a *lot* of hurdles, even during normal operations. Conflicts can and do occur in production systems, especially busy ones.

It wouldn't be reasonable to expect a manual intervention each and every time you need to resolve a conflict. Instead, RavenDB has several conflict resolution strategies that you can use:

◆ If the documents are identical (same change applied on multiple nodes), they can automatically be merged. This also applies if the document was deleted in multiple nodes and we detected a conflict.

◆ You can specify your own conflict resolution behavior by writing a JavaScript function that applies to all conflicts and produces a merged output. We'll see an example of that shortly.

◆ You can designate a node whose changes will be considered authoritative, and all conflicts will be resolved in its favor.

◆ Finally, you can choose to resolve to the latest version based on wall clock time.

The appropriate strategy to use heavily depends on your actual use case. In some cases, just accepting the latest version is perfectly fine. In others, you don't want to lose writes just because they conflicted. Probably the most well known scenario for such a requirement is the notion of the shopping cart.

Listing 6.5 *Two conflicting versions of a shopping cart*

```
// on node A
{
    "Name": "Oren Eini",
    "Items": [
        {
            "ProductId": "products/2134-B",
            "Quantity": 2,
            "Name": "Milk"
        },
        {
            "ProductId": "products/9231-C",
            "Quantity": 1,
            "Name": "Bread"
        }
    ]
}
// on node B
{
    "Name": "Oren Eini",
    "Items": [
        {
            "ProductId": "products/2134-B",
            "Quantity": 1,
            "Name": "Milk"
        },
        {
            "ProductId": "products/8412-B",
            "Quantity": 2,
            "Name": "Eggs"
        }
    ]
}
```

A user's shopping cart document may have gotten into a conflict, but we absolutely don't want the users to have stuff fall out of their cart just because we had a network hiccup. Consider the documents shown in Listing 6.5.

RavenDB, of course, has no idea how to merge such a conflict. But we can teach it. Go back to the Conflict Resolution view that we looked at in Figure 6.14. Click on the Add button to add a conflict resolution script for a particular collection. Listing 6.6 has the code to properly resolve such a conflict on the ShoppingCart collection.

Listing 6.6 *Script to merge conflicting shopping carts*

```
var final = docs[0];

for (var i = 1; i < docs.length; i++)
{
    var currentCart = docs[i];
    for (var j = 0; j < currentCart.Items.length; j++)
    {
        var item = currentCart.Items[j];
        var match = final.Items
            .find(i => i.ProductId == item.ProductId);
        if (!match)
        {
            // not in cart, add
            final.Items.push(item);
        }
        else
        {
            match.Quantity = Math.max(
                item.Quantity,
                match.Quantity);
        }
    }
}

return final;
```

The code in Listing 6.6 will merge the two different versions of the shopping cart, resulting in the document shown in Listing 6.7. With a merge script such as the one in Listing 6.6, RavenDB can automatically resolve conflicts as they happen, with no service interruption. The cart in Listing 6.7 has been intelligently merged, so we don't have any duplicate products and we kept the higher number of milk bottles between the versions of the cart that we merged.

Listing 6.7 *The merged shopping cart*

```
{
    "Name": "Oren Eini",
    "Items": [
      {
         "ProductId": "products/2134-B",
         "Quantity": 2,
         "Name": "Milk"
      },
      {
         "ProductId": "products/9231-C",
         "Quantity": 1,
         "Name": "Bread"
      },
      {
         "ProductId": "products/8412-B",
         "Quantity": 2,
         "Name": "Eggs"
      }
    ]
}
```

Not all collections deserve such attention, of course. For some, you'll choose to only get the latest version or define an authoritative source that will resolve such conflicts. When you need to write such a script, the Studio can be a great help. That's because in addition to just defining the conflict resolution script, you can also debug it inside the Studio.

6.5. Distributed atomic compare exchange operations

In Chapter 2, I introduced the compare exchange feature (sometimes known as `cmpxchg`). This feature allows you to perform atomic compare and swap operations at the cluster level. As you can imagine, this feature relies on the strong consistency available to the RavenDB cluster via the Raft consensus protocol.

Consider the code in Listing 6.8[10], which shows how to use this feature to ensure unique username reservation at the cluster level.

---

10   The same code was already shown in Listing 2.21 from Chapter 2

Listing 6.8 *Using compare exchange to validate unique username in a distributed system*

```
var cmd = new PutCompareExchangeValueOperation<string>(
    key: "names/john",
    value: "users/1-A",
    index: 0);

var result = await store.Operations.SendAsync(cmd);
if (result.Successful)
{
  // users/1-A now owns the username 'john'
}
```

Because this is a cluster level operation, it goes through the full consensus protocol. RavenDB will only answer to such a command after a majority of the nodes in the cluster confirmed its acceptance. This ensures that the cluster as a whole makes this decision. If you attempt a compare exchange operation from a node that cannot reach a majority of the nodes, the compare exchange operation will fail.

This feature is useful when you want to do highly consistent operations at the cluster level, not just the individual node. As already discussed, concurrency in the cluster is complex. Even when you have optimistic concurrency checks, two clients talking to two different nodes may *both* succeed to write to a document. RavenDB will quickly detect and flag this as a conflict, with the usual semantics on how to handle this.

In the vast majority of cases, this is what you want. Cluster-wide operations require coordination of the entire cluster (actually, we only need a majority of the nodes). This means that in a 3 nodes cluster, you'll require the confirmation of at least 2 nodes in order for an operation to succeed. With 5 nodes in the cluster, you'll need 3, etc. See Table 7.1 in the next chapter for full details on this.

As a result, you'll usually save the compare exchange usage for things that must be done in a consistent manner. There are usually fewer of these than you would initially assume. Let's look at a more complex example of using the compare exchange feature in RavenDB.

Consider the following scenario. We have a bunch of support engineers, ready and willing to take on any support calls that come. At the same time, an engineer can take only a certain number of support calls. In order to handle this, we allow engineers to register when they are available to take a new support call. How would we handle this in RavenDB? Assuming that we wanted absolute consistency?

Listing 6.9 shows how an engineer can register to the pool of available engineers.

Listing 6.9 *Using compare exchange to register engineer's availability in a consistent manner*

```
const string key = "engineers/available";

public void RegisterEngineerAvailability(string engineer)
{
    while (true)
    {
        var get = new GetCompareExchangeValueOperation<List<string>>(
            key);
        var getResult = _store.Operations.Send(get);
        if (getResult == null)
        {
            // empty, so create a new one
            getResult = new CompareExchangeValue<List<string>>(
                key,
                index: 0, // new
                value: new List<string> { engineer }
            );
        }
        getResult.Value.Add(engineer);
        var put = new PutCompareExchangeValueOperation<List<string>>(
            key,
            getResult.Value,
            getResult.Index);

        var putResult = _store.Operations.Send(put);
        if (putResult.Successful)
            return;

        // someone pushed a new engineer, retry...
    }
}
```

The code in Listing 6.9 is very similar to how you would write multi-threaded code. You first get the value, then attempt to do an atomic operation to swap the old value with the new one. If we are successful, the operation is done. If not, then we retry. Concurrent calls to RegisterEngineerAvailability will race each other. One of them will succeed and the others will have to retry.

The actual data that we store in the compare exchange value in this case is an array. You can see an example of how that would look in Figure 6.18.

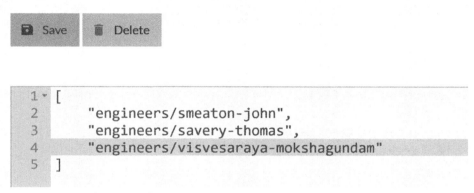

Figure 6.18. *The available engineers compare exchange value in the Studio*

Compare exchange values can be simple values (numbers, strings), arrays or even objects. Any value that can be represented as JSON is valid there. However, the only operation that is allowed on a compare exchange value is a replacement of the whole value.

The code in Listing 6.9 is only doing half of the job. We still need to be able to get an engineer to help us handle a support call. The code to complete this task is shown in Listing 6.10. The code in Listing 6.10 is a bit more complex. Here we read the available engineers from the server. If there are none, we'll wait a bit and try again. If there are available engineers we'll remove the first one and then try to update the value. This can happen for multiple clients at the same time, so we check whether our update was successful and only return the engineer if our change was accepted.

Note that in Listing 6.10 we use two different modes to update the value. If there are still more engineers in the available pool, we'll just remove our engineer and update the value. But if our engineer is the last one, we'll delete the value entirely. In either case, this is an atomic operation that will first check the index of the pre-existing value before performing the write.

It is important to note that when using compare exchange values, you'll typically not act on read. In other words, in Listing 6.10, even if we have an available engineer, we'll not use that knowledge until we successfully wrote the new value. The whole idea with compare exchange values is that they give you atomic operation primitive in the cluster. So a typical usage of them is always to try to do something on write until it is accepted, and only then use whatever value you read.

Listing 6.10 *Getting an available engineer using atomic and distributed compare exchange operations*

```
const string key = "engineers/available";

public string PullAvailableEngineer()
{
    while (true)
    {
        var get = new GetCompareExchangeValueOperation<List<string>>(
            key);
        var getResult = _store.Operations.Send(get);
        if (getResult == null)
        {
            // no support engineers, wait and retry
            Thread.Sleep(500);
            continue;
        }
        string engineer = getResult.Value[0];
        getResult.Value.RemoveAt(0);

        CompareExchangeResult<List<string>> result;
        if (getResult.Value.Count == 0)
        {
            var del =
            new DeleteCompareExchangeValueOperation<List<string>>(
                key,
                getResult.Index);
            result = _store.Operations.Send(del);
        }
        else
        {
        var put =
          new PutCompareExchangeValueOperation<List<string>>(
            key,
            getResult.Value,
            getResult.Index);
        result = _store.Operations.Send(put);
        }
```

```
        if (result.Successful)
            return engineer;


        // someone took an available engineer
        // while we were running, let's try again...
    }
}
```

The acceptance of the write indicates the success of your operation and the ability to rely on whatever values you read. However, it is important to note that compare exchange operations are atomic and independent. That means an operation that modifies a compare exchange value and then does something else needs to take into account that these would run in separate transactions.

For example, if a client pulls an engineer from the available pool but doesn't provide any work (maybe because the client crashed) the engineer will not magically return to the pool. In such cases, the idle engineer should periodically check that the pool still contains the appropriate username.

6.6. Summary

In this chapter, we've touched on most of the distributed portions of RavenDB. We started by spinning up our own cluster, and we played around with creating various databases on it. We looked at how we can manage a database inside the Studio and how RavenDB is actually spreading a database group into multiple database instances on the various cluster nodes.

We talked about how the client API works with a RavenDB cluster, how we can ensure that a write is replicated to a minimum set of replicas before the server will confirm it and how we can ask the client API to load balance our work among the different nodes in the database group.

We discussed the distributed nature of RavenDB at the cluster layer (consensus, majorities required) and at the database layer (multi-master, can act independently) and how it affects our code. If there is a failure that knocks out half of the cluster, we'll not be able to do cluster operations. But reading and writing on each database will proceed normally, and clients will failover silently to any surviving nodes. Certain operations (creating databases or defining new indexes) will not work until the cluster is in a stable state, but the most common day-to-day operations can proceed with each database instance acting on its own and merging its operations with its siblings.

That behavior can lead to conflicts, and we explored some of the options RavenDB has for resolving those conflicts. You can set up automatic conflict resolution based on a preferred node, select the most recent version, or even provide your own logic to merge conflicting versions automatically. The RavenDB Studio also contains a conflicts section that allows you to inspect conflicts and manually resolve them.

We then discussed transaction atomicity in replication, how RavenDB ensures that all changes that happen in the same transaction are always replicated in the same batch and how we can use revisions to ensure that holds true even for documents that were changed later independently. We looked at change vectors and how they are used by RavenDB to piece together the absolute order of events and know what happened where and when.

The final topic we covered was compare exchange values in RavenDB. These allow you to perform distributed and atomic compare and swap operations and are an important primitive for many distributed operations. RavenDB exposes this directly, giving you the ability to manage distributed state in a reliable way by leaning on the consensus protocol that drives the RavenDB cluster.

In the next chapter, we are going to cover how to design your cluster, how to define your topology for geo-distributed environments, and, in general, how to scale your RavenDB cluster.

7. Scaling Distributed Work in RavenDB

In the previous chapter, we covered a lot. We went over how RavenDB clusters and database groups work. We looked at the nitty-gritty details, such as conflicts and change vectors. And we saw how a cluster can handle failover and recovery. But we haven't talked about how to actually make use of a cluster. This is primarily what we'll cover in this chapter: how to properly utilize your RavenDB cluster to best effect.

We'll cover how to grow your cluster to include a large number of nodes, how to host a *lot* of databases in the cluster, how we can automatically have the cluster adjust the nodes a database resides on, which will ensure a minimum number of replicas, and how we can deploy RavenDB in a geo-distributed environment.

But first, we need to go back a bit and discuss the distributed mechanisms in RavenDB – the cluster and the database group. The separation RavenDB makes between a cluster and a database group can be artificial. If you're running a single database on all your nodes, you usually won't make any distinction between the cluster as a whole and the database group. This distinction starts to become much more important if you're working in a system that utilizes many databases.

The simplest example for such a system is a microservice architecture. Each microservice in your system has its own database group that's running on the cluster, and you can define the number of nodes each database group will run on. This tends to be easier to manage, deploy and work with than having a separate cluster per microservice.

Another example of a situation where you'll have multiple databases is multitenancy, where each tenant gets its own separate database. This makes it simple to deal with tenant separation, and you can adjust the number of nodes per tenant easily. This approach will also allow you to scale your system in a way that's convenient. As you have more tenants, you can just add more machines to the cluster and spread the load among them.

That said, note there's a certain cost for running each database instance. It's usually easier for RavenDB to have a single large database than many small ones. The general rule of thumb is that you shouldn't host more than a hundred or so active databases per machine.

7.1. Growing your cluster

RavenDB is using Raft as the underlying consensus protocol for managing the cluster. The Raft Paper is a truly impressive read, mostly because the paper manages to make one of the hardest tasks in distributed programming understandable. I highly recommend reading it, even if you never intend to dig into the details of how RavenDB or other distributed systems do their magic.

The simplest way to explain how Raft works is that the cluster makes decisions based on majority confirmation. This quick explanation does a great injustice to both the algorithm and the Raft Paper, but it simplifies things enough for us to reason about them without deviating *too* much from what's really going on. Majority confirmation is defined as having a particular value on N/2+1 of the nodes, using integer math and assuming that N is the number of nodes. In other words, if your cluster size is three, then a majority would be two. Any value that was confirmed by any two nodes is considered committed.

Table 7.1 shows the majority calculation for several common cluster sizes. Note that even numbers have the same majority as the odd number following them. Because of that, you'll typically have an odd number of nodes in your cluster.

Table 7.1. *Majorities for different-sized clusters*

Cluster size	Majority
2	2
3	2
4	3
5	3
7	4
9	5
15	8
21	11
51	26

This majority behavior has a few very interesting implications you should consider. First, you'll note that if we had a failure condition that took out more than half of our cluster, the cluster as a whole will not be able to make any decisions (even while individual database instances will operate normally). In a cluster of five nodes, if there aren't any three nodes that can communicate with each other, there's no way to reach any decision.

On the other hand, the more nodes there are in your cluster, the more network traffic will be required to reach a consensus. In pathological cases, such as a cluster size of 51, you'll need to contact at least 26 servers to reach any decision. That's going to impose a high latency requirement on anything the cluster is doing.

In practice, you rarely grow the cluster beyond seven members or so. The cost of doing that is usually too high. At that point, you'll either set up multiple independent clusters or use a different method. The cluster size we considered is for voting members in the cluster, but the cluster doesn't have to contain only voting members. We can just add nodes to the cluster as watchers.

Watchers don't take part in the majority calculation and are only there to watch what's going on in the cluster. As far as RavenDB is concerned, they're full-blown members in the cluster. They can be assigned databases and work to be done, but we aren't going to include them in the hot path of making decisions in the cluster.

Using this approach, you can decide that three or five nodes in your cluster are the voting members and all the rest are just watchers. This gives us the ability to make decisions with a majority of only three nodes while the actual size of the cluster can be much higher. Of course, if a majority of the cluster's voting members are unable to talk to one another (because they're down or because the network failed) then the cluster as a whole will not be available.

What are cluster operations?

We've talked extensively about clusters being down. Actually, we've spent more time discussing it than the time most clusters spend being down. A cluster being down means database operations continue normally but we can't perform any cluster operations. And what are all those cluster operations?

Basically, they're anything that requires us to coordinate between multiple nodes. A non-exhaustive list of these[1] includes creating and deleting databases, creating and deleting indexes, handling subscriptions and ETL processes and completing a backup.[2]

In all these cases, the operations need a majority in the cluster to process. The underlying logic behind all these operations is that they aren't generally user-facing. So even in the event of a cluster going down, you'll be able to continue serving requests and operate normally, as far as the external world is concerned, while your operations teams are bringing up the failed nodes.

---

1   The full list can be found in the online documentation
2   Backups *will* happen on their regular schedule when the cluster is down, but they'll fail to be reported to the cluster and may run again after the cluster has recovered.

Figure 7.1 shows a cluster using three member nodes and two watchers. Node E is the leader, and it's managing all of the nodes. Database instances can be allocated on both member nodes and watcher nodes, but only the member nodes A, B or E can become cluster leaders. If two of them are down, the cluster as a whole will also be down, and you'll not be able to perform cluster operations (but your databases will function normally otherwise.)

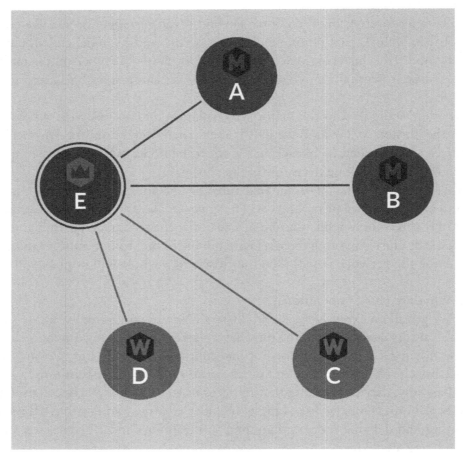

Figure 7.1. *A cluster with members and watchers*

A cluster being unavailable doesn't usually impact ongoing database operations. The actual topology at scale is something the operations team needs to consider. A single large cluster is usually easier to manage, and the cluster can add as many watchers as you need to handle the load you're going to put on it. The databases themselves don't care what node they run on, whether they're voting members or just watchers. And the cluster can manage database instance assignments across all machines with ease.

7.2. Multiple data centers and geo-distribution

It's easy to reason about RavenDB's distributed behavior when you're running on the local network or in the same data center, but what about when you have multiple data centers? And what about when you have geo-distributed data centers? Those are important considerations for the architecture of the system. Because there are so many possible deployment options, I'm going to use AWS as the canonical example, simply because there's so much information about it. You should be able to adapt the advice here to your needs easily enough, even if you aren't using AWS.

Inside the same availability zone (same data center) in Amazon, you can expect ping times of less than a millisecond. Between two availability zones in the same region (separate data centers[3] that are very close by), you'll typically see ping times that are in the single-digit millisecond range.

Each node in the RavenDB cluster expects to get a heartbeat from the leader every 300 milliseconds (that is the default configuration). When running in the same data center, that's typically not a problem unless there's a failure of the leader (or the network), in which case the cluster as a whole will select a new leader. However, what happens when we start talking about geo-distributed data centers? Let's use Table 7.2 as a discussion point.

Table 7.2. *A few AWS data centers and their locations*

Data center	Tag
N. Virginia	us-east-1
Ohio	us-east-2
N. California	us-west-1
London	eu-west-2
Singapore	ap-southeast-1

Ping times[4] between these data centers are quite different. For example, N. Virginia to Ohio is 30 milliseconds, and N. Virginia to N. California is already at around 70 milliseconds. N. California to London is twice that at 140 milliseconds, and Singapore to N. Virginia clocks in at 260 milliseconds.

Given that the default configuration calls for an election if we didn't hear from the leader in 300 milliseconds, it's clear that you can't just throw a cluster with one node each in N. Virginia, Singapore and London. The network latency alone would mean we'd be unable to proceed in most cases. However, that's just the default configuration and is easily changed. The

---

3   Note: this assumes the connection between those data centers doesn't go over the public internet but rather dedicated lines. If the connection between the data centers is over the public internet, expect higher latency and more variance in the timings.

4   The ping times between these data centers were taken from cloudping.co.

reason I'm dedicating so much time to talking about latency here is that it has a huge effect on your systems that you should consider.

If you have the need to run in multiple data centers – or even in geo-distributed data centers – you need to think about the latency between them and what it means for your application. There are two options you should consider. The first is having a data-center-spanning cluster. The second is to have a cluster per data center. Let's review both of these options.

7.2.1. SINGLE CLUSTER, MULTIPLE DATA CENTERS

When you have a single cluster spanning multiple data centers, take note of the expected latency and behavior. The actual configuration of the cluster timeout is easy to set (the configuration option is `Cluster.ElectionTimeoutInMs`, defaulting to 300 milliseconds), but that's the least interesting thing about this scenario.

When running in a geo-distributed cluster, you need to consider the various operations you use. The cluster timeout is merely the maximum amount of time the nodes will wait for a notification from the leader before deciding that there isn't one and an election needs to be held. If there's work the cluster needs to do, it won't wait for the timeout to happen. Instead, it will always execute it as fast as it can.

On the other hand, an excessively high timeout value means the cluster will take longer to detect that there's a failed leader and recover from that. In general, the cluster will typically recover from a failed node in up to three times the timeout value, so that needs to be taken into account. On the WAN, I'd suggest you raise the timeout to three or five seconds and see how stable that is for your environment. A lot of it will depend on the quality of the communication between the various nodes in your cluster.

We've talked a lot so far about the cluster and the effect of latency on the cluster, but most of the time we're going to operate directly with the database, not the cluster. So how does running in a geo-distributed environment affect the database replication?

The answer is that it generally doesn't. The database-level replication was designed for WAN, and there aren't any hard timeouts like there are at the cluster level. The cluster needs to know there's an active leader because, if there isn't, the node needs to step up and suggest itself as the next leader. But at the database level, all nodes are equal. Any disruption in communication between the nodes is handled by merging the data from all the nodes at a later point in time, resolving any conflicts that may have occurred. This means that a database group is much easier to deploy in a geo-distributed environment with high latency; the nodes are fine with delays.

Database instance distribution in the multi-data-center cluster

RavenDB assumes that all nodes in a cluster are roughly equal to one another, and when you create a new database, it will assign instances of this database to nodes in the cluster, regardless of where they're located. If you're running in a multi-data-center cluster, you probably want to explicitly state which nodes this database will reside on so you can ensure they're properly divided between the different data centers.

Another consideration to take into account is that there's also the clients. A client running on the London data center that connects to the Singapore node for all queries is going to suffer. By default, RavenDB assumes that all nodes are equal, and the cluster will arbitrarily choose a node from the database topology for the client to typically work with.

In the previous chapter, we talked about load balancing and how we can ask RavenDB to handle that for us automatically. One of the available load-balancing options is `FastestNode`. This option will make each client determine which node (or nodes) are the fastest, as far as it's concerned, and access them according to speed. This mode, in a geo-distributed configuration, will result in each client talking to the node closest to it. That's usually the best deployment option for such an environment because you're both geo-distributed and able to access a local instance at LAN speeds.

There is a potential issue of consistency to think about when your system is composed of parts far enough apart that it can take hundreds of milliseconds to merely send a packet back and forth. If you're writing a document in one area, it's not guaranteed that you'll see the write in another area. In fact, you'll always have to wait until that write has been replicated.

We talked about write assurances and `WaitForReplicationAfterSaveChanges` in the previous chapter, but it's very relevant here as well. After you make a write with the `FastestNode` option, the next session you open might access a different node. In order to ensure that the next request from the user will be able to read what the user just wrote, you need to call `WaitForReplicationAfterSaveChanges`. Alternatively, if this is a write for which a short delay in replicating to all other nodes is acceptable, you can skip it and avoid the need for confirmation across the entire geo-distributed cluster.

7.2.2. MULTIPLE CLUSTERS, MULTIPLE DATA CENTERS

A single cluster spread over multiple data centers can be convenient for the operations team since there's just one cluster to manage everything. But it can also create headaches. Using the data from Table 7.2 as an example, if we have two nodes in London and one node in N. Virginia, our leader will tend to always be based in London. Any outage between the two data centers will leave the cluster fully functioning in London and unable to complete anything in N. Virginia (since it can't reach the other side).

Another problem is that failover *between* data centers is not something you'll want to do. You might want to fail *to* another data center, but having a web app from the N. Virginia data center go all the way to the database instance in London imposes a very high latency. If a page is making just eight database requests, it's going to take over a second to answer and render a single page. And that's just calculating the network round-trip costs. In such cases, it's often preferable to send the web traffic directly to the London data center until N. Virginia's is fully up again.

In such a scenario, having a single cluster will actually work against us. The problem is that the client API will automatically failover to any available node, but in this case, we don't want that. We can't tell the client not to failover to nodes in our cluster. That doesn't make sense. The appropriate way to handle this is to create separate clusters, one in each data center. In this manner, each data center's cluster is independent and manages only its own nodes. The client API in each data center is configured to point to the nodes in that data center only.

In this case, because failover stops at the cluster boundary, there will be no failover between data centers. But we still need to deal with a tough problem. How are we going to handle sharing the data between the separate clusters?

7.2.3. SHARING DATA BETWEEN CLUSTERS

A RavenDB cluster is a standalone unit. It manages itself and doesn't concern itself much with the outside world. There are situations, however, where you want to have data shared among multiple clusters. This can happen if you want an offsite replica of all your data or if you've decided to have different clusters in each data center rather than a single cross-data-center cluster.

Setting up replication between clusters can be done easily because RavenDB makes a strong distinction between a cluster and database group interactions. In this case, this allows us to define a replication target that's not part of the cluster itself. We can do that in the database by going to `Settings`, `Manage Ongoing Tasks` and then adding an `External Replication` task. You'll need to provide the URL and database name for the destination. Then, save the new replication. If you don't have an additional cluster to test this on, you can specify one of your own nodes and create a separate database to replicate to.

> **Replicating to the same cluster**
>
> On the face of it, it seems strange that we can set up an external replication from the cluster back to itself. Why make it an external replication, then? Well, this can be useful if you want a copy of the data that wouldn't be a failover target for the clients. It may be an offsite copy or just a dedicated database that's set up to do some kind of a job (such as run an ETL process).

Ongoing tasks in general are quite interesting, and we'll discuss them at length in the next section. For now, we'll focus on what the external replication feature means for us. Once we've finished configuring it, the cluster will assign one of the database group nodes to keep that replica up to date at all times.

It's important to remember that, at the database level, we treat the replica as just another destination. The cluster is *not* managing it. That means that cluster-level behaviors – such as conflict resolver definition, failing over for the client and index replication – are not replicated. An external replica is just that: external. You can configure both the source cluster and the destination replica in the same manner, of course, but there's nothing that forces you to do so. In fact, the other common reason to set up an external replica is to have a *different* configuration.

A good example of this is when you want to have expensive indexes and only run them on a particular machine. Maybe you need to run pricey analytics or do certain work on a specific location. Using external replication gives you the ability to control the flow of the data without also dictating how it's going to be processed.

What would it take to have an offsite replica for our cluster? It's quite easy. In the Studio, go to Settings, then to Manage Ongoing Tasks and click Add. Choose External Replication and fill out the URL and database name, and that's pretty much it. The cluster will assign that replication task to one of the database instances in the database group, and it will immediately start replicating the data to the target.

It's important to understand that, for all intents and purposes, this is just the same replication that happens between database group nodes in the same cluster. The nodes don't know (or care) that this particular replication target isn't in their cluster. That's important to know because it means you can use all the replication features, including waiting for offsite replication to occur or ensure distributed transaction boundaries, across disparate geo-distributed clusters.

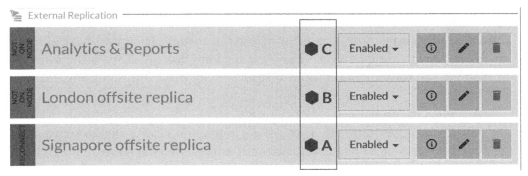

Figure 7.2. *Several external replication tasks and their responsible nodes*

External replication between two clusters will detect conflicts in editing the same documents in separate clusters and will resolve those conflicts according to each cluster conflict resolution policy.[5] Figure 7.2 shows the result of a cluster that has defined several external replications from the cluster, for various purposes.

---

5   The conflict resolution will then flow to the other cluster as well, so it's *highly* recommended that you have the same policy configuration on both clusters – that is, unless you have a specific reason not to, such as one-way replication or a meaningful difference in the tasks that the different clusters perform in your system.

The responsible node portion has been emphasized in Figure 7.2; you can see the node tag that is responsible for keeping each replication target up to date. You can also see that the cluster has assigned each external replication task to a separate node.[6].

We haven't discussed it yet, but that's one of the more important roles of the cluster: deciding what work goes where. Read more about that in section 7.3.

External replication - delayed

One of the use cases for External Replication is to have an off site replica of the data. This works quite nicely in most cases, but it does suffer from an issue. If the problem isn't that your main cluster died but rather that someone deleted an important document or updated a whole bunch of documents in a funny way, the off site replica will reflect these changes. In some cases, that is not desirable, since you want to have some gap between the time the data is modified in the main cluster and when the data is modified in the off site replica.

This can be done by adding a delay to the External Replication Task configuration. The replication task will not send the data immediately, rather, it will replicate the data only after some time has passed. For example, you can configure the External Replication task to delay the data replication by six hours, in which case the off site will be six hours behind the main cluster at all times.

If something happened to the data in the main cluster, you can go to the offsite cluster and get the data from before the change. This can be very useful at times, but it doesn't replace having a backup strategy. This is the kind of thing that you setup in addition to proper backup procedures, not instead of.

A replica isn't a backup

It's tempting to think that an offsite replica is also going to serve as a backup and neglect to pay careful attention to the backup/restore portion of your database strategy. That would be a mistake. RavenDB's external replication provides you with an offsite replica, but it doesn't present good solutions to many backup scenarios. It doesn't, for example, protect you from an accidental collection delete or tell you the state of the system at, say, 9:03 AM last Friday.

An offsite replica gives you an offsite live copy of the data, which is quite useful if you need to shift operations to a secondary data center. But it isn't going to allow you to skimp on backups. We cover backups (and restoring databases) in Chapter 17.

---

6   The cluster will make that determination on its own, and it may not always perfectly distribute the work among the nodes in this fashion. Overall, however, the work will be distributed among all the nodes to create a rough equality of work

7.3. Ongoing tasks and work distribution

The cluster as we know it so far doesn't really seem smart. It gives us the ability to distribute configuration, such as which databases go where, what indexes are defined, etc. But it doesn't seem to actually *do* very much. Well, that's only because we've focused specifically on the flow of *data* inside a database group rather than on the flow of *work*.

What does that mean, to have work assigned to a database group? The simplest example is the one we just talked about: external replication. If we have three nodes in this database group, which node will update the external replica? We don't want to have all three nodes do that. There's no real point in doing so, and it can cause unnecessary network traffic. Instead, the cluster will assign this work to one of the database instances, which will be responsible for keeping the external replica up to date.

Another example of what it means to have work assigned to a database group is an hourly incremental backup of your data, as well as a full backup on a weekly basis. You don't want to have this backup run on all three nodes at the same time. Beside the fact that this will increase the load on the system across the board, we don't really have any use for triplicate backups of the same data. This is where the work assignment portion of the cluster comes into play.

Whenever there's a task for a database group to do, the cluster will decide which node will actually be responsible for it. That seems pretty simple, but there's a bit more to the story. Assigning work is easy, but the cluster is also watching the nodes and checking how healthy they are. If a node is down, the cluster will reassign the work to another node for the duration.

Take the case of a backup, for instance. If the responsible node is down during the scheduled time, another node will shoulder the load and make sure you don't have any gaps in your backups. In the case of external replication, another node will transparently take over keeping the external replica up to date with all the changes that happened in the database group.

Another type of work in the cluster – one we've already talked about in this book – is subscriptions. The cluster will divide all the subscriptions between the various nodes in the database group and reassign them upon failure without your code needing to change anything (or typically even being aware of the failure). Other types of work that we can define for the database group include ETL processes, which are covered in the next chapter.

A fun way to experiment with this is to create some work in your cluster (a few external replications or subscriptions would do just fine) and then close one of the nodes. You'll see that the cluster recognizes the failed node and moves the work around to the surviving nodes. A test you can run, which will give you a taste of RavenDB's failover capabilities, is to have a client writing to the database and a subscription open when you close the node. (Make sure to close the node that the subscription is assigned to.) You shouldn't notice anything happening from the outside. Both subscription and client will silently move to another node, and everything will *just work*. You can monitor all of the work in the database group from the `Ongoing Tasks` page as you run this experiment.

But you aren't the only one watching the state of the cluster. There's another entity in play here. That entity is the supervisor, and it's responsible for making all those separate pieces cooperate seamlessly in the face of error conditions.

7.4. The ever-watching supervisor

The cluster is continuously measuring the health of each of its nodes, using a component known as the supervisor.[7] The supervisor will detect any errors in the cluster, react to a failed node by reassigning work and, in general, keep everything running.

This is important enough to mention here and not in the operations portion of the book because the supervisor also gives you a wealth of information about the state of the different nodes, as well as the database instances that are running on them. In addition to reassigning work to surviving nodes, it's also responsible for a very important role: the promotion and demotion of database instances.

Given that RavenDB is a distributed database and not a military organization, what does that mean, "promotions and demotions"? Consider the case of a database group that has two database instances. We want to increase the number of replicas, so we add a new node to the database group. The process is fairly easy. All we need to do is to click Manage group in the Studio and add the new node.

On large databases, the process of adding a new replica can take a while. During that process, the newly added node isn't really part of the group. It can't take over work in the group (we certainly don't want its backup until it's completely caught up, for example), and we don't want to fail clients over to it (since it doesn't have the full data yet). Because of this, when you add a new node to a database group, it isn't added as a full-fledged member. Instead, it's added as a promotable instance.

But what does "promotable" mean? It means it can't be assigned work for the database group, and that it can't be failed over to. In fact, adding a new node *is* work for the database group since one of the full members will have to start pushing data into this new node until it's fully up to date. This goes on until the supervisor can confirm that the new node is caught up with the state of the database group and that it's finished indexing all the data we sent to it. At this point, the supervisor will promote the node into a full member within the database group, work will be assigned to it and clients will consider it a failover target.

That works when we're talking about new nodes, but what happens when we have an existing node fail? If a member node fails, we don't want to go back into the usual rotation as soon as it recovers. We want it to pull all the changes that happened in the meantime from the other members in the database group. Because of that, the supervisor can send a node to "rehab."

---

7   I always imagine it in bright neon green tights and a cape, flying around and spouting cliches as it keeps everything in order.

A node in rehab isn't a full member of the cluster. It behaves exactly like a promotable node, for the most part. Like a promotable node, one of the other members in the database group will connect to it and update the recovered node until it's fully up to date, at which point the supervisor will promote it to full member again.

The only important distinction between a rehab node and a promotable node is what happens when all the members in a database group are down. This is only relevant in pathological cascading failure scenarios. Consider a cluster of three nodes with a database residing on nodes A and B. First, we have node B failing for some reason. (Perhaps the operations team took it down to apply patches.) The supervisor will detect that and move node B to the rehab group. Node A will assume all duties that were previously assigned to node B. You can see this in Figure 7.3; the red R icon for node B indicates that it is in rehab mode.

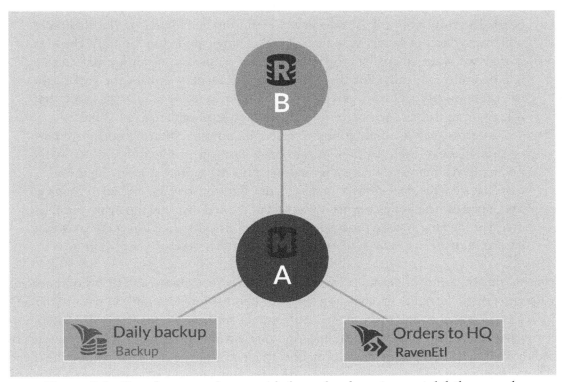

Figure 7.3. *Database topology graph for a database in partial failure mode*

When node B comes back up, node A will send it all the updates it missed. However, we're in somewhat of a pickle if node A is also failing at this point (the operations team is now rebooting that node, without giving it time to get node B fully up to date). On the one hand, we don't have any working members to failover to. On the other hand, node B is functioning, even though it's currently in rehab.

At this point, when there are no more active members in the database group, the supervisor will rehabilitate an active node from the rehab group and mark it as a full member in the database group, restoring functionality to that database. This isn't ideal, of course, because it might be missing writes that happened to node A and haven't been replicated yet, but it's better than losing access to the database completely.

Keep calm and serve requests

You might have noticed that the scenario requiring us to rehabilitate a node in rehab is most easily explained via an operator error. Though rare, such things happen on a fairly regular basis. About a quarter of production failures[8] are the result of human error.

One of the primary goals of RavenDB is that the database should always be up and responding. That means we do automatic failover on the client and will always accept writes as long as there's a single node functioning. The idea is that we want to free the operations team from routine tasks that can be handled automatically. For the same reason, RavenDB utilizes the supervisor to automatically and transparently handle failures for you. Having taken that role upon ourselves, we strive to make the job as complete as possible.

Features such as sending nodes to rehab and rehabilitating nodes are part of that. They're there to handle rare edge cases in production and to avoid getting into situations where a temporary failure becomes a permanent one.

That said, the operations team has a critical role in keeping RavenDB running. The supervisor can only do what it was told to do, and there are too many variables in real production systems to account for them all. The design of RavenDB takes that into account and allows you to override the supervisor decisions to fit your needs.

The clients are also aware of the nodes in rehab, and if they're unable to talk to any of the members, they'll try to talk to the nodes in rehab as a last-ditch effort before returning an error to the caller. A major reason we run this logic on both the clients and the supervisor is that this allows us to respond to errors in a distributed fashion in realtime. And this is without having to wait for the supervisor to find the failure and propagate the information about it throughout the cluster and the clients.

Using demotions and promotions as needed, the supervisor is able to communicate to the clients (and the rest of the cluster) what are the preferred nodes for a particular database group. Note that a failure doesn't have to be just a down node. Something as simple as running out of disk space can also cause a database on a node to fail and be sent to rehab until that situation is fixed.

The supervisor is always running on the leader node, and it operates at the cluster level. In other words, it requires consensus to operate. This protects us from a rogue supervisor deciding that all nodes are unresponsive and taking them down. But as long as it has the majority

---

8   https://journal.uptimeinstitute.com/data-center-outages-incidents-industry-transparency/

of the clusters' votes, the supervisor is the authority on who's up or down in the cluster. Clients will avoid talking to nodes the supervisor can't talk to, even if they can reach them.

7.5. Ensuring a minimum number of replicas

When you create a database, you also specify the number of replicas for that database. This is used by the cluster to decide how many database instances it should create for this database group. One of the roles of the supervisor is to make sure that this value is maintained over time. What do I mean by this?

Well, consider a three-node cluster and a database that was created with a replication factor of two. The cluster assigned this database to nodes A and B. After a while, the supervisor notices that node B is down. It moves the node to the rehab program and hopes that it will recover. However, if it is down for too long (the default value is 15 minutes), the supervisor will decide that it can't assume that node B will come up any time soon and it will need to take action to ensure we have enough replicas for the data in the database.

At this point, the supervisor will create another database instance on another node (C, in this case) and add it to the database group as promotable. At that point, the database group will look like Figure 7.4.

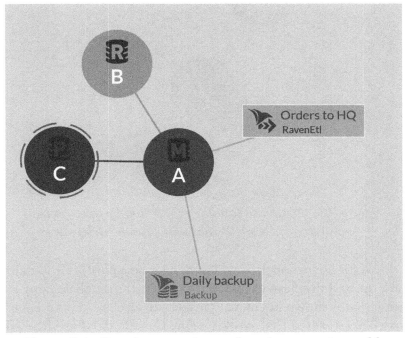

Figure 7.4. *Database topology when the supervisor adds another node to a database group on the fly.*

223

One of the nodes in the database group is a member in full health. This is node A, shown in green in Figure 7.4. We have node B in red in rehab, and we have the new node C, shown as yellow P, that was added as promotable. At this point, we have a race between node B and node C. Node C is getting all the data from the other members in the database group and becoming a full member. Meanwhile, node B is recovering and getting up to date with all the changes it missed.

Either way, one of them will cross the finish line first, and we'll have three full replicas of the data in the database. At that point, the supervisor will delete the extra copy that's now no longer needed. Figure 7.5 shows how the database topology will look if node C has managed to catch up completely while node B wasn't responsive.

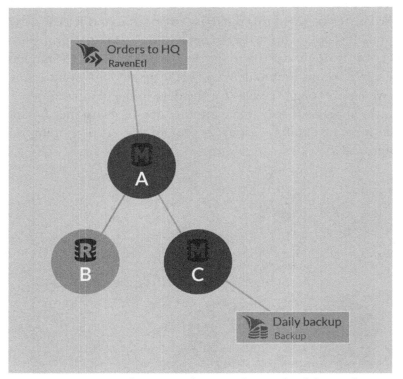

Figure 7.5. *Database topology with two healthy replicas and a failed node B that will soon be deleted.*

If node B is down for long enough, it will no longer be a part of the database group topology when it's back up, and the cluster will tell it to delete the database copy it currently holds. This is the situation that is shown in Figure 7.5. You can also see in both Figure 7.4 and Figure 7.5 that the cluster has ensured that work assigned to the database (the ETL task and the backup) is distributed to working nodes.

On the other hand, if node B recovers in time and catches up to the rest of the members before node C is ready, the supervisor will promote node B to being a database group member again. The supervisor will then let node C know it needs to delete the now-extraneous copy.

Rebalancing of data after recovery is in the hands of the admin

In the scenario outlined above, if node B was down long enough that we removed the database from it and moved it to node C, what would happen when node B recovers? At that point, all of its databases have been redistributed in the cluster, and it's effectively an empty node. RavenDB will not start moving databases back to node B on its own and will instead require the operations team to instruct it to do so. Why is that?

The supervisor has acted to ensure that the number of replicas for a database is maintained, which is why we allow it to just create a new replica on the fly and move the database instance between nodes. However, we don't know what the state of node B is at this point. It may fail again. Even if it's here to stay, the act of moving a database between nodes can be pretty expensive.

It requires a lot of disk and network I/O, and that isn't something that we want to just do on the fly. We only do that automatically to ensure we keep the minimum number of copies required. Once the incident is over, restoring the state is in the hands of the operations team, which can move the database between the nodes according to their own schedule.

The logic behind the supervisor behavior is that a node is allowed to fail for a short amount of time (network partition, reboot for patching, etc.). But if it's gone for a long time, we need to assume it won't be coming back up, and we need to take action. It's important to take this behavior into account during maintenance, and let the supervisor know that it shouldn't take action and get in the way of the actual operator, who is handling things.

The supervisor's decisions can have a serious impact. For that reason, big decisions, such as moving a database between nodes, will generate an alert for the operations team to review. Those alerts can be reviewed in the `Notifications Center`.

7.6. Summary

We started this chapter by talking about how we can grow our RavenDB cluster. We learned that, after a certain size, it doesn't make sense to add more members to a cluster. We should add watchers instead. Those are non-voting nodes in the cluster that are still fully managed by it. The advantage is that we have a single cluster and only a single thing to manage, but we don't suffer from large majorities and the latencies they can incur.

We looked at the implications of working with RavenDB in a geo-distributed environment and considered the pros and cons of having a single cluster span multiple geo-distributed data centers versus having a separate cluster per data center. If we have separate clusters, we need to share data between them, and external replication is the answer to that. External replication allows you to tie separate clusters together by replicating all changes to another database, not necessarily on the same cluster.

This is a good option for offsite replicas and to tie separate clusters together, but it also demarcates a clear line between the database instances that are in the same group and an external replication target. Database instances in the same group share work assignments between them, clients can failover from one instance to another in the same group transparently, etc. With external replication, the only thing that happens is that data flowing to the replication target isn't considered to be a part of the database group at all.

We looked into the kind of work you can assign to databases, such as backups and subscriptions, or filling up promotables or nodes in a rehab mode, to allow them to catch up to the rest of the nodes in the cluster. The supervisor is responsible for assigning the work, and it can reassign work if a node failed.

The supervisor has a critical role in ensuring the proper functioning of a RavenDB cluster. In addition to monitoring the health of the cluster, it's also capable of taking action if there are problems. A failed node will be moved to rehab until it's feeling better, and a node that's down for too long will be automatically replaced by the supervisor.

This was anything but a trivial chapter. I tried to focus on the high-level concepts more than the nitty-gritty details. The purpose of this chapter is to get you to understand how RavenDB operates in a distributed environment. It *isn't* about how to actually run it in such an environment. That's handled in the "Production Deployments" chapter.

Beyond just setting up a cluster, you also need to know how to monitor and manage your systems. That's covered in Chapter 16, which is dedicated to that topic. We'll also talk a bit more about the implementation details that I intentionally skipped here. Your operations team needs to understand what's going on, exactly. This chapter was about the overall concept.

In the next chapter, we'll talk about how we can integrate with other systems in your organization, and we'll introduce the ETL concept [9], which allows RavenDB to write data to external sources automatically.

---

9   Extract, transform, load

8. Sharing Data and Making Friends with ETL

While talking about distributed work with RavenDB so far, we've focused primarily on the work that RavenDB is doing to replicate data between different nodes in the same cluster, either as part of the same database group or between different databases in potentially different clusters. This mode of operation is simple because you just set up the replication and RavenDB takes care of everything else. But there are other modes for distributing data in your systems.

External Replication assumes that you have another RavenDB instance and that you want to replicate *everything* to it. When replicating information, that's what you want, but we also need to be able to share only a part of the data. ETL[1] is the process by which we take data that resides in RavenDB and push it to an external source, potentially transforming it along the way. That external source can be another RavenDB instance or a relational database.

Consider a microservice architecture and a "customer benefits service." This service decides what kind of benefits the customer has. It can be anything from free shipping to a discount on every third jug of milk. And the logic can be as simple as "this customer is in our membership club" and as complex as trying to compute airline miles. Regardless of how the customer benefits service works, it needs to let other parts of the system know about the benefits that this customer has. The shipping service, the help desk service and many others need to have that information.

At the same time, we *really* don't want them to poke around in the customer benefits database (or worse, have a shared database for everything).[2] We could design an API between the systems, but then the shipping service would be dependent on the customer benefits service always being up. A better solution is to define an ETL process between the two services and have the customer benefits service publish updates for the shipping service to consume. Those

---

1   Extract, transform, load
2   Doing so is a great way to ensure that you'll have all the costs of a microservice architecture with none of the benefits.

updates are part of the public contract of those services, mind you. You shouldn't just copy the data between the databases.

Another example is the reporting database. RavenDB is a wonderful database for OLTP scenarios, but for reporting, your organization likely already has a solution. There's little need to replace that. But you can't just dump the data from RavenDB directly into a relational database and expect things to work. We need to transform the data as we send it to match the relational model.

For all of those needs, RavenDB has the notion of ETL processes. RavenDB has built in ETL processes to another RavenDB instance and to a relational database (such as MS SQL Server, Postgres, Oracle, MySQL, etc.). Because RavenDB has native relational ETL, brownfield systems will typically start using RavenDB by replacing a single component at a time. RavenDB is used to speed up the behavior of high value targets, but instead of replacing the whole system, we use ETL processes to write the data to the existing relational database. We'll cover that later in this chapter, discussing the deployment of RavenDB as a write-behind cache.

In most cases, the rest of the system doesn't even need to know that some parts are using RavenDB. This is using RavenDB as the write-behind cache. Some part of your application reads and writes to RavenDB directly, and RavenDB will make sure to update the relational system. We'll start by talking about ETL processes between RavenDB instances because we explore the whole ETL process without introducing another database instance.

8.1. ETL processes to another RavenDB instance

Any nontrivial system is going to have at least a few ETL processes, and RavenDB has a good way to handle those. The simplest ETL process between two RavenDB nodes is when we tell RavenDB we want to send just a single collection to the other side. We first need to configure the connection string we'll use. The RavenDB connection string defines the destination database and the destination database-group nodes URLs. Since there can be multiple URLs, it's more convenient to put it all in one single location.

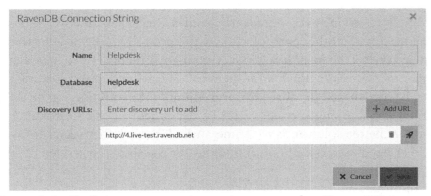

Figure 8.1. *Defining a connection string to another RavenDB instance.*

Go to Settings and then to Connection Strings and create a new RavenDB connection string. As you can see in Figure 8.1, I've defined a connection string to the helpdesk database in the live-test instance.

With the connection string defined, we can now go ahead and build the actual ETL process to the remote instance. Go to Settings and then to Manage Ongoing Tasks. Click the Add Task button and then select RavenDB ETL. You can see how this looks in Figure 8.2. Give it a name and select the previously defined connection string.

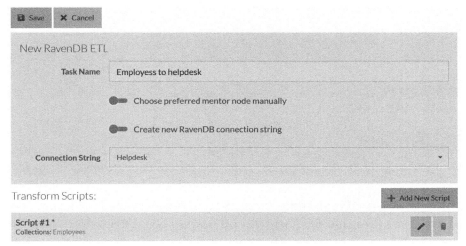

Figure 8.2. *Defining an ETL process to another RavenDB instance*

Now we need to let RavenDB know what will be ETL'ed to the other side. We do that by defining scripts that control the ETL process. Click Add New Script and give it a name, such as "Employees to Helpdesk." Then select the employees collection below, click on Add Collection and then on Save. The result should look like Figure 8.3.

What about security?

We'll cover security in depth in Chapter 13, but given that we've shown a connection string, I wanted to address a not-so-minor issue that you probably noticed. We don't have a place here to define credentials. This is because we're talking to another RavenDB server, and for that we use x509 certificates.

In practice, this means that inside the same cluster, ETL processes don't need any special configuration. (Nodes within the same cluster already trust one another.) Outside the cluster, you'll need to register the cluster's certificate with the remote cluster to allow the ETL process to work. You can read the full details of that in the security chapter.

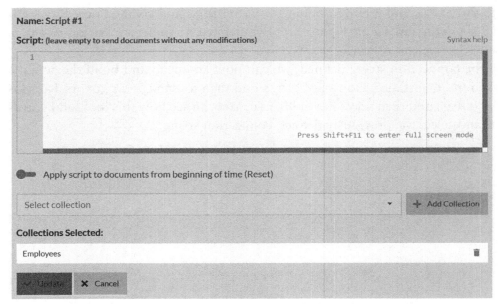

Figure 8.3. *Defining a simple "copy the whole collection" ETL script*

Because we didn't specify anything in the ETL script, RavenDB will just copy the entire collection as is to the other side. That's useful on its own because it allows us to share a single collection (or a few collections) with other parties with very little work.

> **ETL is a database task, with bidirectional failover**
>
> In the previous chapter, we learned about database tasks and how the cluster will distribute such work among the different database instances. If a node fails, then the responsibility for the ETL task will be assigned to another node.
>
> Take note that in cases where we ETL to another RavenDB instance, we also have failover on the receiving end. Instead of specifying a single URL, we can specify all the nodes in the remote cluster. If one of the destination nodes is down, RavenDB will just run the ETL process against another node in the database group topology.

It's very important to remember that ETL is quite different from replication. When a RavenDB node performs ETL to another node, it's not replicating the data – it's *writing* it. In other words, there are no conflicts and thus no attempts to handle conflicts. Instead, we'll always *overwrite* whatever exists on the other side. As far as the destination node is concerned, the ETL process is just another client writing data to the database. That's done because the data is *not* the same. This is important because of a concept we haven't touched on so far: data ownership.

Data ownership in distributed systems

One of the key differences between a centralized system and a distributed system is that, in a distributed environment, different parts of the system can act on their local information without coordination from other parts of the system. In a centralized system, you can take a lock or use transactions to ensure consistency. But in a distributed system, that's not possible, or it's prohibitively expensive to do so. Because of this limitation, the concept of data ownership is very important.

Ideally, you want every piece of data to have a single well-defined owner and to only mutate that data through that owner. This allows you to put all the validation and business rules in a single place and ensure overall consistency. Everything else in the system will update that data through its owner.

A database group, for example, needs to handle the issue of data ownership. Conceptually, it's the database group as a whole that owns the data stored in the document. However, different database instances can mutate the data. RavenDB handles that using change vectors and conflict detection and resolution. That solution works for replication inside the database group, because all nodes in the group share ownership of the data. But it doesn't work for ETL.

The ETL source is the owner of the data, and it distributes updates to interested parties. Given that it's the owner, it's expected that the ETL source can just update it to the latest version it has. So if you made any modifications to the ETL'ed data, they would be lost. Instead of modifying the ETL'ed data directly, you should create, in the destination database, a companion document that you own. In other words, for ETL'ed data, the rule is that you can look but not touch.

An example of such a companion document is when you have ETL for help desk system users. The `users/123-B` document is owned by the users' database, and the help desk system will store all the information it needs about the user in the `users/123-B/helpdesk` document, ensuring there's no contention over the ownership of documents.

So far, we've only done ETL at the collection level, but we can also modify the data as it's going out. Let's see how we can do that – and why we'd want to.

8.1.1. ETL SCRIPTS

Sometimes you don't want to send full documents through the ETL process. Sometimes you want to filter them or modify their shape. This matters, since ETL processes compose a part of your public interface. Instead of just sending your documents to a remote destination willy nilly, you'll typically only send data you're interested in sharing, and in a well-defined format.

Consider the employees we sent over the wire. We sent them as is, potentially exposing our own internal document structure and making it harder to modify in the future. Let's create a new ETL process that will send just the relevant details and add a script for sending redacted employee information over the wire. You can see what this looks like in Figure 8.4.

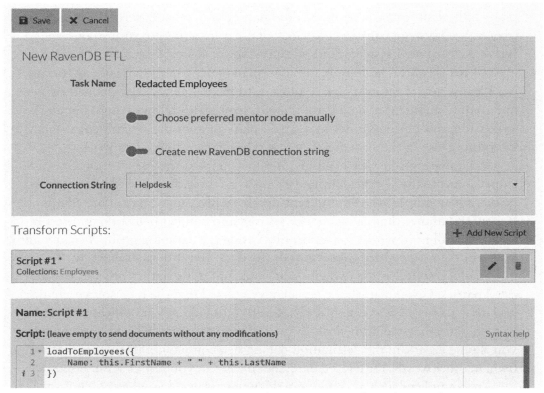

Figure 8.4. *Using ETL with a script to redact the results*

When we're using an ETL script to modify what's sent, it's essential to take into account that RavenDB will send only what we told it to. This seems obvious, but it can catch people unaware. If you don't have a script, the data sent to the other side will include attachments and go to the same collection as the source data.

However, when you provide your own script, you need to take responsibility for this yourself. Listing 8.1 shows a slightly more complex example.

The script in Listing 8.1 will send the employees, their title, their birth year and their manager over to the other side. You can see that the script is actually a full-blown JavaScript that allows you complete freedom as to how you extract the data to load into the remote server. A word of caution is required about using functions such as load in this context, though. While this will work just fine, the referencing document will not be updated if the referenced document has been updated. In other words, if the manager's name has been updated, it will not trigger an update to the employees that report to this manager.

Listing 8.1 *Creating a subscription to process customers*

```
let managerName = null;
if (this.ReportsTo !== null)
{
    let manager = load(this.ReportsTo);
    managerName = manager.FirstName + " " + manager.LastName;
}

loadToEmployees({
    Name: this.FirstName + " " + this.LastName,
    Title: this.Title,
    BornOn: new Date(this.Birthday).getFullYear(),
    Manager: managerName
});
```

A good solution is to limit yourself to just the data from that particular document. That makes it easy to ensure that whenever the document is changed, the ETL process will reflect that change completely on the other side.

Resetting the ETL process after update

It's common to test out the ETL process as you develop it, but by default, updates to the ETL script will not be applied to documents that were already sent. This is done to avoid an expensive reset that would force RavenDB to send all the data all over again for a minor change. You can use the "Apply script to documents from beginning of time" option during the script update, as shown in Figure 8.5, to let RavenDB know that it needs to start the ETL process for this script from scratch, rather than apply the update only to new or updated documents.

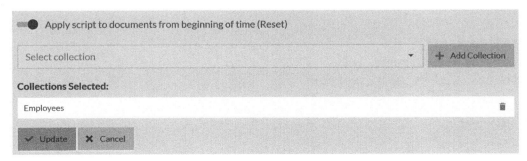

Figure 8.5. *Resetting the ETL process after a script update*

Looking on the other side, you'll be able to see the ETL'ed document, as shown in Listing 8.2.

Listing 8.2 *ETL'ed document on the destination*

```
{
    "BornOn": 1966,
    "Manager": "Steven Buchanan",
    "Name": "Anne Dodsworth",
    "Title": "Sales Representative",
    "@metadata": {
        "@collection": "Employees",
        "@change-vector": "A:84-4Xmt8lVCrkiCDii/CfyaWQ",
        "@id": "employees/9-A",
        "@last-modified": "2017-12-04T12:02:53.8561852Z"
    }
}
```

There are a few interesting things in the document in Figure 8.2. First, we can see that it has only a single change vector entry (for the destination database). Also, the last modified date is when it was written to the destination, not when it was updated on the source.

8.1.2. MULTIPLE DOCUMENTS FROM A SINGLE DOCUMENT

Another interesting ETL example is when we want to push multiple values out of a single document, as shown in Listing 8.3.

Listing 8.3 *Sending multiple documents from a single source document in ETL*

```
loadToEmployees({
    Name: this.FirstName + " " + this.LastName,
    Title: this.Title,
    BornOn: new Date(this.Birthday).getFullYear(),
});

loadToAddresses({
    City: this.Address.City,
    Country: this.Address.Country,
    Address: this.Address.Line1
});
```

The results of the script in Listing 8.3 can be seen in Figure 8.6. You can see that the `Employees` documents were sent, but there are also the addresses documents. For those, we use the prefix of the source document to be able to identify them.

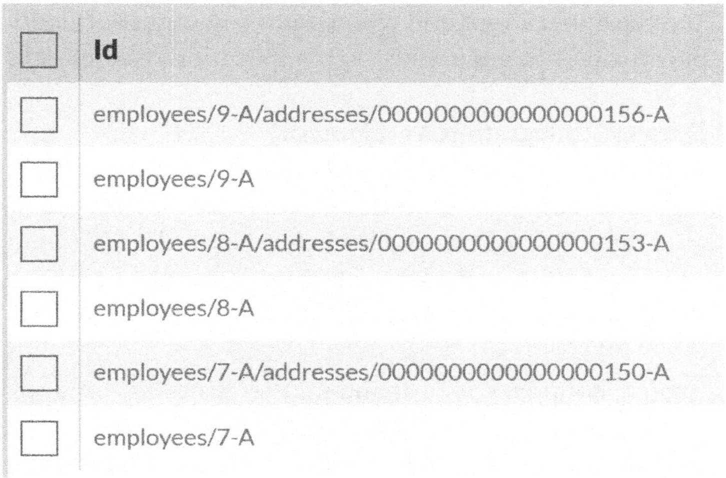

	Id
☐	employees/9-A/addresses/0000000000000000156-A
☐	employees/9-A
☐	employees/8-A/addresses/0000000000000000153-A
☐	employees/8-A
☐	employees/7-A/addresses/0000000000000000150-A
☐	employees/7-A

Figure 8.6. *Multiple outputs from a single source document on the destination*

An important consideration for sending multiple documents from a single source document is that on every update to the source document, *all* the documents created from this one are refreshed. In addition, you don't have control over the IDs being generated and shouldn't assume that they're fixed.

Attachments and Revisions with RavenDB ETL

Attachments are sent automatically over the wire when you send a full collection to the destination. If you do use a script, there's currently no way to indicate that attachments should also be sent. This feature is planned, but it wasn't completed in time for the 4.0 RTM release. Revisions are also not sent automatically, and another upcoming feature is support for ETL processes on top of the revision data, similar to how it's possible to use subscriptions with the `current` and `previous` versions of the document.

8.2. Use cases for ETL between RavenDB instances

When you have a complex system, composed of more than a single application, it's considered bad form to just go peek inside another application's database. Such behavior leads to sharing way too much between the applications and will require constant coordination between them as you develop and deploy them. A boundary between applications is required to avoid such issues.

> **Shared Database Integration Anti-Pattern**
>
> This kind of behavior is called the shared database integration and is considered to be an anti-pattern. For more information on why you should avoid such a system, I refer you to Martin Fowler's post on the matter and in particular to the summary, "most software architects that I respect take the view that *integration databases should be avoided*."

One way to create such a boundary is to mandate that any time an application needs some data from another application, it will ask that application. In concrete terms, whenever the help desk system needs to look up a user, it will go to the user's application and ask it to get that user's data. This is often referred to as a service boundary.

The problem with such a system is that many interactions inside a particular service require information owned by another service. Any support ticket opened by a user will require a call from the help desk service to the user management service for details and updates. As you can imagine, such a system still requires a lot of work. In particular, even though we have a clear boundary between the services and the division of responsibility between them, there's still a strong temporal coupling between them.

Taking down the user management service for maintenance will require taking down everything else that needs to call to it. A better alternative in this case is to not rely on making remote calls to a separate service but to pull the data directly from our own database. This way, if the user management service is down, it doesn't impact operations for the help desk service.

Note a key difference here between this type of architecture and the shared database model. You don't have a single shared database. Instead, the help desk database contains a section that's updated by the user management service. In this manner, the ownership of the data is retained by the user management service, but the responsibility for maintaining it and keeping it up is that of the help desk service.

If the user management service is taken down for maintenance, it has no impact on the help desk service, which can continue with all operations normally. The design of the ETL processes in RavenDB is meant to allow such a system to be deployed and operated with a minimum of hassle. That's also partly why the ownership rules and responsibility for changes is built the way it is.

ETL is explicitly about sending data you own to a third party that's interested in it but doesn't own it. As such, any change you make will, by necessity, overwrite any local changes in the destination. If you're interested in a shared ownership model, ETL is not the method you should use. Rather, you should choose external replication, discussed in the previous chapter.

8.2.1. MODELING CONCERNS FOR ETL PROCESSES

An important aspect of using ETL processes in a multi-service environment is the fact that the ETL process itself is part of the service contract that needs to be deployed, versioned and managed as such. In particular, the format of the documents that are sent via the ETL process compose part of the public interface of the service. Because of this, you should think carefully about the shape of the data you expose and the versioning considerations around that.

Listing 8.1 is a good example of exposing just enough information to be useful to the other side without leaking implementation details or other aspects that may change over time. The ETL process design accommodates for the fact that you may have different processes and different outputs for different destinations. In this way, you may collaborate with another service to update your contract while maintaining the same behavior for all others.

Another option is to only allow additive changes; adding a property would be fine but removing one wouldn't. That *usually* works, but unfortunately Hyrum's Law applies. Even such innocuous changes can break a third-party application.

8.2.2. CONTROLLED EXPOSURE OF DATA VIA ETL

Beyond using ETL for disseminating documents between services, there are a few other scenarios in which it can be useful. A typical usage scenario for ETL is sending data from production (after redacting any sensitive information) to UAT or CI instances, allowing you to test realistic data sizes – and with real-world data.

Sending redacted data from production to UAT is just one application of a larger concept: controlling the degree to which you expose data to outside parties. We'll discuss authorization in detail in Chapter 13, but for now, know that RavenDB allows you to define permissions at the database level.

Sometimes, you need to apply such permissions on a per-collection or a per-document level. In some cases, it's per field or even dependent on the exact data in the document to control who sees the data. The ETL process in RavenDB offers a nice way to manage that using the customization scripts. You can select exactly which collections you want to send, and you're free to decide what data to send and what data to hold back.

The target database in this case will usually be another database in the same cluster, which you'll allow access to based on your own internal policies. This gives the operations team a lot of freedom in designing and implementing data exposure processes and policies.

8.2.3. Case study: ETL usage in point-of-sales systems

Another ETL usage example is data aggregation. One use case we've seen many times is the embedding of RavenDB inside a larger application. In this manner, each instance of the application also has its own instance of RavenDB. Consider a point-of-sales system in a supermarket, running its own copy of the store management application and talking directly to its own local database.

In such a case, we want to send some of the information we have (the new sales generated on that particular POS system) to the central server. At the same time, we have the central server send updates to each of the POS systems with new prices, products, etc. However, there's no need to send all the data back to the server or to have each POS system contain all the sales across the system. Figure 8.7 shows the data flow between the various components of the system in such a scenario.

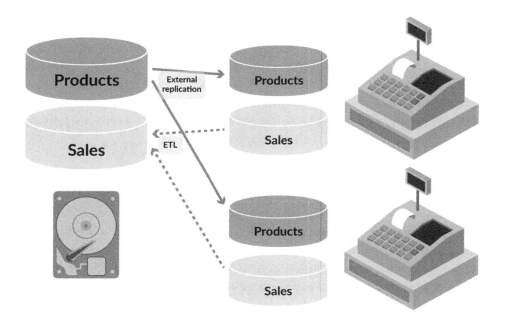

Figure 8.7. *Data flow diagram for a POS system with replication and ETL processes.*

The central server in the store will send updates using external replication to all the POS machines. In turn, whenever there's a new sale, the POS will use an ETL process to update the central server in the store, telling it about the new sales that were rung up on the machine. You can also imagine the same architecture writ large when you zoom out, with the central server of the supermarket chain updating each store in turn and aggregating all the sales across its stores.

8.2.4. FAILOVER AND RECOVERY WITH ETL IN DISTRIBUTED SYSTEMS

The ETL feature in RavenDB, like any other feature, was designed with the knowledge that networks fail, have outages and can slow you down. In general, networks are *not* something that you can rely on. The ETL process was designed to be like the replication process in that it's resilient in the face of such issues.

In the worst case scenario, when the ETL process has no way to communicate with the other side, it will wait until the destination is reachable again and proceed from where it left off. In other words, it's a fully offline, async process. If the other side is not responding for any reason, we'll catch up when we can.

That is the worst case, but we can usually do better. An ETL process is an ongoing task in the cluster, and that means that while the task is assigned to a single node, the cluster as a whole is still responsible for it. If the node that was assigned to the ETL process is down for whatever reason, the cluster will move the task assignment[3] to another node, and the ETL process will proceed from there.

Being robust on just the sender side is all well and good, but we're also robust on the receiving end. Part of defining the RavenDB connection string in Figure 8.1 was to add the URL of the destination. In this case, we have just one server. But if we have a cluster on the other side, we can list all the nodes in the cluster, and RavenDB will ensure that even if a node goes down on the other end, the ETL process will proceed smoothly.

8.3. Sending data to a relational database

In addition to supporting ETL processes to another RavenDB instance, there's also support for the ETL process to relational databases (Microsoft SQL, Oracle, PostgreSQL, MySQL, etc.). The idea here is that RavenDB holds the master copy of the data and wants to send the data to a relational database. This is desirable for many reasons.

You probably already have a reporting infrastructure in your organization. Instead of having to build one from scratch for use with your data inside of RavenDB, you can just let RavenDB schlep all that data to a relational database and use your pre-existing infrastructure. It's also common to use this feature during migrations from a relational database to RavenDB. Instead of trying to do it in a big bang sort of way, you'll slowly move features away from the relational database; but you'll use the ETL feature in RavenDB to make sure that the rest of the system is not actually aware that anything has changed.

Finally, a really interesting deployment model for RavenDB is as a write-behind cache. Because of RavenDB's speed and the different model, it's often *much* faster than a relational database for many types of queries. That makes it ideal for the kind of user-facing pages that need speedy reactions. Instead of moving the entire application to RavenDB, you can move just the few pages that have the most impact for users.

---

3   Assuming that your license allows dynamic task distribution, that is.

In many cases, you can use RavenDB in this manner as a read-only cache, albeit one that's much smarter than the usual cache and has excellent querying capabilities. But it often makes sense to use RavenDB for writes as well, if the scenario demands it. And in this case, you'll write directly to RavenDB and let RavenDB write to the relational database behind the scenes. That can be very helpful if your relational database is struggling under the load since a large portion of it will now be handled by RavenDB instead.

The impedance mismatch strikes back

Translating between the document model and the relational model isn't trivial. Let's use the sample data as an example. We have the notion of an `Order` document, which contains an array of `Lines`. However, there's no good way to represent such an entity in a single table in the relational model. In order to bridge the gap in the models, we can use the ETL script to transform the data. Instead of sending it to a single table, we'll send the data from a single document to multiple tables.

The concept of data ownership can also complicate things. As with RavenDB ETL, we need to be the owners of the data. In particular, the way that RavenDB implements updates to the data is via `DELETE` and `INSERT` calls, not via an `UPDATE`. This is because we don't know the current state in the relational data, and we need to make sure we have a clean slate for each write.

That means you need to modify your foreign keys on the destination tables because they may be violated temporarily during the ETL operation until RavenDB makes it all whole again. If you're using Oracle or PostgreSQL, you can set such constraints as `deferrable` so they'll be checked only on commit. If you're using a database that doesn't support this feature (such as Microsoft SQL), you'll likely need to forgo foreign key constraints for the tables that RavenDB is writing to.

We'll start with a simple ETL process for `Employees` as a way to explore the SQL ETL feature. Before we can start, we need to have created data in Microsoft SQL with the appropriate table. You can see the table creation script in Listing 8.4.

Listing 8.4 *Table creation script for the sample ETL process*

```
CREATE TABLE Employees
(
    DocumentId NVARCHAR(50) NOT NULL PRIMARY KEY,
    Name NVARCHAR(50) NOT NULL,
    Birthday DATETIME NOT NULL
)
```

Once you have created this table in the relational database, go into the RavenDB management Studio, then to `Settings` and then to `Connection Strings`. Create a new SQL connection string, as shown in Figure 8.8. You'll need to provide your own connection string. Note that you can test that the connection string is valid directly from the Studio.

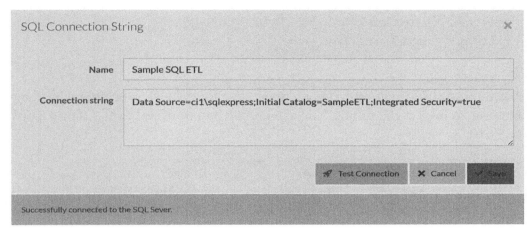

Figure 8.8. *Creating a new SQL connection string*

Note the identity issue

In Figure 8.8, you can see a SQL connection string that uses `Integrated Security=true`. This is possible because the user that RavenDB is running under has permissions for the database in question. In this case, it's running as if it were in debug mode under my own user. In production, RavenDB will often run as a service account, and you'll either need the operations team to allow the service account access to the relational database or use a username and password to authenticate.

You can now go to `Settings` and then `Manage Ongoing Tasks`. Click `Add Task` and select `SQL ETL`. You can name the ETL process and select the appropriate connection string to use here. Before we can really start, we need to let RavenDB know which tables are going to be used in the ETL process and what column in the destination table is going to be used as the document ID column. Note that this doesn't have to be the primary key of the table in question. It just needs to be a column RavenDB can use to place its document ID in. You can see such a configuration in Figure 8.9.

Figure 8.9. *Specifying a table to be used in the ETL process*

Select the `Employees` collection on the transformation script on the right and use the script from Listing 8.5.

Listing 8.5 *Simple ETL script to send employees to SQL*

```
loadToEmployees({
    Name: this.FirstName + " " + this.LastName,
    Birthday: this.Birthday
});
```

Click `Add` on the transformation script and then `Save` for the ETL process and head into your SQL database to inspect the results. You can see the output of `select * from Employees` in Figure 8.10.

DocumentId	Name	Birthday
employees/1-A	Nancy Davolio	1948-12-08 00:00:00
employees/2-A	Andrew Fuller	1952-02-19 00:00:00
employees/3-A	Janet Leverling	1963-08-30 00:00:00
employees/4-A	Margaret Peacock	1937-09-19 00:00:00
employees/5-A	Steven Buchanan	1955-03-04 00:00:00
employees/6-A	Michael Suyama	1963-07-02 00:00:00
employees/7-A	Robert King	1960-05-29 00:00:00
employees/8-A	Laura Callahan	1958-01-29 00:00:00
employees/9-A	Anne Dodsworth	1966-01-27 00:00:00

Figure 8.10. *Result of SQL ETL script on the relational database side*

You can now play with the data, modifying and creating employees as you wish. RavenDB will make updates to the relational database whenever a document is changed. This is done in an async and resilient manner. If the relational database is slow or not responding for any reason, it won't impact operations for RavenDB and we'll retry the ETL operation until we're successful.

8.3.1. MULTI-TABLE SQL ETL PROCESSES

The example in Listing 8.5 is pretty simple. We have a one-to-one match between the documents and the rows that represent them. We did have a bit of fun with the concatenation of the first and last name into a single field, but nothing really interesting was going on there. Let's tackle a more complex problem: sending the `Orders` documents to the relational database.

Here, we can't just rely on one-to-one mapping between a document and a row. An `Order` document can contain any number of lines, and we need to faithfully represent that in the SQL destination. We'll start by first defining the tables that we need on the receiving end, as shown in Listing 8.6.

Listing 8.6 *Table creation script for multiple tables ETL process*

```
CREATE TABLE Orders
(
    OrderId NVARCHAR(50) NOT NULL PRIMARY KEY,
    Company NVARCHAR(50) NOT NuLL,
    OrderedAt DATETIME NOT NULL,
    Total FLOAT NOT NULL,
    ShipToCountry NVARCHAR(50) NOT NULL
)

CREATE TABLE OrderLines
(
    OrderLIneId int identity NOT NULL PRIMARY KEY NONCLUSTERED,
    OrderId NVARCHAR(50) NOT NULL INDEX IX_OrderLines_OrderId CLUSTERED,
    Price FLOAT NOT NULL,
    Product NVARCHAR(50) NOT NULL,
    Quantity INT NOT NULL
)
```

Once we've created the tables in Listing 8.6, we can proceed to actually define the ETL process for orders. First, we need to add the new tables, as you can see in Figure 8.11.

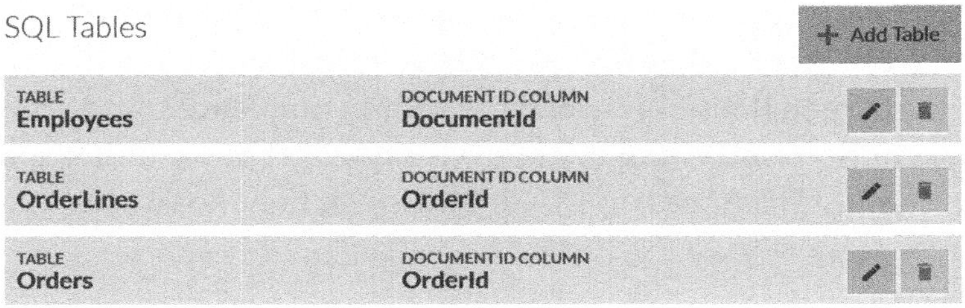

Figure 8.11. *Adding additional tables to the SQL ETL process*

Once we've configured the additional tables for the ETL process, we can get started on sending the data over. We need to let RavenDB know both that we're going to be using these two tables and that it needs to send multiple values to the OrderLines table. This turns out to be easy to do. The reason we need to define the tables upfront for SQL ETL is that we're generating matching functions to be called from the script. In the case of the script to send the Orders to the relational database, these are loadToOrderLines and loadToOrders, as you can see in Listing 8.7.

Listing 8.7 *ETL Script for sending the Orders documents*
to the Orders and OrderLines tables

```
let total = 0;

for (let i = 0; i < this.Lines.length; i++) {
    let line = this.Lines[i];
    total += line.PricePerUnit * line.Quantity * (1 - line.Discount);
    loadToOrderLines({
        Quantity: line.Quantity,
        Product: line.Product,
        Price: line.PricePerUnit
    });
}

loadToOrders({
    Company: this.Company,
    OrderedAt: this.OrderedAt,
    ShipToCountry: this.ShipTo.Country,
    Total: total,
});
```

The script in Listing 8.7 iterates over the Lines in the order, telling RavenDB that we need to send the object to that table as well as compute a running total of the order. Lastly, it calls loadToOrders with the final tally for the Orders table. RavenDB will actually call into the relational database and update it only when the script completes.

You might have noticed in Listing 8.7 and Listing 8.5 that we didn't specify the OrderId or DocumentId columns. That's because we implicitly define those when we set up the tables that the SQL ETL process will use.

8.3.2. THE CARE AND FEEDING OF PRODUCTION-WORTHY SQL ETL PROCESSES

With RavenDB ETL, there isn't a lot that you need to verify to get things right. But with SQL ETL, there are a few common pitfalls that you need to be aware of. Probably the most important one is the notion of indexes. Unlike RavenDB, relational databases usually don't learn from experience, and they require you to define indexes explicitly. You should define indexes on the relevant tables on at least the column used to hold the document ID.

Whenever RavenDB updates a document, it issues a set of DELETE statements for each of the relevant tables. For example, such a DELETE statement might look like the code in Listing 8.8.

Listing 8.8 *First step when updating a document is to delete its existing data*

```
DELETE FROM OrderLines WHERE OrderId = 'orders/830-A';
DELETE FROM Orders WHERE OrderId = 'orders/830-A';
```

As you can imagine, such statements are sent frequently during normal operations. That means that the relational database is going to be doing a lot of queries on the OrderId field (which is the one RavenDB is using to store the document ID). If the field in question isn't indexed, that can cause a *lot* of table scans, having a negative impact on the performance of the relational server and slow down the ETL process.

If you look at the tables creation script in Listing 8.6, you'll note that we explicitly handled that. In the Orders table, the OrderId field is marked as the primary key (which is clustered by default on SQL Server). This means that searches on that field are going to be very fast. With the OrderLines table, the situation is a bit more complex.

Here, we can't use the OrderId as a primary key because a single order has multiple lines. We define a throwaway primary key using identity, but we mark it as NONCLUSTERED and define a clustered indexed on the OrderId. This kind of setup is ideal for the RavenDB ETL process. All deletes and writes from RavenDB will always use a clustered index, and that minimizes the amount of operations that the relational database needs to perform.

> **Append-only systems**
>
> Sometimes you have a system that's built to never delete data – in fact, a regulator might require you to keep all data. In such cases, you can configure the SQL ETL process to use inserts only. This is configurable on a per-table basis. And it can also be a performance boost in some cases because we can directly insert the data without first running a set of DELETE statements to clean up the previous incarnation of the document we're sending over.

8.3.3. ERRORS AND TROUBLESHOOTING

As usual, we can't close a topic without discussing the error-handling strategy. Just like the RavenDB ETL process, the SQL ETL process is a task at the cluster level that's always assigned to a node. If the node in question fails, the cluster will assign the task to another node, which will proceed from the same place the previous node stopped at.

There are two more general classes of issues that need addressing, the first of which is when the relational database cannot be accessed, for whatever reason. If the relational database is down, too slow to respond or inaccessible, that would halt the entire ETL process and cause RavenDB to keep retrying the process until we've successfully connected to the relational database.

Another type of error is when we fail to complete the ETL process for a single statement. For example, in Listing 8.5, we're sending a Name field that is composed of the FirstName and

LastName of an employee. If the length of the employee's name in question exceeds 50 characters (as defined in the table creation script in Listing 8.4), we'll not be able to process that document. In such a case, when there is an error that pertains only to a particular document, RavenDB will *proceed* with the ETL process, rather than halting it entirely.

An alert will be raised and the admin will need to resolve the issue, either by limiting the size of the name we send or by extending the size of the column on the relational table. The example of the column length is a simple one and illustrates the issue quite nicely. There is a non-recoverable error in the document that prevents us from completing the ETL process for that particular document but doesn't halt it for others. Other examples include a violation of not-null constraints and violations of foreign keys.

Because they don't halt the ETL process, it can be easy to miss the fact that some documents haven't been sent over. RavenDB generates an alert when this type of error occurs. You can see such an error by going to one of the Employees documents and increasing the size of the FirstName field until it is over 50 characters and saving. RavenDB will attempt to send the update over but will fail, and you'll get the error shown in Figure 8.12.

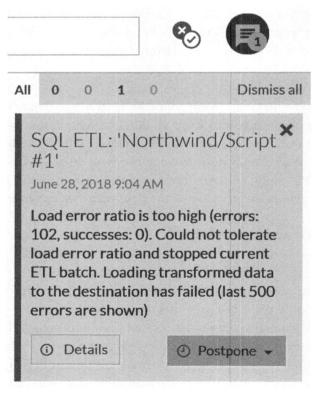

Figure 8.12. *Error in the SQL ETL process*

The error-handling strategy RavenDB uses in such a scenario is based on the assumption that as long as we're making progress, it's better to alert than to fail completely. But if the number of errors exceeds a certain threshold, we consider the entire ETL process to be failing and stop processing it until an admin tells us otherwise. The reasoning behind this behavior is that we want to ensure proper progress, but we don't want to limp along, failing on each and every document that we try to send.

Handling deletes in ETL

In both RavenDB ETL and SQL ETL, dealing with document changes is actually relatively easy. What's more complex is handling deletes. This is because we need to propagate the delete to the other side, but the delete is an absence of something. So how do we know what isn't there?

RavenDB needs to deal with this problem in many different forms. It's relevant for replication between databases (both inside the same cluster and external replication between clusters), for ETL processes, for indexes and even for backups. In all cases, this is handled via the tombstone concept. A tombstone is an entry that marks the absence of a document.

Usually you don't care about tombstones; they're an internal implementation detail. For ETL, what you need to know is that a deletion of a document will trigger the ETL process as usual, and it will remove the matching records on the destination side.

8.4. Summary

In this chapter, we went over the ETL processes supported by RavenDB. An ETL process allows you to take the documents residing in RavenDB and send them over to another location. This can be another RavenDB node or even a relational database. Along the way, you have the chance to mutate and filter the data, which opens up a lot of avenues for interesting use cases.

We looked at a few such examples. One was relying on RavenDB ETL to distribute a set of records to related services so they'll have their own copy of the data and can access it without making a cross-service call. In this case, the ETL process is part and parcel of the service public interface and needs to be treated as such. Another option is to provide partial views of the data. Access to production-grade data can be given to developers without allowing them to be exposed to details that should remain private, for example. We also looked at the reversed example, seeing how we can send data from multiple locations (the point-of-sales systems) to a central server that will aggregate all that data.

RavenDB also supports automatic ETL processes to a relational database. You can use scripts to decide how RavenDB will transform the document model into the table model, including non-trivial logic. This allows you to use RavenDB in a number of interesting ways:

- As an OLTP database while your reports are handled by the ETL target
- As a cache, for both reads and writes, with RavenDB sending updates to the back-end relational database.
- As part of a migration strategy, where you move different segments of your applications to RavenDB while others continue to operate with no change.

We looked at some of the details of the ETL processes: how they handle failure and recovery and what kind of response you should expect from them. With ETL processes between RavenDB instances, you get failover on both the source and destination, with each cluster being able to route the ETL process to the right location even if some of the nodes have failed. With SQL ETL, a RavenDB node going down will cause the cluster to move the task to another node, while a problem with the relational database will halt the ETL process until the remote database is up and running.

RavenDB employs a sophisticated error-handling strategy with regards to errors writing to relational databases, trying to figure out whether a particular error is transient and relevant for a single record or should impact the entire ETL process. In the first case, we'll alert you about the error and continue forward, while in the latter, after alerting, we'll stop the ETL process until an admin has resolved the issue.

We looked into some of the more common options for utilizing ETL processes in your system, and I tried giving you a taste of the kind of deployments and topologies that are involved. It's important to note that this is just to give you some initial ideas. The ETL features are quite powerful, and they can be used to great effect in your environment. I encourage you to think about them not just as a feature to be used in the tactical sense but how they play in the grand architecture of your system.

In the next part of the book, we're going to start on an exciting topic: queries and indexes in RavenDB. This has been a long time coming, and I'm almost more excited than you are at this point.

III. Querying and Indexing in RavenDB

We are pretty far into this book, but we haven't yet really talked about one of the most important aspects of a database: queries. We've mentioned queries in passing in previous chapters, but we've been focused on other details.

This is because as important as querying is, getting your data model right and understanding the distributed nature of RavenDB is of paramount importance for a successful system. These are often somewhat amorphous topics that are quite hard to relate to, whereas queries are much easier to talk about, primarily because it is so very easy to look at a query and then look at its results.

This book is meant to give you an *in-depth* view of how RavenDB is working, so we'll start by actually looking into the query engine and how RavenDB processes queries. We'll dig into the query optimizer and the index generation process, as well as how queries are handled, optimized, executed and sent to clients. These details are important if you're going to make the most of your queries, so I'm going to go through all them before actually diving into what you can do with queries in RavenDB.

I suggest at least skimming the next chapter (which talks about the RavenDB query engine) before heading into the one after (which teaches you how to actually query). This is especially important for those trying to analyze the behavior of RavenDB or find a good way to handle a specific scenario.

Personally, I consider this kind of discussion fascinating, but I realize that I might be in the minority here. I expect that most readers will have a lot more fun when we get to actually running queries. RavenDB has a powerful query language and some unique features around querying, indexing and managing your data that make it easier to find exactly what you want and shape it just the right way. MapReduce indexes allow you to perform aggregation queries with very little cost, regardless of the data size.

Advanced features such as facets allow to slice and dice the data as you show it to the user, and suggestions allow you to correct the user if they are searching for something that isn't quite right. RavenDB also allows you to perform full text queries on the cheap, execute geo spatial searches and gain fine-grained control over indexed data.

After talking about the query engine, we are going to tackle simple queries using the RavenDB query language to get you familiarized with the way queries work in RavenDB. Next, we are going to look into some of the more advanced features, such as full text search and various querying options.

We are going to discuss how to use RQL for projections and transformation of the data on the server to select just what you are going to get from the query. This allows you to get exactly what you need with very little effort, reducing the number of remote operations you have to make.

Following all of that, we are going to dive directly into *how* RavenDB indexes data, how you can gain control over that and when it makes sense to do so. The layered design of RavenDB also shows itself with indexing and querying; you have several levels you can plug yourself into, depending on exactly what you need.

Here we'll also discuss how you can use patching and queries together to update your documents en masse, migrate between versions and perform operational tasks such as correcting data or adding new behavior to the system.

We'll tie it all together with a discussion of how you can use these features in your application to get the most out of your data. Simply knowing that specific features are possible isn't enough; you have to consider what will happen when you start using several of these features at all the same time, taking you several levels higher in one shot.

This part of the book targets developers using RavenDB and operations teams supporting RavenDB-based systems, whether from inside your applications or while you are trawling the data to figure out what's going on in there.

9. Querying in RavenDB

Queries in RavenDB use a SQL-like language called "RavenDB Query Language,"[1] hence-forth known as RQL.[2]

You've already run into the RavenDB Query Language when using subscriptions, even if I didn't explicitly call it out as such. Both subscriptions and queries use RQL, although there are a few differences between the two supported options. The idea with RQL is to directly expose the inner workings of the RavenDB query pipeline in a way that won't overwhelm users.

If you're interested in a simple listing of query capabilities and how to do certain queries, head over to the online documentation, where all of that information is found. I find it incredibly boring to list all that stuff. So instead, we'll cover the material by examining it in a way that gives you insight into not only how to query RavenDB but also what RavenDB actually needs to do to answer the query.

> **Where is the code?**
> This chapter is going to focus solely on the query behavior of RavenDB. As such, we'll be working in the Studio, generating queries and looking at documents. We'll look at code to consume such queries from the client API in later chapters.

Here, we'll first take a brief look at how RavenDB is processing queries. Then we'll get started on actually *running* queries. We'll start from the simplest scenarios and explore all the nooks and crannies of what you can do with RavenDB queries. And the place to start is with the query optimizer.

---

1   Aren't you surprised?
2   Pronounced "Rachel," like my wife, and because it's funny.

9.1. The query optimizer

When a query hits a RavenDB instance, the very first thing that happens is that it will be analyzed by the query optimizer. The role of the query optimizer is to determine what indexes should be used by this particular query. This is pretty much par for the course for databases. However, with RavenDB, there are two types of queries. You may have a dynamic query, such as `from Orders where ...`, which gives the query optimizer full freedom with regards to which index that query will use. Alternatively, a query can specify a specific index to be used, such as `from index "Orders/ByCompany" where ...`, which instructs RavenDB to use the `Orders/ByCompany` index.

> **Queries are always going to use an index**
>
> You might have noticed that we're only talking about the selection of the index to use. While with other databases, the query optimizer may fail to find a suitable index and fall back into querying using a full scan, RavenDB doesn't include support for full scans, and that's by design.
>
> Queries in RavenDB are fast, and they will always use an index. Using full scans is excellent for when the size of your data is very small, but as it starts to grow, you're going to experience ever-increasing query times. In contrast, RavenDB queries always use an index and can return results with the same speed regardless of the size of the data.

What happens when the query optimizer is unable to find an index that can satisfy this query? Instead of scanning all of the documents, inspecting each one in turn and including it in the query or discarding it as an unsuccessful match, the query optimizer takes a different route. It will *create* an index for this query, on the fly.

If you're familiar with relational databases, you might want to take a deep breath and check your pulse. Adding an index to a relational database in production is fraught with danger. It *is* possible, but it needs to be handled carefully. In contrast, RavenDB indexes won't lock the data, and they're designed to not consume all the system resources while they're running. This means adding a new index isn't the world-shattering spectacle that you might be used to. In RavenDB, it's such a routine event that we let the query optimizer run it on its own, as needed.

Now, creating an index per query is going to result in quite a few indexes in your database, which is still not a great idea. It's a good thing the query optimizer doesn't do that. Instead, when it gets a query, the optimizer analyzes the query and sees what index can answer it. If there isn't one, the query optimizer creates an index that can answer this query and *all previous queries* on that collection.

Indexing in RavenDB is a background operation, which means the new query will be waiting for the index to complete indexing (or timeout). But at the same time, queries that can be answered using the existing indexes will proceed normally using these indexes. When the new index has caught up, RavenDB will clean up all the old indexes that are now superseded by the new one.

In short, over time, the query optimizer will analyze the set of queries you make to your database and will generate the optimal set of indexes to answer those queries. Changes in your queries will also trigger a change in the indexes on your database as it adjusts to the new requirements.

Practically speaking, this means that deploying a new version of your application won't invalidate all the hard work the DBA has put in to make sure all the queries are optimized.

> **Learning on the side**
>
> You don't have to do the new version adjustment on the production system. You can run the new version of your system on a test instance of RavenDB and let it learn what kind of queries will be performed. Then, you can export that knowledge into the production system during a quiet time, so by the time the new system is actually deployed, the database is already familiar and ready for the new workload.

Let's get started with actual queries. In the Studio, create a new database. Go to `Settings`, then to `Create Sample Data`, and click the big `Create` button. This will create a sample database (the Northwind online shop data) that we can query. Now, go to `Indexes` and then `List of Indexes`. You'll note that there are three indexes defined in the sample database. We're going to switch back and forth between `List of Indexes` and `Query` quite often in the instructions that follow, so you might want to open the `Query` in a separate tab and switch between the two.

Go to `Query` and issue the following query:

```
from Employees
```

You'll get a list of employees in the Studio, which you can inspect. You can view the full document JSON by clicking on the eye icon next to each document. If you look at the list of indexes, you'll see that no new index was created, even though there are no existing indexes on the `Employees` collection. This is because there isn't any filtering used in this query, so the query optimizer can just use the raw collection documents as the source for this query – no need to do any work.

The same is true for querying by document ID or IDs, as you can see in Listing 9.1. The query optimizer doesn't need an index to handle these queries. It can answer them directly.

Listing 9.1 *Querying based on the document ID will not create an index*

```
from Employees
where id() = 'employees/1-A'

from Employees
where id() in ('employees/1-A','employees/2-A')
```

However, what happens when we start querying using the data itself? You can see the result in Figure 9.1. In particular, you'll note that RavenDB reports that this query used the `Auto/Employees/ByFirstName` index.

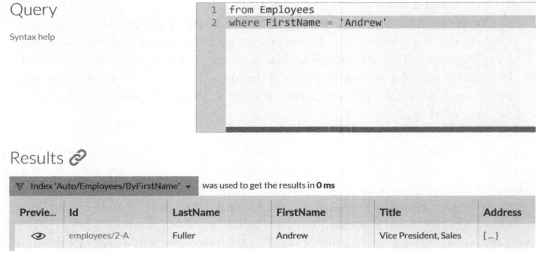

Figure 9.1. *RQL query for employees named Andrew*

Switching over to the indexes listing will show you that, indeed, a new auto index was created to answer these kinds of queries. Let's test this further and query by *last* name now, using the following:

```
from Employees where LastName = 'Fuller'
```

You can see the index that was created as a result of running this query in Figure 9.2.

The query optimizer has detected that there's no index for this query, looked at the previous history of queries on the `Employees` collection and created an index that can satisfy all such queries in the future. If you were fast enough, you might have managed to catch the `Auto/Employees/ByFirstName` index disappearing as it was superseded by the new index.

Employees

Figure 9.2. *The merged auto index can answer queries by first name or last name or both*

Now that you've experienced the query optimizer firsthand, let's give it a bit of a workout, shall we? Let's see what kind of queries we can do with RavenDB.

9.2. The RavenDB Query Language

We decided to require that all queries must always use an index, and that decision has a few interesting results. It means that queries tend to be *really* fast because there's always an index backing the query and you don't need to go through full scans. Another aspect of this decision is that RavenDB only supports query operations that *can* be answered quickly using an index. For example, consider the following query:

```
from Employees where FirstName = 'Andrew'
```

This kind of query is easy to answer using an index that has indexed the FirstName field because we can find the Andrew entry and get all the documents that have this value. However, a query like the following is not permitted:

```
from Employees where years(now() - Birthday) > 18
```

This query would require RavenDB to perform computation during execution, forcing us to do a full scan of the results and evaluate each one in turn. That isn't a good idea if you want fast queries, and RavenDB simply does not allow them. You can rewrite the previous query to efficiently use the index by slightly modifying what you're searching for:

```
from Employees where Birthday < $eighteenYearsAgo
```

The $eighteenYearsAgo variable would be set for the proper time, and that would allow the database to find the results by merely seeking in the index and returning all the results smaller than the given date. That's cheap to do, and it's the proper way to run such queries. In general, you can usually do a straightforward translation between queries that require computations and queries that don't, as above. Sometimes you can't just modify the query. You need to tell RavenDB it needs to do some computation during the indexing process. We'll see how that's done in Chapter 10.

Queries can also use more then a single field, as you can see in Listing 9.2.

Listing 9.2 *Querying over several fields at the same time*

```
from Employees
where (FirstName = 'Andrew' or LastName = 'Callahan')
and Address.Country = 'USA'
```

Using the sample data set, this should give two results, as shown in Figure 9.3. In that figure, you can also see some of the options available to inspect the index behavior. Viewing the index definition will tell you what is indexed and how. And the indexing performance statistics will give you all the details about the costs of indexing, broken down by step and action. This is very important if you're trying to understand what is consuming system resources, but that will be covered in the next part of the book, discussing production deployments and how to monitor and manage RavenDB in production.

Figure 9.3. *Available operations for inspecting the index state*

Far more important for us at this point is the View index terms page, which exposes the internal index structure. This is helpful when you need to understand how RavenDB is processing a query. If you click the View index terms link, you'll be taken to the index terms page, where you'll see the index fields. Clicking this will show you what was actually indexed, as illustrated in Figure 9.4.

Why is this so important? Even though Figure 9.4 doesn't show all the values, it shows enough to explain how RavenDB will actually process the query. The first thing to understand is that RavenDB is going to treat each field in the query separately. The query is broken into three clauses, and you can see the result of each in Table 9.1.

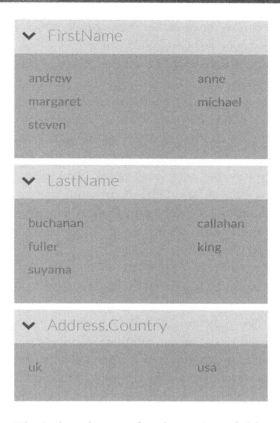

Figure 9.4. *The indexed terms for the various fields in the index*

Table 9.1. *Query clauses and their individual results*

Query	Results
FirstName = 'Andrew'	employees/2-A
LastName = 'Callahan'	employees/8-A
Address.Country = 'USA'	employees/1-A, employees/2-A, employees/3-A, employees/4-A, employees/8-A

The reason that RavenDB deals with each field separately is because it stores the indexed data for each field independently. This allows us a lot more freedom at query time, at the expense of having to do a bit more work.

RavenDB's indexes aren't single-purpose

If you're familiar with common indexing techniques in databases, you know there's a major importance to the order of the fields in the index. The simplest example I can think of is the phone book, which is basically an index to search for people by "LastName, FirstName."

If you have both a first and last name, then the phone book is easy to search. If you need to search just by last name, the phone book is still useful. If you only have a first name, however, the phone book is basically useless. You'll have to go through the entire thing to find any results.

In the same way, indexes that mash all fields together into a single key and then allow searching on the result are very efficient in answering that particular kind of query, but they can't really be used for anything else. With RavenDB, we index each field independently and merge the results at query time. That means that our indexes can be used in a more versatile manner, and they're able to answer a much wider range of queries at a small cost of additional work to merge them at query time.

To answer the query in Listing 9.2, RavenDB will find the matching documents for each of the clauses, as shown in Table 9.1. At that point, we can use set operations to find the final result of the query. We have an `OR` between the `FirstName` and `LastName` query, so the result of both clauses is the union of their results. In other words, the answer to `FirstName = 'Andrew' or LastName = 'Callahan'` is (employees/2-A, employees/8-A).

The next step in the query is to evaluate the `and` with the `Address.Country = 'USA'` clause. Because we have an `and` here, we'll use set intersection instead of a union (which we use for `or`). The result of that will be (employees/2-A, employees/8-A), which appear on both sides of the `and`. Similarly, `and not` uses set difference.

The end result is that a single index in RavenDB is able to be used by far more types of queries than a similar index in a relational database. This is at the cost of doing set operations on queries that have multiple clauses. Since set operations are quite cheap and have been carefully optimized, that's a pretty good tradeoff to make.

9.2.1. OPERATIONS IN QUERIES

As I mentioned, queries in RavenDB do not allow computation. We saw some simple queries earlier using equality and range queries at a glance. In this section, I want to talk about what kinds of queries you can make in RavenDB and dig a bit into how they're actually implemented.

The standard query operations you would expect are here, of course, as well as a few more, as shown in Table 9.2.

Table 9.2. *Operators and methods that can be used in queries*

Operation	Operators / Methods
Equality	=, ==, !=, <>, IN, ALL IN
Range queries	>, <, >=, <=, BETWEEN

Operation	Operators / Methods
Text search	Exact, `StartsWith`, `EndsWith`, `Search`
Aggregation	Count, Sum, Avg
Spatial	`spatial.Contains`, `spatial.Within`, `spatial.Intersects`
Other	Exists, Lucene, Boost

9.2.1.1. Equality comparisons

The first and most obvious operators are equality comparisons ('=' or '=='). As you can imagine, these are the easiest ones for us to find since we can just check the index for the value we compare against. It is important to note that we only allow the comparison of fields against values or parameters. This kind of query is fine: where `FirstName = 'Andrew'` as well as this: where `FirstName = $name`. However, this is not allowed: where `FirstName = LastName`.

These type of queries count as computation during a query and can't be expressed directly in RQL. Don't worry – you can still make such queries, but you need to use a static index to do that. This will be discussed in Chapter 10, which is dedicated just to this topic.

Inequality queries are more interesting. Remember that RavenDB uses set operations to compute query results. A query such as where `FirstName != 'Andrew'` is actually translated to: where `exists(FirstName) and not FirstName = 'Andrew'`. In other words, you're saying, "Find all the documents that have a `FirstName` field and exclude all the documents where that `FirstName` is set to `'Andrew'`."

There's also `IN`, which can be used in queries such as where `Address.City IN ('London', 'New York')` – a shorter way to write where `Address.City = 'London' or Address.City = 'New York'`. However, `IN` also allows you to send an array argument and write the query simply as where `Address.City IN ($cities)`, which is quite nice. `ALL IN`, on the other hand, is a much stranger beast. Quite simply, if we used `ALL IN` instead of `IN`, the query it would match is where `Address.City = 'London' and Address.City = 'New York'`. In other words, it'll use and instead of or. This is a strange and seemingly useless feature. How can a value be equal to multiple different values?

The answer is that a single value can't, but an array most certainly can. Consider the document shown in Figure 9.5, with an array of territories. We can use `ALL IN` in our query to find all the regions that have multiple territories in them, like so: from Regions where `Territories[].Name ALL IN ('Wilton', 'Neward')`

This query shows two new features. First, we have `ALL IN`, which shows how we can match multiple values against an array. A common usage of this feature is to filter documents by tags. The user can select what tags they're interested in, and you use `ALL IN` to find all the documents that match the requested tags.

The second new feature is the usage of the `Territories[].Name` path and, in particular, the use of `[]` in the path. Within RQL, the use of the `[]` suffix in a property indicates that this is an array and the rest of the expression is nested into the values of the array. This is useful both in the `where` clause and when doing projections using `select`, as we'll see later in this chapter.

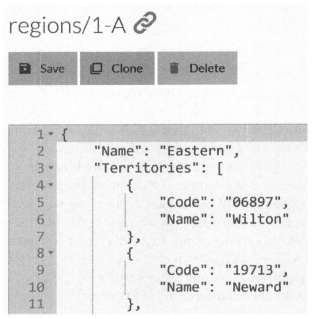

Figure 9.5. *The* `regions/1-A` *document contains an array of* `Territories`

9.2.1.2. Range queries

For range queries, things like > or <= are fairly self explanatory, with BETWEEN as a nicer mechanism for actually querying over a specific range. BETWEEN is inclusive on the low and high ends. In other words, consider the query in Listing 9.3.

Listing 9.3 *Querying date ranges using BETWEEN*

```
from Employees
where HiredAt.Year BETWEEN 1992 AND 1994
```

The results of the query in Listing 9.3 will include employees hired in 1992, 1993 and 1994. We could have also written the same query with string matches, as shown in Listing 9.4.

Listing 9.4 *Querying date ranges using BETWEEN with string prefixes*

```
from Employees
where HiredAt BETWEEN '1992' AND '1995'
```

The query in Listing 9.4 will also match all the employees hired in 1992, 1993 and 1994. But why? It's because of a minor trick we use here. The actual date format used by RavenDB is ISO 8601, so technically speaking, the query in Listing 9.4 is supposed to look like this:

```
HiredAt BETWEEN '1992-01-01T00:00:00.0000000'
AND '1995-01-01T00:00:00.0000000'
```

In practice, RavenDB considers such queries as string operations and allows us to do the BETWEEN operation using just the prefix.

This is because of the way RavenDB processes range queries. For non-numeric values, range queries use lexical comparisons, which means that just specifying the prefix is enough for us to get the required results. That's why RavenDB uses ISO 8601 dates. They sort lexically, which makes things easier all around at querying time.

For numeric values, we use the actual number, of course. That too, however, has some details you should be familiar with. When RavenDB indexes a numeric value, it will actually index that value multiple times: once as a string, which allows it to take part in lexical comparisons, and once as a numeric value. Actually, it's even more complex than that. The problem is that when we deal with computers, defining a number is actually a bit complex.

> **Range queries on mixed numeric types**
>
> If you use the wrong numeric type when querying, you'll encounter an interesting pitfall. For example, consider the products/68-A document in the sample dataset. Its PricePerUnit is set to 12.5; yet if we query for from Products where PricePerUnit > 12 and PricePerUnit < 13, RavenDB finds no results.
>
> The problem is that we're using an int64 with a range query, but PricePerUnit is actually a double. In this case, RavenDB indexed the PricePerUnit field as both double and int64. However, when indexing the 12.5 value as int64, the value was naturally truncated to 12, and the query clearly states that we want to search for values greater than 12, so RavenDB skips it.
>
> A small change to the query,
> from Products where PricePerUnit > 12.0 and PricePerUnit < 13.0
>   will fix this issue.

RavenDB supports two numeric types: 64-bit integers and IEEE 754 double-precision floating-points. When RavenDB indexes a numeric field, it actually indexes it three times: once as a string, once as a double and once as an int64. And it allows you to query over all of them without really caring what you use to find your results.

9.2.1.3. Full text searching

So far, we've looked at querying the data exactly as it is. But what would happen if we ran the following query?

```
from Employees where FirstName = 'ANDREW'
```

Unlike the previous times we ran this query, now the FirstName is using a different case than the value of the field in the document. But we'd still get the expected result. Queries that require you to match case have their place, but they tend to be quite frustrating for users. So RavenDB defaults to using case-insensitive matching in queries.

On the other hand, you could have written the query as shown in Listing 9.5 and found only the results that match the value and the casing used.

Listing 9.5 *Case sensitive queries using the exact() method*

```
from Employees
where exact(FirstName = 'Andrew')
```

Within the scope of the exact, you'll find that all comparisons are using case-sensitive matches. This can be useful if you're comparing BASE64 encoded strings that are case sensitive, but it's rarely useful otherwise.

By default, queries in RavenDB are case insensitive, which helps a lot. But what happens when we need more than a match? Well, we can use StartsWith and EndsWith to deal with such queries. Consider the following query:

```
from Employees where StartsWith(FirstName, 'An')
```

This will find all the employees whose names start with 'An'. The same can be done with where EndsWith(LastName, 'er') for the other side.

Note that queries using StartsWith can use the index efficiently to perform prefix search, but EndsWith is something that will cause RavenDB to perform a full index scan. As such, EndsWith isn't recommended for general use. If you really need this feature, you can use a static index to index the reverse of the field you're searching on and use StartsWith, which will be much faster.

Of more interest to us is the ability to perform full text searches on the data. Full text search allows us to search for a particular term (or terms) in a set of documents and find results without having an exact match. For example, examine Figure 9.6, where we're searching for a company that has the word 'stop' in its name.

Query

Syntax help

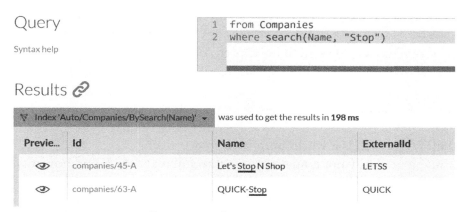

```
1  from Companies
2  where search(Name, "Stop")
```

Results 🔗

Index 'Auto/Companies/BySearch(Name)' ▾   was used to get the results in **198 ms**

Previe...	Id	Name	ExternalId
👁	companies/45-A	Let's Stop N Shop	LETSS
👁	companies/63-A	QUICK-Stop	QUICK

Figure 9.6. *Full text search queries on companies' name*

The result of this query is that we're able to find two results. What makes this interesting is that, unlike the EndsWith case, RavenDB didn't have to go through the entire result set. Let's go into the terms for the Auto/Companies/BySearch(Name) index and see how this works.

We have two fields indexed here. The first is Name, and if you click on that, you'll see 91 results – one for each of the companies we have in the sample dataset. The other one is named search(Name) and is far more interesting. Clicking on it shows 223 results, and the terms that are indexed are *not* the names of the companies. Figure 9.7 shows a comparison of the two fields.

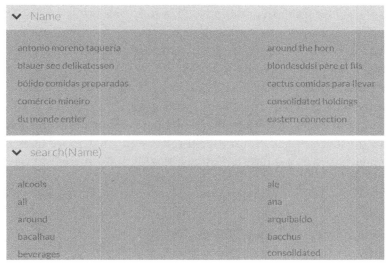

Figure 9.7. *List of indexed terms for Name and search(Name) fields*

When we do a simple equality query, such as where Name = 'Consolidated Holdings', it's easy to understand how the database will execute this query. The Name field's terms are sorted, and we can do a binary search on the data to find all the documents whose name is equal to "Consolidated Holdings". But what happens when we query using search(Name)?

The answer is in the way RavenDB indexes the data. Instead of indexing the Name field as a single value, RavenDB will break it into separate tokens, which you can see in Figure 9.7. This means that we can search for individual words inside the terms. We search not the full field but rather the indexed tokens, and from there, we get to the matching documents.

> **Full text search is a world unto itself**
>
> I'm intentionally not going too deep into full text search and how it works. If you're interested in learning more about full text search, and I personally find the topic fascinating, I recommend reading Lucene in Action and Managing Gigabytes. They're both good books that can give you insight into how full text search works. Lucene in Action will give you a practical overview. Managing Gigabytes is older (it was written about twenty years ago), but it's more digestible for handling the theory of full text search. These books aren't required reading for understanding how to use RavenDB, though.

Most of the work was already done during the indexing process, so queries tend to be very fast. Full text search in RavenDB also allows us to do some fascinating things. For example, consider the following query:

```
from Companies where search(Address, "London Sweden")
```

The Address property on the Companies documents isn't a simple string; it's actually a nested object. But RavenDB has no problems indexing the entire object. The results of this query include companies that reside in the city of London or in the country of Sweden. This powerful option allows you to search across complex objects easily.

It's worth noting the order in which the results have returned from the query. In order to better see that, we'll use a select clause (we'll talk about that more later in this chapter) to fetch just the information we're interested in. See Listing 9.6 for the full query.

Listing 9.6 *Full text search and projection on the relevant fields*

```
from Companies
where search(Address, "London Sweden")
select Address.City, Address.Country
```

The results of the query in Listing 9.6 are really interesting. First, we have six companies that are located in London. Then we have two that are based in Sweden. Here's the interesting part: this isn't accidental. RavenDB ranks the results based on their quality. A match on London would rank higher than a match on Sweden since London was the first term in the query. (Switch them around and see the change in results). This means the more relevant results are nearer to the top and more likely to be seen by a user.

9.2.1.4. Lucene

RavenDB uses the Apache Lucene library for indexing, which means that there's quite a bit of power packed behind these indexes. Lucene is a full text search library that can support complex queries and is considered to be the de facto leader in the area of search and indexing.

Unfortunately, Lucene is also temperamental. It's tricky to get quite right, and it's not known for its ease of use or robustness in production systems. Even still, this library is amazing, and whenever you run into search *anywhere*, it's a safe bet that Lucene is the core engine behind it. For that reason, it's common to consume Lucene using a solution that wraps and handles all of the details of managing it (such as Apache Solr or ElasticSearch).

In the case of RavenDB, a major factor in our Lucene usage is that we're able to have our storage engine (Voron) provide transactional guarantees, which means our Lucene indexes are also properly ACID and safe from corruption without us needing to sacrifice expected performance. In general, all the operational aspects of running Lucene indexes are handled for you, and they shouldn't really concern you. We'll discuss Lucene in more depth in Chapter 10. But for now, I want to focus on the querying capabilities that Lucene provides.

If you're familiar with Lucene, you might have noticed that RQL is nothing like the Lucene query syntax. This is intentional. Lucene queries only find matches, while all else, like sorting of projections, is handled via code. This makes it a great tool for finding information but a poor tool for actual queries. That said, you can use an RQL query and the Lucene method as an escape hatch to send queries directly to Lucene.

The following query uses the Lucene method to query with wildcards, which isn't supported by RavenDB.

```
from Companies where Lucene (ExternalId, "AL?K?")
```

There are some scenarios where this is required, particularly if you're upgrading an application from older versions of RavenDB, which exposed the Lucene syntax directly to users. But in general, RQL should be sufficient and is the recommended approach. Typically, you'd only use Lucene on static indexes where you have control over what fields are indexed.

> **Built-in methods in RQL are case insensitive**
>
> Built-in methods (such as the ones listed in Table 9.2) are case insensitive, and you can call where startsWith(Name, 'An') or where StartsWith(Name, 'AN') without issue. Note that field names are case sensitive, though.

Most of what you can do with Lucene is available natively in RQL. For example, we can use the Boost() method to change the way queries are evaluated. Consider the query in Listing 9.7, which expresses a fairly complex conditional and ranking requirement using Boost()

Listing 9.7 *Using boost to modify query results ranking*

```
from Companies
where Boost(Address.City = 'London', 3) or
      Boost(Address.City = 'Paris', 2) or
      Address.Country IN ('Germany', 'Sweden')
```

The query in Listing 9.7 will select companies based in London, Paris or anywhere in Germany or Sweden. The effect of Boost() on the results is that a document matching on London would be given a boost factor in the ranking. This means that the query in Listing 9.6 will first get results for London, then Paris and then Germany and Sweden.

This may seem silly, but there are many search scenarios where this can be a crucial feature. Consider searching on messages. A match on the Subject field is more important than matches on the Body field, but we want to get results from both.

An interesting issue with boosting is that it isn't quite as obvious as you may think. Consider the query in Listing 9.7. If we change the last clause to be Address.Country IN ('Germany', 'France'), we'll start getting Parisian companies first, even though the boost on London-based companies is higher. The reason for that is because the Parisian companies will have two matches to their names (both Paris and France) while the London companies will only have one. The results from Paris will be considered higher quality and be ranked first.

> **Exposing the raw score**
>
> The query result also includes the @index-score metadata property that exposes the scoring of each result. You can inspect this to figure out why the final sort order of a query is the way it is.

We could adjust that by increasing the boost factor for the London-based companies, but in more complex scenarios, it can be hard to figure out the appropriate ratios. In practice, when using such techniques, we aren't usually too concerned with absolute ordering. The expected consumer of these sorts of queries is the end user, who can scan and interpret the information as long as the ranking more or less makes sense.

9.2.2. PROJECTING RESULTS

We've looked into how to filter the results of a query, but so far, we've always pulled the full document back from the server. In many cases, this is what you want to do. In Chapter 3, we spent a lot of time discussing how you should think about documents. One element of the trifecta of document modeling (cohesive, coherent and isolated) is the notion that a document is cohesive. From a modeling perspective, it doesn't usually make sense to just grab some pieces of data from a document without having it all there.

At least, it doesn't make sense until you realize that you often need to *display* the data to the user, picking and choosing what will be shown. For example, an order without its order lines may not be very meaningful in a business sense to the user. But knowing that an order was made on December 17th is probably enough information to recall they required expedited shipping on their last-minute holiday shopping to get it in time.

In this section, we're going to take documents apart and then mash them together. In almost all cases, projection queries are used for either subscriptions or for feeding the data into some sort of a user interface. If you need to actually *work* with the data, it's generally better to get the full document from the server and use that. It's also important to remember that on the client side, projections are *not* tracked by the session, and modifications to a projection will not modify the document when SaveChanges is called.

The simplest query projection can be seen in Listing 9.8.

Listing 9.8 *Projecting only some parts of the document*

```
from Companies
select Name, Address.City, Address.Country as Country
```

The query in Listing 9.8 will produce the results with three fields: Name, Address.City and Country. A single simple projection of fields and the use of aliases from this query is demonstrated in Figure 9.8. You can see that we didn't specify an alias for the Address.City field and that the full name was used in the resulting projection. On the other hand, the use of aliases, as we can see in the case of Country, allows us to control the name of the field that would be returned.

```
{
    "Name": "Alfreds Futterkiste",
    "Address.City": "Berlin",
    "Country": "Germany",
    "@metadata": {
        "@id": "companies/1-A",
        "@last-modified": "2018-06-22T10:21:47.5510292Z",
        "@change-vector": "A:2-CAEHH/djXUuc1inHWX8vIQ",
        "@projection": true,
        "@index-score": 0
    }
}
```

Figure 9.8. *A single document result in a projection query*

In the case of the query in Listing 9.8, we're only projecting simple fields, but RQL is capable of much more. Listing 9.9 has a more complex projection example, projecting both objects and arrays.

Listing 9.9 *Projecting arrays and objects using RQL*

```
from Orders
select ShipTo, Lines[].ProductName as Products
```

A single projection from the results of the query in Listing 9.8 is shown in Figure 9.9. This query is a lot more fun. You can see that there's no need to flatten out the query and that we can send complex results back. The projection of `Lines[].ProductName` is more interesting. Not only are we projecting an array, but we're actually projecting a *single* value from the array back to the user. I don't think that I need to expand on how powerful such a feature can be.

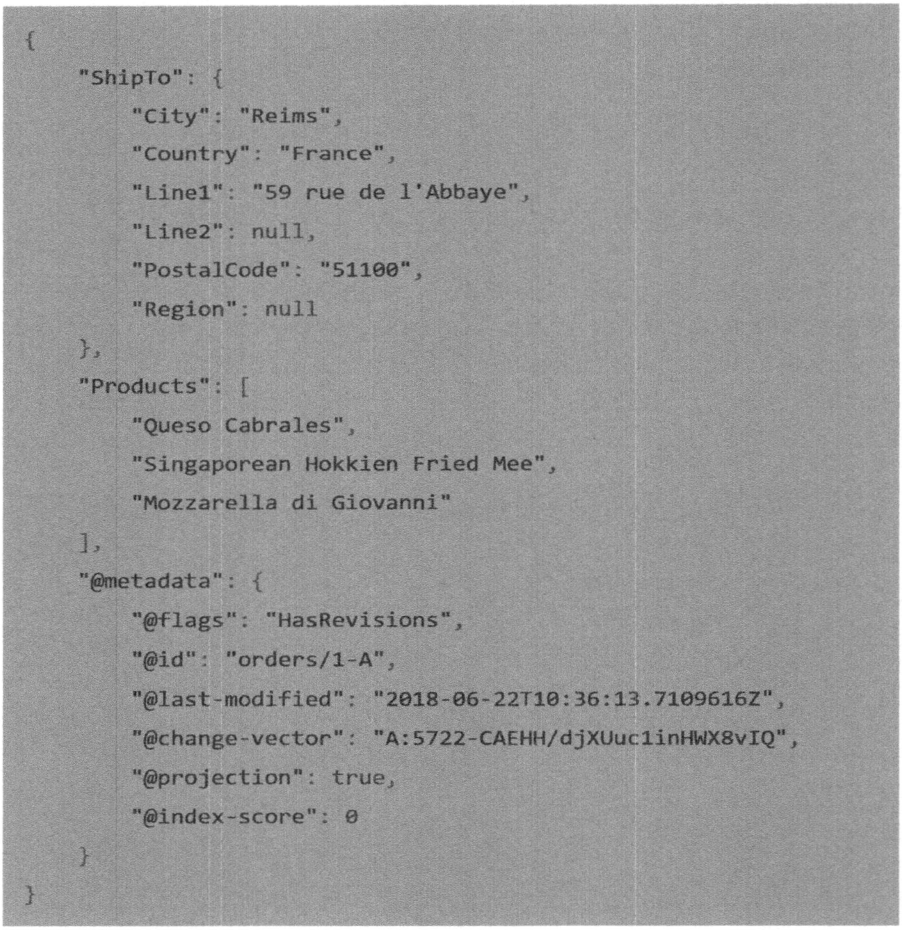

```json
{
    "ShipTo": {
        "City": "Reims",
        "Country": "France",
        "Line1": "59 rue de l'Abbaye",
        "Line2": null,
        "PostalCode": "51100",
        "Region": null
    },
    "Products": [
        "Queso Cabrales",
        "Singaporean Hokkien Fried Mee",
        "Mozzarella di Giovanni"
    ],
    "@metadata": {
        "@flags": "HasRevisions",
        "@id": "orders/1-A",
        "@last-modified": "2018-06-22T10:36:13.7109616Z",
        "@change-vector": "A:5722-CAEHH/djXUuc1inHWX8vIQ",
        "@projection": true,
        "@index-score": 0
    }
}
```

Figure 9.9. *Projecting array and complex object from a document*

The `select` clause listing is an easy, familiar way to get a specific piece of data out. But it only lets us select what we're getting back and rename it using aliases. RavenDB is a JSON database, and as smart as the `select` is, it's best for dealing with mostly flat data. That's why we have the ability to project object literals.

9.2.2.1. *Projecting with object literals*

SQL was meant to handle tabular data. As such, it's great in *expressing* tabular data but not so great when we need to work with anything but the most trivial of documents. With RQL, you aren't limited to simply selecting the flat list of properties from the document. You can also project a complex result with the object literal syntax. Let's look at a simple example of using object literals to query in Listing 9.10.

Listing 9.10 *RQL projection using object literal syntax*

```
from Orders as o
select {
    Country: o.ShipTo.Country,
    FirstProduct: o.Lines[0].ProductName,
    LastProduct:  o.Lines[o.Lines.length - 1].ProductName,
}
```

The result of the query in Listing 9.10 for document `orders/1-A` is shown in Listing 9.11. As you can see, we're able to project the data out not only using property paths but also using complex expression, pulling the first and last products from the order.

> **Alias is required with the object literal syntax**
>
> The query in Listing 9.10 is using `from Orders as o`, defining the alias o for the `Orders` collection. This is required when using the object literal syntax since we need to know the root object the expression starts from.

Listing 9.11 *Result of projection from Listing 9.10*

```
{
    "Country": "France",
    "FirstProduct": "Queso Cabrales",
    "LastProduct": "Mozzarella di Giovanni",
    "@metadata": {
        "@id": "orders/1-A",
    }
}
```

The key to the object literal syntax is that this isn't a JSON expression; it's a JavaScript object literal, and any valid JavaScript expression is going to work. For example, let's take a look at Listing 9.12, which shows a slightly more complex example.

Listing 9.12 *Projections of JavaScript metohd calls*

```
from Orders as o
select {
    Year: new Date(o.ShippedAt).getFullYear(),
    Id: id(o)
}
```

Because JSON doesn't have a way to express dates natively, we can use the `new Date()` `.getFullYear()` to handle date parsing and extracting of the year portion of the date. You can see the projection of the document identifier as well. In addition to the usual JavaScript methods, you also have access to functions defined by RavenDB itself, such as `id`. A full list of the functions available for your use can be found in RavenDB's online documentation.

We'll look at one final example of the kind of projections you can make with the object literal syntax, mostly because I think it's a beautiful example of what you can do. Listing 9.13 shows a query that will get the two most expensive products and the total value of the order.

Listing 9.13 *Making non trival calculations in projections*

```
from Orders as o
select {
    TopProducts: o.Lines
        .sort((a, b) =>
            (b.PricePerUnit * b.Quantity) -
                (a.PricePerUnit * a.Quantity))
        .map(x => x.ProductName)
        .slice(0, 2),
    Total: o.Lines.reduce(
        (acc, l) => acc += l.PricePerUnit * l.Quantity, 0)
}
```

There's a lot going on in this small bit of code, so let's break it into its individual pieces. First, we use the object literal syntax and define two properties that we'll return. For `TopProducts`, we sort the lines by the `PricePerUnit * Quantity` in descending order, grabbing just the names, and then take the first two items. For `Total`, we simply use the JavaScript `reduce` method to calculate the total price on the order during the query. If you're familiar with JavaScript, this is nothing special, but it expresses a lot of the power available to you when you project using the object literal syntax.

The object literal syntax is quite flexible, but it has a few limits. In particular, take a look at Listing 9.13 and how we compute the cost of a particular product by using the following formula: `l.PricePerUnit * l.Quantity`. However, I forgot to also include the discount that may be applied here. The formula for the discount is simple. The new way to compute the price of a product is simply `l.PricePerUnit * l.Quantity * (1 -l.Discount)`. That's easy enough, but it repeats three times in Listing 9.13, making it a perfect example of a violation of the "don't repeat yourself" principle. If we were writing code using any standard programming language, we would wrap this in a function call to make it easier to understand and so that we would only need to change it in a single location. Luckily, RQL also has such a provision, and it allows you to define functions.

Listing 9.14 shows how we can use the function declaration to properly compute the product price while avoiding repetition.

Listing 9.14 *Using functions to consolidate logic*

```
declare function lineItemPrice(l) {
    return l.PricePerUnit * l.Quantity * (1 - l.Discount);
}

from Orders as o
select {
    TopProducts: o.Lines
        .sort((a, b) => lineItemPrice(b) - lineItemPrice(a))
        .map(x => x.ProductName)
        .slice(0, 2),
    Total: o.Lines.reduce((acc, l) => acc + lineItemPrice(l), 0)
}
```

In Listing 9.14, we first declared the function `lineItemPrice`. This took the line item and computed the total amount you would pay for it. Once this was declared, you could then use the function inside the object literal.

Declaring functions in queries

You can declare zero or more functions as part of the query, and they will be visible both to each other and to the object literal expression. Such functions can do anything you want, subject to the usual limits of projections. (You can't take too long to run since it will time out the query).

Inside the function, all the usual JavaScript rules apply, with the exception that we'll ignore missing properties by default. In other words, you can write code such as `l.Who.Is.There`, and instead of throwing a `TypeError`, the entire expression will be evaluated to `undefined`.

Declared functions can only be used from inside the object literal expression and are not available for the simple select expression syntax.

I'm sure you can imagine the kind of queries that declaring functions make possible. You can tailor the results of the query specifically to what you want, and you can do all that work on the server side without having to send a lot of data over the wire.

Projections are applied as the last stage in the query

It's important to understand that projections – either simple via select Name, Address.City, Address.Country as Country or more complex using the object literal syntax – are applied as the last stage in the query pipeline. In other words, they're applied after the query has been processed, filtered, sorted and paged. This means that the projection doesn't apply to all the documents in the database, only to the results that are actually returned.

This reduces the load on the server significantly since we can avoid doing work only to throw it out immediately after. And it also means that we can't do any filtering work as part of the projection. You can filter what will be returned but not which documents will be returned. That has already been determined earlier in the query pipeline.

Another consideration to take into account is the cost of running the projection. It's possible to make the projection query expensive to run, especially with object literal syntax and with method declarations that we'll soon explore. RavenDB has limits to the amount of time it will spend evaluating the projection, and exceeding these (quite generous) limits will fail the query.

I want to emphasize that you shouldn't be reluctant to use projections or the object literal syntax in particular. This can significantly reduce the amount of data that's sent over the network, and it's usually preferred when you need to return a list of documents showing only partial data for display purposes.

In fact, there's one more way to project data from queries: using a function directly. This method is usually employed when you want to return objects with a different shape in the query. Before we see how this can be done, a word of caution; it's usually hard to deal with heterogeneous query results, with each object being a potentially different shape. There are some cases where this is exactly what you want, but it usually complicates the client code and shouldn't be overused.

Listing 9.15 shows how we can project a method directly to the client, doing what's probably the world's most ridiculous localization effort.

Listing 9.15 *Returning differently shaped results based on the document data*

```
declare function localizedResults(c) {
    switch(c.Address.Country)
    {
        case "France":
            return { Nom: c.Name };
        case "Brazil":
            return { Nome: c.Name };
        default:
            return { Name: c.Name };
    }
}
from Companies as c
where id() in ('companies/15-A', 'companies/14-A', 'companies/9-A')
select localizedResults(c)
```

The result of this query can be seen in Figure 9.10, where you can see that different documents have different shapes. I had a lot of fun writing the query in Listing 9.15, but I wouldn't want to have to deal with it in my code. It would probably be too confusing.

Id	Name	Nome	Nom
companies/14-A	Chop-suey Chinese		
companies/15-A		Comércio Mineiro	
companies/9-A			Bon app'

Figure 9.10. *RQL query results for the projecting via a method call*

To summarize projections, we have the following options available to us when we query RavenDB.

◆ Getting the whole document back. This can be done by omitting the select clause entirely or using select o or select *, with o being the root alias of the query.

♦ Projecting values from the document using simple select expressions, such as `select Name, Address.City, Address.Country as Country`. This allows us to control what's sent back and lets us rename fields. We can also project nested values and dig into arrays and objects, but this is intentionally made simple to ensure that we can process it quickly and efficiently.

♦ Projecting values from the document using object literal expression gives you far more power and flexibility. You can utilize JavaScript expressions to get the results just the way you want them. This includes doing computation on the returned result set and even declaring functions and doing more work inside the function to avoid repetition and to make it easy to build complex queries.

♦ Projection values as the result of a single method call in the select, such as `select localizedResults(c)`. In this case, the shape and structure that will be returned is completely up to you. You can even return `null` or `undefined` from the method call, and that will be sent to the client (where you'll need to be careful about handling it, of course).

Of the four options we have, you need to remember that only the first option will give you the full document back. In all other cases, you'll be returning a projection. This is important from the client side because the client API won't be tracking a projection, and changes to the projection will not be saved back to the server when you call `SaveChanges`.

Querying by ID

If you look at Listing 9.15, you'll see an interesting type of query. There, we're querying by document ID and specifying a projection. This may seem like a strange thing to do. Surely it'd be better to just get the documents directly if we know what their IDs are, no?

Querying by ID is handled differently. If the query optimizer can see that your query is using an ID, then instead of going through an index, it'll fetch the relevant documents directly using their IDs and pass them to the rest of the query for processing. This applies when you're querying by ID and don't have additional filters, sorting or the like that would require the use of an index.

This allows us to define projections on a single document (or a group of them) and use all the power of RQL projections to get back the results we want. For large documents, this can be significant savings in the amount of data that goes over the network. And that's without the server having to make any additional effort since this is an exception to the rule that queries without an index to cover them will have an index created for them. In this case, the query optimizer can use the internal storage indexes and avoid creating another one.

We looked into all the different ways we can project results from a document as part of a query, but there's still more we can do. We can use RQL to work with *multiple* documents. That's the topic of the next section.

9.2.3. LOADING AND INCLUDING RELATED DOCUMENTS

In general, queries in RavenDB apply only to a single document. That is, you can ask questions about a single document and not about other documents.

Querying on relations

The previous statement isn't quite true. You can actually query on related documents and even across heterogeneous document collections using RavenDB, but only when you're the one who's defining the index. We'll discuss static indexes in the next chapter, so I'll hold discussion of that until then.

In other words, you can query on every aspect of a document quite easily, but it's not trivial to query on related data. If you're used to SQL, then the simple answer is that RavenDB doesn't allow joins. Recall the three tenets of document design: coherent, cohesive and independent. With proper modeling, you shouldn't usually want to join. But RavenDB has ways to enable that scenario, and they're discussed in the next chapter.

That said, it can be very useful to grab some data from related documents during the query. Consider a query to show the list of recent orders. We can query it using `from Orders where Company = 'companies/1-A'`, and the result is shown in Figure 9.11.

Id	Company	Employee	OrderedAt
orders/396-A	companies/1-A	employees/6-A	1997-08-25T00:00:0...
orders/445-A	companies/1-A	employees/4-A	1997-10-03T00:00:0...
orders/455-A	companies/1-A	employees/4-A	1997-10-13T00:00:0...

Figure 9.11. *The results of simple query on orders*

As you can see in Figure 9.11, the output is the document. That document includes useful fields such as `Company` and `Employee`. This is great, but if we intend to show it to a user, showing `employees/6-A` is not considered a friendly act. We can ask RavenDB to include the related documents as well, as you can see in Listing 9.16.

Listing 9.16 *Including related documents in RQL*

```
from Orders
where Company = 'companies/1-A'
include Company, Employee
```

Figure 9.12 shows the output of this in the Studio, and you can see that we've gotten the company and the employees back from the query. We've already talked about the include feature in Chapter 4 at length. It allows us to ask RavenDB to send us related documents as well as the query results themselves, saving us the network roundtrip to fetch the additional information.

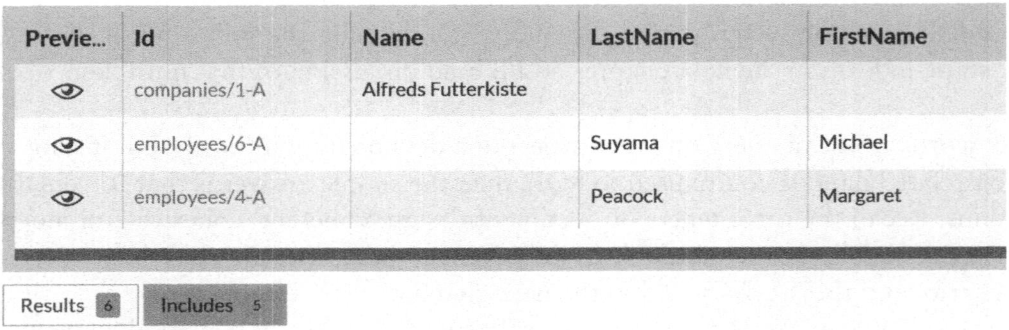

Previe...	Id	Name	LastName	FirstName
👁	companies/1-A	Alfreds Futterkiste		
👁	employees/6-A		Suyama	Michael
👁	employees/4-A		Peacock	Margaret

Results 6   Includes 5

Figure 9.12. *Viewing included results in the Studio*

Including related documents is very useful, but if we just intend to show the information to the user, sending the full documents back can be a waste. We can do better by using load. In Listing 9.17, you can see a small example of pulling data from multiple documents and returning that to the user.

Listing 9.17 *Using load to fetch data from related documents*

```
from Orders as o
where Company = 'companies/1-A'
load o.Company as c, o.Employee as e
select {
    CompanyName: c.Name,
    EmployeeName: e.FirstName + " " + e.LastName,
    ShippedAt: o.ShippedAt
}
```

It's important to remember that the load clause is not a join; it's applied *after* the query has already run and before we send the interim results to the projection for the final result. Thus, it can't be used to filter the results of the query by loading related documents and filtering on their properties. It also means that load doesn't impact the cost of the query, and the database will only need to handle a single page of results to send back to the client.

You can also use the load() method inside declared functions or inside the object literal. We could have skipped the load o.Company as c and used CompanyName: load(o.Company).Name instead and gotten the same results. Load is also supported for collections, as you can see in Listing 9.18.

Listing 9.18 *Loading data using arrays*

```
from Orders as o
where Company = 'companies/1-A'
load o.Employee as e, o.Lines[].Product as products[]
select {
    CompanyName: load(o.Company).Name,
    EmployeeName: e.FirstName + " " + e.LastName,
    ShippedAt: o.ShippedAt,
    Products: products
}
```

In Listing 9.18 we pull all the related products from the lines. Note that we indicate to RavenDB that the result is an array by using products[], but we use products in the object literal (since it's an array instance value there). The same would be the case for simple select. We don't need to specify the [] postfix for RavenDB to know that this is an array.

Loading documents in such a manner allows you to bring together a complete picture for the user. This is typically done as a way to feed the results directly from RavenDB to the UI, with minimal involvement of middleware between the UI and the results of the query. For includes, you're actually getting the real documents back. Modifications on them will be sent to the server when you call SaveChanges. But when you're using load, you'll typically get a projection back, which isn't tracked.

With load, you typically have fewer bytes going over the network, but sometimes it's easier to do certain things in your own code. Even though load and object literals allow you to shape your results in some pretty nifty ways, don't try to push too much into the database layer, especially if this is business logic. That road rarely leads to maintainable software systems.

9.2.4. SORTING QUERY RESULTS

All the queries we've made so far have neglected to specify the sort order. As such, the order in which results are returned isn't well defined. It'll usually be whatever RavenDB thinks is the most suitable match for the query. That works if you're using queries that match over complex conditionals, but it's usually a poor user experience if you query for the orders a user made in the past six months.

RQL supports the order by clause, which allows you to dictate how results are sorted. Take a look at Listing 9.19 for an example.

Listing 9.19 *Sorting by multiple fields in RQL*

```
from Employees
where Address.Country = 'USA'
order by FirstName asc, LastName asc
```

The query in Listing 9.19 reads like a typical SQL one, and that's by design. However, you need to be aware of a very important distinction. Consider the query in Listing 9.20.

Listing 9.20 *Sorting by multiple fields in RQL with different orders*

```
from Employees
where Address.Country = 'USA'
order by LastName asc, FirstName asc
```

The query in Listing 9.20 is very nearly the same exact query as the one in Listing 9.19. However, the sort order is different. Why does this matter? It matters because, in both cases, we used the same index: "Auto/Employees/ByAddress.CountryAndFirstNameAndLastName," in this case. This is one of those cases where you needed to have experienced the pain to understand why this is such an important detail.

Typically, databases will use an indexing format that allows the database to quickly answer specific order by clauses. Similar to the phone book we discussed earlier in the chapter, they can only be used for the purpose for which they were created. It's possible to use the phone book index to answer the query in Listing 9.20, but it isn't in Listing 9.19. RavenDB, however, doesn't use such single purpose indexes. It indexes each field independently. That means it's able to answer both queries (and any combination thereof) using a single index.

The more flexible index and sorting behavior makes little difference if the size of the data is small. But as the size of the data increases, this means that you can still offer flexible sorting to the users, while other databases will typically be forced to do full table scans.

Another important factor of sorting in RavenDB is that it's applied *after* the filters. In fact, the RQL syntax has been designed so each step in the query pipeline corresponds to its place in the query as you type it. You can see that, in the queries in Listing 9.19 and 9.20, the order by comes after the where clause. That's because we first filter the result, and then we sort them.

This is more flexible, but it has a downside. If you're querying over a large dataset without a filter and you apply sorting, then RavenDB needs to sort all of the results and give you back just the first few records. This is usually only a problem if your query has hundreds of thousands of results to sort through. In such cases, it's usually advisable to filter the query to reduce the number of results that RavenDB needs to sort.

You aren't limited to sorting by the fields on the document. You also have the following sorting options:

◆ `order by score()` – order the results by how closely they match the `where` clause (useful if you are using full text search or using `OR` in the `where` clause).
◆ `order by random()` – random order, useful for selecting a random result from the query.
◆ `order by spatial.distance()` – useful for spatial queries which will be discussed later in this chapter.
◆ `order by count()` / `order by sum()` – allows ordering the results of queries using `group by`, discussed later in this chapter.

The sort order can also be impacted by how you want RavenDB to sort the fields. For example, consider the following query: `from Products order by PricePerUnit desc`. If you run it, you'll get some peculiar results, as shown in Figure 9.13.

Id	Name	PricePerUnit
products/52-A	Filo Mix	7
products/18-A	Carnarvon Tigers	62,5
products/13-A	Konbu	6
products/59-A	Raclette Courdavault	55
products/51-A	Manjimup Dried Appl...	53

Figure 9.13. *Unexpected ordering with numeric order by*

The issue is that RavenDB doesn't know the type of the `PricePerUnit` field, and therefore it defaults to lexical ordering, which means that 7 will show before 62.5. In order to get the actual descending results from our `order by` clause, we need to let RavenDB know what kind of sorting we want to do. An example of how to do just that can be seen in Listing 9.21.

Listing 9.21 *Sorting by numeric data in RQL*

```
from Products
order by PricePerUnit as double desc
```

The `as double` in Listing 9.21 instructs RavenDB to sort the results as doubles. You can also use `as long` to specify that the data should be sorted as natural integers, truncating any fractional values. The way as long and as double work is they direct RavenDB to use a dedicated field with the numeric values in the index instead of using the string value for sorting. There's also the ability to sort using as alphanumeric, which will do exactly what you expect and apply alphanumeric sorting to the query.

** Deep paging is discouraged **

Sorting and paging usually go together. Paging is actually specified outside of RQL, so we won't be seeing it in this chapter. However, paging in RavenDB is pretty simple, in general. You specify the number of results you want and the number of results you want to skip. The first option, the number of results you want to get back, is obvious and easy for RavenDB to deal with. The second, not so much.

For example, if you want to get the first page, you specify start as 0 and pageSize as 10. If you want the second page, you specify that start is 10, and so on. This works well as long as the depth of your paging isn't too excessive. What do I mean by that?

If you expect to be issuing queries in which the start is very high (thousands or higher), you need to be aware that paging will happen during the sorting portion of processing the query. We'll get all the matching results for the query, sort them, and then select the relevant matches based on the page required.

However, the more deeply you page, the more work you force RavenDB to do. If you need to page deeply into a result set, it's typically much better to do the paging in the where clause. For example, if we were looking at recent orders for a customer and we expected customers to want to look at very old orders, we'd be better off specifying that the pages we show are actually dates. So the query will become where OrderedAt < $cutoffPoint. This will significantly reduce the amount of work required from RavenDB.

There isn't much more to say about sorting In RavenDB. It works pretty much as you would expect it to.

9.3. Spatial queries

Spatial searches allow you to search using geographical data. We'll explore them in more depth in Chapter 10, but we can do quite a lot with spatial queries without any special preparation. Spatial queries require that you have spatial data, of course, such as a lng/lat position on the globe. Luckily for us, the sample data set also contains the spatial location for many of the addresses in the database.

Spatial queries are expressed using the following basic spatial operations: spatial.within(), spatial.intersects(), spatial.contains() and spatial.disjoint(). You can read more about the kind of spatial queries that are supported by RavenDB in the online documentation. For now, let's have some fun. The spatial coordinates of the Seattle-Tacoma International Airport (SEA) are 47.448 latitude and -122.309 longitude. We can use that information to query for nearby employees that can pick you up if you come through the Seattle airport. Listing 9.22 shows just how to tickle RavenDB to divulge this information.

Listing 9.22 *Find all employees within 20 km from SEA airport*

```
from Employees
where spatial.within(
    spatial.point(Address.Location.Latitude,
      Address.Location.Longitude),
    spatial.circle(20, 47.448, -122.309, 'kilometers')
)
```

The query in Listing 9.22 results in two matches: Nancy and Andrew. It's pretty simple to understand what the query is doing, and I wish most spatial queries were that simple. Unfortunately, in the real world, we have to deal with much more complex systems. A good example of that would be the London Orbital motorway (M25). It's *sort of* a circle that surrounds London. I drew it out on a map as a polygon and then asked RavenDB to find all the employees that live within that area. You can see the polygon on a map in Figure 9.14.

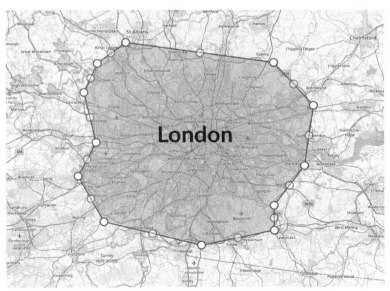

Figure 9.14. *Polygon for the London Orbital*

You can see how we query RavenDB using this polygon in Listing 9.23.

Listing 9.23 *Find all employees inside the London M25 motorway*

```
from Employees
where spatial.within(
    spatial.point(Address.Location.Latitude, Address.Location.Longitude),
    spatial.wkt("POLYGON((-0.38726806640625 51.72477396651261,
        0.1483154296875 51.67881439742299,0.2911376953125 51.579928527080114,
        0.2581787109375 51.439756376733676,0.1483154296875 51.347212267024645,
        0.1483154296875 51.288847685894844,-0.1153564453125 51.25448088572911,
        -0.4669189453125 51.3094554292733,-0.560302734375 51.41578143396663,
        -0.494384765625 51.494509016952534,-0.538330078125 51.61064031418932,
        -0.490264892578125 51.677111294565,-0.38726806640625 51.72477396651261
        ))")
)
```

The actual polygon in Listing 9.23 is unlikely to be a very accurate representation of the London Orbital (I drew it by hand, and quite roughly, too) but it's a good demonstration of RavenDB's spatial query capabilities. As it turns out, of all the employees in our dataset, only Steven lives in London.

I find that pretty much the only way to reason about spatial queries is to draw them out on a map. Otherwise, I'm completely lost. Typically, when you have the need for spatial queries, you also have a good idea of what you actually need and can translate that need into the appropriate operation using the basic building blocks that RavenDB provides. We'll touch more on spatial queries in Chapter 10, and they're covered in detail in the online documentation.

9.4. Aggregation queries

Aggregation in RavenDB can be used either directly from RQL using group by or by building your own MapReduce indexes. In both cases, however, the underlying implementation is the same. Aggregation in RavenDB happens during indexing, not during query, and as such it is much cheaper than aggregation queries in other databases.

Let's start by looking at the simple aggregation query in Listing 9.24.

Listing 9.24 *Simple group by query in RQL*

```
from Orders
group by Company
where count() > 25
order by count() as long desc
select count(), Company
```

This query is quite trivial: listing the companies with the most orders in descending rank if they have more than 25 orders in total. Simple and obvious. But there's a lot going on behind the scenes. As usual, the query optimizer will generate an index for us to answer this query. This index will serve all queries on Orders that group by Company.

The interesting bit is that the index is going to handle the actual aggregation for us. In other words, during indexing, we're going to do the grouping and write the already computed results to the index. When we query, we don't need to do any additional work – only look up all the companies in the index with more than 25 orders and return that immediately.

When there's a new order, the index will not need to recompute the entire aggregation from scratch but will be able to just update the relevant details. We'll discuss this in detail in the next chapter, so for now I'm going to defer further explanations.

RQL aggregation support is pretty basic. You can do most simple queries directly in RQL, but as the complexity grows, you'll likely find it easier to define a static index and handle MapReduce in that fashion.

Regardless of what you're using – a group by in your queries or a MapReduce index – the idea that aggregation queries are cheap has some really interesting implications for your system. When using an aggregation query you don't need to handle caching or have a scheduler to recompute results, all that is done for you.

Let's see why this is so important. Consider the query in Listing 9.24. In a relational database, this kind of query is actually quite expensive. Even assuming we have an index on the Company field, the relational database will need to go over all the results and count them, filter those that don't have enough, order and sort them. If the number of orders is high, that effectively means that the relational database needs to read through all the orders (or at least the entire index on the Company column).

RavenDB, on the other hand, already did this work during indexing, so when you make the query, RavenDB just grabs all the companies that have more than 25 orders, sorts them and gives them back to you. This is significantly cheaper – cheap enough that you don't need to worry about how up to date your reports are. Unlike other databases, RavenDB can help you avoid the need to only do aggregation during off hours, leaving you with data that's usually 24 hours old. Instead, you can have an aggregation that keeps up with the incoming flow of the data and is very close to real time.

9.5. Indexing in the background

Indexing in RavenDB will always happen in the background. This has been mentioned a few times in this book, but it's important to call it out explicitly and explain what it means. When you write a new document or update an existing one, RavenDB doesn't wait to update all the indexes before it completes the write operation. Instead, it writes the document data and completes the write operation as soon as the transaction is written to disk, scheduling any index updates to occur in an async manner.

Why is RavenDB doing this? There are several reasons for this behavior. First, it means that writes aren't going to be held up by the indexes, so adding an index will not negatively impact your write performance. This changes the equations of `more indexes = slower writes` and `fewer indexes = slower reads` in favor of another alternative: more indexes impact indexing speed, not write speed.

Another reason for this behavior is performance. RavenDB can apply multiple optimizations to indexes that are running in an async manner to start with. Instead of having to update all the indexes on every write, we can update them in batches. A single slow or expensive index isn't going to impact any other index or the overall writes in the system.

There are a few additional reasons, such as being able to add indexes dynamically and on the fly to busy production systems and being able to update indexes in a side-by-side manner. In the next chapter, we'll discuss a bit more about the actual indexing architecture of RavenDB and how it operates. For now, let's focus on the implications of this design choice.

Writes are faster and indexes are operating independently. However, a client that's fast enough can modify the data and then query on that data before it's been indexed. This is called a stale read, and there are several strategies to handle it.

Stale queries, documents and replication, oh my!

From the point of view of a single node, a stale read can only occur when you're querying an index. Loading a document or querying by ID is always going to use the internal collection and can never result in a stale read. So a query such as `from Orders where id() ='orders/1-A'` will always return a non-stale result.

RavenDB makes a distinction between indexes (which allow stale reads) and document access (via `Load` or query by ID), which can never yield stale results.

This applies when you're running on a single node. When running in a cluster, you need to take into account that a write request to a particular node may not have been propagated to the node that you're currently using. This may result in what's globally a stale read, even though the data you received is the most recent the queried node has.

For both replication lag and indexing lag, there are similar strategies. `WaitForIndexesAfterSaveChanges` and `WaitForReplicationAfterSaveChanges` allow the client to wait until the operation has been processed by additional nodes or by the relevant indexes. This means that you get a choice. You can ask RavenDB to wait until the operation is complete or accept that the updates will happen shortly in the background.

Stale reads sound scary, but most of the time you don't really need to pay the full cost of getting up-to-the-nanosecond updates. By the time you show the information to the user, that information might have already been modified, after all. And the cost of ensuring you'll never see stale data is very high indeed. That's why caches are introduced so often. It's usually better to get a response out, even if the information is slightly out of date, than to wait until we get an authoritative answer that's not relevant by the time we hand it to the end user.

RavenDB ensures that if you're getting a stale response to a query, you'll know it. The query statistic's IsStale result will be set to true, allowing you to make decisions based on this fact. In addition to knowing that the query result is stale, you'll also know the timestamp for this information.

You can also request that RavenDB waits until the index is up to date with the current changes by calling WaitForNonStaleResults on the query. This option will ensure that you get the most up to date information, but at a slight delay. Finally, you can choose to wait at write time by calling WaitForIndexesAfterSaveChanges, which will cause RavenDB to wait until the indexing process for these changes has completed before acknowledging the write.

Choosing the appropriate option depends on your specific needs, so let's explore a few examples.

> ### The indexing lag is usually *very* short
>
> On most systems, the time between a document write and the indexes applying it measures in single-digit milliseconds. We talk a lot about that in this section, but in most cases, you need to issue a write immediately after a query before you can encounter a stale result from the index.

The most problematic scenario for stale indexes is the Create/List pattern. The application makes a change (such as adding a new order) and then shows the list of items that should include the newly created document (the customer's recent orders). In this case, the user has a reasonable expectation to see the change they just made, and the query immediately after the save might be fast enough that it gets the index before it had a chance to complete indexing the new data.

This is a good place to use WaitForIndexesAfterSaveChanges. In addition to saving the value, you'll also wait for the index. And only then will you query for the new data. But why not do this all the time? The reason this isn't the default is that it's almost always not what you want in terms of performance.

Creating or modifying a document is not always followed by an immediate query for a list of items. In all of those cases, there's no real reason for you to wait until the indexes are done indexing. Your data is now on RavenDB, and the ACID nature of the database ensures that it's safely stored on disk.

In addition to waiting on the write, you can also wait on the read, using WaitForNonStaleResults. This is usually not a good idea. If you need to wait, do the wait on the write (which is far rarer than reads). The problem with waiting on the read side of things is that you may be waiting for something that isn't related to you. Consider the case of showing the list of recent orders for a customer that didn't just create a new order. Is there any sense in waiting for all the *other* orders (by other customers) to complete indexing before you get the results? Until the new documents have been indexed, RavenDB doesn't know to which customer they belong, so it will mark the results as stale. But the same results will be returned after the index is up to date anyway.

RavenDB lets you avoid paying for what you don't use

This section can be complex to understand, particularly with regards to why we chose to have async index by default. It's because not doing so would mean you'd have to wait for the indexes to complete on every write, and they'd require coordination with the queries to ensure you're reading the latest information.

The part about slowing the write is not so hot, but the part about getting the latest information is surely what you want, right? Well, that depends on what this costs. A study of relational databases[3] shows that they spend over 30% of their time just managing locks of various kinds. This is a truly stupendous amount of effort to spend on managing locks, and a large part of that is to ensure you get the properly consistent guarantees.

In contrast, RavenDB has chosen to avoid this entirely. Writes aren't held up because of indexes, queries don't wait for indexes to complete and indexes can do their own work without waiting for each other or for document writes. For the vast majority of cases, what you'll notice is that things are faster and don't take as many resources.

However, someone must pay the piper at some point, which is why RavenDB allows you to choose to pay the price and wait for these tasks on a case-by-case basis. This way, you don't pay the full cost when you almost never need the benefits.

Async indexing also works with hard resets, shutdowns and the like. Indexes and documents are actually stored in separate stores, each of them fully transactional. If the database restarted for any reason after a document was modified but before it was indexed, the indexing process will just pick up from where it left off and complete the work.

One of the major advantages that RavenDB has for production usage is that all indexes are always built in an online fashion. That means that adding an index doesn't take any locks and can be done even on busy systems. This allows RavenDB to create new indexes while the system is working, and it's one of the key reasons why the RavenDB query optimizer is able to do its work in this manner. Adding a new index in production is no longer a task you

---

3   "OLTP – Through the Looking Glass, and What We Found There" by Stavros Harizopoulos, Daniel Abadi, Samuel Madden, Michael Stonebraker.

schedule for late at night over the weekend. Rather, it's something that can happen during normal operations.

This lets RavenDB analyze and optimize your queries and indexes on an ongoing basis. This also applies to indexes you create manually. We'll discuss them in detail in the next chapter, but it's worth noting that when you update an index, the existing one is going to be kept around while the new version of the index is being built – only to be automatically (and atomically) replaced when the updated version has fully caught up.

9.6. Summary

In this chapter, we looked at how to query in RavenDB. We started by looking at the way RavenDB processes queries using the query optimizer, including the way RavenDB is able to generate indexes on the fly to optimize your queries. We then looked into RQL and all the nice things that we can do with it to query your data.

Beyond the simple equality and range queries, we showed how you can use advanced features such as full text search and spatial queries. All of the queries that we looked at in this chapter used RavenDB's automatic indexes, and while their features are quite rich, in the next chapter we'll introduce user-defined indexes that allow you to take the kind of queries you can make to the next level.

Queries in RavenDB do not allow any computation to occur during the query phase. This is done to ensure that queries in RavenDB can always use an index to answer the query promptly and efficiently. RQL does allow you to perform computation inside the select, either to project specific fields out or to massage the data from the query in every way imaginable. RQL is flexible enough that, using the object literal syntax, you can transform the result from the document into just the right shape you need, including pulling data from other documents using the `load` option.

The query language is quite rich, and you can do a lot of transformations using its capabilities. But be aware that while computation during projection is allowed, it *does* add to the cost of the query, as we need to run the JavaScript code on the results. Usually this is not an issue, but if you have a very complex logic or computation, that can impact the query performance.

Queries in RavenDB can project data from other documents or include the whole document on the way back from the server, reducing the need to do another network round trip to the database. This can be done using `load`, which gives you access to a related document, or using `include`, which lets RavenDB know that you'll need this related document in the client shortly so we might as well send it now.

From plain queries, we moved to talk about aggregation, using `group by` in RQL to aggregate information about our documents. Aggregation in RavenDB is done using MapReduce, which we'll explore more thoroughly in the next chapter. Aggregation is done in the background and in an incremental fashion, allowing the database to perform aggregation queries not when you're actually waiting for the results but rather beforehand. This makes aggregation queries in RavenDB *very* fast and enables a whole new set of features because you no longer have to work so hard to get an aggregated value from the server.

Where typically you'll worry that an aggregation query can consume too many resources and cache it (requiring you to manage the cache, the updates to it, etc.), with RavenDB, you can just make the query. The database will take care of returning the results and update the final tally whenever documents are modified or inserted.

Finally, we talked about the async nature of RavenDB indexes. This nature allows us to optimize many aspects of RavenDB, allowing us to use batches, enabling online index builds and opening the path to the query optimizer's ability to define indexes on the fly. It does mean that you need to be aware that, by default, writes will complete without waiting for indexes, but there are ways to wait for the indexes to complete as part of the write or even during the read (although that is not recommended).

In the next chapter, we're going to talk about customer indexes (called static indexes in RavenDB) that you'll define. We'll also cover what kind of fun we can have with them and what features and queries they enable.

10. Static Indexes and Other Advanced Options

In the previous chapter, we looked at how we can query RavenDB, while letting the query optimizer handle the indexing for us. In the next chapter, we'll talk about MapReduce indexes and in the one after that, we'll dive into the actual details of how indexes are implemented in RavenDB and the wealth of metrics that show how indexes work and behave, which is very useful for performance monitoring and troubleshooting issues. This chapter, however, will primarily focus on how you can define your own indexes, why you would want to do that and what options this provides you.

Indexes in RavenDB are split across multiple axes:

◆ Auto (dynamic) indexes vs. static indexes.
◆ Map-only indexes vs. MapReduce indexes.
◆ Single collection indexes vs. multi-collection indexes.

Indexes offer quite a bit of features and capabilities, it's a big topic to cover – but it's also one that gives you a tremendous amount of power and flexibility.

10.1. What are indexes?

Indexes allow RavenDB to answer questions about your documents without scanning the entire dataset each and every time. An index can be created by the query optimizer or by the user directly. The way an index works is by iterating over the documents and building a map between the terms that are indexed and the actual documents that contain them - a process that is called indexing. After the first indexing run, the index will keep that map current as updates and deletes happen in the database.

Listing 10.1 shows a simple way to construct an index. The code in Listing 10.1 has nothing to do with RavenDB but is provided so we'll have a baseline from which to discuss how indexes work.

Listing 10.1 *Creating an index over users' names*

```
Func<string, List<User>> BuildIndexOnUsers(List<User> users)
{
    var index = new Dictionary<string, List<int>>();
    for (var i = 0; i < users.Count; i++)
    {
        if (index.TryGetValue(users[i].Name, out var list) == false)
        {
            list = new List<int>();
            index[users[i].Name] = list;
        }
        list.Add(i);
    }

    return username =>
    {
        var results = new List<User>();
        if (index.TryGetValue(username, out var matches))
        {
            foreach (var match in matches)
                results.Add(users[match]);
        }
        return results;
    };
}
```

The code in Listing 10.1 is meant to convey a sense of what's going on. We're given a list of users, and we iterate over the list, building a dictionary that would allow fast access to the user by name. This is all an index is, effectively. It trades the cost of building the index with a significant reduction in the cost of the query.

If there's a query you only want to perform once, you're probably better off just scanning through the entire dataset since you'll do that anyway when creating an index. But if you intend to query more than once, an index is a fine investment. Consider the two options shown in Listing 10.2.

Listing 10.2 *The right and wrong way to use an index*

```
// the right way
Func<string, List<User>> findUserByName =
    BuildIndexOnUsers(largeNumberOfUsers);
List<User> usersNamedOren = findUserByName("Oren");
List<User> usersNamedArava = findUserByName("Arava");

// the wrong way
List<User> usersNamedOren =
    BuildIndexOnUsers(largeNumberOfUsers)("Oren");
List<User> usersNamedArava =
    BuildIndexOnUsers(largeNumberOfUsers)("Arava");
```

In the first section in Listing 10.2, we generate the index and then use it multiple times. In the second section, we create the index for each query, dramatically increasing the overall cost of making the query.

The code in Listing 10.1 and Listing 10.2 is about as primitive an index as you can imagine. Real world indexes are quite a bit more complex, but there's a surprising number of details that are actually unchanged between the toy index we have here and the real-world indexes used in RavenDB.

Indexes in RavenDB are implemented via the Lucene search library, hosted inside Voron, RavenDB's storage engine. An index in RavenDB can contain multiple fields, and a query can be composed of any number of clauses that operate on these fields. But in the end, we end up with a simple search from the queried term to the list of documents that contain the term in the specified field, just like our dictionary usage in Listing 10.1.

10.1.1. INDEXES COME IN LAYERS — AND WITH AN IDENTITY CRISIS

I'll be the first to admit that this can be quite confusing, but RavenDB actually has several different things called "index" internally. At the lowest level, we have Voron indexes, which is how RavenDB organizes the data in persistent storage. As a user, you don't have any control over Voron indexes. A Voron index is used to find a document by ID, for example, or to return a list of documents that belong to a particular collection, without any further filters.

A Voron index is updated by the storage engine directly as part of the transaction and is always kept in sync with the data. Unlike the async nature of higher level indexes in RavenDB, these Voron indexes (sometimes also called storage indexes) guarantee full consistency to the reader. You'll rarely be able to see them in use or affect them in any way, but they're crucial for the well being and performance of RavenDB.

I *did* mention this is confusing, right? Because while we call these Voron indexes, our regular (exposed to the user) indexes are also stored in Voron, to ensure the index data is transactionally safe and can recover from an error such as an abrupt shutdown.

Even for the user-visible indexes (what you'll generally mean when you're talking about indexes), there are several different levels. At the outer edge of the system, you have the index that was defined for you by the query optimizer or that you manually created. This, however, is not the actual index but rather the index *definition*. It merely tells RavenDB how you want to index the data.

Then, we have the actual process of indexing the data (which resides in the Index class and its derived classes) and the actual output of the indexing process, which is also called an index.

The good news about this naming mess is that you're rarely going to need to think about any of that. As far as the outside world can tell, RavenDB allows you to define indexes, and that's pretty much it. But if you're reading the code or interested in the implementation details, you need to remember that when we're talking about an index, you might want to verify *what* index we're talking about.

For this chapter, we'll use the term `index definition` for the definition of what's going to be indexed and the term `index` for the actual indexed data generated from the indexing process.

10.1.2. THE FIRST INDEX

In the Studio, go to the `Indexes` section and then to `List of Indexes`. Click the `New index` button and give the index the name "MyFirstIndex". This screen allows you to define an index by writing the transformation function from the document format to the actual indexed data.

RavenDB uses C# and Linq to define indexes, and Figure 10.1 shows the simplest possible index: indexing the `FirstName` and `LastName` from the `Employees` collection.

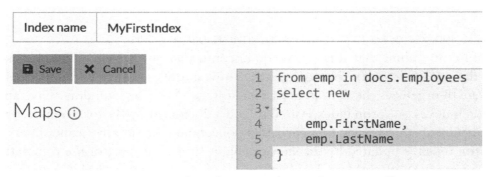

Figure 10.1. *A simple index over the* Employees *collection*

An index is just a C# Linq expression on a collection that outputs the values we want to index. The index in Figure 10.1 isn't a really interesting one, and it usually won't be a good candidate for a static index. There's nothing there that can't be done using an auto index the query optimizer will create for us. Nevertheless, let's see how we use such an index.

Listing 10.3 shows how we can query this index. Instead of specifying that we'll use a collection, which will cause the query optimizer to take over and select the best index to use, we're explicitly specifying that we want to use the "MyFirstIndex" index.

Listing 10.3 *RQL query using an explicit index*

```
from index 'MyFirstIndex' where FirstName = 'Andrew'
```

Except for the explicit index, the rest of the query looks familiar. Indeed, everything that we've gone over in the previous chapter still applies. The difference is that, in this case, we have an index that defines the shape of the result in a strict fashion. That doesn't seem like such a good idea until you realize the shape of the index and the shape of the source document don't have to be the same. Consider Listing 10.4, which shows an updated definition for "MyFirstIndex". It indexes a computed value rather than actual values from the document. Also consider Listing 10.5, which shows how to query the new index.

Listing 10.4 *Indexing a computation allow us to query over the computed value*

```
from emp in docs.Employees
select new
{
    Name = emp.FirstName + " " + emp.LastName
}
```

Listing 10.5 *Querying over the computed field*

```
from index 'MyFirstIndex' where Name = "Nancy Davolio"
```

The result of Listing 10.4 and Listing 10.5 is quite interesting, so it's worth examining further. In Listing 10.4, we define an index whose output is a computed field ("Name"), which in turn is the result of a concatenation of two values from the document. In Listing 10.5, you can see that we're querying over the index and finding a result, even though the source document never contained such a field.

The example here is silly; I'll be the first to admit it. But it nicely shows off an important feature. You can run computation during the indexing process and then query over the result of the said computation. This is quite powerful because it allows you to do some pretty cool things. For example, consider Listing 10.6, which shows an index ("Orders/Total" in the sample dataset) that does a more interesting computation.

Listing 10.6 *Computation during indexing can be arbitrarily complex*

```
from order in docs.Orders
select new {
    order.Employee,
    order.Company,
    Total = order.Lines.Sum(l =>
                        (l.Quantity * l.PricePerUnit) * (1 - l.Discount))
}
```

In Listing 10.6, we've computed the total value of an order. The formula we used isn't too complex, but it's also not trivial. What makes it interesting is that this allows us to run a query such as the one in Listing 10.7.

Listing 10.7 *Querying over computed field as well as sorting by it*

```
from index 'Orders/Totals'
where Total > 100
order by Total as double desc
```

The query in Listing 10.7 demonstrates a few key concepts. Once the indexing process is done, the computed field is just that: a field. It means that you can filter using this field as well as sort by it. The computation has already happened at indexing time, and the cost of the query in Listing 10.7 is the cost of a seek to the relevant location in the index, plus the cost of sorting the results according to the indexed value.

Most importantly, this query involves *no* computation during its execution, only index operations. In contrast to a comparable query in SQL, which would have to sum all of the order lines for each `Orders` table, we can take an enormous shortcut by running the computation once during indexing and reusing it in our queries. We're going to spend quite some time exploring what kind of fun we can have with this feature.

Computation during indexing vs. computation during query

In the previous chapter, we mentioned that RavenDB does not allow you to perform queries that will require computation during the query, such as `from Employees where FirstName = LastName`. In order to answer such a query, RavenDB will need to check each individual document, which is incredibly expensive.

You can get an answer to the question you actually want to ask, though, which is "Do I have users whose first and last name match?" You do that using a static index, such as

```
// Employees/FirstAndLastNameMatch index definition
  from employee in docs.Employees select new
  {
      FirstAndLastNameMatch = employee.FirstName ==
                                        employee.LastName
  }
```

And you can query this index using the following query:

```
from index 'Employees/FirstAndLastNameMatch' where
    FirstAndLastNameMatch == true
```

This query can be performed as a simple indexing operation instead of an expensive full scan. This is a common thing to do with RavenDB: shift the cost of the computation to indexing time as much as possible. Queries are far more frequent than updates, so this kind of cost-shifting makes a lot of sense. Of course, even so, if you have several operations you want to do on a specific collection, you're better off having them all on a single index rather than having a separate index for each.

Doing computation during indexing is a neat trick, but how does RavenDB handle the case where a document was updated? That's quite simple, as it turns out. All RavenDB needs to do is simply run the updated document through the indexing function again and index the resulting values.

Index definition must be a pure function

RavenDB places several limitations on the index definition. Primarily, it requires that the index definition be a pure function. This means that for the same input, the index definition will always produce the same output. One of the reasons that RavenDB uses Linq for defining indexes is that it's quite easy to define a pure function using Linq. In fact, you need to go out of your way to get a nondeterministic output from a Linq expression. And the syntax is quite nice, too, of course.

In particular, usage of date time functions or `random`, as well as trying to access external resources, is not allowed. This lets RavenDB assume that identical inputs will produce identical outputs and is important for reindexing and updates.

10.1.3. HOW THE INDEX ACTUALLY WORKS

There are a lot of moving parts here, so we need to clearly define what the terms we use mean:

◆ Document – the RavenDB JSON document.
◆ Index entry – all of the fields and values that have been indexed from a particular document. Frequently, it will be a subset of the fields from the document that is being indexed, but it can be some computed fields as well.

◆ Term – the actual indexed value that's stored in the index. This is usually the same as the value of the field being indexed, but it can be different if you're applying full text search.

For example, let's assume we have the JSON document in Listing 10.8 and we query using `from Dogs where search(Name, "Arava")`.

Listing 10.8 *Sample document that is about to be indexed*

```
{
    "Name": "Arava Eini",
    "Nick": "Dawg",
    "@metadata": {
        "@id": "dogs/1",
        "@collection": "Dogs"
    }
}
```

What will happen is that RavenDB will produce an index entry from this document that will have the structure `{"Name": "Arava Eini"}` and will mark the Name field as using full text search. This requires additional processing, and the actual terms that will be indexed are shown in Listing 10.9.

Listing 10.9 *Index terms after the analyzing for full text search*

```
index = {
    "Name": {
        "arava": ["dogs/1"],
        "eini": ["dogs/1"]
    }
}
```

The `search(Name, "Arava")` will then be translated into what's effectively a search on `index.Name["arava"]` to get the proper matches.

This isn't how the index works *at all*. But it's a very good lie because it allows you to reason about what's going on and make intuitive guesses about the behavior of the system without actually having to deal with the full complexity of managing an index. For example, you can see from the data we keep in the index in Listing 10.9 that we aren't storing the full document in the index. Instead, we only store the document ID.

This means that the query pipeline first needs to run the query on the index and get the list of document IDs that are a match for this query and then go to the document storage to load the actual documents from there.

Queries, stale indexes and ACID documents, oh my!

In the previous chapter, we talked about async indexes and the possibility that a query will read from an index before it's done indexing new or modified documents. An interesting wrinkle here is that the index doesn't contain the actual document data, so after the index is done giving us the document IDs, we need to go to the document storage and load the documents.

One of the promises that RavenDB provides is that document reading is always ACID and must be consistent (within a single node, at least). That means that even if the index itself hasn't caught up to changes, the data it pulls from the document store will have everything up to date.

Another important aspect of how queries work in RavenDB, which you can see in Listing 10.9, is that the Name field was not indexed as a single term. In other words, if we looked for index.Name["Arava Eini"], we wouldn't find anything in the index. This is because we search for the terms in the index. And during indexing, the terms were created by breaking the name to its constituents' parts and making all letters lowercase. At query time, we can apply the same transformation and be able to find the individual terms.

If we were indexing the name *without* full text search, we'd index the term arava eini. So the only thing this will allow is for us to run a non-case-sensitive query. Using exact(), of course, will store the term in the index as is and will require a case-sensitive match.

We already saw, in Figure 9.4 in the previous chapter, that you can pull the terms that are actually indexed from RavenDB and inspect them, which can help you understand why your queries return the results they do.

All of this explanation is here to hammer home the fact that at the index level, we aren't querying on your documents' properties. We're querying on the output of the indexing function, and that may bear little resemblance to how your index looks. The Total field in Listing 10.6 serves as a good example for this feature. The documents don't have a Total property, but we can compute it during indexing and query on it.

Security considerations

It's worth noting that a static index is just a C# Linq statement, which means you have a lot of power in your hands. An index can transform a document into an index entry in some pretty interesting ways. Combine this with the fact that the shape of the index entry and the shape of the data can be completely disconnected from one another and it's easy to understand why we'll spend most of this chapter just skimming over all that you can do with indexes.

This power has a downside. Static indexes can do everything, including running arbitrary code. In fact, they are arbitrary code. Defining static indexes is an operation that's limited to database administrators for that reason. Auto indexes defined by the query optimizer do not have this issue, obviously, and will be defined for users of all permissions levels.

You can also use the `Additional Sources` feature in indexes to expose additional classes and methods to the index definition. This goes beyond having a simple Linq expression and allows you to run any code whatsoever on the server. It's mostly meant to allow you to perform complex logic in the indexing and enable advanced scenarios (using custom data types on client and server, with their own logic, like `NodaTime`). You can read more about the `Additional Sources` feature in the online documentation.

We can also *filter* data out during indexing. The indexing function takes a collection of documents and returns a collection of index entries. It can also return *no* index entries, in which case the document will not be indexed. This can be done using a `where` in the Linq expression that composes the index definition. Listing 10.10 shows an example of filtering out employees without a manager for the "Employees/ByManager" index.[1]

Listing 10.10 *Filtering documents during indexing*

```
from employee in docs.Employees
where employee.ReportsTo != null
select new
{
    employee.ReportsTo
}
```

Only employees who have someone to report to will be included in this index. There isn't usually a good reason to filter things during the indexing process. The reduction in the index data size isn't meaningful, and you're usually better off having this in the query itself, where you can make such decisions on a per query basis. We'll see another use case for filtering the raw data in the index in a bit, when we discuss multimap indexes.

10.1.4. STORING DATA IN THE INDEX

A query in RavenDB will go to the index to find the results (and the order in which to return them) and then will usually grab the document IDs from the results and load the documents from the document store. Since the typical query will return full documents back, that's usually what you'll want to do.

Sometimes, such as with the `Total` field in Listing 10.6, you want to compute a value during indexing and use it in your projection. By default, RavenDB will store only enough

---

1   The general recommendation is that you have a single index per collection with all the fields that you want to search defined on that index. It's better to have fewer and bigger indexes than many smaller indexes.

information in the index to handle the query – not to get data out of the index. So as it stands, we'll need to recompute the `Total` after the query.

We can ask RavenDB to store the field. Go to `Indexes`, `List of Indexes`, and click the `Orders/Totals` index. This will take you to the index edit screen. Click `Add Field` and then set `Total` as the field name. Next, set `Store` to `Yes`. You can now save the index. This setting tells RavenDB that it needs to store the value itself (and not just the parts that it indexed) in such a way that we can later retrieve it.

We can project the `Total` field from the query, as you can see in Listing 10.11.

Listing 10.11 *Projection of a stored computed field*

```
from index 'Orders/Totals'
where Total > 10.0
select Total, Company, OrderedAt
```

Listing 10.11 also shows that we can project a standard field, `Company`, without storing it. This works because if the value isn't stored in the index we'll try to get it from the document. Last, we also project the `OrderedAt`, which follows the same logic. It isn't stored in the index, so it's fetched directly from the document.

Stored fields are used primarily to store the result of such computations. There's a small performance advantage in projecting everything from the index. We don't need to do the document load, and in some very specific circumstances, that might be helpful. But document load is a *very* cheap process in RavenDB. It happens so frequently that it's been heavily optimized, so there's usually not much point trying to store fields in the index.

Storing data in the index will also increase its size and the time it takes to actually index since it needs to do more work. Unless you actually need to get the projection out, it's usually not worth it.

10.2. Querying many sources at once with multimap indexes

Sometimes, just querying a single source isn't enough. In the sample database, we have several types of users. We have `Employees`, the `Contact` person on `Companies` and the `Contact` person for `Suppliers`. If an application needed to allow a free-form search over all of these users, how would that work? Would we need to perform three separate queries? We *could* do that, but it would be pretty complex. Instead, we can define an index that will use more than a single source of data.

Go to `Indexes` and then to `List of Indexes`. Click `New Index`. Then, name the new index "People/Search" and click `Add map` twice. You can see the content of the map functions in Listing 10.12.

Listing 10.12 *These map functions allow us to query over multiple sources with ease*

```
from e in docs.Employees
select new
{
    Name = e.FirstName + " " + e.LastName
}

from c in docs.Companies
select new
{
    c.Contact.Name
}

from s in docs.Suppliers
select new
{
    s.Contact.Name
}
```

The three map functions in Listing 10.12 each point to a different collection. RavenDB will use the information from all three map functions to generate a single index. This means that you can now query on all of these collections as a single unit. There are a few things to notice, though. First, multimap indexes require that all the maps in the index have the same output. Note that we indexed a Name field in all three maps even though the Employees collection has no such field.

The other important factor is that it's usually awkward to have to deal with a heterogeneous result set. When you're querying, it's nice to know what shape of data to expect. A query on a multimap can return any of the collections that the multimap index covers. Because of that, it's usually best to project the data out into a common shape, as you can see in Listing 10.13.

Listing 10.13 *Projecting data from multiple collections into a common shape*

```
from index 'People/Search' as p
where Name in ('Mary Saveley', 'Nancy Davolio', 'Wendy Mackenzie')
select
{
    Collection: p["@metadata"]["@collection"],
    ContactName: (p.Contact ||
                        { Name: p.FirstName + " " + p.LastName }).Name
}
```

The output of the query in Listing 10.13 can be seen in Figure 10.2. You can also remove the `select` clause for this query to see how the results will change when you get three different types of documents back from a single query.

Id	Collection	ContactName
companies/84-A	Companies	Mary Saveley
employees/1-A	Employees	Nancy Davolio
suppliers/24-A	Suppliers	Wendy Mackenzie

Figure 10.2. *Common output shape for results from multimap index*

In a way, the multimap feature is similar to a union in a relational database. It allows you to query over multiple sources and get the results back from any of them. However, there's no limit on the shape of the results like there would be with a union, although that's quite convenient.

10.3. Full text indexes

The query in Listing 10.13 is nice, but it's awkward. We wouldn't want to ask our users to specify the full name of the person they're trying to find. We'll typically want to do a smarter search...a *full text search*, one might even say.

In the previous chapter, we looked at some full text search queries. They looked like `search(Name, 'Nancy')` and allowed us to efficiently search for results without the expense of scanning all of them. Listing 10.9 is a good example of how RavenDB breaks up the terms during indexing for quick lookups and speedy searches. But so far, we only looked at it with dynamic queries. How do I make use of the full text search capabilities of RavenDB using static indexes?

Full text search in RavenDB is composed of the following elements:

◆ The analyzer you've selected.
◆ The values and manner in which you're querying.
◆ The field or fields you're indexing.

The analyzer for full text search is defined on a field or fields in the index, and it determines how RavenDB will break apart the text into individual terms. We've seen such an example in Listing 10.9, but let's consider the following string: `"The white knight is running to the princess's tower to slay the dragon"`. How would full text search operate on such a string?

10.3.1. FULL TEXT SEARCH ANALYSIS

RavenDB will hand over this string to the analyzer and get a list of terms back. This is an extremely simplistic view of what's actually happening. But it's important to understand it so you'll have the proper mental model of what's actually going on under the hood. The simplest analyzer will do nothing to the text provided to it, and you'll get it back as is. This is what `exact()` does with dynamic queries – it lets RavenDB know that we should use the no-op analyzer, which does case-sensitive matches.

The default analyzer that RavenDB uses isn't doing much more than that, merely allowing us to query in a case-insensitive manner. This is done by converting the input string to lowercase (with all the usual casing required for Unicode-aware programs, of course). It's important to note that the analyzer runs during indexing *and* during query time. In this way, what ends up querying the actual index data structures is a value that's been passed through the analyzer during the query and compared to a value that was passed through the analyzer during the indexing.

Just changing strings to lowercase isn't that interesting, I'll admit, but analyzers can do much more. When you use `search()`, you'll use something called the "standard analyzer," and that's when things start to get interesting. The analyzer will break the input string into individual terms on a word boundary. So the previous string will be broken up to the following terms:

- the (3x)
- white
- knight
- is
- running
- to (2x)
- princess's
- tower
- slay
- dragon

Note that we have made the terms lowercase and that the term `the` appears three times and `to` appears twice. In many languages, there are certain words that appear so frequently that they're meaningless noise in most cases. In English, those would be words like `a`, `the`, `to`, `from`, `is`, `are`, etc. These are called stop words and are stripped from the terms the analyzers return because they add no semantic value to the search results.

The terms we end up with are

- white
- knight
- running
- princess
- tower
- slay
- dragon

Note that the possessive "s" in `princess's` is something that the standard analyzer has removed. We could also reduce words to their stems, such as turn `running` into `run`. The standard analyzer doesn't do this, but you can select an analyzer that would do that. Analyzers are usually specific to the language (and sometimes even the specific business domain) that you're working on. The standard analyzer is a good default for English and most Latin-based languages, but sometimes you'll need more. In that case, you can look at the available analyzers and use them. A full list of the analyzers available by default with RavenDB can be found in the online documentation. Because RavenDB uses Lucene behind the scenes, it's quite easy to find analyzers for most needs that can be readily used by RavenDB. You can also define your own custom analyzers quite easily as well.

Let's look at how analyzers modify how RavenDB indexes documents. Figure 10.3 shows a sample document that we'll focus on.

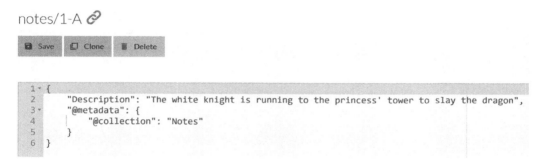

Figure 10.3. *Sample document for playing with full text search*

Go ahead and create this document, and then create an index named `test/search` with the index definition in Listing 10.14.

Listing 10.14 *This index definition uses the same field three times, to allow different indexing*

```
from n in docs.Notes
select new
{
    Plain = n.Description,
    Exact = n.Description,
    Search = n.Description
}
```

After adding the index definition, you'll need to customize the way RavenDB will index these fields. Click the `Add field` button and enter "Search" as the field name, then click `Advanced` and select `Search` as the value for the `Indexing` dropdown. Add another field and enter "Exact" in the name field. Then click `Advanced` and select `Exact` as the value for the `Indexing` dropdown. You can see how this should look in Figure 10.4.

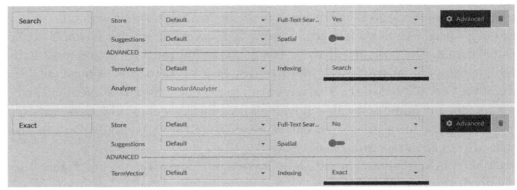

Figure 10.4. *Configuring the* test/search *index fields with different analyzers*

And with that, you can click Save, and we're done. You can now go to the index Terms to see the different indexing methods that were used on each of these fields. The results are shown in Figure 10.5.

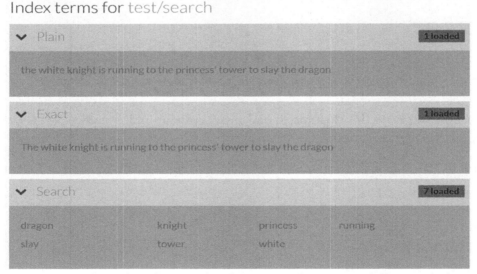

Figure 10.5. *The indexed terms for the same values using different analyzers*

The Plain field was indexed as is, but in lowercase. (Note the first the in the string). The Exact field is almost the same, but it preserves the casing. (Again, notice the The at the beginning.) And the Search field is probably the most interesting one. There, we can see the whole process of breaking it up into individual terms, filtering out stop words and stripping the possessive "s" out.

Now, let's do some queries on this index.

10.3.2. FULL TEXT SEARCH QUERIES

Querying a full text search field is an interesting experience because what we think we're doing and what's actually happening is so often drastically different, yet the end result is the same. Consider the query:

```
from index 'test/search' as n
where search(n.Search, "princess flower tower")
```

If you run this query, you'll find that this actually matches the document, even though the word `flower` is nowhere to be found. That's because of the way RavenDB processes queries on full text search. It's enough that we have *any* match to be considered enough to return the result. More advanced options, such as phrase queries, are also available when using Lucene directly, such as the following queries:

◆ `where lucene(n.Search, ' "princess tower" ')`
  Phrase query match (note the " in the query) because there's a `princess` followed by a `tower` in the text, even though we don't have the ' in the query.
◆ `where lucene(n.Search, ' "running princess" ')`
  Also a match because the word `running` is followed by a `princess` (with the stop words removed).
◆ `where lucene(n.Search, ' "running knight" ')`
  Not a match. There's no `running` followed by `knight` in the text.

As you probably remember, the `lucene()` method allows you to drop down directly into the Lucene syntax and compose complex full text search queries. I'm using it here primarily because it allows me to demonstrate the way full text search matches work. They're not quite so simple. You can read more about the full power of Lucene in the online documentation, but I want to focus on understanding how the queries work. Let's take, for example, the `search()` method and see how it operates.

The `search()` method accepts the query string you're looking for and passes it to the analyzer for the specified field. It then compares the terms the analyzer returned with the terms already in the index, and if there's a match on any of them, it's considered to be a match for the query. There's also the ranking of the results to take into account. The more terms that are matched by a particular document from the query, the higher it will be in the results. This is affected by such things as the term frequency, the size of the document and a lot of other things that I'm not going to cover but are quite interesting to read about.[2]

What happens when we're making a query on a full text field (one with an analyzer defined) without using `search()`? Let's see:

---

2   See the *Lucene in Action* and *Managing Gigabytes* books, recommended in the previous chapter.

- ◆ where n.Search = "princess tower"
  No match. There's no term princess tower for this field.
- ◆ where n.Search = "dragon"
  Match. There's a term dragon for this field.

This is really strange, isn't it? But take a closer look at Figure 10.5, and it will be clear what's going on. There's a term dragon there, and when we use equality comparison, we compare against the terms directly, so we find a dragon but we don't find a single term princess tower. When we use search() or lucene(), we're performing more complex operations, which allows us to do more interesting queries.

For the same reason, it's not meaningful to talk about *sorting* on a full text field. The value you're sorting on can be any of the terms that were generated by the analyzer for this field. If you want to sort on such a field, you need to index it twice: once as a full text field and once as a normal field. You'll search on the full text field and sort on the normal field.

This leads us nicely to an important discussion: how to work with fields in the index.

10.3.3. FULL TEXT SEARCH FIELDS

RavenDB doesn't require anything to match between the source document and its index entry. We saw that previously in Listing 10.14, when we indexed a single field from the document three different times, with different analyzers for each field. In many cases, you'll use the same field names, but there's no requirement to do that. This behavior is intentional because it gives you a lot of freedom with regards to how you're able to build your index and perform queries.

Listing 10.14 showed an example of how we can index a single field multiple times. Listing 10.15 shows the index definition for Companies/Search, which allows for the reverse scenario, where we're searching over multiple fields in the document using a single field in the index entry.

Listing 10.15 *Combining several document fields in a single index field*

```
from c in docs.Companies
select new
{
    Query = new[] {
        c.ExternalId,
        c.Name,
        c.Contact.Name
    }
}
```

The index definition in Listing 10.15 adds three different fields to the Query field on the index entry. When creating this index definition, you also need to register the Query field as full text search (as we've done with the `Search` field in the previous example). The question is, what does this give us?

This type of index is typically used to serve search pages directly. For example, we can run the following queries on this index:

- `from index 'Companies/Search' where search(Query, "ALFKI")`
  Search companies using the external ID.
- `from index 'Companies/Search' where search(Query, "Alfreds")`
  Search companies by full text search on the company name.
- `from index 'Companies/Search' where search(Query, "Anders")`
  Search companies by full text search on the contact person's name.

Note that in all cases, we get the same result (`companies/1-A`). A user can type any of the above into the search text box and get the result they're looking for. Gone are the days of search pages with dozens of fields and extra long waiting times. You can search on any of the interesting fields that a client may remember without any hassle.

This is something that's quite easy to do but can significantly improve the life of our users. Now they have much greater freedom in querying, and they don't need to limit themselves to knowing exactly what value to search in what field. One of the things I recommend you do in such pages is to directly go into the details page, if there's just one result. This gives the users the impression that they can type just enough for your system to recognize who they're talking about and take them to the right place. It may seem like a small thing, but these are the kind of things that make a user really appreciate a system.

Of course, it's not always this easy. What happens if I know what I'm searching for but I can't quite get it right enough for the index to find it? There's a lot more that you can do with indexes in RavenDB.

10.4. Getting the most out of your indexes

Indexes are typically used to answer very specific questions, such as "Give me all the documents that match this criteria in this order." But RavenDB indexes are actually capable of doing much more. In this section, I want to highlight three of the more interesting capabilities of the indexes in RavenDB.

- Suggestions – allowing you to ask RavenDB what the user probably *meant* to ask about.
- More like this – suggesting similar documents to an existing one.
- Facets – slicing and dicing of the data to provide you with detailed insights into what's going on in large result sets.

I'm going to cover them briefly here, mostly to introduce them and explain where and how they should be used. I'll leave the details on all the myriads of options and advanced features they have to the online documentation.

10.4.1. SUGGESTIONS

In the sample data, we have the companies/8-A document. It's for a company in Spain, whose owner name is: Martín Sommer. Note that diacritic over the i. It's reasonable for someone to not notice that and search for Martin. In this case, they'd find nothing. This can be frustrating, so we have a few ways in which we can help the user find what they're looking for.

In the same way we'll automatically go to the details page if there's only a single result, we'll also ask RavenDB if it can think of what the user meant to ask for. This can be done using the suggestions feature. Before we can use it, though, we need to enable it in the index, as shown in Figure 10.6.

Figure 10.6. *Marking a field as having the suggestions feature*

With this change, we let RavenDB know that we'll be asking it to suggest options to queries the user has made. This typically requires RavenDB to spend more time in indexing, preparing all the options that a user can misspell in a search query, but the results can be astounding to users. Consider the query in Listing 10.16.

Listing 10.16 *Querying for suggestions for a misspelled term*

```
from index 'Companies/Search'
select suggest(Query, "Martin")
```

We're asking RavenDB, "What could the user have meant by 'Martin' in the Query field?" RavenDB will try to look at the data in the index for this field and infer the intent of the user. If you care to know the details, RavenDB breaks the terms into pieces during the indexing process and scrambles them to simulate common errors. Those all go into an index that's used during query. This does increase the cost of indexing, but the cost of querying suggestions is typically very low. I wouldn't suggest[3] applying this globally, but for user-facing searches, the dataset is typically pretty stable, so that works out great.

The result of the query in Listing 10.16 can be seen in Figure 10.7.

---

3   Pun intended.

```json
{
    "Name": "Query",
    "Suggestions": [
        "wartian",
        "martine",
        "martin",
        "cartrain",
        "warth"
    ],
    "@metadata": {
        "@attachments": []
    }
}
```

Figure 10.7. *Suggested alternatives for "Martin"*

You can use the results of the suggestion query to show results to the user, or you can ask them what they meant, similar to how Google does it. This feature tends to get enthusiastic responses when users run into it.

I gave an example in Unicode because it's clear how it would be hard to use, but the same is possible using any type of misspelling, such as that in listing 10.17.

Listing 10.17 *Asking RavenDB to suggest other options for 'Summer' from the terms in the index*

```
from index 'Companies/Search'
select suggest(Query, "Summer")
```

The query in Listing 10.17 will give sommer and cramer as the possible suggestions for summer.

I focused heavily on finding what the user meant when they misspelled something and didn't find anything, but suggestions can also be useful when you *did* find something but want to let the user know there are additional alternatives they might want to explore. Sometimes, this can give the user a reason to go exploring, although the "more like this" feature is more appropriate there.

10.4.2. MORE LIKE THIS

My toddler likes playing "what looks like this" and it's a lot of fun. In a more serious setting, there are a lot of use cases for "find me more stuff that looks like this." In bug tracking, it might be finding a previous occurrence of a bug. With a product catalog, that might be finding another item that's roughly the same.

What the "more like this" feature is and isn't

The way "more like this" works beneath the surface is quite simple. You mark a field as full text search and define it to have a term vector. These two things together provide RavenDB the ability to build a query to find similar documents. There is a bit of smarts around how we decided the query should actually look, but that's the basis of how it works.

In many cases, this simple approach works well to find similar and related documents, especially if your dataset is large and the documents and data you're indexing are complex. In this case, the more data you have, the more information RavenDB has to decide upon a similar document vs. what's just random noise, common in your domain.

This isn't the basis of a recommendation engine, though. It's a good start and allows you to hit the ground running and demonstrate a feature quickly. But while there's quite a lot of tuning that you can do (see the online documentation for the full details), it's a feature that was developed to find documents based on shared indexed terms and nothing beyond that. True recommendation engines can do much more.

To make true use of the "more like this" feature, we typically use a large dataset and utilize large text fields that give us enough information to distinguish between noise and what's of real value. This is especially true when we're talking about user-generated content, such as comments, posts, emails and the like. It's of somewhat less use for static fields, but there are still quite a few interesting use cases for this feature.

We'll start by defining the `Orders/Search` index, as shown in Listing 10.18.

Listing 10.18 *Index definition to use as more like this target to find similar orders*

```
from o in docs.Orders
select new{
    Address = new[]{o.ShipTo.City, o.ShipTo.Country},
    Products = o.Lines.Select(x => x.Product)
}
```

Before we can start performing a "more like this" query, we need to configure a term vector for these fields, as shown in Figure 10.8.

Setting a field to use a term vector tells RavenDB we need to store enough information about each index entry to not only be able to tell from a term what index entries contained it but also to be able to go from an index entry to all the terms that it contained. A term may appear multiple times in an index entry (common when we're using full text search). For example, the word `term` has appeared multiple times in this paragraph. A term vector for the paragraph will contain a list of all unique words and how often they appeared.

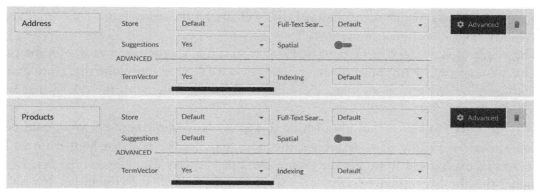

Figure 10.8. *Defining term vectors (for use with more like this) in the* `Orders/Search` *index*

Why didn't we define full text search on the fields in `Orders/Search`?

You might have noticed in Figure 10.8 that we didn't set the fields to use full text search. Why is that? The values we're going to put into these fields (a city, a country or a product ID) are all terms that we don't want to break up. In this case, using full text search on those fields would break them apart too much. For example, if we have a city named "New York," that is the city name. We don't want to break it into "New" and "York".

Another thing to note is that the `Address` field in the index is actually using an array to store multiple values in the same field. It's similar to using an analyzer, but for one-off operations, this is often easier. You can look at the index terms to see what got indexed.

With all of the preparations complete, we can now actually make our first "more like this" query, which is shown in Listing 10.19.

Listing 10.19 *Finding similar orders to 'orders/535-A' based on products ordered and the city and country it was shipped to*

```
from index 'Orders/Search'
where morelikethis(id() = 'orders/535-A')
```

The query asks RavenDB to find similar orders to `orders/535-A` based on the `Orders/Search` index. This index has two fields marked with term vectors, which are used for this purpose. The `orders/535-A` document has a single purchased product (products/31-A) and was shipped to Buenos Aires, Argentina. Based on this, RavenDB will construct a query similar to this one: where Address = 'argentina' or Address = 'buenos aires' or Products = 'products/31-a'

Note that the casing on the query parameters is intentional because the data comes directly from the index terms, which were changed to lowercase by the default analyzer. I'm doing this to explicitly show the source of the data.

The result of the query in Listing 10.19 is 65 results. It's the same as if we replaced the morelikethis() call with the equivalent query that we figured out manually. Note that issuing the query on orders/830-A, for example, will have 25 items in the query that will be generated.

Why go into so much detail about how this is actually implemented? Well, consider the implications. As we know, in such queries, the more matches we have, the higher the rank of a result. So this explains how we get the "more like this" aspect. We query on the matches, and the higher the number of matches, the more we'll consider it similar to the target and return it. It's magic demystified but hopefully still pretty cool and a nice way to give the user something to follow up on.

I'm not going to cover all the options of morelikethis() here, but I wanted to point out that you have a great deal of control over exactly how RavenDB is going to match these documents. Take a look at Listing 10.20, where we want to apply the morelikethis() only on the Address field.

Listing 10.20 *Querying with* morelikethis() *on a specific field*

```
from index 'Orders/Search'
where morelikethis(id() = 'orders/535-a', '{ "Fields": ["Address"] }')
```

The results of the query in Listing 10.20 is just 15 similar orders: those that were sent to the same city and country. Other options allow you to decide what terms will be considered for the morelikethis() query based on their frequency of use and overall popularity. You can find the full details in the online documentation.

We're now going to look at another element of the RavenDB querying capabilities: facets and how we can use them to get all *sorts* of information about the result set for your queries.

10.4.3. Facets

To query is to ask a question about something. Usually the questions we ask are some variant of "give me all the documents matching this pattern", such as when we ask to get the last 50 orders from a particular customer. This is easy to understand and reason about. We run into problems when the size of the result set is so big that it's not meaningful for the user.

Consider the case of a support engineer fielding a phone call. The customer reports an error, so the engineer searches the knowledge base for all articles with "error" in them.

As you can imagine, there are likely going to be quite a few of these. The poor engineer is unlikely to find something meaningful using such a strategy. On the other hand, very often we have a pretty good idea about the general query we want but not a clue how to narrow it down.

Facets are widely used, but they're the sort of feature that you don't really pay attention to. A good example of that would be YouTube. As you can see in Figure 10.9, searching YouTube for "Dancing" is an interesting experience. How would I be able to choose from over 280 million different videos?

Figure 10.9. *Faceted search in YouTube*

Facets allow me to narrow down the search quite easily by exposing the inner structure of the data. There are two searches shown in Figure 10.9: the first doesn't have any filters applied, and the second filters for 4K and uploaded today. This reduces the results to a far more manageable number. It also gives me additional information, such as the fact that there are no matches with the type "Show" in the results. You can see another good example of facets in commerce. If I want to buy a new phone, I have way too many options. Searching eBay for "phone" gives me over 300,000 results. Figure 10.10 shows how eBay uses facets to help you narrow down the selection to just the right one.

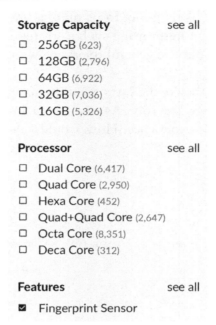

Storage Capacity   see all

☐ **256GB** (623)
☐ **128GB** (2,796)
☐ **64GB** (6,922)
☐ **32GB** (7,036)
☐ **16GB** (5,326)

Processor   see all

☐ **Dual Core** (6,417)
☐ **Quad Core** (2,950)
☐ **Hexa Core** (452)
☐ **Quad+Quad Core** (2,647)
☐ **Octa Core** (8,351)
☐ **Deca Core** (312)

Features   see all

☑ **Fingerprint Sensor**

Figure 10.10. *Facets can help a customer to narrow down to the exact product they want*

In some cases, this is just there to help you feed the system the exact query it needs. In many other cases, facets actively assist the user in figuring out what kind of questions they need to ask. The feedback from the numbers in Figure 10.10, in contrast to the match / no match indication in Figure 10.9 is another factor, giving the user the ability to guide their searches.

Facets are a cool feature indeed. Let's see how you can use them in RavenDB. Facets require that you define an index for the fields you want to query and apply facets on. In this case, we'll use the Product/Search index in the sample data set. We'll start with the simple faceted query shown in Listing 10.21.

Listing 10.21 *Range and field facets on product search*

```
from index 'Product/Search'
select
    facet(
        PricePerUnit < 10,
        PricePerUnit between 10 and 50,
        PricePerUnit between 51 and 100,
        PricePerUnit  > 100
    ) as Price,
    facet(Category),
    facet(Supplier)
```

The results of the query shown in Listing 10.21 can be seen in Figure 10.11. The query itself is composed of three facets: a range facet on the PricePerUnit field and two field facets on Category and Supplier. As you can see, in the case of the range facets, we grouped all the matches in each particular range. And in the case of the field facet, we group by each individual value.

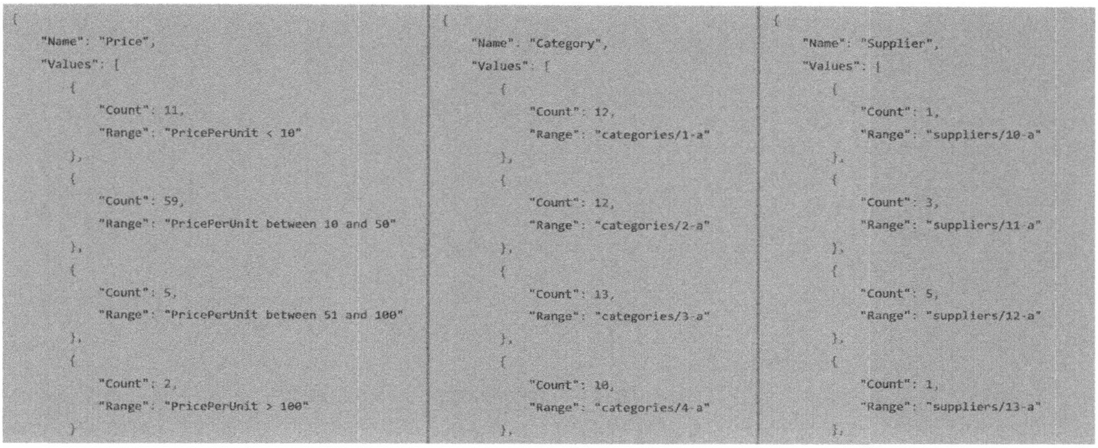

Figure 10.11. *Faceted query results*

The query in Listing 10.21 is simple since it has no where clause. This is where you'll typically start – just giving the user some indication of the options they have for queries. Let's say the user picked suppliers 11 and 12 as the ones they want to drill down into. The query will then look like the one in Listing 10.22.

Listing 10.22 *Faceted search over particular suppliers*

```
from index 'Product/Search'
where Supplier in ('suppliers/11-a', 'suppliers/12-a')
select
    facet(
        PricePerUnit < 10,
        PricePerUnit between 10 and 50,
        PricePerUnit between 51 and 100,
        PricePerUnit  > 100
    ) as Price,
    facet(Category),
    facet(Supplier)
```

In Listing 10.22, we're querying over the same facets, but we're now also limiting it to just particular suppliers. The output of the Price facet will change, as shown in Listing 10.23.

Listing 10.23 *'Price' facet output from the query in Listing 10.22*

```
{
    "Name": "Price",
    "Values": [
        {
            "Count": 1,
            "Range": "PricePerUnit < 10"
        },
        {
            "Count": 6,
            "Range": "PricePerUnit between 10 and 50"
        },
        {
            "Count": 0,
            "Range": "PricePerUnit between 51 and 100"
        },
        {
            "Count": 1,
            "Range": "PricePerUnit > 100"
        }
    ]
}
```

As you can see, the number of results per each range has changed to reflect the new filtering done on the query.

The facets portion of the query is the very last thing that happens, after the entire query has been processed. This means that you can use any where clause you want and filter the results accordingly. However, any query that uses facet() must return *only* facet() results and cannot use clauses such as include or load.

Faceted queries are typically combined with the same query, sans the facets, to show the user the first page of the results as they keep narrowing down their selections. You'll typically use the Lazy feature to combine such multiple queries, as was discussed in Chapter 4.

10.5. Spatial indexes

In Chapter 9, we discussed spatial queries and used them with automatic indexes. Using a static index gives you a high degree of control over the spatial indexing that RavenDB will perform on your data. Let's create a new index called Companies/Spatial, as shown in Listing 10.24.

Listing 10.24 *Defining an index with spatial support*

```
from c in docs.Companies
select new
{
    Name = c.Name,
    Coordinates = CreateSpatialField(
            c.Address.Location.Latitude,
            c.Address.Location.Longitude)
}
```

The `CreateSpatialField` method instructs RavenDB to use the provided latitude and longitude to create a spatial field named `Coordinates`. As usual, even though there are some companies with a null `Address.Location`, we can safely ignore that. RavenDB will handle null propagation during the indexes and save us from all those null checks.

With this index, we can now perform spatial queries. You can see such a query in Listing 10.25, querying for companies within a mile of 605 5th Ave. S., Seattle, Washington.

Listing 10.25 *Spatial querying for companies using a static index*

```
from index 'Companies/Spatial'
where spatial.within(Coordinates,
    spatial.circle(1, 47.5970, -122.3286, 'miles'))
```

The query in Listing 10.25 has a single result: the White Clover Markets company. You can also use the `CreateSpatialField` to pass a WKT string representing any arbitrary shape that will be indexed by RavenDB. So far, this seems to be pretty much the same as we've previously done with auto indexes. Static indexes allow you to customize the spatial indexing behavior. So let's see how.

Go to the `Companies/Spatial` edit index page and click on the `Add field` button. Set the `Field name` to `Coordinates` and click on the `Spatial` toggle. The result should be similar to Figure 10.12.

You can use these options to have fine-grained control over exactly how RavenDB will index your spatial data and process spatial queries. Of particular interest is the `Max Tree Level` field, which controls how precise the spatial queries are going to be and directly relates to the cost of spatial indexing.

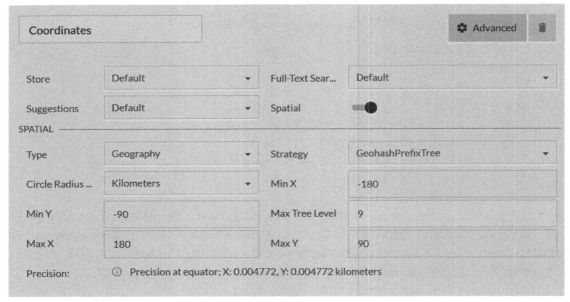

Figure 10.12. *Spatial field indexing options*

10.5.1. How RavenDB handles spatial indexing and queries

This section isn't going to be an exhaustive study of how spatial indexing works, nor will it dive too deeply into the actual implementation. The first topic is too broad for this book (and there are excellent resources online), and the second topic is unlikely to be of much interest to anyone who isn't actually implementing the querying support. Full details on the spatial behaviors and options are available in the online documentation. What this section *is* going to do is to give you a good idea of how RavenDB performs spatial queries – enough so that you'll be able to reason about the impact of the decisions you're making.

RavenDB offers three different spatial indexing strategies:

- ◆ Bounding box
- ◆ Geohash prefix tree
- ◆ Quad prefix tree

To demonstrate the difference between these strategies, we'll use the Terms feature to see what's actually going on underneath it all. Go into Companies/Spatial and edit the Coordinates field to the BoundingBox strategy. Click Save and then go into the index terms. You should see something similar to Figure 10.13.

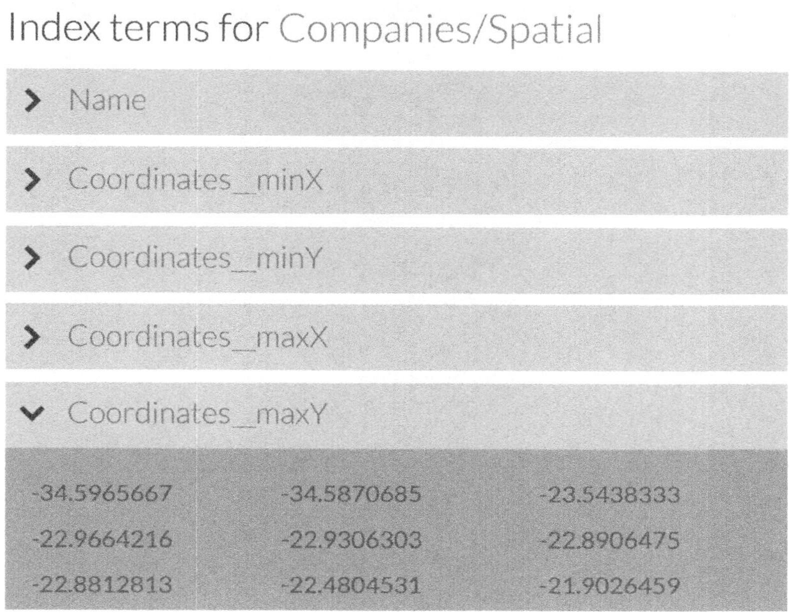

Index terms for Companies/Spatial

> Name

> Coordinates__minX

> Coordinates__minY

> Coordinates__maxX

∨ Coordinates__maxY

-34.5965667	-34.5870685	-23.5438333
-22.9664216	-22.9306303	-22.8906475
-22.8812813	-22.4804531	-21.9026459

Figure 10.13. *Bounding box indexing behind the scenes*

The bounding box strategy is the simplest one. Given a spatial shape, such as a point, a circle or a polygon, it computes that shape's bounding box and indexes its location. These are the `Coordinates__minX`, `Coordinates__minY`, `Coordinates__maxX` and `Coordinates__maxY` fields that you can see in Figure 10.13.

As for the actual values of these fields, these are the spatial coordinates that match the bounding box. Whenever you make a query, RavenDB will translate it to the same bounding box system. You can see a sample of this query translation in Listing 10.26.

Listing 10.26 *Translated spatial query using bounding box*

```
// actual query
from index 'Companies/Spatial'
where spatial.within(Coordinates, spatial.circle(1, 47.5970,
-122.3286, 'miles'))

// what actually gets executed
from index 'Companies/Spatial'
where Coordinates__minX >= -125.3341 and
    Coordinates__maxX <= -119.3230 and
    Coordinates__minY >= 45.5707 and
    Coordinates__maxY <= 49.623237136915
```

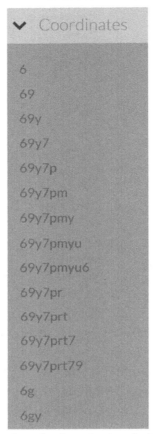

Figure 10.14. *Geo hash indexing behind the scenes*

As you can imagine, this is a pretty cheap way to handle spatial queries, both during the indexing portion and at the time of the query. However, it suffers from a number of issues related to the accuracy of the solution. In many cases, you wing it and get by with a bounding box, but in truth it's limited in the kind of queries it can perform and how well it can answer them. In particular, the bounding box assumes that the world is flat (or at least that the bounding box is small enough that it can ignore the curvature of the earth).

Let's move to the next option and look at the geohash strategy. Go to the index, update the spatial option to GeohashPrefixTree and save the index. Now, go to the index terms, and you'll find something similar to Figure 10.14.

The pyramids you see are the actual geohashes, but before we can start talking about how RavenDB uses them, we need to explain what they *are*. The way geohashes work is by dividing the world into a grid with 32 buckets. They then divide each bucket in the grid further into another 32 buckets, and so on. You can play with geohashing in an interactive manner using the following sites:

http://geohash.gofreerange.com/
https://rawgit.com/rzanato/geohashgrid/master/geohashgrid.html

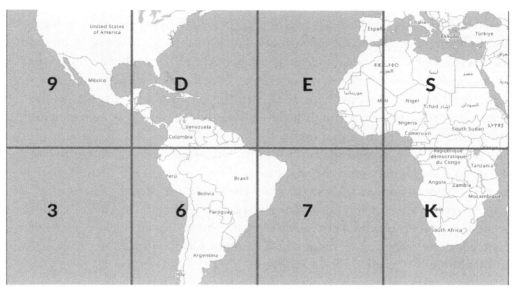

Figure 10.15. *A map showing the top level of geohash*

By looking at the map in Figure 10.15 and the terms from Figure 10.14, we can see that the prefix 6 covers most of South America. The next level we have, 69, is mostly Argentina, and 69y is Buenos Aires. In other words, the longer the geohash, the more precise it is.

Figure 10.16. *A map showing multiple levels of geohash*

Look at the spatial indexing options in Figure 10.12. You can see the `Max Tree Level` there, which determines the accuracy of the spatial indexing. This, in turn, determines the length of the geohash. A tree level of 9 (the default) gives us a resolution of about 2.5 meters. That somewhat depends on the exact location on the earth that you are searching.

When indexing a shape, RavenDB will pixelate it to the required resolution and enter the geohashes that cover it. The more irregular the shape and the higher the precision required, the more work that's needed to generate the terms that match the query. At query time, we do the reverse and find the matches. Note that with the geohash strategy, the geohash indexing creates the relevant shapes in a rough fashion, after which we check whether all the shapes inside the geohash match our actual query.

In other words, with spatial queries using geohash (or quad), there are two stages to the query. First, do a rough match on the shapes. This is what you see in the index terms. Second, have the actual spatial geometry check to see if the shape matches the query.

The quad tree strategy is similar in many respects to the geohash but uses a different coordinate system (a grid of four buckets, hence the name quad). Quad buckets are always squares, while geohash buckets can be rectangular. This might make a difference if you're using heatmaps and want a more predictable zoom in/out.

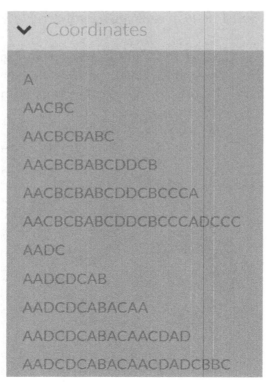

Figure 10.17. *Coordinates terms when indexing using quad prefix tree*

Geohash is more widely used, and it's supported by many platforms and tools. The selection of geohash or quad typically doesn't have any major effect on indexing speed or queries; it primarily depends on what you're going to be using this for. If you're going to display spatial data, you'll probably want to select a mode that works best with whatever mapping component you're using.

Bounding box strategy is much cheaper at indexing time and can produce very quick queries, but that's at the expense of the level of accuracy you can get. This is good if what you typically care about is rough matches. For example, if your query is something like "find me the nearest restaurants", you likely don't care too much about the shape. On the other hand, if you're asking for "give me all the schools in this district", that's something quite different, and you'll care about the exact shape the query is processing.

The performance cost of spatial indexing is directly related to the tree level you chose, and a very granular level with complex shapes can cause long indexing times. You'll usually not notice that, because indexing is async and doesn't hold up other tasks, but it can impact operations when you are creating a new index or storing large number of entities to the database all at once. In particular, if you have an expensive spatial index, it is usually better to avoid indexing documents that have very high rate of change since RavenDB will need to re-index them every time, even if the spatial fields didn't change.

In such cases, it might be better to move the spatial data to a dedicated collection containing just that, so only the documents with the spatial data will be indexed if they change. This is typically not required, since even with spatial indexing, the indexing is fast enough for most cases, but it can be a valid approach if you need to speed up indexing times and are getting held up by the spatial indexing level you require.

Splitting the spatial data to a separate collection brings up an interesting issue, though. How do we deal with indexing of data that is located on multiple documents?

10.6. Indexing referenced data

The document modeling rules we've reviewed so far call for documents to be independent, isolated and coherent. Documents should be able to stand on their own without referencing other documents. Sometimes, however, you need data from a related document to create a good search experience.

For example, using the sample dataset, you want to search for employees using the name of their *manager*. In general, I dislike such requirements. I would much rather have the user first search for the appropriate manager and then find all the employees that report to this manager. From many perspectives, from the purity of the model to the user experience you can provide, this is the better choice.

In particular, searching employees by a manager's name leads to confusion about which manager you're talking about if more than one manager have the same name. Even so, sometimes this is something you just have to do. The users may require it to behave in this manner because the old system did it this way, or maybe the model they use actually calls for this. So how *would* you do it?

One way to handle this requirement is to store the document field on the related entity. In other words, you'd store the manager's name in the employee document. That *works*, but it will rightly raise eyebrows when you look at your model. This isn't a value we want to freeze in time, such as a product's price or its name in the `Orders` collection. A manager's name is their own, and they're free to modify it as they wish. If we stored that name in the employee document, it would mean we'd have to update the employee document whenever we updated the manager. That is…not so nice, even if RQL makes it easy, as you can see the patching done in Listing 10.27.

Listing 10.27 *Using RQL to update the manager's name in all the managed employees*

```
from Employees as e
where e.ReportsTo = $managerId
update {
    e.ManagerName = $managerName;
}
```

The only thing that's of interest in Listing 10.27 is the passing of parameters to both the query and the `update` clause. Other than that, it's a perfectly ordinary patch. However, having to do such things will likely result in the ghost of "you shoulda normalized that" haunting you. In particular, while this can be a viable solution for certain things, it isn't elegant, and it goes against the grain of the usual thinking in database design.

Another option is to ask RavenDB to handle this explicitly during the indexing process, as you can see in Listing 10.28.

Listing 10.28 *Getting values from a related document at indexing time*

```
from e in docs.Employees
let manager = LoadDocument(e.ReportsTo, "Employees")
select new
{
    e.FirstName,
    e.LastName,
    ManagerFirstName = manager.FirstName,
    ManagerLastName = manager.LastName
}
```

I've created Listing 10.28 as an index named `Employees/Search`. And I can query it as shown in Listing 10.29:

Listing 10.29 *Querying information from a related document*

```
from index 'Employees/Search'
where ManagerLastName = 'fuller'
```

As you can see, we're able to query the related information. But how does this work? In Listing 10.28, you can see the use of an unfamiliar function: `LoadDocument(e.ReportsTo, "Employees")`. This is the key for this feature. At indexing time, RavenDB will load the relevant document and allow you to index its values. Note that we need to specify which collection we're loading the document from.

This is all well and good, but what happens when the manager's name changes? Go ahead and change `employees/2-A`'s `LastName` to `Smith`. Then execute the query in Listing 10.29 again. You'll find no results. But if you run it on `ManagerLastName = 'Smith'`, you'll find the missing documents.

In other words, when using `LoadDocument` in the index, you can index data from a related document, and it's *RavenDB*'s responsibility to keep such related data up to date. In fact, this is why we need to know which collection you're loading the document from: so we can watch it for changes (in a similar way to how we watch the collection that we're indexing). The loaded documents can be from the collection we're already indexing (as is the case in Listing 10.28) or an unrelated collection.

The cost of tracking related documents

The `LoadDocument` behavior doesn't come without costs. And these costs come in two areas. First, during indexing, we need to load the relevant document. That may require us to read a document that currently resides on the disk, skipping many of the performance optimizations (such as prefetching) that we apply when we need to index a batch of documents. This cost is usually not large and is rarely an issue.

Of more concern is the fact that whenever any document in a collection that's referenced by `LoadDocument` is changed, the index needs to scan and assess whether any references need to be reindexed. This is usually the more expensive portion of this feature.

When you consider using the `LoadDocument` feature, first consider whether this is used to paper over modeling issues. In particular, `LoadDocument` allows you to do "joins" during the indexing process. That can be very useful or lead you down a problematic road, depending on your usage. In particular, if a large number of documents reference a single document (or a small set of them), then whenever that referenced document is changed, *all* the documents referencing it will also need to be reindexed. In other words, the amount of work that an index has to do because of a single document change can be extremely large and may cause delays in indexing.

These delays will only impact the specific index using LoadDocument and will have the effect of making it do more work. But other work on the server will continue normally, and queries (including to this particular index) can run as usual (but may show outdated results). Other indexes or operations on the server will not be impacted.

The whole referenced document vs. referencing documents can be a bit confusing, so an example might be in order. In Listing 10.28, we have the Employee referencing the manager using the ReportsTo field. In other words, the referencing document is the Employee and the referenced document is the manager. (In this case, it's also a document in the Employees collection.) The topology of the references is critical in this case.

If the number of employees that report to the same manager is small, everything will work just fine. Whenever the manager document is updated, the employees managed by this document will be reindexed. However, consider the case where all employees report to the same manager and that manager's document is updated. We'd now need to index *everything* that referenced it, which can be a huge number of documents.

Remember that the reindexing will happen on any change in the referenced document. In Listing 10.28, we are only using the manager's FirstName and LastName, but RavenDB will reindex the referencing employees even if the only change was an updated phone number.

LoadDocument is a very powerful feature, and it deserve its place in your toolbox. But you should be aware of its limitations and costs. Unfortunately, it's used all too often as a means to avoid changing the model, which will usually just defer a problem rather than fix the modeling issues. All of that being said, if you aren't going to have a large number of references to a single document and you do want a query based on data from related documents, LoadDocument is a really nice way to do so.

10.7. Dynamic data

RavenDB is schemaless. You can store any kind of data in any way you want – to a point. This flexibility doesn't extend to querying. You do need to know what you're querying on, right? Of course, you can query on fields in a dynamic fashion, and it will work because the query optimizer will add the new field you just queried onto the index. But adding a field to an index requires us to reindex it, and that isn't quite what we want. We want to be able to say, "This index will cover any of the fields I'm interested in" and have that done regardless of the shape of the data we index.

We can do that in RavenDB quite easily with a bit of pre-planning. Let's look at Listing 10.30, showing the Employees/DynamicFields index and how RavenDB allows us to index dynamic fields.

Listing 10.30 *'Employees/DynamicFields' index, using dynamic fields*

```
from e in docs.Employees
select new
{
    _ = e.Address.Select(field =>
            CreateField(field.Key, field.Value)
    ),
    __ = CreateField(e.FirstName, e.LastName),
    Name = e.FirstName + " " + e.LastName
}
```

There are several things going on with the `Employees/DynamicFields` index in Listing 10.30. First, we used the `_` variable name as an index output to indicate that this index is using dynamic field indexes. (Otherwise, RavenDB will error with an invalid field name when you query.)[4] You can see that you can mix and match dynamic index names with static field names. RavenDB doesn't mind, it just works.

We also used the `CreateField` method twice. The first time, we used it to index all the fields inside the `Address` object. In this way, we aren't explicitly listing them one at a time, and if different documents have different fields for the `Address` object, each document will have different fields indexed.

The second time we called `CreateField` is much stranger. This created a completely dynamic field whose name is the employee's `FirstName` and whose value is the employee's `LastName`. This is an example of dynamic fields that are created explicitly. With the index defined, we can now start querying it, as you can see in Listing 10.31.

Listing 10.31 *Querying over dynamic fields*

```
from index 'Employeess/DynamicFields'
where City = 'London'
```

Even though the index doesn't have an explicit field named `City`, we can still query on it. For that matter, we can also query using `where Nancy='Davolio'`. You can add any field that you want to the `Address` object, and it will be indexed. No two documents must have the same fields; the `Employees/DynamicFields` shown in Listing 10.30 can accept any structure you want. Dynamic fields complete the schemaless nature of RavenDB and allow for complete freedom of operations.

It's still recommended that you mostly use static indexing, mostly because it's easier to reason about and work with. While RavenDB doesn't actually care for the field names you

---

4   We can only use `_` once in an index output, and the name of the field doesn't matter when you use `CreateField`, so we typically just use `__`, `___`, etc. for the dynamic field names.

have, it's usually easier if you use dynamic fields only when needed. In particular, we've seen users that used dynamic fields to index every single field in their documents. That *works*, and sometimes you'd want to do this. But in most cases, it's an issue of "we might need this in the future" and is rarely, if ever, used.

Indexing documents has a cost that is proportional to the number of indexed fields, so indexing things that you'll likely not need will end up costing time and disk space for no return.

10.8. Summary

We started this chapter by discussing *what* indexes are in RavenDB. We saw that, like an onion,[5] indexes come in layers. There's the index definition, specifying what and how we should index, the index on disk and the actual indexing process. We started working with indexes explicitly by defining indexes using Linq expressions. Such expressions give us the ability to select the fields (and computed values) that we want to be able to index.

We looked into how the indexes actually work, starting from a document being transformed into the index entry by the index definition all the way to the actual processing that happens for the data being indexed. We looked at how the values we index are broken into terms according to the specified analyzer and then are stored in a way that allows quick retrieval of the associated documents. We also saw that we can store information directly in the index, although that's reserved for special cases.

Once we covered what indexes are, we started to look at how we can use static indexes in RavenDB. Multimap indexes allow us to index more than a single collection in one index, giving us the ability to merge results from different sources in a single query. Full text search is a world unto itself, but RavenDB contains everything you can wish for in this regard.

We looked at how full text search analysis processes text and how it's exposed in the index terms in the Studio. RavenDB allows you to utilize full text search using both purpose-built methods (such as StartsWith(), Search(), etc.) and a lower level interface exposed via the Lucene() method that lets you interface directly with the Lucene engine.

A nice trick you can use in indexing is to merge multiple fields from the index into a single field in the index entry, which allows you to query over all these fields at once. This kind of behavior is perfect for building search pages, avoiding the need to have a field for each option and simplifying the user interface to a single textbox. In the area of search, your users will surely appreciate you looking like Google, and RavenDB makes such behavior quite easy to implement.

In fact, as we have seen, indexes aren't limited to just plain searching. Features such as suggestions allow RavenDB to analyze your data and guess what the user actually meant to search for, and "more like this" can be used to find similar documents to the one the user is looking at.

Facets are a way to dissect the result set you get from a query and gather additional information from it. Instead of forcing your users to go through thousands or millions of results,

---

5   Or an ogre.

you can have RavenDB slice and dice the results so the users can dig deeper and find exactly what they're looking for. These last three features (suggestions, "more like this" and facets) are primarily used when you need to directly expose search operations to the users. They allow you to provide an intelligent and easy-to-use interface to expose the data from your system in a way that can be easily consumed, without having to work hard to do so.

RavenDB also supports spatial queries, allowing you to find documents based on their location on the globe. We looked at how such indexes are defined and what you can do with them. We also dove into how they're actually implemented and the varying costs of the levels of accuracy you can get from spatial queries.

We peeked into how RavenDB allows you to query related data by calling `LoadDocument` at indexing time. This moves the responsibility of updating the indexed data from related documents to RavenDB, which may increase the indexing time but has no impact on the cost of querying the information.

Finally, we looked at how RavenDB allows you to define indexes on dynamic data without needing *any* common structure between the indexed documents. This is useful for user generated data and when you're working on highly dynamic systems. Instead of the usual complexity involved in such systems, with RavenDB, you can just make everything work. The database will allow you to store, retrieve and query the data in any way you want.

In the next chapter, we'll look into RavenDB's MapReduce indexes, what they can do for you and how they actually work.

11. MapReduce and Aggregations in RavenDB

MapReduce is an old term. It came from Lisp and was used as early as the 1960s. For a long time, it was primarily known only by functional language aficionados, and it was rarely seen outside their circles. In 2004, the Google paper "MapReduce: Simplified Data Processing on Large Clusters" was released, and MapReduce was instantly a big hit in the distributed programming circles. Everyone had to have a distributed MapReduce implementation.

RavenDB is a distributed database, and it uses MapReduce. However, it doesn't do so in the context of distributed computing. Instead, RavenDB uses MapReduce for aggregation of data on each node independently. If you're used to MapReduce jobs that run on large clusters processing terrabytes of data, this might look very strange. But RavenDB isn't using MapReduce to break apart large computations across different machines. Instead, it uses MapReduce to break apart computations across *time*.

It's usually easier to explain with an example, so let's jump into that.

11.1. Executing simple aggregations

Listing 11.1 shows a simple aggregation query, giving us the total number of orders and items purchased by a particular company.

Listing 11.1 A simple aggregation query in RavenDB

```
from Orders as o
group by o.Company
where o.Company = 'companies/1-A'
select count() as NumberOfOrders,
       sum(o.Lines[].Quantity) as ItemsPurchased,
       o.Company
```

The query in Listing 11.1 should be familiar to anyone who's used SQL before. Now, let's analyze what RavenDB must do in order to answer this kind of query:

◆ Find all the `Orders` documents where the `Company` field is set to `'companies/1-A'`.
◆ Iterate over these documents, count their number and sum the quantity of items in each.
◆ Return the results to the client.

This seems quite straightforward, but it has a couple of issues – in particular, the first two steps. The sample data we're using is a little over a thousand documents in the database. There isn't much we can do to make any query expensive over this sample dataset. However, with real-world datasets, we'll typically deal with collections that contain hundreds of thousands to many millions of documents.

Consider the first step, which is finding all the `Orders` documents with the `Company` field set to a value. If I have a few million documents to scan, that alone can be quite expensive, both in I/O (to read the data from disk) and computation (to check equality so often). This is obviously something that we can optimize with an index. It's the next step that's hard to work with.

If a company has a *lot* of orders, then the process of iterating over each of these orders can be extraordinarily expensive. Consider the case where you want to show the number of orders and the number of items purchased on the company page. This is a small amount of information that can tell you how important this particular customer is.

However, if we need to repeat the second step each time we run the query, that can get expensive very quickly. What's worse is that the more important the company, the more orders and items this particular customer purchased from us and the slower things will become. This method won't work. It's punishing success, and that isn't something we want.

Typically, you won't run such queries directly because of their cost and time to run. Instead, you'll write a job that will run these queries at idle times and cache the results. Then you only have to deal with cache invalidation, making sure that this job is never run under load, explaining to users that the results are delayed and so on and so forth. Suddenly, this is a big task. It's complex and will take time to complete.

But all you really wanted was to put a couple numbers on a page, and suddenly you need to deploy a background job, monitor its cost and execution and wait until the daily or weekly run to get updated numbers. Such a high cost of aggregation will usually cause such features to be dropped.

And even if you don't have enough data to require such measures, aggregation queries are still typically costly for the database – enough so that they're used sparingly in most systems.

RavenDB's aggregation doesn't work like this.

11.1.1. THE GORY DETAILS OF AGGREGATION IN RAVENDB

Instead of gathering all the data and then aggregating it all in place, RavenDB uses MapReduce to break apart the aggregation computation into discrete steps: the "map" and the "reduce."

Let's look at how RavenDB *actually* processes the query in Listing 11.1. Run the query in the listing and then click on the index button in the results, as shown in Figure 11.1.

We're going to go deep into how RavenDB is handling aggregations. You'll not typically need to know this level of detail, and you can feel free to just skip this section if you don't think you need such knowledge. I'm including it here because it's important to understand the implications of how things work and that aggregation queries in RavenDB are *very* cheap.

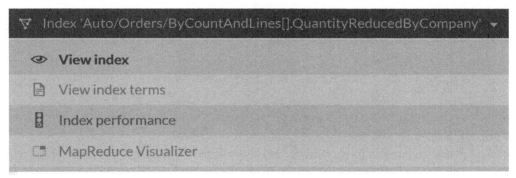

Figure 11.1. *Getting to the index details on the query page*

You can already see that an aggregation query in RavenDB is also using an index. In addition to the usual options, such as the index terms and performance statistics, there's also the MapReduce visualizer, which we'll look at in more detail later. For now, click on the View Index option, which should open the index details page shown in Figure 11.2.

Figure 11.2 shows the structure of the index. Operating over Orders, it groups by the Company and aggregates over them. One thing to note here is that there's no mention anywhere of companies/1-A. Even though the query in Listing 11.1 mentioned it, the index isn't operating on that particular value but rather on the generic concept of aggregating by the Company field.

In other words, as usual, RavenDB looked at the query and generalized the operation to answer any question using Company. But what about the aggregation?

Aggregation is actually handled via two separate actions, map and reduce. The first stage runs a map operation on each of the documents, grabbing just Company, sum(Lines[].Quantity) and Count = 1 from each of the Orders documents. The second stage is to group them all by Company and run the reduce operation to get the final result by each of the Company field values.

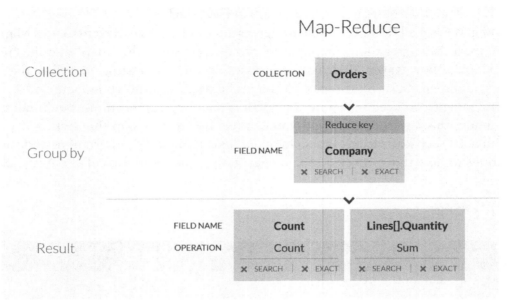

Figure 11.2. *A MapReduce index aggregation* Orders *by* Company

If this doesn't make sense to you, don't worry. RavenDB contains a few tools specifically to help you understand how the MapReduce process works.

In the Indexes menu item, go to Map-Reduce Visualizer and then select the Auto/Orders/ByCountAndLines[].QuantityReducedByCompany index from the drop-down. Then search for the following document IDs: orders/396-A and orders/445-A. The result should look similar to Figure 11.3.

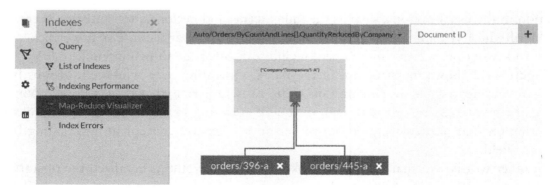

Figure 11.3. *The MapReduce visualizer allows us to inspect the internal structure of the index*

Clicking on the {"Company":"companies/1-A"} rectangle in Figure 11.3 will give us more details about that particular value, as you can see in Figure 11.4.

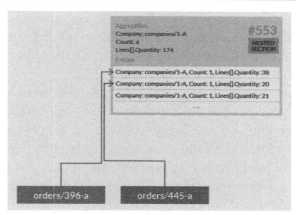

Figure 11.4. *A single reduce result and the total reduced value for a MapReduce index*

With the details in Figures 11.3 and 11.4, you can now see exactly what I mean when I talk about map output and the resulting aggregation. The documents we selected (orders/396-A and orders/445-A) both belong to companies/1-A, and we can see that for orders/396-A, the map output was {"Company": "companies/1-A","Count": 1,"Lines[].Quantity": 38}. Indeed, if we go and inspect the document, we'll see three line items, with quantities of 15, 21 and 2, totaling 38. For orders/445-A, we can see that the total quantity is 20, with a single line item.

This is interesting, but what's even *more* interesting is the aggregated value. For companies/1-A, you can see the aggregated values of a total of six orders for this company, with a final quantity of 174 items ordered. Clicking on the aggregation summary will take us even further down, into the individual page entries, as you can see in Figure 11.5.

In Figure 11.5, you can see all the details for each of the entries for companies/1-A. This is the lowest level we need to inspect as well as the reason why RavenDB implements aggregation in such a manner. I've already spent several pages now just explaining what's going on. Why is the aggregation implementation for RavenDB so *complex*?

MapReduce Page Entries			✕
Company	**Count**	**Lines[].Quantity**	**Source Document**
companies/1-A	1	38	orders/396-a
companies/1-A	1	20	orders/445-a
companies/1-A	1	21	-
companies/1-A	1	17	-
companies/1-A	1	18	-
companies/1-A	1	60	-

Figure 11.5. *Individual mapped entries for* companies/1-A

The reason is quite simple, actually. We don't run aggregation queries once; instead, we compute the aggregation result once, and then we store it. When we issued the query in Listing 11.1, we queried only for results for `companies/1-A`, but the index that the query optimizer generated for us applies to all companies.

In fact, if we now run the same query but for `companies/2-A`, we'll be able to reuse the same index. And in fact, we'll have to do very little work. The query will use the existing index and fetch the already precomputed results for `companies/2-A`. It won't have to actually perform any aggregation whatsoever. All the work has already been done.

As great as that is, you might be asking yourself why there's this level of complexity. After all, surely we could have done the same thing without so many moving parts, right? That's correct, but there's one additional item that you need to consider. How are we going to handle updates?

The MapReduce indexes in RavenDB aren't simply a cache of the already computed results. Instead, we store the data in such a way that makes it cheap to also update the results. Consider what will happen inside RavenDB when a new order comes in. We'll run the map portion of the index, getting the `Company`, `sum(Lines[].Quantity)` and `Count = 1` from the newly created document.

The easiest way to visualize that is to add another row to Figure 11.5. At this point, RavenDB can then just aggregate the new results alongside the already existing result and get to the final tally. In other words, the complexity here exists in order to allow RavenDB to efficiently update MapReduce results when documents are created or updated.

This works great when we have a small number of items to aggregate. Such is the case with `companies/1-A`. But what happens when the number of items grow? Let's increase the number of documents we're aggregating by a hundred fold and see where that takes us. Go to `Documents` and then `Patch` and run the update script in Listing 11.2.

Listing 11.2 *Increase the number of Orders documents by a hundred*

```
from Orders
update {
    for (var i = 0; i < 100; i++ ){
        put("orders/", this);
    }
}
```

After running this script, we should have 83,830 Orders documents in the database (830 original Orders and ten times that number that we just entered). Where we previously had six entries for `companies/1-A`, we now have 606. Let's look at how that works.

Go back to the MapReduce visualizer and select the `Auto/Orders/ByCountAndLines[].`
`QuantityReducedByCompany` index. Then add the `orders/396-A` and `orders/445-A` documents. The result is shown in Figure 11.6

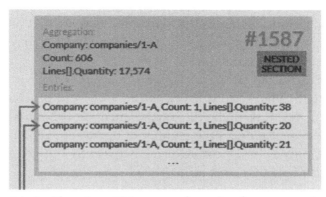

Figure 11.6. *Showing* 606 *mapped entries for* `companies/1-A`

This is very similar to how it looked before, and indeed, the structure of the data is exactly
the same. This is because the number of entries for `companies/1-A` is still quite small. Let's
select another pair of documents, this time belonging to `companies/77-A` and see what kind
of structure we have there. Add `orders/77-A` and `orders/146-A` to the visualizer and take a
look at the results, as shown in Figure 11.7.

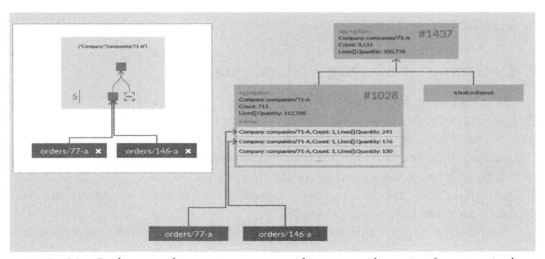

Figure 11.7. *MapReduce works as a tree once we have enough entries for a particular value*

On the left in Figure 11.7, you can see that, unlike for `companies/1-A` in Figure 11.3 where we had a flat list, Figure 11.7 shows a tree structure. Indeed, once we're past a certain size, RavenDB will start processing MapReduce entries in a treelike fashion.

Consider an update to `orders/77-A` and how RavenDB will apply it. First, we'll run the `map` on the updated document, giving us the map entry to write to #1028. Then, we'll run the `reduce` on that page, giving us the final tally for this page. We'll then recurse upward, toward #1437, where we'll also run the `reduce`.

The end result is that an update operation will take us a single `map` invocation and two `reduce` calls to update the final result for `companies/77-A`. In other words, if we have a lot of data for a particular key, RavenDB will start segmenting this data and apply aggregation operations in such a way that reduces the number of operations required to a minimum. This ensures that we're not only able to answer queries efficiently but are also able to update the MapReduce results with very little cost.

Using aggregation in RavenDB

Aggregation operations in RavenDB are cheap, both to compute and to query. This is in stark contrast to the usual behavior of aggregation queries in other databases. The more data you have to go through, the more efficiently will RavenDB be able to actually process and aggregate it.

While typically you'll run aggregation as a daily or weekly report (usually during off hours) and store these results for use later, RavenDB allows you to just query the aggregated data. RavenDB will provide the answers you need, as well as keep everything up to date.

11.2. Defining your own MapReduce indexes

We've seen from Listing 11.1 how we can query using `group by` and RavenDB will generate a MapReduce index for us behind the scenes. This works quite nicely, but there's only so much that you can do with a dynamic query before the query optimizer will give up.

The query optimizer can do quite a lot, but in order to make sure that it's predictable, it's currently limited to recognizing and being able to generate MapReduce indexes from a fairly small list of predictable patterns. For more complex things, you'll need to create your own MapReduce index. Luckily, this is easy to do.

Let's say we want to get the total number of sales and the total amount we made on each product. We can't express this as a simple query, so we'll need to create a MapReduce index of our own for that. Go to the `Indexes` page and click on `New Index`. Name the index `Products/Sales`, then click the `Add Reduction` button. Listing 11.3 has the contents of the `Map` and `Reduce` fields. After you're done filling these in, click `Save` to create the new index.

Listing 11.3 *Compute total number of sales and revenue per product*

```
// map
from o in docs.Orders
from l in o.Lines
select new
{
    l.Product,
    l.Quantity,
    Total = (l.Quantity * l.PricePerUnit) * (1 - l.Discount)
}


// reduce
from r in results
group r by r.Product into g
select new
{
    Product = g.Key,
    Quantity = g.Sum(x => x.Quantity),
    Total = g.Sum(x => x.Total)
}
```

Before we get to investigating how this index works, let's talk about what it does. The map portion runs over all the orders and all the line items for each order. Then, for each of the line items, we output an entry with the quantity sold and the amount of money we made on this product. The reduce will group all these results based on the Product field and then sum up all the final numbers for the Total and Quantity sold.

Now that we've really seen map and reduce, it should be easier to grasp how they're truly two separate operations. It's also important to understand that we aren't actually running the map or the reduce on the full results all the time. Instead, we break the results apart internally and apply map and reduce to portions of the data each time. This leads to several important restrictions on MapReduce indexes:

◆ Both the map and reduce functions must be *pure* functions. In other words, they should have no external input, and calling them with the same input must always return the same output. In particular, usage of Random or DateTime.Now and similar calls is not allowed.

- ◆ The output of the `map` is fed into the `reduce`. This should be obvious, but what may not be obvious is that the output of the `reduce` is *also* fed into the `reduce`, recursively. In particular, you should make no assumptions in the `reduce` about the number of calls or the amount of data that you have to process in each invocation of `reduce`.
- ◆ The output of the `reduce` must match the output of the map. (Because both are being fed back into the `reduce`, they must have the same structure.) RavenDB will error if you have a different shape for each of the functions.

Because of these restrictions, RavenDB can apply the `map` and `reduce` functions in an incremental fashion and generate the results that we've already seen. This is the key to RavenDB's ability to compute aggregation cheaply over time.

We can now run the query in Listing 11.4 to find the top grossing products:

Listing 11.4 *Finding the top grossing products across all orders*

```
from index 'Products/Sales'
order by Total as double desc
```

You'll note that the results of this query are instantaneous. Even though we have tens of thousands of records, RavenDB only needs to look through 77 precomputed results. We can also sort by `Quantity` to find the most popular products.

Go into the `Map-Reduce Visualizer` and select the `Products/Sales` index. Then, enter `orders/6-A` and `orders/10-A` to see the internal structure of the MapReduce index, as shown in Figure 11.8.

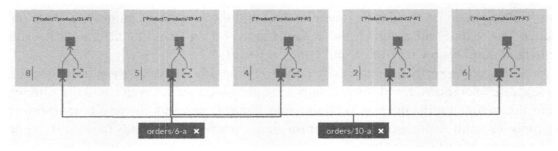

Figure 11.8. *Internal structure of the* `Products/Sales` *index in the MapReduce visualizer*

As you can see in Figure 11.8, all of the entries are big enough to require a tree structure. Let's take a closer look at `products/39-A`, with Figure 11.9 zooming in on a single page inside that tree.

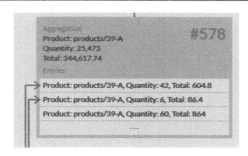

Figure 11.9. *A single page holding over 25,000 map entries, due to high compression rate*

Page #578 holds over 25,000 entries for this product. How can a single page hold so many? The answer is that RavenDB applies compression to the mapped entries. Since they're mostly similar, they have a high compression rate, allowing us to pack a *lot* of entries into a small amount of space. This also adds to performance of the updating entries in the tree, since we don't have to do as much work and the depth of the tree is much smaller.

This is about as low-level as we'll get when discussing the MapReduce implementation. You should now have a good feel for the relative costs of using aggregation in general – and MapReduce in particular – in RavenDB. With that knowledge under your belt, let's explore some of the more interesting things that we can do with MapReduce indexes in RavenDB.

11.2.1. COMMON PITFALLS WITH MAPREDUCE INDEXES

Certain operations are not easy to perform using the limits on the map and reduce functions that RavenDB has. Probably the most obvious example here is the problem with calculating an average. Let's edit the Products/Sales index to add an average. Listing 11.5 shows the updated definition with the most obvious (and wrong) way to do so:

Listing 11.5 *Computing average (wrongly) in MapReduce index*

```
// map
from o in docs.Orders
from l in o.Lines
select new
{
    l.Product,
    l.Quantity,
    Count = 1,
    Total = (l.Quantity * l.PricePerUnit) * (1 - l.Discount),
    Average = 0, // so we'll have the same shape as the reduce
    Debug = new object[0] // same shape as reduce
}
```

```
// reduce
from r in results
group r by r.Product into g
select new
{
    Product = g.Key,
    Quantity = g.Sum(x => x.Quantity),
    Count = g.Sum(x => x.Count),
    Total = g.Sum(x => x.Total),
    Average = g.Average(x => x.Total),
    Debug = g.Select(x => x.Total).ToArray()
}
```

Save the updated index and then run the following query: from index 'Products/Sales' where Product = 'products/1-A'. The result is showed in Figure 11.10.

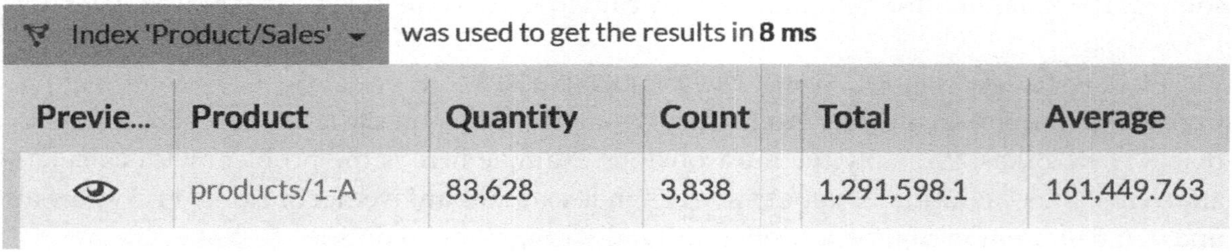

Previe...	Product	Quantity	Count	Total	Average
👁	products/1-A	83,628	3,838	1,291,598.1	161,449.763

Index 'Product/Sales' ▼ was used to get the results in **8 ms**

Figure 11.10. *The wrong results shown for an average computation*

The results shown in Figure 11.10 are wrong. The average price for a box of chai (which is what products/1-A is) is not $161,449.793. So why are we getting this result?

The answer is simple. The Average call isn't complex: it sums the input elements and then divides that sum by the number of elements. But remember that map and reduce are not called on each individual value. Instead, they're called in batches. This means by the time the final call to reduce happened, it didn't get a flat list of all the results. Instead, it got an aggregated list. Figure 11.11 shows the Debug field from the index, which can allow us to better understand what's going on.

```json
{
    "Product": "products/1-A",
    "Quantity": 83628,
    "Count": 3838,
    "Total": 1291598.1,
    "Average": 161449.7625,
    "Debug": [
        151359.3,
        148996.8,
        91692,
        196200,
        262440,
        210528,
        133632,
        96750
    ],
    "@metadata": {
        "@change-vector": null
    }
}
```

Figure 11.11. *The debug field from the* Products/Sales *index demonstrating the recursive nature of* reduce *operations*

As you can see, the computation of the Average is correct for the input it received. Because we executed the reduce multiple times, by the time the final round came, we fed it seven results, each of them aggregating about 500 documents. In other words, when we write a MapReduce index, we need to take into account the fact that we never have access to the total result set. This make sense, when you think about it. You don't want to have a single function invocation that has to go through many tens of thousands of documents (or many more, on realistic datasets).

Don't assume that the order is fixed, either

If your MapReduce index does work that relies on the order of operations or the order of items passed to the map or reduce function, it's going to fail in a similar manner. This is common when you have calls to First or use arrays in the MapReduce index. If you care about the order of operations, you'll need to ensure the order as part of the MapReduce index and remember that the calls are made in a recursive manner.

So how *can* we compute an average? The answer is obvious when you know it, we need to keep track of the Count and Total as we are reducing the data and compute the Average using these. You can see it in Listing 11.6.

Listing 11.6 *Properly computing average in a MapReduce index*

```
// reduce
from r in results
group r by r.Product into g
let qty = g.Sum(x => x.Quantity)
let total = g.Sum(x => x.Total)
select new
{
    Product = g.Key,
    Quantity = qty,
    Count = g.Sum(x => x.Count),
    Total = total,
    Average = total / qty
}
```

All we need to do for the proper computation is make sure we aren't assuming the total dataset is passed to the reduce call. In this case, we already have all the data we need, and we can just compute the final average. Note that we'll still need to have a field called Average in the map function because the shape must match. But since we're never reading this field, we don't have to give it any special value and can just initialize it to any value we want.

Similarly to Average, we can't use Count() in the reduce either, for the exact same reason. That's why we use Count = 1 in the map and sum it in the reduce: to allow us to start the recursive computation of the total amount of items.

11.2.2. COMPLEX MAPREDUCE INDEXES

So far, the MapReduce indexes we've built were pretty simple, mostly doing trivial aggregation on numbers. To be fair, that's usually what you'll do with MapReduce indexes. But you can also do more with them.

A good example would be to compute the total sales per company. This sounds like just taking the Products/Sales index and changing what we're grouping on, so let's make this more interesting. What we want to do is to get, per company, the total sales per product.

Listing 11.7 shows the Companies/Purchases index, which does just that.

Listing 11.7 *Computing the total products sold for each company*

```
//map
from o in docs.Orders
from l in o.Lines
select new
{
    o.Company,
    Products = new [] { new { l.Product, l.Quantity } },
    Total = l.Quantity
}

//reduce
from r in results
group r by r.Company into g
select new
{
    Company = g.Key,
    Products = g.SelectMany(x => x.Products)
        .GroupBy(x => x.Product)
        .Select(p => new
        {
            Product = p.Key,
            Quantity = p.Sum(x => x.Quantity)
        }),
    Total = g.Sum(x => x.Total)
}
```

Looking at Listing 11.7, we can see that the map function looks pretty normal, but there's a considerable amount of work going on in the reduce. Let's break it apart into its components and examine each independently.

First, the map generates an entry per line item, and the entry contains a single element Products array with the product's ID and the quantity sold. The reason we create the array in the map is that we need to match the shape of the reduce. In the reduce function, we group the results by the Company and then generate the results for that particular company. The most interesting tidbit happens when building the Products field.

There, we apply *another* GroupBy call to aggregate the data inside the Company once again. We use this to get the total numbers of items purchased for each product, and this mechanism allows us to aggregate the data across multiple invocations to reduce safely and in a natural manner.

```json
{
    "Company": "companies/13-A",
    "Products": [
        {
            "Product": "products/21-A",
            "Quantity": 1010
        },
        {
            "Product": "products/37-A",
            "Quantity": 101
        }
    ],
    "Total": 1111,
    "@metadata": {
        "@change-vector": null
    }
}
```

Figure 11.12. *Complex output from the index, showing aggregation inside the reduced result*

Now, let's see what this index actually generates. Execute the following query: from index 'Companies/Purchases' where Company = 'companies/13-A' and observe the results. You can also see this in Figure 11.12.

This kind of index can be used to prepare complex computations ahead of time, leaning on RavenDB's ability to compute this beforehand. RavenDB will then be in charge of keeping such details up to date, and your client code can simply query the output of the index.

Reduce should...*reduce* the size of the data

A somewhat overlooked requirement for the reduce function is that the amount of data going out of the reduce function should be smaller than the amount of data going in. All the examples we've seen so far have done this properly, mostly because they aggregated information.

Let's look at an example where the amount of information that passed through reduce doesn't go down and discuss its implications. In the Companies/Purchases index, if the Products field was defined just as

Products = g.SelectMany(x => x.Products), we would have a problem. Calling reduce won't actually reduce the amount of data we're working with and, as time goes by, the reduce function will have to operate on larger and larger values.

This isn't an efficient way to do things, and since we need to keep track of intermediate values, it will lead to a marked increased in memory utilization and disk space usage, and it will overall be quite expensive.

11.3. Querying MapReduce indexes

When talking about MapReduce indexes, we typically focus on the Reduce portion of them – the aggregation and computation being done. This, however, is only part of the story. While a lot of stuff is going on in the Reduce portion of the index, in the end, the data is still being written to the index in exactly the same way as we've seen in the previous chapter.

This means that you can execute any of the usual operations you would normally run. As a good example, let's look at Figure 11.12. The output of the query is pretty bare bones: what *is* products/21-A, for example. Listing 11.8 shows a nice way to get more information at very little cost.

Listing 11.8 *Using functions to enrich the results from a MapReduce index*

```
declare function addProductName(result) {
    for (var i = 0; i < result.Products.length; i++) {
        var p = load(result.Products[i].Product);
        result.Products[i].ProductName = p.Name;
    }
    return result;
}
from index 'Companies/Purchases' as result
where result.Company = 'companies/13-A'
select addProductName(result)
```

The result of the query in Listing 11.8 is shown in Listing 11.9.

Listing 11.9 *Output of the query in Listing 11.8,
showing enriched result set of MapReduce index*

```
{
    "Company": "companies/13-A",
    "Products": [
        {
            "Product": "products/21-A",
            "Quantity": 1010,
            "ProductName": "Sir Rodney's Scones"
        },
        {
            "Product": "products/37-A",
            "Quantity": 101,
            "ProductName": "Gravad lax"
        }
    ],
    "Total": 1111
}
```

The query in Listing 11.8 should serve as a nice example of the kind of things we can do, but it's just the first taste. In addition to using projections in this manner, you can also define MapReduce fields to support full text search, apply suggestions and "more like this."

You can even query using facets on MapReduce indexes, an example of which you can see in Listing 11.10.

Listing 11.10 *Facets also apply to MapReduce indexes*

```
from index 'Companies/Purchases'
select facet(
    Total < 5000,
    Total between 5_000 and 9_999,
    Total between 10_000 and 24_999,
    Total between 25_000 and 49_999,
    Total between 50_000 and 74_999,
    Total > 75_000,
    avg(Total)
    )
```

Applying facets, which can do their own aggregation, to MapReduce is an interesting experience. It allows us to do things like build a MapReduce operation to aggregate some of the data in a static fashion, then allow faceted queries to slice and dice it further. If you look at the results of the query in Listing 11.10, you'll note that the faceted results also include an average value for each facet, and we have support for the usual (min, max, sum, avg) aggregation methods.

In fact, that's not the only way to aggregate the data in multiple ways. There's also recursive MapReduce operations.

11.4. Recursive MapReduce

The sample dataset that we used consists of orders representing sales to companies. This is the typical e-commerce model and should be pretty familiar to you. A common requirement in such a system is reporting – in particular, pulling sales data on a daily, monthly and yearly basis.

Listing 11.11 shows the `Products/DailySales` index, which gives us the details of sales by product by day.

Listing 11.11 *Computing total daily sales by product for all orders*

```
//map
from o in docs.Orders
from l in o.Lines
select new
{
    o.OrderedAt.Date,
    l.Product,
    Count = l.Quantity
}

//reduce
from r in results
group r by new { r.Date, r.Product } into g
select new
{
    g.Key.Date,
    g.Key.Product,
    Count = g.Sum(x => x.Count)
}
```

The output of the `Products/DailySales` index can be seen in Figure 11.13. The only new thing we have in Listing 11.11 is the group by on multiple fields, the Date and the Product.

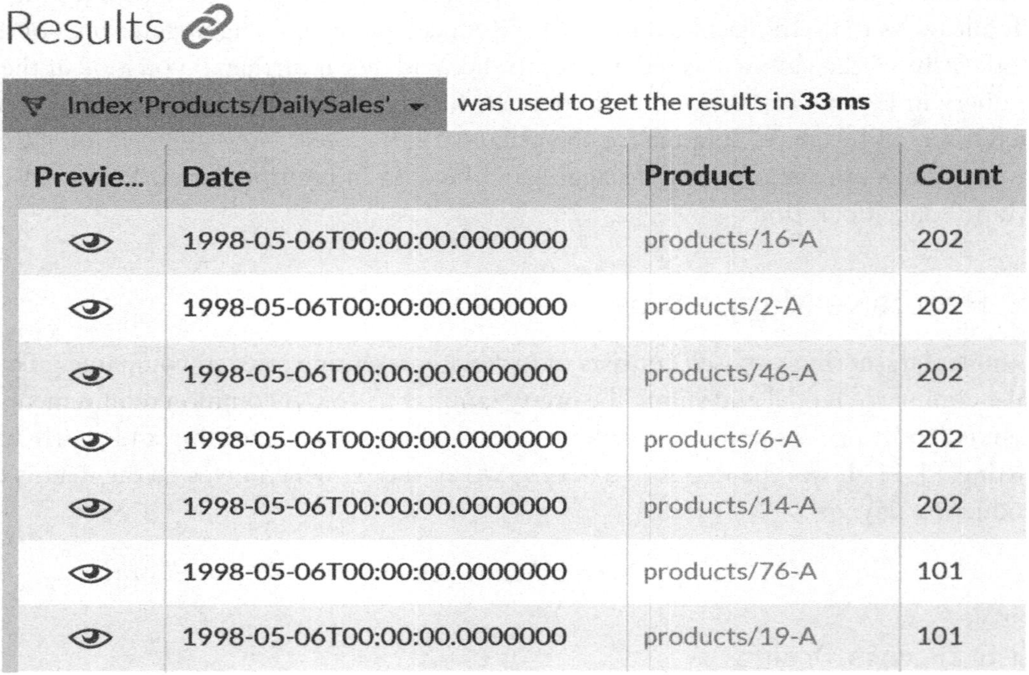

Results 🔗

| Index 'Products/DailySales' ▾ | was used to get the results in **33 ms** | | |

Previe...	Date	Product	Count
👁	1998-05-06T00:00:00.0000000	products/16-A	202
👁	1998-05-06T00:00:00.0000000	products/2-A	202
👁	1998-05-06T00:00:00.0000000	products/46-A	202
👁	1998-05-06T00:00:00.0000000	products/6-A	202
👁	1998-05-06T00:00:00.0000000	products/14-A	202
👁	1998-05-06T00:00:00.0000000	products/76-A	101
👁	1998-05-06T00:00:00.0000000	products/19-A	101

Figure 11.13. *Showing the daily sales for each product on May 6th, 1998*

Next, we need to compute the same values per month and then per year. We can define the same index again and run the exact same computation but this time group by the product, year and month and then just by the product and year. But we currently have 83,830 orders in the database, and we'll likely have more. Doing the same operation on all these values again and again seems...inefficient.

RavenDB supports the notion of outputting a MapReduce output from an index to a dedicated collection. Set the `Output reduce to collection` to `DailyProductSales`. Figure 11.14 shows how this can be done.

☑ Output reduce to the collection   **DailyProductSales**

Figure 11.14. *Configuring MapReduce index to write the output of the index to a dedicated collection*

Make the modification to the `Products/DailySales` index and save it. Then head to the `Documents` tab and look at the collections in the database. You can see the results in Figure 11.15.

DailyProductSales/3183876884104958208

[💾 Save]   [🗐 Clone]   [🗑 Delete]

```
1 ▾ {
2       "Date": "1998-05-06T00:00:00.0000000",
3       "Product": "products/75-A",
4       "Count": 101,
5 ▾     "@metadata": {
6           "@collection": "DailyProductSales",
7           "@flags": "Artificial, FromIndex"
8       }
9   }
```

Figure 11.15. *An artificial document created as a result of a MapReduce's output collection*

In many respects, these artificial documents will behave just like standard documents. You can load them, query them and even save modifications to them. Note that modifying an artificial document by hand is *not* recommended, as the next update to the index will overwrite any changes you have made to the document, after all. Artificial documents are *not* replicated. Since they're being created by the index directly, they'll also be created in the remote node, so there's no point in sending them over the wire.

Artificial documents are updated whenever the index completes a batch of documents, so there's very little lag time between the index picking up changes and the artificial documents' update. If this were the only thing artificial documents were good for, that wouldn't be of much use. After all, we already have the results as the output of the MapReduce index. So why do we need artificial documents?

The primary reason that artificial documents exist is so you can set up indexes on top of them. And that includes *additional MapReduce indexes*. Take a look at Listing 11.12, showing just such an example of the Products/MonthlySales index, computing the monthly totals from the daily totals.

Listing 11.12 *Recursive MapReduce index using artificial documents*

```
//map
from ds in docs.DailyProductSales
select new
{
    ds.Product,
    Year =  ds.Date.Year,
    Month = ds.Date.Month,
    ds.Count
}

//reduce
from result in results
group result by new
{
    result.Product,
    result.Year,
    result.Month
}
into g
select new
{
    g.Key.Year,
    g.Key.Month,
    g.Key.Product,
    Count = g.Sum(x => x.Count)
}
```

You can see that the map of the Products/MonthlySales index is using the DailyProductSales collection as it source, and the reduce aggregates the data by product on a monthly basis. Let's examine what's actually going on here in a little more depth.

Whenever an order is created or modified, the Products/DailySales index will run, computing the updated daily totals for the products in the new order. As a result of this index running, artificial documents will be created (with IDs such as DailyProductSales/3183876884104958208).

Because a DailyProductSales document was created, the Products/MonthlySales index will run on the changed daily tallies to update its own numbers. We can even set things up so we'll have an output collection for the MonthlyProductsSales as well, and then define a `Products/YearlySales`. The recursive nature of the indexing naturally extends in this manner.

Artificial documents do have a few limitations that you should be aware of:

◆ RavenDB will detect and generate an error if you have a cycle of artificial documents. In other words, you can't define another index that will output artificial documents if that will trigger (directly or indirectly) the same index. Otherwise, you might set up a situation where the indexes run in an infinite loop.

◆ You must choose an empty collection. RavenDB will not allow you to output artificial documents into a preexisting collection. This is done because RavenDB will overwrite any document in the collection, so it prevents the option of overwriting existing documents.

◆ The document identifiers for the artificial documents are generated by RavenDB (based on the hash of the reduce key), and you don't have any control over them.

◆ Artificial documents are not sent over replication and cannot use revisions or attachments.

Artificial documents and subscriptions

You can use subscriptions and artificial documents together. (In fact, along with recursive MapReduce, that's one of the primary reasons they exist.) But you need to be aware of a small wrinkle in this setup. Because artificial documents aren't sent via replication, each node in the database group is going to have its own (independent) copy of the results. The contents are the same, but the subscription has no way of knowing this.

Because of this issue, it's recommended to use artificial documents with subscriptions only on a single node. Failover of the subscription to another node may cause the subscription to send artificial documents that the subscription has already acknowledged. You can configure this by disabling the dynamic task distribution as part of the subscription configuration.

Artificial documents and recursive MapReduce are a good match, but before you turn your RavenDB instances into a reporting powerhouse, there's another possible topology to consider. Instead of defining these indexes and processes on the main database, you can set up external replication to a dedicated database (on the same cluster or on a separate one) and run all that work there.

This can simplify distribution of work as the application grows. If you have many such indexes and a high rate of changes, being able to isolate the work to a particular database group (and thus specific nodes) can be very helpful.

11.5. MultimapReduce indexes

In the previous chapter, Listing 10.12 demonstrated the usage of multimap indexes to index several collections and unite the results into a single index. This can be great for when you want to search over several things at the same time. The example we looked at in Chapter 10 searched for a person by name, where the person can be an Employee, a Contact on a Company or a Contact for a Supplier. Regardless, we were able to search for that person easily and in a convenient manner.

MultimapReduce indexes allow us to extend that behavior to also include aggregation across multiple sources in a natural way. Let's first look at Listing 11.13, showing off this feature, and then explore what this means.

Go to the Indexes page and create a new index. Click on Add map twice and create the three maps. Then click Add Reduction and add the reduce. Name the new index Cities/Details and click Save.

Listing 11.13 *MultimapReduce index that sums the points of interest in each city*

```
// map #1
from c in docs.Companies
select new
{
    c.Address.City,
    Companies = 1,
    Suppliers = 0,
    Employees = 0
}



// map #2
from s in docs.Suppliers
select new
{
    s.Address.City,
    Companies = 0,
    Suppliers = 1,
    Employees = 0
}
```

```
// map 3
from e in docs.Employees
select new{
    e.Address.City,
    Companies = 0,
    Suppliers = 0,
    Employees = 1
}

//reduce
from result in results
group result by result.City
into g
select new
{
    City = g.Key,
    Companies = g.Sum(x => x.Companies),
    Suppliers = g.Sum(x => x.Suppliers),
    Employees = g.Sum(x => x.Employees),
}
```

Take a few minutes to look at Listing 11.13. There's a lot of stuff going on there. We define three maps, on the Companies, Suppliers and Employees. And for each, we output a count for the type of the document we're mapping, as well as the relevant City. Finally, on the reduce, we simply group by City and then sum up all the results from all the intermediate steps to get the final tally. Listing 11.14 shows the output from this index for London.

Listing 11.14 *Output of the 'Cities/Details' index for London*

```
{
    "City": "London",
    "Companies": 6,
    "Suppliers": 1,
    "Employees": 4
}
```

The Cities/Details index is interesting, in the sense that it shows off capabilities, but it isn't really that exciting. It also operates on a small dataset, even if it touches multiple collections. Let's modify the index by having it operate also on orders.

We'll first add another entry for each of the existing maps: `OrderTotal = 0`. And we'll add the same logic for the reduce function: `OrderTotal = g.Sum(x => x.OrderTotal)`. The first step is required because all the maps and reduces in an index must have the same output. The second is required to actually sum up the information we'll shortly add. Now click on the `Add map` button on the index edit page and add the map shown in Listing 11.15.

Listing 11.15 *Adding total order per city to the 'Cities/Details' index*

```
from o in docs.Orders
select new
{
    o.ShipTo.City,
    Companies = 0,
    Suppliers = 0,
    Employees = 0,
    OrderTotal =  o.Lines.Sum(
        x => x.Quantity * x.PricePerUnit
    )
}
```

We now have an index that can give us a lot of interesting details about each city. Listing 11.16 shows the updated output for London in the database.

Listing 11.16 *London's information now includes the total revenue for orders shipped to it*

```
{
    "City": "London",
    "Companies": 6,
    "Suppliers": 1,
    "Employees": 4,
    "OrderTotal": 4107034.71
}
```

As you can imagine, this kind of behavior is powerful because it allows you to pull data from disparate parts of your system and aggregate it with very little work. Querying this information is effectively free, so that also makes it much easier to consume and work with.

> **MapReduce indexes are also just indexes**
> It bears repeating that a Reduce index is also just an index. We focused heavily in this chapter on the Reduce portion of such indexes, but it's important to remember that they're also capable of doing everything that a map-only index can do.

In other words, if we had a `Cities` collection that also had the coordinates of each city, we would be able to modify the `Cities/Details` index to be a MultimapReduce index that also provides spatial queries. You can use facets on a MapReduce index, apply suggestions, run full text queries, etc. All too often, I see users assume the Reduce part of the index is where the functionality stops. In fact, this is where it begins.

11.6. Dynamic aggregation with MapReduce indexes

MapReduce indexes are a wonderful way to handle aggregation. RavenDB's ability to pre-compute and answer complex aggregation cheaply can make a world of difference in your ability to deliver features in your applications. The fact that showing an aggregated value doesn't require you to set up an off-hours job, monitor it, clear caches, etc. is a force multiplier for your application's capabilities.

However, while the MapReduce operation can seem magical at times, it's a tool fit for a purpose. Trying to use it for a different purpose than it's intended for will produce suboptimal results. MapReduce indexes are great when

◆ The fields you're aggregating by are known in advance.
◆ The source data you're aggregating is known in advance.

In other words, MapReduce is great for static aggregation. If you want to get the daily totals by product, MapReduce is the perfect solution. The data source (all orders) is known. What you're aggregating by (the date and the product) is known in advance, too. RavenDB is able to generate the appropriate MapReduce operation, compute the result and allow you to query it easily and cheaply.

But what happens if we want to aggregate daily sales by product only for London? Well, that's easy. We can define another MapReduce index that aggregates the results by date, product and city. We get the same benefits, and everyone is happy. But the next request is to get the daily sales by city based on the supplier, not the product. And the *next* request after that is to aggregate the sales by the employee on a monthly basis, and the one after that is to see the yearly sales by product only for specific customers, and then...

I think you get the picture. MapReduce indexes are great when the type of aggregation is known in advance. In this case, RavenDB is able to prepare everything and have an answer ready for you by the time you query. But if your queries are dynamic and fluid, and if you're changing what you're querying on and how you're doing the aggregation, this is much more complex.

One option would be to define a MapReduce index for each type of aggregation you need. This works, but you might end up with a *lot* of MapReduce indexes. That can be fine.

RavenDB is *very* efficient in the handling of MapReduce indexes (they're typically *cheaper* to run than a map-only index, actually), but a large number of indexes still means that we need to execute some amount of work times the number of indexes for each change.

A better approach for dynamic aggregation is to use facets. To see the total sales for egg noodles and cheese in the first week of July 1996, we can run the query in Listing 11.17.

Listing 11.17 *Using facets on top of a MapReduce index to achieve dynamic aggregation*

```
from index 'Products/DailySales'
    where Date between '1996-07-01' and '1996-07-07'
    and Product in ('products/11-A', 'products/42-A')
    select facet(Product, sum(Count))
```

Let's break the query in Listing 11.17 apart, one clause at a time. First, we select the MapReduce index `Products/DailySales`, which we've already seen in Listing 11.11. The `where` clause specifies the date range we want to query and the particular products we're interested in. Note that the `Date` query is using `between` and relies on the fact that we do lexical comparisons to get a clear syntax for the date range.

The `select` clause is using facets, but unlike the facets queries we looked at in the previous chapter, we're now adding a new wrinkle in the form of `sum(Count)`. This allows us to do an aggregation operation over the query results. In this way, we can dynamically control what will be aggregated.

Cost analysis for dynamic aggregation (facets) vs. static aggregation (MapReduce)

An important distinction needs to be made about the cost structures of using aggregation in MapReduce vs. facets. For MapReduce, by the time you're querying the information, it's already been aggregated. You're actually doing a search on top of the already precomputed results.

Aggregation with facets (which is sometimes also called dynamic aggregation) requires us to run over the results of the query and compute the final aggregated values. Note that the amount of results the faceted query needs to aggregate is just the query results, not the total size of the source data.

This can be confusing, so we'll use the example of the `Products/DailySales` index and the faceted query in Listing 11.17 to clear things up. We have the following values:

❖ `D` – the total number of orders. In this database, after running the patch operation in Listing 11.2, the number is 83,830 documents.

❖ `R` – the unique reduce keys after the MapReduce aggregation. In the case of the `Products/DailySales` index, that's the unique (date, product) pairs that we're grouping by. This value is 2,106 unique reduce keys for the dataset we have.

❖ Q – the number of results matched in the query. For the query in Listing 11.7 (sans facets), that number is two.

With these values, we can now give proper estimates of the costs of making various queries. A typical cost of a MapReduce query is $O(\log R)$. So the cost for a query on `Products/DailySales` would be about 11 operations.

A faceted query on all orders will have a cost of $O(D)$, with D equal to 83,830. This computation is done each time the query is run. However, the only reason the cost is $O(D)$ is that we queried over all orders. Because the number of results for the query in Listing 11.7 is two, the cost of actually aggregating them is effectively nil.

It's a great way to handle such scenarios: use MapReduce to do the first level of the aggregation, and then use dynamic aggregation using facets to further slice and dice the data as you need.

The result of the faceted query is affected by the matches for the query, and that can change dynamically with very little cost, opening the way to more dynamic aggregation queries. Dynamic aggregation also has a pretty straightforward cost, since it varies linearly with the amount of matches for the query.

That's a great thing since it simplifies dynamic queries. But it also means that if you want to run a faceted query with aggregation on a very large result set, it's going to take time to process. A MapReduce on the same (or much larger) amount of data will be much faster at querying time, but it's limited in the amount of flexibility it allows for each query.

Combining MapReduce and facets to handle this is a great way to reduce[1] the amount of data the facets need to go through. It's easiest to consider this kind of approach as feeding the facets baby food, already pre-chewed. That dramatically cuts down the amount of effort required to get the final result.

11.7. Multi-step aggregation processes

We've looked at all sorts of MapReduce indexes in this chapter, and we also looked at how we can use dynamic aggregation to build dynamic aggregated queries. Now I want to apply all that knowledge to a more complex example, utilizing many of the features we explored in this chapter.

Here's the requirement: we want to be able to get a monthly report of sales by supplier per city. It might be easier to understand if we start from the point of view of the user interface. Take a look at Figure 11.16, which shows a mockup of the search interface and the results we want to see.

---

1 Pun very much intended here.

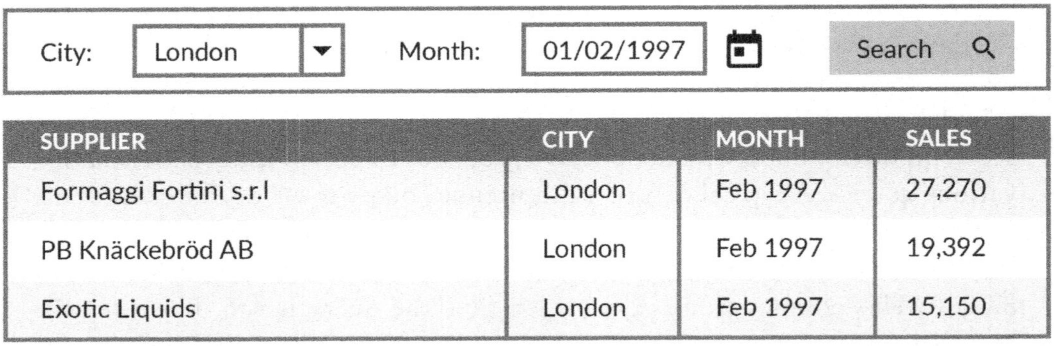

City:	London ▼	Month:	01/02/1997 📅	Search 🔍

SUPPLIER	CITY	MONTH	SALES
Formaggi Fortini s.r.l	London	Feb 1997	27,270
PB Knäckebröd AB	London	Feb 1997	19,392
Exotic Liquids	London	Feb 1997	15,150

Figure 11.16. *Mockup of the user interface for the kind of data we want*

The simplest way to be able to answer this query is to use LoadDocument in the map phase of the index. You can see how this is done in Listing 11.18.

Listing 11.18 *MapReduce index using 'LoadDocument' can pull data from related documents*

```
//map
from o in docs.Orders
from l in o.Lines
let product = LoadDocument(l.Product, "Products")
select new
{
    o.ShipTo.City,
    o.ShippedAt.Month,
    o.ShippedAt.Year,
    Supplier = product.Supplier,
    Total = l.PricePerUnit * l.Quantity
}
// reduce
from result in results
group result by new
{
    result.City,
    result.Supplier,
    result.Month,
    result.Year
}
```

```
into g
select new
{
    g.Key.City,
    g.Key.Supplier,
    g.Key.Month,
    g.Key.Year,
    Total = g.Sum(x => x.Total)
}
```

The interesting bit in Listing 11.18 is the `LoadDocument` call in the map. Everything else is pretty much the same as we've done throughout this chapter. We looked at `LoadDocument` in the previous chapter, and it serves mostly the same role in MapReduce indexes as well. If the product document has changed, we'll have to re-index all the documents that referenced it. Because of this, the `LoadDocument` option is only available during the map phase of a MapReduce index. You can't call `LoadDocument` from the reduce.

A sample query for this index can be seen in Listing 11.19.

Listing 11.19 *This query can be used to render the results in Figure 11.16.*

```
from index 'Sales/ByCityAndSupplier' as t
where t.City = 'London' and t.Month = 2 and t.Year = 1997
order by t.Total as double desc
load t.Supplier as s
select s.Name, t.City, t.Supplier , t.Month, t.Year, t.Total
```

This works. It generates the results you see in Figure 11.16. However, there's a problem here. `LoadDocument` requires that RavenDB updates the index if the referenced document (the product's document, in this case) is updated. This means that an update to a product can force RavenDB to re-index all the orders that have this product. If it's a popular product, this may require RavenDB to re-index a large number of orders.

Ideally, we want to have `LoadDocument` where the number of referencing documents is bounded and small. Is there a better way to handle this? We can change the index in Listing 11.18 so it doesn't include the `Supplier`, and instead groups things only by (product, city, month, year). We'll also define an output collection for the results. The output collection is then used in another index where we'll use a `LoadDocument` to achieve the same output.

Why all of this complexity? Aren't we in exactly the same position as we were before? An update to a product document will force us to re-index, after all. And the answer is yes, it will force us to re-index, but the question is *what*. In the case of Listing 11.18, any change to a product will force re-indexing of all the `Orders` documents that referenced it. But in the case where we had an intermediate artificial documents collection, we'll only need to re-index those that referenced the modified product.

Those documents have already gone through a MapReduce process, and there are likely to be far fewer of them than there are orders, so this is a net win in terms of the total amount of work that has to be done.

11.8. Summary

This chapter covered a *lot* of ground. I tried to strike the right balance between giving you enough information about what's actually going on behind the scenes and drowning everything in implementation details.

The key takeaway I hope you'll get from this chapter is that aggregation in RavenDB is cheap and plentiful, so have at it. This is in direct contrast to the way things usually work with other databases. Aggregation is often expensive and hard, so it gets pushed to dedicated solutions (nightly runs, reporting databases, cached queries, etc.). None of this is needed with RavenDB.

We started this chapter by writing some simple RQL queries using group by, and it just worked. The query optimizer recognized the query and generated the appropriate MapReduce index, and we were off to the races. We then took a deep, hard look at what was actually going on there, analyzing what the index was doing and how MapReduce works inside RavenDB.

In order to better understand that, RavenDB has a few tools built in to help you. Chief among them is the MapReduce visualizer, which lets you peek deep into the heart of how RavenDB executes MapReduce operations. We looked at the different behaviors that happen when we have a small amount of items to aggregate for a particular reduce key (all items are reduced in a single group) and when we have a very large amount of items (reduce is handled in a recursive tree fashion).

This means that updates to MapReduce indexes are very fast because we usually need to do a minimal amount of work to get the updated results. After learning how RavenDB processes MapReduce indexes, we learned how we can define our own, with complete freedom of how we want to structure the data and aggregate it.

We also learned there are some things to remember when you build your indexes, such as making sure that the map and reduce functions are pure, that your reduce function can handle being called recursively and that the reduce outputs less data than we put in.

We then upped the ante and looked at more complex MapReduce indexes, grouping all the results by company. Inside each company, we grouped things again by product to get a detailed summary of the results. These kinds of indexes can allow you to do sophisticated aggregation, rollups and computation during the indexing. Then they expose the whole thing, readily consumable, to your application.

MapReduce indexes can do amazing things, but they're also indexes in RavenDB. That means that, in addition to whatever you're doing in the MapReduce operation, all the usual stuff you can do with indexes is also there. We looked at how we can use JavaScript projections to enrich the MapReduce output during query, use facets on the data (including additional aggregation) and the many more options (full text search, spatial, etc.).

If a single MapReduce index isn't enough, you can always try things recursively. Indeed, RavenDB allows MapReduce indexes to output artificial documents back to the database, and these documents are a key part of allowing RavenDB to handle recursive MapReduce indexes. We looked at how we can do a daily and monthly rollup of sales per product by creating a MapReduce index that's fed off the artificial documents collection that's created by another MapReduce index. This opens up the option to do some really cool things because you can pipeline the work and take advantage of what's already been done.

Another cool option we looked at was the ability to use MultimapReduce indexes. Instead of just aggregating data from a single collection, we can aggregate the data from several of them at once. That allows you to, with very little effort, paint a picture of what's actually going on in your database and gain insight into what you're doing. We saw a good example of that when we looked at what was going on in each city and were able to tell how many companies, employees, suppliers and sales we had in each location.

MapReduce is fantastic when you have a static aggregation scenario – when you know what you're aggregating ahead of time. Otherwise, you'll need to (either directly or via the query optimizer) generate MapReduce indexes for each permutation that you want to query. Another alternative to that is the notion of dynamic aggregation, using facets to slice and dice the information dynamically. This tends to be less efficient than a MapReduce index, but it has less upfront costs.

It's common to do that in two stages: first defining the rough shape of the aggregation in a MapReduce index, efficiently doing the aggregation, and then using facets and dynamic aggregation on that much smaller result set to narrow down things more accurately. This gives you both fast aggregations and more flexibility in the queries.

We finished the chapter by looking at aggregating documents by a *related* document, using `LoadDocument` in a MapReduce index. This works, and it can be quite an elegant solution for some scenarios. But it's also possible to get into trouble with this approach because an update to a referenced document requires re-indexing of all the referencing documents. Instead, we can utilize artificial documents and two MapReduce indexes to reduce the amount of work required when we need to re-index.

The MapReduce engine inside RavenDB is very flexible, and it's been used to great effect over the years – including in many scenarios that surprised RavenDB's own development team. Aggregation of results is only the most obvious of the options that are available to you.

In the next chapter, we'll switch gears a bit and move to a more practical mindset, talking about how to utilize and work with indexes in your applications.

12. Working with Indexes

We've spent the last three chapters examining how querying works in RavenDB, as well as what indexes are, how they operate and what they can do. We looked at everything from simple map indexes to spatial queries, from performing full text queries to aggregating large amounts of data using MapReduce. What we haven't talked about is how you'll work with indexes in a typical business application.

This chapter will focus on that, discussing how to create and manage indexes from the client side, how to perform queries and what options are available for us on the client API. We explored some basic queries in Chapter 4, but we only touched on queries briefly – just enough to get by while we learn more about RavenDB. Now we're going to dig deep and see everything we can do with indexes and queries in RavenDB.

12.1. Creating and managing indexes

RavenDB is schemaless. You can have documents in any shape, way or form that you like. However, indexes are one of the ways to bring back structure to such a system. An index will take the documents as input and then output the index entries in a fixed format. Queries on this index must use the fields defined on the index (unless the index is doing dynamic field generation), and there's typically a strong tie between the structure of the index, the output of queries and the client code using it.

That's interesting because it means that changing the index might cause client code to break, and that strongly brings to mind the usual issues you run into with a fixed schema. This often leads to complexities when developing and working with schemas because versioning, deploying and keeping them in sync with your code is a hassle.

RavenDB allows you to define your indexes directly in your code, which in turn allows you to version the indexes as a single unit with the rest of your system. In order to see how this works, we'll use a C# application. Open PowerShell and run the commands shown in Listing 12.1.

Listing 12.1 *Creating a new RavenDB project*

```
dotnet new console -n Northwind
dotnet add .\Northwind\ package RavenDB.Client
dotnet restore .\Northwind\
```

The commands in Listing 12.1 just create a new console application and add the RavenDB client package to the project. Now, go to RavenDB and create a new database named Northwind. Go to Settings and then Create Sample Data and click the Create button. Click the View C# Classes link, copy the code to a file called Entities.cs and save it in the Northwind app folder.

We're now ready to start working with real indexes from the client side.

12.1.1. WORKING WITH INDEXES FROM THE CLIENT

Before we get to defining new indexes, let's start with an easier step: querying on an existing index. Your Program.cs file should be similar to Listing 12.2.

The code in Listing 12.2 is the equivalent of "Hello World," but it will serve as our basic structure for the rest of this chapter.

The query we have in Listing 12.2 is a pretty simple dynamic query, the likes of which we already saw in Chapter 4. This is translated to the following RQL: FROM Employees WHERE Address.City = $p0. So far, there are no surprises, and if you check the indexes on the database, you should find that the Auto/Employees/ByAddress.City index was automatically created to satisfy the query. How can we select the index we want to use for a query from the client side? You can see the answer in Listing 12.3.

Listing 12.2 *This console application queries RavenDB for all London based employees*

```csharp
using System;
using System.Linq;
using Raven.Client.Documents;
using Orders;

namespace Northwind
{
    class Program
    {
        static void Main(string[] args)
        {
            var store = new DocumentStore
            {
                Urls = new []
                {
                    "http://localhost:8080"
                },
                Database = "Northwind"
            };
            store.Initialize();

            using (var session = store.OpenSession())
            {
                var londonEmployees =
                    from emp in session.Query<Employee>()
                    where emp.Address.City == "London"
                    select emp;

                foreach (var emp in londonEmployees)
                {
                    Console.WriteLine(emp.FirstName);
                }
            }
        }
    }
}
```

Listing 12.3 *Specifying the index to use for a query (using strings)*

```
var ordersForEmployee1A =
   from order in session.Query<Order>("Orders/Totals")
   where order.Employee == "employees/1-A"
   select order;

foreach (var order in ordersForEmployee1A)
{
   Console.WriteLine(order.Id);
}
```

As you can see, the major difference is that we're now querying on the `Orders/Totals` index and we pass that as a string to the `Query` method. Using this method means that we need to define the index somewhere, which leads to the deployment and versioning issues that I already discussed. RavenDB has a better solution.

12.1.2. DEFINING SIMPLE INDEXES VIA CLIENT CODE

When using a strongly typed language, we can often do better than just passing strings. We can use the features of the language itself to provide a strongly typed answer for that. We'll recreate the `Orders/Totals` index in our C# code, as shown in Listing 12.4. (You'll need to add a using `Raven.Client.Documents.Indexes`; to the file.)

We use `My/Orders/Totals` as the index name in Listing 12.4 to avoid overwriting the existing index. This way, we can compare the new index to the existing one. There are a few interesting features shown in Listing 12.4. First, we have a class definition that inherits from `AbstractIndexCreationTask<T>`. This is how we let RavenDB know this is actually an index definition and what type it will be working on.

The generic parameter for the `My_Orders_Totals` class is quite important. That's the source collection for this index. In the class constructor, we set the `Map` property to a Linq expression, transforming the documents into the index entries. The `orders` variable is of type `IEnumerable<Order>`, using the same generic parameter as was passed to the index class. Now we just need to actually create this index. There are two ways of doing that. Both are shown in Listing 12.5.

Listing 12.4 *The index is defined using a strongly typed class*

```
public class My_Orders_Totals : AbstractIndexCreationTask<Order>
{
    public My_Orders_Totals()
    {
        Map = orders =>
            from o in orders
            select new
            {
                o.Employee,
                o.Company,
                Total = o.Lines.Sum(l =>
                    (l.Quantity * l.PricePerUnit) * (1 - l.Discount))
            };
    }
}
```

Listing 12.5 *Creating indexes from the client side*

```
// create a single index
new My_Orders_Totals().Execute(store);

// scan the assembly and create all the indexes in
// the assembly as a single operation
var indexesAssembly = typeof(My_Orders_Totals).Assembly;
IndexCreation.CreateIndexes(indexesAssembly, store);
```

The first option in Listing 12.5 shows how we can create a single index. The second tells RavenDB to scan the assembly provided and create *all* the indexes defined there.

Automatically creating indexes

The `IndexCreation.CreateIndexes` option is a good way to avoid managing indexes manually. You can stick this call somewhere in your application's startup during development and as an admin action in production. This way, you can muck about with the index definitions as you wish, and they'll always match what the code is expecting.

In other words, you can check out your code and run the application, and the appropriate indexes for this version of the code will be there for you, without you really having to think about it. For production, you might want to avoid automatic index creation on application startup and put that behind an admin screen or something similar. But you'll still have the option of ensuring the expected indexes are actually there. This makes deployments much easier because you don't have to manage the "schema" outside of your code.

After running the code in Listing 12.5, you'll see that there is an index named My/Orders/Totals in the database. By convention, we replace _ with / in the index name. Now is the time to try to query this index, in a strongly typed manner, as you can see in Listing 12.6.

Listing 12.6 *Specifying the index to use for a query (strongly typed)*

```
var ordersForEmployee1A =
    from order in session.Query<Order, My_Orders_Totals>()
    where order.Employee == "employees/1-A"
    select order;
```

The second generic parameter to Query is the index we want to use, and the first one is the item we're querying on. Note that in this case, what we query on and what we're getting back is the same thing, so we can use Order as both the item we query on and the return type. But that isn't always the case.

12.1.3. WORKING WITH COMPLEX INDEXES USING STRONGLY TYPED CODE

As we've seen in previous chapters, there isn't any required correlation between the shape of the document being indexed and the output of the index entry. In fact, there *can't* be if we want to support dynamic data and schemaless documents. That means that when we're talking about indexing, we're actually talking about several models that are usually either the same or very similar, but they don't have to be.

There are the following models to consider:

◆ The documents to be indexed.
◆ The index entry that was outputted from the index.
◆ The actual queryable fields in the index.
◆ The result of the query.

Consider the case of the following query: from Orders where ShipTo.City = 'London'. In this case, all four models behave as if we're querying on the Orders collection directly. But even in such a simple scenario, that isn't the case.

The documents to be indexed are the documents in the Orders collection, but what is actually being indexed here? In the simplest case, it's an index entry such as {"ShipTo.City": "London", "@id": "orders/42-A"}. When we query, we actually try to find a match for ShipTo.City = 'London', and from there we fetch the document and return it.

Consider the query in Listing 12.7, on the other hand, which adds a couple of interesting wrinkles.

Listing 12.7 *Using projections and query on array to show*
the difference between various models

```
from Orders as o
where o.Lines[].Product == "products/3-A"
select {
    Company: o.Company,
    Quantity: o.Lines
        .reduce((sum, l) => sum + l.Quantity, 0)
}
```

The Lines[].Product is a field that's used differently during indexing and querying. In the index entry generated from the documents, the Lines[].Product is an array. But during queries, we use it in an equality comparison as if it was a normal value. This is because the array in the index entry was flattened to allow us to query any of the values on it.

The shape of the results of the query in Listing 12.7 is very different than the shape of the documents. That's because of the projection in the select. As long as we're working with RQL directly, we don't really notice, but how do we deal with such different shapes on the client side?

When using a strongly typed language such as C#, for example, we need some way to convey the differences. We can do that using explicit and implicit types. Consider the index My/Orders/Totals that we defined in Listing 12.4. Look at the Total field that we computed in the index. How are we going to be able to query on that?

We need to introduce a type, just for querying, to satisfy the compiler. An example of such a query is shown in Listing 12.8.

The code in Listing 12.8 shows a common usage pattern in RavenDB. First, we define a nested type inside the index class to represent the result of the index. This is commonly called Result, IndexEntry or Entry. There's no real requirement for this to be a nested class, by the way. It can be any type that simply has the required fields. The idea here is that we just need the compiler to be happy with us.

The problem with using the My_Orders_Totals.Result class is that, while we can now use it in the where clause, we aren't actually going to get this class in the results. We'll get the full Order document. We can tell the compiler that we'll be getting a list of Order by calling OfType<Order>(). This is a client-side-only behavior, which only converts the type being used in the query and has no effect on the server-side query that will be generated.

Listing 12.8 *Using a dedicate type for strongly typed queries*

```
public class My_Orders_Totals :
    AbstractIndexCreationTask<Order, My_Orders_Totals.Result>
{
    public class Result
    {
        public string Employee;
        public string Company;
        public double Total;
    }

    // class constructor shown in Listing 12.4
}

var bigOrdersForEmployee1A =
(
    from  o in session.Query<My_Orders_Totals.Result, My_Orders_Totals>()
    where o.Employee == "employees/1-A" &&
        o.Total > 1000
    select o
).OfType<Order>().ToList();
```

Calling OfType doesn't close the query. We can still continue to add behavior to the query to project the relevant data or to select the sort order for the results, as you can see in Listing 12.9.

Listing 12.9 *Adding projection and sorting after calling OfType*

```
var bigOrdersForEmployee1A =
(
    from  o in session.Query<My_Orders_Totals.Result, My_Orders_Totals>()
    where o.Employee == "employees/1-A" &&
        o.Total > 1000
    orderby o.Total descending
    select o
).OfType<Order>();
```

```
var results =
    from o in bigOrdersForEmployee1A
    orderby o.Employee
    select new
    {
        o.Company,
        Total = o.Lines.Sum(x => x.Quantity)
    };
```

The RQL generated by the query in Listing 12.9 is shown in Listing 12.10.

Listing 12.10 *The RQL generated by the query in Listing 12.9*

```
from index 'My/Orders/Totals' as o
where o.Employee = $p0 and o.Total > $p1
order by Total as double desc, Employee
select {
    Company : o.Company,
    Total : o.Lines.map(function(x) { return x.Quantity; })
        .reduce(function(a, b) { return a + b; }, 0)
}
```

As you can see, even though Listing 12.9 has the orderby clauses in different locations and operating on different types, the RQL generated doesn't care about that and has the proper sorting.

The last part is *important*. It's easy to get caught up with the code you have sitting in front of you while forgetting that, underneath it all, what's sent to the server is RQL. In many respects, we torture the type system in these cases to get it to both agree on the right types and to allow us to generate the right queries to the server.

Listing 12.4 shows how we can create a simple index from the client. But we're still missing a few bits. This kind of approach only lets us create very simple indexes. How are we going to handle the creation of a MapReduce index?

12.1.4. DEFINING MAPREDUCE INDEXES VIA CLIENT CODE

On the client side, a MapReduce index is very similar to the simple indexes that we've already seen. The only difference is that we have an issue with the strongly typed nature of the language. In Listing 12.4, we defined index My_Orders_Totals and used a generic parameter to indicate that the source collection (and the type this index is operating on) is Order.

However, with a MapReduce index, we have two types. One is the type that the Map will operate on, just the same as we had before. But there's another type, which is the type that the Reduce is going to work on. As you probably expected, we'll also pass the second type as a generic argument to the index. Listing 12.11 shows such a MapReduce index using strongly typed code.

Listing 12.11 *Defining a map-reduce index from code*

```
public class My_Products_Sales :
    AbstractIndexCreationTask<Order, My_Products_Sales.Result>
{
    public class Result
    {
        public string Product;
        public int Count;
        public double Total;
    }

    public My_Products_Sales()
    {
        Map = orders =>
            from order in orders
            from line in order.Lines
            select new
            {
                Product = line.Product,
                Count = 1,
                Total = (line.Quantity * line.PricePerUnit)
            };

        Reduce = results =>
            from result in results
            group result by result.Product
            into g
            select new
            {
                Product = g.Key,
                Count = g.Sum(x => x.Count),
                Total = g.Sum(x => x.Total)
            }
    }
}
```

The index `My_Products_Sales` in Listing 12.11 defined the `Map` as we have previously seen in the `My_Orders_Totals` index. We also have another nested class called `Result`. (Again, using a nested class is a mere convention because it keeps the `Result` class near the index using it). However, we're also using the nested class for this type as the generic argument for the base type.

This might look strange at first, but it's actually quite a natural way to specify a few things: first, that this index's `Map`'s source collection is `Order`, and second, that the output of the `Map` and the input (and output) of the `Reduce` are in the shape of the `Result` class. Note that I'm using the phrase "in the shape of" and not "of type." This is because, as you can see in the `select new` clauses, we aren't actually returning the types there. We're returning an anonymous type.

As long as the shape matches (and the server will verify that), RavenDB doesn't care. The actual execution of the index is done on the server side and is not subject to any of the type rules that you saw in the code listing so far. It's important to remember that the purpose of all the index classes and Linq queries is to generate code that will be sent to the server. And as long as the *server* understands what's expected, it doesn't matter what's actually being sent.

You can create the index in Listing 12.11 using either `new My_Products_Sales().Execute(store)` or by running the `IndexCreation.CreateIndexes(assembly, store)` again. Go ahead and inspect the new index in the Studio. Remember, the index name in the RavenDB Studio is `My/Products/Sales`.

With the index on the server, we can now see how we can query a MapReduce index from the client side. This turns out to be pretty much the same as we've already seen. Listing 12.12 has the full details.

Listing 12.12 *Querying a map-reduce index using Linq*

```
var salesSummaryForProduct1A =
    from s in session.Query<My_Products_Sales.Result, My_Products_Sales>()
    where s.Product == "products/1-A"
    select s;
```

The `Query` method in Listing 12.12 takes two generic parameters. The first is the type of the query – in this case, the `Result` class, which we also used in the index itself as the input (and output) of the `Reduce` function. The second generic parameter is the index that we'll use. In the case of the query in Listing 12.12, the output of the query is also the value emitted by the MapReduce index, so we don't have to play any more games with types.

Strong types and weak lies

RavenDB goes to great lengths to pretend that it actually cares about types when you're writing code in a strongly typed language. The idea is that from the client code, you'll gain the benefits of strongly typed languages, including IntelliSense, compiler checks of types, etc.

That isn't what's actually being sent to the server, though. And while the vast majority of the cases are covered with a strongly typed API, there are some things that either cannot be done or are awkward to do. For such scenarios, you can drop down a level in the API and use the string-based APIs that give you maximum flexibility.

We've seen how to create simple indexes and MapReduce indexes, but we also have multimap indexes in RavenDB. How are we going to work with those from the client side?

12.1.5. MULTIMAP INDEXES FROM THE CLIENT

An index can have any number of Map functions defined on it, but the code we explored so far in Listing 12.4 and Listing 12.11 only shows us how to define a single map. This is because the AbstractIndexCreationTask<T> base class is meant for the common case where you have only a single Map in your index. If you want to define a multimap index from the client, you need to use the appropriate base class, AbstractMultiMapIndexCreationTask<T>, as you can see in Listing 12.13.

Listing 12.13 *Defining a multimap index from the client side*

```
public class People_Search :
    AbstractMultiMapIndexCreationTask<People_Search.Result>
{
    public class Result
    {
        public string Name;
    }

    public People_Search()
    {
        AddMap<Employee>(employees =>
            from e in employees
            select new
            {
                Name = e.FirstName + " " + e.LastName
            }
        );
        AddMap<Company>(companies =>
            from c in companies
            select new
            {
                c.Contact.Name
            }
        );
```

```
AddMap<Supplier>(suppliers =>
    from s in suppliers
    select new
    {
        s.Contact.Name
    }
);
    }
}
```

The index in Listing 12.13 is using multimap to index Employees, Companies and Suppliers. We already ran into this index before, in Listing 10.12. At the time, I commented that dealing with a heterogeneous result set can be challenging – not for RavenDB or the client API, but for your code.

You can see that, in Listing 12.13, we also have a Result class that's used as a generic parameter. Technically, since we don't have a Reduce function in this index, we don't actually need it. But it's useful to have because the shape the index entry will take is explicit. We call AddMap<T> for each collection that we want to index, and all of the AddMap<T> calls must have the output in the same shape.

How about actually using such an index? Before we look at the client code, let's first consider a use case for this. The index allows me to query across multiple collections and fetch results from any of the matches. Consider the case of querying for all the results where the name starts with Mar. You can see a mockup of how this will look in the UI in Figure 12.1.

Find contact...

🔍 Mar

Margaret Peacock
Employee id: employees/4-A

Marria Anders from Alfreds Futterkiste
Company id: companies/1-A   *ALFKI*

Martin Somer from Bólido Comidas preparadas
Company id: companies/8-A   *BOLID*

Marie Delamare from Escargots Nouveaux
Supplier id: suppliers/27-A

Figure 12.1. *Getting the UI to display heterogeneous results from the* People/Search *index*

To query this successfully from the client, we need to specify both the type of the index and the shape we're querying on. Luckily for us, we already defined that shape: the `People_Search.Result` nested class. You can see the query in Listing 12.14.

Listing 12.14 *Querying a multimap index with heterogeneous results from the client*

```
var results = session.Query<People_Search.Result, People_Search>()
    .Where(item => item.Name.StartsWith("Mar"))
    .OfType<object>();

foreach (var result in results)
{
    switch(result)
    {
        case Employee e:
            RenderEmployee(e);
            break;
        case Supplier s:
            RenderSupplier(s);
            break;
        case Company c:
            RenderCompany(c);
            break;
    }
}
```

In Listing 12.14, we're issuing the query on results in the shape of `People_Search.Result` and then telling the compiler that the result can be of any type. If we had a shared interface or base class, we could have used that as the common type for the query. The rest of the code just does an in-memory type check and routes each result to the relevant rendering code.

Linq isn't the only game in town

The RavenDB query API is built in layers. At the top of the stack, you have Linq, which gives you strongly typed queries with full support from the compiler. Below Linq, you have the `DocumentQuery` API, which is a bit lower level and gives the user a programmatic way to build queries.

You can access the `DocumentQuery` API through `session.Advanced.DocumentQuery<T>`, as shown in the following query:

```
var results = session.Advanced
        .DocumentQuery<object>("People/Search")
        .WhereStartsWith("Name", "Mar")
        .ToList();
```

This query is functionally identical to the one in Listing 12.14, except that we're weakly typed here. This kind of API is meant for programmatically building queries, working with users' input, and the like. It's often easier to build such scenarios without the constraints of the type system. The DocumentQuery API is capable of any query that Linq can perform. Indeed, since Linq is implemented on top of DocumentQuery, that's fairly obvious.

You can read more about the options available to you with DocumentQuery in the online documentation.

We could have also projected fields from the index and gotten all the results in the same shape from the server. Writing such a query using C# is *possible*, but it's awkward and full of type trickery. In most cases, it's better to use RQL directly for such a scenario.

12.1.6. USING RQL FROM THE CLIENT

Within RavenDB, RQL queries give you the most flexibility and power. Any other API ends up being translated to RQL, after all. Features such as Language Integrated Query make most queries a joy to build, and the DocumentQuery API gives us much better control over programmatically building queries. But at some point, you'll want to just write raw RQL and get things done.

There are several levels at which you can use RQL from your code. You can just write the full query in RQL, you can add RQL snippets to a query and you can define the projection manually. Let's look at each of these in turn. All of the queries we'll use in this section will use the SearchResult class defined in Listing 12.15.

Listing 12.15 *A simple data class to hold the results of queries*

```
public class SearchResult
{
    public string ContactName;
    public string Collection;
}
```

Listing 12.16 shows how we can work directly with RQL. This is very similar to the query we used in Listing 10.13 a few chapters ago.

Listing 12.16 *Querying using raw RQL*

```
List<SearchResult> results = session.Advanced
    .RawQuery<SearchResults>(@"
        from index 'People/Search' as p
        where StartsWith(Name, $name)
        select
        {
            Collection: p['@metadata']['@collection'],
            ContactName: (
                p.Contact || { Name: p.FirstName + ' ' + p.LastName }
            ).Name
        }
    ")
    .AddParameter("$name", "Mar")
    .ToList();
```

There are a few items of interest in the query in Listing 12.16. First, you can see that we specify the entire query using a single string. The generic parameter that's used in the RawQuery method is the type of the *results* for the query. This is because we're actually specifying the query as a string, so we don't need to play hard to get with the type system and can just specify what we want in an upfront manner.

The query itself is something we've already encountered before. The only surprising part there is the projection that checks if there's a Contact property on the object or creates a new object for the Employees documents (which don't have this property).

Query parameters and RQL

In Listing 12.16, there's something that's both obvious and important to call out, and it's the use of query parameters. We use the $name parameter and add it to the query using the AddParameter method.

It's strongly recommended that you only use parameters and you don't build queries using string concatenation (especially when it involves users' input). If you need to dynamically build queries, using the DocumentQuery is preferred. And users' input should always be sent using AddParameter so it can be properly processed and not be part of the query.

See also SQL Injection Attacks in your favorite search engine.

Listing 12.16 required us to write the full query as a string, which means that it's opaque to the compiler. We don't have to go full bore with RQL strings; we can ask the RavenDB

Linq provider to do most of the heavy lifting and just plug in our custom extension when it's needed.

Consider the code in Listing 12.17, which uses RavenQuery.Raw to carefully inject an RQL snippet into the Linq query.

Listing 12.17 *Using Linq queries with a bit of RQL sprinkled in*

```
List<SearchResult> results =
    from item in session.Query<People_Search.Result, People_Search>()
    where item.Name.StartsWith("Mar")
    select new SearchResult
    {
        Collection = RavenQuery.Raw("item['@metadata']['@collection']"),
        ContactName = RavenQuery.Raw(@"(
          item.Contact || { Name: item.FirstName + ' ' + item.LastName }
        ).Name")
    }
```

Listing 12.17 isn't a representative example, mostly because it's probably easier to write it as a RQL query directly. But it serves as a good example of a non-trivial query and how you can utilize advanced techniques in your queries.

It's more likely that you'll want to use a variant of this technique when using the DocumentQuery API. This is because you'll typically compose queries programmatically using this API and then want to do complex projections from the query. This is easy to do, as you can see in Listing 12.18.

Listing 12.18 *Using a custom projection with the 'DocumentQuery' API*

```
List<SearchResult> results =
    session.Advanced.DocumentQuery<People_Search.Result, People_Search>()
    .WhereStartsWith(x => x.Name, "Mar")
    .SelectFields<SearchResult>(QueryData.CustomFunction(
        alias: "item",
        func: @"{
            Collection: item['@metadata']['@collection'],
            ContactName: (
              p.Contact || { Name: item.FirstName + ' ' + item.LastName }
            ).Name
        }")
    ).ToList();
```

The queries in Listing 12.16, 12.17 and 12.18 produce the exact same query and the same results, so it's your choice when to use either option. Myself, I tend to use RQL for complex queries where I need the full power of RQL behind me and when I can't express the query that I want to write in a natural manner using Linq.

I use the DocumentQuery API mostly when I want to build queries programmatically, such as search pages or queries that are composed dynamically.

12.1.7. CONTROLLING ADVANCED INDEXING OPTIONS FROM THE CLIENT SIDE

In the previous section, we explored a lot of ways to project data from the People/Search index, but our query was a simple StartsWith(Name, $name). So if $name is equal to "Mar", we'll find an employee named Margaret Peacock. However, what would happen if we tried to search for "Pea"?

If you try it, you'll find there are no results. You can check the index's terms to explore why this is the case, as shown in Figure 12.2.

When you look at the terms in Figure 12.2, it's obvious why we haven't been able to find anything when searching for the "Pea" prefix. There's no term that starts with it. Our index is simply indexing the terms as is, with minimal work done on them. (It's just lowercasing them so we can run a case-insensitive search.)

Figure 12.2. *The terms list for the* People/Search *index near* Margaret Peacock

We already looked at this in Chapter 10, in the section about full text indexes, so this shouldn't come as a great surprise. We need to mark the Name field as a full text search field. But how can we do that from the client side? Listing 12.19 shows the way to do it.

Listing 12.19 *Configuring index fields options via code*

```
public class People_Search :
  AbstractMultiMapIndexCreationTask<People_Search.Result>
{
    public People_Search()
    {
        // AddMap calls from Listing 12.13
        // removed for brevity

        Index(x => x.Name, FieldIndexing.Search);
        Suggestion(x => x.Name);
    }
}
```

In Listing 12.19, you can see the Index method. It configures the indexing option for the Name field to full text search mode. And the Suggestion method is used, unsurprisingly enough, to indicate that this field should have suggestions applied to it.

Creating weakly typed indexes

In addition to the strongly typed API exposed by AbstractMultiMapIndex CreationTask and AbstractIndexCreationTask you can also use the weakly typed API to control every aspect of the index creation, such as with the following code:

```
public class People_Search  : AbstractIndexCreationTask
{
    public override IndexDefinition CreateIndexDefinition()
    {
        return new IndexDefinition()
        {
            Maps = {
                @"from e in docs.Employees select new {
                    Name = e.FirstName + ' ' + e.LastName
                }",
                @"from c in docs.Companies select new {
                    c.Contact.Name
                }",
```

```
            @"from s in docs.Suppliers select new {
                s.Contact.Name
            }"
        },
        Fields = {
            ["Name"] = new IndexFieldOptions {
                Indexing = FieldIndexing.Search
            }
        }
    };
}
}
```

You're probably sick of the People/Search index by now, with all its permutations. The index definition above behaves just the same as all the other People/Search indexes we looked at, including being picked up by IndexCreation automatically. It just gives us the maximum amount of flexibility in all aspects of the index.

There are other options available, such as using Store to store the fields, Spatial for geographical indexing and a few more advanced options that you can read more about in the online documentation. Anything that can be configured through the Studio can also be configured from code.

12.1.8. MULTIMAPREDUCE INDEXES FROM THE CLIENT

The last task we have to do with building indexes from client code is to build a Multimap-Reduce index. This is pretty straightforward, given what we've done so far. We need to define an index class inheriting from AbstractMultiMapIndexCreationTask, define the Maps using the AddMap methods and finally define the Reduce function. Listing 12.20 shows how this is done.

Listing 12.20 *MultimapReduce index to compute details about each city*

```
public class Cities_Details :
    AbstractMultiMapIndexCreationTask<Cities_Details.Result>
{
    public class Result
    {
        public string City;
        public int Companies, Employees, Suppliers;
    }
```

```
public Cities_Details()
{
    AddMap<Employee>(emps =>
        from e in emps
        select new Result
        {
            City = e.Address.City,
            Companies = 0,
            Suppliers = 0,
            Employees = 1
        }
    );

    AddMap<Company>(companies =>
        from c in companies
        select new Result
        {
            City = c.Address.City,
            Companies = 1,
            Suppliers = 0,
            Employees = 0
        }
    );

    AddMap<Suppplier>(suppliers =>
        from s in suppliers
        select new Result
        {
            City = s.Address.City,
            Companies = 0,
            Suppliers = 1,
            Employees = 0
        }
    );
```

```
            Reduce = results =>
                from result in results
                group result by result.City
                into g
                select new Result
        {
                City = g.Key,
                Companies = g.Sum(x => x.Companies),
                Suppliers = g.Sum(x => x.Suppliers),
                Employees = g.Sum(x => x.Employees)
        }
    }
}
```

Listing 12.20 is a bit long, but it matches up to the index we defined in the previous chapter, in Listing 11.13. And the only new thing in the `Cities_Details` index class is the use of `select new Result` instead of using `select new` to create an anonymous class. This can be helpful when you want to ensure that all the `Maps` and the `Reduce` are using the same output. RavenDB strips the `Result` class when it creates the index, so the server doesn't care about it. This is simply here to make our lives easier.

12.2. Deploying indexes

I briefly mentioned earlier that it's typical to deploy indexes using `IndexCreation.CreateIndexes` or its async equivalent `IndexCreation.CreateIndexesAsync`. These methods take an assembly and the document store you're using and scan the assembly for all the index classes. Then they create all the indexes they found in the database.

During development, it's often best to call one of these methods in your application startup. This way, you can modify an index and run the application, and the index definition is automatically updated for you. It also works great when you pull changes from another developer. You don't have to do anything to get the right environment set up.

Attempting to create an index that already exists on the server (same name and index definition) is ignored and has no effect on the server or the cluster. So if nothing changed in your indexes, the entire `IndexCreation.CreateIndexes` call does nothing at all. Only when there are changes to the indexes will it actually take effect.

Locking indexes

Sometimes you need to make a change to your index definition directly on your server. That's possible, of course, but you have to be aware that if you're using `IndexCreation` to automatically generate your indexes, the next time your application starts, it will reset the index definition to the original.

That can be somewhat annoying because changing the index definition on the server can be a hotfix to solve a problem or introduce a new behavior, and the index reset will just make it go away, apparently randomly.

In order to handle this, RavenDB allows the option of locking an index. An index can be unlocked, locked or locked (error). In the unlocked mode, any change to the index would be accepted, and if the new index definition is different than the one stored on the server, the index would be updated and re-index the data using the new index definition. In the locked mode, creating a new index definition would return successfully but would not actually change anything on the server. And in the locked (error) mode, trying to change the index will raise an error.

Usually you'll just mark the index as locked, which will make the server ignore any changes to the index. The idea is that we don't want to break your calls to `IndexCreation` by throwing an error.

Note that this is not a security measure. It's a way for the operations team to make a change in the index and prevent the application from mindlessly setting it back. Any user that can create an index can also modify the lock mode on the index.

Index creation is a cluster operation, which means that you can run the command against any node in the database group and RavenDB will make sure that it's created in all the database's nodes. The same also applies for automatic indexes. If the query optimizer decides that a query requires an index to be created, that index is going to be created in all the database instances, not just the one that processed this query.

This means that the experience of each node can be shared among all of them and you don't have to worry about a failover from a node that has already created the indexes you're using to one that didn't accept any queries yet. All of the nodes in a database group will have the same indexes.

Failure modes and external replication

Being a cluster operation means that index creation is reliable; it goes through the Raft protocol and a majority of the nodes must agree to accept it before it's acknowledged to the client. If, however, a majority of the nodes in the cluster are not reachable, the index creation will fail. This applies to both manual and automatic index creation in the case of network partition or majority failure. Index creation is rare, though, so even if there's a failure of this magnitude, it will not typically affect day-to-day operations.

External replication allows us to replicate data (documents, attachments, revisions, etc.) to another node that may or may not be in the same cluster. This is often used as a separate hot spare, offsite backup, etc. It's important to remember that external replication does not replicate indexes. Indexes are only sent as a cluster operation for the database group. This allows you to have the data replicated to different databases and potentially run different indexes on the documents.

There are other considerations to deploying indexes, especially in production. In the next section, we'll explore another side of indexing: how indexes actually work.

12.2.1. How do indexes do their work?

This section is the equivalent of popping the hood on a car and examining the engine. For the most part, you shouldn't have to do that, but it can be helpful to understand what is actually going on.

An index in RavenDB is composed of

◆ Index definition and configuration options (Maps and Reduce, fields, spatial, full text, etc.).
◆ Data on disk (where we store the results of the indexing operation).
◆ Various caches for portions of the data, to make it faster to process queries.
◆ A dedicated index thread that does all the work for the index.

What's probably the most important from a user perspective is to understand how this all plays together. An index in RavenDB has a dedicated thread for all indexing work. This allows us to isolate any work being done to this thread and give the admin better accountability and control. In the Studio, you can go to Manage Server and then click Advanced and you'll see the Threads Runtime Info. You can see a sample of that in Figure 12.3.

Name	Thread Id	Start Time	Duration
Indexing of Orders/ByCompany of Northwind	84 (23976)	2018 June 22nd, 10:57 AM	3 s 437 ms

Figure 12.3. *Showing the details on the* Orders/ByCompany *index's thread*

In Figure 12.3, you can see how much processing time is taken by the Orders/ByCompany indexing thread.

A dedicated thread per instance greatly simplifies operational behaviors and allows us to apply several important optimizations. It means that no index can interfere with any other index. A slow index can only affect itself, instead of having a global effect on the system. It simplifies the code and algorithms required for indexing because there's no need to write thread safe code. This design decision also allows RavenDB to prioritize tasks more easily. RavenDB uses thread priorities at the operating system level to hint what should be done first. Setting the index priority will affect the indexing thread priority at the operating system level. You can see how to change the index priority in Figure 12.4.

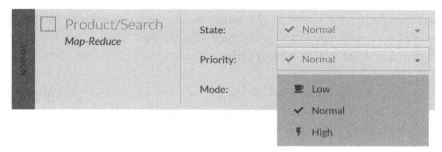

Figure 12.4. *Changing the indexing priority will update the indexing thread priority*

By default, RavenDB prioritizes request processing over indexing, so indexing threads start with a lower priority than request-processing threads. That means requests complete faster and indexes get to run when there's capacity for them (with the usual starvation prevention mechanisms). You can increase or lower the index priority and RavenDB will update the indexing thread accordingly.

RavenDB also uses this to set the I/O priority for requests generated by indexing. In this way, we can be sure that indexing will not overwhelm the system by taking too much CPU or saturating the I/O bandwidth we have available.

The last point is important because RavenDB's indexes are always built online, in conjunction with normal operations on the server. And this request I/O priority scheme applies to both indexing creation and updates with each change to the data. We don't make distinctions between the two modes.

What keeps the indexing thread up at night?

When you create a new index, RavenDB will spawn a thread that will start indexing all the documents covered by the index. It will go through the documents in batches, trying to index as many of them in one go as it can, until all are indexed. What happens then?

The index will then go to sleep, waiting for a new or updated document in one of the collections that this index cares about. In other words, until there's such a document, the thread is not going to be runnable. It isn't going to compete for CPU time and takes very few resources from the system.

If the indexing thread detects that it's been idle for a while, it will actively work to release any resources it currently holds and then go back to sleep until it's woken by a new document showing up.

Indexing in batches

RavenDB typically needs to balance throughput vs. freshness when it comes to indexing. The bigger the batch, the faster documents get indexed.

But we only see the updates to the index when we complete the batch. During initial creation, RavenDB typically favors bigger batches (as much as the available resources allow) and will attempt to index as many documents as it can at once.

After the index completes indexing all the documents it covers, it will watch for any new or updated documents and index them as soon as possible, without waiting for more updates to come. The typical indexing latency (the time between when a document updates and when the index has committed the batch including this document) is measured in milliseconds on most systems.

The query optimizer's capability to create new indexes on the fly depends on making sure the new index isn't breaking things while it's being built. Because of this requirement, RavenDB is very careful about resource allocations to indexing. We talked about CPU and I/O priorities, but there's also a memory budget applied. All in all, this has been tested in production for many years and has proven to be an extremely valuable feature.

The ability to deploy, in production, a new index (or a set of indexes) is key for operational agility. Otherwise, you'll have to schedule downtime whenever your application changes even the most minor of queries. This kind of flexibility is offered not just for new indexes but also for when you're updating existing ones.

12.2.2. SIDE BY SIDE

During development, you'll likely not notice the indexing update times. The amount of data you have in a development database is typically quite small, and the machine is not usually too busy in handling production traffic. In production, the opposite is true. There's a *lot* of data, and your machines are already busy doing their normal routine. This means that an index deploy can take a while.

Let's assume we have an index deploy duration (from the time it's created to the time it's done indexing all the relevant documents) of five minutes. An updated index definition can't just pick up from where the old index definition left off. For example, we might have added new fields to the index, so in addition to indexing new documents, we need to re-index all the documents that are already indexed. But if we have a five-minute period in which we're busy indexing, what will happen to queries made to the index during that time frame?

All index updates in RavenDB are done using the side-by-side strategy. Go to the Studio and update the `Orders/Totals` index by changing the `Total` field computation and save the document. Then immediately go to the indexes page. You should see something similar to what's shown in Figure 12.5.

Figure 12.5. *Updating an index keeps the old definition alive until the new index is caught up.*

Figure 12.5 shows an index midway through an update. But instead of deleting the old index and starting the indexing from scratch (which will impact queries), RavenDB keeps the old index around (for answering queries and indexing new documents) until the new version of the index has caught up and indexed everything.

This way, you can minimize the effects of updating an index in production. Once the updated version of the index has completed its work, it will automatically replace the old version. Of course, you can also force an immediate replacement if you really need to. (Swap now will do it.)

12.3. Auto indexes and the query optimizer

We talked about the query optimizer creating indexes on the fly several times, but now I want to shine a light on the kind of heuristics that the query optimizer uses and the logic that guides it.

At the most basic level, the query optimizer analyzes all the queries that don't specify an explicit index to use (anything that doesn't start with from index ... is fair game for the query optimizer). The query optimizer will attempt to find an index that can answer the query being asked, but if it fails to find any appropriate indexes, it will go ahead and create a new one.

One very important aspect is that the query optimizer isn't going to create an index blindly. Instead of only considering the current query when it's time to create a new index, the query optimizer is also going to weigh the *history* of the queries that were made against the database.

In other words, the logic that guides the query analyzer looks something like this:

1. Is there an index that can match this query? If so, use that.
2. If there's no such index, we need to create one.
3. Let's take a look at all the queries that were made against the same collection as the one that's now being queried and see what would be the optimal index to answer all of these queries, including the new query.

4. We need to create this new optimal index and wait for it to complete indexing.

5. We should retire all the automatic indexes that have been created so far that are now covered by the new index.

The idea here is that RavenDB uses your queries as a learning opportunity to figure out more about the operational environment, and the query optimizer is able to use that knowledge when it needs to create a new index.

Over time, this means that we'll generate the optimal set of indexes to answer any query that doesn't use an explicit index. Furthermore, it means that operational changes, such as deploying a new version of your application with slightly different queries, will be met with equanimity by RavenDB. The query optimizer will recognize the new queries and figure out if they can use the existing indexes. If they can't, the optimizer will create a new index for them. All existing queries will continue to use the existing indexes until the new indexes are ready. Then they'll switch.

All of this will be done for you, without anyone needing to tell RavenDB what needs to be done or babysit it. The fact that index modifications are cluster-wide also means that all the nodes in the cluster will be able to benefit from this knowledge.

12.3.1. IMPORTING AND EXPORTING INDEXES

RavenDB's ability to learn as it goes is valuable, but even so, you don't always want to do that kind of operation *directly* in production. If you have a large amount of data, you don't want to wait until you already deployed your application to production for RavenDB to start learning about the kind of queries that it's going to generate. During the learning process, there might be several paths taken that you want to skip.

You can now run your application in a test environment, running a set of load tests and making the application issue all its queries to your test RavenDB instance. That instance will apply the same logic and create the optimal set of indexes to answer the kind of queries it saw.

You can now export that knowledge from the test machine and import it into the production cluster. The new indexes will be built, and by the time you're ready to actually deploy your application to production, all the work has already been done and the indexes are ready for the new queries in the updated version of your application.

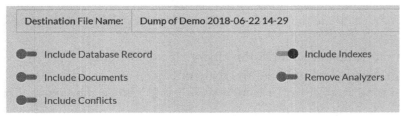

Figure 12.6. *Exporting just the indexes from our database.*

Let's see how that can work, shall we? In the Studio, go to `Settings` and then to `Export Database`. Ensure that only the `Include Indexes` is selected and click the `Export Database` button. You can see what this looks like in Figure 12.6.

You can then take the resulting file and import that into the production instance (`Settings` and then `Import Database`) and the new indexes will be created. The query optimizer will then take them into account when it needs to decide which index is going to handle which query.

12.4. Indexing and querying performance

When it comes time to understand what's going on with your indexes, you won't face a black box. RavenDB tracks and externalizes a *lot* of information about the indexing processes and makes it available to you, mostly via the Studio in `Indexes` and then the `Indexing Performance` page. You can see a sample of what it looks like when the system is indexing in Figure 12.7.

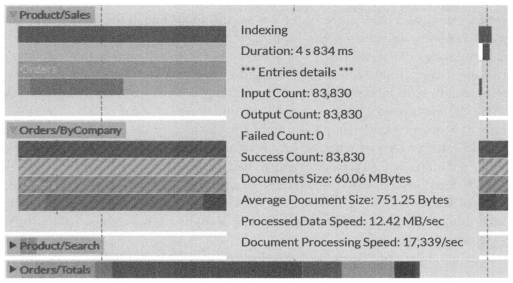

Figure 12.7. *Visually exploring details about the indexing actions (and their costs)*

The timeline view in Figure 12.7 shows several indexes running concurrently (and independently). (Solid colors mean the index batch is complete, stripes mean this is an actively executing index.) And you can hover over each of the steps to get more information, such as the number of documents indexed or the indexing rate, as shown in Figure 12.8.

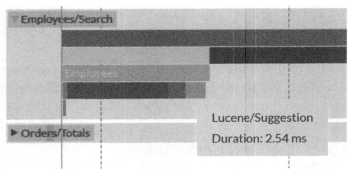

Figure 12.8. *Drilling down into particular operations (such as "Suggestions")*
can provide insight into what's costly

This graph can be very useful for investigating what exactly is going on inside RavenDB without having to look through a pile of log files. For example, look at the thread details that we previously discussed (see Figure 12.3 for what this looks like in the Studio) and notice that a particular indexing thread is using a lot of CPU time.

You can go into the Indexing Performance window and simply look at what's taking so much time. For example, you may be using the "Suggestions" feature, which can be fairly compute-intensive with high update rates. An example of this is shown in Figure 12.8, where you can see the exact costs of suggestions during indexing.

Figure 12.8 shows a fairly simple example, but the kind of details exposed in the timeline can give you a better idea of what exactly is going on inside RavenDB. As part of ongoing efforts to be a database that's actively trying to help the operations team, RavenDB is externalizing all such decisions explicitly. I encourage you to look at each of these boxes. The tooltips reveal a lot of what's going on, and this kind of view should quickly give you a feeling about how much things *should* cost. That way, you can recognize when things are out of whack if you are exploring some issue.

Having a good idea of what's going on during indexing is just half the job. We also need to be able to monitor the other side: what's going on when we query the database. RavenDB actively monitors such actions and will bring it to the operator's attention when there are issues, as shown in Figure 12.9.

Figure 12.9 shows the large result set alert, generated when a query returns a very large number of results while not using streaming. (Streaming queries were discussed in Chapter 4.) This can lead to higher memory utilization on both client and server and is considered bad practice. RavenDB will alert you to this issue and provide the exact time and the query that caused it so you can fix the problem.

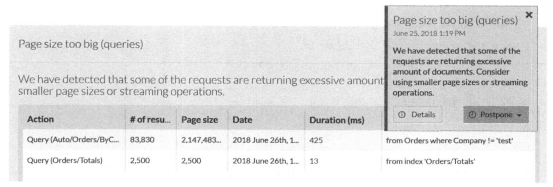

Figure 12.9. *RavenDB will generate operational alerts*
for slow queries and very large results sets.

In the same vein, very slow queries are also made explicitly visible to the operators because they're something they probably need to investigate. There are other operational conditions that RavenDB monitors and will bring to your attention – anything from slow disk I/O to running out of disk space to network latency issues. We'll discuss alerts and monitoring in RavenDB in much more depth in the next part of the book, so I'll save it till then.

12.5. Error handling in indexing

Sometimes, your index runs into an error. RavenDB actually goes to great lengths to avoid that. Property access inside the index will propagate nulls transitively. In other words, you can write the index shown in Listing 12.21 and you won't get a `NullReferenceException`.

The `employees/2-A` document has null as the value of `ReportsTo`. What do you think will happen when the index shown in Listing 12.21 is busy indexing this document? `LoadDocument` will return `null` (because the document ID it got was `null`) and the value of `HasManager` is going to be false because there's no manager for `employees/2-A`. However, just one line below, we access the `manager` instance, which we know is `null`.

Usually, such an operation will throw a `NullReferencException`. RavenDB, however, rewrites all references so they use null propagation. The actual mechanism by which this is done is a bit complex and out of scope for this topic, but you can imagine that RavenDB actually uses `Manager = manager?.FirstName + " " + manager?.LastName` everywhere. Did you notice the `?.` usage? This means "if the value is `null`, return `null`; otherwise, access the property."

In this way, a whole class of common issues is simply averted. On the other hand, the index *will* contain a name for a manager for `employees/2-A`. It will be `" "` because the space is always concatenated with the values, and `null` concatenated with a string is the string.

Listing 12.21 *Accessing a null 'manager' instance will not throw an exception*

```
public class Employees_Managers
    : AbstractIndexCreationTask<Employee>
{
    public Employees_Managers()
    {
      Map = emps =>
        from e in emps
        let manager = LoadDocument<Employee>(e.ReportsTo)
        select new
        {
            Name = e.FirstName + " " + e.LastName,
            HasManager = manager != null,
            Manager = manager.FirstName + " " + manager.LastName
        };
    }
}
```

Some kinds of errors don't really let us recover. Consider the code in Listing 12.22. The index itself isn't very interesting, but we have an int.Parse call there on the PostalCode property.

Listing 12.22 *Parsing UK 'PostalCode' as 'int' will throw an exception*

```
public class Employees_PostalCode
    : AbstractIndexCreationTask<Employee>
{
    public Employees_PostalCode()
    {
        Map = emps =>
            from e in emps
            select new
            {
                Name = e.FirstName + " " + e.LastName,
                Postal = int.Parse(e.Address.PostalCode)
            };
    }
}
```

The `PostalCode` property in the sample data set is numeric for employees from Seattle and alphanumeric for employees in London. This means that for about half of the documents in the relevant collection, this index is going to fail. Let's see how RavenDB behaves in such a case. Figure 12.10 shows how this looks in the Studio.

Figure 12.10. *Indexing errors and an errored index in the Studio*

We can see that the index as a whole is marked as errored. We'll ignore that for the moment and focus on the `Index Errors` page. If you click on it, you'll see a list of the errors that happened during indexing. You can click on the eye icon to see the full details. In this case, the error is "Failed to execute mapping function on `employees/5-A`. Exception: `System.FormatException`: Input string was not in a correct format. ... `System.Number.ParseInt32` ..."

There are two important details in that error message: we know what document caused this error and we know what this issue is. These details make it easy to figure out what the problem is. Indeed, looking at `employees/5-A`, we can see that the value of the `PostalCode` property is `"SW1 8JR"`. It's not really something that `int.Parse` can deal with.

So the indexing errors give us enough information to figure out what happened. That's great. But what about the state of the index? Why is it marked as errored? The easiest way to answer that question is to query the index and see what kind of error RavenDB returns. Executing the following query `from index 'Employees/PostalCode'` will give us this error: "Index 'Employees/PostalCode' is marked as errored. Index Employees/PostalCode is invalid, out of 9 map attempts, 4 has failed. Error rate of 44.44% exceeds allowed 15% error rate."

Now things become much clearer. An index is allowed to fail processing only *some* documents. Because of the dynamic nature of documents in RavenDB, you may get such failures. However, allowing such failures to go unattended is dangerous. An error in indexing a document means that this particular document is not indexed. That may seem like a tautology, but it has important operational implications. If the document isn't indexed, you aren't going to see it in the results. It is "gone".

While the indexing error is intentionally very visible, if you're running in an unattended mode, which is common, it may be a while before your users' complaints of "I can't find that record" make you check the database. What would be worse is if you had some change in the application or behavior that caused *all* new documents to fail to index. Because of that, an index is only allowed a certain failure rate. We'll mark the entire index as errored when that happens.

An index in an error state cannot be queried and will return an immediate error (similar to the error text above) with an explanation of what's going on. With an explicit error, it's much easier to figure out what's wrong and then fix it.

12.6. Summary

We started this chapter by discussing index deployments, from the baseline of defining indexes using strongly typed classes to the ease of use of `IndexCreation.CreateIndexes` to create all those indexes on the database.

We re-implemented many features and scenarios that we already encountered, but this time we implemented them from the client's code perspective. Building indexes using Linq queries is an interesting experience. We started from simple indexes and MapReduce indexes with `AbstractIndexCreationTask<T>` and then moved to multimap and MultimapReduce indexes with `AbstractMultiMapIndexCreationTask<T>` base classes.

We explored how to query RavenDB from the client side, starting with the simplest of Linq queries and building toward more flexibility with some more complex queries. With both Linq queries and the strong typed indexes, we talked about the fact that RavenDB isn't actually aware of your client-side types, nor does it really care about them.

All the work done to make strongly typed indexes and queries on the client side is purely there so you'll have good compiler, IntelliSense and refactoring support inside your application. In the end, both queries and indexes are turned into RQL strings and sent to the server.

We looked at how we can directly control the `IndexDefinition` sent to the server, giving us absolute power to play with and modify any option that we wish. This can be done by using the non-generic `AbstractIndexCreationTask` class and implementing the `CreateIndexDefinition()` method.

In a similar sense, all the queries we run are just fancy ways to generate RQL queries. We looked into all sorts of different ways of using RQL queries in your applications, from using RQL directly by calling `RawQuery` (and remembering to pass parameters only through `AddParameter`) to poking holes in Linq queries using `RavenQuery.Raw` method to using a `CustomFunction` to take complete control over the projection when using `DocumentQuery`.

Following the discussion on managing the indexes, we looked into how indexes are deployed on the cluster (as a reliable cluster operation, with a majority consensus using Raft) and what this means (they're not available for external replication and they require a majority of the nodes to be reachable to create/modify an index).

We dived into the execution environment of an index and the dedicated thread that RavenDB assigns to it. Such a thread makes managing an index simpler because it gives us a scope for prioritizing CPU and I/O operations, as well as defines a memory budget to control how much RAM this index will use. This is one of the key ways that RavenDB is able to implement online index building. Being able to limit the amount of system resources that an index is using is crucial to ensure that we aren't overwhelming the system and hurting ongoing operations.

The process of updating an index definition got particular attention since this can be of critical importance in production systems. RavenDB updates indexes in a side-by-side manner. The old index is retained (and can even index new updates) while the new index is being built.

Once the building process is done, the old index is removed in favor of the new one in an atomic fashion.

We briefly looked at the query optimizer, not so much to understand what it's doing but to understand what it *means*. The query optimizer routinely analyzes all queries and is able to create indexes on the fly, but the key aspect of that is that it uses that information to continuously optimize the set of indexes you have. After a while, the query optimizer will produce the optimal set of indexes for the queries your application generates.

You can even run a test instance of your application to teach a RavenDB node about the kind of queries it should expect and then export that knowledge to production ahead of your application deployment. In this way, RavenDB will prepare itself ahead of time for the new version and any changes in behavior that it might have.

We then moved to performance and monitoring. RavenDB exposes a lot of details about how it indexes documents in an easy-to-consume manner, using the `Index Performance` page, and it actively monitors queries for bad practices such as queries that return too many results or are very slow. The result of this level of monitoring is that the operations team is made aware that there are issues that they might want to take into account and resolve, even if they aren't currently critical.

We want to head things off as soon as possible, after all, and not wait until the sky has fallen to start figuring out that there were warning signs all along the way. At the same time, these alerts aren't going to spam your operations team. *That* kind of behavior builds tolerance to any kind of alerts because they effectively become noise.

We closed the chapter with a discussion of error handling. How does RavenDB handle indexing errors? How are they made visible to the operators, and what kind of behavior can you expect from the system? RavenDB will tolerate some level of errors from the index, but if there are too many indexing issues, it will decide that's not acceptable and mark the whole index as failing, resulting in any query against this index throwing an exception.

This chapter has marked the end of theory and high-level discussion and moved toward a more practical discussion on how to operate RavenDB. In the next part of the book, we're going to focus on exactly that: the care and feeding of a RavenDB cluster in production. In other words, operations, here we come.

IV. Security, encryption and authentication

Databases are very tempting targets for intruders. They typically contain all sort of juicy bits of info (your data and, more importantly, your *customers'* data); attacking them is very much like attacking the heart of an organization. In fact, the end goal of many intrusions is to get to the database and the data it holds.

The goal of an information security attack is often to steal data, either for espionage purposes or for resale purposes. In many cases, the entity purchasing the stolen data is the same organization it was stolen from, either because they don't have the data anymore or in order to prevent it from being leaked elsewhere. Some intruders have noticed this and shorten the feedback loop by creating ransomware, which forces organizations to pay ransom to get their own data back. This is often done by encrypting the data in the database and then holding the decryption key until a ransom is paid (usually in bitcoin or similar cryptocurrency).

Given that we've seen repeated intrusions and widely publicized breaches with severe consequences for the organizations that suffered them, you half expect to see a database holding production data stored in a hole in the ground, surrounded by laser-bearing sharks and vicious, hug-hungry puppies. Or at least the digital equivalent of such a setting.

In truth, many databases are properly deployed, but security has become so complex that it is actually common for people to give up on it completely. I'm not sure if this is done intentionally, out of ignorance or due to inattention, but the end result is that there are literally hundreds of thousands of databases running on publicly visible networks, containing production data and having *no security whatsoever*.

In 2017, there were several waves of attacks on such databases that encrypted data and demanded ransom in order to decrypt it. This included databases containing medical and patient records, recordings of conversations between children and parents and pretty much everything you *don't* want to fall into unauthorized hands.

A large part of the reason for these attacks, I believe, is that security has gotten so hard, obtuse and complex that people often put it off until "later". Of course, eventually they go to production. But at this point, it is easy to forget that all the doors are opened and there is a welcome mat for every Joe and Harry who wants to go into the database and ransack it. Securing the database is a task that is easy to defer for later, when we "really" need it. In some cases, it is deferred until right after the point when the entire database is in the hands of Mr. Unsavory and the rest of his gang.

Security is a hard requirement; if you are properly deployed, but not secured, you *aren't* properly deployed. RavenDB offers both encryption in transit and at rest, has several layers of protection for your data and was designed to make it easy for mere mortals to get the system up securely.[1]

We invested a lot of time not just in our security infrastructure, but also in making it approachable, easy to use and switched on by default. Instead of having to go through a 60-page document detailing all the steps you need to go through to secure your database, RavenDB is secure by default.

We'll cover how RavenDB ensures the safety of your data as it travels the network, using strong encryption to ensure that no outside party can read what is being sent, even when the traffic is sent through channels you don't own. Another important piece of security is knowing who you're talking to; after all, if you're securely sending secrets to a bad guy, the most sophisticated encryption in the world won't help you. RavenDB uses X509 certificates to mutually authenticate both clients and servers, ensuring that your data goes only to those it was authorized to go to.

Beyond encryption of data in transit, we'll also look at how RavenDB can protect your data at rest, encrypting all data on disk and ensuring that even if your hard disk is stolen, the thief will end up with seemingly random bits on the disk and without a way to actually get to your data.

Proper security is *important*, which is why we cover this topic in detail before we get to actual deployment scenarios. I believe that you should first have a good grounding in running a secure system before you take it out into the wild, chaotic environment that is production.

---

1   At the same time, we also designed RavenDB so that it would be harder to deploy when it is set in an unsecured mode.

13. Securing your Ravens

The internet is often seen as a magical grove where you have the sum total of human knowledge at your fingertips, a land of unlimited opportunities. But if you dig down just a little bit, you'll find that this is not a magic grove, but haunted woods. The internet is a hostile place where very little trust is given or expected. A network packet traveling between two machines is likely to be intercepted, inspected, logged and modified before it reaches its destination.

With rewritten links that download malware and phishing sites that steal your passwords and then your identity, the ideal of a safe-to-browse network is very far from reality. You might not typically notice this because the baseline assumption is, and has been for a while, that the internet is hostile. Websites use certificates and top-of-the-line encryption to identify themselves and hide the content of requests and responses over the wire; digital signatures are sent and validated automatically by your browser and platform.

There is so much encryption around us that we barely notice it. We've reached the stage where we need to use military-grade encryption to upload a lunch selfie to the cloud. We've gotten used to the green lock icon in the address bar and the end-to-end encryption, forward security and authentication employed by common chat platforms. Since the network is assumed to be hostile, only the foolish would go forth without the armor of encryption.

This chapter is not meant to be a thorough discussion of security practices in general. There have been many books published on the subject, guides on topics ranging from how to protect your data and services to how to break into insufficiently protected locations and ransack their contents.

Instead, we are going to focus on understanding the threat models your RavenDB instances face and what kinds of features RavenDB has to deal with such threats. This chapter is all about controlling who can access the data inside your databases, protecting the conversation between client applications and the database from being eavesdropped on or modified as well as protecting the data on disk from being usable if it is stolen.

Running RavenDB in an unsecured mode

You might find this surprising, but it is very common to run RavenDB with no security whatsoever. This typically happens when RavenDB is running on a developer machine. By default, this mode is only allowed as long as RavenDB is listening to either `127.0.0.1`, `::1` or `localhost`. In other words, as long as RavenDB is not listening on the network.[2]

In such a mode, none of the security features of RavenDB are accessible. You can neither authenticate users (anyone listening on the network would be able to hijack the connection, after all) nor create or use encrypted databases (anyone can access the server and get the encrypted data, so why bother).

Note that even in development mode, we still strongly recommend that you run in a secured configuration. The RavenDB team has worked hard to make sure that running in a secured mode is easy. Your default mode should be secured.

Even if you're not running development work in a secure network, you'll want to run RavenDB in a secured mode. Security is a core part of the design of RavenDB; we've made it easy for you to run RavenDB in a secured mode, so secured should be your default.

13.1. Introduction to transport-level security and authentication

I'm going to assume that you have little-to-no knowledge of security. This is likely false, but it's better to give you information you already have than risk missing something critical. Securing a RavenDB server requires that you do the following:

1. Allow the client to verify that the database server is indeed the one it wants to talk to.
2. Allow the server to verify that the client is valid and decide what access the client should have.
3. Prevent anyone else from eavesdropping on the communication between server and client, hijacking the client credentials, etc.

RavenDB is not the first to have this set of requirements. Instead of rolling our system[3], RavenDB uses the TLS 1.2 protocol.[4] You might not be familiar with the term; a more common use name for this is HTTPS. RavenDB uses TLS 1.2 in the following ways:

---

2   RavenDB will *refuse* to run in this mode while listening to other IPs unless you explicitly tell it that you are fine with an unsecured setup.

3   Roll your own is usually a *bad* idea with security practices.

4   TLS - Transport Level Security, the successor to SSL and what is actually used when you are using HTTPS

- The database server identifies itself to clients with a X509 certificate.
- Clients use the X509 client certificate to identify themselves to the server.
- All traffic between the database and clients is encrypted.

TLS 1.2 is the recommended protocol for secure communication by NIST and PCI 3.1, and in Dec 2017, it was the chosen protocol for close to 90% of all encrypted web traffic worldwide.

If you have previously deployed a website or application using HTTPS, you're already familiar with the key problem that arises from using TLS/HTTPS: certificates. Or more to the point: *getting* certificates.

A certificate, according to Wikipedia, is "an electronic document used to prove the ownership of a public key", but that might not mean much to a layperson. Basically, it's a way for a service to identify itself in a cryptographically secured manner. There are two types of certificates that interest us: self-signed certificates and certificates signed by a certificate authority (CA).

A self-signed certificate is similar to a name tag at a class reunion, while a certificate signed by a CA is more like an official government ID. Figure 13.1 might make this easier to understand.

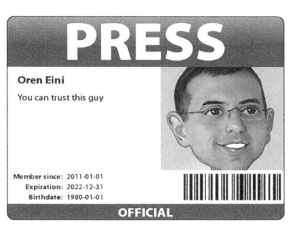

Figure 13.1. *Self signed vs. CA certificates, in real world terms*

Certificates use cryptographic signatures to identify themselves. You can assume that if a connection is using a certificate, then no outside party can listen to the contents of the traffic between the client and the server. But that, as it turns out, is just half the issue. Imagine going to your class reunion, seeing a name tag that says "Your Best Friend From High School", and then whispering a dire secret to the person wearing that name tag.

You know that your secret has only reached that person's ears, but the mere fact that they have a name tag doesn't guarantee that they *are* the person you think they are. In the real world, you typically use a government-issued ID to verify someone's identity. There's a much higher level of trust given to a driver's license than to a hand-written name tag.

In the same sense, you have a self-signed certificate (which ensures that the connection is private but doesn't guarantee who you are talking to) and you have a CA-signed certificate. A CA does some level of validation before issuing a certificate. And a CA will sign the certificate using its own cryptographic signature. This way, if you have a list of trusted CAs (called root CAs), by default you'll trust that certificates signed by those CAs are valid.

What does that mean, CA validation?

There are different types of certificates that you can use. They range from domain validation (DV), code signing, extended validation (EV) and many more. For the purpose of RavenDB, we only care about DV certificates, which allow you to verify that the server you are talking to is actually the server you think you are talking to.

A DV certificate ensures that when you type `https://db.example.org`, your client will validate that the certificate served from the server is actually for the right domain and that it is signed by a trusted party (root CA).

It's important to note that this is all a DV certificate does. Most CAs will only check that you have control over a domain before issuing a certificate for it. And if you have the certificate for a site, you can absolutely pretend to be that site. If you have bought the domain `example.org`, you can get a certificate for `db.example.org`, but unless you have really good eyes and a good font choice, you wouldn't know that the a character in the domain is not U+0061 but actually U+0251, a completely different letter, resulting in a different domain.

I'm using the Unicode letters because they are so sneaky, but the same rules apply to, say, `exampel.org` and `examp1e.org`. The first can mislead you with a typo, and the second with 1 instead of l. At the time of writing, both domains were actually available for purchase, by the way.

Another aspect of security to consider is whom you trust. For example, inside an organization, the admins usually have a root certificate installed on all machines so they can generate certificates for any sites they wish to.

A CA can be one of the global root CAs (such as Comodo, IdenTrust, DigiCert or Let's Encrypt), which are trusted by most browsers and operating systems, or it can be a local CA. For example, your operations team might define a root certificate that is trusted by all your machines and use that root CA to generate more certificates. A real-world parallel for having a local root CA would be accepting employee ID cards as proof of identity inside a company.

13.1.1. CERTIFICATE USAGE INSIDE RAVENDB

RavenDB uses certificates for all communication and authentication needs. This has the advantage that *everything* can talk to RavenDB because HTTPS is so widely supported. Operations teams are also familiar with handling certificates, securely storing them, renewal, revocation, etc.

By default, the client API will trust the server if the server's certificate is a match to the expected URL, the certificate is valid and the certificate is signed by a trusted party. You can override the client API's decision by setting `RequestExecutor.ServerCertificateCustomValidationCallback` and doing your validation logic there. This is useful if you are using self-signed certificates that aren't trusted by the client, or if you want to verify additional properties on the certificate.

When running in a secured mode, RavenDB requires that the client also authenticates using a `X509` certificate. This is called a client certificate, and it allows the client and server to establish a mutually authenticated channel between them. A client trusts the server because the server's certificate is signed by a trusted party. For the server to trust a client's certificate, that certificate needs to be *explicitly* registered in the cluster. RavenDB does not delegate trust to 3rd parties or the PKI infrastructure.

> **Reducing optional attack surface**
>
> RavenDB's security was designed with a single on/off switch. The unsecured mode for RavenDB uses plain text transport only (HTTP), supports no authentication and cannot use encrypted databases. It can also only talk to other unsecured servers and be part of an unsecured cluster.
>
> On the other hand, the secured mode uses HTTPS and TLS 1.2 for all communications, requires authentication for all operations (using client certificates) and can only talk to other secured servers and be part of a secured cluster. This also allows us to have encrypted databases.
>
> We require secured servers to have authentication in order to prevent operator mistakes from exposing production machines to the world. Sadly, this is a very common occurrence and something that we have strived to make difficult to do by accident.

Client certificates are easy to get: the only thing that needs to trust them is RavenDB, and we can either register certificates with the cluster directly or ask the cluster to generate them for us. Server certificates are usually much more complex to get ahold of because you're dealing with issues of trust. In many organizations, the ability to generate trusted certificates is tightly controlled (and rightly so).

Let's us see what RavenDB does to make secured setup easier.

13.2. Setting RavenDB up in a secured mode

Setting up RavenDB in a secured mode is a fairly simple process. You can do it yourself by setting the right configuration values and deploying it directly. In this case, we'll be using the setup wizard to get things going. This simplifies the process of setting up a secured RavenDB instance because the setup wizard takes care of all the details for you.

The first time you start a RavenDB instance, you'll be directed to the setup wizard where you will be asked to make important decisions about how RavenDB will be deployed. You can see what this looks like in Figure 13.2.

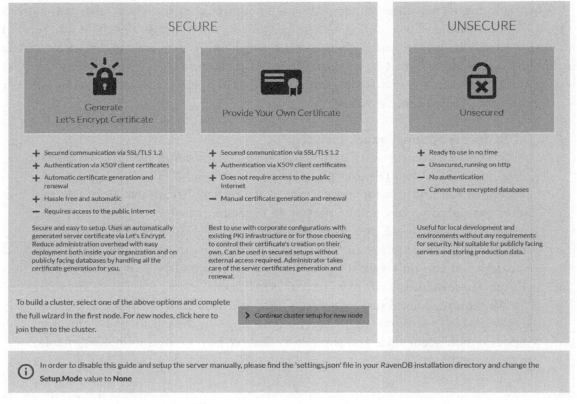

Figure 13.2. *The setup wizard is the first screen you'll see when accessing RavenDB for the first time*

You have four setup options available. You can generate a certificate through Let's Encrypt, use your own certificate, set up RavenDB in an *unsecured* mode or complete the setup process for a cluster node that was started on another instance.

Using `Let's Encrypt`

One of the reasons TLS and HTTPS aren't used everywhere is that they require certificates. In order for a certificate to be useful, you need it to be trusted, which means that you need to get it from one of the root CAs. Up until recently, that was something that you could only get in a commercial setting, which severely limited HTTPS adoption.

Enter `Let's Encrypt`. Its mission is to bring HTTPS everywhere by providing free, trusted, fully automated certificates to all. The only requirement of `Let's Encrypt` is that you must prove that you own the domain for which you are requesting a certificate.

The online documentation does an excellent job of walking you through all the ways you can set up RavenDB, so I'm not going to go into detail on each and every option. Instead, I'm going to guide you through the process of setting up a RavenDB cluster in production mode in as few steps as possible. Right now, my focus is on the security aspects of the solution; we'll talk a lot more about deployment options in later chapters.

First, uncompress the RavenDB server package (available on the "https://ravendb.net/downloads") three times to `raven/srv-a`, `raven/srv-b` and `raven/srv-c`. We are going to run three instances of RavenDB on a single machine, but you can follow the exact same steps to set up RavenDB on multiple machines. Just be sure to get the IP addresses correct and open the relevant ports in the firewalls.

`Let's Encrypt` **is completely optional**

It's important to note that this part of the process is entirely optional. Certificate and domain management is the bread and butter of most operations teams, and RavenDB couldn't care less about where you got your certificate from. You can run your RavenDB instance using your own certificates and your own domains. You can use the same setup process with your own certificates by selecting the `Provide Your Own Certificate` option. `Let's Encrypt` is available to make it easier for you to set up RavenDB in a secure manner, should you choose to use it.

First, run the `raven/srv-a/run.sh` (Linux) or `raven/srv-a/run.ps1` (Windows) script. This should start the RavenDB instance and open your browser automatically. If this does not happen, look for the `"Server available on: <url>"` line on the command line and go the the specified URL.

You should see a screen similar to the one in Figure 13.2.

Automatic certificate generation requires a (free) license

Let's Encrypt's free certificate generation is helpful, but to be able to actually generate a certificate, you need to use a domain that you own. In many cases, you are only deploying internally without having any external access.

To alleviate much of the complexity of such a deployment, RavenDB takes it upon itself to handle the details of updating DNS records and generating the certificate. The RavenDB team is managing a set of root-level domains from which it allocates subdomains to users; RavenDB uses these subdomains to create certificates.

These domains looks like <name>.development.run or <name>.ravendb.community. You can provide any <name> you want as long as it hasn't been taken by someone else.[5]

Names are provided on a first come, first served basis, and once they have been given to a user, they are associated with that user permanently. This is to avoid the possibility of two users having certificates to the same domain, which would allow them to capture traffic meant for the other.

You can request a free license from the RavenDB site, use that license during the setup process to register your domain name and then get a certificate to run RavenDB securely. That license is then tied to the domain and can be used later to modify the domain's settings and to generate another certificate.

On the setup screen, select Generate Let's Encrypt Certificate, provide the license that you received over email (you can get a free license by registering on the RavenDB website) and click next. You can see the next screen in Figure 13.3.

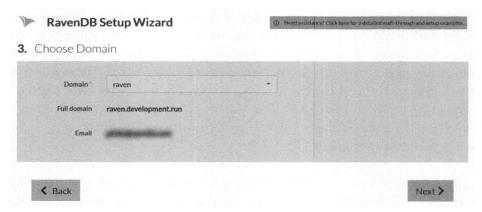

Figure 13.3. *The domain selection page allows you to select the name of your domain.*

---

5   The exact domain you'll get depends on the the license you are using. If you're using a development license, you'll get development.run; if you're are using a community license, you'll get ravendb.community; and if you're using a commercial license, you'll get ravendb.run.

The domain selection screen in Figure 13.3 shows the screen where you'll select your domain name. This will also be how you'll typically refer to your cluster. If this is the first time you're running through the process, you'll need to select a name. As long as it hasn't already been taken by someone else, you will be granted the name. If you have already set up RavenDB, you'll be able to select from the domain names you have previous registered. After selecting a domain name, click next.

You'll be faced with the cluster setup, as shown in Figure 13.4. We're setting a local cluster, so set the HTTP Port to 443 and the IP Address to 127.0.1.1 for node A. Note that this is 127.0.1.1, *not* 127.0.0.1, which you are more used to. In this case, we are relying on the fact that the entire 127.x.x.x IP range has been reserved for the loopback device. Why use 127.0.1.1, then? Because we want to bind to the HTTPS port 443 by default, and it is unlikely that someone has already bound to 127.0.1.1:443.

For production, you obviously won't need to fight some other program for access to a port – I'm looking at you, Skype – but I'm assuming that you will run this exercise on your own machine to start with. You can see what this should look like in Figure 13.4.

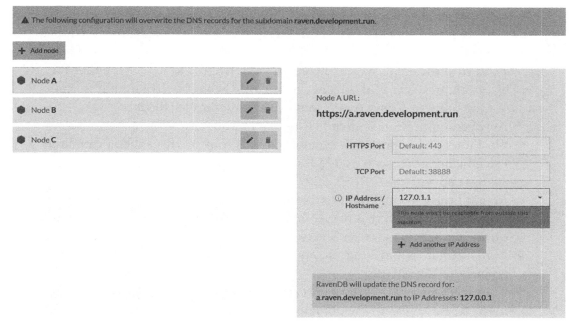

Figure 13.4. *Setting up a cluster of three machines, including setting of DNS records*

If you look at the left portion of Figure 13.4, you'll see a list of nodes (A, B and C). As we have already seen in Chapter 6, we usually use the letters of the alphabet to name the nodes in the cluster. Click on Add node to add node B on your system and give it the IP 127.0.1.2. Then do this again for node C with the IP 127.0.1.3.

If you are deploying to multiple machines, make sure that the IPs are correct, that the ports are available and that the firewall permits the machines to talk to one another. In particular, note that RavenDB actually uses two ports: one for HTTPS (usually 443) and one for TCP (usually 38888). You'll need to open both ports for incoming connections in the firewall. The setup process supports binding to an internal IP and registering the DNS name to an external IP (common in cloud platforms such as AWS, Azure, etc.).

Assuming you went with `127.0.1.1` and a local cluster, you are now ready and can hit the next button. The next little bit should take about a minute or two, as RavenDB contacts `Let's Encrypt` and completes the DNS challenge to prove that you are in control of the domain you have selected. (In my case, this is `raven.development.run`; yours will be different and unique to you, of course.) Along with generating the certificate via `Let's Encrypt`, RavenDB does something else that's very important: it updates the *global* DNS records to set up the domain name you have chosen with the IPs you have set up.

Troubleshooting the setup

As mentioned previously, this isn't going to be a step-by-step guide to setting up RavenDB. The online documentation goes through that process in great detail. The following quick list should cover the most common issues you may run into during setup, and the online docs have full troubleshooting for anything not covered here.

First, read the error. We have gone to great lengths to make sure that RavenDB errors are clear and concise, telling you what is wrong and, in many cases, how to fix it. Common reasons for setup failure include:

- ❖ Another application is already listening on the port.
- ❖ On Linux, using port 443 usually requires root privileges. You can either use a higher port (such as 8443) or use
`sudo setcap CAP_NET_BIND_SERVICE=+eip /path/to/Raven.Server`
  to grant the RavenDB binary the right to bind to a low-numbered port.
- ❖ Your antivirus / proxy is preventing RavenDB from binding to the network or preventing clients from accessing it.
- ❖ Your firewall is blocking incoming network connections, so you cannot connect to RavenDB.
- ❖ Your DNS server is aggressively caching and you can't see the DNS updates made by RavenDB to the domain you have chosen. You can set your DNS server to `8.8.8.8` to avoid that, or you can wait about 30 minutes for the usual refresh cycle.

Upon successful completion of the setup, you'll see a message with details about your newly defined cluster. Your browser will have also downloaded a `.zip` file. This file is critical and should be saved carefully. You can see the contents of this file in Figure 13.5.

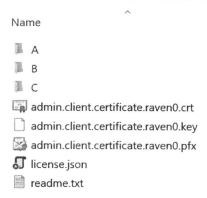

Figure 13.5. *Contents of the setup* .zip *file with everything you need to get your cluster started.*

The file contains a client certificate with admin-level privileges to the cluster (`admin.client.certificate.raven`), the license used and a README file with additional setup instructions. In Figure 13.5, you can also see that there are three directories there: A,B and C. These contain the configuration *and the server certificate* for each of the nodes in the cluster. Depending on your organization's policies, you might need to store them separately. We'll touch on that towards the end of this chapter.

You should install the admin client certificate into your browser. If you are using Chrome, double clicking on the certificate will usually prompt the wizard to begin installation. If it doesn't, go to `Settings`, `Manage certificates`, `Import...` inside Chrome to import the client certificate.

The certificate is generated locally

This info regarding the security of the generated certificate is for the technically inclined. The RavenDB setup process is running locally on your machine. The only involvement of an external party (aside from `Let's Encrypt`, of course) comes when the `api.ravendb.net` service registers the `Let's Encrypt` challenge in the DNS.

The actual certificate sign request (CSR) is generated on your local machine, as is the private key for the certificate. Neither `Let's Encrypt` nor `api.ravendb.net` are exposed to your private key, and neither party can recreate the certificate / private key. The certificate is generated locally under your own control, which means the safety of the certificate is in your hands. We'll discuss some security management strategies for your certificates toward the end of this chapter.

Once you've installed the admin client certificate, you can click on the `Restart Server` button at the end of the setup screen. The browser should then redirect you to the RavenDB management Studio. At this point in the process, you are actually running a secured server, which means you need to authenticate yourself to the server. This is the purpose of installing the admin certificate. You should get a dialog similar to the one shown in Figure 13.6 and you should select the appropriate certificate (if you have more than one).[6]

Figure 13.6. *Chrome certificate selection dialog for your RavenDB instance*

You should now see the Studio's dashboard. A new feature that is now available is the "Who am I?" notification. Look at the bottom of the window and you'll see a bright green lock icon. Hovering over that icon will reveal what certificate you are using and what permissions are available to you. You can see an example of this in Figure 13.7.

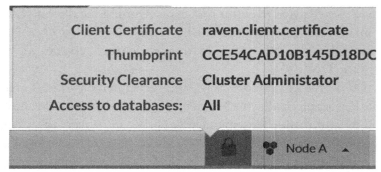

Figure 13.7. *The "Who am I" feature gives you details about how you authenticated to the server and the permissions you've been granted.*

---

6   If you make a mistake and choose the wrong certificate (or cancel the dialog), you'll need to close Chrome and restart it to make it forget this decision. Creating an incognito window also works, and might be easier.

At this point, we've finished setting up a single node. But we haven't actually set up the cluster, have we? In the Studio, go to `Manage Server` and then `Cluster` and you'll see that node A is up, but both B and C are showing up red. This is because we haven't even started setting up B or C.

13.2.1. SETTING UP THE REST OF THE CLUSTER

You can now run the `raven/srv-b/run.sh` (Linux) or `raven/srv-b/run.ps1` (Windows) script. This will start up a new instance of RavenDB, also in initial setup mode. Unlike the when we set up the first node, we don't need to do much this time. At the bottom of the setup window, you'll see `Continue cluster setup for new node`, as you can see in Figure 13.2. Click on that button and then upload the `.zip` file that you got from the first node, select node B in the drop-down, and then click `next`. You can see what this looks like in Figure 13.8.

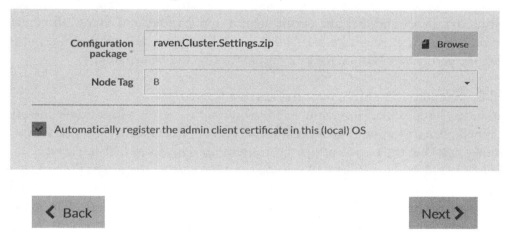

Figure 13.8. *Completing the setup process for the second node in the cluster*

You should see the success screen again with details about the setup. Click on `Restart server` at the bottom, and you're done. If you look under `Manage Server` and `Cluster` in node A, you'll see that the server has recognized that node B is functional, connected to it, and joined it to the cluster. You can now repeat the process with node C to complete the cluster setup.

This is it: you now have a cluster of three nodes. You have a valid certificate that is broadly trusted and is being used to secure all access to the cluster. Authentication to the cluster is done via the generated admin client certificate (you'll learn more about authentication in RavenDB later in this chapter). The setup process has also updated the DNS system for your cluster, so you can put `https://a.raven.development.run` to go to node A, or `https://b.raven.development.run` to go to node B, etc.[7]

---

7   Your URLs will obviously be a bit different.

Updating the certificate over time

A certificate has a time limit built into it. Let's Encrypt generates certificates for a maximum of 90 days. This means, operationally speaking, that you'll need to replace your certificates. But don't worry: just like RavenDB automatically generates certificates for you during setup, RavenDB will make sure to update your certificates when needed (with plenty of buffer time to avoid any issues).

RavenDB will take care of updating certificates, distributing new certificates to the rest of the cluster and orchestrating certificate replacement (done live, without any downtime) when all the nodes have the new certificate.

If there are any issues during the process, RavenDB will alert the operations team so that you have plenty of time to resolve it. It will also retry on regular basis to avoid being blocked by any transient errors.

In other words: you are pretty much done as far as setup is concerned. Your remaining steps are creating databases and creating certificates so applications and users can connect to the cluster (and not as the cluster admin!). And that's *it*. Even ongoing maintenance in the form of refreshing the certificates is done for you automatically and transparently.

13.2.2. SECURITY CONCERNS WITH THE AUTOMATED SETUP

The automated setup is nice. I'm really happy about how it saves a lot of time and effort. It's a feature aimed primarily at developers running a secure system locally. It is also useful for small applications that don't get a lot of operator attention. However, that has a cost. In order to make this process seamless, RavenDB uses api.ravendb.net to answer the Let's Encrypt DNS challenge and update the DNS records to point to your server.

This service is provided (free of charge) as a courtesy to RavenDB users. For mission critical systems, we recommend that your operations team takes ownership of the process. The actual certificate is generated on *your* machine, not on a machine owned by us. But given that you don't own the domain name for your cluster, you will have to go through api.ravendb.net to make changes.

We are not in the business of providing hosting, nor do we offer 24/7 support for issues like, "I need to change the server IP address on this node". For production systems, you are encouraged to run RavenDB on your own DNS and use your own certificates.

A security audit of your system will also point out that since we own the domain name, we can generate our own certificates for your cluster domain. We obviously promise not to (and you can check the certificate transparency logs to verify that), but running a critical system is best done on your own systems and under your control.

Certificate transparency

Each certificate generated by a root CA is registered in the public certificate transparency logs. This means that in order for a certificate to be trusted, it must be logged. We have carefully designed the structure of the RavenDB default domain name so we can't generate certificates for your cluster's domain without them becoming immediately visible in the certificate transparency logs.

The technical details are as follows. Your nodes' URLs look like `<node-tag>.<cluster-name>.development.run`, where RavenDB controls the `development.run` domain. We can generate a wildcard certificate for `*.development.run`, but that will not be valid for nested domains. In the case of the `raven` cluster name, you'll need a certificate that will be valid for URLs such as `https://a.raven.development.run`. A wildcard certificate on the root domain will not do; only a certificate for `*.raven.development.run` will be acceptable, which will be very visible in the certificate transparent logs.

Consider the automated setup to be something akin to training wheels on a bicycle: really useful to get you going, but something that you intend to grow out of in time.

The setup process is actually *faster* when you provide your own certificate. It offers the same user experience without you having to worry about third parties.

13.3. Authentication and authorization

We now have a RavenDB cluster set up with encrypted channels of communication and strong authentication methods for clients. We can use the admin client certificate that was generated during setup to authenticate ourselves to the cluster as the admin, which gives us the ability to create additional certificates and manage permissions.

Certificates are not users

It's tempting to consider a certificate as a simple replacement for a user/pass, just another way for a user to authenticate. I would suggest avoiding this line of thinking. Instead, think about granting access to the cluster (and specific databases inside it) on a per-application basis, rather than a per-user basis.

In other words, don't give out certificates to specific users, but to applications (for example, `orders.northwind` or `fulfilment.northwind`). This strategy can have profound implications for the way you view the security of the system.

The problem with trying to model security on a per-user basis is that your users aren't (and shouldn't be) accessing and manipulating the data directly. Instead they are going through your application where business rules and validation and authorization decisions are made taking into account full knowledge of your domain and application.

Here's an example I like to use: consider an employee management system and a `VacationRequest`. Any employee can create a `VacationRequest` document at any time, modify it freely and put it in the Submit state. At this point, the employee's manager can then Approve or Deny the request. From the point of view of the database, all of the operations (Request, Submit, Approve and Deny) are business operations. As far as the database is concerned, those are all just reads and writes.

Attempting to push business-level authorization decisions (such as "only an employee's manager can Approve a VacationRequest") to the database can lead to a lot of complexity for both the application and the database and can cause data security leaks.

Managing certificates and permissions is done via the Studio in the Manage Server, Certificates page. (Naturally, you can also define certificates through an API, so this is easily automated.) You can see what this looks like in Figure 13.9.

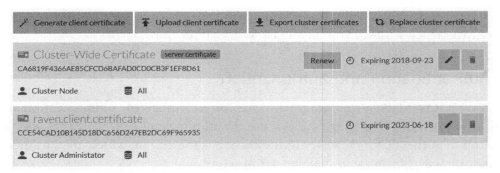

Figure 13.9. *Client certificate screen in the RavenDB Studio*

In order for RavenDB to accept a client certificate as valid, it *must* be registered with the cluster.[8] Note that as long as the certificate has been registered with RavenDB, RavenDB does not validate the certificate aside from verifying that it has not expired.

To be more specific: RavenDB does not check the certificate chain of trust or the validity period of the certificate that signed the client certificate. RavenDB does not place any requirements at all on the certificate or its properties aside from that it must be usable for Client Authentication. This is important because the generated admin client certificate, for example, is signed by the server certificate that RavenDB is using.

In the case of the Let's Encrypt setup that we ran in the previous section, the generated server certificate is only valid for three months, but the admin client certificate (which is signed by the generated server certificate) is valid for five years. Even if the signing server certificate has expired (and has since been replaced), RavenDB will continue to accept the admin client certificate until the client certificate itself expires.

---

8   The one exception to this rule is that the server's own certificate is always acceptable as a client certificate.

Plan for certificates to expire

RavenDB generates client certificates with a default validity period of five years. If you need a different duration, you can generate your own client certificates and set different time limits. But regardless of a certificate's validity period, it is important to recognize that certificates can and do expire. A certificate that smoothly runs in production for years could expire one day, causing you to scramble to figure out exactly where it is stored and how to register a new certificate.

RavenDB will warn you about soon-to-be-expired certificates (both cluster certificates and client certificates), but you should have a plan in place to ensure rotation of certificates at regular intervals. It's not only a good security practice, but a good operations practice; it means that your operations team is in the habit of actually replacing certificates so they will be ready to do so when needed.

Creating a new client certificate is easy. Click on the Generate client certificate button, and you should see a screen similar to that shown in Figure 13.10.

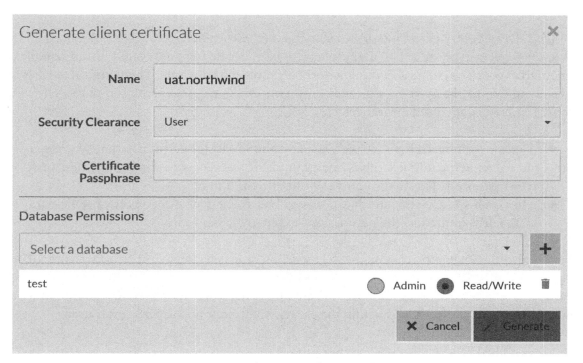

Figure 13.10. *Generate a new client certificate and assign permissions to it.*

In Figure 13.10, you can see the creation of a new certificate, `uat.northwind`, and that we have granted it read/write access to the `test` database. Once you click on the `Generate` button, the new certificate will be generated on the server and registered with the appropriate permissions. The browser will download the newly generated certificate file.

It's important to understand that on the server side, RavenDB only keeps track of the certificate's *public* information. In other words, RavenDB does not require the private key of the client certificate. If you want to register an existing client certificate with RavenDB, you can do so with `Upload client certificate`; you don't need to upload the private key, only the public information about the certificate.

> **Certificates and permissions are cluster-wide**
>
> You can make modifications to your trusted certificates and to the permissions assigned to them from any node in the system. Modifying a certificate is a cluster operation and will be reflected on every node in the cluster.

Internally, the only certificate details that RavenDB keeps are the certificate's subject, expiration date and most importantly, its thumbprint, which is used to identify the certificate when a connection comes in.

13.3.1. SECURITY CLEARANCES AND PERMISSIONS IN RavenDB

A complex security system has many places where it can fail simply due to its complexity. RavenDB's security system was designed to be simple and obvious. There are three clearance levels available to the system, although only two of them are generally applicable for your needs. The commonly used clearances are:

◆ Cluster Administrator - That's you. The admin cluster certificate that was generated during the initial setup is one example. It has access to *everything* and can do *any* operation. This is the equivalent of `root` in Linux.
◆ User - This is a certificate that needs to be assigned permissions to specific databases. It is limited to the permissions explicitly given to it.

There is also the `Operator` clearance level, which is similar to the `Cluster Administrator` in scope but is limited in terms of the kinds of operations it can perform on the cluster. The `Operator` clearance level is typically only used in cloud environments where the host manages the cluster and the operator can modify settings within the cluster, but cannot impact the cluster itself.

> **The `Cluster Node` clearance alias**
>
> If you look closely at Figure 13.9, you'll see that there is another clearance level that I didn't mention: `Cluster Node`. What's the story there? The `Cluster Node`

is basically an alias for the `Cluster Administrator` role. It exists because communication between different RavenDB servers also requires authentication (discussed in more detail in the next section) and we wanted a clear distinction between operations initiated by a user and operations initiated directly by a node.

For instance, a node may decide to forward a request to another node, and that is done with the node's own certificate. RavenDB ensures that all validation and authorization checks have been made on the original node *before* forwarding the request, using the original node's own certificate to authorize it.

Permissions in RavenDB apply only to certificates with the `User` security clearance level. Permissions apply to a particular database or group of databases and determine whether a certificate has access to that database and, if so, at what level. The available permissions are:

◆ Database admin - Can read and write documents, query, create static indexes, set up backups, engage ETL processes, define revisions retention and the conflict resolution policies, etc. Basically, this user can perform any operation that is in scope to the single database for which they are the administrator.

◆ Read/Write - Can read and write documents, query over documents and existing indexes, define and use subscriptions and in general perform any non-maintenance task on the databases to which this user has access. The ability to query also includes the ability of the query optimizer to generate automatic indexes on the fly. It does not include the ability to define new indexes manually. That is reserved to the database administrator.

Typically, a certificate will have access to a single database (its own application database). It might also have access to a shared database for ETL, etc.

RavenDB explicitly does not offer a read only access mode. If you want a user to be able to access your data without being able to modify it, set up external replication (or even RavenDB ETL, to decide exactly what is going to be exposed) and give access to that. This way, the user cannot read or modify your source data; instead they have their own copy of the data that they can work with in isolation.

Reminder: Only database admins can create static indexes

An important note: a static index allows you to write code that will be executed as part of the indexing process. If a user has permission to create a static index, they have the ability to write code that does *anything at all*.

For this reason, static index creation is limited to database administrators only. But that still means that a sufficiently motivated user with database admin access can access *other* databases. For the most part, we've assumed that if you've given a database administrator access, you trust that user.

If you require a true security boundary between administrators of different databases, we recommend that you split the databases into independent clusters so that the first administrator only has access to their own cluster.

Because static index creation requires higher security privileges, it is common to use the Read/Write permissions in production and split the static index creation function off into a separate tool that will run with elevated permissions.

13.3.2. SERVER-TO-SERVER AUTHENTICATION

We have talked about how RavenDB uses certificates to identify clients, but what about servers? How do the different servers in the cluster decide whether to trust each other?

The answer is simple. Any time a RavenDB server talks to a remote node, it will identify itself using its local server certificate. We just need to recognize that certificate, and from then on the server can be handled just like any other client.

> **I lost the keys to the kingdom, what now?**
>
> Edge cases are always the hardest things to deal with in development. You need to consider what will happen if you manage to lose all the keys to your security system. What will happen if you lose the client certificate that talks to RavenDB? RavenDB will have no way of recognizing you and will (rightly) reject any requests as unauthorized.
>
> There are two ways to handle this. First, you can use the rvn admin-channel tool, which uses the operating system to confirm that you should have access to the RavenDB process. This tool gives the root user (or Administrator on Windows) a back channel into RavenDB and the ability to run a few commands to get you back on your feet (such as trustClientCert to register a new certificate with Cluster Administrator clearance). If you have access to the server, you can also get the server's certificate and use that, since RavenDB always trusts clients that connect using the same certificate as the server.

When running in a cluster, we typically use a wildcard certificate (such as *.raven .development.run) or a certificate that contains multiple Subject Alternative Names such as:

- a.raven.development.run
- b.raven.development.run
- c.raven.development.run

This means that all the nodes in the cluster are using the *same* certificate. That leads to some interesting behavior when a client connects to a server and is authenticating using the same certificate that the server itself is using. When this happens, we consider the connection to be trusted and grant it `Cluster Node` privileges. There's no need to register the certificate for this to work.

So if you need to connect to the server and don't have a client certificate registered, but you do have access to the certificate that the server is using, you can use the server's certificate and your connection will be trusted without the admin having to take any action.

Putting these two facts together, you can see that when we bring up a new node in the cluster that has the same certificate as the other nodes, the new node intrinsically knows that it can trust the other side. This greatly simplifies the process of setting up a secured cluster.

You *can* run a RavenDB cluster with a different certificate for each node, but you'll need to register all the certificates in the cluster. That presents a bit of a chicken-and-egg problem because you can't *have* a cluster until the nodes trust each other. The `rvn admin-channel` tool solves this issue by providing the `trustServerCertificate` command that you can run on each of the nodes, instructing each node to trust the others.

Updating the cluster certificate at runtime is a delicate dance. You need to first distribute the new certificate (including the private key) to all the nodes, then register the new certificate as a `Cluster Node`, then start switching over all new connections to use the new certificate. Different nodes may do that at different times, which is why we need to ensure that the new certificate is registered explicitly.

RavenDB manages this dance for you. When you are using `Let's Encrypt`, RavenDB will automatically refresh the cluster certificate about a month before it is due to expire. Then the actual certificate replacement will take place once all the nodes are confirmed to have the new certificate. You can also trigger this process manually with your own certificate using the `Replace cluster certificate` button, as shown in Figure 13.9.

13.3.3. AUTHENTICATION BETWEEN CLUSTERS

We've talked so far about certificates and trust within a single cluster. We also need to talk about how certificates and authentication work when you're running multiple clusters that need to communicate securely among themselves. Whenever a RavenDB server communicates with the outside world, it uses its own server certificate as the client certificate so that it will be properly identified on the other side.

Within the same cluster, the nodes know that they can trust the connection. But when we are dealing with separate clusters, we'll need to explicitly tell the remote cluster that it can trust our cluster.

In Figure 13.9, you can see the `Export cluster certificates` button. Clicking this button will download a `.pfx` file containing the certificates of all the nodes in the cluster sans their private keys (everything that has a `Cluster Node` clearance level). You can take that `.pfx` file to a different cluster, register it using `Upload client certificate` and give it the appropriate permissions for your needs.

Cross-cluster authentication is often used as part of external replication and RavenDB ETL processes. Note that you don't have to specify credentials as part of the ETL connection string or when you're setting up external replication. The credentials are implicit in the cluster itself.

Handling automatic certificate refresh in cross-cluster authentication
You will encounter a wrinkle if you're using cross-cluster authentication and also automatically updating your certificates. In this case, the remote cluster will not be familiar with the new certificates, and you'll need to manually add the new certificates to the remote cluster.

13.4. Externalizing certificate management

Certificates are of high importance. If you have the certificate for a domain, you can eavesdrop on communication to that domain, modify responses, pretend to *be* that domain and in general do a whole bunch of pretty nasty stuff from a security point of view.

In many organizations, there are strict policies regarding how you are expected to manage certificates, due to their sensitive nature. These policies range from, "Let's not put them on publicly shared folders" to, "Only store certificates on hardware security modules with level 4 certification".

There is an astounding variety of policies regarding certificate management, and RavenDB makes no attempt to accommodate all of them. Instead, we provide the following options:

- ◆ Store the certificate on the file system (potentially secured via file system permissions).
- ◆ Use your own policy for certificate storage and provide a script that RavenDB will call to fetch the certificate as needed.

In the `Let's Encrypt` scenario we've explored, the actual certificate is located in the server's folder with the `Security.Certificate.Path` configuration parameter pointing to the file. The certificate file is not encrypted on the disk.

Default security of the certificate
We could have added additional security measures to the `Let's Encrypt` certificate, such as storing it in an encrypted form on the file system. But then we would have needed to store the certificate password somewhere. RavenDB does support encrypted certificates and you can provide passwords using the `Security.Certificate.Password` configuration option. But this just shifts the problem to how to secure the certificate password.

Given that this certificate is routinely refreshed by RavenDB and can be regenerated at will using the license file (which is also typically sitting right next to the certificate), there is no need to put overdue efforts into securing it. If your threat model calls for securing the certificate from an attacker that has physical access to the files on disk, you should not be using the Let's Encrypt setup mode. Instead, you should use more advanced methods to provide your own certificate, as we'll soon explore.

If you need a more sophisticated setup than a certificate file on disk (with an optional password), you need to tell RavenDB how to get the certificate yourself. This can be done by two configuration options: Security.Certificate.Exec and Security.Certificate.Exec.Arguments.

You can see an example of how this can be done in Listing 13.1.

Listing 13.1 *Partial configuration of shelling out to a user defined method for obtaining the certificate*

```
{
    "ServerUrl": "https://0.0.0.0",
    "PublicServerUrl": "https://a.raven.development.run",
    "Security.Certificate.Exec": "powershell",
    "Security.Certificate.Exec.Arguments":
            "get-cert-by-id.ps1 90F4BC16CA5E5CB535A6CD8DD78CBD3E88FC6FEA"
}
```

The idea is that instead of RavenDB having to support all the various options, policies and rules around the storing of certificates, you tell RavenDB that whenever it wants to get a certificate, it just needs to run the specified process and read the certificate from the standard output. Listing 13.2 shows the implementation of the get-cert-by-id.ps1.

Listing 13.2 *script to get a certificate by id from the current user's key store*

```
try
{
    $thumbprint = $args[0]
    $cert = gci "cert:\CurrentUser\my\$thumbprint"
    $exportedCertBinary = $cert.Export("Pfx")
    $stdout = [System.Console]::OpenStandardOutput()
    $stdout.Write($exportedCertBinary, 0,
        $exportedCertBinary.Length)
}
catch
{
    write-error $_.Exception
    exit 3
}
```

The output of the script is the `.pfx` binary data, sent to the standard output. You can report errors using the standard error, which will be included in the RavenDB error message. In this way, you can integrate RavenDB into your existing policies with very little hassle.

For example, if you wanted to get a certificate from Azure Vault, you'd use: `Get-AzureKeyVaultSecret` cmdlet. You're also not limited to just using PowerShell; you're free to shell out to any process or method you'd like.

13.4.1. REFRESHING THE CERTIFICATES MANUALLY

If you can tolerate the certificate being store on disk, then refreshing a certificate is easy. Either RavenDB will handle this for you on its own if you are using the `Let's Encrypt` mode, or you can trigger the refresh manually by using `Replace cluster certificate`. But how do you handle a server certificate refresh if your certificate cannot be stored on disk?

RavenDB will periodically (once an hour) reload the certificate from store (either the file on disk or using the executable command you specified) and compare it to the certificate that is already in memory. If the certificate has been updated, RavenDB will begin to use the new certificate instead.

But before we can replace the certificate, we need to register the new certificate in the cluster. You should only replace the certificate once that registration is complete. The reason being, you don't want some of the servers to load the new certificate, immediately start using it and then not be able to talk to the other nodes that haven't noticed the new certificate yet.

This two-step approach – first registering the certificate in the cluster as a known entity, then replacing it and letting each node pick it up in its own time – ensures that there will be no interruption in service while a server certificate is being updated.

13.5. Auditing accesses to RavenDB

Controlling who can get into RavenDB and what they can access is just one part of the security story. We also need to be able to keep track of who has connected to the system and when. RavenDB supports the process of auditing accesses at the level of database connection.

Configuring auditing is easy. You need to set the `Security.AuditLog.FolderPath` and optionally the `Security.AuditLog.RetentionTimeInHours` (which defaults to a year). Once these values are set, RavenDB will record the following events in a dedicated audit log:

- A connection was made to RavenDB, including what certificate was used and what privileges it was granted;
- A connection was rejected by RavenDB as invalid;
- A database was created or removed (from all nodes or a single node);
- An index was created or removed.

The audit log folder will contain the audit entries and is usually loaded into centralized audit and analysis by dedicated tools. RavenDB does nothing with the audit logs except write to them.

It is important to understand that the audit logs are also local (local to the originator node). That is, if we have a database residing on node C that is removed by a command originating on node B, the audit entry will be in the audit log of node B, not node C.

Another important consideration is that RavenDB writes *connections* to the audit log, not *requests*. This is done for performance and manageability reasons; otherwise, you'd have extremely large and unwieldy audit logs. With HTTP 1.1, a single TCP connection is used for many different requests. The only items you'll find in the audit log are the time of the TCP connection, the certificate being used and the level of access granted to this certificate at the time of the connection.

If you require more detailed logs (at the level of individual HTTP requests), you can use a proxy in front of RavenDB that will log the appropriate requests as they are being made.

13.6. Summary

This topic ended up taking significantly more time than I intended it to. I'm talking both about the time it took to write the chapter (and the length of the topic) and the time it took us to properly implement authentication and authorization in RavenDB.

Security is a *big* topic, one that needs to be taken seriously and handled with care. Recognizing this, we ran RavenDB through an external security audit in January 2018 and made the resulting report public.[9]

We started this chapter with a brief review of the state of the network under the baseline assumption that the network is *hostile* and we should take explicit steps to protect ourselves, our systems and our data. RavenDB handles this requirement by using TLS 1.2 for communications and using X509 for mutual authentication between clients and servers. We touched briefly on the notion of trust and how that is conferred using digital signatures from trusted parties, the root CAs (either the global list or specific CAs for your organization). We then moved to discussed what this means for deploying RavenDB.

One of the more common causes of security breaches is security systems that are so complex that they are either never enabled or enabled with poor defaults that offer nothing but a security theater. RavenDB's system was carefully designed to be both simple and secure.

Instead of offering a lot of options and configurations and tweaks, RavenDB has a simple on/off mode for security. If you don't need security (for example, if you're working locally on a development machine), you can choose to run in an unsecured mode. In that case, you will use HTTP and unencrypted TCP, have no authentication, be unable to use encrypted databases and be unable to be part of secure clusters or replication.

---

9   You can get the security report at: https://tinyurl.com/rvn-sec-rpt

The secured mode, on the other hand, uses HTTPS and TCP encrypted using TLS 1.2 for all remote communications, requires authentication of clients using X509 client certificates, can use encrypted databases and can only be part of secure clusters and replications.

The automated setup mode via Let's Encrypt takes you through the entire process of setting up a RavenDB cluster and takes upon itself the task of setting up *everything*. This includes generating a certificate, setting up DNS entries so your servers will have nice URLs, generating a configuration package to complete the setup of the other nodes in the cluster and everything else that is required to properly set things up.

We also talked in this chapter about how the automated setup, while very convenient, represents a loss of control for your system (the DNS entries are not owned by your organization, for example) and is most suitable for development and small applications. If you're setting up everything yourself, you can use the same setup process; the only difference will be that you'll be the one to take care of the DNS entries and the certificate generation.

Next, we dived into authentication and authorization and how they work inside RavenDB. We learned how RavenDB maps certificates internally handling security clearances and permissions for specific databases, and that the server's own certificate can also be used as a client certificate (with admin privileges). This fact makes it very easy for us to run clusters since all the nodes in the cluster share the same certificate.

We then talked about server-to-server authentication both within the same cluster, where RavenDB manages this almost entirely for you, and between clusters, where it's the administrator's job to ensure that the clusters trust each other and have the right permissions for the tasks that they need to do.

We talked about how to actually manage certificates, from just storing the plain text certificate on the disk to using hardware security modules or relying on external secret services (such as the machine key store or Azure Vault). RavenDB allows you to define exactly how it will fetch certificates, though remember that this approach makes certificate refresh a somewhat manual process. We also talked about what is required from the administrator to enable online certificate refresh with no downtime, as well as the reasoning behind these steps.

Finally, we discussed how you can audit access to your RavenDB cluster by configuring RavenDB to log all connections and the security clearance that these connections are granted.

In this chapter, we talked about security in transit: encrypting data as it goes through the network, authenticating who we are talking to and authorizing that users and systems are allowed to perform the operations they've requested. In the next chapter, we are going to talk about encryption at rest: how we can ensure that our data is safe, even if our hard disk is not.

14. Encrypting your data

There are three states of data: data in transit (when it flows through the network), data in use (when it's actively being read and modified) and data at rest (when it's in a stable storage). In the previous chapter, we discussed securing your data in transit using TLS 1.2 and strong encryption. In this chapter, we will focus on securing your data at rest.

Some data is intrinsically public, such as a press release. In contrast, some data is very private, such as healthcare, financial and personally identifiable information. Part of any security consideration is the notion of "defense in depth": Even if your servers are protected (physically and virtually), you must still consider the case that someone will be able to get their hands on your data.

RavenDB supports strong encryption (XChaCha20Poly1305 with a 256 bit key) to allow for full and transparent protection of your entire database. This feature ensures that nothing unencrypted is ever written to the disk, and that even in memory, outside of a running transaction, everything is encrypted.

In many industries, data encryption is a regulatory requirement. (PCI and HIPAA come to mind.) Even if an application doesn't require it, encryption is a fairly routine request that can provide you with the benefit of additional safety. Encrypting data at rest doesn't replace other security measures (such as limiting access to your database, encrypting the communication lines, protecting your access credentials, etc.) but it does complement them.

The major advantage of having encryption at the database level is that you don't need to change anything in your applications or clients. RavenDB will take care of this encryption behind the scenes – with no external changes for you to deal with. A user with access to this encrypted database can simply log in, query documents, modify them, etc., while RavenDB handles encrypting and decrypting the data as needed. RavenDB requires that any access to an encrypted database will use HTTPS, which takes care of the data in transit portion as well.

What *doesn't* database encryption protect you from?

Encrypting the database means that if you open your database file, the data inside it will appear indistinguishable from random noise unless you have the key. This means that if the hard disk is lost or stolen, you can be confident that the data on it will be inaccessible to others. But that's just one threat vector.

Encrypting the database will not protect you from breaches through authorized credentials; if a user has permissions to your database, RavenDB will decrypt the information from the disk and hand it over to this authorized user.

Such encryption will also place only a few hurdles in the path of someone who can execute code on the database machine (as the database user or as root) because he or she will be able to connect to RavenDB using the `rvn admin-channel` and register a certificate, then just access the data normally.

RavenDB goes to great lengths to ensure that on disk, and even in memory, your data is encrypted. In fact, the data is only decrypted when there is an active transaction – and even then, only the pieces that are touched by that transaction are left unprotected. Once the transaction is complete, RavenDB will zero the memory to erase the sensitive data.

Database encryption should be deployed as part of a comprehensive security strategy, including controlled access to the machines, a secure backup strategy (addressing security concerns with your high-availability and off-site deployment), management of your keys, and the appropriate audit and monitoring tools. This is a much wider topic than can be covered in this book, so I'll focus here only on the details of data encryption in RavenDB.

Before we get into the details, I want to be sure to mention that encryption has a cost. In terms of database performance, this cost is usually around 15% to 20%, depending on the exact load. In most cases, that's a reasonable price to pay for the additional security afforded. But there are also additional costs in managing encrypted databases: key management and backup, secure backups, being able to get the encryption key when you need to restore the database, etc.

Together, these can add up to a significant operational overhead (as much as RavenDB strives to reduce it). I suggest confirming that you actually need the benefits of database encryption before using this feature in RavenDB, rather than just saying "encryption is good" and pressing forward needlessly.

To get started, we'll review how to define an encrypted database through the Studio. Then, we'll dive into what goes on behind the scenes and how RavenDB actively protects your data.

14.1. Setting up an encrypted database

The first step of creating an encrypted database is to verify that your cluster is running in a secured mode. There's no point in securing the data on disk if anyone on the network can see the data going in and out. In the previous chapter we reviewed the steps required for a such a setup, so we can skip the details here.

A database in RavenDB can be marked as encrypted when it's first created. You can see how this looks in the Studio in Figure 14.1.

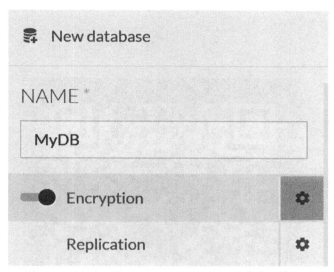

Figure 14.1. *Creating an encrypted database*

An encrypted database uses a 256 bit key to protect all its data. Without this key, the data only appears as random noise. (So, as you can imagine, your key is *important*. More on that later.) RavenDB's design also offers no way for a person to obtain the encryption key of an existing database. You'd have to know the key in advance. The properties of the key are also important. The key is a 256 bit value, generated using a cryptographically strong random number generator. While you *can* provide your own key, in general, there is little reason to bother.

Regardless, you should be sure to keep a copy of the encryption key somewhere safe, so that you can access it and the database later on if needed. RavenDB makes such a decision explicit, as shown in Figure 14.2.

In RavenDB, you must confirm that you have a copy of the key saved somewhere. For convenience, RavenDB even lets you print the key and its QR code. The idea is that you can print this page and then file it away in a locked cabinet somewhere – as even the most sophisticated computer attack will have a hard time reaching information stored on paper! Plus, a hard-copy backup is beyond easy as a protection step to implement.

Of course, many organizations already have policies for encryption key usage, storage and backup. Sometimes it's with a hardware security modules. Sometimes it's using "vault" services such as Microsoft Azure Key Vault, Keywhiz or HashiCorp Vault. Whether part of a formal policy or not, you as the admin should ensure that there's a copy of the encryption key.

Encryption Configuration

Key (Base64 Encoding)

gvdfghsxb78kP2RO135s/CLToWBlweVTtlttA9fu9q0=

QR Code:

Copy to clipboard   Download encryption key   Print encryption key

I have saved the encryption key.

⚠ Save this key in a safe place. It will not be available again.
If you lose this key you could lose access to your data!

Figure 14.2. *The encryption configuration includes just the key and requires that you store a copy of it.*

What can an admin do with the encryption key?

Given the emphasis I have just placed on the admin holding a copy of the encryption key, you might think you'll be using it often. But that can't be further from the truth. During normal operations, there are no cases where the key is needed. Instead, the key is needed when you're restoring the database from a snapshot backup (for example, if the machine is lost and you need to move the data elsewhere) or if you're adding a node to the encrypted database group and want all the nodes to use the same key (which is suggested, but not required).

Another requirement for encrypted databases is that the admin *must* select which nodes to include in the encrypted database group. Usually, RavenDB can select these nodes based on its own preferences. But for encrypted databases, an admin must specify them directly. This distinction is designed to handle the cases where servers might have different security zones in the same cluster.

> **Storing the encryption keys**
>
> Only the nodes participating in the database group will have the encryption key for that database. When you first create the encrypted database, RavenDB will contact each node hosting the database and identify the encryption key to use – over an encrypted HTTPS request, of course.
>
> This is why admins must manually select the nodes that will participate. These nodes must be up and available during the database's launch so that they can accept the new key.

Once the database is created, what I've described here is pretty much it – at least as far as deviations from the standard usage and configuration of databases.

14.2. Full database encryption

Caesar, about 21 centuries ago, used a cipher to send messages securely, by shifting the letters of his messages by three characters. When most of the population was illiterate, this approach was probably sufficient by way of security. Today, the science of cryptography and cryptoanalysis is a *bit* more sophisticated.

The goal of encryption is to take your input and a key, and then generate a random-looking pattern of bytes from it. This offers no way of going back to the original input without the key. But that's only part of what a good encryption scheme must deal with today. Modern cryptography should handle other things, such as the timing (and other side channels) of an attack, forward secrecy, authenticated encryption and many other details that are crucial for the security of the system but tend to be rather obtuse, onerous and obscure to non-experts.

RavenDB uses Daniel J. Bernstein's `XChaCha20Poly1305` algorithm to encrypt your databases, as implemented by the `libsodium` library. Both the algorithm and the library have been analyzed and audited by cryptographic experts. Both passed with flying colors.

I'm not going to discuss the actual encryption algorithm here, which would be quite out of scope for this book. You can find the gory details elsewhere. But I am going to focus on the way RavenDB uses encryption to protect your data. You can safely skip this section if you'd like, as it has a very little impact on using and operating RavenDB.

Internally, RavenDB holds your data inside a data file (usually called `Raven.voron`) that's memory-mapped to the RavenDB process. We also use temporary files[1], which are typically found in the Temp directory and have names such as: `Temp/scratch.0000000000.buffers` and `Temp/compression.0000000000.buffers`. There are also the write-ahead journals, which are the key to RavenDB's transactional nature and ACID capabilities. These are stored in the Journals directory with names such as `Journals/0000000000000000001.journal` and `Journals/0000000000000000002.journal`.

All these files contain some portion of your document data. As such, they need to be encrypted. Let's see how we deal with encrypting each of them in turn in the next section.

14.2.1. ENCRYPTING THE WRITE-AHEAD JOURNAL

The write-ahead journal is a set of files (`Journals/0000000000000000001.journal`, `Journals/0000000000000000002.journal`, etc.) that RavenDB uses to maintain its ACID guarantees. Each journal file is allocated in advance (typically 256 MB at a time), and a new transaction is written to the file whenever it's committed. Indeed, a transaction cannot be considered committed unless it's been successfully written to the journal file.[2]

A journal file is a set of consecutive transactions. When RavenDB opens a database, it will read the journal file, find all the transactions that haven't yet been synced to disk and apply them to the data file. In this way, we can be certain - even after a crash - that no data has been lost. Without encryption, a transaction is protected using a non-cryptographic hash (`XXHash64`) to ensure that the full transaction has been written to disk. This lets us verify whether a transaction was committed or not.

Authenticated encryption

If I took the following text `{"User": "Oren", "Admin': "N"}` and "encrypted" it using the Caesar cipher, I would get the following output text: `{"Xvhu": "Ruhq", "Dgplq": "Q"}`. Figure 14.3 shows the encryption key for this cipher.

I'm using the Caesar cipher here because it makes it easier to talk about encryption, while staying simple enough that we don't need to delve into complex mathematics to discuss the details.

A common use pattern for encrypted data is to hand it to an untrusted party, then accept it back from that party later on. A good example of this

---

1   These files are also memory-mapped, but they aren't persistent, as far as RavenDB is concerned. Instead, we are using memory-mapped files to avoid using too much private memory and give the operating system well-known backing store for this temporary memory. It also allows RavenDB to have fine-grained control over the memory usage required by the storage requirements.

2   RavenDB uses direct and unbuffered I/O to write to the disk, ensuring that writes are persistent, skipping the caches in the middle.

is the cookies in your browser. The text above would be used as the session cookie to remember the user among different HTTP requests – but obviously with a better encryption algorithm.

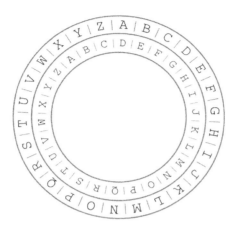

Figure 14.3. *The encryption key for the Caesar cipher*

Now, imagine that somewhere in your code you have a line such as `isAdmin = GetSessionCookieData().Admin != 'N'`. We give the cookie to the browser, and the user is free to modify it. What happens if we change the encrypted text to `{"Xvhu": "Ruhq", "Dgplq": "R"}`? The only change we made was to flip the `"Q"` at the end to `"R"`. When decrypted, the output will be `{"User": "Oren", "Admin": "O"}`, and suddenly the user is considered an admin.

In other words, just because the encrypted text was decrypted successfully doesn't mean that its original value remains – this text might have been tampered with. There have been real attacks using this angle.

Because of this risk, all modern encryption algorithms use a mode called Authenticated Encryption (with Additional Data), which is usually shortened to AEAD. In this mode, the algorithm not only encrypts the data but also computes a cryptographically secure hash over it (and potentially over additional data as well) – and then signs it.

Similarly, during decryption, the signature is checked first and the decryption fails if the signature doesn't match. Any tampering with the data will be caught this way. RavenDB uses only AEAD encryption to protect your data, so any attempt to modify it will be immediately detected. Such modification can be done maliciously or as a result of a hardware failure (bit flipping in storage, for example).

During encryption, we store only the transaction header unencrypted in the journal file. The transaction data itself is encrypted using XChaCha20Poly1305. This is an authenticated encryption algorithm, giving us cryptographic assurance that if the decryption was successful, the data we got matches the data we encrypted. Since we're already verifying the integrity of the data, we don't bother to also use XXHash64 on the transaction when using encryption. Each transaction is encrypted with a different key, derived from the master key, the transaction ID and a 192 bits random nonce.

14.2.2. ENCRYPTING THE MAIN DATA FILE

The main data file (Raven.voron) contains all the data in your database. Unlike the journals, which are written to in a consecutive manner – one transaction at a time – the data file is written to and read from using random I/O. To handle this mode of operations, the data file is split into 8 KB pages[3] that can be treated as independent of one another. If there's a value over 8 KB in size, then the file will use as many consecutive pages as needed and will be treated as a single page, as only the first of those pages will have a page header.

Each page is encrypted independently. This means that when we need to read a page, we can go directly to that page, decrypt it and read its content without having to touch anything else in the database. This process grants us the ability to do random reads and writes through the database. The structure of a page is shown in Figure 14.4.

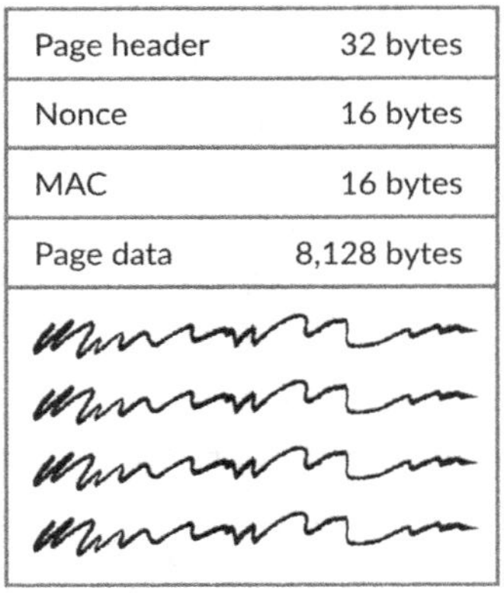

Page header	32 bytes
Nonce	16 bytes
MAC	16 bytes
Page data	8,128 bytes

Figure 14.4. *The internal structure of an encrypted page in RavenDB*

As you can see in Figure 14.4, the page is composed of a header, nonce, MAC and the data itself. You're already familiar with the nonce. But what is the MAC field for? This is the

---

3 There are a lot of other reasons why the data is divided into pages, and this is how RavenDB works without encryption as well. It just happens that it also plays very nicely into the requirements for using the data while keeping it encrypted.

message authentication code, which is used to verify that the page hasn't been modified (see the section on authentication encryption earlier in this chapter). Another interesting tidbit is that the space we have for the nonce is only 128 bits (16 bytes), but we know that the XChaCha20Poly1305 algorithm uses a 192 bits (24 bytes) nonce. Listing 14.1 shows what's actually going on.

Listing 14.1 *Internal structure of the page header and the full nonce usage*

```
+--------+
|Page    |
|Header  |
|        |
|32 bytes| <-------+
+--------+         |
|Nonce   |     Actual nonce
|16 bytes|        |24 bytes
+--------+ <-------+
|MAC     |
|16 bytes|
+--------+
```

When RavenDB needs to encrypt a page, it will generate a 128 bits random value and store it in the nonce portion of the page header. However, when we need to pass a nonce to XChaCha20Poly1305, we will pass a value that is 24 bytes in size, starting 8 bytes before the nonce. In other words, the nonce also contains 8 bytes from the page header. In practice, this means that the nonce is using 128 bits of randomness with an additional 64 bits that will change as RavenDB sees fit. Each page is encrypted using a dedicated key, derived from the master key and the page number. The page header is stored unencrypted, of course, but the page's contents are encrypted.

14.2.3. HOW DOES RavenDB ACCESS ENCRYPTED DATA?

RavenDB keeps all the data in the database encrypted at all times, both on disk and in memory. Whenever a transaction requires access to a particular page, that page is decrypted into memory owned by that transaction. For the duration of the transaction, the unencrypted values touched by this transaction will be kept in memory. When the transaction is over, that memory will be securely wiped.

To further protect your data, RavenDB will attempt to lock the unencrypted data in memory, so that it will not be written to a page file and will not be visible in core dumps. This is done by calling mlock or VirtualLock, depending on the system in question.

Locking memory into physical RAM is subject to certain limitations and may require you to change the system configuration to let RavenDB lock enough memory to handle routine operations. If your threat model doesn't include worrying about attackers digging into the page file, you can tell RavenDB that failing to lock memory is fine by using the following configuration option:

`Security.DoNotConsiderMemoryLockFailureAsCatastrophicError`.

This might be a valid choice if the system doesn't have a swap or page file defined, for example, or if you're using encrypted swap already and don't need to worry about data leaks from there.

RavenDB also uses a few temporary files (`Temp/scratch.0000000000.buffers` and `Temp/compression.0000000000.buffers`, for example). In terms of encryption, there are two file types that we care about. First are the scratch files. This is the place where RavenDB writes your data until it's written to the data file. These files are encrypted in the exact same way as the data file itself. Whenever you need to access data from one of these files, they're decrypted on temporary storage during the transaction and then wiped after it's completed. The other set of files are used as temporary buffers and are wiped immediately after use. The compression set of files, for example, is used as part of writing to the journal. We write the transaction data to the memory-mapped compression file and then compress, encrypt and write it to the disk. Once that's done, we securely wipe the compression file to remove all traces of your data from memory.

So, what's encrypted, you ask? Everything stored in the database file. This includes:

◆ Documents
◆ Revisions
◆ Conflicts
◆ Attachments
◆ Tombstones

What's *not* encrypted? Values that are stored at the cluster level. These are:

◆ Identities
◆ Compare exchange values
◆ The database record

Identities aren't generally considered sensitive information. But compare exchange values most certainly can contain data you'll want to keep private. Most important, the database record might contain connection strings to other databases. This is relevant only if you're using ETL SQL and providing the password in the connection string. In that case, the full connection string is stored at the cluster level and is not affected by your database's encryption mode.

To enable encryption at the cluster level, you'll need to take additional steps, as we'll see now.

Notice the logs output

In an encrypted database – likely storing high-value data – be sure to pay attention to the output of the log. RavenDB doesn't generally log documents' data to the log file, even on the most verbose mode, but it can certainly write document IDs in certain cases. If document IDs themselves are sensitive data, you should either ensure that the logs directory is encrypted or disable logging entirely.

14.2.4. ENCRYPTING THE CLUSTER INFORMATION

In addition to storing your database-level data, RavenDB also stores data at the cluster level. Data stored at the cluster level is usually referred to as the server store and is managed independently by any node in the cluster. The data stored there includes all the databases' records, identities, compare exchange values, etc. These are stored in all the nodes in the clusters, including for databases that don't reside on this particular node.

You can also encrypt the information on the server store. Although, doing so is a bit more involved than the process of encrypting a database, and you must repeat this operation on *all* the nodes in the cluster. Here's how:

1. Shutdown the RavenDB node
2. Run `rvn offline-operation encrypt /path/to/system-db`
3. Restart the RavenDB node

The key here is in the second step. This action loads the existing server store (which typically resides in the `System` directory), generates a new key (see the section on key management later in this chapter) and then encrypts the server store using this key.

This process should be done on all the nodes in the cluster, and it will typically result in a different key being generated for each node. Note that RavenDB does *not* enforce a server store encryption on every node. This is to allow for a rolling migration of encrypting the server store (taking one node at a time, encrypting it and restarting it). If you do decide to encrypt your server store, make sure to involve all nodes in the cluster – including when you are adding *new* nodes. You can also run the `rvn offline-operation encrypt` command before adding any new nodes to the cluster so that it won't ever write unencrypted data to the disk.

14.2.5. ENCRYPTING INDEXES

In addition to the main data file, there are indexes to consider. Each index has a separate `Raven.voron` file, its own `Scratch` and `compression` files, etc. And just like the main data file, indexes are encrypted on all levels, using the exact same techniques we just discussed.

Key derivation and additional security

You might have noticed that pages and transactions aren't encrypted using the master key. Instead, each time you need to encrypt a value, RavenDB generates a derived key for that specific purpose. The idea is that even if – due to some unforeseeable error – an attacker were able to figure out the key for a particular page or transaction, all your other data would remain protected.

The key derivation function we use ensures that attackers can't go back to the master key from which a derived key was generated. This way, even full key exposure for a particular part of the data won't expose your entire database.

During queries, the indexing transaction decrypts the relevant pages so that you can perform searches normally. It then wipes the data from the memory when the query is completed. There's one exception to this rule: in memory caches that the indexing engine uses for optimization purposes.

These caches contain the indexed terms as memory arrays and are kept outside the transaction boundary. This is because creating them can be quite expensive, in terms of time and number of allocations. Because of that, they are created once and retained for as long as they are useful. They're never written to the disk, but they might be written to the page file.

If you're concerned about the safety of this type of data, either make sure your page file or swap is encrypted or don't index any sensitive information. (There's rarely a need to run a query using a full credit card number, for example; the last four digits will usually suffice.) Document data that hasn't been indexed isn't included in the cache!

During indexing, we also write temporary files to the indexing directory, containing the indexed data. These files are also encrypted using XChaCha20Poly1305, with a random key RavenDB generates.

Even index *definitions* are encrypted. So, you can rest assured that with RavenDB everything going to a persistent medium is encrypted and safe.

Now, what about what goes on the network?

14.3. Encrypted data on the wire

Different nodes in the cluster may use different keys to encrypt the database. That means that we can't just send raw encrypted data from one node to another. Indeed, whenever RavenDB sends data over the network – whether as a response to a client's query or to replicate data for another node – we must first decrypt the data before sending it.

This may sound worrisome, but remember that an encrypted database can only reside on a node that's running in a secured mode – and, all communication uses HTTPS and TLS 1.2 which is both strongly encrypted and authenticated. Let's explore a few of the ways this is put into practice.

Aside from a client querying the database, there are few other ways to get data from RavenDB. Replication, external replication and ETL are the most common ones. Backups should also be considered; these are handled later in this chapter.

Replication is done between different database instances in the same database group – all of them will be encrypted (usually, but not always, with the same key). See the key management section later in this chapter for more details. External replication lets us copy data to a different database, either in the same or a different cluster. While RavenDB requires that any external replication from an encrypted database go to a secure server, it does not require the destination to be an encrypted database.

The lost (encrypted) laptop

Why doesn't RavenDB require that external replication from an encrypted database also goes to an encrypted database? Because the other side is the one that controls the server. We wouldn't gain anything by creating such a requirement, and there are several desirable scenarios where we wouldn't want or need it.

Consider the case of a salesperson who travels to pitch his product to customers. He needs to carry data on his laptop (to be able to fill new orders, etc.) but this data might be sensitive in nature. So, we set up the database on his laptop as an encrypted database. We also set up external replication to the master cluster in our data center.

We assume that our data center is locked - so we don't want to encrypt the data in the master cluster. Thus, encrypting the database on the salesperson's laptop only protects us from a loss or theft of this laptop. That way, data that goes out and travels is encrypted, while the data we store in a secure location is not. This distinction allows for better performance and makes specific operational tasks easier (see the discussion on backups later in this chapter).

In addition to external replication, it's common to use ETL processes to extract data out of a RavenDB database. A good example is on a system that stores payment information. Given PCI[4] compliance issues, data must be stored in an encrypted way. But imagine we set up the RavenDB ETL process on a separate database to let us work with the data more easily. In doing so, we removed the sensitive payment details and were effectively left with just the orders history. Since this (non-sensitive) information isn't required to be encrypted, it's left alone here. In the same way, we can also use ETL SQL to transfer some of the (non-sensitive) data to a reporting database for later analysis.

One thing to note at this point is that, while RavenDB will insist that the ETL process use a secure mode (HTTPS), we don't always have a good way to detect whether your SQL ETL connection string is itself encrypted. It's therefore the admin's responsibility to ensure that this

---

4   Payment Card Industry.

communication channel is safe from eavesdropping. For that matter, regardless of whether your communication channel is encrypted, admins should be aware of the data flow inside the system, making sure that sensitive information is not sent to an unencrypted store and potentially exposing data that shouldn't be stored in plain text.[5]

14.4. Key management

This section is *important*. In fact, it's probably the most important aspect for an admin to read. This is because, to understand the security of the system, you ultimately need to be aware of where your keys are. You can encrypt your data using the strongest encryption methods, using post-quantum algorithms, for example. But in the end, everything still hinges on the security of your keys. If the key leaks in any way, it's game over for you as far as your system's security is concerned.

As you can imagine, we put a lot of thought into key management at RavenDB. And yet we recognize competing concerns here: The more secure your system is, the harder it is to use. As you've already seen earlier in this chapter, not much is required to set up an encrypted database using RavenDB. Our software generates a key for you automatically. So, aside from writing this key down, you can just sit back and let run everything normally.

But this leads to an interesting question: Where is the key stored on our end, and how?

In fact, there isn't a key in the singular sense; there might be more than one. RavenDB uses the following two keys[6]:

◆ Database encryption key - a per-database key, used as the master encryption key for the entire database and stored on the server store
◆ Server master key - a server-wide value used for encrypting the databases encryption keys

By default, the server store as a whole is not encrypted. To prevent an attacker from simply reading the database encryption keys from the file system and then accessing your data, we encrypt the database encryption keys themselves a second time, using a server master key.

Of course, as a smart reader, you know that this just moves the attack vector. So, you may be wondering: How is the server master key being protected?

While RavenDB could encrypt the server master key as well, doing so would just lead to a need for a third encryption key, and then a fourth. And if we encrypt that, then we'll discover that it's turtles all the way down.

This isn't a problem that's unique or new to RavenDB. Your organization is also likely to have policies in place for protecting the encryption key: through safe storage. We'll discuss

---

5   You can force RavenDB to accept ETL tasks that use non encrypted channels using the `AllowEtlOnNonEncryptedChannel` option.
6   Both the database keys and the server master key are local to a node, not shared across the cluster.

how RavenDB can fit into those policies later on. But for now, let's see how RavenDB stores the server master key by default.

On Windows, a data protection API (DPAPI) lets RavenDB piggyback the encryption of the key on top of a Windows password. (Conceptually, Windows uses a value derived from the logged-in user's password to encrypt or decrypt values.) This means that RavenDB doesn't even need a server master key; we can rely on DPAPI to manage things for us.

So, whenever we need to store the database encryption keys for Windows, we'll call DPAPI, which will encrypt each key and store its encrypted value. Whenever we open an encrypted database, we'll hand the encrypted value back to DPAPI and get the key in return, which we can then use to open the encrypted database.

This process has the advantage of being pretty seamless and (usually) good enough as a security measure. The disadvantage is that this security is tied to your Windows password.[7] For example, an admin resetting a password will cause DPAPI to fail at decrypting any values encrypted with the old password. (Note that changing your password, which requires entering the current password, is safe in this regard. Only a password reset will lose us access to previously encrypted DPAPI values.)

On Linux, the situation is a lot more complex. There isn't a single solution like DPAPI on Linux. Instead, there are many solutions that can be used: libsecret, Gnome Keyring, KDE Vallet, etc.

Because there's no universally accepted approach – and to avoid dependencies that might not exist for all deployments – RavenDB doesn't use any of these solutions for Linux (see the next section for how you can customize that). Instead, we use the operating system permissions to securely hold the key. This key is stored in the ~/.ravendb/secret.key file with permissions set to only allow the RavenDB user access to it.

On Linux, if you have a single hard disk that stores both the secret.key file and the encrypted database, then you can plug it into a separate system where you have root privileges and skip any permissions checks on the file-system level. (On Windows, there are tools such as DPAPick that can decrypt DPAPI values, given offline access to a machine.)

So, by default, RavenDB uses these operating-system level mechanisms to secure the server master key. But recognizing that doing so gives you only up to a certain level of security, we let you customize the way in which RavenDB gets the encryption key.

14.4.1. CUSTOMIZING KEY MANAGEMENT IN RAVENDB

Your master encryption key is the holy grail of your database security. RavenDB has reasonable defaults to store it – using DPAPI or file system permissions, depending on which operating system you're running on. But there's a limit to how much these methods can protect your data. In many organizations, there are strict security policies around key management, and RavenDB lets you follow them easily.

---

7   In this case, the relevant password is for the user account that is running the RavenDB process. That will usually not be a normal user, but a service account.

In much the same way that you can customize how RavenDB gets the X509 certificate to ensure that your communication is safe, we also let you specify an executable that will fetch the key from some secret store. This process is controlled using the `Security.MasterKey.Exec` configuration value.

Listing 14.2 shows an example of a PowerShell script that can be invoked to fetch the encryption key from Azure Vault.

Listing 14.2 *Getting the encryption key from Azure Vault and sending it to RavenDB*

```
$secret = Get-AzureKeyVaultSecret -VaultName 'AllMySecrets' -Name
'RavenMasterEncKey'
$key = [System.Convert]::FromBase64String($secret.SecretValueText)
$stdout = [System.Console]::OpenStandardOutput()
$stdout.Write($key, 0, $key.Length)
```

RavenDB will invoke this script, read the key from the standard output and use it as the server master key. In this way, you retain complete control over key storage, access control, etc.

Changing the key

You *can* change the server master key, but it takes a bit of work. Effectively, you have to decrypt and re-encrypt the server store with the new key. This is actually reasonable to do because the server store is usually fairly small. Changing the database encryption key, on the other hand, isn't really possible without a full export/import, which can take a lot of time for a large database.

Since different servers can use different keys, you might want to create the new key on a new server, then tell RavenDB to move the databases over. That way, you have an online process and won't need to take the system down while it's all happening. But in practice, changing the key is rare, and isn't usually needed.

It is important to note that failing to retrieve the server master key - or getting the wrong key - will cause a failure when loading any encrypted database. And if the server store is encrypted, starting RavenDB will result in a failure as well.

14.4.2. MANAGING THE DATABASE ENCRYPTION KEY

So far we've talked primarily about the server master key. But the database encryption key also deserves some attention. Earlier in this chapter, we walked through creating an encrypted database, and as part of that, we also got the encryption key to safely store away (Figure 14.2).

Encryption keys are not part of the global cluster state, nor are they usually sent over the wire. Instead, at database creation time, the server generates a key and then contacts each of the nodes configured for hosting this database and tells them the key for this database. Only then is the actual database created.

If you created an encrypted database on Node A, and later on you want to expand the database group to also reside on Node C, how does that work? After all, the encryption key isn't available on Node C. So, just trying to expand the database group at this point will result in an error, as setting up a key for an encrypted database is a separate action from setting up the database.

The database creation wizard makes this process seamless. But it's important to understand what's going on beneath the surface.

Getting the encryption keys from RavenDB

As an administrator, you can get the server master encryption key by using `rvn offline-operation get-key` and providing the path to the server store folder. This is typically used if you need to move the database between machines.

To get the database encryption key, you would go to `Manage Server` and then to `Admin JS Console`. Choose `Database` as the type, and select the database you want to get the key for. Now you can run the following command to get the key: `return database.DocumentsStorage.Options.MasterKey;`.

You can see an example of this process in Figure 14.5.

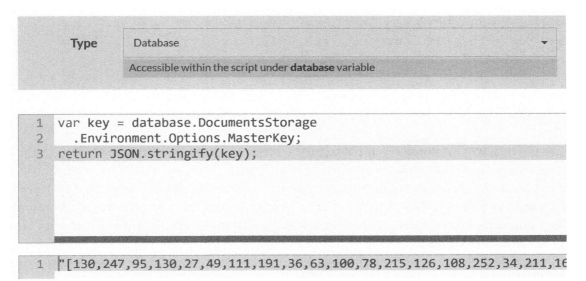

Figure 14.5. *Getting the encryption key from an active database using an admin script*

This technique uses the admin scripting functionality, which is only available to the cluster administrator and lets you execute arbitrary scripts in the context of RavenDB itself. The same functionality is also exposed through the `rvn` tool – using `rvn admin-channel` and then the `script` command.

Note that getting the server master encryption key is an offline operation, while the only way to get the database encryption key is when the database server is up and running.

Because different nodes don't necessarily have the same encryption key for the same database – and because the encryption key is *important* – we require an administrator action to create the key on a node before RavenDB loads an encrypted database. This can be done through a REST call, as you can see in Listing 14.3.

Listing 14.3 *Pushing a database encryption key to a node*

```
$baseUrl = "https://c.raven.development.run"
$dbName = "Northwind"

$spm = [System.Net.ServicePointManager]
$spm::SecurityProtocol = [System.Net.SecurityProtocolType]::Tls12
$rng = [System.Security.Cryptography.RNGCryptoServiceProvider]
$key = New-Object byte[] 32
$rng::Create().GetBytes($key)
$payload = [System.Convert]::ToBase64String($key)
$cert = Get-PfxCertificate -FilePath admin.cert.pfx

Invoke-WebRequest "$baseUrl/admin/secrets?name=$dbName" `
    -Certificate $cert -Method POST -Body $payload
```

There is actually a lot going on in Listing 14.3. First, we define which node we'll push the key to and which database whose encryption key we'll push. Then, we ask PowerShell to use TLS 1.2 to talk to the server. (Sometimes it defaults to TLS 1.0, which isn't supported by RavenDB for security reasons.) `RNGCryptoServiceProvider` is then used to generate a cryptographically secured random number. We convert it to Base64 and then use a certificate with cluster administrator privileges to send it to the node.

Once this is done, we can now expand the Northwind database from Node A to Node C as well. The database will be created on the new node, and the previously pushed encryption key will be in use.

An admin can decide whether to use the same key on all nodes – which may simplify some operations, such as restoring from backup – or use different keys. We'll speak more about backup later in this book. But there are some things about backing up an encrypted database that require special attention here. Let's go over them.

14.5. Backing up encrypted databases

Just because a database is encrypted doesn't mean that it doesn't need all the usual care and maintenance you give to other data. In particular, I'm thinking about backups, restores and high-availability considerations.

We'll discuss backups in full in the next part of this book, so I won't get too deep into the details now of how to work with them. Instead, I'll just discuss the details that are important to remember when dealing with encrypted databases.

RavenDB supports the following forms of backups:

◆ Snapshot - a compressed binary view of the database files at a given point in time, as well as additional data from the cluster level that belongs to the database (identities, compare exchange values, etc.)
◆ Full backup - a compressed JSON of all data in the database, as well as all the cluster-level data for this database
◆ Incremental backup - a compressed JSON of all data in the database since the last full backup, as well as all the cluster-level data for this database.

For an encrypted database, it's important to consider what parts of the backup are encrypted, and in what manner. With a Snapshot backup, the entire snapshot is encrypted using the database encryption key. Conceptually, you're getting the raw file from the disk-as is[8].

As a result, you *must* have the appropriate encryption key if you ever want to restore the snapshot. Without this key, there's no way to restore the database, access the data or really do anything at all.

Alongside the snapshot data, there's also the cluster-level data. This set of data is typically much smaller, but it is *not* encrypted in the case of a snapshot. While it is compressed, this data is available to anyone who can read the backup media.

Full and incremental backups are always completely unencrypted, so you should be aware of your backup strategy and where you'll back up your encrypted databases. RavenDB is equipped to push backups to a local or shared directory, to an FTP/SFTP site, to Azure Blob storage, to Amazon S3 and to Amazon Glacier.

In any of these cases, if you have an encrypted database, you need to consider where you will store the data. You can back up to an encrypted folder, or you can enable data-at-rest encryption settings when uploading to the cloud (exactly how depends on which

---

8   Note that this is just a conceptual model. You can't just copy the file out of the way while RavenDB is running and consider this a backup

system you're using, but all have some level of support for automatic encryption of uploaded content).

We'll discuss backup management at length in Chapter 17, later in this book. But I want to emphasize that, for encrypted databases, in addition to backing up the data for the document itself, it's important to have a copy of the encryption key. Not only is this step important for restoring snapshot data, but it also can be very relevant if an admin has ever reset a password for a user, resulting in DPAPI failure to decrypt the database encryption key at startup.

This error can happen pretty far down the line. If the admin resets the password on Monday, but RavenDB had already gotten the encryption key in memory, then no issue will appear until the moment when RavenDB unloads the database and needs to reload it – potentially several days or weeks later. At that point, your being able to quickly and easily grab the encryption key from a locked drawer and provide it to RavenDB for loading the encrypted database is much preferred to a forced restore of everything.

14.6. Summary

This chapter might have been hard to decipher, but I hope you got the right keys out of it. In a more serious tone, we've gone over a lot of information about how RavenDB is using high-end encryption to safely protect your data. RavenDB uses the XChaCha20Poly1305 algorithm to encrypt any and all data on disk. Decrypting information is done only during an active transaction. The memory holding the decrypted data is locked into memory, so it won't be written to a page file or a swap partition. RavenDB will immediately wipe the decrypted contents in memory upon transaction closure, reducing the time that sensitive information is available.

We went over the details of how RavenDB encrypts every part of the system, from how transactions are encrypted as they're written to the disk to how each individual page in the database is encrypted with its own unique key. We saw what's encrypted on RavenDB (documents, attachments, revisions, indexes) and what isn't - even if the database itself is encrypted (identities and compare exchange values). We then saw how we can encrypt cluster-level data by encrypting the server store and met for the first time the rvn tool.

After that, we looked at what's probably the most important topic for you in this chapter: how the encryption keys are being managed by RavenDB. By default, RavenDB encrypts the database encryption keys using the server master key. This master key is then encrypted using DPAPI on Windows or protected using file system permissions on Linux. You also have the option of telling RavenDB how to fetch the master key from a hardware security module, a vault or any other method that fits your security policies using the Security.MasterKey.Exec option.

Finally, we discussed backup concerns for encrypted databases, and in particular, the safe-keeping of your encryption keys. I find it ironic that the most secure backup method is probably just printing a hard copy of the encryption key and storing it offline in a locked cupboard at your offices. Nonetheless, I've found this approach to be one of the most efficient ways to handle the issue of a lost or stolen key. Having the key tucked away like this means that you won't have to think about it too much – but if you do have a need, the key is available to you.

You might have noticed some emphasis on my part on the topic of keeping the encryption key safe. This is because the key is *important*. Without it, you have zero access to the database. You may think this emphasis is obvious as a basic property of an encrypted database. And yet, we've gotten support calls with some variant of "we lost the key, how do we get the data back?". This scenario can occur due to a password reset invalidating a `DPAPI`-encrypted value, losing the main hard disk of the machine while still having the database drive up, or many other reasons.

Regardless of the cause, the key was lost. If there's no key, then there's no way to access your data. That is the *point* of encryption! So, please remember that when you create an encrypted database, keep your encryption keys somewhere safe - just in the off case that you'll need them.

This chapter also closes our discussion on security inside RavenDB. The next topic on the table is an in-depth dive into operations, deployments and monitoring your production clusters.

V. Running in production

We have spent a lot of time talking about what RavenDB can do in this book. We've talked about the best way to put data into it and get data out, how indexes work, how RavenDB runs as a distributed cluster and how to work with the database from your applications. What we haven't talked about, except for a few tidbits here and there, is how you are actually going to run RavenDB in production.

The production environment differs from running in development mode in several key areas. You typically have *much* more data that's more important, may need protection from prying eyes and (most importantly) definitely needs to be there at all times. Production systems should be available, speedy and functional.

Production systems also run under heavy constraints, from limited network access to air-gapped systems to (true story) an old PC that is thrown in an unventilated cupboard and expected to serve business-critical functionality. The common thread is that what you can do in production is limited. You can't just attach a debugger, run invasive procedures or even assume that there is a person monitoring the system who can react when it beeps.

With cloud deployments thrown in, you might not even know what kind of machines you're running on and issues can arise because of a noisy neighbour on the same hardware that impacts your operations. Regardless of the environment and the hurdles you need to clear, your operations team needs to deliver reliability, performance, security and agility.

RavenDB was designed with an explicit focus on production. We already saw some of this earlier in the book when talking about different kinds of alerts and behaviors; in this part, we are going to be taking a deep dive into some yet unexplored parts of RavenDB.

We'll cover deployments at length: in house and on the cloud, on your own machines and as a database as a service (DBaaS). We'll explore topologies that range from single-production servers to clusters spanning the globe and talk about how to manage your databases for optimal resource usage and maximum survivability. In particular, we'll focus on what RavenDB is expecting from the underlying platform, what kind of optimizations you can apply at the deployment level and the kinds of resources you should give to your RavenDB instances.

We'll discuss monitoring, both as part of ongoing metrics gathering and analysis and as it applies to when you need to gather information about what is going with a specific issue. There is a wealth of information that RavenDB externalizes specifically to make such investigation easier and ongoing monitoring will give you a good feel for the "heartbeat" of the system, meaning you'll be able to notice changes from expected patterns and head off problems early.

Routine and preventive maintenance is also an important topic that we'll go over. From proper backup and restore procedures to disaster recovery strategies, it pays to be prepared in case trouble lands in your lap. We'll see how to troubleshoot issues in production, covering additional tools available at the operating system level and dedicated tools and features meant to help you manage and operate RavenDB. We'll discuss ways to manipulate the internal state of RavenDB, impact decision making and behavior at runtime and always keep your application running.

This part is meant for the operations team that will support your RavenDB cluster in production, but it's also very useful for developers and architects who want to understand at least the rudimentaries of how RavenDB is being run in the production environment and the options you have to inspect and manage it. The content of this part of the book was composed after over a decade's work supporting RavenDB deployments in production in a variety of environments. You'll note that the general approach we took is that if there's an error RavenDB can do something about, it will.

That doesn't mean your operations team has nothing to do. There is quite a lot of work to do, but most of it should be done before the system is anywhere near a production deployment. We'll cover in detail the notion of capacity planning, setting service-level agreements (SLAs) for RavenDB and your system (and measuring compliance with them) and the kinds of machines and systems you should expect to use to meet these goals.

15. Production deployments

The day you deploy to production can be a very scary day. It is the culmination of months or years of work; the time where you actually get to see the results of your work bearing fruit. Of course, sometimes the fruit is unripe because you pushed the big red button too soon. There is no riskier time in production than just after a new version has been deployed.

I want to recommend the Release It! book by Michael T. Nygard. I read it for the first time over a decade ago, and it made an impact on how I think about production systems. It had a big effect on the design and implementation of RavenDB as well. This chapter will cover topics specific to RavenDB, but you might want to read the Release It! book to understand how to apply some of these patterns to your application as a whole.

There are quite a few concerns that you need to deal with when looking at your deployment plan and strategy. These start with any constraints you have, such as a specific budget or regulatory concerns about the data and how and where you may store it. The good thing about these constraints is that most of the time, they're clearly stated and understood. You also have requirements, such as how responsive the system should be, how many users are expected to use it and what kind of load you have to plan for. Unfortunately, these requirements are often unstated, assumed or kept at such a high enough level that they become meaningless.

You *need* the numbers

In 2007, I was asked by a client to make sure that the project we were working on would be "as fast as Google." I took him at his word and gave him a quote for 11.5 billion dollars (which was the Google budget for that year). While I didn't get that quote approved, I made my point, and we were able to hammer down what we actually needed from the application.

Giving a quote for $11,509,586,000 is a cry for help. I don't know what "fast" means. That's not how you measure things in a meaningful way. A much better way to state such a request would be to use a similar format to that in Table 15.1.

Table 15.1. *SLA table allowing for max response time for requests under different loads*

Reqs / sec	%	Max duration (ms)
100	99%	100
100	99.99%	200
200	99%	150
200	99.9%	250
200	99.99%	350

Table 15.1 is actional. It tells us that under a load of 100 requests per second, we should complete 99% of requests in under 100ms and 99.99% requests in under 200ms. If the number of concurrent requests goes up, we also have an SLA set for that. We can measure that and see whether we match the actual requirement.

Developers typically view production as the end of the project. If it's in production, it stays there, and the developers can turn to the next feature or maybe even a different project entirely. The operations team usually has the opposite view. Now that the system's in production, it's their job to babysit it. I don't intend for this to be a discussion of the benefits of having both operations and development insight during the design and development of a system, or even a discussion about closer collaboration in general. You can search for the term "DevOps" and read reams about that.

Instead, I'm going to assume that you are early enough in the process that you can use some of the notions and tools in this chapter to affect how your system is being designed and deployed. If you're farther along, you can start shifting to a point where you match the recommended practices.

And with that, let's dive in and talk about the first thing you need to figure out.

15.1. System resources usage

You must have a 386DX, 20MHz or higher processor, 4MB of memory (8MB recommended) and at least 70MB of available hard disk space. Oh, wait. That's wrong. These are actually the system requirements if you want to install Windows 95.

I want to refer you back to Table 15.1. Before you can make any decisions, you need to know what kind of requirements are going to be placed on *your* system. Is this a user-facing system or B2B? How much data will it need to handle? How many requests are expected? Are there different *types* of requests? This is important enough concept that it's worth repeating. There are a lot of good materials about how to go about your system's requirements; I'll point you again to the Release It! book for more details.

There is an obvious correlation between the load on your system and the resources it consumes to handle this load. Figure 15.1 shows a couple of graphs from a production system. This isn't peak load, but it isn't idle either.[1]

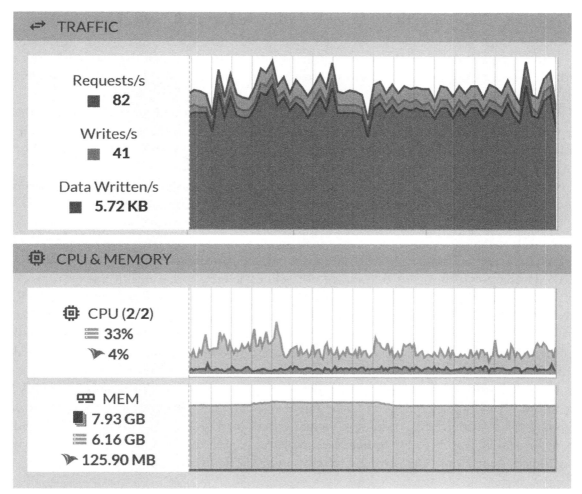

Figure 15.1. *Load and resource graphs from the RavenDB dashboard on production system*

---

1   All the stats and monitoring details are directly from the RavenDB Studio. We'll go over where they are located and what you can deduce from them in the next chapter.

This particular machine is running on an Amazon EC2 `t2.large` instance with 2 cores and 8 GB of memory. The machine isn't particularly loaded, with enough spare capacity to handle peaks of three to four times as many requests per second. Of course, this is just a very coarse view of what is going on, since it is missing the request latencies. We can get that information as well, as you can see in Figure 15.2. (In the Studio go to `Manage Server` and then `Traffic Watch`).

Requests:	Minimum duration:	Average duration:	Maximum duration:
10,200	**0 ms**	**2.68 ms**	**163 ms**

Figure 15.2. *Request latencies tracked using the RavenDB Traffic Watch feature*

Things seems to be fine: the average request time is low, and even the maximum isn't too bad. We can dive into percentiles and metrics and all sort of details, but at this point getting too specific won't be of much relevance for this book.

If you're already in production, the RavenDB Studio has already surfaced these numbers for you, which means that you can act upon them. For one thing, the correlation between the requests on the server and the load on the server can be clearly seen in Figure 15.1, and that can help you figure out what kind of system you want to run this on.

Given that you are not likely to have an infinite budget, let's go over how RavenDB uses the machine's resources and what kind of impact that is likely to have on your system.

15.1.1. DISK

By far the most important factor affecting RavenDB performance is the disk. RavenDB is an ACID database, which means that it will not acknowledge a write until it has been properly sent to the disk and confirmed to be stored in a persistent manner. A slow disk can make RavenDB wait for quite a while until it has disk confirmation, and that will slow down writes.

RavenDB is quite proactive in this manner and will parallelize writes whenever possible, but there is a limit to how much we can play with the hardware. At the end of the day, the disk is the final arbiter of when RavenDB can actually declare a transaction successful.

If you are using physical drives, then the order of preference at this time is to use NVMe if you can. Failing that, use a good SSD. Only if you can't get these (and you should), go for a high-end HDD. Running a production database load on a typical HDD is not recommended. It's *possible*, but you'll likely see high latencies and contention in writing to the disk, which may impact operations. This strongly relates to your actual write load.

What kind of request are you?

It's easy to lump everything into a single value – requests per second – but not all requests are made equal. Some requests ask to load a document by id (cheap), others may involve big projections over a result set containing dozens of documents (expensive). Some requests are writes, which will have to wait for the disk, and some are reads, which can be infinitely parallel.

When doing capacity planning, it's important to try to split the different types of requests so we can estimate what kind of resource usage they're going to need. In Figure 15.1, you can see that RavenDB divides requests into the total number (`Requests/s`) and then the number of writes out of that total. This gives us a good indication of the split in requests and the relative costs associated with such requests.

If you're using network or cloud disks, be sure to provision enough IOPS for the database to run. In particular, when using a SAN, do *not* deploy a cluster where all the nodes use the same SAN. This can lead to trouble. Even though the SAN may have high capacity, under load, all nodes will be writing to it and will compete for the same resources. Effectively, this will turn into a denial of service attack against your SAN. The write load for RavenDB is distributed among the nodes in the cluster. Each node writes its own copy of the data, but all data ends up in the same place.

I strongly recommend that when you deploy a RavenDB cluster, you use independent disks and I/O channels. RavenDB assumes that each node is independent of the others and that the load one node generates shouldn't impact operations on another.

You might have noticed that so far I was talking about the disk and its impact on writes, but didn't mention reads at all. This is because RavenDB uses memory-mapped I/O, so reads are usually served from the system memory directly.

15.1.2. MEMORY

The general principle of memory with RavenDB is that the more memory you have, the better everything is. In the ideal case, your entire database can fit in memory, which means that the only time that RavenDB will need to go to disk is when it ensures a write is fully persisted. In more realistic scenarios, when you have a database that is larger than your memory, RavenDB will try to keep as much of the database as you are actively using in memory.

In addition to memory-mapped files, RavenDB also uses memory for internal operations. This can be divided into managed memory (that goes through the .NET GC) and unmanaged memory (that is managed by RavenDB directly). Typically, the amount of memory being allocated will only be large if RavenDB is busy doing heavy indexing, such as when rebuilding an index from scratch.

For good performance and stability, it's important to ensure that the working set of RavenDB (the amount of data that is routinely accessed and operated on at any given time) is less than the total memory on the machine. Under low memory conditions, RavenDB will start scaling down operations and use a more conservative strategy for many internal operations in an attempt to reduce the memory pressure.

If you are running on a machine with a non-uniform memory access (NUMA) node, that can cause issues. RavenDB doesn't use NUMA-aware addressing for requests or operations, which can cause memory to jump between NUMA nodes, as well as high CPU usage and increased latencies. We recommend that you configure the machine to behave in a non-NUMA-aware fashion. Alternatively, you could run multiple instances of RavenDB on the machine, each bound to a specific NUMA node.

15.1.3. CPU

Given an unlimited budget, I want the fastest CPU with the most cores. Reads in RavenDB scale linearly with the number of cores that a machine has, but sequential operations such as JSON parsing are usually bounded by the speed of the individual cores.

RavenDB makes heavy use of async operations internally to reduce the overall number of context switches. But the decision to prioritize more cores over faster cores is one you have to make based on your requirements. More cores means that RavenDB can have a higher concurrent number of requests, but will also have higher latency. Fewer and faster cores means faster responses, but also fewer concurrent requests.

The choice between faster cores or more cores is largely academic in nature. RavenDB is a *very* efficent database. We have tested RavenDB with a Raspberry Pi 3, a \$25 computer that uses a quad-core 1.2GHz ARM CPU and 1GB of RAM. On that machine, we were able to process a little over 13,000 document reads per second. Those were simple document loads without complex queries or projections, but that should still give you some idea about the expected performance of your production systems.

15.1.4. NETWORK

As you can imagine, network usage in RavenDB is important. With enough load, RavenDB can saturate a 10GB connection, sending out gigabytes of data per second. But if you get to this point, I suggest taking a look at your application to see what it's doing. Very often, such network saturation is the result of the application asking for much more data than is required.

A good example is wanting to load the list of orders for a customer and needing to show a grid of the date, total order value and the status of the order. In some cases, the application will pull the full documents from the server, even though it uses only a small amount of the data from them. Changing the application to project only the relevant information is usually a better overall strategy than plugging in a 20GB card.

An important consideration for network usage is that RavenDB will not compress the outgoing data by default when using HTTPS. If you are talking to RavenDB from a nearby machine (same rack in the data center), there is usually enough network capacity that RavenDB can avoid spending time compressing the responses. There is also the BREACH attack for compressed HTTPS to consider, which is why automatic compression is off by default.

Compression on the wire is controlled via `Http.UseResponseCompression` and `Http.AllowResponseCompressionOverHttps` settings. You can also control the compression level using the `Http.GzipResponseCompressionLevel` setting, favoring speed over compression rate or vice versa. On a local network, it is probably best to not enable that; the CPU's time is better spent handling requests, not compressing responses.

15.2. Common cluster topologies

RavenDB is quite flexible in the ways it allows you to set itself up for production. In this section, we are going to look at a few common configuration topologies for RavenDB, giving you the option to pick and chose what is best for your environment and needs. These aren't the only options, and you can usually mix and match them.

> **A RavenDB cluster and what it's good for**
>
> A cluster in RavenDB is a group of machines that is managed as a single unit. A cluster can contain any number of databases that are spread across its nodes. Each database can have multiple copies which are are replicated to some (or all) of the nodes, depending on the replication factor for the specific database.
>
> RavenDB doesn't split the database data among the various nodes, but replicates *all* the data in the database to each of the nodes in the database group.[2]

You'll typically use a dedicated database per application, potentially with some data flows (ETL and external replication) between them. These databases are hosted on a single cluster, which simplifies management and operations. Let's see how we actually deploy RavenDB in various scenarios and the pros and cons of each option.

15.2.1. A SINGLE NODE

The single node option is the simplest one. Just have one single node and run everything on top of that. You can see an example of this topology in Figure 15.3.

a.raven.development.run

Figure 15.3. *A single node option hosting multiple databases*

In this mode, all the databases you use are on the same node. Note that this can change over time. Any RavenDB node is always part of a cluster. It may be a cluster that only contains itself,

---

2   See Chapters 6 and 7 for full details on how RavenDB clusters behave.

but it is still a cluster. In operational terms, this means that you can expand this cluster at any point by adding more nodes to it and then decide how to arrange the databases on the cluster.

This mode is popular for development, UAT, CI and other such systems. While possible, it is *not* recommended that you use a single node configuration for production because it has a single point of failure. If this single node is down, there is no one else around that can take its duties, and that makes any issues with the node high priority by definition.

The better alternative by far is a proper cluster.

15.2.2. THE CLASSIC CLUSTER

The classic cluster has either three or five nodes. The databases are spread across the cluster, typically with a replication factor of two or three. Figure 15.4 shows a three-node cluster where the 'Helpdesk' and 'Users' databases have a replication factor of three, while 'Fulfillment', 'Ledger' and 'Orders' databases have a replication factor of two.

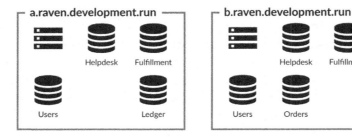

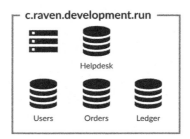

Figure 15.4. *A three-node cluster with each database residing on two or three nodes.*

In the three-node cluster mode shown in Figure 15.4, we know that we can lose any node in the cluster and have no issue continuing operations as normal. This is because at the cluster level, we have a majority (2 out of 3) and we are guaranteed to have all the databases available as well.

In this way, we've reduced the density from five databases per server to four. Not a huge reduction, but it means that we have more resource available for each database, and with that we've gained higher security.

You don't need a majority

The topologies shown in Figure 15.4 and Figure 15.5 showcase a deployment method that ensures that as long as a majority of the nodes are up, there will be no interruption of service. This is pretty common with distributed systems, but it isn't actually required for RavenDB.

Cluster-wide operations (such as creating and deleting databases, assigning tasks to nodes in the cluster or creating indexes) require a majority to be accessible. But these tend to be rare operations. The most common operations are the reads and writes to documents, and these can operate quite nicely even with just a single surviving node. The mesh replication between the different databases uses a gossip protocol (discussed in more depth in Chapter 6) with a multi-master architecture.

All reads and writes can go to any database in the database group and they will be accepted and processed normally. This gives the operations team a bit more freedom with how they design the system and the ability to choose how much of a safety margin is needed compared to the resources required.

Another classic setup is the five-node cluster, as shown in Figure 15.5. Each node in the cluster contains three databases and the cluster can survive up to two nodes being down with no interruption in service. At this point, you need to consider whether you actually need this level of redundancy.

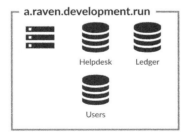
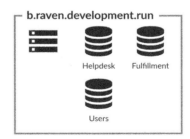

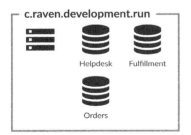
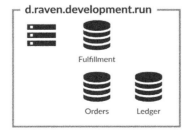
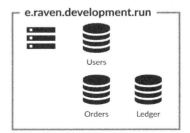

Figure 15.5. *A five node cluster with each database residing on three nodes.*

There are many cases where you can live with a lower redundancy level than the one shown in Figure 15.5. Having a five-node cluster with each of the databases having a replication factor of two is also an option. Of course, in this mode, losing two specific nodes in the cluster may mean that you'll lose access to a particular database. What happens exactly depends on your specific failure. If you lose two nodes immediately, the database will become inaccessible.

If there is enough time between the two nodes failures for the cluster to react, it will spread the database whose node went down to other nodes in the cluster to maintain the replication factor. This ensures that a second node failure will not make a database inaccessible.

High availability clusters

RavenDB clusters and their highly available properties were discussed at length in Chapters 6 and 7. Here it is important to remember that the cluster will automatically work around a failed node, redirecting clients to another node, re-assigning its tasks and starting active monitoring for its health.

If the node is down for long enough, the cluster may decide to add extra copies of the databases that resided on the failed node to ensure the proper number of replicas is kept, according to the configured replication factor.

This particular feature is nice when you have a five-node cluster, but most times you'll use a replication factor of three and not have to think about the cluster moving databases around. This is far more likely to be a consideration when the number of nodes you have in the cluster grows much higher.

15.2.3. SOME NODES ARE MORE EQUAL THAN OTHERS

RavenDB uses a consensus protocol to manage the cluster. This means that any cluster-wide operation requires acknowledgment from a majority of the nodes in the cluster. For a five-node cluster, this means that each decision requires the leader's confirmation as well as the confirmation of two other nodes to be accepted. As the size of the cluster grows, so does the size of the majority. For example, with a seven–node cluster, you need a majority of four.

Because of this, you typically won't increase the size of your cluster whenever you need more capacity. If you have enough databases and load to need a 20-node cluster, each decision will require 11 confirmations. That… is quite high. Instead, we arrange the cluster in two ranks.

In the first rank, we have the cluster members. These are nodes that can vote and become the cluster leader. You'll typically have three, five or seven of them, but no more than that. The higher the number of member nodes, the more redundancy you'll have in the cluster. But what about the rest of the cluster nodes?

The rest of the cluster nodes aren't going to be full members. Instead, they are marked as watchers in the cluster. You can see how this topology looks like in Figure 15.6.

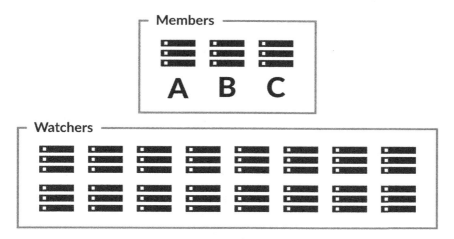

Figure 15.6. *A large cluster divided into full members and watchers*

A watcher in the cluster is a fully fledged cluster node. The node hosts databases and is managed by the cluster, just like any other node. However, it cannot be voted as the leader, and while it is informed about any cluster decision, the cluster doesn't count a watcher's vote towards the majority. A cluster majority is always computed as: `floor(MembersCount / 2) + 1`, disregarding the watchers (which are just silent observers).

A watcher node can be promoted to a member node (and vice versa), so the decision to mark a node as a member or watcher doesn't have long-term implications. If a member node is down and you want to maintain the same number of active members, you can promote a watcher to be a member. But keep in mind that promoting a node is a cluster operation that requires a majority confirmation among the cluster members, so you can't promote a node if the majority of the members is down.

15.2.4. PRIMARY/SECONDARY MODE

The primary/secondary topology is a common topology to achieve high availability. A good example of this topology can be seen in Figure 15.7. You have a primary server that does all the work and a secondary server that replicates the data. This is also called active/passive topology.

Figure 15.7. *A primary server replicating to a secondary*

With RavenDB, using a two-node cluster is not a good idea. The majority of two is still two, after all, so even a single node failure will make the cluster unavailable.[3] A two-node cluster is sometimes chosen as the selected topology when you want to manually control failover behavior for some reason. We'll cover this option in the next section.

15.3. Database group topologies

We've talked about the topology of the cluster, but most of the work done with RavenDB is at the database level. Let's zoom in to see how we should deploy our databases in production.

> **Reminder: database groups and database instances**
> A database group is the set of nodes that holds the individual instances of the database. Each one of the database instances will replicate all its data to any of its sibling instances on the other nodes in the database group.
>
> The database group as a whole is being managed by the cluster: assigning tasks to various nodes in the group, determining the nodes' priority order for clients, etc. At the same time, each instance constantly gossips with other members of the group, sharing new and updated information and reconciling any changes that have happened in the meantime.
>
> This gossip is done *independently* from the cluster behavior and continues even under error conditions that cause the cluster to become inoperable. Clients know the database group topology and will try another node if the node they tried talking to isn't responding. This leads to a robust system in which the cluster, the database group members and the clients are all working together to achieve maximum uptime.

There a few considerations to take into account about the database topology. First, we need to decide the appropriate replication factor for the database. The more copies of the data we have, the safer we are against catastrophe. On the other hand, at some point, we are safe enough and increasing the replication factor any further is just burning through disk space.

Second, we need to consider what kind of access pattern the client should use. By default, clients will access the database instances in a database group in the order they are defined on the server. You can see that in Figure 15.8 and on the Studio under `Settings` and then `Manage Database Group`.

As you can see in Figure 15.8, the admin can control this order. This is designed not just to comply with some people's OCD tendencies – no, I'll not call it CDO, even though that is the *proper* way to alphabetize it – the order of nodes in this list matters. This list forms the nodes' priority order by which the clients will access a database instance by default.

---

3   Although the *databases* inside that cluster will continue to be available from the remaining node.

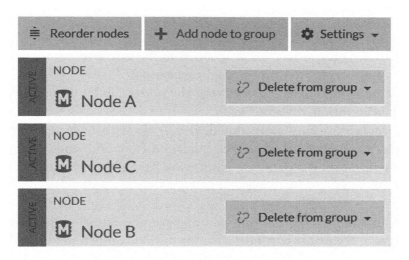

Figure 15.8. *Showing the priority order for clients to access nodes in a database group*

If a client cannot talk to the first node in the list, it will try the second, etc. Reordering the nodes will cause the server to inform the clients about the new topology for the next requests they make.

Aside from the operations team manually routing traffic, there is also the cluster itself that can decide to change the order of nodes based on its own cognizance, to handle failures, to distribute load in the cluster, etc. You can also ask clients to use a round robin strategy (configured via Settings, Client Configuration and then selected from the Read balance behavior dropdown) in order to spread the read load among the nodes.

In addition to defining a database group inside a single cluster, you also have the option of connecting databases from *different* clusters. This can be done in a one–way or bidirectional manner.

15.3.1. USING REPLICATION OUTSIDE THE CLUSTER

Database groups have fairly rigid structures. Except for determining which nodes the databases reside on, you can't configure much on a per-node basis. Sometimes, you want to go beyond that. Maybe you want different indexes on different nodes, or to have a "firebreak" type of failover where only if you manually switch things over will clients fail over to a secondary node. Or maybe you just need a higher degree of control in general.

At that point, you will no longer use the cluster to manage things; you'll take the reins yourself. You'll do this by manually defining the data flow between databases using external replication. We covered external replication in Chapter 7. Using external replication, you can control exactly where and how the data will travel. You aren't limited to just defining the data flow between different database instances in the same cluster.

When using external replication, you need to remember:

◆ Clients will *not* follow external replication in the case of failure.
◆ Indexes are not replicated via external replication.
◆ The configuration and settings between the nodes can be different (this impacts things like expiration, revisions, etc.).
◆ External replication is unidirectional. If you want to have documents flowing both ways, you'll have to define the replication from both ends.
◆ External replication is a database group-wide task that is managed by the cluster with automatic failure handling and failover on both source and destination.

These properties of external replication open up several interesting deployment options for your operations team. Probably the most obvious option is offsite replicas. An offsite replica can be used as part of your disaster recovery plans so that you have a totally separate copy of the data that isn't directly accessed from anywhere else.

This is also where the delayed replication feature comes into play. Configuring a delay into external replication gives you time to react in case something bad happens to your database (such as when you've run an update command without using a where clause).

The fact that external replication is a database group-wide operation and that its target is a database group in another RavenDB cluster (not a single node) is also very important. Consider the topology in Figure 15.9.

Figure 15.9. *Two clusters in different data centers connected via external replication*

In Figure 15.9, you have two independent clusters deployed to different parts of the world. These clusters are connected via bidirectional external replication. Any change that happens on one of these clusters will be reflected in the other. Your application, on the other hand, is configured to use the cluster in the same data center as the application itself. There is no cross-data center failover happening here. But the data is fully shared.

This is a good way to ensure high availability within the same data center, global availability with a geo-distributed system and good locality for all data access since the application will only talk to its own local nodes. In this case, we *rely* on the fact that clients will not fail over across external replication. This way if we lose a whole data center, we'll simply route traffic from your application to the surviving data center rather than try to connect from one data center to another for all our database calls.

15.3.2. IDEAL NUMBER OF DATABASES PER NODE

It's rare that you'll only have a single database inside your cluster. Typically, you'll have each application using its own database. Even inside a single application, there are many good reasons for having separate pieces store information separately. This leads to an obvious question: how many databases can we squeeze onto each node?

There is no generic answer to this question. But we can break down what RavenDB does with each database and then see how much load that will take. Each database that RavenDB hosts uses resources that can be broken up into memory, disk and threads. It might seem obvious, but it's worth repeating: the more databases you have on a single node, the more disk space you're using. If all these databases are active at once, they are going to use memory.

I've seen customers packing 800-900 databases into a single server, who were then surprised to find that the server was struggling to manage. Sure, each of those databases was quite small, 1-5GB in size, but when clients started to access all of them, the database server was consuming a lot of resources and often failed to keep up with the demand. A good rule of thumb is that it's better to have fewer, larger databases than many small databases.

Each database holds a set of resources with dedicated threads to apply transactions, run indexes, replicate data to other instances, etc. All of that requires CPU, memory, time and I/O. RavenDB can do quite nicely with a decent number of databases on a single node, but do try to avoid packing them too tightly.

A better alternative if you have a lot of databases is to simply break the node into multiple nodes and spread the load across the cluster. This way, your databases aren't all competing for the same resources, which makes it much easier to manage things.

15.3.3. INCREASING THE DATABASE GROUP CAPACITY

A database group is not just used for keeping extra copies of your data, although that is certainly nice. Database groups can also distribute the load on the system at large. There are many tasks that can be done at the database group level. We've already looked at how `Read balance` behavior shares the query load between the nodes, but that's just the beginning.

Subscriptions, ETL processes, backups and external replication are all tasks that the cluster will distribute around the database group. You can also define such tasks to be sticky so they'll always reside on the same node. The idea is that you can distribute the load among all the instances you have. You can see how that works in Figure 15.10.

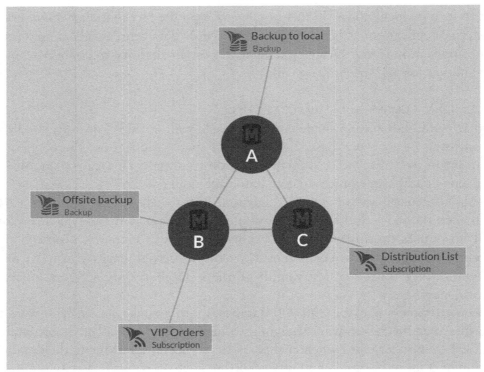

Figure 15.10. *The database group topology and task distribution among the nodes*

If needed, you can increase the number of nodes a database group resides on, giving you more resource to distribute among the various tasks that the database group is responsible for. This can be done via the `Settings`, `Manage Database Group` page by clicking on `Add node to group` and selecting an available node from the cluster. This will cause RavenDB to create the database in the new node in a `promotable` state. The cluster will assign one of the existing nodes as the mentor, replicating the current database state to the new database.

Once the new database is all caught up (which for large databases can take a bit of time) the cluster will promote the node to a normal member and redistribute the tasks in the database group in a fair manner. You need to be aware that for the duration of the expansion, the mentor node is going to be busier than usual. Normally, it's not busy enough to impact operations, but you still probably don't want to be doing it if your cluster is at absolute full capacity.

15.4. Databases, drives and directories

I already talked about the importance of good I/O for RavenDB earlier in this chapter. That was in the context of deploying a cluster; now I want to focus on the I/O behavior of a single node and even a single database inside that node.

Using a database's data directory as the base, RavenDB uses the format shown in Listing 15.1.

Listing 15.1 *On disk structure of the* Northwind *database folder in RavenDB*

```
*-- Indexes
| *-- Orders_ByCompany
| | *-- Journals
| | | *-- 0000000000000000001.journal
| | *- Raven.voron
| *-- Orders_Totals
| | *-- Journals
| | | *-- 0000000000000000001.journal
| | | *-- 0000000000000000002.journal
| | *-- Raven.voron
| *-- Product_Search
| *-- Journals
| | *-- 0000000000000000002.journal
| *-- Raven.voron
*-- Journals
| *-- 0000000000000000003.journal
| *-- 0000000000000000004.journal
*-- Raven.voron
```

You can see that the most important details are Raven.voron (the root data file), Journals (where the transaction write ahead journals live) and Indexes (where the indexes details are kept). Interestingly, you can also see that the Indexes structure actually mimics the structure of the database as a whole. RavenDB uses Voron to store the database itself and its indexes (in separate locations).

This is done intentionally because it gives the operations team the chance to play some interesting games. This split allows you to define where the data will actually reside. It doesn't have to all sit on the same drive. In fact, for high-end systems, it probably shouldn't.

Using the operating system tools

Splitting data and journals into separate physical devices gives us better concurrency and helps us avoid traffic jams at the storage level.

Instead of having to configure separate paths for journals, data and indexes, RavenDB relies on the operating system to handle all that. On Linux, you can use soft links or mount points to get RavenDB to write to a particular device or path. On Windows, junction points and mount points serve the same purpose.

The Journals directory files are typically only ever written to. This is done in a sequential manner, and there is only ever a single write pending at any given time. Journals always use unbuffered writes and direct I/O to ensure that the write bypasses all caches and writes directly to the underlying drive. This is important when making sure that the transaction is properly persisted. It's also in the hot path for a transaction commit, since we can't confirm that the transaction has actually been committed until the disk has acknowledged it.

The Raven.voron file is written to in a random manner, typically using memory-mapped I/O. Occasionally an fsync is called on it. These writes to the memory-mapped file and the fsync are not in the hot path of any operation, but if they're too slow, they can cause RavenDB to use memory to hold the modified data in the file while waiting for it to sync to disk. In particular, after a large set of writes, fsync can swamp the I/O on the drive, slowing down other operations (such as journal writes).

Each of the directories inside the Indexes directory holds a single index, and the same rules about Raven.voron and Journals apply to those as well, with the exception that each of them is operating independently and concurrently with the others. This means that there may be many concurrent writes to the disk (either for the indexes' Journals or for the writes to the Raven.voron files for the indexes).

You can use this knowledge to move the Indexes to a separate drive to avoid congesting the drive that the database is writing to. You can also have the Journals use a separate drive, maybe one that is set up to be optimal for the kind of access the journals have.

The idea is that you'll split the I/O work between different drives, having journals, indexes and the main data file all on separate physical hardware. In so doing, you'll avoid having them fighting each other for I/O access.

15.4.1. Paths in the clusters

In a cluster, you'll often use machines that are identical to one another. That means that paths, drives and setup configurations are identical. This makes it easier to work in the cluster because you don't have to worry about the difference between nodes. There's nothing in RavenDB that actually demands this; you can have a database node with a drive D: running Windows and another couple running Ubuntu with different mount point configurations, all in the same cluster.

However, when you need to define paths in the cluster, you should take into account that whatever path you define is not only applicable for the current node, but may be used on any node in the cluster. For that reason, if you define an absolute path, choose one that is valid on all nodes.

For relative paths, RavenDB uses the DataDir configuration value to determine the base directory from which it will start computing. In general, I would recommend using only relative paths, since this simplifies management in most cases.

15.5. Network and firewall considerations

RavenDB doesn't require much from the network in order to operate successfully. All the nodes need to be able to talk to each other; this refers to both the HTTPS port used for external communication and the TCP port that is mostly used for internal communication. These are configured via `ServerUrl` and `ServerUrl.Tcp` configuration options, respectively.

If you don't have to worry about firewall configurations, you can skip setting the `ServerUrl.Tcp` value, in which case RavenDB will use a random port (the nodes negotiate how to connect to each other using the HTTPS channel first, so this is fine as long as nothing blocks the connection). But for production settings, I would strongly recommend setting a specific port and configuring things properly. At some point, there *will* be a firewall, and you don't want to chase things.

Most of the communication to the outside world is done via HTTPS, but RavenDB also does a fair bit of server-to-server communication over a dedicated TCP channel. This can be between different members of the same cluster, external replication between different clusters or even subscription connections from clients. As discussed in Chapter 13, all communication channels used when RavenDB is running in a secured mode are using TLS 1.2 to secure the traffic.

RavenDB will also connect to `api.ravendb.net` to get notifications about version updates and check the support and licensing statuses. During setup and certificate renewal, we'll also contact `api.ravendb.net` to manage the automatic certificate generation if you're using RavenDB's Let's Encrypt integration (see Chapter 13). For these reasons, you should ensure that your firewall is configured to allow outgoing connections to this URL.

In many cases, using certificates will check the Authority Information Access (AIA) and Certification Revocation List (CRL). This is usually controlled by system-level configuration and security policies and is basically a way to ensure trust in all levels of the certificate. These checks are usually done over HTTP (*not* HTTPS), and failing to allow them through the firewall can cause slow connections or failure to connect.

15.6. Configuring the operating system

I want to point out a few of the more common configuration options and their impacts on production deployments. The online documentation has full details on all different options you might want to play with.

On Linux, the number of open file descriptors can often be a stumbling block. RavenDB doesn't actually use that many file descriptors.[4] However, network connections are also using file descriptors, and under load, it's easy to run out of them. You can configure this with `ulimit -n 10000`.

---

4   See Listing 15.1 to get a good idea of the number of files RavenDB will typically have open.

Another common issue on Linux is wanting to bind to a port that is lower than 1024 (such as 443 for HTTPS). In cases like this, since we want to avoid running as root, you'll need to use `setcap` to allow RavenDB to listen to the port. This can be done using `sudo setcap CAP_NET_BIND_SERVICE=+eip /path/to/Raven.Server`.

When using encryption, you may need to increase the amount of memory that RavenDB is allowed to lock into memory. On Linux, this is handled via `/etc/security/limits.conf` and increasing the `memlock` values. For Windows, you may need to give the RavenDB user the right to `Lock pages in memory`.

15.7. Summary

We started this chapter talking about capacity planning and, most importantly, measurable SLAs, without which operations teams resort to hand waving, imprecise language and the over-provisioning of resources. It's important to get as precise an idea as possible of what your system is expected to handle and in what manner. Once you have these numbers, you can plan the best way to actually deploy your system.

We went over the kinds of resources RavenDB uses and how we should evaluate and provision for them. We took a very brief look at the kinds of details we'll need for production. We talked about the kinds of disks on which you should run RavenDB (and the kind you should *not*). I/O is very important for RavenDB, and we'll go back to this topic in the next chapter as well. We covered how RavenDB uses memory, CPU and the network. In particular, we went over some of the settings (such as HTTP compression) that are only really meaningful for production.

We then talked about different cluster topologies and what they are good for. We looked at the single-node setup that is mostly suitable for development (and *not* suitable for production) and highly available clusters that can handle node failures without requiring any outside involvement. We went over the considerations for replication factors in our cluster, which depend on the value of the data, how much extra disk space we can afford and the results of being offline.

We then talked about large clusters composed of many nodes in tiers. We covered members nodes that form the "ruling council" of the cluster and can vote on decisions and become the leader, as well as the watcher nodes (the "plebs") that cannot vote but are still being managed by the cluster. Separating clusters into member and watcher nodes is a typical configuration when you have a very large number of databases and want to scale out the number of resources that will be used.

We then narrowed our focus to the database level, talking about database group topologies and how they relate to the behavior of the system in production. As an administrator of a RavenDB system, you can use database topology to dictate which node the clients will prefer to talk to, whether they will use a single node or spread their load across multiple nodes and how tasks should be assigned within the group.

Beyond the database group, you can also use external replication to bridge different databases, including databases in different clusters. We looked at an example that shared data between London and New York data centers in two separate clusters. The option to bridge databases in different clusters gives you better control over exactly how clients will behave if an entire data center goes down.

We then talked about the number of databases we want to have per node. RavenDB can support a decent number of databases without issue, but in general, we prefer fewer and larger databases over more and smaller. We also looked into what is involved in expanding the database group and adding more nodes (and capacity) to the database.

Following that, we dove into how RavenDB stores data on disk and what access patterns are used. You can use this information during deployment to split the data, indexes and the journals to separate physical drives, resulting in lower contentions on the I/O devices and giving you higher overall performance.

We ended the chapter by discussing some of the minor details involved in deploying to production, the kinds of firewall and network settings to watch out for and the configuration changes we should make to the operating system.

This chapter is meant to give you a broad overview of deploying RavenDB, and I recommend following it up by going over the detailed instructions in the online documentation. Now that your RavenDB cluster is up and running, you need to know how to maintain it. Next topic: monitoring, troubleshooting and disaster recovery.

16. Monitoring, troubleshooting and disaster recovery

We talked about deploying to production in the previous chapter, but just *being* in production is only half the job. The other half is ensuring that your systems are up, running and answering queries faster than your SLA thresholds.

In this chapter, we'll cover how to tell that your RavenDB cluster is healthy, how to monitor its state over time and what to do if any issues pop up.

Even before getting the production deployment ready, you need to plan how you'll monitor what's going on in RavenDB. The first thing you see when you go to the RavenDB Studio in a browser is the dashboard view, giving you the most-important details about what's going on in this specific RavenDB instance. This dashboard shows you crucial details, such as the number of requests, CPU load, memory utilization, indexing rate, etc.

The dashboard view was designed so you can just throw it on a monitor somewhere and take a peek every so often to measure the health of your system. If you have nothing else to guide you, just looking at the dashboard should still give you some idea about what's happening on a particular node.

The problem with relying on *only* the RavenDB dashboard is that it's limited to what's going on only right now, and only on one node. This view isn't so useful if you want to capture aggregated statistics across your cluster, for example, including historical information and an analysis of the patterns over time. For that, you need a dedicated monitoring system.

RavenDB doesn't attempt to build a full-blown monitoring solution in the dashboard, only to show you the most-pertinent information. The expectation is that you'll plug RavenDB into your existing monitoring solutions. Let's now explore what kind of hooks are provided for you to do just that.

16.1. Ongoing monitoring

The most obvious monitoring option is to use SNMP.[1] To configure SNMP in RavenDB you'll need to set it up in the way shown in Listing 16.1.

Listing 16.1 *Setting up SNMP using the settings.json configuration file*

```
{
    "Monitoring.Snmp.Enabled": true,
    "Monitoring.Snmp.Port": 161,
    "Monitoring.Snmp.Community": "password"
}
```

Once you have the configuration options from Listing 16.1 in the settings.json file, restart the node. You can now start querying RavenDB's internal state using SNMP. For example, the command in Listing 16.2 fetches the server update from the public RavenDB test instance.

Listing 16.2 *Getting the live instance server update via SNMP*

```
$ snmpget -v 2c -c ravendb live-test.ravendb.net
1.3.6.1.4.1.45751.1.1.1.3

iso.3.6.1.4.1.45751.1.1.1.3 = Timeticks: (84790246) 9 days, 19:31:42.46
```

The key parts of these commands are:

- -v 2c - the protocol version (RavenDB uses RFCs 1901-1908)
- -c ravendb - the community string, which in this case is -c password, etc. (in the case of the public instance, the default ravendb is used)
- live-test.ravendb.net - the hostname, which in this case is the live instance (plug your own instance URL here, of course)
- 1.3.6.1.4.1.45751.1.1.1.3 - the OID to query, which in this case is the server uptime

The output of the command in Listing 16.2 is the server uptime, fetched via SNMP. We told RavenDB that we wanted this particular value using the OID in the command. OID stands for Object Identifier, which is a way to globally name a particular value. The 1.3.6.1.4.1.45751 prefix belongs to RavenDB, and anything nested under it denotes a particular value that can be queried. Don't worry, you don't have to memorize all these OIDs. Instead, you can simply ask RavenDB for a list of any that are supported for a particular instance, by calling the

---

1   Simple Network Management Protocol

`/monitoring/snmp/oids` endpoint on your server. For the live test server, that would be http://live-test.ravendb.net/monitoring/snmp/oids.

The `/monitoring/snmp/oids` endpoint can be very helpful because it also gives you the OID for specific values in specific databases. For example, the `1.3.6.1.4.1.45751.1.1.5.2.2.2.1` OID can be used to tell us the size (in megabytes) of a particular database. This can make it very easy to plot all sorts of interesting values over time. You can also use SNMP to monitor the index rate of a specific index in a specific database. The amount of details and control you have is extensive.

Of course, you won't usually be querying SNMP OIDs using `snmpget`. You'll instead plug in directly a monitoring solution like Zabbix, Nagios, SCOM, OpenView, etc. The online documentation has a few walkthroughs for setting up common scenarios, but I'll assume you're familiar with your own monitoring systems and skip any further hand-holding at this point.

> **RavenDB isn't the only source of monitoring data.**
>
> RavenDB exposes a lot of information about its internal state to make it easier to figure out what's going on. Yet we don't bother to expose the *machine* state via SNMP. RavenDB assumes that you can get that information directly from the machine using standard monitoring metrics (the `1.3.6.1.2.1.25.3.3` OID to get per-core CPU load, for example).
>
> When setting up monitoring, be sure to include metrics for anything that is useful; CPU load, memory, network and I/O are among the most-common values that should be tracked. In most systems, these are part of the standard templates and require very little effort to set up. I mention this explicitly because tracking only the values that RavenDB provides will paint only part of the picture.

Beyond using SNMP, RavenDB also exposes a lot of the state in REST endpoints, outputting JSON that you can use. These are meant both for humans to look at during troubleshooting and for automated systems to scrape and store over time. Most monitoring solutions have a way for you to provide a URL and a way to fetch the interesting values from the response. For example, Zabbix supports JSON Path queries from JSON data sources.

You can get the full list of the debug endpoints from your server's `/debug/routes` endpoint. (For the live test server this URL would be http://live-test.ravendb.net/debug/routes.) Just like any other endpoint in RavenDB, when running in a secure mode, you'll need to provide authentication using a client certificate. Each monitoring solution has a different way of specifying this authentication, so check your user's manual for more details.

16.1.1. WHAT SHOULD BE MONITORED?

Now that we know how to *get* the values to monitor, the obvious question is: What *should* be monitored? I'm afraid that this is a hard question to answer, as it depends on your actual usage and needs. CPU load, memory, network and disk I/O are the most obvious things that you want to pay attention to. The numbers of requests and writes are also very interesting in most cases.

> **Why not just monitor *everything*?**
>
> You can most certainly capture and store all the values that RavenDB and the machines expose. The problem there is that most of this information isn't relevant for most scenarios. So, you might end up with a needle-in-a-haystack situation when you're looking for something specific. The pertinent information would be easily overlooked when drowning in so many other details.

At the very least, you definitely want to monitor values like the number of alerts for each of your databases. But seeing the time since the last query for each index is probably not worth it.

The general recommendation is to start with the basic template (see the online documentation for more on that) and add more details as you see fit. A lot of these details depend on whether you're seeing any signs of trouble and are hoping to head them off early on.

This is a vague advice, I realize. But the problem is that good advice is hard to give when speaking in generalities. One scenario may call for a B2B system with a fairly constant load, so that seeing the CPU percentage go too low or too high would be a a strong indicator of an issue. But for another scenario, such as a user-facing system with hardly any activity at lunchtime, a spike in CPU usage at 9 AM every single workday would be normal.

There is simply no substitution for knowing your environment and what's expected. Once you know that, you can set thresholds for alerting the operations team when the monitored values go out of their expected range. Some monitoring tools can even analyze the data on their own and detect and report when there are irregularities for you.

16.1.2. PERFORMANCE HINTS AND ALERTS

RavenDB itself is constantly monitoring its own health. This includes measuring I/O latencies, connectivity to other nodes in the cluster, the amount of memory and disk available, etc. For some of these values, RavenDB will take action on its own. For example, if the memory is low, RavenDB will switch gears and actively try to reduce its memory usage to avoid running out of space completely.

Most of the time, however, there isn't much that RavenDB *can* do. For example, if the backup folder is out of free space or if RavenDB is experiencing slow I/O, all RavenDB can do is alert you to these troublesome details. Such issues appear as performance hints and alerts, as shown in red in Figure 16.1.

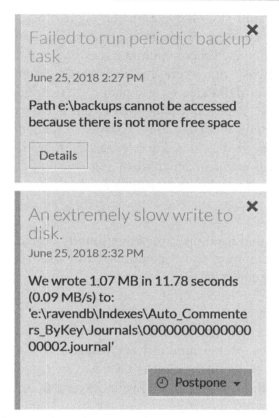

Figure 16.1. *Alerts and performance hints give your operations team ideas about what to look into.*

Alerts are issues that RavenDB encounters that require some sort of manual intervention. These may be something simple, such as running out of disk space or network issues with talking to a particular database. Sometimes the errors are transient, which is common in network scenarios. Alerts are also generated for your perusal even if the actual error was already fixed (a connection resumed between the nodes, for example) because investigating what happened after the fact can still be useful.

Alerts are node-local.
An alert isn't a cluster-wide notification. Indeed, in many cases, you'll be alerted that a node is unable to talk to the rest of the cluster. As such, you need to monitor each node in the cluster and check its state whenever an alert appears.

Performance hints, on the other hand, are different (see the blue in Figure 16.1). While they don't denote errors, they do very likely warrant your attention. RavenDB generates such hints for various reasons, such as the slow I/O example in Figure 16.1. Other reasons include queries that return very large numbers of results without using streaming, slow requests, high fanout during indexing and a few other common issues.

These issues aren't typically too severe, but they're still better to address early on. Hints are generated whenever RavenDB detects a use pattern that is known to be problematic. For example, if your queries have a very large page size or your documents are unusually large, then RavenDB identifies a potential for issues and is proactive in bringing these to your attention.

In general, alerts are designed as an acknowledgement that no one reads the logs until it's too late. So, instead of hiding errors in a text file that no one reads, RavenDB ensures that your operations team knows about any big stuff as they need to.

16.1.3. THE DEBUG LOG

Alerts are high-level items that need operator attention. By design, very few things rise to the level of alerts, to avoid spamming your operations team with too many cries for attention. That's where the debug log comes in.

RavenDB has just two log levels: Operations and Information. By default, RavenDB will log only messages with the Operations label. Operational log messages are things that the operations team needs to pay attention to or be aware of, such as updating certificates, a failure to process commands, background tasks errors, etc.

At the Operations level, the log output is meant to be readable and fairly shallow. You aren't informed about anything that goes on inside RavenDB, only things that matter to the operations team. These are mostly errors and issues, even if they were transient or already worked around by RavenDB.

> **The audit log**
>
> In addition to the Operations level, RavenDB also supports an explicit audit mode, where RavenDB records all database connections, their sources, the certificates used and their level of access granted.
>
> Certain special actions, such as the creation of a database or index, are also written to the audit log. To enable the audit log, you can set a path to Security.AuditLog.FolderPath. For more details, see Chapter 13.

The Information level, on the other hand, is much more detailed and will include anything that goes in the database. This level can be helpful when tracking down a specific issue, but it generally results in a *lot* of data. On a busy server, you can easily see a log file roll over after reaching its 256 MB limit in five to ten minutes.

By default, RavenDB retains log files for 72 hours. After that, these files are deleted. In many cases, you'll have a logs agent that monitors the directory and sends the logs to a central location, which means you can delete the logs file as soon as RavenDB starts a new one.

The logs location is controlled by the Logs.Path configuration option, and the general recommendation is to have RavenDB write the logs to a separate hard disk. This is to avoid the case of setting the Logs.Mode to the Information level and having the logs fill up the RavenDB data disk completely. If you do change the logs path or mode, a server restart is required.

But these logs aren't the only ways to get information from RavenDB.

16.2. Finding out what your server is doing

If you run into issues with RavenDB, it might be too late to set up logging and monitoring. Recognizing this reality, RavenDB is designed to have a lot of knobs to tweak and places to peek into under the hood on a regular basis. But this does *not* mean you can skip setting up a proper monitoring regime. The techniques outlined in this section are nonetheless very useful when trying to understand the behavior of RavenDB.

In many cases, these techniques can help you pinpoint what's going on very quickly. Monitoring, on the other hand, gives you insight into the behavior of the system over time and alerts you if something is out of whack. Any production cluster is expected to have a proper monitoring strategy.

The RavenDB Studio does provide explicit support to help you figure out what's going on. The first place to look is inside Manage Server and the Debug section, shown in Figure 16.2.

Figure 16.2. *The* Debug *section is your first stop to figure out what's going on inside.*

These options are only available to the operations team (requiring Operator or Cluster Admin privileges). This is because they contain data for the entire server, not for a particular database. A standard user will not be able to use these features.

Let's explore each one of these options in turn.

16.2.1. THE ADMIN LOGS VIEW

The easiest way to figure out what's going on inside RavenDB is to use the `Admin Logs` feature. This lets you hook into the logs stream generated by RavenDB and view it in a browser – a very convient option, because it doesn't require you to do anything to the server.

Even if the server is configured to not log anything, going to the `Admin Logs` page will start streaming the log entries to you at the `Information` level. This means that you can enable the logs and watch them only during interesting periods, instead of having them on all the time (or having to restart the server to change the logs mode).

> `rvn logstream`
> From the command line, if you're running on the same machine as RavenDB, you can use the `rvn logstream` command to have the same effect of seeing the logs stream on the console, but only for the pre-configured logging. The `rvn admin-channel` command has an option to enable logging on a live server on a temporary basis.

Errors will be highlighted in red, but note that many of them are actually expected and are handled by RavenDB. So, don't let seeing some errors here alarm you.

Note that debug level logging can cause the server to have to do a *lot* more work. While convenient, this feature comes with a potential performance penalty. In most cases, that isn't something to worry about. RavenDB uses a purpose built logging system that was design for low overhead and high throughput. But if your system is on the verge of resource exhaustion, enabling the debug logs can cause noticeable effect on the system.

16.2.2. THE TRAFFIC-WATCH VIEW

Looking at the logs can be fairly tedious, given how much information is being generated. In some cases, it's easier to figure out what's going on by just looking at the requests being made. RavenDB offers a dedicated view for that, as shown in Figure 16.3.

Timestamp	Status	Database Name	Duration	Method	URI
2018 June 26th, 12:03 PM	201	Users	3	POST	https://a.prod.rvn/databases/Users/bulk_docs
2018 June 26th, 12:03 PM	200	Users	0	GET	https://a.prod.rvn/databases/Users/docs?id=trackings%2F03...

Figure 16.3. *Watching live requests on a production database can be helpful in many cases.*

In Figure 16.3 you can see each individual request, how much time it took and some statistics about all the requests captured during a specific session (number, min., avg., max.

duration). This information can be very helpful if you want to figure out why something is slow or resulting in an error. You can also export the traffic capture for later analysis.

16.2.3. THE DEBUG INFO PACKAGE

By far, the most valuable tool for inspecting the state of RavenDB is the `Gather Debug Info` page. You can see how this looks in Figure 16.4.

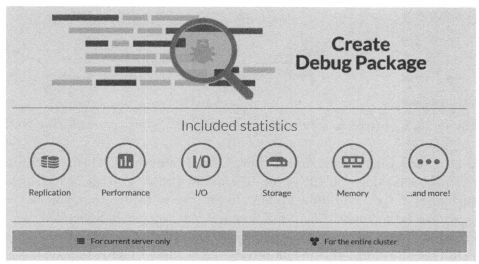

Figure 16.4. *The* Debug Info *package gives us access to all the RavenDB debug endpoints.*

What this page does is give us the ability to generate – at the click of a single button – a snapshot of the current state of the RavenDB instance or even the whole cluster. The result is a single `zip` file that you can send along with your support ticket or analyze offline at a later date.

I mentioned a few times before that RavenDB goes to great lengths to externalize its state. Even with this chapter – dedicated entirely to helping you figure out what RavenDB is doing – I won't have enough time or space to go over all the details that are available. Some of them are extremely useful for a single, specific case. But usually you don't need to go over each and every one of them.

The ability to so easily capture the entire state at once means that if you *are* in a bad state, you can quickly see the current status of the system and immediately take potentially invasive action to fix it. The classic example is rebooting the system, which will "fix" many issues. The problem is that if you do so, you'll also typically lose crucial information about what went wrong and how to prevent it in the future.

The Debug Info package allows you to retain all of that knowledge. It's also very useful if you need to contact the RavenDB support team, since it saves a *lot* of back and forth.

16.2.4. ADVANCED DETAILS

The last item in Figure 16.2 is the Advanced option. This is where RavenDB puts details that can be very interesting but aren't usually needed. Among them, we have two views, as shown in Figure 16.5.

Threads Runtime Info	Memory Mapped Files	Cluster Observer Log		

		Threads Count: 168	Dedicated threads Count: 126	

Name	Thread Id	Start Time	Duration	State
Voron Global Flushing Thread	29 (23904)	2018 June 25th, 8:41 AM	18 m 27 s 656 ms	Ready
Indexing of UsersByCountry of U...	3 (24232)	2018 June 25th, 8:52 AM	10 m 27 s 687 ms	Ready

Figure 16.5. *Advanced information about what's going on inside RavenDB*

Figure 16.5 shows the details on the threads inside RavenDB. This information can tell you what exactly is costing you CPU time. The list is sorted by usage order, so threads that burn through a lot of CPU will show up first. In the case of Figure 16.5, you can see that the most costly thread is the Voron Global Flushing Thread (we'll discuss I/O, which is what this thread is doing, later in this chapter), followed by an indexing thread.

RavenDB typically names threads intuitively – according to what they do – which makes it easier for the operations team to quickly figure out what's costing you and to take action.

Another interesting peek into the inside of RavenDB is offered by the Cluster Observer Log view. In Chapter 7 we discussed how the RavenDB cluster observer assigns work and even automatically moves databases between nodes. Figure 16.6 shows the logs of such a decision, allowing you to examine and understand them.

Threads Runtime Info	Memory Mapped Files	Cluster Observer Log	

Refresh	Term: 175,321		⊛ Suspend cluster observer

Date	Database	Message
2018 June 25th, 10:19 AM	Users	Node B was recovered from rehabilitation and promoted back to member
2018 June 25th, 10:19 AM	Users	The database 'Users' on B not ready to be promoted, because the mentor hasn't sent all of the documents

Figure 16.6. *The cluster observer log explains how the cluster makes decisions.*

The logs in Figure 16.6 show that Node B was down, as well as at what point the cluster detected that this node's databases caught up with the rest of the nodes in the database group. This allowed the cluster to move Node B from a rehab state to a normal member state.

Operational stability

Two of the worst things a piece of software can do to an operations team is surprise and mystify them. Surprises are almost never a good idea in production. And a good mystery is wonderful when it comes in book form, but not when you're trying to figure out what blew out in production.

The cluster observer routinely monitors the health of the entire cluster, making decisions about where traffic should go and which nodes are reliable. By default, it will only take action if a node is down for a long time (15 minutes or more).

This means that it won't start taking action before you can react. You can also ask the cluster observer to suspend any actions for a while, if, for example, you know that you will be doing maintenance that would normally trigger it to act. This is done using the Suspend cluster observer button shown in Figure 16.6.

This view can be very useful for understanding how the system got into its current state and what has led the cluster observer to make the decisions it did. This information is also logged, of course, but is usually much easier to see in a condensed form here than by searching through the log files.

16.3. I/O operations in RavenDB

As a critical part of its database, I/O *matters* to RavenDB. In particular, I/O performance matters. A lot of problems in production can be tied directly to issues with I/O. And these issues typically come with one (or both) of the following:

◆ insufficient depth - when the I/O system can't handle the amount of data (read/write) fast enough
◆ insufficient width - when the I/O system can't handle the number of concurrent read/write requests fast enough

Both these issues will end up looking like slow I/O. But their root causes are different. In the case of insufficient depth, we have an I/O system getting requests that are too big for it. A good example is when you're trying to make a large write (greater than the buffer size, typically) and seeing very high latency.

Imagine I/O bandwidth as a shipping channel.

I use the terms depth and width here because of the following metaphor. Imagine a water channel that has ships going through it. If you have a ship that's heavily loaded, it would be sitting deep in the water. If the channel doesn't have enough depth, then this ship will repeatedly hit the bottom. Bringing this idea back to our case, a "heavy" I/O request will usually still work, but *very* slowly.

As for width, imagine a water channel with a lot of canoes going through it. The wider the channel, the greater number of canoes that can go through it at the same time. But if the channel has insufficient width, you're sure to see a traffic jam. The same with I/O: If you have a lot of requests (even if they are individually very small) the I/O system might struggle to serve them all.

If you're running on an HDD and making a lot of random reads, this task requires seeking, which is slow. For a single continuous write, the HDD is wonderful (high depth). But for concurrent work, not so much (insufficient width).

If you ever wonder how to better spend your hardware budget, get better I/O – it will almost always be a good idea. Given the way RavenDB handles memory, if you have a fast-enough disk (NVMe comes to mind) you can even get a machine with less RAM in favor of getting higher end drives and faster I/O. For some scenarios, getting the memory-mapped data from NVMe disk can usually happen quickly enough that it doesn't *have* to be in main memory for acceptable performance.

What should you look out for?

Watch the disk queue length. If this length grows, it's usually a sign that requests are waiting on the I/O system. If this length is high for long period of time, then there's a starvation of your I/O and your database is likely suffering.

High disk queue length means that some form of action is required (upgrading hardware, increasing IOPS, changing the load pattern, etc).

RavenDB will alert you if it detects slow I/O for writes (as you already saw in Figure 16.1). But for more detailed I/O monitoring, you'll need to look in a few additional places. RavenDB makes this easy by gathering all I/O statistics on writes in one place. In the RavenDB Studio, go to your database, then `Stats`, then `IO Stats`. You can see how this looks in Figure 16.7.

There's an abundance of details in Figure 16.7, and it probably won't make sense in isolation. In the Studio, however, you can zoom in and out to inspect every detail in the performance graph. Doing so can give you tremendous insight into any specific operation that RavenDB made.

The green bar at the bottom is the most important piece of data. There, you can see the costs of writes to the journal file over time. Since a transaction can't be completed before writing its changes to the journal file, that's the critical hot path for any performance issues with slow writes. Any delay in completing the journal write will be translated to delays in returning write results to the users.

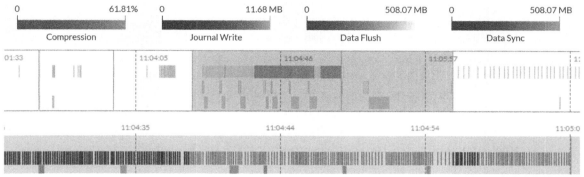

Figure 16.7. *RavenDB's internal stats for I/O write operations, for a production database*

The size of each write indicates how long it took, and the color tells you how big it was. The darker the value, the bigger the write. In general, you want to see a healthy situation, involving mostly small (and therefore shown using light colors) and thin writes. Having a few wider and darker spots is also fine (although writing more may take longer, obviously), but if you see wider areas that are bright (small writes that took a long time), then these are usually signs that the I/O system is saturated.

In such cases, you want to turn to the operating system's own tools to figure out what's going on. Some ideas about what you should be looking for and how to retrieve them are shown in Table 16.1.

Table 16.1. *I/O monitoring tools and what metrics to look at*

	Windows	Linux
Tool	perfmon	iostat
Counters	Disk Reads/sec	r/s
	Disk Writes/sec	w/s
	Avg. Disk Queue Length	avgqusz
	Avg. Disk sec/Transfer	await

Table 16.1 is a good starting place to investigate why your system is showing slow I/O symptoms. You can also use the Resource Monitor tool on Windows and iotop / sysdig on Linux to figure out what files exactly are taking up all your I/O.

Do you have enough IOPS?

When running on the cloud, a surprisingly common mistake is to forget to reserve enough IOPS for your data disks. With many cloud providers, you have some sort of burst capability, after which you'll be throttled. In that case, you'll see a good performance initially (until the burst window is closed) – and then a sharp drop. This is the very first thing to check for I/O issues when running on a cloud.

When running on your own hardware, talk to the storage team to make sure that the database server has a high enough quality of service (QoS) rating to support the workload you have on it. I've seen cases where RavenDB was put on a powerful server, backed by a SAN full of speedy drives, and the QoS setting it had restricted the database to about 5% of the available resources.

In this section so far, we looked at how to gather information about what's going on – whatever it is – via RavenDB and the I/O Stats graphs or through the operating system tools. Yet we're still missing how to make this information actionable. To know what to do when you have I/O issues, we need to first understand how RavenDB uses I/O.

16.3.1. RAVENDB I/O BEHAVIOR

The graph in Figure 16.7 shows how RavenDB keeps track of its writes. In general, RavenDB writes mostly to documents and indexes. Each write goes first to the journal (the green bar in Figure 16.7) and then is flushed to the data file (blue bar). Every now and then RavenDB will sync the data to the disk (using fsync) to allow for reusing the journal files.

Flushing data and syncing to disk

RavenDB uses the term data flush to describe the process of copying modified transaction data to the memory-mapped data file. This operation is typically very fast, since it works by copying *from* memory *to* memory, involving no disk I/O. Periodically, RavenDB will ensure that the data written to the data file actually resides on disk by calling fsync. This is called a data sync, and it's typically much more costly as an operation.

It is important to understand that within a given storage environment (the documents store for a database, or each individual index), there can only be a single outstanding write, a single data flush and a single file sync. However, writing to the disk, flushing the data and syncing to disk can all run at the same time.

Each index is also a full-blown storage environment, meaning that each will have its own cycle of journal writes, data flushes and fsync calls. Each index also runs completely independently from other indexes and the documents store – when you have multiple databases inside the same server, each database and index will also operate independently of and concurrently with the others.

What about reads?

So far we've covered a lot of details about how RavenDB writes data. But what about reads? How are those handled?

All I/O operations in RavenDB use memory-mapped I/O. In other words, we let the operating system buffer the cache, to manage what lives in memory and when to read from the disk. In most cases, the operating system will know how to select an effective working set that will minimize the amount of I/O required for RavenDB.

If that isn't the case – for example, if you don't have enough memory for your workload – you'll start seeing a high number of page faults. In particular, pay attention to *hard* page faults. A few of these are to be expected, but seeing a spike in the hard page faults per second counter indicates a possible issue.

If you're using a faster disk, you might not care about this issue. NVMe reads, for example, are fast enough that in some cases they replace the main memory. Or, you might be reading cold data because a new index was created that needs to go over existing documents. But in most cases, seeing high hard page faults per second indicates an issue and requires investigation.

By default, RavenDB limits the number of concurrent syncs and flushes that are performed on a specific device, to avoid overwhelming the disk with too many writes at the same time. This is controlled by the `Storage.MaxConcurrentFlushes` and `Storage.NumberOfConcurrentSyncsPerPhysicalDrive` options.

For best performance, we recommend having each database use its own device. That way, they don't have to fight for the same hardware resources. For the same reason, you can also dedicate specific drives for indexes or journals by using symbolic links and junction points, as discussed in the previous chapter.

16.3.2. HOW THE DATA IS LAID OUT ON DISK

After looking at how RavenDB uses I/O, the next obvious step is to look at how the data is actually stored on disk. Table 16.2 lists the files that are stored and how RavenDB uses each of them.

Table 16.2. *File structure of a RavenDB database on disk*

Path	Purpose
Raven.voron	The main data file for a database
headers.*	Snapshot of the global state of the database

Path	Purpose
Scratch/	Directory to hold temporary data while the database is opened, such as compression buffers, uncommitted data, etc.
Journal/	Holds the write-ahead log (transaction journals) that are key to ensuring ACID behavior
Indexes/	Recursively holds the same structure (Raven.voron, headers.one, Scratch, Journal) for each of the indexes.

You can go to the RavenDB database directory to look at these files, but they won't really mean much. They hold binary data and are opaque to the user.

Exclude the RavenDB directories from indexing services and from antivirus scans.

If your machines have any kind of antivirus or file indexing services, you should exclude the RavenDB directories from them. That's because these services often add significant latency to the I/O.

It's also common for these services to lock files, cause I/O failures and, in general, mess around in what RavenDB considers its own backyard. Please keep anything (whether a noisy antivirus program or a curious user) from dealing with the RavenDB directory directly.

You can't really learn anything about the file structure from the file system. But you *can* learn quite a bit from asking RavenDB what's going on directly. In the RavenDB Studio, go to your database, then to `Stats`, then `Storage Report`. Figure 16.8 shows what this storage breakdown looks like for the blog database.

Figure 16.8. *Internal storage details for the blog database*

The tree map in Figure 16.8 should help you figure out at a glance what's taking up space in your database. Below the tree map, you'll see a table similar to our Table 16.3.

Table 16.3. *Detailed breakdown of disk size for each item inside a RavenDB database*

Type	Name	Size (SUM 567.62 MB)	% Total
Documents	blog.ayende.com	320 MB	56.38%
Index	PostComments/CreationDate	68 MB	11.98%
Index	Auto/Commenters/ByKey	34 MB	5.99%
Index	Posts/ByTag	33 MB	5.81%

You might notice that the numbers here are nice and round. That's quite intentional. An index in RavenDB reserves a minimum of 16 MB on the disk. RavenDB also uses a pre-allocation pattern when requesting disk space from the operating system. What does *that* mean, you ask?

Asking the operating system for more disk space in small increments will result in major fragmentation of your files. Instead, RavenDB asks for a file size increase upfront – starting with doubling the size of the data file on disk every time more space is needed, until 1 GB is reached. After that, the data file grows by 1 GB at a time. This pattern gives the operating system the best chance for allocating continuous disk space for the file (and it reduces metadata I/O overhead in most cases).

You can see how the space is used in a particular item by clicking on it in the Studio, where the breakdown is shown between journals and data for that storage environment. Journals are used whenever a transaction is committed. These files are where RavenDB writes all the changes that happen in a transaction, ensuring that the data is stored in a persistent way and that the hot path of I/O is sequential writes, which is the fastest option.

Journal files are also pre-allocated in terms of space (starting at 64 KB and doubling in size to a max of 256 MB[2]). Whenever RavenDB is finished using a particular journal file, it will not delete it, but instead reuse it, as needed. This saves the amount of on-disk space allocated to the journals. RavenDB does rename the files to maintain consistent numbering, but the reuse of journals makes sure that the file system allocation is otherwise unchanged.

Going back to the tree map, you can click on the `Datafile` entry to see the breakdown inside the actual database. Table 16.4 shows what this looks like for the blog database.

Table 16.4. *Space usage breakdown for a 256 MB database hosting a blog*

Type	Name	Size (SUM 256 MB)	% Total
Tables	Tables	156.22 MB	61.03%
Free	Free	93.70 MB	36.60%
Trees	Trees	2.28 MB	0.89%
Reserved	Pre-allocated Buffers	8 KB (out of 6.00 MB)	0.00%

---

2   All these sizes, as well as the max size of database's growth are configurable, of course.

The information about space in this table is interesting. It's divided into tables, trees, reserved and free. Let's talk about what each of these mean.

A table in this context is not a relational table, but rather an internal structure inside the low-level Voron storage engine. This is how RavenDB stores data internally. You can click `Tables` to see more about how much space is used by each one, as shown in Table 16.5.

Table 16.5. *Space breakdown of the storage tables inside the blog database*

Type	Name	Entries	Size (SUM 156.22 MB)	% Total
Table	Collection.Documents.postcomments	6,604	50.65 MB	32.42%
Table	Collection.Documents.posts	6,589	40.21 MB	25.74%
Table	Collection.Documents.commenters	10,714	8.18 MB	5.24%
Table	Collection.Revisions.posts	363	4.18 MB	2.68%
Table	Collection.Revisions.postcomments	369	3.50 MB	2.24%
Table	AttachmentsMetadata	0	2.25 MB	1.45%
Table	Collections	9	2.25 MB	1.45%
Table	Collection.Tombstones.postcomments	0	2.13 MB	1.37%
Table	Collection.Tombstones.posts	0	2.13 MB	1.37%
Table	Attachments.Tombstones	0	2.13 MB	1.37%

As you can see, a storage table is part of how RavenDB implements collections (for example, the `posts` collection is using `Collection.Documents.posts`, `Collection.Tombstones.posts` and `Collection.Revisions.posts`). There are also other tables, such as `Collections` and `AttachmentMetadata`, that are used inside RavenDB to implement its functionality. In general, you won't need to worry about how this is structured. Usually you'll look at this view only to figure out why you might be using this much disk space.

The `Trees` section is Table 16.4 is the amount of space used by internal storage indexes. Clicking on `Trees` shows you more details, but these details tend not to be interesting to operations people, since the indexes are only a small fraction of the data size and thus rarely matter.

The `Reserved` section is reserved by RavenDB to ensure a high locality of reference internally – an implementation detail that's used for optimizing access patterns. This section will never be very big, and you can safely ignore it.

What's left in Table 16.4 is `free` space. And that takes a whopping 36.6% of the data. In this case, RavenDB is pre-allocating data from the file system. But the section can also refer to free space that RavenDB reclaims once data is deleted.

In general, you don't need to concern yourself with the actual management of the free space inside RavenDB. This process is handled completely internally, and deleted data will free space up for RavenDB to reuse as needed. This means that deleting a lot of documents and then inserting them again will result in disk space reuse.

However, it's important to note that RavenDB does *not* release free space back to the operating system itself. In other words, if you delete all the data inside a very large database, you won't get any on-disk space back. RavenDB will simply reuse this space as needed.

If you do want RavenDB to give up this space, you'll need to take actually manually by compacting the database.

16.3.3. DATABASE COMPACTION
You can ask RavenDB to compact the database to its smallest possible size by using the `Compact database` option on the database page (see Figure 16.9).

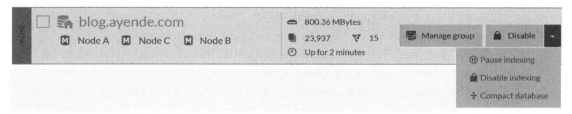

Figure 16.9. *You can start a database compaction from the* `Databases` *view.*

Compaction is an offline process, meaning it will take the database down temporarily (only on the node where you actually run the compaction) and re-create the database files from scratch. Note that this has the effect of reading and writing the entire database and can cause a significant amount of I/O. The process also requires enough disk space to create the compacted database clone in addition to the current database.

Compaction reserves no additional free space from the operating system and can arrange the data on disk in a more optimal way. But unless you have an explicit need for the disk space that this process will free up, it's probably best to leave well enough alone. After all, RavenDB is designed run off as little operational overhead as possible, and managing the data on disk is one of its primary tasks. Any free space inside the data file is already going to be reused by RavenDB, so manual compaction is typically not worth the time.

16.4. Troubleshooting connection issues
After talking at length about disk I/O, let's turn our eyes to other I/O sources. In particular, the network which is well-known for being a troublesome and finicky beast in this arena.

Actually delving into all the things that can go wrong in the modern network environment will take multiple books, so I'm going to assume that you're at least familiar with the usual concepts.

The common network issues with RavenDB include:

♦ Firewalls, both at the network and machine level - Remember that RavenDB uses two ports for communication: one for HTTP(S) and one for TCP communication. If you didn't explicitly use the configuration `ServerUrl.Tcp`, RavenDB will use a dynamic port, which works inside a data center. In the cloud, for example, you'll instead need to set a fixed port and define the firewall rules to allow it.

♦ Latency - If you're deploying in a geo-distributed manner or have high latency between nodes, you'll need to account for it in the RavenDB configuration. The setting `Cluster.ElectionTimeoutInMs` controls this behavior and is set to 300 ms by default. Note that this setting is meant for nodes deployed in the same data center, so you'll need to set it to a higher value on other configurations. Replication between database instances on different nodes isn't too sensitive to delays and was designed for deployment in high-latency situations, so you won't need to change anything there.

♦ Intrusive middleboxes - In many environments, a network connection goes through multiple network appliances, often called middleboxes. These can be firewalls, intrusion detection systems, WAN optimizers, load balancers, etc. The problem with these middleboxes is that they often add behavior (and even modify the payload) which can result in unexpected results. Because RavenDB is almost always deployed in a secure configuration while in production, the communication to and from the server is encrypted and cannot be modified. This reduces the number of times that a network appliance can apply a transformation to the TCP connection and break things.

♦ SSL termination - A special case of a middlebox is the SSL-terminating appliance. This is when a client uses SSL to connect to the endpoint, where the SSL connection is terminated and a plain HTTP connection is made from the appliance to RavenDB. This process is only possible when RavenDB is run without security – authentication requires a client certificate to reach the RavenDB server, which obviously cannot happen if the SSL connection was terminated at the appliance level.

♦ TLS downgrade - Some appliances can only accept certain versions of SSL/TLS connections. RavenDB *requires* you to use TLS 1.2 to connect and will show an error if a connection is attempted using TLS 1.0 or 1.1.

Troubleshooting issues on the network usually means using low-level tools, such as packet inspectors likes `WireShark`. While I'm not going to go into the details of such tools, I want to point out that in many cases – especially for resolving issues in TLS/SSL connections – using `openssl s_client`[3] can be much easier. The full command is:

```
$ openssl s_client -connect a.oren.ravendb.run:443 \
    -cert client.pem -key client.pem.
```

---

3   Full documentation for this feature can be found in the OpenSSL Cookbook..

The output of this command can tell you quite a lot about the connection. In particular, it can tell you whether the client successfully created a secured connection to the server, mutually authenticated and which certificates were used by either side. This command is a good way to pinpoint or rule out common issues at the beginning of your troubleshooting search.

16.4.1. INTERNAL, EXTERNAL AND MULTIPLE IPs

When you run on your own hardware, the situation is pretty simple: Your server has *one* IP address to listen to and that clients will use to talk to it. But when you run in the cloud, things get more complicated. Your server has both an internal IP to listen to (such as `172.31.25.240`) and a public IP (such as `52.9.72.38`)[4].

The server can't actually bind to `52.9.72.38`, because it isn't directly exposed to the network. Instead, any connection to this IP will be routed to the server by the cloud's network appliances. This leads to an interesting problem, because the server needs to bind to an IP address so it can listen to incoming packets. This is the logic behind the `ServerUrl` and `PublicServerUrl` configuration settings.

Normally, you'll want to set the `ServerUrl` to `0.0.0.0:443` to have RavenDB bind to all available network interfaces. However, the server often needs to tell clients and other servers how to talk to it, so we also need to provide the server with its publicly visible details. This is where the `PublicServerUrl` setting (as well as `PublicServerUrl.Tcp`) come into play. It's important to remember to calibrate this setting properly – or else the server will tell clients to use its internal IP, which the outside world can't reach. (You'll usually establish this configuration during your initial setup. But if you're doing things manually, it can be easier to forget this step.)

RavenDB uses HTTPS for securing the communication, which means we also validate that the hostname used matches the hostname on the certificate. Issues can occur if you attempt to connect to the server using a different hostname. For example, if your certificate was issued for `a.oren.ravendb.run`, any connection made with `https://rvn-srv-01` will fail, due to this hostname mismatch. On the client side, you can ignore this validation step, whether from the browser or client API (although doing so is not recommended). But on the server side, RavenDB will always validate the hostname, so it *must* match the certificate's hostname for any server-to-server communication.

16.5. The Admin JavaScript console

We've already covered quite a few of the ways that RavenDB externalizes its state and lets you poke around inside the server. Yet even beyond everything described above, RavenDB contains another option that's very powerful. As they say, with great power comes great responsibility.

Here's what you do: In the RavenDB Studio, go to `Manage Server` and then `Admin JS Console`. You can see how this looks in Figure 16.10.

---

4   These are real internal and external IPs from one of our AWS machines.

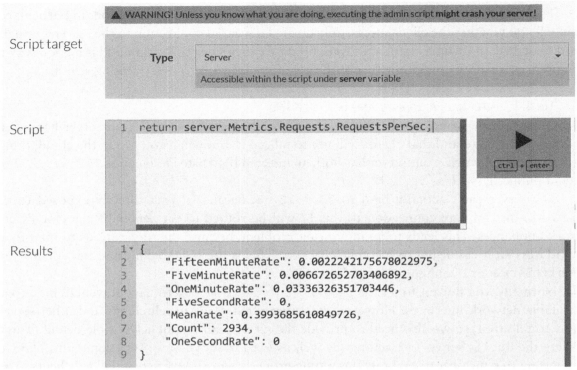

Figure 16.10. *The Admin JS Console lets you run scripts against the current server instance.*

This console unlocks a way to run scripts inside the server itself, giving you full access to anything going on inside. Figure 16.10 shows how we can use this process to retrieve data from the server. But much more is possible: You can also mutate the state of the server, including calling methods and interfering with the internal state.

The Admin JS Console comes with no safety net, nor a harness. You are absolutely able to do things there that would crash the sserver or merely stop it from accepting additional requests. (This option is available to those who are experts in the internals of RavenDB. There's no documentation available on the API specifically – but there's also no promise of the compatibility of your scripts between releases.) This tool is mostly meant to be used during support incidents, when you'll get directions for which scripts to run from a RavenDB support engineer, and when the ability to make changes to the server on the fly is invaluable. Otherwise, we don't recommend touching this tool in production. Nonetheless, it's always available via `rvn admin-channel`, which can connect to a running instance of RavenDB and perform operations directly from inside the server, bypassing the network layer.

The `rvn` tool was mentioned briefly before, but I think it's time to talk about it now in more depth, as it's part of a larger disaster recovery strategy for RavenDB.

16.6. Disaster recovery strategies

RavenDB is used in mission-critical systems and holds valuable information. Part of the very core of its design is to consider failure modes and reactions to them. There have been quite a few of such failures that we took into account, including both hardware issues and losing the admin certificate to your RavenDB instances.

> **Maximize survivability: Run on a cluster, and avoid single points of failure.**
>
> At a minimum – if you care about being up at all – you should always run RavenDB in a multi-node cluster. Running RavenDB on a single node is something that should only be done during development or testing. In fact, all of RavenDB's high-availability features assume that you have multiple nodes to function.
>
> Using the same logic, try to avoid having any single points of failure, such as a single SAN that all the nodes use for storing their data. If the SAN is down, then the entire cluster is down.

It goes without saying that you should always develop a proper backup strategy (see the next chapter, dedicated to this topic). But just having backups isn't enough. If you have a large database, even the time it takes to copy the backed-up data to the machine can take hours. Instead, you need multiple layers of defense to ensure that you'll always be online.

The first layer is running in a multi-node cluster and ensuring that each database has a high-enough replication factor to survive the loss of a node or two. The exact value of this replication factor depends on the size of your cluster and the importance of your data. The more important the data and the continued operation of the system, the more resources you should use.

The next layer of defense is having an offsite clone of the data. This is usually defined using external replication and is meant to serve as a live server that holds all your data – allowing you to manually fail over to it if you happen to lose *all* the nodes in the cluster.

> **Paranoia? You mean common sense.**
>
> For high-value production systems, paranoia is just the way things are. You don't necessarily have to follow all the suggestions in this section. But know that we're safeguarding systems that must always be up and that seek to survive even the most unlikely scenarios.
>
> We also know that a cost is associated with such duplicated measures (an offsite hot node, backups, additional nodes in the cluster, etc). Part of any operations team's job is to weigh these costs against the acceptable level of risk to see if they're worth it. At some point, the risks become negligible and the costs prohibitive. To my knowledge, no one has yet set up a server farm on the moon

to handle the case of a thermonuclear war, for example. You need to make your own determination in the matter.

One other thing to note on this topic is that you can also set up a delay in external replication, which can give you time to react if you happen to run a query that modifies data that shouldn't get across the cluster.

16.6.1. ADMIN ACCESS WITHOUT THE ADMIN CERTIFICATE

Imagine trying to get into your house, only to discover that you lost your keys. The same can happen to RavenDB if you lose the admin certificate. A basic example is when an employee goes on vacation – with the admin client certificate locked on his or her machine. You don't have access to the certificate, but you desperately need to perform some admin operation. What can you do?

RavenDB follows a simple rule: If you have admin or `root` privileges on the box, then you can access RavenDB. As a root user, you have a few options available to help you access RavenDB: You can use your root privileges to get the server certificate that RavenDB itself is using to run. This certificate can also be used for client authentication. If you authenticate as a client using the server's own certificate, RavenDB will always give you a full unrestricted access to the server.

In other words, if you can access the machine RavenDB is running on as root or administrator, then you can get the certificate that RavenDB is using and then access RavenDB directly as admin. At this point, you could generate a new admin client certificate or perform any other action as needed.

The security of allowing root access

This kind of access raises the obvious question: Isn't this a security risk? Why should it be so easy for a root user to have full access to RavenDB?

The answer is that it doesn't actually matter. If attackers have enough privileges to run as root users, then they also have enough access to do whatever else they want – inject code into the RavenDB process, read and write to its memory, etc.

If there's no protection from the root user, then there's no point in making the operations team work any harder than necessary.

In addition to getting the server certificate for client authentication, there's also the option to use the `rvn` tool. This tool is used for various tasks (such as the `rvn offline-operation` described in Chapter 13 for encrypting the server store) and in this case can also be run in the `rvn admin-channel` mode to use a named pipe for connecting to the server.

In particular, you can run commands that let you do thing like add a new client certificate, dig into statistics, force a GC collection, restart the server and even access the Admin JS Console discussed earlier in this chapter.

The `rvn admin-channel` uses a named pipe, controlled by the operating system permissions. Only those with root or admin privileges and the user who is running the RavenDB process have access to this named pipe and can send such commands to RavenDB.

16.6.2. DEALING WITH DATA CORRUPTION

Hardware does break and disks do fail – eventually, entropy will take us all. Yet I'll assume that you can get over the depressing reality of the previous statement and actually want to do something when such things happen. The scenario we'll deal with in this case is a bad sector, hardware failure or something similar that resulted in data corruption of the RavenDB on-disk files.

RavenDB uses hashing to ensure that the data has been successfully written to the disk. This allows RavenDB to detect if there have been unexpected changes to the data.[5] In this way, data corruption can be detected and handled early on – before it has the chance to spread. RavenDB will mark a database with such an error as corrupted and shut it down.

If you're running in a cluster, the usual – and easiest – way to handle such a scenario is to replace the hard disk on the faulty node and just let RavenDB replicate the data back to the node. But if you don't have the data on another node, you might need to take additional steps.

The `Voron.Recovery` tool is designed for such cases. This tool reads a RavenDB database (data file and journals) and goes over all the data – one byte at a time. It doesn't rely on a file's structure and *assumes* that the file is corrupted. It tries to recover as much data as possible by going over the raw data with a fine-tooth comb.

The output of this process is a set of `.ravendump` files (gzipped json, essentially) that contain all the recovered data as well as the list of errors that the tool encountered. You can import these `.ravendump` files into a new database to recover the documents.

16.7. Routine maintenance

By design, RavenDB is not one to require regular maintenance. For most things, RavenDB will quite happily clean up after itself and not require any human involvement in the process. Monitoring is the way to go here, to only alert you when things arise that RavenDB can't recover from automatically. Things like running out of disk space or having an index definition that

---

5   By default the hash function used is XXHash64, which is non-cryptographic. It doesn't provide any level of authentication. A malicious user that can modify RavenDB's on disk files can update the data and the hash without RavenDB ever knowing. When using an encrypted database, RavenDB uses cryptographic authentication to ensure that the data was modified only by someone who holds the secret encryption key.

failed to index too many documents are two examples of such issues. For those, you need monitoring, alerts and a human in the loop to actually fix things.

Most tasks, such as backups and ETL jobs, are defined only once and then executed by the cluster on its own, without the need for a babysitter.

The most common task for an admin to do, in fact, is to go over the cluster's own to-do list and see whether all its tasks are still relevant. For example, the number of subscriptions on a database may be very large, but many of them haven't had a client connecting to them for weeks or months. This doesn't actually *hurt* anything, but it can be nice to trim such subscriptions to make it easier to see what's actually going on in your cluster.

16.8. Summary

In this chapter, we've gone through the core details of keeping RavenDB running in production. A lot of these details involve simply setting up proper monitoring and alerts – if something happens that RavenDB isn't actually able to fix on its own. RavenDB doesn't need a lot of regular maintenance, as it does most things automatically. However, when something does break, you want to have a red light flashing somewhere and a person to investigate it and help RavenDB recover. As a result, RavenDB offers a lot of features aimed specifically at enabling proper monitoring and externalizing its internal state to make the operations team's job easier.

The first topic we discussed was SNMP monitoring, a protocol that is used by all operational monitoring systems to check the state of servers and network services. RavenDB supports this protocol and exposes quite a bit of data to it for observation and analysis. You also have more detailed information available in JSON endpoints, giving you multiple ways to access and act on the data.

Beyond exposing its state, RavenDB also continuously performs analysis on itself and makes decisions on what to do. In most cases, these actions are internal and reflect RavenDB's automatic adjustment to the environment. There are also cases where RavenDB will issue alerts and performance hints for the operators to look at.

The performance hints in particular should interest the operations team, because they can usually head off the system taking a problematic direction. The alerts are of more immediate concern, of course, but at that point the problem is likely more severe. Because the performance hints that show up today point to problems that may happen in a few weeks or months, it's best to take advantage of this lead time and take action on them early – before you have a crisis on your hands.

Routine monitoring of your application will let your team know when something is … *off*. But you might need more information. So, we looked at how to figure out what's going on inside the server. Tools such as admin logs and traffic watch give you immediate insight into what's going on. Admin logs can enable logs to run on the fly, even if logging was disabled in the server configuration. Traffic watch lets you to observe the incoming requests and monitor latency and usage.

In most troubleshooting scenarios, however, you'll head directly to the debug info package. This view captures a snapshot of all the details about the running server (or even the entire cluster) and puts them in a single zip file. The package makes it very convenient to explore the entire state of RavenDB at a given point in time. It's also useful to first capture the state of the server, then restart it (which fixes most problems). You can do offline analysis of the package at your leisure, while restoring the system to full functionality as soon as possible.

We then discussed network and connection issues. We went over some common problems that may occur in your environment, in particular related to firewalls and other network appliances. The `openssl s_client` command is very useful in such scenarios, since it gives you a simple place to start your investigation. We also discussed internal and external IPs and how to resolve a potential identity crisis for RavenDB when running in such an environment. We have to explicitly tell RavenDB what IP to bind to and what hostname to direct clients to for their server connections. Otherwise we're likely to create confusion.

The Admin JS Console is a way for you to run scripts directly inside RavenDB. Here, you can even mutate the internal state of RavenDB (for example, enable logging to a file without having to do a restart), but this access can also be dangerous, since you're literally modifying RavenDB in real time.

The final topic we covered in this chapter is how to deal with disasters. RavenDB was explicitly designed to run in a hostile environment, where nodes may go down and hardware may fail. We went over several strategies to deal with such cases, mostly by adding redundancies to handle these failures. There's also the `Voron.Recovery` tool that can extract data from a partially corrupted RavenDB database if the hard disk itself has suffered a failure.

Even though we talked about disaster recovery, we haven't yet covered one crucial topic: the backup (and restore) of RavenDB. This is because the backup process is an important topic on its own and deserves a proper forum for discussion. The next chapter is dedicated to backups, and even more important, to how to restore your systems afterward.

17. Backups and restores

Backups are *important*. I don't really think I need to tell you just how important. Still, it's worth discussing why we have backups. There are two reasons to have backups:

◆ Restoring the database after losing data.
◆ Recovering data from an earlier point in time.

Let's consider each reason independently. Restoration after data loss can be necessary because an operator accidentally deleted the wrong database, because the hard disk or the entire server died, etc. I intentionally picked these two examples because they represent very different scenarios. In the latter case – a hardware failure resulting in the loss of a node – the other members in the cluster will just pick up the slack. You can set up a new node or recover the old one and let the cluster fill in any missing details automatically.[1]

The case of accidental deletion of the database is more worrying. In this case, the database has been erased from all the nodes in the cluster. At this point, you can be saved by an offsite replica: a database to which you had set up external replication. Because that database isn't part of the same database group, it will not be impacted by the deletion, and you can manually fail over to it while you replicate the data back to the original cluster.

Restoring databases can take time

The potential that you could delete a database or lose a whole cluster is the perfect reason to have a backup. Why wouldn't we just restore from backup at this point? The answer is simple: *time*.

---

1   Remember that a single–node system cannot have any uptime SLA, since a single node failure will bring the whole thing down.

Imagine that we have a decent-sized database, 250GB in size. Just copying the raw data from the backup destination to the machine on which we want to restore can take a long time. Let's assume that we have a Provisioned IOPS SSD on Amazon Web Services (a high speed hard disk recommended for demanding database loads). Ignoring any transport/decompression costs, it will take about 10 minutes just to copy the backup to the local disk and another 10 minutes (with just I/O costs, ignoring everything else) for the actual restore.

That gives us a minimum of 20 minutes for the restore, assuming we are using a high end disk and are only limited by the speed of the disk itself. But the actual restore time *will* be higher. Plus, the I/O costs aren't the only costs to consider. Most of the cost of restoring a database is actually spent on getting the data to the machine. Backups are often optimized for long-term storage, and speed of access is not prioritized (such as with tape storage, for example).

So if you're interested in minimizing downtime in such scenarios, you would need access to a separate offsite replica (which we discussed at length in the previous chapter). There is a balance between how much protection you want and how much you are willing to pay for. If your threat scenario does not include an admin deleting a database by mistake or losing the entire cluster in one go, you probably don't need an offsite replica. Alternatively, you may decide that if those issues do come up, the time it will take to restore from backup is acceptable.

It's more common to restore a database to a particular point of time than to restore after data loss. You might want to restore from backup on an independent machine, to try to troubleshoot a particular problem, or to see what was in the database at a given time. In many cases, there are regulatory requirements dictating that backups should be kept for a certain period of time (often a minimum of seven years).

In short, backups are *important*. But I said that already. This is why I'm dedicating a full chapter to this topic, and why RavenDB has a whole suite of features around scheduling, managing and monitoring backups. We'll start by going over how backups work in RavenDB to make sure that you understand what your options are and the implications of the choices you make. Only after that will we start setting up backups and performing restores.

17.1. How backups work in RavenDB

Backups are often stored for long periods of time (years) and as such, their size matters quite a lot. The standard backup option for RavenDB is a gzipped JSON dump of all the documents and other data (such as attachments) inside the database. This backup option gives you the smallest possible size for your data and makes it easier and cheaper to store the backup files.

On the other hand, when you need to restore, RavenDB will need to reinsert and re-index all the data. This can increase the time that it takes to restore the database.

Avoid backing up at the level of files on disk

It can be tempting to try to back up the database at the file system level. Just copy the directory to the side and store it somewhere. While this seems easy, it is *not* supported and is likely to cause failures down the line. RavenDB has an involved set of interactions with the file system with a carefully choreographed set of calls to ensure ACID compliance.

Copying the directory to the side will usually not capture the data at a point in time and is likely to cause issues, while the RavenDB backup handles such a scenario and ensures that there is a point in time freeze of the database. In the same manner, you should avoid using full disk snapshots for backups. Depending on exactly what technology and manner of disk snapshotting you use, it may or may not work.

In short, you should be using RavenDB's own backup system, not relying on the file system for that.

An alternative to the backup option is the snapshot. A snapshot is a binary copy of the database and journals at a given point in time. Like the regular backup, snapshots are compressed. But aside from that, they're pretty much ready to go as far as the database is concerned. The restoration process of a snapshot involves extracting the data and journal files from the archive and starting the database normally.

The advantage here is that it's *much* faster to restore the database using a snapshot. But a snapshot is also typically much larger than a regular backup. In most cases, you'll have both a regular backup defined for long-term storage (where the restore speed doesn't matter) and a snapshot backup written to immediately accessible storage (such as local SAN) for quick restores.

Both backups and snapshots save full clones of the database from specific points in time. However, there are many cases where you don't want to have a full backup everytime. You might just want just the changes that have happened since the last backup. This is called an incremental backup and is available for both backups and snapshots.

An incremental backup is defined as the set of changes that have happened since the last backup/snapshot. Regardless of the backup mode you choose, an incremental backup will always use gzipped JSON (since RavenDB doesn't do incremental snapshots). The reason for this is that applying incremental backups to a snapshot is typically very quick and won't significantly increase the time needed to restore the database, while incremental snapshots can be very big. One of the primary reasons incremental backups exist in the first place is to reduce the cost of taking backups, after all. Figure 17.1 shows the interplay between snapshots, full backups and incremental backups from a real production database (my blog).

Size	Name
	> This PC > Data (D:) > Backups > 2018-04-17-02-00.ravendb-blog.ayende.com-A-snapshot

Size	Name
43,414 KB	2018-04-17-02-00.ravendb-snapshot
4 KB	2018-04-17-12-15.ravendb-incremental-backup
5 KB	2018-04-17-21-15.ravendb-incremental-backup

Size	Name
	> This PC > Data (D:) > Backups > 2018-04-16-02-00.ravendb-blog.ayende.com-A-backup

Size	Name
17,142 KB	2018-04-16-02-00.ravendb-full-backup
12 KB	2018-04-16-16-00.ravendb-incremental-backup
11 KB	2018-04-16-18-00.ravendb-incremental-backup

Figure 17.1. *Snapshot, full backup and ensuing incremental backups for the* blog.ayende.com *database*

In Figure 17.1, you can see a snapshot taken April 17 at 2 a.m. on node A as well as two incremental backups after that. The second folder shows a full backup on April 16 at 2 a.m. and two incremental backups after that. In both cases, the database is blog.ayende.com, which powers my personal blog. The database size on disk is 790MB, so you can see that even for snapshots, we have quite a big space saved. And keep in mind, this is a pretty small database. Figure 17.2 shows the same snapshot/backup division for a database that is about 14GB in size.

The reason why snapshots are so much smaller than the raw data is that the backup is compressed, even for snapshots. The cost of decompressing the backup is far overshadowed by the cost of I/O at such sizes. However, encrypted databases typically cannot be compressed, so you need to be prepared for snapshots that are the same size as the database (*very* big).

In Figure 17.1, you can see that there are only a couple of incremental backups; in Figure 17.2, we have a lot more. This is because while both backups were defined with roughly the same incremental backup duration, they represent very different databases. The blog database is seeing infrequent writes; when the incremental backup runs and sees that there have been no changes since the last time, there's nothing for it to do, so it skips out on its backup run. On the other hand, whenever a full backup gets run, it produces a full copy of the entire database even if no changes have been recently made.

In Figure 17.2, we are backing up a database that is under relatively constant write load. This means that we'll get an incremental backup on every run, although you can see that there are significant differences between the sizes of these incremental backups.

	Name ↑≡	Last modified ↑≡	Size ↑≡
☐	🗋 2018-02-07-11-49.ravendb-snapshot	Feb 7, 2018 11:55:40 AM GMT+0200	1.2 GB
☐	🗋 2018-02-07-12-15.ravendb-incremental-backup	Feb 7, 2018 12:15:02 PM GMT+0200	660.3 KB

	Name ↑≡	Last modified ↑≡	Size ↑≡
☐	🗋 2018-04-10-12-15.ravendb-full-backup	Apr 10, 2018 3:18:16 PM GMT+0300	191.8 MB
☐	🗋 2018-04-10-12-18.ravendb-incremental-backup	Apr 10, 2018 3:18:24 PM GMT+0300	237.6 KB
☐	🗋 2018-04-10-15-15.ravendb-incremental-backup	Apr 10, 2018 6:15:03 PM GMT+0300	2.0 MB
☐	🗋 2018-04-10-18-14.ravendb-incremental-backup	Apr 10, 2018 9:15:03 PM GMT+0300	2.2 MB
☐	🗋 2018-04-10-18-15.ravendb-incremental-backup	Apr 10, 2018 9:15:04 PM GMT+0300	8.8 KB
☐	🗋 2018-04-10-21-15.ravendb-incremental-backup	Apr 11, 2018 12:15:05 AM GMT+0300	2.2 MB
☐	🗋 2018-04-11-00-15.ravendb-incremental-backup	Apr 11, 2018 3:15:07 AM GMT+0300	2.1 MB

Figure 17.2. *Snapshot and backup for a large database on S3*

Incremental backups record the current state

An important consideration for the size of an incremental backup is the fact that the *number* of writes doesn't matter as much as the number of *documents* that have been written to. In other words, if a single document was modified a thousand times, when the incremental backup runs, the latest version of the document will be written to the backup. If a thousand different documents were written, we'll need to write all of them to the backup. That kind of difference in behavior can produce signficant size changes between incremental backups.

Backups record the current state of documents, but if you want to get all the changes that have been made in between, you need to use revisions. Just like documents, revisions are included in backups. This means that even if you store revisions inside your database for only a short period of time, you can still restore a document to any point in time by finding relevant revision from the historical backups.

17.1.1. WHAT IS IN THE BACKUP?

A backup (or a snapshot) contains everything that is needed to restore the database to full functionality. Table 17.1 shows all the gory details about what exactly is being backed up. This requires us to understand a bit more about where RavenDB stores different information about a database.

Table 17.1. *What is backed up for a database and at what level.*

Database	Cluster
Documents	Database Record (including tasks)
Attachments	Compare-exchange values
Revisions	Identities
Tombstones	Indexes
Conflicts	Tasks state (snapshot only)

We already discussed the differences between database groups and the cluster (see Chapter 7). At the database level, we manage documents and any node in the database group can accept writes. At the cluster level, we use a consensus algorithm to ensure consistency of the cluster-level operations. Such operations include identities, creating indexes, etc. These details are stored at the cluster level and are managed by the cluster as a whole, instead of independently on each node.

> **Incremental backup of the cluster-level state**
>
> At the cluster level, RavenDB backs up the entire cluster-level state of a database (on both full and incremental backups). If you have a *lot* of identities (very rare) or many compare-exchange values (more common), you might want to take that into account when defining the backup frequency.

Identities and compare-exchange values can be very important for certain type of usages, and they are stored outside of the database itself. When we back up a database, the cluster-level values are also backed up. The database tasks are another important factor to consider: backup definitions and schedules, ETL tasks, subscriptions, etc.

17.1.2. IMPORTANT CONSIDERATIONS

When a database is restored, the tasks that were defined to it are also restored. In other words, if you have an ETL task defined for a production database and you restore the backup on a development machine, you need to disable the task. Otherwise, assuming your development server can reach the ETL targets, your database might start running this task and writing to places you don't want it to write to.

The same applies to external replication, backups and any other tasks that were defined for the database. The restore includes all these tasks. That's what you want when restoring a node after failure, but it's something to note if you're restoring a backup on the side. During restoration, you have the option of disabling all such tasks so you can restore the database cleanly. But you'll have to manually select which tasks to re-enable. You should set that option when you're not restoring the backup to the same environment (or purpose) as before.

If you're using encrypted databases, you need to be aware that a snapshot backup keeps the actual data encrypted, but all the cluster-level data are stored in plain text (even if the server store itself is encrypted). And regular backups are always in plain text. As part of your backup strategy, you need to consider the security of the backups themselves. You can read more about backups and encrypted databases in Chapter 14.

17.1.3. BACKING UP THE CLUSTER ITSELF

We've talked about backing up databases, but what about backing the cluster as a whole? In general, the cluster is mostly concerned with managing databases; there isn't a persistent state beyond the database data that needs backing up. If you look at Table 17.1, you'll see that all the details therein – whether they are stored at the cluster level or the database level – are for a particular database.

The only details at the cluster level that aren't directly related to a database are details about the cluster itself (nodes, topology, task assignments, history of health checks, etc). All of that data isn't going to be meaningful if you lost the entire cluster, so there is no real point to preserve it.

Backups in RavenDB are always done at the database level. Recreating the cluster from scratch takes very little time, after all. Once completed, you can restore the individual databases on the new cluster.

17.1.4. WHO IS DOING THE BACKUP?

A database in RavenDB is usually hosted on multiple nodes in the cluster. When it comes to backups, we need to ask a very important question: who is actually going to run the backups? Individual database instances in a database group are independent of each other but hold the same data. We don't want to have each of the nodes in a database group create its own backup. We would wind up duplicating our backups and wasting a lot of resources.

A backup task, just like ETL tasks or subscriptions, is a task that is set for the entire database group. The cluster decides which node in the database group is the owner of this task and that node will be the one in charge of running backups. The cluster knows to pick an up-to-date node and will move responsibility for backups to another node if the owner node has failed.

For full backups, which node is selected doesn't matter. Any node will perform the backup from its current state as usual. If the cluster decides that a different node will execute the backup, that node's backup will be clearly marked and timestamped. From an operational perspective, there is no difference between the nodes in this regard.

For incremental backups, the situation is a bit different. You can only apply an incremental backup on top of a full backup from the *same* node that took the full backup. When the cluster decides that incremental backup ownership should switch because the owner node is down, the new node will not run an incremental backup. Instead, it will create a *full* backup first, and only when that is complete will it start creating incremental backups.

> **Backups from different nodes to the same location**
>
> RavenDB encodes the node ID in the backup folder name. This way, even if you have a backup triggered from multiple nodes at the same time, you'll be able to tell which node is responsible for which backup. This scenario can happen if there is a split in the network when the owner node of the backup is still functional but is unable to communicate with the cluster.
>
> At this point, the cluster will assign another node as the owner for the backup (since the original node is missing in action, as far as the cluster is concerned). But since the original node can't communicate with the cluster, it won't be notified of the ownership change. This can cause both the original owner and the new owner to run the backup. This behavior is in place because backups are important; it's better to have extra backups than to go without.

Consider the case of a three-node cluster and a database that is configured to take a full backup every midnight and an incremental backup every four hours. Node C is the node that is usually assigned to do the backups, and indeed at midnight, it takes a full backup. It also dutifully creates incremental backups at 4 a.m. and 8 a.m. However, at noon, node C goes down and the cluster moves responsibility for the backups to node A.

Node A cannot create an incremental backup on top of node C's full backup, so node A starts its own full backup. If node C is still down at 4 p.m., node A will still own the backup task and will create an incremental backup of all changes that took place since noon. When node C comes back up at 6 p.m., the cluster transfers backup ownership back to it. At 8 p.m., node C creates an incremental backup of everything that happened since 8 a.m., the last time node C performed an incremental backup.

There are a few interesting behaviors that you might want to pay attention to with this example:

◆ The cluster ensures that the minimum backup definition is always respected. In other words, every four hours we have an incremental backup of the database's state.

◆ Only nodes that are up to date are considered appropriate candidates for backup ownership. Since node C was down for so long, the cluster considered it out of date. The cluster only transferred ownership of the backup task (as well as any other tasks) back to node C when node C had finally caught up with any changes that happened while it was down.

◆ The backup schedule is shared among all members of the cluster. In other words, the fact that one node fails doesns't automatically trigger a backup in another node. Only after the appropriate time has passed since the last successful backup will the cluster trigger a backup on a substitute node.

◆ Incremental backups apply from the last backup (incremental or full) on that particular node. This means that you can use a single-node backup to fully restore the database state.

◆ When the cluster moves the ownership of a backup from node to node, the new owner will first run a full backup even if only an incremental backup was scheduled to run. This is a good rule of thumb to remember, but in practice it's actually a bit more complex. When a new node is assigned the backup task, it will check to see if it has done a full backup on schedule. If it is not yet time to run a new full backup, it will only run an incremental backup (from the last full backup this node did).

The last two points are important for a simple reason: even though you may schedule your full backup to happen during off hours, a change in ownership could result in a full backup running when you only expect an incremental backup. This can be an issue because the cost of a full backup can be high in terms of disk I/O, CPU, etc. If you are running a full backup when you're are under high load – especially if you've already lost at least one node – this can put additional pressure on the server.

To handle this issue, RavenDB controls the amount of resources a backup can take. The I/O and CPU priority for the backup task is equal to the normal request processing priority, which is higher than the usual indexing priority. This will likely only be an issue if your system is teetering on resource exhaustion as it is.

Now that we know how backups behave in RavenDB, let's go ahead and see how to configure backups in RavenDB.

17.2. Setting up backups

Backups in RavenDB are set up using the Studio by going to Settings, Manage Ongoing Tasks, clicking on Add Task and selecting Backup.[2] You can see what the backup screen looks like in Figure 17.3.

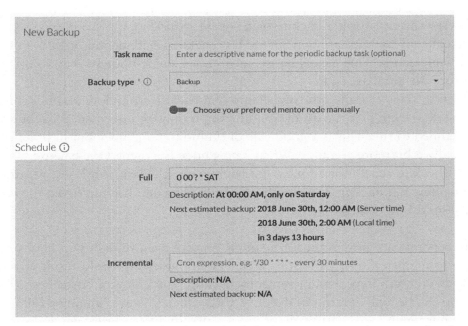

Figure 17.3. *Defining a backup schedule for every Saturday at midnight*

In Figure 17.3, we have defined a backup that is scheduled to run in full at 00:00 a.m. every Saturday. As you can see, RavenDB uses cron expressions to define recurring backup schedules. In the case of Figure 17.3, we have defined only one weekly full backup. The incremental backup duration is empty, so no incremental backups will be generated.

> **Manual backups aren't a thing for RavenDB**
>
> RavenDB doesn't have a way to specify a one-time backup. You can define a backup schedule, force it to run immediately and then discard it, but all backup operations in RavenDB are intrinsically tied to a schedule. This is because we treat backups not as something that the admin needs to remember to do, but as something that should be on a regular schedule. Once scheduled, RavenDB takes care of everything.

---

2   You can also set up backups through the API, of course.

You can see in Figure 17.3 that we didn't select the preferred mentor node, which means we've let the server assign any node to the backup task. Even if we were to choose a preferred node, if that node were to go down at the time of the backup, the cluster would still re-assign that task to another node to ensure that the backup happens.

When will my backup run?

Time is an awkward concept. In the case of a backup schedule, we have a few conflicting definitions of time:

The server's local time

The admin's local time

The user's local time

In some cases, you'll have a match between at least some of those definitions, but in many cases, you won't. When you define a backup schedule for RavenDB remember that RavenDB *always* uses the server local time. This can be confusing. You can see that Figure 17.3 lists the next estimated backup time in triplicate: once in the server local time (the time you actually used in your definition), once in the admin's own time and once as a time interval until the next backup.

RavenDB also expects that your servers' clock will be (more or less) in sync. There is no actual requirement for this to be the case, but since we use the server's local time to schedule backups, one node's midnight might be middle of the business day for you. In general, it is easier if all nodes agree to follow same timezone and sync their clocks on a regular basis.

You can save the backup task definition as it stands, but that won't really do much since no destinations have been defined yet. In order to be able to use the backup task, we need to tell the system where it should write backups to. RavenDB supports the following destinations:

- Local/network paths
- FTP/SFTP
- Amazon S3
- Azure Storage
- Amazon Glacier

Figure 17.4 shows how you can define a backup task that will write to a local folder as well as to an Amazon S3 account. The backup will run *once* each time it is executed, and the backup files will be sent to all the specified destinations from that single source.

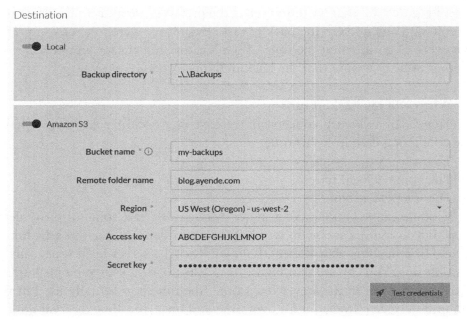

Figure 17.4. *Setting up multiple destinations for a single backup task*

The backup process will first write the backup to the local path (or to a temporary path if the local path is not specified). Once that's done, the backup owner will start uploading the backup to all remote destinations in parallel. If any of the remote destinations fail, the entire backup will be considered to have failed.

Removing old backups

RavenDB does not remove old backups. Instead, RavenDB relies on the operations team to set things up properly. That can take the shape of a cron job that deletes backup folders that are too old, which can be as simple adding the following to your crontab:

```
0 4 * * * find /path/to/backup/* -type d -mtime +14 -delete
```

This will run a backup every day at 4 a.m. and delete all directories over 14 days-old. If you don't set up a process something similar to this, backups will accrue until you run out of disk space. In particular, be *very* careful about setting backups to the same volume your database is using. There have been many not-so-humorous incidents where backups took up whole disk spaces and caused RavenDB to reject writes because there was no more space for them.

You'll need to decide your own policy for remote backups. It is fairly common to never delete backups in the interest of always being able to go back to a specific moment in time. Given how cheap disk space is today, that can be a valid strategy.

The local backup option also supports network paths (so you can mount an NFS volume or use \\remote\directory) and it treats them as if they are local files. If you define both a local path and a remote one (for example, Azure Storage), RavenDB will first write to the local path and then upload from there. If the local path is actually remote and only being treated as local, that can increase the time it takes to complete the backup.

When selecting a local path, take into account that the backup task may run on different nodes. It is usually better to use either an absolute path (after verifying that it is valid on all machines) or a relative path. In the latter case, the path is relative to the RavenDB executable, not to the database location.

I'm going to skip going over the details of each of the backup options; the online documentation does a good job of covering them, and you can probably figure out how to use them even without reading the docs. Instead, let's look at what the backups look like after we have defined them.

17.2.1. YOUR DATABASE BACKUP STATUS

After defining the backup schedule and the backup destinations, you can click Save and the Studio will take you back to the Manage Ongoing Tasks page where you'll see the tasks distribution across the cluster, as is shown in Figure 17.5.

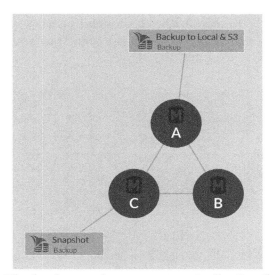

Figure 17.5. *The backup tasks are automatically distributed between the nodes in the database group*

Figure 17.5 shows the nodes on which each task will run. Click the details icon to expand and see the full details for each backup task defined for the database, as can be seen in Figure 17.6.

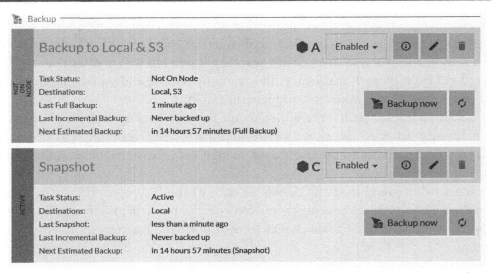

Figure 17.6. *The status for each of the backup tasks defined for this database*

Figure 17.6 shows the most recent successful full and incremental backups, as well as the time of the next scheduled backup. You can also see that you have the option to trigger a backup immediately. Note that the backup will run on the assigned node, not on the node opened in the Studio view. So in this case, even though I'm accessing this view from node C, if I press Backup now on the first backup (which is assigned to node A), it will be executed on node A.

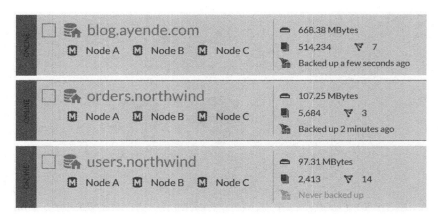

Figure 17.7. *The backup status for each database is shown as an integral part of the database details*

Backup tasks are always defined as scheduled tasks that run automatically. If you haven't scheduled them, RavenDB will make it clearly visible to you in the databases list view, as shown in Figure 17.7. You can see that the users.northwind database has never been backed up, while the status of most recent backups for the other databases is also shown.

This is an important piece of information, and RavenDB makes sure that it is clearly visible to the operator.

This concludes the topic of backups. You now know everything there is to know about how to set up and schedule backups in RavenDB. But we aren't actually done. Backups are just half the job; we now need to talk about how we actually handle restores.

17.3. Restoring databases

We've talked about how to generate backups, but the most important thing about backups is actually restoring a database from a backup. RavenDB attempts to make the restore process simple and obvious. To start the restore process, go to the Databases view in the Studio and click on the chevron near the New database button, then select New database from backup. The result is shown in Figure 17.8.

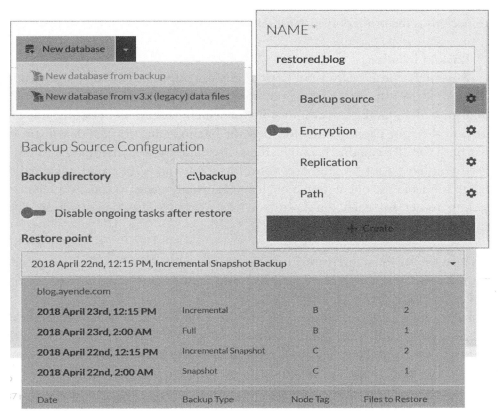

Figure 17.8. *How to restore a database in RavenDB*

Figure 17.8 shows the basic structure of restoring a RavenDB database. You create a new database from backup, then provide the name for the new database (the name is cropped from Figure 17.8 for space reasons) and the path for the backup. Once you have provided the path, RavenDB will inspect the directory and list the backups that can be restored from that path.

You can see that in this case, we have a snapshot from node C from April 22 at 2 a.m. and an incremental snapshot from the same node from 12:15 p.m. of the same day. The next day, April 23, we have a full backup at 2 a.m. from node B and an incremental backup at 12:15 p.m. RavenDB makes it easy to decide to which point in time you will restore. RavenDB also knows how to start from a full backup or a snapshot and then apply the incremental backups up to the point you have specified.

Figure 17.8 also contains a bit more information. Some slicing and dicing was required to make everything fit into the pages of this book, but it should be clear enough. Of great importance is the `Disable ongoing tasks after restore` flag. If this is set, RavenDB will disable all ongoing tasks (backups, subscriptions, ETL processes, etc.) in the database. This is what you want if you are restoring a database for a secondary purpose (i.e., you want another copy of the database, but you don't want the same behavior). You want to disable this flag if you're restoring to replace the database. Since this is the primary reason for database restoration, this flag is disabled by default.

Backup locations

RavenDB doesn't care if all your databases put their backups in the same location; it uses the database name as part of the backup folder name to distinguish which database is responsible for which backup. On restore, you can provide the root backup path for all your backups and RavenDB will probe that path for all available backups, then sort them by their database and date.

If you have a lot of databases (or a lot of backups), it can be awkward to search for a specific one within a big list. It is usually easier to specify a separate backup folder for each database (such as `e:\backups\blog.ayende.com`, `e:\backups\users.northwind`, etc).

Figure 17.8 also shows some interesting options. If you are using a full backup option, you can specify that the new database will be encrypted (and set up a new key).[3] Figure 17.9 shows the result of the restoration process.

The restoration process can take a *long* time. In Figure 17.9, you can see that the process took two seconds or so when the database size was about 700MB, and you can see the details about each part of the database that was restored from the backup. This is a very small database. For databases that range in the hundreds of GB or more, you can expect much longer

---

3   This option is not available for snapshots. A snapshot is a binary copy of the database at a given point in time. Either it is already encrypted and has its own key, or it is unencrypted and will require an import/export cycle for encryption.

restore durations. Snapshots speed up the process significantly, but the cost in I/O is significant and should be accounted for. You should practice your restores to see how much of a toll they take on your hardware and account for that in any disaster recovery plans you make.

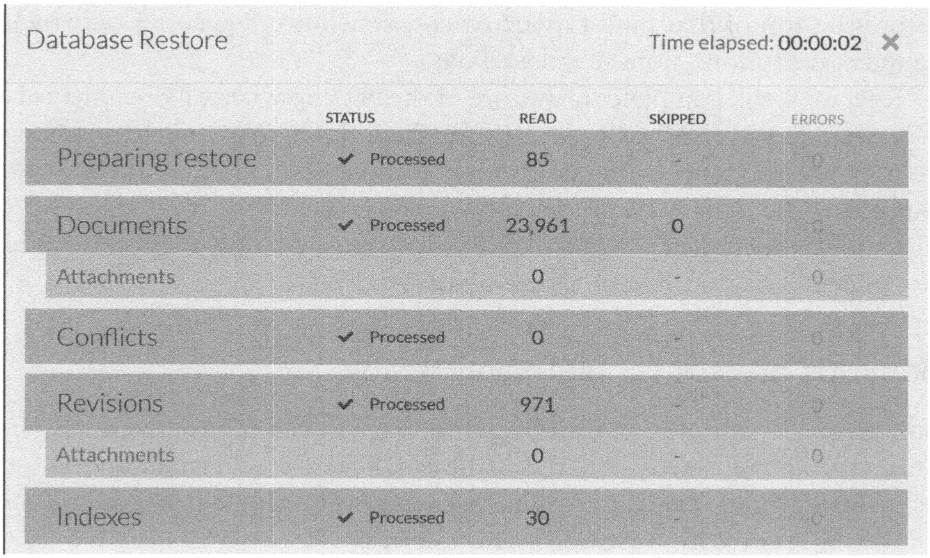

Database Restore	STATUS	READ	SKIPPED	ERRORS	Time elapsed: 00:00:02 ✕
Preparing restore	✔ Processed	85	-	0	
Documents	✔ Processed	23,961	0	0	
Attachments		0	-	0	
Conflicts	✔ Processed	0	-	0	
Revisions	✔ Processed	971	-	0	
Attachments		0	-	0	
Indexes	✔ Processed	30	-	0	

Figure 17.9. *Setting out to restore a database*

In particular, you need to account for the fact that you must have the backup files accessible to the machine. Consider a backup strategy that backs up to a local folder (retained one week), Amazon S3 (retained one year) and Amazon Glacier (retained forever).

Assuming that you want to restore from a recent backup, you can expect a pretty speedy restore time. I have tested this on an AWS machine (t2.large with 2 cores, 8GB of RAM and an EBS volume with 2,000 IOPS). Restoring a full backup from a 5GB backup file had a restore time of about three hours. A full backup that is 5GB in size is compressed JSON, which usually has *really* good compression properties. Such a backup expanded to a database whose size exceeded 350GB. That takes *time* to insert to the database. A snapshot can usually be restored more quickly. But the same 350GB database will have a snapshot of about 30GB, which on the t2.large machine took just under an hour.

I intentionally took the numbers in the above example from a relatively low-powered machine; your real production machines are likely to be more powerful. But even on a more powerful machine, you will still have a length of time during which the server will be restoring the database. And remember that this is when the backup is available on the local machine. If you need to restore from Amazon S3, you also need to account for the time it will take to fetch the data from S3 (which can be significant for large databases). Using a service like Amazon Glacier has a minimum latency of *days*. These time lags have to play a part in your disaster recovery plans.

Remember to account for indexing time as well

When measuring the restore time, you need to take into account that indexes will need to be updated as well. A snapshot restore includes the database state (with all the indexes) at the time of the snapshot, but incremental restores on top of that (and full/incremental backups in general) only include the index definitions, not the indexed data.

RavenDB will complete the restore of the backup when all documents have been written; RavenDB will not wait for the indexes to complete. Indexing of the data is then done normally through async tasks and may take a while to complete, depending on how much there is to index. This is done to give you access to the documents and to enable you to start defining a replication factor for the new database as soon as possible.

17.4. Backups are not for high availability

I've emphasized the length of time restoring from backup can take a few times already, and I feel like I need to explain exactly why this is the case. There is a (mistaken) belief within some operations teams that they can get away with having just a single instance and handling any reliability issues that come up by restoring from backup.

To a certain extent, this is true, but only if you don't care about the availability of your system. Relying on restoring from backup could mean that you get stranded without a database for a long time. This is especially likely if you don't have a regularly practiced process for restoring the data.

Conversely, if you have a cluster and a database that spans multiple nodes, that does not mean you can just ignore making backups. Spreading the database on multiple nodes ensures that any single node (or even multiple nodes) going down will not affect your ability to access and modify your data. However, it does absolutely nothing to protect you from accidental data modifications or deletes. That is what a backup gives you: the ability to roll back the clock on a mistake and revert to a previous state of the database.

There's another option available to you that somewhat combines these two options: delayed external replication. You can set up a replication target that has a certain amount of lag built in. For example, you can specify that you want a six-hour delay in replication. This means that any change made to your system will not be reflected on the replica for six hours. This gives you a hot node that you can refer to and from which you can recover lost or modified data.

17.4.1. Restoring is done locally

When you restore a database, you always provide a file path. This is a path for the *specific* node that you are restoring from, and the path is local to this node. The database will also be restored only to that specific node. This local restoration has several interesting implications.

First, you need a file path: a way to expose the backups to RavenDB. This is easy enough when you are backing up to a local path in the first place, but what happens if you have backed up to Azure Blob Storage or to Amazon S3? In those cases, you will usually download the files to your local machine and then restore them from the local path.

Alternatively, you can use projects such as S3FS-FUSE and BlobFUSE to mount cloud storage as a normal volume in your system. This will allow RavenDB to access the data directly from these systems without having to first download it to the local machine, and that can save some time in the restoration process.

The second implication of the local restore is that if you want to restore a database to multiple nodes, the typical process is to restore it on one node and then modify the database group topology to spread it to the other nodes. Part of the reason that we make the database available immediately after backup, even before the indexes have had a chance to run, is that doing so allows us to start replicating the data to other nodes in the cluster as soon as possible.

17.5. Restoring to multiple nodes at the same time

As already mentioned previously, restoring from a backup can be a lengthy process. Even though we don't recommend treating backups as time-sensitive operations, you are likely to want to spend as little time on them as possible. One option for decreasing the time backups take is restoring databases to multiple nodes at the same time.

The idea is that restoring to multiple nodes at once cuts out the secondary step of replicating data to the other nodes in the cluster after the initial node restore is completed. The problem with this approach is that it ignores the real cost of data transfer. In most cases, you'll restore to the node where you have the latest backup because that is the node that will take the least amount of time to restore on. Then, once you have the database up and running, you can expand it at your leisure.

Restoring the database on other nodes simultaneously will require copying all the backup data to the other nodes and then restoring there as well. This is doable, but it rarely speeds up the entire process in any significant way, and it usually adds overhead. There are other issues as well. When restoring from a full backup to multiple nodes, each instance will generate its own separate change vectors for each document. RavenDB is able to handle that and can reconcile such changes automatically, but it still means that each of the nodes will have to send all the data to all the other nodes to compare between them.

The process is slightly different when using snapshots. Because snapshots are binary clones of the database from a specified time, restoring on multiple nodes can be done without generating different change vectors. This means that the databases can detect early on that the data they have is identical without even having to send it over the network. For this reason, I'm only going to explain how to perform a multiple node restore for snapshots (and still, it's probably not something that you should usually do). Here is what you'll need to do:

- Ensure that on all the nodes in the cluster you want to restore on, you have a way to access the data. You could do this by copying it to each machine, having it shared on the network or using mount tools such as S3FS-FUSE and the like. If you are using some sort of shared option (such as network drive, NAS or some form of a cloud drive) you have to take into account that the nodes might compete with one another for the I/O resources to read from the shared resource.
- On the first node (node A), restore the database using the original name (users.northwind, for example). On the other nodes (B and C), restore the database using different names (users.northwind.1, users.northwind.2).
- Wait for the restore process to complete on all the nodes.
- *Soft* delete the additional databases on each of the nodes. This will remove the databases from the cluster but retain the data files on disk.
- On each of these nodes, rename the database folder on file to the proper database name (users.northwind).
- Expand the database group to all the other relevant nodes (so users.northwind will be on nodes A, B and C).

What does this process do? First, it restores the database on all the nodes in parallel, under different names. Because a snapshot is a binary copy of the database, the nodes end up with the same data on disk. We then soft delete the databases on all but one of the nodes and rename the database folders to the proper name on disk. When we add new nodes to the database, the new topology will be sent to all the nodes in the database group. Each of these nodes will open the database at the specified path and find the already restored data there.

For large restores, following these steps can save you quite a bit of time, though it will be at the expense of giving more work to the operator. You'll need to decide whether that's worth it for your scenario or not.

This process works because the change vectors across all the databases instances are the same, so there is no need to reconcile the data between the nodes. Since you're looking to reduce restoration time, I'm assuming you have a non-trivial amount of data. If you use a full backup instead of a snapshot, each node will generate different change vectors and each database instance will have to compare its documents to the other nodes' documents. This will *work*, mind you, but it can take time and a *lot* of network traffic.

It's true that any incremental backups that are applied to the snapshot restore will have the exact same problem. But I'm assuming that the amount of modified documents in this case is small enough that it effectively won't matter. The nodes will just need to reconcile the differences between the change vectors of the documents that were changed since the last full snapshot. That is unlikely to be a significant number of documents, so the process should finish quickly.

17.5.1. RESTORING ENCRYPTED DATABASES

We talked about encryption in detail in Chapter 14, so I'm going to focus here on just the practical details of handling the restoration of encrypted databases. In practice, there are three scenarios that interest us in this regard:

- ◆ Restoring a full backup.
- ◆ Restoring an encrypted snapshot.
- ◆ Restoring a non-encrypted snapshot.

If you look at Figure 17.8, you'll see that the restore dialog has an Encryption dialog, which is how you'll define the encryption options for the restored database. For a database restored from backup, the data isn't encrypted in the backup file. Defining an encryption key will encrypt the newly restored database.

When you restore from an encrypted snapshot, you *must* provide the encryption key (in the Encryption dialog) during the restore process. The encryption key is not stored in the snapshot, and you must retrieve it from your own records. (When creating a new database with encryption, you are prompted to save the encryption key in a safe location.) Once you provide the encryption key for the snapshot, the database will be restored normally and any incremental updates that happened after the snapshot was taken will also be encrypted and stored in the database.[4]

When restoring an unencrypted snapshot, you cannot provide an encryption key. You must first restore the snapshot and then export/import the data to a separate encrypted database.

17.6. Summary

In this chapter, we have gone over the backup and restore procedures for RavenDB. More importantly, we started by understanding how the RavenDB backup process works by looking into exactly what backup options are available to you with RavenDB. The first choice you have is between a backup and a snapshot. A snapshot is a full binary clone of the database at a particular point in time. Although compressed, it is typically fairly large. A backup (full or incremental), on the other hand, is a compressed JSON format that tends to be much smaller than a snapshot. Snapshots reduce restoration time, while backups take up a lot less space (particularly important for backups that you might retain for years).

---

4   It's important to remember that while the snapshot itself is encrypted, the incremental updates made since the snapshot was taken are *not* encrypted and are storing the data in plain text mode.

We discussed what exactly is included in a backup or snapshot, from obvious things like documents and attachments to less-obvious things like data that is usually stored at the cluster level (such as indexes, identities and compare exchange values). All of these are bundled into a single location and can be restored as a single unit.

Then we delved into who actually runs backup tasks, which led to an exploration of the way the RavenDB cluster assigns ownership of backup tasks and how tasks get executed. In general, RavenDB will always ensure that *someone* is going to run the backup process to keep your data safe. That includes moving ownership of the backup task between nodes if there are failures and gracefully recovering from such failures.

We then turned to how backups get scheduled. RavenDB expects the administrator to set up a backup schedule and leave everything else at the hands of RavenDB. The automatic scheduling of full and incremental backups alongside the ability to shift backup ownership means that the administrator can relax and let RavenDB do its job. The only thing the administrator really needs to consider is what kind of cleanup policy should be in place for old backups. Everything else is handled for you.

RavenDB goes to great lengths to make sure that you're aware of the backup state of your database, and it will explicitly warn you if a database hasn't been backed up properly. You can also inspect quite a lot of details about backups to verify what is going on in this regard.

The other side of backups is actually restoring databases to their previous state. We talked about how to use the RavenDB Studio to restore a backup to a node and how to select the appropriate point in time to which the database will restore. Remember, restoring a database from backup takes time and can impact operations; you should not rely on "let's restore from backup" as a failover strategy.

Restoring a database is done on a single node, typically reading from local storage.[5] After the database restore has completed, you can expand the database group to additional nodes in the cluster. It's also important that you remember to disable ongoing tasks during restoration if you're restoring for a secondary purpose (such as checking the state of the database at a particular point in time), rather than recovering from losing a database.

Databases are usually restored to a single node, but we also discussed some options for reducing recovery time by restoring a database to multiple nodes at once. This is a manual operation that has quite a few moving steps. If you can avoid it, restoring to a single node and then replicating the data from that node is often easier, simpler and in some cases, even faster.

We concluded the chapter with a short discussion on restoring encrypted databases, although the topic was covered in more depth in Chapter 14. Our next (and last) chapter is right around the corner, where we'll discuss operational recipes – specific scenarios you might run into in your day-to-day work maintaining RavenDB clusters – and how best to deal with them.

---

5   You can also set up cloud storage mount volumes using external tools, which will be exposed to RavenDB as a local path.

18. Operational recipes

This chapter mostly consists of walkthroughs of particular tasks that you might need to do when operating a RavenDB cluster. This isn't meant to replace the online documentation, but to complement it. I tried to cover most of the common scenarios that you might run into in your systems. Beyond using this as a reference, I also suggest going through the various recipes to get some insights about how such issues are resolved.

Many of the methods listed in this chapter aren't new; we have covered them in previous chapters. Here they are just laid out in practical terms as a set of operations to achieve a specific goal.

Before we start, I want to mention something quite important. Each of these recipes is meant to be used to solve the specific problem for which it is introduced. These recipes often include deep assumptions about what is going on, and it is *not safe* to blindly apply these techniques to other situations or without following the exact same procedures listed here.

This chapter is where we learn how to make fixes to the system while it is running. RavenDB was explicitly designed to allow for such things. However, you are still modifying a live system, often when it is already stressed or in partial/full failure mode. The recipes here will help you escape such scenarios, but mistakes can cause hard failures.

Now that I've finished scaring you, let's get to the real meat of this chapter. I included specific warnings for common issues that you might want to pay attention to, and you'll probably conclude that it isn't *that* scary.

18.1. Cluster recipes

The cluster is the workhorse that users of RavenDB rarely think about. The cluster is responsible for managing all the nodes in the cluster, assigning work, monitoring the health of the nodes, etc. Most of the time, you set up the cluster once and then let it do its thing.

This section discusses when you need to go in and intervene. The usual reason for intervention is that you want to modify your cluster topology. The cluster topology isn't meant to be static, and RavenDB explicitly supports online modifications of the topology, so there isn't a high level of complexity involved. But there are some details that you should take into account.

18.1.1. ADDING A NEW NODE TO THE CLUSTER

At some point, you're going to want to add a new node to your cluster. Most of the time, you set up the cluster as a whole using the setup wizard, so you might not even be aware how to add a node.

> **Prerequisites for the new node**
>
> I'm assuming that you are running in a secured mode (the only reason you wouldn't be is if you're playing around on the local machine). Running in secured mode means that in order to add the new node, you need to have mutual trust between the new node and the existing cluster. The easiest way to establish this trust is to use a single wildcard certificate for all the nodes in the cluster. Because the new node is using the same certificate as the rest of the cluster, the cluster will intrinsically trust the remote node and accept it. If you don't have the same certificate for all nodes, you'll need to register the cluster certificate in the new node using `rvn admin-channel` and then the `trustServerCert` command.

You'll have to take care of the certificate (it is easiest to use a single wildcard certificate for all the nodes in the cluster, although that is not required), DNS updates, firewall configuration, etc. I'm assuming that all of this has been properly set up ahead of time. There's nothing special about that part of the preparation.

When you start a new node for the first time, it defaults to using `Setup.Mode=Initial` and will start the setup wizard. This is *not* what you want in this case. Take a look at the `settings.json` file from one of your existing cluster nodes and use that as the template for the configuration of the new node. You'll have to change the `ServerUrl`, `PublicServerUrl`, `ServerUrl.Tcp` and `PublicServerUrl.Tcp` options to match the new node location. Beyond that, keep the configuration identical. While it is *possible* to run with different configurations on different nodes, it is not recommended; too high a variance of some options will cause errors.

Once you are done with the configuration, you can start the new node. Connect to it and you'll see the Studio as usual, but obviously without any databases or documents in there. This new node is currently running in `passive` mode, indicating that it has not yet been determined whether the new node will be joined to an existing cluster or form a completely new cluster. A new cluster will be formed if you create a new database or set up client certificates: basically, if you do anything that shows you are preparing this node to stand on its own.

Once you have verified that the new node is up, running and accessible – but remember: don't perform any actions on the new node! – go to an *existing* node and head to `Manage Server`, `Cluster` and then to `Add Node to cluster`. You can see how this will look in Figure 18.1.

Figure 18.1. *Adding a new node to an existing cluster*

Figure 18.1 shows the new node screen. There isn't much there, because you don't need to do much beyond providing the URL of the new node to add to the cluster. Once you click on the `Add` button, the cluster will connect to the new node, add it to the cluster topology and start updating it with the current state of the system. The node will switch to the `Promotable` state.

In the `Promotable` state, the node is part of the cluster in the sense that it is getting updates, but does not take part in votes and cannot be elected for the cluster leadership. When the cluster is finished updating the new node with the existing cluster state, the cluster will move the node into the `Member` state. At this point, the new node will be able to become a leader and its vote will be counted by the cluster.

Even though the node has been added to the cluster and can potentially become the leader, it is still missing something. It has no databases. RavenDB will not auto-move databases between nodes when you add or remove a node from the cluster. This is left to the discretion of the operations team. New databases created on the cluster will take the new node into account, and the cluster may decide to migrate databases from a failed node to the new node, but these are rather exceptional circumstances.

You'll typically wait until the node is fully joined to the cluster and then tell RavenDB to start migrating specific databases to the new node yourself. Remember that this process is transparent to the client and will not impact the usual operations in any manner.

18.1.2. REMOVING A NODE FROM THE CLUSTER

The flip side of adding a node to the cluster is removing a node. The *how* of this is pretty simple, as you can see in Figure 18.2.

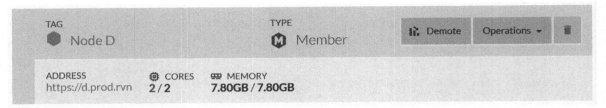

Figure 18.2. *Cluster node in the* Cluster *view; the red trash icon allows you to remove the node from the cluster*

In Figure 18.2, you can see the nodes in the cluster view in the Studio. The red trash icon at the top right allows you to remove the node from the cluster. Clicking it will cause the cluster to remove the node. But what does this mean?

At the cluster level, it means that the node will be removed (obviously). Any database groups that contain this node will have the node removed from the database group and the replication factor adjusted accordingly. Any databases that reside only on this node will be removed from the cluster entirely.

At the removed node level, the node will revert back to passive mode. It will still be accessible, but the databases that reside on the node will be unloaded. You'll need to either rejoin the node to the cluster or let it know that it should form a new cluster in order for the databases on this node to become available again. This is done to avoid having clients or ETL tasks talk to the now isolated database instance on the node that was removed from the cluster.

Forming a new cluster is a one-way option. After the new node has been moved away from being passive, you cannot add it back to the previous cluster – or any other cluster, for that matter. A cluster can only add empty nodes or nodes that were previously attached to that same cluster.

When a new cluster is formed on the formerly passive node, the topology of all the database groups is adjusted. All database groups that include the current node are shrunk to include just the current node. All database groups that do not contain the current node are removed.

Don't create a new cluster with the old URL

Forming a new cluster on the removed node is fine, but you should make sure that this is done with a *new* URL. This is to avoid the case of a client using an old URL or ETL task that hasn't been updated. The new cluster will share the same security configuration, and you'll want to avoid existing clients and tasks talking to the newly independent node while thinking they are talking to the cluster as a whole.

All other cluster-wide settings, such as the certificates and database access authorization, remain the same. You should take that into account if you intend to keep the node around after removing it from the cluster.

18.1.3. MIGRATING A NODE BETWEEN MACHINES

Node migration can happen for any number of reasons. The most obvious one is that the server IP has changed, and you need to update the cluster topology. For this reason, among many others, it is not recommended to use raw IPs in the cluster topology. Instead, use proper URLs and DNS to control the name resolution.

This way, moving node C from `10.0.0.28` to `10.0.0.32` can be done simply by updating the DNS of `c.prod.rvn` to the new value and forcing a DNS flush. You can do that with machine names, of course, but that would just shift the problem if you need to change the host machine. A good example is if you set up a RavenDB node on `prodsrv1` and you need to move it to `prodsrv3`. Since `prodsrv1` is used for other services, you cannot just change the DNS.

> **Use dedicated DNS entries for RavenDB nodes**
>
> Avoid using IPs or hostnames for RavenDB nodes. The easiest option is to have a DNS entry for each RavenDB node that can be changed directly if needed. This can make changing the physical topology of the cluster as easy as running a DNS update. This section focuses on how to handle cases when you did *not* do that.

I'm assuming that you have to move the node by updating the cluster topology, not just updating the DNS. There are a few things you need to do to ensure that the transition is handled properly, starting with obtaining a certificate for the new node URL. Once that's done, the process is simple.

We'll assume that you have a cluster of three nodes – A, B and C – and that you want to move node C to a different machine. The first thing to do is to shut down node C. Then go to one of the other nodes and remove node C from the cluster. You can also do things in the reverse order (first remove node C and then shut it down). It doesn't really matter.

Move node C to another machine, set up the certificate and update the `ServerUrl`, `PublicServerUrl`, `ServerUrl.Tcp` and `PublicServerUrl.Tcp` options in the `settings.json` file. Then go to node A or B and follow the same procedure to add a new node to the cluster. This node will be re-added to the cluster (while still being called node C). RavenDB will remember the node and perform all the necessary hookups to make sure that the newly added node returns to its rightful place in the cluster.

18.1.4. Replacing a node on the fly

What happens if a node in the cluster suffers a catastrophic failure? For example, let's assume that node C had a hard disk failure and went down completely. You restore the machine, but all the cluster data and databases on node C are gone. What's the best way to handle this scenario?

Because node C is effectively suffering from amnesia, the first thing we need to do is go to the cluster and demote it from a full member to a watcher. We'll discuss this in more detail in the next section, but the core idea here is that we want to avoid giving node C any decision-making power (which, as a full member node, it has) until it recovers from its period of forgetfulness.

Once node C has been demoted to a watcher, we can let the cluster handle the rest. Just start up RavenDB again, and since node C has no data, it will start up as a passive node. Because it will be using an existing node URL, the cluster will connect to it and update it with the cluster's current state, including any databases that should reside on node C. The other nodes with databases that also reside on C will start replicating the data back to node C.

In short order, the cluster will make sure that node C is restored to full functionality, has all of its relevant data, is up to speed and can once again be a contributing member of the cluster. At this point, you can promote it to a full member again.

We talked about members and watchers in Chapter 7, but I figure a refresher is probably in order.

18.1.5. Promoting and demoting nodes in the cluster

The nodes in a RavenDB cluster can be in the following states: `Member`, `Promotable`, and `Watcher`. A member node is a fully functional part of the cluster, able to cast votes and be elected as the leader. Typically, a cluster will have up to seven members at any given time. A promotable member is one that is currently in the process of catching up with the state of the cluster and is typically only seen when you add a new node to the cluster.

A watcher is a member of the cluster that is managed by the cluster (assigned work, monitored, etc.) but has no way of impacting the cluster. It isn't asked to vote on commands and it can't be elected leader. Once your cluster grows beyond seven nodes, you'll typically start adding new nodes as watchers instead of as full members. This is to reduce latency for cluster-wide operations by involving a smaller number of nodes.

In Figure 18.1, you can see the `Add node as Watcher` option, which will add a new node to the cluster as a watcher. You can also demote member nodes to watchers and promote watchers to be full members. Figure 18.2 shows the `Demote` button for node D.

You'll typically only demote a node when you are recovering from some sort of fatal error that caused amnesia, as was discussed in the previous section. Alternatively, you might want to shift the responsibility of the cluster to the newer, more powerful nodes. The nodes in RavenDB are all homogenous; the only difference is the roles they are assigned. Any watcher node can become a member node and vice versa.

18.1.6. BRINGING UP A CLUSTER FROM A SINGLE SURVIVING NODE

All the cluster-wide operations (adding/removing nodes) require that the cluster itself be healthy. A healthy cluster is one where a majority of the nodes are able to communicate with one another. There are certain disastrous cases where that doesn't hold. In a three-node cluster, if you lose two of the nodes, your cluster goes down until one of the failed nodes recovers.

However, what happens if the cluster *can't* recover? Imagine that you have a hard failure on both of your machines, leaving you with a sole surviving node. What do you do? You can't remove the failed node from the cluster because there is no majority of surviving nodes to confirm this decision.

At this point, there's a nuclear option you can use: unilaterally seceding from the cluster. As you can imagine, this is considered to be a *rude* operation and not something to be handled lightly. This feature exists to deal only with these specific circumstances. It will forcibly update the internal cluster topology on a node without waiting for a majority vote on the cluster and create a new single-node cluster.

This can be achieved only through the Admin JS Console that we discussed in Chapter 16. Go to `Manager Server`, `Admin JS Console` and ensure that you are running in the context of the server, then run the command in Listing 18.1.

Listing 18.1 *Emergency command to initiate cluster secession on the current node*

```
return server.ServerStore.Engine.HardResetToNewCluster();
```

This command will output the new topology ID. You can now go to the `Cluster` view and see that there is only a single node in this cluster now and that the current node is the leader. At this point, you'll be able to run cluster-wide operations, such as adding a new node to the cluster.

A small wrinkle here is that RavenDB validates that a node added to the cluster is either a brand new node or was previously part of the same cluster. Because the node has seceded, it is now its own cluster. This can be an issue if you lost three out of five nodes in a cluster. In this case, you have two nodes that are up, but you don't have a majority to change the cluster topology.

Do *not* pull the emergency handbrake

Calling `HardResetToNewCluster()`, like everything else under the Admin JS Console, is provided with an important caveat. The hard reset will modify the internal structure of RavenDB in a very invasive way. It's meant to be used only in the most dire of emergencies.

Before calling `HardResetToNewCluster()`, you should verify that there is no other usage of the system. This kind of operation should be done in isolation from outside interference; if not, you might see bad system behavior or unexpected results.

In order to recover from permanently losing three out of five nodes in the cluster, you must cause one of the nodes to secede from the cluster. But when you cause a node to secede, it will form its own single-node cluster. Let's assume that you have only nodes A and B remaining from a five-nodes cluster. We can't just move to a single-node cluster, because each of them will be its own *separate* cluster. We need to take a slightly more complex series of steps.

On node A, run the `HardResetToNewCluster` command and note the topology ID that is provided. On node B, in the Admin JS Console, you'll need to execute the command shown in Listing 18.2 (remember to update the topology ID from the previous step).

Listing 18.2 *Emergency cluster secession in favor of a particular cluster topology*

```
server.ServerStore.Engine.HardResetToPassive(
    // the topology id from Listing 18.1 goes here
    "xxxxxxxx-c4d2-494e-bc36-02274ccc6e4c"
);
```

Listing 18.2 shows the command to secede from the existing cluster in favor of a new one. This will also mark node B, where this command was run, as passive. You'll need to go to node A (where `HardResetToNewCluster` was run) and add node B to the cluster again. If the live nodes aren't named nodes A and B, by the way, this process will rename them to be nodes A and B.

Which node should be made passive?

In such a disaster scenario, it is not uncommon to have different surviving nodes each with its own specific view of the state of the cluster and the command log. It is imperative that you select the node with the most up-to-date command log to be the one that resets to a new topology.

You can use the `/admin/cluster/log` endpoint to check the status of the command log on each of the nodes. The node with the highest `CommitIndex` and the latest log in the `Entries` array is the one you should run `HardResetToNewCluster` on; `HardResetToPassive` should be run on the other(s).

At this point, you'll have a two-node cluster and can start adding brand new nodes as usual. This process is only valid for nodes that are part of the same cluster. It is not possible to use this process to merge clusters. In general, this should be treated as an option of last resort.

18.2. Database recipes

So far, we've talked a lot about all the things that happen to RavenDB at the cluster level. These are important to understand, but they're not things you'll have to deal with on a day-to-day basis. It is far more common to deal with operations at the individual database level.

To clarify the terminology: a database in RavenDB can refer to a database group (a named database in the cluster, which resides on one or more nodes) or a database instance (a named databased on a particular node in the cluster). We don't usually have to distinguish between them because RavenDB lets you work at the database group- or database instance-level transparently.

We can look at the databases from any node without needing to specify which node we are talking to for each database. Topology updates are handled automatically, and you usually don't care what database instance you are talking to for a particular operation. RavenDB handles all of that for you behind the scenes.

This is all thanks to the fact that RavenDB stores the database group topology on all the nodes in the cluster. This is what allows any node in the cluster to tell a client where to find the database, regardless of if this particular node hosts an instance of this database or not.

18.2.1. REORDERING NODES AND WHY IT MATTERS

You can see the database group topology in the Studio by clicking on the `Manage group` button on the `Databases` page. This will take you to the `Manage Database Group` page, as you can see in Figure 18.3.

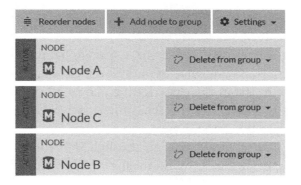

Figure 18.3. *Examining the database group topology in the Studio*

If you look closely at Figure 18.3, you might notice something odd. The order of the nodes there is *wrong*. It goes [`A, C, B`] but *obviously* it should be sorted alphabetically, no? What is going on?

The order of the elements in the topology matters, and RavenDB allows you to control that order using the `Reorder nodes` button. But why is the order of nodes so important? Put simply: this is the priority list that clients will use when deciding which node in the database group they will talk to.

Usually, RavenDB will manage the list on its own, deciding the order in which clients should talk to the different nodes as well as the other tasks that are assigned to this database group. If the cluster detects that a node is down, it will drop that node to the bottom of the list and alert the clients.

Clients, for their part, will use the list to decide which node to call whenever they need to query RavenDB. If the node they choose is down, they will automatically fail over to the next node on the list. Note that in this case, both the cluster and the clients are working both cooperatively and independently of one another. The cluster gives its opinion on the best node to use at any given point. If the cluster is able to reach a node and the client isn't, the client can still fail over to the other nodes in the topology.

After the topology of the database groups has changed, the client will update their topology for the next request. This is done by the server setting a header (in the response of a request) that lets the client know the database-group topology on the server has changed. In practice, this means that any change to the topology is usually visible to all clients within a very short amount of time.

That leads to interesting options. For example, you can use this feature to shape the way the clients will talk to a particular node. You can move a node to the bottom of the list to keep clients from talking to it (assuming no round robin or fastest node options are in place). You can also move a node to the top so that clients will prefer to use that particular node.

This is useful if you need to take a node down and want to gracefully move traffic away from it instead of having clients fail (and then recover by failing over to another node in the database group).

18.2.2. MOVING A DATABASE BETWEEN NODES

A database instance is the term used to refer to a specific database inside a particular node. Sometimes, for whatever reason, you want to move a database instance between nodes. There are a few ways of doing this, from the easy (letting RavenDB do it for you) to the less easy (when you do everything yourself). We'll discuss the easy way to do things in just a bit, but right now I want to focus on the manual mode.

If there's an easy way, why would you go through the trouble of doing this manually? Mostly because in some *specific* cases (by no means all of them, mind) it can be faster to do things directly. Walking you through the manual process of moving the database between nodes also gives you good exposure of how RavenDB is actually managing databases internally and may be helpful in other situations.

The way RavenDB is actually managing your databases across the cluster is interesting. At the cluster level, RavenDB coordinates between the various nodes to achieve consensus on the Database Record. The Database Record is a JSON document that describes a particular database. You can see it by going into one of the databases, then to Settings, Database Record. Listing 18.3 shows a (simplified) example of such a database record.

Listing 18.3 *A database record example*

```json
{
    "DatabaseName": "Northwind.Orders",
    "Disabled": false,
    "Encrypted": false,
    "Topology": {
        "Members": [
            "A",
            "B"
        ],
        "DynamicNodesDistribution": false,
        "ReplicationFactor": 2
    },
    "Indexes": {
        "Orders/ByCompany": {
            "Name": "Orders/ByCompany",
            "Priority": "Normal",
            "LockMode": "Unlock",
            "Maps": [
                "from order in docs.Orders /* redacted */"
            ],
            "Reduce": "from result in results /* redacted */",
            "Type": "MapReduce"
        }
    },
    "Revisions": {
        "Collections": {
            "Orders": {
                "Disabled": false,
                "PurgeOnDelete": false
            }
        }
    },
    "PeriodicBackups": [],
    "ExternalReplications": [],
    "RavenEtls": [],
    "SqlEtls": [],
    "Etag": 113
}
```

What you see in Listing 18.3 is what goes on behind the scenes. You have the database topology (the members of the database group), you have the index definitions and revisions configurations and you can see where we define tasks for the database. When I talk about the cluster managing the database, what I mean is that the cluster mutates this document and ensures that all nodes in the cluster have consistent views of it.

The database instance managed at the node level is, to use a very crude definition, just the set of files that make up the data on that node. How does all of this relate to moving a database between nodes? Well, let's see.

Pay no attention to the man behind the curtain

This isn't magic. RavenDB uses the `Database Record` to tell databases where they need to go, and when a database is assigned to a node, the node will create an instance. A database instance is the set of files, threads and in-memory data structures required to handle queries and operations.

The first thing to do when manually moving a database between nodes is to actually remove the database from the original node. You can either soft delete the database (if it exists on only a single node) or remove it (using soft delete) from the database group. This can be done in the `Manage Database Group` view under the database's `Settings`. You can see how this looks in Figure 18.4.

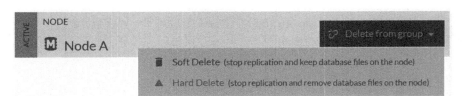

Figure 18.4. *Removing a database from a node can be done using soft delete, leaving the database files untouched*

This soft delete measure leaves the database files on the disk. Furthermore, it also means that the RavenDB server on the original node will close all the file handles and release any resources associated with this database. At this point and at this point *only*, we can take the database folder and move it to another machine.

Don't make a habit of schlepping databases around manually

It is generally *not safe* to muck about in the RavenDB directory. That is true for users in general as well as other things like antiviruses, file system indexing, file monitoring, etc. RavenDB has firm ideas about how it interacts with the disk. Interfering with its I/O can cause issues.

In this case, we have started off by explicitly shutting down the database (by soft deleting it). This gives RavenDB the chance to do a graceful shutdown: closing all the file handles and freeing all related resources. This is the only reason it is OK for us to muck about in RavenDB's data directory.

You're going through all this trouble because you want to move the database folder to another machine. This presupposes that you have some way to get the data from one machine to the other that's faster than sending it over the network. This can happen when you have so large a database that it's faster to literally move the disk from one machine to another.

Another scenario is when your "disk" is actually a cloud storage volume. This allows you to detach it from one machine and then attach it to another with relative ease. In this case, moving the data manually might be worth this hassle. Otherwise, just use RavenDB's built-in replication for this scenario.

> **This is *not* going to work to clone a database**
>
> You might be tempted to use this approach to quickly clone a new database when you want to add a new node to the database group. This will not work because the internal database ID will be the same across multiple nodes, something that is not allowed and can cause complex issues down the road. RavenDB will not be able to tell where exactly a specific change happens, so it will not be able to tell if documents should be replicated to the other nodes or not.
>
> This approach is only valid if you remove the data from the old node entirely so there is just one copy of the database with the same database ID.

Once you have the database directory on the other machine, make sure that it is in the expected path on the destination and add it to the new node. When updating the `Database Record`, RavenDB will open the directory and find the pre-existing files there. From that point on, it will just proceed normally.

18.2.3. RENAMING A DATABASE

Given the previous topic, can you guess how you'll rename a database with RavenDB? All you need to do is soft delete the database and then recreate it on the same path but with a new name.

There are a few things that you need to pay attention to when renaming databases. Only the *database-level* data is going to be preserved in this scenario. Tasks and data at the cluster level will *not* be retained, which includes tasks such as subscriptions, backups, ETLs, etc. This also includes database *data* that is stored at the cluster level, such as identities and compare-exchange values.

In short, don't do this. If you want to rename a database, the proper way to do it is to back up and restore the database under a different name.

18.2.4. EXPANDING AND SHRINKING THE DATABASE GROUP

I mentioned earlier that there is an easy way to move a database between nodes. It's quite simple: first expand the database group to include the new node, wait for replication to complete and then remove the node you want from the group.

You can do this from the Settings, Manage Database Group view. Expanding the Database Group to include a new node is as simple as clicking on Add node to group and selecting which node you want to add. Once that is done, the RavenDB cluster will create the database on the new node and assign one of the existing nodes in the database group for the initial seeding of data.

The Manage Database Group view will allow you to monitor the status of the initial seeding until the cluster detects that the new node is up to speed and promotes it to full member status. At this point, you can remove another node from the database group and the cluster will adjust accordingly.

Given what we've already learned, you'll probably first take the node that is about to be removed from the database group and move it lower in the priority list, then wait a bit to give clients the chance to learn about the new topology and connect to another server. This way, when you eventually do remove the node, no client will be talking to it.

> **Removing the last node in the group will delete the database**
>
> Removing a node can be done as either a soft delete (you keep the files, as we previously discussed) or a hard delete. If the node you're removing is the last node in the database group, the database will be removed from the cluster even if you choose a soft delete. The same rules about the cluster-level data apply as when we talked about the wrong way to rename a database.
>
> A soft delete of the last node in a database group will keep the database-level data intact on that node, but all the cluster data (tasks, identities, compare exchange values, etc.) will be removed from the cluster.

The advantage of this method for the operations team is obvious: very little hand-holding is required. Expanding the group means that RavenDB will handle all the details of moving the data to the other node(s) and setting everything up.

The downside is that it requires RavenDB to do a fair amount of work: effectively read the entire database, send it over the network and on the other side, write out the entire database. This is intentionally handled in such a way that will not impact overall operations too much. The idea is that the stability of the cluster is more important than raw speed.

This might sound like we'ved intentionally throttled things down, but nothing could be further from the truth. We've taken care to ensure that adding a new node won't consume so many resources as to be prohibitively expensive. After all, the most common reason for adding another node is wanting to share an already high load.

18.2.5. SCALING DATABASE UNDER LOAD

RavenDB contains several features that allow you to scale your systems easily. Among the abilities available to you are distribution of tasks across the nodes in the database group and load balancing between the nodes.

If you start seeing a very high load on your system, what options do you have? The first thing you sould do is to look at the kind of client configuration you have. This is available in Settings, Client Configuration, as shown in Figure 18.5.

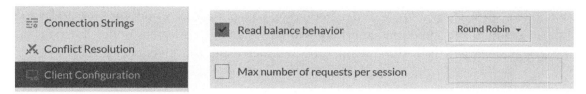

Figure 18.5. *The client configuration allows you to change clients' load balancing behavior on the fly*

Client configuration, just like the cluster topology, is defined on the cluster and disseminated to clients automatically. This means that if the configuration isn't set, the first thing you should do is to set the Read balance behavior to Round Robin and wait a bit. You'll see how clients start distributing their reads across the entire database group.

> **Changing the load balancing behavior can change system behavior**
>
> This may sounds obvious, but if you change the Read balance behavior to Round Robin (or Fastest Node), you'll change the behavior of the system. Of course this is what you want, so why am I mentioning this?
>
> Because this also changes externally observed behavior. A write to one server followed by a load-balanced read from another may cause you to read the data from another server. That can cause you to miss the just written value because it hasn't been replicated yet. This isn't just a "make things faster" setting; you need to understand what this means to your application before setting it.
>
> Under the gun, you may accept the potential of this (likely to be very rare) issue until you can come back from the precipice. But in general, you want to change to this setting with full understanding of the impact it will have on your system. We discussed this setting in more detail in Chapter 6.

If you do have this value already set up and RavenDB seems to be struggling even with the load split among the different nodes of the database group, the obvious next step is to add new nodes to the group. This specific scenario is why RavenDB favors stability over speed when you add a new node. Only one single node in the group will be in charge of updating the new node, and even on that single node, we'll ensure that we send the data at a rate that both sender and receiver can handle without choking.

So while it's possible to scale under load, it's (quite obviously) not recommended. If you have a large database, the initial seeding may take a while. During this time, you don't have any extra capacity; in fact, the replication is actually taking (some limited amount) of system resources. If at all possible, try to scale your systems ahead of time or during idle periods, rather than under the highest load.

If you do find yourself in this situation, remember that because the initial seeding of a new node happens from a single designated node, you can actually add *multiple* nodes to the database group at the same time and they will be assigned to different nodes. In some cases, this can significantly help with reducing time and increasing overall capacity.

18.3. Miscellaneous operational tasks

Beyond managing the cluster and the databases, you also have operational concerns inside particular databases. This section touches on some of the issues that can come up in these cases and will provide you with options on how to resolve them.

We're going to go over some RavenDB features we've already discussed. This time around, we're going to see how these features can be applied and chained together to achieve some really nice results.

18.3.1. OFFLINE QUERY OPTIMIZATION

We discussed RavenDB's query optimizer and its ability to detect changes to the operational environment (such as deployment of a new release of your software with different queries). Under such conditions, the query optimizer will adjust the indexes on the database to better serve the new behavior.

You *can* do this in production on live deploy; in fact, this feature is explicitly meant to be used in such a scenario. However, in many cases, it is valuable to avoid having the adjustment period take place during live production. Instead, we recommend doing this on the side and introducing the changes to production at an early enough date such that by the time the new code is deployed, the database is already expecting the changes. So, how do you go about doing this?

Use a separate instance of your database (such as the UAT/QA instance) and run the new version of your application against that instance. At this point, I suggest running your load test procedure and encouraging users to click around randomly. Basically, exercise your system to make it query the database.

The query optimizer on the database will analyze all this activity and create the relevant indexes for you. After a while, you'll see that the system reaches a steady state. There is enough information now that all the queries in use are being properly served by indexes.

At this point, go to the database and export *just the indexes*. This will export any static indexes you have created on the database, but most importantly, it will export any automatic indexes that were created by the query optimizer. You can now take the indexes export and import it on your production system.

This will introduce the new indexes to production. RavenDB will start building them on the fly, replacing older indexes once the indexing is done. You can monitor that process and wait until all the additional indexing activity has completed. Because your application isn't going to be using the new indexes, there will be very little impact while they are being built.[1] Once the indexes are done, you can deploy your new version to production knowing that you already taught the database what to expect.

18.3.2. DAISY-CHAINING DATA

In Chapter 11, we talked about using MapReduce indexes and their ability to output results to a collection. In Chapter 8, we talked about ETL processes and how we can use them to push some data to another database (a RavenDB database or a relational one). Bringing these two features together can be surprisingly useful when you start talking about global distributed processing.

A concrete example might make this easier to understand. Imagine a shoe store (we'll go with Gary's Shoes) that needs to track sales across a large number of locations. Because sales must be processed regardless of the connection status, each store hosts a RavenDB server to record its sales. Figure 18.6 shows the geographic distribution of the stores.

Figure 18.6. *Gary's Shoes locations (and the locations of the servers)*

To properly manage this chain of stores, we need to be able to look at data across all stores. One way of doing this is to set up external replication from each store location to a central server.

---

1   Make sure that any changes to the static indexes you make are backward compatible, otherwise queries may fail once the indexes complete and the side-by-side index is promoted to be the active index.

This way, all the data is aggregated into a single location. In most cases, this would be the natural thing to do. In fact, you would probably want two-way replication of most of the data so you could figure out if a given store has a specific shoe in stock by just looking at the local copy of its inventory.

But for the purpose of this discussion, we'll assume that there are enough shoe sales that we don't actually want to have all the sales replicated. We just want some aggregated data. But we want this data aggregated across all stores, not just at one individual store. Here's how we can handle this: we'll define an index that would aggregate the sales across the dimensions that we care about (model, date, demographic, etc.).

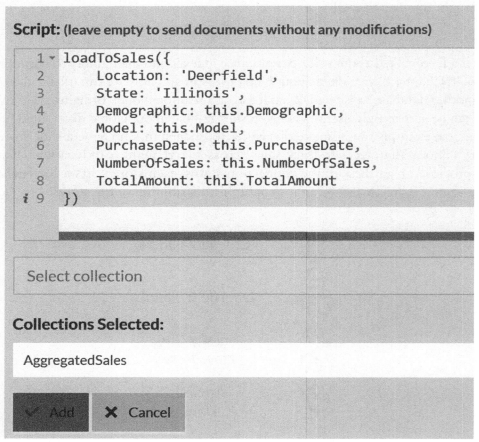

Figure 18.7. *ETL script to send aggregated sales to a central server*

This index can answer the kind of queries we want, but it is defined on the database for each store so it can only provide information about local sales, not what happens across all the stores. Let's fix that. We'll change the index to have an output collection. This will cause it to write all its output as documents to a dedicated collection.

Why does this matter? These documents will be written to solely by the index, but given that they are documents, they obey all the usual rules and can be acted upon like any other document. In particular, this means that we can apply an ETL process to them. Figure 18.7 shows what this ETL script would look like.

The script sends the aggregated sales (the collection generated by the MapReduce index) to a central server. Note that we also added some static fields that will be helpful on the remote server so as to be able to tell which store each aggregated sale came from. At the central server, you can work with these aggregated sales documents to each store's details, or you can aggregate them again to see the state across the entire chain.

The nice things about this approach are the combination of features and their end result. At the local level, you have independent servers that can work seamlessly with an unreliable network. They also give store managers a good overview of their local states and what is going on inside their own stores. At the same time, across the entire chain, we have ETL processes that will update the central server with details about sales statuses on an ongoing basis.

If there is a network failure, there will be no interruption in service (except that the sales details for a particular store will obviously not be up to date). When the network issue is resolved, the central server will accept all the missing data and update its reports. The entire process relies entirely on features that already exist in RavenDB and are easily accessible.

The end result is a distributed, highly reliable and fault tolerant MapReduce process that gives you aggregated view of sales across the entire chain with very little cost.

18.3.3. DISCONNECT EXTERNAL REPLICATION/ETL FROM A REMOTE SOURCE

The bad thing about push-based ETL processes and replication is that sometimes, you want to disable them on the destination side.[2] That can be a bit awkward when you only have access to the destination and not the source.

For example, you might want to disable the Jersey City shoe store from the aggregation process we outlined in the previous section. That store has been sold and is no longer part of the chain, so you don't want its reports, but it'll take some time before the new owner's IT staff will get around to replacing the internal systems. During that time, you want to ignore the pushed data from that store.

The obvious way to do that would be to shut down the ETL process at the source, but let's assume that's not an option currently available to you. How do you disable the data push at the *destination*? The answer is quite simple: remove the credentials of the certificate this store is using. With the credentials no longer being valid, the Jersey City store will fail to connect to the central server and will be blocked from pushing any additional data.

Note that the certificate's credentials are checked during connection setup, not on each individual request. You might need to drop an already established connection to complete the process.

---

2   Push-based in this context refers to the fact that they are defined in the source and they push the data to the destination.

18.4. Summary

This is an odd chapter. I wanted to give you detailed recipes and steps for what to do if you run into particular issues in production; adding a node, expanding a database group and moving a node between machines are all tasks you may find yourself doing. At the same time, all of these tasks (and more) are covered in detail in the online documentation.

This chapter isn't meant to replace the online documentation, but to complement it. I intentionally chose some of the most common scenarios and then talked not just about the list of steps that you'd take to work through them, but also the kinds of things you'd need to watch out for and how they play into the overall architecture of RavenDB.

The cluster recipes we have gone over should also help you better understand how the cluster is put together. Beyond simply knowing about the Raft protocol and consensus algorithms, I wanted to give you an idea of what is actually happening within the system. For example, the interaction between nodes as they are added and removed from the cluster gives a lot of insight into what is going on at the node level.

Removing the magic behind what is going on with RavenDB is very important. Having a sense of what's going on behind the scenes means that you'll be able to predict what RavenDB will do and, more importantly, *why*.

After working through some cluster recipes, we moved on to discuss how databases are composed. It's crucial to understand the notion of the `Database Record` that is managed at the cluster level, with each node holding the databases instances that are assigned to it. We looked at how this can be useful if we want to physically move a database between machines (for example, moving the disk volume directly).

We also talked about some scale and performance tricks: how to expand your database group and load balance work between nodes. This is something that you should be doing ahead of time, but it's not a perfect world. RavenDB understands and expects that you'll probably be doing this kind of thing under fire, so to speak. Expanding the database group to add more capacity is a controlled operation so as to limit the amount of additional load it generates.

Speaking of things that should be done ahead of time, we talked about how you can take the results of the query optimizer from your load testing machine and apply them to your production systems ahead of new version deployment. This will allow the production cluster to benefit from the experience of the test server. This allows you to smooth the process of introducing new behaviors in production.

We finished the chapter with an interesting challenge: distributed aggregation of data across many physically separated locations using several distinct features in tandem. This kind of usage is pretty common. One of the strengths of RavenDB is its ability to treat features in an orthogonal manner; you can mix, match and combine them to get to some really nice results.

VI. Appendix

Index

D

Made in the USA
Coppell, TX
26 September 2022

83644732R00308